16th Annual Edition
KNIVES '96

Edited by
Ken Warner

DBI BOOKS, INC.

STAFF

EDITOR
Ken Warner

ASSOCIATE EDITORS
Robert S.L. Anderson
Harold A. Murtz
Ray Ordorica

ASSISTANT TO THE EDITOR
Lilo Anderson

PRODUCTION MANAGER
John L. Duoba

EDITORIAL/PRODUCTION ASSOCIATE
Holly J. Porter

EDITORIAL/PRODUCTION ASSISTANT
Laura M. Mielzynski

ELECTRONIC PUBLISHING MANAGER
Nancy J. Mellem

ELECTRONIC PUBLISHING ASSOCIATE
Larry Levine

COVER PHOTOGRAPHY
John Hanusin

MANAGING EDITOR
Pamela J. Johnson

PUBLISHER
Sheldon L. Factor

DBI BOOKS, INC.

PRESIDENT
Charles T. Hartigan

VICE PRESIDENT & PUBLISHER
Sheldon L. Factor

VICE PRESIDENT—SALES
John G. Strauss

VICE PRESIDENT/MANAGING EDITOR
Pamela J. Johnson

TREASURER
Frank R. Serpone

THE COVER KNIVES

Atop the other five rests Don Lozier's handsome Persian-styled dagger. To its right is W.D. Pease's nice big folder in Damascus and fossil ivory, engraved by Chris Meyer. Then, clockwise, is Harold Corby's big Sheffieldian Bowie replica, a V.J. McCrackin dagger in Damascus and glowing fossil walrus ivory, and an ebony-gripped hunter by D'Alton Holder, with Bruce Shaw engraving. At bottom is a Roy D. Cutchin liner-lock folder, brush-finished anodized titanium and all.

Photo by John Hanusin.

KW

ISBN 0-87349-174-2   Library of Congress Catalog Card #80-67744

CONTENTS

INTRODUCTION 5

FEATURES

MATT HELM'S KNIVES & MINE
by Donald Hamilton 6

THE AX IN THE MODERN WOODS
by Steven Dick 10

THE FUNCTIONAL CHARACTERISTICS OF SWORDS
by Tom Maringer 15

A PERPLEXITY OF POCKET TOOLS
by Joseph Rychetnik 21

THE SHAPES OF JAPANESE BLADES
by Allan H. Pressley 30

SPECIAL BLADES FOR SPECIAL JOBS
by Bernard R. Levine 38

THE KNIVES OF CORSICA
by Raymond Caranta 44

FINALLY...ONE GOOD POCKETKNIFE
by Jim Foral 48

TRENDS

NO PLOWSHARES YET 54
SMALL KNIVES 58
BACKWOODS CUTLERY 63
THE FOLDING KNIFE 66
FIELD-GRADE KNIVES 77
THE OVERSEAS CONTRIBUTION 84
BIG KNIVES 92
MEDIUM KNIVES 102
REALLY SMALL IS STILL BIG 115
MORE AUTOMATICS THAN EVER 119
INVESTMENT-GRADE KNIVES 122
THE ELEGANT KNIFE 125
MISCELLANY 132

STATE OF THE ART

INTERESTING KNIVES 134
STUDY OF STEEL AND SHAPE AND STUFF 140
EMBELLISHMENT 148
LEATHERWORK 160

FACTORY TRENDS

NEW KNIVES IN PRODUCTION 166
SABATIER AGAIN 178

DIRECTORY

CUSTOM KNIFEMAKERS 180
KNIFEMAKERS STATE-BY-STATE 269
KNIFEMAKERS MEMBERSHIP LISTS 277
KNIFE PHOTO INDEX
    Knives '96 281
    Knives '91-'95 283
SPECIALTY CUTLERS 290
GENERAL CUTLERS 291
IMPORTERS & FOREIGN CUTLERS 291
KNIFEMAKING SUPPLIES 293
MAIL-ORDER SALES 295
KNIFE SERVICES 297
ORGANIZATIONS & PUBLICATIONS 304

INTRODUCTION

WE'VE SAID IT before. We'll say it again: You see here the best knives ever made. Last year you also saw the best knives ever made.

Yes. This year's crop is better than last year's, and next year's will beat these. One would think there would be an end to it sometime, but one would be wrong.

For instance, here and there throughout this book, you'll see knives by a dozen or so Netherlanders and Scandinavians. They are remarkable knives, splendid, in fact—leading designs. Ten years ago, though, the knives of Holland and Norway and Sweden had gone about as far as they could go. Everyone thought so.

Your reporter here was around when some people still at work today were grinding with spinning rocks and polishing with giant sewed cotton wheels. It is not just the gleam in the eye that produced all this excellence.

In fact, knifemakers today work with the best tools cutlers ever saw. And when these tools showed up, there was an explosion of revealed talent.

It is commonplace for veterans to say of younger knifemakers, fellows with three or five years' experience, "If these guys were around back then, I'd never have got started."

It's commonplace, but it ain't so. I know those old guys. They can be had, sure, but none of them are easy money. Nor are the young ones.

Any of them will admit they're in a group activity. There are no artistic vacuums. And darned little reluctance to share ideas and experience.

After that, however, it's the devil take the hindmost. And we get the knives that result.

Ken Warner

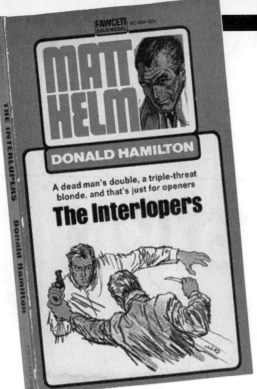

In *The Interlopers*, lead character Helm gets into knife work big-time. He started with a pocket-sized lock-blade, switched to a Buck 110, and finally wound up with a Boy Scout knife—and did permanent things with all of them.

The Devastators was early on when Helm used a small lockblade, but "I always had it in my hand in my pocket." He uses it twice in this book, and once only to cut a lady out of some rope.

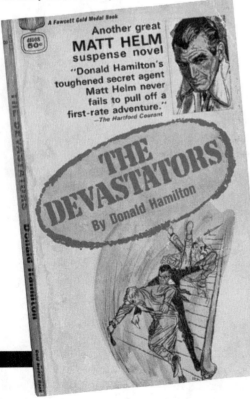

MATT KNIVES

by DONALD HAMILTON

Unlike his firearms, the knives carried by my fictional character, Matt Helm, are mostly the knives I carry myself. Granted, I don't often wear a belt that uses a knuckle-knife as a buckle—although I own one—and I don't strap cutlery to my arms or legs except to check it out for fictional purposes, but I always do carry some kind of an edged implement. With modern packaging the way it is, I can't see how anybody can get along without one. These days, it practically takes an ax or saber to get into a box of dog food.

Frankly, I can't remember just what knife Matt Helm was wearing at any given time in any given book; except for the few occasions when something truly lethal was required (all knives are, of course, lethal to some extent), what he carried in his pocket was probably what I was carrying when I wrote the book. So a history of my own knives seems appropriate.

Of course, Matt Helm, as I wrote him, was born in this country, although his parents came from overseas. So he was never, like me, a little Swedish immigrant boy heading off for his first day in an American public school. I suppose my clothes were kind of odd, and I may have been a little concerned about them, but I felt basically well-dressed because I had the one essential item that every Swedish schoolboy carried at that time—he'd sooner go to school without his trousers than leave his sheath

HELM'S & MINE

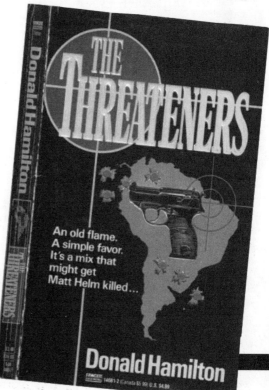

knife at home. So I had mine on my left hip. As I recall, it had a slim blade of about 4 inches—kept sharp, of course—and the grip was birch with an ornate pommel of some kind. It was the standard Scandinavian knife, and it can, I believe, still be found in any tourist shop over there.

Well, I needn't have worried about my foreign clothes. Nobody even noticed my clothes; what they saw was the knife. The first teacher who spotted it called up reinforcements, just in case I proved truly homicidal, and they whipped me into the principal's office faster than you can say "Dagger." I couldn't understand what all the uproar was about—remember that at the time I didn't understand much English.

Well, my parents were summoned and were just as surprised by the commotion as I. Fortunately, they spoke good English, and they explained that I was carrying the weapon, as the principal called it, with their full permission because all schoolboys carried such knives in Sweden. (I'd be interested to hear if they still do.) My parents said they hadn't realized that customs were different here. Were they to understand that knives were totally forbidden? How in the world did a boy get along without some kind of a knife?

The principal said, well, ha, hum, a small pocketknife, perhaps, or a Boy Scout knife....

(Today, as the school systems have improved, even the small pocketknife is forbidden—Editor.)

So I spent my boyhood in the company of various Scout knives. They kept getting lost, of course, as boys'

In *The Frighteners*, Helm has his Russell One-Hand knife and a Latina colleague has her cuchillo, and they're both good stalkers. Helm observes a that a One-Hand knife gets all bloody sometimes, because it's so small.

The Threateners goes to the wall in the knife department, starting with a "wall-hanger" Bowie pressed into service, then a Swiss army knife in a hotel room, a carving knife in a big hacienda, and finally a machete out in the night.

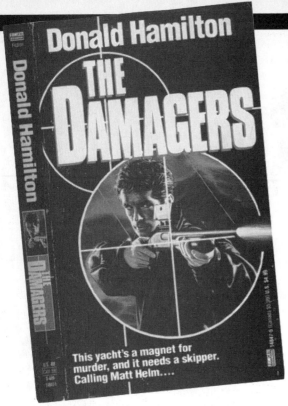

The Damagers takes place mostly on boats, and the action starts with a Chef's knife, then switches to Swiss army knives and Russells hidden all over the boat and used as tools and as weapons. Fun stuff.

The Two-Shoot Gun is a great Western about an 1870s Eastern quail shooter with a Purdey. The only time he uses a knife is to clean a mess of desert quail, and to do it, he takes out a Barlow. Perfect!

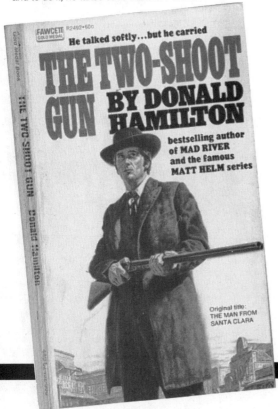

belongings do, although some lasted long enough for the staghorn to be worn fairly smooth. I would mourn my old friend, then go out and get another just like it, until one Christmas my father gave me a lovely little pearl-handled pocketknife with two spring-loaded blades. I looked at it with some doubt. For one thing it looked kind of, well, sissy, and for another it lacked the features I'd come to consider essential: It didn't have a screwdriver, can opener, leather punch or bottle opener. However, the push-button, click-open feature was intriguing, so I gave it a try anyway.

I found it a revelation. It seemed that I was always getting into a spot where a knife that could be opened one-handed was practically a lifesaver, whether I was hanging onto a plunging boat to cut some snarled fishing line or climbing a tall tree to free a tangled kite. I grew to love that pretty little knife, and it broke my heart when my father asked for it back, apologetically. He explained that a law had just been passed making spring-operated "switchblade" knives illegal, and he was afraid that my little knife (largest blade 2 inches!) fell under this prohibition.

I went back to my Scout knives—well, actually, I got fancy, or my father did. By way of making amends for taking my spring-knife away, he got me a glorified version of the knives I'd been carrying: a bright red Swiss army knife with every gadget in the world. I carried this and its successors (my knives still had that knack of disappearing occasionally) well out of boyhood and on into middle age.

Then I read an article describing how to open a folding knife one-handed. I still remembered the ancient hurt inflicted upon me by those legislators; now I was going to show them how little their law really meant. I dug out a folding Buck hunting knife I'd picked up somewhere and got to work. There was nothing to it, with a knife that size. Grab the back of the blade and snap the wrist, and the heavy handle flipped open of its own weight. It worked better, of course, after the knife had been well oiled and broken in. It was a big knife to carry in the pocket, and it may even have been illegal, but it made me happy to thumb my nose at Washington. I wore out a number of pockets lugging that big Buck around, discovering once more that when I needed to drive a screw or open a bottle there was generally a suitable implement around; I didn't really need one on my knife. The blade was the important thing, and the Buck had plenty of that.

But one day a small package arrived in the mail. Opening it, I found a letter from the well-known knifemaker, A.G. Russell, who said he'd read and enjoyed my Matt Helm books, which was nice to hear. In return for the pleasure they'd given him, he went on, he was sending me

On a pronghorn hunt some years ago, author Hamilton settled in for some long-range shooting of his own.

one of his knives. Opening the box, I found a handsome little single-bladed folding knife, quite flat since it was made entirely of stainless steel except for a brass stud set into the base of the blade. The instructions described how that stud should be used to open the knife one-handed. This was a much simpler and more efficient system than the violent flip-open method I'd been using. (I wondered if, perhaps, Mr. Russell had read the book in which Matt Helm describes that technique and decided to show me how it could be improved upon.)

The knife even had my name engraved on it; how could I reject such a thoughtful present? The Buck was retired to hunting duty, and the Russell—much more comfortable to carry—took its place in my pocket, where it still resides.

Strangely enough, in my latest book, Matt Helm seems to have found a nice little stainless Russell knife somewhere, I can't imagine where.   •

Editor's Note

Serious Hamilton readers, such as this writer and A.G. Russell—those who save the books so they may read each several times—will miss several knives from this account. Never fear; they are still in the books; I checked.

The Solingen folding hunter that came back from World War II; the "specially ordered" gift from a rich lady, made in Florida; the borrowed machete used in a saber-style duel—all are safely and permanently there.

In fact, there are *a lot* of knives in Don Hamilton's novels, even those that don't involve Matt Helm. There are a lot of guns, too—specific guns, used specifically. But those are another story for another DBI book.

Ken Warner

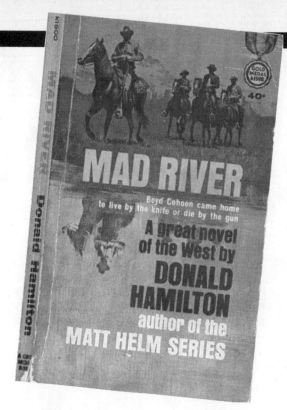

On *Mad River's* cover, it says "He came back to live by the knife or die by the gun," and so it proved. The knife was his mountain man Dad's, ranch-made from a file, and he uses it like his Daddy taught him.

Assassins Have Starry Eyes' finale turns on the fact that the un-Helm-like hero has the stuff to stash a hunting knife in his boot and then finds the nerve to use it when it counts. He also gets the girl—and deserves her.

The AX In The MODERN WOODS

by STEVEN DICK

Over the years, many different styles of ax head have evolved for varying uses: (left to right) the standard 3$\frac{1}{2}$-pound-head single bit on a 36-inch handle, a 2$\frac{1}{2}$-pound cruiser on a 28-inch haft, an antique Puget Sound faller on a 38-inch haft, a modern 3$\frac{1}{2}$-pound swamper on a 36-inch haft, an unusual 3$\frac{1}{2}$-pound Snow and Nealley on a 28-inch haft, my twenty-year-old Hudson Bay, and a 2$\frac{1}{4}$-pound boy's ax.

KNOWING MY FORESTRY background, a friend recently asked me what the real woods pros considered the Rolex of axes. He seemed somewhat surprised when I told him the chainsaw had pretty much eliminated the need for an ax in logging. Old-time loggers used to spend evenings in the bunkhouse carefully honing their prize double bits. Modern timber beasts carry axes mainly because state forestry fire rules mandate it. These fire box axes see little or no use for months at a time. As a result, few loggers give much thought to ax quality and often buy whatever is cheapest.

Timber fallers do use a special "falling ax," bearing no resemblance to the pre-chainsaw falling axes. Instead of a long-handle double bit, the modern faller is a $3^1/_2$- to 5-pound single-bit head with a flat poll and a relatively short handle. I inquired at the local saw shop about how these axes were used and was told they were mostly mauls to drive falling wedges, that most loggers pick up falling axes to see if the poll is flat and smooth. He had never seen any of them examine the edge for sharpness.

There were once dozens of manufacturers in the United States producing scores of different ax patterns. Each area of the country had its own favored head style suited to the timber found there. In the Northwest, the legendary tool of the timber faller was the Puget Sound-pattern double-bit ax. The Puget Sound had an extra wide head with thin narrow cutting edges well suited to putting an undercut on a giant Douglas fir. A misery whip—a crosscut saw—was then used to make the backcut that actually dropped the

tree. The Puget Sound ax pattern disappeared almost overnight when chainsaws replaced axes in the big timber.

Practically every full-size double bit produced today is actually what was once known as a swamping ax. *Swamping* was a term used for cutting all the smaller saplings, brush and limbs around a large tree for safety reasons. Not only was the wide, flaring edge better suited to slashing cuts at small targets, the swamper absorbed the abuse of hitting rocks and hard objects that would have destroyed the fine ground edge of the falling ax.

Most camping and woodcraft guides are quick to point out the double-bit ax is strictly a tool for the experts. This is probably true, but I'm not entirely sure who the experts are anymore. As I mentioned earlier, our state Department of Natural Resources requires double-bit swampers as part of all logging and forestry fire-fighting tool boxes. On small forest fires, this usually works OK as crews tend to be made up of full-time foresters. Major fires require large amounts of manpower in a hurry, so timber companies normally hire contract crews comprised of assorted marginal-lifestyle types. From my point of view, this puts the expert tool in the hands of the least experienced people available. Even the U.S. Forest Service's much-touted "hotshot crews" are largely made up of college kids on break. They are tough, but not skilled ax users. Ax cuts happen, but what seems to be most common is for the inexperienced to break the handles out of the swampers.

When I was around nine or ten years old, my Dad gave me a three-quarter or "boy's" ax for use around the farm.

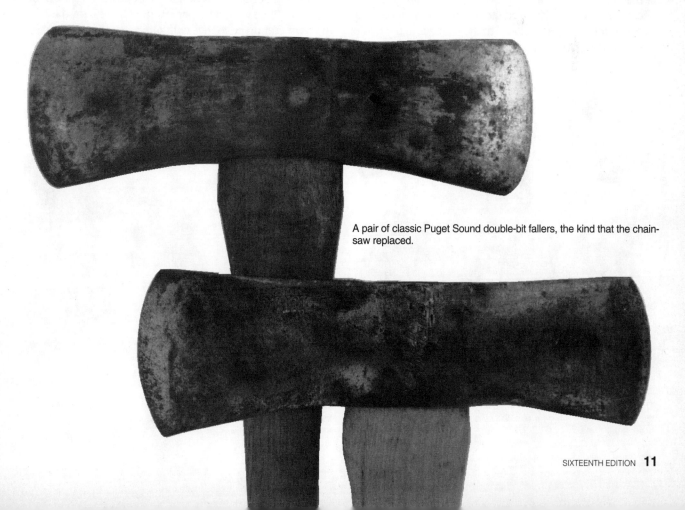

A pair of classic Puget Sound double-bit fallers, the kind that the chainsaw replaced.

Such an ax normally has a 2¼-pound single-bit head, flat poll and a 28-inch handle. Later, when I landed a summer job on a Forest Service timber cruising crew, I was handed a Collins three-quarter poll ax for sounding trees to see if they had heart rot and as a general survival tool. After college, I moved on to a private timber company assignment involving the selection of parent trees for a genetic improvement project. Each candidate had to be limbed up to above head height, and the tool was again a Swedish-made three-quarter ax. After Mount St. Helens erupted, I spent a little over a year on a wood's engineering crew putting in logging road locations through the blown-down timber. Along with a compass, 300-foot chain and plastic ribbon by the mile, our primary tools were Collins three-quarter axes. With this background, it's probably only natural that I think very highly of the three-quarter ax as a professional woodsman's tool.

Another ax closely related to the three-quarter is the classic Hudson Bay pattern. This is a slightly lighter polled-head ax, averaging around 2 pounds, with a wide, thin bit on a 28-inch handle. I bought my Norland Hudson Bay while my wife and I were on our honeymoon twenty years ago. We spent the next thirty days backpacking and camping our way around the Cascades. The Hudson Bay saw constant use building cooking and warm-up fires, and has been a standard part of our pickup equipment ever since. It has earned its keep at scores of camp sites and survived a couple of deep wilderness canoe trips. I've replaced the handle twice and the sheath three times. Other than making sure the edge is sharp, and oiling it on rare occasions, I've never babied the tool in any way. As often as not, it rode around exposed to the weather in the bed of my pickup. It's not good-looking anymore, but it's the one cutting tool I would want with me if I were dropped into any North American wilderness.

A third but less common ax pattern of three-quarter size is the cruiser double bit. I find the "cruiser" designation strange, as no timber cruiser I've known ever carried one. Possibly, things were different in the old days. The narrow 2½-pound head and its two cutting edges can be handy when a compact ax suited to serious chopping jobs is desirable. I often put mine, a Collins I picked up at a flea market, in the pickup on days when I don't feel like loading a chainsaw. More than once, I've had a tree fall across the road blocking my way into or out of a job. The chainsaw or a good sharp ax then becomes an absolute necessity.

Recently, I acquired a hybrid Snow and Nealley single-bit poll with a three-quarter-size 28-inch handle and a full 3½-pound head. I didn't realize this ax wasn't mounted on a standard 36-inch handle until it was delivered, but now that I've tried it, I think it too may soon find a home in my pickup gear. While it's a bit heavy for extended carrying, it packs a lot of chopping power in a fairly compact tool without giving up the utility of a flat poll.

A few years ago, while walking the fireline of a forest fire I had been on the previous summer, I found the head of an unmarked 3½-pound double-bit swamper. Other than a little rust, it seemed to be in basically good condition, so I took it home and mounted it on a 36-inch handle. This isn't a tool for splitting firewood, and I personally wouldn't want to use it to clear brush, but if you need to drop a tree without starting a chainsaw, it has few modern equals. Unlike the average hardware store single bit, the edges on this swamper taper from well back on the head to a thin cutting edge that will take a serious bite out of a tree with each swing.

The falling ax on top as compared to a modern double-bit swamper—the faller bit deep in big targets, the swamper's broader edge misses fewer small ones.

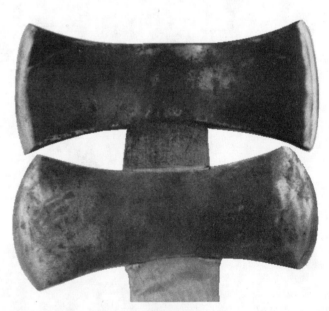

The Sager ax on the bottom looked something like the swamper above before long, hard use took 12 ounces of steel from its head. Bill Harsey thinks the Sager is one of the better old-time axes.

Getting back to the original question—what is the professional's choice in ax brands?—Collins seems to be the dominant stamp in forestry and logging supply shops around the Northwest. Most large hardware stores have gone over to the Taiwan and Chinese axes that have flooded the market. These low-cost imported axes are also finding homes in lots of firetool boxes out in the woods, though most will never see much use. Timber King is another popular brand with Northwest professionals, though I suspect this is a private distributor label. Though Snow and Nealley of Maine is often called the premium ax by camping supply catalogs, that company doesn't seem to market their product to professional users on the West Coast.

Believe it or not, the first choice of competition choppers are the speed axes made in Australia and New Zealand. Custom knifemaker Bill Harsey, who has a sideline of sharpening and polishing competition axes, tells me the Tuatahi brand from New Zealand (imported by Bailey's) are highly thought of. At $230 an ax, they had better be good! Harsey is from a logging family, so I asked him what brand of American ax he thought was best. He thinks axes are no longer very important in the woods and said there really weren't any premium brands anymore.

Of the older axes, Harsey preferred the "Sager" brand double bits. An antique store I sometimes visit usually has a box of ax heads sitting in a corner, so I pawed through the pile of rusty steel looking for a Sager. Down around the bottom, I came up with a smallish double bit I assumed was an older version of the cruiser marked "Sager, Warren Ax & Tool Co?"

At home, I cleaned the rust off the blade and found the reverse side was stamped 3½ pounds. The kitchen scale showed the ax head now weighed 28 ounces. In other

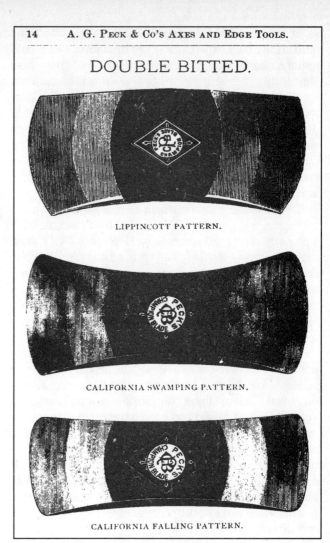

DOUBLE BITTED.

LIPPINCOTT PATTERN.

CALIFORNIA SWAMPING PATTERN.

CALIFORNIA FALLING PATTERN.

This page from an 1891 ax catalog shows three double-bit patterns. The Lippincott is basically a cruiser, the California Falling is very close to the Puget Sound, and the Swamper is a swamper.

The 2½-pound double bit is generally labeled a cruiser by ax companies, but I have never known a timber cruiser to carry one. Most carry a standard three-quarter single-bit poll ax like this Collins.

words, someone had sharpened 12 ounces of steel off this head! If my own experience is any indication, this would require years of heavy everyday use. As Harsey had warned me, the steel in the head was much harder than most modern axes and a file barely touched it. After mounting it in a new handle and spending considerable time and labor resharpening it, I found the head had been worn down to the point it no longer cut very well. The thick bevels might make for a good splitting ax, but I'm not sure that high Rockwell edge would stand up to striking the ground or other hard objects.

If there is one point on which all professional ax users will agree, it is that few if any single-bit heads come with a properly sharpened cutting edge. Everyone I've known who uses an ax on a daily basis ground and filed the edge down to a far thinner and keener profile than the factory supplied. One of the reasons I am so fond of my Hudson Bay is that twenty years of sharpening has thinned the blade to a much better edge than I could ever find on a new head.

Most single-bit axes seem to be ground more for splitting than for cutting wood. As anyone heating with wood probably knows, wood splitting is best done with a splitting maul. The first thing I do with any new ax is to take a large file or belt sander and grind a flatter bevel $1/4$- to $1/2$-inch back from the edge. I polish the file marks and burrs off the blade, and have a tool that will actually cut. I keep working the bevels back each time I sharpen the ax, and it only gets better with use—better, that is, if you stay away from the ground, rocks and knots with it. I keep a full-size Collins sharpened to a steeper edge especially for jobs that require cutting into the ground.

While I'm on the subject of ax sharpening, I might mention one bit of conventional wisdom about double-bit axes I've never found to be true. It is often said the pros sharpen one edge thin for chopping and the other thick for splitting. All the old fallers I've handled had two very thin ground edges to extend the axes' working time between resharpenings. The same goes for the swampers in all the fireboxes I've opened over the years. A double-bit head tends to be a so-so splitting tool no matter how you grind it.

Though the chainsaw has pretty much replaced them for professional use in the timber, the ax is still one of man's oldest tools. Even if they are obsolete, there is still something to say for a tool that doesn't require gas and oil, never needs a new chain, and doesn't wake up the whole county with its roar. We may not have the choices the old-time logger had, but a well-sharpened modern ax is a relatively inexpensive tool that will last its owner a lifetime. ●

Most full-size single bits come with a 3½ head like this Snow and Nealley and the Collins. The Collins serves as my ground chopping ax and is now on its third handle. The Snow and Nealley will probably be honed to a finer edge and join my old Hudson Bay as part of my permanent pick-up gear.

Probably the two best ax patterns for the average woodsman are the Hudson Bay (top) and the standard three-quarter or boy's ax. I've used both most of my life with total satisfaction. Either makes a fine wilderness survival tool.

The Functional Characteristics Of Swords

by TOM MARINGER

THERE IS NO way to get around this: The design function of a sword is to cleave human flesh and bone. It may be repugnant to contemplate, but all swords of whatever ethnic background or method of manufacture have this feature in common. They are long slivers of steel specifically designed to kill or dismember human beings in the quickest, most efficient manner possible. Any sword-like item which cannot perform this function is not a sword, but merely a visual representation of a sword.

That paragraph concluded swordmaker Maringer's "Thoughts on Swords" *in* KNIVES '95. *His thoughts on the features and construction of modern swords follow.*

Swords are distinguishable from knives not only by their size, but also by the manner in which they are used. Swords are primarily weapons, while knives are basically tools, used in everyday life for a wide variety of simple tasks. There are, of course, the so-called "fighting knives," but such knives have always been back-up or supplementary weapons. Traditionally, and for practical reasons, primary weapons have always had more range and power, such as the spear, bow, sling or sword.

Let's take a look at the seven factors that make a sword what it is, then we'll take each in turn and examine it more closely. Some of the obvious working characteristics of a sword are:

Cutting Edge: A working sword must be able to cut, deeply and often, keep its edge and cut some more. This is basically a function of the steel used, the heat-treatment, and the edge geometry.

Weight: A sword must have some weight to it in order to be effective, but the weight should not be excessive.

Balance: The importance of balance is far greater in a sword than in a knife. Different types of swords will be balanced differently, depending on the intended fighting style. Balance affects the ease with which the sword can be moved during use and also determines the location of the "sweet spot"—the point of maximum cutting power on the blade.

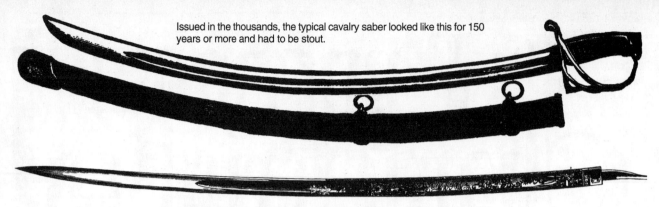

Issued in the thousands, the typical cavalry saber looked like this for 150 years or more and had to be stout.

Purveyors cataloged blades alone, which enables us to see the forged tang, normally peened over the pommel. (From a Schuyler, Hartley & Graham catalog.)

Grip: The handle must be shaped and/or textured so the orientation of the blade can be known by feel alone, and so the handle will not slip from the user's grip in use.

Construction: The sword must be assembled in such a way that it will withstand repeated hard usage without the blade breaking off at the guard, the handle flying apart, or the steel becoming permanently bent.

Scabbard: A sword without a scabbard is a danger to the owner and is susceptible to accidental damage. A good blade should never be purchased without provision for carrying and/or storage.

Workmanship: A sword may have all of the above features and still be poorly made. Such a sword may be "practical" in a utilitarian sense, but it lacks beauty. The mystique of swords is caught up with concepts such as honor, chivalry and courage. Some degree of workmanship is necessary to invoke a pride of ownership and an appreciation of beauty, otherwise the sword is no better than a machete, thrown in the corner of the garage to rust.

Without all of these seven functional characteristics, a so-called sword becomes either useless, dangerous or not a sword at all. Each deserves closer scrutiny.

Cutting Edge

The cutting edge is what it's all about, where the real action takes place. To be effective, a sword must be *sharp*. The edge must be capable of cutting through flesh and bone without dulling appreciably, thus it must be *hard*. The blade must be able to withstand the shock of a full-power blow without breaking, thus it must be *tough*. The edge must be able to penetrate into the cut with a minimum of drag, thus it must be *thin*. Still, it should do so without curling or chipping the edge, thus it must be *stout*.

If these features seem to you to be mutually exclusive, then you are learning the lesson that must be understood by all aspiring swordmakers: Tradeoffs and compromises must sometimes be made.

Steel heat-treated to its maximum hardness will be too brittle. At its maximum toughness, it will be too soft. A blade made as stout as it can be will be too thick to cut efficiently and will be of more use as a crowbar. A blade

ground ultra-thin for cutting ease will be too floppy in use and susceptible to severe edge damage.

The "perfect" sword will have a blade hard enough to take and hold a good edge, yet tough enough to withstand severe abuse without breaking, chipping or taking a permanent bend. It should be thin enough to have some flexibility and a minimum of drag when cutting, yet stiff enough for stoutness and control. The ideal blade would have a combination of all these features in a union that provides symmetry and utility of design.

Weight

Swords are cutting weapons that depend partly on momentum to move the blade through the cut. Still, anyone who has handled some custom swords knows there are some pretty chunky ones being made out there. I'm responsible for a few of those myself. Excessive weight does nothing for the usefulness of a sword, merely making it harder to maneuver and less effective in cutting. The most common problem is the use of steel blade stock that is too thick. The second most common weight problem is the use of furniture (guard, pommel, etc.) that is overly massive.

When I first began making swords, I contemplated steel thickness for use in the blades. I fell into the trap that has snared many would-be swordmakers and assumed that a blade five times as long as a knife should likewise be thicker. (Maybe not five times thicker, but thicker, nonetheless.) Some of my earliest swords were made with blades as thick as .375-inch (about 9.5mm)! This makes for a very heavy blade that has the feel of a lead pipe. I now use .250-inch (about 6mm) steel as the maximum thickness for sword blades, with most falling in the range between .160- (about 4mm) and .200-inch (about 5mm). Steel thinner than .125-inch (about 3mm) should probably not be used for sword blades due to its lack of stiffness.

I even had one client who wanted to order a sword from me and specified the blade thickness as 1.125 inches! After consulting with him to be sure that it was not an error and determining that he really did want a sword with

a blade more than 1-inch thick, I promptly turned down the commission.

The proper weight range for swords should be between $1^1/_4$ pounds (about 600 grams) for a small sword (that's a type, not a description) up to a maximum of about 6 pounds (about 2700 grams) for a very large two-handed sword. Most swords will fall in the range between 2 and 4 pounds (1000-2000 grams).

Balance

The easiest way to understand the "balance" of a sword is simply to find its center of gravity by balancing it on a finger. Most swords will have this balance point on the blade somewhere in front of the guard. The exact distance to that point from the guard is one of the most useful ways of describing a sword to someone who can't see it. A very common range is for the balance point to be from 2 to 4 inches bladeward of the guard.

In general, a sword designed strictly as a thrusting weapon (such as the epee) should have the balance point relatively close to the guard. This allows the strength of the wrist to move the point around with comparative ease and quickness. On the other hand, a sword designed solely for cutting (such as the darn-do) should have the balance farther forward for increased momentum and "tracking." Dual-use cut-and-thrust weapons would have the balance point in an intermediate location.

In making a sword, the balance is primarily a function of the basic design of the sword: the relationship between the mass of the blade and handle. However, it can be altered somewhat by the adjustment of the size and weight of the pommel. This is commonly found in the longer bladed thrusting weapons such as the rapier, in which a heavy pommel is used to offset a longer blade and still provide acceptable wrist action.

Balance also affects the location of the so-called "sweet spot," one of the two primary nodes of vibration. This is primarily of significance for cutting rather than thrusting-type weapons.

Many of us who played baseball are familiar with that magical spot on the bat called the sweet spot, which is in fact a vibration node. When a baseball is struck exactly on the sweet spot, there is almost no vibration induced in the bat, while the ball sails an unusually long distance. Swords share some of the same characteristics as baseball bats, including the sweet spot.

The significance of the nodes of vibration are dual. Ideally, the controlling hand should be holding the sword at one node, while the target is struck with the other. In this way, a minimum of energy is absorbed by the vibration of the blade, and a maximum is transferred to the target through the edge of the blade.

The nodes of vibration of any sword may easily be found by holding the sword by the handle with the point straight up toward the sky, then striking the pommel with the heel of the other hand. You can see the blade vibrate and should note the place where it seems to stay still. This is your sweet spot. Likewise, you will be able to feel the vibration in your other hand—move your hand up and down the handle until the vibration is at a minimum. Now you have the ideal position for your controlling hand for that sword.

Increasing the weight of the pommel will move the handle node downward toward the pommel, while lightening it will move it forward toward the guard, without

Even so grand an ensemble as this mameluke style by Wilkinson would contain, below the ornament, the time-tested construction.

Serious swordsmen fussed over the hang of their swords as dandies over their lapels—this was a traveler's outfit.

appreciably changing the location of the other sweet spot—the point of maximum cutting power. Similarly, a blade that grows wider and heavier towards the point will have a sweet spot farther from the guard, while a thin tapering blade will have one that is farther back, closer to the handle.

Grip

The handle of a sword is much more than merely a place for embellishment or a canvas for the engraver's art. The warrior's hand upon the grip of a sword constitutes the necessary link between flesh and steel. The handle of a sword (sometimes called the "hilt") should provide a non-slip gripping surface even when wet and must allow the orientation of the blade to be sensed by feel alone.

The handle may be made of any of a number of materials, so long as a rough enough surface is provided, yet it needs to be smooth enough for quick changing of grip style. A classic technique is the wrapped handle. The wrapping may be of silk braid in the Japanese style or of twisted wire in the European style, but in either case it provides a smooth yet roughened surface for the hand to contact when gripping the handle. Wood, ivory or horn materials may also be used, but care should be taken to see that the handle design is such that they will not slip from the grasp in a moment of need.

The user must know by feel alone exactly where the edge is, so lathe-turned handles should never be used on a sword unless the shape is modified with respect to the blade orientation. Handles for double-edged blades will generally have handles of a roughly elliptical cross-section, while single-edge blades should have grips with a slightly "egg-shaped" cross-section, having the small side toward the edge.

Handle furniture almost always includes a guard (sometimes also called a "hilt") and a pommel (also known as the "butt"). The guard is the fitting that separates the handle from the blade and is almost always found on a fighting sword. Its function is double, being designed both to keep the user's hands from sliding forward onto his own blade and to block an opponent's blade from cutting the user's hands. The guard should be made of a material sturdy and thick enough to prevent an opponent's blade from cutting through it. The pommel functions as a stop at the handle's end to prevent loss of the sword in combat. It also may be used as a counterweight to help balance a sword design.

Construction

Basically, any sword-like item being offered for sale as a sword should be soundly constructed so that it will not fall to pieces the first time it is used. The construction of a sword is fundamentally a description of the way the handle is attached to the blade. There are several common methods of construction for real swords, and they are here described by the shape and function of the tang. The blade

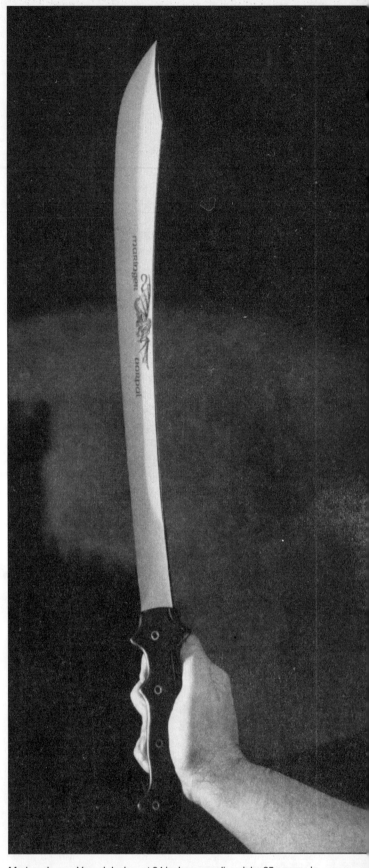

Maringer's own Vorpal design, at 24 inches overall, weighs 25 ounces in full-tang all-purpose design. Blackjack's factory in Effingham, Illinois, makes 1000 knives, but just five Vorpals, a day. The Cutlery Shoppe sells them. (Cutlery Shoppe photo)

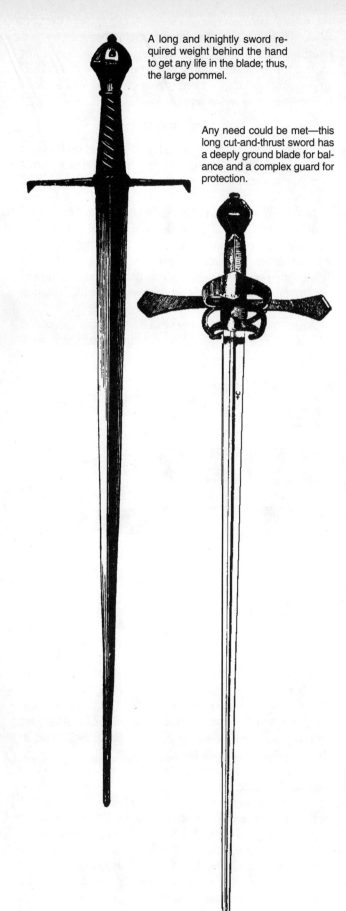

A long and knightly sword required weight behind the hand to get any life in the blade; thus, the large pommel.

Any need could be met—this long cut-and-thrust sword has a deeply ground blade for balance and a complex guard for protection.

tang is that portion of the steel blade which is part of or within the handle.

The commonly seen types of sword construction include stick and through tangs, full tangs, the Japanese type and some hybrids thereof. The sword may either be a permanent assembly or may be so made that it is possible to disassemble it into its constituent pieces for cleaning, refitting or repairs. Each style of construction has its own merits.

The stick tang is shorter than the handle. It is not screwed or pinned, but generally just "stuck" there with glue or resin, forming a permanent assembly. This is a common style of knife construction, but is generally considered unsuitable for swordmaking due to its reliance on the adhesive substance. The only ethnic swords which are commonly of stick-tang construction are the Malay Krisses. The merit? It's quick, but it is not recommended for those pursuing modern swordmaking.

The through tang literally goes "through" the handle and emerges on the pommel end. On many older European swords, the tang end was hammered (peened) over, forming a permanent assembly. A more modern method is to thread the end of the tang and screw a pommel onto it, resulting in a takedown style. This is a commonly seen style of construction and, if well done, results in a sturdy, usable sword.

More common as a method of knife construction, the full-tang style features a wide, flat tang that is visible all the way around the handle of the finished sword. It has the advantage of extreme strength, but allows the maker less freedom in handle shape and texture. The handle slabs of a full-tang sword must be attached more positively than would be necessary for an ordinary knife, or the shock and vibration of a full-power blow could pop the scales right off. Generally, the full tang is used for permanent assemblies only. It's commonly seen in some Middle Eastern and Russian sword designs. This style can be reliably used to create a fine weapon.

The Japanese-tang style is germane to the famous fighting swords of the Samurai. It features a very wide tang that extends only partway into the handle and is secured by one or two pegs whose ends are exposed on the surface of the handle. This is the traditional method of constructing a Japanese-style sword and, when correctly done, is extremely reliable in battle, yet still amenable to full takedown for cleaning or storage.

This style of construction depends on the strength of the handle for its integrity, therefore the handles are almost always wrapped, either with braid or wire, in order to give them the strength and flexibility necessary to withstand the forces encountered in use. Highly recommended for modern makers of custom swords, this style is demanding of the maker's time and talent. It is an integrated method in which each part has a definite purpose.

There is a catch-all group of tangs that considers the merits of some construction methods either unavailable to

the ancients or are not covered by the above classifications.

My personal favorite hybrid style is what I call a "modified Japanese-tang" construction, in which the wide, short tang is pinned to a "toggle" rather than to the handle. This toggle is threaded internally and anchors a screw inserted through the pommel to secure the sword. Other hybrid styles might include a welded all-steel construction, partial full tangs, wrapped full tangs and many others.

Scabbard

I include the scabbard as a necessary part of a sword because without it a real sword is simply too dangerous to have lying around. You can't carry it without inadvertently cutting something, and you can't just leave it sitting in a corner for fear that someone will hurt himself or others. Remember, a sword is *never* unloaded, nor does it ever run out of ammunition. A wise person would never carry a pistol with a loaded chamber, the hammer cocked, and

blade when inserting the sword. It should be so strong that even a strong blow on the scabbarded weapon will not expose the blade. Finally, it should be made so that the all-important edge of the sword is protected and kept at maximum sharpness while scabbarded.

Workmanship

It may be true that as a weapon of war the sword is all but obsolete. Still, if we look at the history and function of war in early societies, we can see the practical value of workmanship.

In the old days, rulers kept only small forces of permanent military troops. Then in times of war, an army would be raised from the populace. Young men would be drafted into service, handed a cheap sword or spear, given a few days of training, and sent into battle. Imagine the terror of being sent into conflict with an unfamiliar weapon out of some storeroom.

Now imagine the fellow who has thought ahead and has purchased a high-quality sword that suits him well.

When bronze was the metal, the best choice was the full tang—these are the remnants of Celtic Bronze Age weapons.

the safety off! Yet that is exactly the constant state of readiness for battle that characterizes a good, sharp sword. In this sense, the scabbard is the "safety" on a sword. The scabbard allows the sword to be stored or carried from place to place without danger and without damage to the sword, especially the edge.

Scabbard is defined here as: A sheath or covering for a sword blade made of a stiff material and capable of rendering the sword "safe" for storage or transport, yet from which the sword may quickly be drawn at need.

Notice that a "scabbard" is made of a stiff material, as opposed to a "sheath" which may be soft. Soft sheaths such as leather do not necessarily render the sword safe as they may be cut through too easily. A scabbard is easily distinguished from a "case," which commonly encloses the entire sword and must be opened in some way before the sword may be drawn.

A good scabbard will allow the sword to be drawn freely and quickly, and yet will not permit the sword to fall out if turned upside-down. It should be so stiff that it is impossible to accidentally pierce the scabbard with the

He now has more self-confidence; he knows his abilities and his equipment. He now has the mental stamina and pride to prevail on the battlefield and get home upright.

To someone facing a life-and-death conflict, the cost of weapons is immaterial. Such a person will want the best possible weapon, no matter the price. The value of workmanship is in the result. A fine sword not only works, but inspires pride and confidence by its beauty and grace, its embellishment or clean flowing design.

It is my experience that when a person seeks out a custom swordmaker to order that special weapon, the customer wants a *real* sword. They are looking for a true weapon, not merely a sword look-alike. Many customers are embarrassed about this desire and apologetic when explaining their wants, but it is a visceral striving for something *real* in a world that is quickly becoming only a video simulation of reality. Wrapping your hand around the grip of a well-made sword is a "grounding" experience. Heaven may await, but we yet dwell in a material and strife-torn world. ●

SOG Micro Tool Clip—a handy size and effective plier jaws. Open file blade is also a good-sized scewdriver.

Our writer never found the end of...

A Perplexity of POCKET TOOLS

MY INTRODUCTION TO the pocket tool knife was long ago when I first entered the realm of scouting. I was a Cub Scout at nine and went through the wonderful world of Boy Scouting and Explorer Scouting until World War II took my attention. My "Scout" knife was given to me by a cousin.

This was somewhat frowned on, as Boy Scouts looked down on Cub Scouts in those days, and for me to carry one of their knives was taboo. But I did, and in summer camp one July I even plaited a red, white and blue lanyard for it. If I had not lost it, that Remington Official Boy Scout knife would be worth about a hundred dollars. I think my sister, who was into girl scouting, swiped it when I went off to war.

The utility knife, as these three- or four-bladed equal-ended pocketknives are described, had been around in one form or another for many years. The idea of a folding tool knife must go back to the Roman Empire as broken-tip jackknives have been found in the ruins, and what is a broken-tipped jackknife but a mishandled tool?

The knives with broken points must run in the billions, as men who carried pocketknives—and up until the 1950s, most men did—often found themselves needing a screwdriver or small pry tool, and blade tips were broken with regularity. Even my dear wife, a woman who should know better, was once seen prying open a stout cardboard box with a sterling silver fruit knife that was valued in the high three figures, but happened to be handy. It's a common death for a fine knife, prying with it. I caught her in time and we sold the knife.

Utility knives burgeoned in the 19th century when folding knives of many styles included leather punching blades and screwdrivers. Soon other blade forms became popular with can openers, corkscrews, files and dozens of other specialty tool shapes. The utility knife business took a turn for the better when the Swiss Master Cutlers Association was formed in 1890. The purpose was to gather a group of highly skilled knifemakers who would design and manufacture knives for the Swiss army. Up until that time, the Swiss government was buying odd lots from the makers in Solingen, Germany.

The first Swiss Army knife was a product of the fertile mind of Karl Elsener, assisted by the technology of thirty local cutlers working under him. He produced the Soldiers' knife in 1891 and followed that with the Officers' knife in 1897. The Soldiers' knife contained the bare-bones blades that all troops needed—a good spear blade, a stout screwdriver (for tightening ski screws), a leather punch (for adding holes to equipment straps) and a can opener. This knife was part of every Swiss soldier's kit. The handle was wood, a quite plain but serviceable knife.

The Officers' model had to be more elaborate and added to the four basic blades (officers were on skis, too!)—the corkscrew for informal wining while dining and a small blade called the erasing blade. In those days, orders were handwritten in ink. Once down, any correc-

Prior to the onset of perplexity, Rychetnik's Victorinox Craftsman was about as complex as he got.

tion entailed scraping, and a sharp blade that would do it perfectly was called for, as mistakes were frequent, I'm told. Especially after using the corkscrew.

Both the Soldiers' knife and the Officers' knife became quite popular outside the Swiss army. The Elseners added more models of the Officers' style, and in 1909 they added the Swiss White Cross to the red scale material to identify their superior product from the flood of imitators, mainly from Germany. The Solingen cutlers were very imitative and eager.

The world-famous trademark name Victorinox was added to the Swiss company's growing list of cutlery in 1921 when stainless steel replaced the high carbon steel blades, and in Europe such steel had the common name of Inox. This term, added to Karl Elsener's mother's given name of Victoria, has lasted to this day as the official trademark of the Swiss Army knife business run by the Elseners at their plant in Ibach.

Since being the sole provider of issue knives to the Swiss army had proven more than profitable, and others sought to profit, the Swiss government, in fairness, split the business with another Swiss pocket cutlery firm producing similar knives, the Wenger firm. Both of them do very well, but I'm told the Victorinox label is the best selling and most recognizable knife trademark in the world.

With everything from student's pocketknives to elaborate multi-bladed sportsmen's knives in production, the Swiss Army knife idea became a symbol of Swiss precision and quality, and no traveler passing through Switzerland was truly equipped if he did not purchase one of these for himself and perhaps another for a son or good friend. Never cheap but always in good taste, the red-handled white-crossed pocketknives became indispensable to many and a staple in every airport shop. I used to go positively "ape" in Hoffritz stores as there were so many styles I wanted to own. It's an expensive hobby!

I have been a Swiss Army knife collector and user for nearly half a century, and find them (one has to be selective!) a most useful carry-around pocket tool. There is a Swiss Army Knife Society headquartered in San Diego whose publication regularly features an article contributed by some user on how the Swiss Army knife saved his bacon, day, or life, whatever.

They are most useful, and the idea of a very portable pocket tool kit has spawned dozens of similar devices—some quite useful, others just attractive, some just junque.

One of the factors facing any user of the utility knife is that, as rugged as the best of them are built, they still lack the beef to do workaday jobs on the ranch, farm or shop. Not too much torque can be applied or damage will result. And the size of the largest of them still leaves much to be desired for the leverage offered. Don't get me wrong. My bacon has been saved dozens of times by the screw I could tighten, the wire I could cut and strip, or the item I

(Above) The Original Leatherman delivered twelve tools in stainless steel and made the market happen.

(Above) Jimmy Jack Liberacki takes his Super Leatherman tool on horseback every day; the pliers and cutters are large enough for wire. (Hamblin photo)

(Left) The Leatherman Super Tool is now in center stage, providing a pliers and ten locking blades.

(Below) Now it's Leatherman's PST II, which includes tough-looking scissors and convenient size.

could snip from the print media with a handy Swiss Army knife.

A Wenger I once used had a pair of pliers on it that saved a fishing day. I have seen dedicated fly-fishers working in wilderness situations tying just the fly the local trout anticipated; Ike Walton had the Swiss Army knife blade jammed into a eye-high branch, the pliers of his "Craftsman" model tightly held shut by a rubber band, and a fly hook snugly grasped in this rig close to his eye for just that bit of color that success demanded. This fisher told me in the future he will carry two SAKs as he really preferred the fine scissors for trimming his feathery handiwork, but had to use his nail clippers instead. The magnifier on some SAKs gives an oldster like me a chance to see what we are doing when messing with flies and tiny hooks, or extracting a sliver, or reading directions on maps.

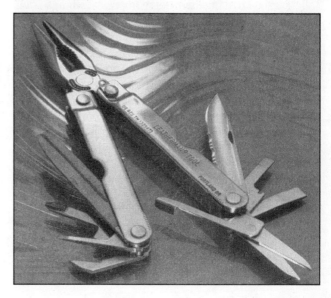

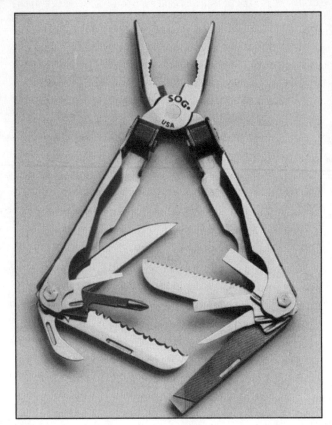

The author found SOG's Tool Clip handy for working on a stereo speaker system.

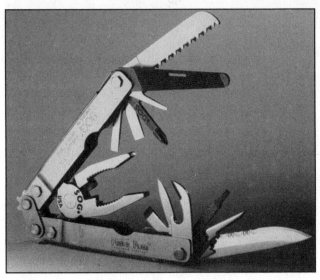

First there was the SOG Tool Clip, now SOG's Para Tool has a plier head that folds and nine other blades in a 4-inch package.

SOG pumped up their line with the Power Plier—nine blades and a pliers that grabs hard and holds hard.

My wife has an SAK in her purse at all times as she can't live without the scissors or the file. I have just about all the models made in recent years and find them a collector's delight. I carry a Champion on a lanyard snap hanging into my right pocket from a belt loop. Very handy tool, I say.

The limits of pocketknife tools were reached when folks started breaking them doing impossible things—and complaining about the knife. I once left my corkscrew "blade" in a bottle of Napa Valley Merlot when I couldn't free the cork after a waitress had failed, and with my red-handled SAK attached, they took the bottle to the kitchen where Gargantua, the sculleryman, had a try. He broke off the corkscrew and then knocked the bottle off the work table, leaving me with a dilemma. They couldn't fix my SAK nor did they have another bottle of that vintage. We got the dinners on the house, but it wasn't such a good trade.

I see corkscrews on knives that are the property of mere children—there should be a requirement that no corkscrew be issued to anyone under 21 or so. I know, I know: W.C. Fields once lost his corkscrew and nearly starved to death, and that his life would have been made more comfortable if one of the lads now carrying corkscrewed pocketknives came by.

Tools of pocketable size lately have been designed and created by a number of cutlery and hand tool makers, each hoping theirs would be the next hot item on the gift and gimmick market. I have, over the years, rounded up a few of the many available today. I have tested each one of the described pocket tools in my own feeble way around the house, and during hunting and fishing adventures.

I have also submitted some of them to friends in the field who would give the pocket tool a real workout in their workaday situation. I won't mention who they are, as they asked that I not expose them to dire threats. But to establish them as bona fide hard workers, one is a rancher in the piney hill country of East Texas, one is a nursery-man here in the Coachella Valley, and another is a fellow living in the bush of Alaska whose everyday life is one rugged trial after another—he's a pilot and fishing guide. He lives in a log house and considers the knife an essential tool.

My criteria to discuss these pocket tools in a knife publication as learned as KNIVES '96 is they must, somewhere, have a knife blade. I don't think I found all the pocket tools that possess a blade of sorts, as every catalog that comes in the mailbox has offered another type, but I do think I am covering the more popular styles and makes.

I will not recite word for word what the field testers have told me, as some of the comments are still not able to be entered into the U.S. Mails. My testers were pithy, to say the least, and more than one was bitten by a bad design and told me in no uncertain terms what they thought as blood ran down their body. If nothing else, a pocket tool should be safe and, incidentally, perform some task.

The pocket tool idea comes in various forms, some not knife-like at all. The photos illustrating some of the styles offered will show the interesting designs that have become successful. I did not find one style of pocket tool that received four stars from all the testers and myself. Taste and other personal needs have a lot to do with selection.

The most unlikely pocket tool (remember they all are supposed to have blades somewhere) was a black plastic-handled ZAP 18-in-One All Purpose Survival Tool from

Zona Alta Products in Miami, Florida. The folks there said it was designed in England, made in Taiwan, and sold by them only. I hated it on sight, but being a fair guy I did pack it around for a week and found women of all ages eyeballing my sexual zone as it appeared I was in heat. It is bulky. It had some good ideas built in.

The survival handful includes a typical spear-point knife blade, compass, fish hook remover, can opener, cap lifter, eating fork, magnifier, wire stripper, and (would you believe) a flashlight, telescope and whistle! There is even a hiding place which contains some feeble fish hooks and line, but which would be a wonderful place to hide a $20 bill for emergencies and your ID sticker. I can't see a time when all those things would come to play, because if you are in that much trouble, you need a heli-copter!

As I said, I didn't like it much, but when I showed it to my wife, she went wild over it and said she wanted it! The idea of a flashlight and whistle plus the folding telescope for seeing miscreants at a distance, no doubt, appealed to her. She carries an SAK with a few female tools in her purse, but she added this ZAP to her "outdoor" equipage. The other testers refused to deal with it, but, remember, half of us humans are women.

I am always suspicious of tiny compasses. All compasses are a problem and of little help if you have no idea where you are or where safety is. I tested the tiny compass against three performers from my kit. It was within 15 degrees of my $250 Brunton professional compass, within 10 degrees of the Leupold and Stevens Foresters' compass I carried on patrol in Alaska years ago, and right on target with the Swiss Army Recta DP-6 backpackers compass. Not bad at all. But using the compass in the ZAP is frustrated by the opposite side of the tool having anything but a flat surface for placement. I told her that

(Above) The Gerber Multi-Plier tool fully opened showing two knife blades (both serrated and regular edge), excellent file, screwdriver and lanyard ring. Note the stubby Phillips-head screwdriver which serves to function the Gerber Tool Kit.

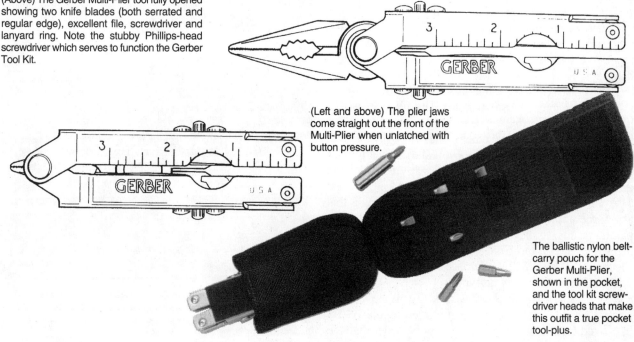

(Left and above) The plier jaws come straight out the front of the Multi-Plier when unlatched with button pressure.

The ballistic nylon belt-carry pouch for the Gerber Multi-Plier, shown in the pocket, and the tool kit screw-driver heads that make this outfit a true pocket tool-plus.

when she got that lost to use the whistle or scan the horizon with the telescope. She normally can find a shopping mall without any optical help.

One of the most popular pocket tools is the Gerber Multi-Plier and Tool Kit. This is a very complete system, as one would expect from Gerber, costing $60 for the basic model. As with anything else in today's world, you get what you pay for. The standard Multi-Plier has two knives (one a serrated blade), an excellent file, Phillips screwdriver, flat-head screwdriver, bottle cap lifter—all sprouting from the handles of the powerful pliers and wire cutter. The supplemental tool kit snaps onto the Phillips screwdriver and offers six other "bits" for driving screws. A ballistic nylon case is offered, and the handle has a 3-inch ruler inscribed.

The tool opens easily. Pushing side buttons drops the pliers into play. In use, the tool offered no hazards to the user, which is not the case with other pocket tools I tested. My nurseryman said he had his Gerber "for years" and carried it in the belt pouch when he worked and in the motorcycle saddle bag when he traveled. He rated it his favorite of all.

His long usage brings up another factor in pocket tool use—you must have it with you to make it work. Too many such gadgets come from the Christmas stockings and end up in some drawer, never doing what they were designed to do.

Folks who use tools daily will always have their belt pouch filled with their favorites, and no all-in-one pocket tool will suffice. Electricians, linemen and installers know their tools like old friends. The electronics repair guys carry an expensive attache case filled to the brim with the best of just the right tool. These kits cost up to $500 and offer precision tools for their jobs. The kind of people who should carry pocket tools are those who do not have this need.

The Gerber was highly rated by my other testers and top rated by the nurseryman, who said he uses it all the time and it once saved him from being stranded when he repaired a motorcycle breakdown. I liked it very much, but....

Brainstorms of Skokie, Illinois, offers the fourteen-tool Pocket Mechanic, a plastic-handled flat-knife tool with a black nylon pouch that "appears" to be an answer. The serrated blade and the two other blades were fine, as was the saw, but the tool was just too small to do many plier jobs, wire cutting, or even much screwdriving, since the drivers are on the ends of a serrated-edged knife in one case and on a small cap lifter in another. My feeling is that any force applied would fold the blades, perhaps with painful results. Brainstorm would *not* send me a sample to offer my testers, but I did get to see and use a Pocket Mechanic offered me by a furnace repairman. He said it was just OK—a gift from his wife.

The Leatherman Pocket Survival Tools have been around for ages and are being improved regularly. By improved I mean new models seem much better than the

older styles. All my testers fell madly in love with the new Super Leatherman. It is a very well-made and easy-to-use tool, for sure. But so is $70! Folded into two handles that then capture the plier/wire cutter head, the item opens easily and offers all the contained tools both safely and easily—not so with many others tested.

In a fine leather pouch, this stainless steel gem offers full-sized pliers with combination needlenose and standard jaws with wire cutter, three screwdrivers (one small enough to repair eyeglass screws), Phillips head, awl, can and bottle opener, file (that works!), saw for metal and wood, and regular 2½-inch knife blade. The handle has an inscribed 8-inch ruler that would get service at many of my trout expeditions. The Original Leatherman goes for $38 and offers twelve tool items, again a rugged tool.

The Texas rancher, who uses a pocketknife a dozen times a day on his chores, loved the Super Tool. He called it a one-hand tool, as it was that easy to use. He carried it

The ZAP 18-In-One kit offers eighteen functions, including storage space.

The author's wife fell in love with ZAP 18-in-One knife for its blade, whistle and flashlight, as shown. The ZAP also contains a telescope to identify suspicious characters, a spoon for frozen yogurt, and compass for finding the way home from the shopping center.

Stephanie Klein snips cactus needles with Chinese surgical scissors that seem to cut everything and cost about $5. Why cut cactus? They snag people here.

The author's wife trims salmon steaks with heavy-duty game shears—more efficient than knives for many tasks.

for several weeks without any other tool in his saddlebag or Jeep. He has now abandoned his Buck belt knife for the Super.

In the testing, he installed a stereo in his office, serviced hand weapons on his pistol range, rescued a partially paralyzed cow from a barbed wire/bramble ravine, and found jobs around the ranch house and barn that, prior to packing the Super Tool, he would have had to return to with other tools.

"This is the only tool that I have tested that I can place into immediate service with one hand—all the tools are readily accessed with my fingers. It was the right size to do real work, and after a day on my belt I found I was completely unaware of it being there. The nose on the pliers was of near surgical precision, and I could use it to hold a suture needle when I repaired one of my torn cows. The knife blades were large enough, very sharp and did not fall short of any task I tried.

"The tiny screwdriver was ideal for adjusting the sights on the S&W revolvers we have at our pistol range. The only suggestion I would make to improve this Super Tool would be to point the awl for serious leather work, which I did quickly on the tool room grinder. Anyone who uses this tool for a day will find he can't live without it—at least not on a ranch."

The Alaskan bush pilot loved it, too, but felt it was rather large to carry in the pocket and too cold when worn on the belt outside. He preferred the Super Tool to the Original, as every other tester did, but said $70 was a bit pricey. I am certain the Super Tool will supplant the Original in years to come, the $20 difference absorbed by those who need quality.

SOG Specialty Knives offers several models of SOG pocket tools, covering a wide price range as well as utility. I tested the SOG ParaTool at $60, the Tool Clip at $80, and

the Micro Tool Clip at $50, and came up with some across-the-board comments of the same kind from all my testers.

The belt-clip idea may sell the Tool Clip tools, but everyone attempting to wear this device on his belt said they could have skipped that idea. It fit none of their belts, being too small and accommodating only 1 1/4-inch belts or narrower. My guys wore He-Man 1 3/4- to 2-inch belts. And even on their belts they all found the tool clip was uncomfortable to wear all day and offered another thing to catch on brush or outer wear, and, in two cases, poke into their tender ribs.

I found the clip idea fine only because it allowed the tool to be fastened to a pocket of my camera bag and never be lost. One man clipped the Micro to his shirt pocket. SOG offers a nylon carry belt case that would solve the carry problem, so I sent along a nylon belt case with a Velcro flap fastener. The testers liked it.

My bush pilot said he would carry the Para Tool only, as too much stuff hauled tends to make an airplane fall from the sky. I like the Micro because my photo repair needs are met by this small and well-finished tool. Very handy. The fellows who needed a heavier pliers and larger knife blade were not happy with the small-sized tools. The razor-sharp serrated blade was rated tops by all, though. There is a definite appeal for the Micro, for sure, but both Tool Clips lacked the power for heavy work.

The SOG Para Tool was a more serious device, but the testers felt it was still not in the blue-collar class with either the Leatherman Super Tool or the Gerber. The bush pilot said that he would carry the Para instead of the pair of 5-inch Vice Grips that have filled his back pocket for the past thirty years. He finds the variety of tool heads or blades helpful when doing work on snowmobiles and airplanes away from home.

The Texas cow chaser said the individual blades were

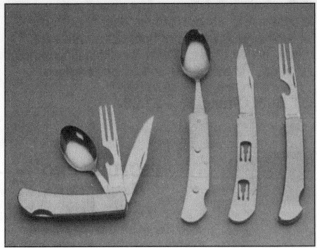

The author likes a key-chain-sized adjustable wrench from Sporty's and—naturally—some very portable eating tools.

too difficult to open. He was also unhappy that the big and little Tool Clips could not cut barbed wire and other fence wire as he has to do several times a week. Holding the tool in the wrong way, he punctured his thumb while cutting single-strand barbed wire with the Para. The other tools tucked into the handle bit him.

He rated the serrated blade very high, but too short. The saw was too short, too.

"Here we have a tool made for convenience about one inch too short in many ways to be that," he said. The nurseryman said it was OK, but he would stay with the Gerber. The Para Tool's flexible pliers head was rated an excellent idea by the rancher, and he said it was just large enough to handle fence wire tasks, too. Every tool had something good.

Now, I want you to know that A.G. Russell and I have been friends since the early 1970s, and there isn't a better knife man in the country. My kitchen is fully equipped with A.G. Russell kitchen cutlery. However, the A.G. Russell Toolbox is a good idea that went awry in order to maintain compactness. So we're not going to discuss it further.

The Bud-K 11-in-1 Master Tool, a $13 copy of a better tool, was poorly made (in China) and did not elicit any comment from anyone that could be printed. Crude, almost unusable, junk. Again, one gets what one pays for. Bud-K's $28 Pocket Toolchest was a poor copy of the SOG Tool Clips, and for that reason none of my people would test it. Everything can be made cheaper, and since we are talking about carry tools to save a job in an emergency, junk doesn't make it.

I want to mention several items I received too late to pass around to the boys in the field, but that impressed me as quality goods. Sporty's Tool Shop in Batavia, Ohio, offers a lot of great tools, and in the pocket tool department the interchangeable-blade pocket knife ($90) offers lock-blade styles of clip-point, drop-point, saw and fillet. They are a tad small for most work—3 inches—but again

they may fit someone's exact needs. A leather belt pouch comes with it.

A made-in-Japan wrench-knife in stainless steel has a super-sharp blade, a file with screwdriver head, and $1/2$-inch monkey wrench, and is even more useful as it has a key ring! From my viewpoint, this little tool would fit the needs of a lot of guys I know, for $25.

And finally, Shorty's offers the most important tools of all—eating tools, made of stainless in Japan. There used to be all sorts of clip-together knife/fork/spoon combos made for picnics and camping. I don't see them any more as plastic throwaway "silver" has replaced the metal eating tool. I love to eat, and one set, which snaps into a knife-sized and -shaped article, would be my choice for "emergency gear"—easy to clean and ready for soup, steak or pie.

I started this piece knowing I couldn't and wouldn't cover all the pocket tools. I have had for too long a time in my collection one of those U.S. Army Camillus Utility knives. I traded some GI for it in Korea too many years ago. A.G. still offers them for about $16, and they do the job as well as any. Spear-point blade, can opener, cap lifter/screwdriver, and leather punch—sort of the U.S. version of the Swiss Soldiers' knife. The shackle allows a lanyard to be attached, making it a never-lose knife, one of my sore points with good knives. My knife losses would make a fine collection.

There's another factor in this tool-knife thing. We could call it the love bug, maybe. To illustrate: My wife was in a quandary about what to put in the traditional Christmas stocking we still hang from the mantle on December 24th. I know I am nearly seventy, but I still believe in Tooth Fairies, Friday the 13th, and Santa Claus—and they have never let me down. Having seen me test and play with a dozen or more pocket tools and knives during the months before the holiday season, she had too many ideas. But she had what the distaff side calls Women's Intuition, and I was surprised.

I did play with a lot of tools, and read and edited the

SWISS KNIFE SANITATION

People often ask me how to keep the SAK-style knives clean. They, with all their machinery, offer fine lodging for all sorts of crud, lint, plain old dirt and more. I open all my blades and pour a tad of dish washing soap into the guts and then run very hot water into the knife for a while. This removes most of the debris. A toothpick and Kleenex will get what remains out of the blade spaces. Rinse in very hot water and turn upside-down to dry hot in a dish basket. I lube with fine gun oil like CLP Break-Free or the oil from Remington. The job takes five minutes and will prolong the knife's life.

While we are on the topic of knife preservation, and I have too many these days to maintain, I also recommend a good cleaning with WD-40 or similar stuff and wiped dry, the blade and other exposed steel coated lightly with A.G. Russell's Rustfree, which is a non-petroleum liquid that comes in a plastic squeeze bottle and lasts forever.

A.G., who must have fingers like a brick layer after fifty years of knifemaking and sales, says to place a small drop on the blade and spread the Rustfree around with your finger tips. A little Rustfree goes a long way, but I found a box of Band-Aids should be nearby as the slippery stuff will certainly put a finger or two or three in harm's way, and blood and Rustfree do not a pretty picture make. I use a Q-Tip to spread the stuff, and

This lithesome lad—he's in there—once braved Alaska in a cop suit; now he knows how to keep a pocket tool clean.

when my fingers heal, I will be able to do it better. I expect to use his wee bottle of Rustfree until the turn of the century!

One of the main problems with sheath knives kept in sheaths is the green gunk that builds up from leather chemicals around any brass guards and pommels. Blitz-clothing the brass is a constant chore. My knives with brassy parts get wrapped in a plastic sandwich bag before placement in a leather sheath. Enough about the chores—it's suppose to be a fun hobby! I'll never separate knives and sheaths, though.

Joseph Rychetnik

reports from my field testers, and seemed to favor this one and that one, and ended up rewarding the field testers with a tool each, leaving none for myself except the SOG Micro Tool Clip, which found a home in my camera bag.

On Christmas morn, I found a wrapped lump of something heavy—a smallish package and good things do come in small packages (she wanted an emerald necklace but...). I opened up the wrapping and the blue box, and found the Gerber Multi-Plier complete with Toolkit in the black nylon belt carry case. WOW! We are talking big money now, almost a C-Note, and I didn't spend anywhere near that much on all her stuff. I started to function the neat device and asked her how she knew, of all the tools I played with in the past few months, that this was my favorite, after all.

"Well, I watched you fondle and open and close this one more than any other. You seemed to enjoy pushing

the buttons, letting it open up, and snapping all those tool bits on and off. I gathered that you enjoyed doing it, so I made the big plunge. The guy at the store said he would exchange it for anything else if you didn't want it," she added. The Gerber tool was hard to lay down. I smiled at her and thanked her.

The kitchen was flooded from the rains the day before. I felt so warm inside with my Gerber on my belt that I took over the mopping duties. The Gerber outfit seemed to hang on well, and before long I was used to it.

It couldn't repair the leaky roof (I found out that $15,000 was needed as the rains persisted—the original roof had held back the tide for 25 years), but it did a lot of things around the house and on the Jeep. Now I had to decide if I wanted to give up the slick SOG knife that served as a car-key holder, the Swiss Army Champ or carry all three!

●

The Shapes of JAPANESE BLADES

LENGTH

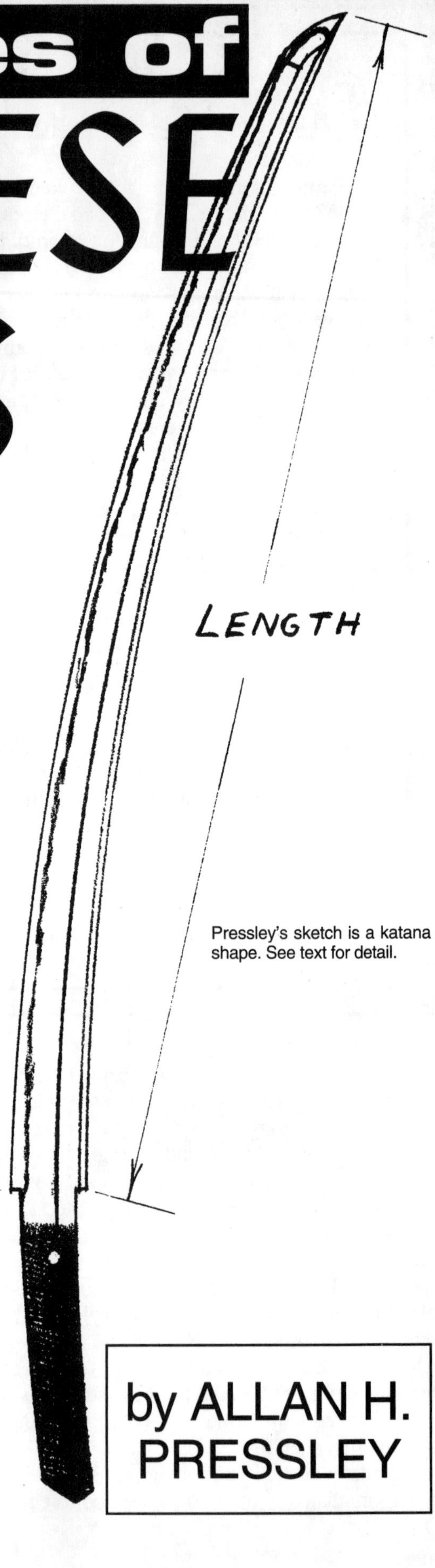

Pressley's sketch is a katana
shape. See text for detail.

by ALLAN H. PRESSLEY

JAPANESE LONG SWORD and short sword blades generally have the same shape characteristics. We have sketched a typical long sword blade which notes these traits. This type of blade is called *shinogi zukuri* in Japanese, which means "ridge-line style." Long swords are called *katana* or *tachi*, depending on their style of mountings. Short swords are called *wakazashi*. They will almost always have the same shape as the katana we show, but they will be shorter in comparison to their width.

The length of a Japanese sword is defined as the straight-line distance from the point to the shoulder at the start of the tang, probably because this is the only practical way to measure the length. Long swords are more than 24 inches long by correct length measurement; wakazashi are between 12 and 24 inches in length.

In days gone by, a Samurai left his long sword in a rack by the door when he entered a building; he kept his wakazashi with him at all times. It is believed this was because the wakazashi was a much more practical sword to use indoors. It would have been easy to get the tip of a katana stuck into the ceiling when swinging it. Samurai committed *seppuku* (vulgarly called *hari-kiri*) with their wakazashi.

There was a third type of blade, made in the early koto period, called a *ko-dachi* (small *tachi*), which was 24 inches long and looked like a smaller tachi blade. Tachi were carried by two rings on the scabbard and slung edge-down like Western swords. Katana were carried thrust in the sash edge-up. Apparently, the ko-dachi was an auxiliary small blade to the tachi. They are extremely rare. Tachi blades are generally longer and more curved than katana blades.

One interesting thing about a Japanese sword: When you hold it up, the graceful curve makes it look like it's already in motion. The true Japanese sword had evolved in its final technology and basic form by the 10th century.

Both long swords and wakazashi have curvature which

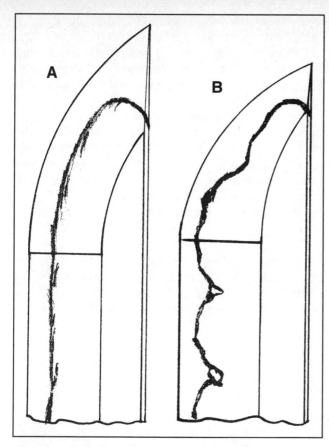

Good and bad kissaki or points. The arcs at A are parallel; those at B are not, therefore deficient.

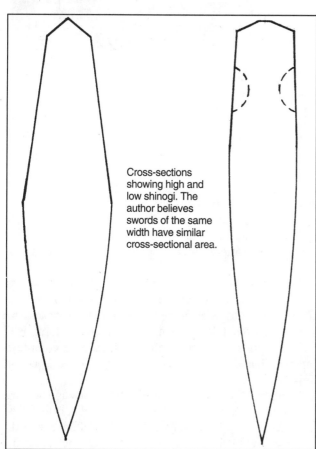

Cross-sections showing high and low shinogi. The author believes swords of the same width have similar cross-sectional area.

is called *sori* in Japanese. The percentage of curvature can be defined by depth of curvature divided by length (*nagasa*). Typical figures for curvature range from about 4.5 percent for very old swords from about 1000 years ago to almost zero for some atypical abnormally straight swords. However, the most commonly occurring straightest swords will have about 2 percent of curvature. The sword we sketched actually has 5 percent curvature, which is a little too much, but I can't draw it with any less curvature with my beam compass. Therefore, real swords you will see have less curvature than our sketch.

The Japanese sword is a cutting sword meant either to cut the enemy in two or to cut a major piece off him, with a slashing, slicing motion. The sword is not used to chop; it is used to cut. The Japanese swordsman pulls his arms back as he makes the cut to impart a slicing motion. Curvature helps this motion. The Japanese sword was almost never used to stab.

When the unhardened sword is first made, the blank is straight. When the hardened edge is made, the sword takes its characteristic curvature. There was a fascinating article in "The Japanese Sword Society Newsletter" by William Weins and Peter Bleed about this subject. They took a late koto sword which had flaws and used it for various scientific tests. They found that the martensite in the hardened edge was under extreme compression, up to 100,000 psi. This imparted the curve to the blank and also put the back under compression. Because the hardened edge is under such compression, the brittle martensite does not crack and break as it normally would. The change to martensite involves a volume expansion which causes both curve and compression. They also found that the edge was about Rockwell C60 in hardness.

All Japanese swords, and most other blades discussed later, have a single edge because, as previously mentioned, they were used to cut, not to stab. The edge is called the *ha* in Japanese. Later, I will discuss an unusual type of blade, called the *ken*, that is not single-edged.

All Japanese blades have hardened edges. While this isn't strictly a shape consideration, it is a fundamental trait of Japanese blades and is tied to the single edge and traits of the point discussed later. The hardened edge follows around the point of the sword as shown in the various drawings. The hardened edge is called the *hamon* in Japanese.

The back of the blade—that is, the edge opposite the cutting edge—usually has a ridged shape. Some have a three-cornered shape, but this is very rare. Both of these types are shown in the cross-section sketches. There is a third type of back which is rounded, but this type is extremely rare. The back of the blade is called the *mune*.

Virtually all long and short swords have ridge lines which impart specific cross-sections to the swords. It was found that this allows more efficient cutting through flesh and bones, apparently by reducing the friction on the side of the blade. It also makes the blade look much better— long blades without the ridge line look very awkward.

The ridge line is called a *shinogi* in Japanese, which is

why this type of blade is called a shinogi zukuri. One sketch here shows two typical cross-sections—low and high shinogi. The width of the space between the shinogi and the *mune*, called the *shinogi-ji* (the space between the edge and the shinogi is called the *ji*), varies with different schools of sword making. In some schools, the shinogi-ji can be almost 50 percent of the width of the blade, although this extreme is not seen very often. In other schools, the shinogi-ji can be as little as 20 percent of the width of the blade.

Swords with a high shinogi tend to have a wide shinogi-ji. Swords with a low shinogi tend to have a narrow shinogi-ji. I believe these combinations tend to keep the cross-sectional area the same on swords of the same width. The cross-sectional area from the shinogi to the edge bounded by the ji on both sides tends to be clam-shaped on older swords. Later, the ji tended to be straighter. We show both of these conditions.

Most blades with ridge lines have an arc-segment point

sword collectors say, "Poor swords hurt your eyes." I think you can see this in that sketch.

The hardened edge must be present following around the curve of the kissaki, its absence is a very serious flaw. This part of the hardened edge is called the *boshi*, which means cap in Japanese.

The sword tang is tapered as we show it, but it is also tapered looking down from the top so it is thinnest at the end of the tang. This gives what is basically a self-locking taper to the tang. The hilt is made in two halves glued together and then thrust onto the tang until it locks on the taper. I believe this is what really holds the sword together. I think the peg is just a safety device to hold it together in case the tapered fit comes loose.

The tang is called the *nakago* in Japanese. It is allowed to rust naturally. The quality of the patina of the nakago, if it is original, helps to date the sword. Swords made in the 1300s have usually lost the filemarks, and the patina is a rich blackish, purplish, dark-chocolate brown which is

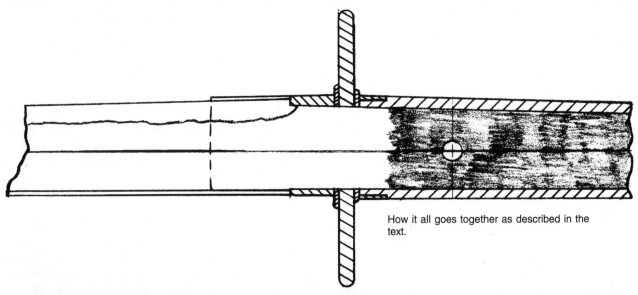

How it all goes together as described in the text.

as we sketch here. I believe this is just a manifestation of the Japanese desire for perfection. It allows a logical finish to the end of the blade and gives a nice looking point to a blade with a ridge line. The point is called the *kissaki*. Points can be short, medium or long. The long kissaki is sketched because I like that type.

The two radii that define the arc section in the point should have the same common radius point. If different, this means either the tip of the point has been broken off and the polisher who reshaped the point did not have the skill, or would not take the time, to do it right, or the blade was not shaped right in the first place.

The quality of the kissaki, its shape, the hardened edge, and the forging as defined by the grain of the steel are what separate great swords from lesser quality swords. Low-quality modern swords made in the 1930s and '40s usually have very poorly shaped kissaki; I can almost always tell one of these swords just by looking at it. We show a poorly shaped kissaki in one sketch. Experienced

very beautiful. As the swords become newer, the patina fades to a lighter chocolate brown. Blades made in this century usually have only some spots of rust; of course, new-made blades have no rust at all.

You will see nakago with more than one peg hole. This usually occurs because the blade was shortened—the number of shortenings corresponding to the number of peg holes.

The nakago has filemarks to finish it. The filemarks are sharper and more distinct when they are newer. There is a controversy as to whether the filemarks help the nakago to grip the wooden hilt. I personally think it is just for finish. Even the most inconsequential surface on a complete Japanese blade and its mounts has some sort of specific finish.

There are five or six slightly different nakago shapes with as many different end shapes. These all help to determine what school the blade belongs to. Often, a sword-smith signed his blades by incising the characters of his

name on one side of the nakago. He might also put his province, village, personal name (different than his professional name), school name and date. Tachi and katana are signed on different sides of the nakago. Ownership, presentations, cutting tests and other information may be placed there.

If a blade does not have a signature, there may be two reasons for it. First, the blade may have been shortened and lost its signature; if so, the nakago is always cut straight across at the end. Secondly, the smith just may not have signed it. There are a number of plausible reasons why. If a sword has the signature of a famous smith, then it is very highly probable that it is a fake signature. People were not honest in the old days, either.

One of the major areas of expertise in Japanese swords is to be able to tell what school and time period an unsigned sword belongs to, perhaps even which smith made it. There were more than 156 schools of sword making and 33,000 recorded sword smiths. The top 1700 smiths are considered exceptionally good, and a Japanese sword expert should usually be able to tell, in the majority of cases, which one of the 1700 famous smiths made a blade.

A collar abuts onto the shoulders at the blade/tang joint, and the roughly circular guard, with washers on either side of it, abuts the collar. The hilt abuts the guard/washer sandwich and holds it all snug. These notches are called *machi* in Japanese and are either *ha machi* or the *mune machi*, depending on their location. Our sketch shows how the parts fit together. Japanese blades are always mounted with this collar, called a *habaki*. They never have a ricasso; the blade cross-section always goes to the notches (the machi).

The shapes of the blade changed subtly over the centuries. Swords of the *koto* (old sword) period—806 A.D. to 1596 A.D.—were light, long and highly tapered. Early koto had the greatest curvature near the hilt, which is called *koshi-zori* in Japanese. (*Sori* is changed to *zori* when it follows another word.) They were relatively straight near the tip, with a very high degree of taper. The total width at the kissaki was about 50 percent of the width of the sword at the notches. The swords that have survived are all very high quality swords used by high-status Samurai. Made to be used from horseback, they were all probably mounted as tachi. Original swords of this shape are one of the most subtle and beautiful man-made shapes I know of, ranking with Purdey shotguns, Supermarine Spitfires, early Griffin and Howe rifles, and Ferrari Barchettas.

This curvature, with the deepest part of the curvature nearest the hilt, continued to be used in later times, especially by some prolific schools. In the mid-koto period, the curvature was usually an even or constant radius, called *torii-zori* after the red archways you see at the entrances of Japanese temples. They also had less taper.

Our sketched sword has a mid-koto shape with even curvature and medium taper. A sword of this shape could be made anytime after this period, however. I drew the mid-koto shape with torii-zori because this is the only shape I could draw neatly on a drawing board using a beam compass. One fascinating thing I learned doing this sketch: The radius for the mune and the edge are the same, they only have different pivot points. I had to fuss around with different radii and pivot points until the sword looked right, and that is what came up. I believe that the shapes of these blades are governed by some principles of physics.

In the late koto period, there was less taper yet, and the sword tended to have the greatest curvature near the point, called *saki-zori*. This was supposed to allow the sword to be drawn quicker. Also during the same period, Samurai started carrying their swords edge-up and thrust into their sashes. The ability to draw the sword quickly was very important to staying alive. They were also shorter, because some time earlier fighting on foot became more prevalent, even for high-status Samurai.

These three types of curvature are very subtle and hard to discern for beginning collectors and students. The only way you can really learn about the shapes of Japanese swords is to study many of them, in hand, with an expert at your side. The figures accompanying this article were carefully drawn, or rubbings were taken of actual blades, but the processes of reproduction and printing may change the shapes. It would take full-size rubbings and incredibly good full-size reproductions to learn about shape from paper.

A Japanese sword should always be looked at naked. That is, the hilt, guard and collar should be stripped off. The sword is held vertically at arms length by the nakago with the edge to the left. This gives you a uniform technique and allows you to compare shape more easily from blade to blade. This is the only practical way to look in a crowded area. Another way to look at a blade is to lay the stripped blade on a table and back up about 10 feet or so, then bend over and look at it from a very shallow angle. This foreshortens the blade and exaggerates the shape. Unfortunately, this is almost impossible to do at a crowded show.

Swords of the *shinto* (new sword) period—1597 A.D. to 1780 A.D.—were shorter and heavier, and had even less taper than the late koto period. Swords of earlier shapes were made at later times right up to the present, which is often confusing to students. However, later swords are always thicker and heavier than older swords, which helps to date the blades. This constant increase in tip width made the sword heavier, especially at the tip, probably in order to counter the constant improvements in armour and helmets.

Japanese long and short swords always taper smaller towards the point; the amount of taper may fluctuate, but there is always taper towards the point by all the arcs and surfaces. Later, I will discuss the only exception to this rule, the *naginata*. Sometimes you will see

swords that are extremely crude, but they superficially look like Japanese swords. These were made by people of various nationalities (probably including Americans) to sell to rear area G.I.s as real Japanese swords. Supposedly, a lot of these fake swords were made by Australians.

The polish of a Japanese sword is an integral part of its shape. If a sword is properly polished, the surfaces will appear to be optically perfect to the naked eye. The arcs of the edge, shinogi and mune will be perfect. There can be no ripples or wavers in the lines or surfaces of a correctly polished Japanese sword. If you see a poorly polished Japanese sword, it means it was given a cheap polish and was not well thought of by the person who had it polished. This is a pretty good indication that it is not a good sword. It takes at least a five-year apprenticeship in Japan under a Japanese master polisher to learn how to polish a blade properly. If you try it without this knowledge, you could ruin the blade, and you might be ruining a very valuable piece. You might also ruin an art object, which is even worse.

You can observe the polish by pointing the blade at a source of light such as an unshaded light bulb and catching the reflection of the bulb on the surface of the blade. Then, above and below the reflection, you can see the surfaces very well.

Some swords are out of shape, that is, their arcs are not perfectly converging, or there is a shallow scallop in an arc or surface. A sword that is even $1/32$-inch out of true will look out of shape to an experienced collector.

The nakago is allowed to rust naturally because this is where the bare blade is grasped when the sword is taken apart. You *never* touch the polished part of the blade with your bare hand, or you will put fingerprints on it that will rust in rapidly. Blades were always shortened from the tang end, never the point end, because the hardened edge wraps around the kissaki. If a sword loses its original kissaki, it is no longer considered a collectible sword unless it is very old and very intact otherwise. Since so many older long swords were shortened to fit new, later styles of fighting, there are few katana from before 1400 A.D. that have intact nakago. It is rare to see a koto katana at a gun show that has the original nakago. Swords of any time period were shortened to fit the stature of the person carrying it. Some swords were shortened just because their owners wanted to carry them as wakazashi.

Daggers are called *tanto* in Japanese. They are almost always made with flat sides, called *hira zukuri*. They are shallow wedges with one of the three standard mune on the top. Usually straight along the top, some tanto curve very slightly downward toward the edge, called *uchi-zori*. Some have the normal curve of katana and are also called *saki-zori* even though the curvature is even, like *torii-zori*.

These three shapes were fashionable at various times during the 1000-year history of the Japanese sword and

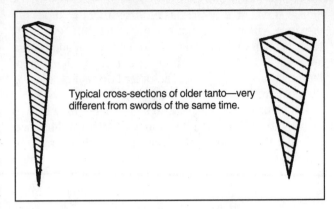

Typical cross-sections of older tanto—very different from swords of the same time.

help to date the blade. If you see a tanto in shinogi-zukuri style (with ridge line), it was probably the tip of a katana or wakazashi that had broken off in combat. It was recycled as a tanto by putting a new nakago on it.

The "tanto" made by American knifemakers with the wedge-shaped tips are historically inaccurate, and their shapes are incredibly poor to someone who has intensely studied Japanese swords. A certain style of tanto was developed in late koto times called a *yoroi-doshi* or armor-piercer. It was used in close combat to pierce the armor of an opponent. They have extremely wide mune and a strong triangular cross-section. Our sketch shows normal and yoroi-doshi cross-sections.

The best way to let you see the shapes of some actual tanto is to show rubbings taken off actual blades. We show an unsigned blade which has a certificate from a Japanese expert in Japanese swords attributing it to a famous swordsmith, Enju Kunitoshi, who started his career in 1319. It has a very straight mune. There is some downward curve, but not much. Its length is $10^{1}/_{2}$ inches. Since it is so old, the ha machi has disappeared from the many polishings it has had.

We also show a signed blade apparently made by a very famous swordsmith, Sa Yasuyoshi, who started his career in 1346. Note that this blade has saki-zori. In the time period since the Enju Kunitoshi was made, the fashion had gone to longer curved blades. This blade is $11^{13}/_{16}$ inches long. Note that the ha machi is very shallow because of repeated polishings.

And there is a signed and dated blade. It is the signature of a school of swordsmiths, thirty of whom had the same name, called the Bizen Kiyomitsu school. It is dated 1552 and is very fresh with a deep ha machi. It was not polished very much and is $8^{1}/_{16}$ inches long. This blade has very strong uchi-zori.

Those are the three standard types of hira-zukuri tanto blades. You will note that they all have two or more peg holes, but I do not believe they were shortened. This is common in koto tanto. My personal theory is that tanto used a different style of mounting in koto times. Then the style of mounting changed to be like the katana and wakazashi, and a second hole had to be added nearer the end of the nakago, so that a peg could be inserted.

Attributed to Enju Kunitoshi, who began his career in 1319, it's 10½ inches long.

This tanto was made by Sa Yasuyoshi, whose career dates from 1346 when fashion called for more curve.

This is a blade of the Bizen Kiyomitsu dated 1552. It remains strongly marked.

Tanto wore blades less than 12 inches long. A few katana blades were made in hira-zukuri style, but they are very awkward looking and not at all pleasing to the eye. I have only seen two out of the many thousands of blades I've looked at. On the other hand, a fair amount of hira-zukuri wakazashi were made. Those blades close to 12 inches in length are called large tanto, probably because tanto are more valuable than wakazashi, all other things being equal. Surprisingly, there are few tanto compared to the numbers of katana and wakazashi. I believe the wakazashi developed from the tanto. As they made tanto longer and longer in the 1300s, they started to look awkward, with the flat-sided hira-zukuri shape, so they went to shinogi-zukuri wakazashi around 1400 A.D. Therefore, if you see a shinogi-zukuri wakazashi dated much before then, it almost has to be a fake.

There is another type of rare short sword called a *ken*. This is straight, double-edged, with a diamond cross-section. This type of ken apparently evolved after the true Japanese sword and is made with the same technology, but with both edges hardened. The ken is believed to have evolved from Chinese swords that came to Japan with Buddhism around 600 A.D. Later, tanto were also made in this form.

Very early swords made in the eighth century were also called ken, and are single-edged and perfectly straight. This style was made in China and may also have come over from China, as did most of Japanese culture. This sword apparently evolved into the modern Japanese sword with curvature and a shinogi. The Japanese word *to-ken* is a generic word for swords. Fencing schools are called *ken-jutsu* and *kendo*. As far as I know, only a very few single-edged ken exist in Japan; I don't think you will ever see one in the U.S.A., unless it is a later replica.

There were other shapes of tanto and wakazashi made, but they are quite rare. Some were also used for katana and polearm shapes. I personally believe they are rare because they are not nearly as nice looking as the standard shapes—shinongi zukuri for katana and wakazashi, with an arc-shaped point, and hira zukuri for tanto—and very few people wanted them.

We show these various other shapes and their cross-sections. Their Japanese names are:

Shobu zukuri—This style blade has a cross-section like a normal shinogi-zukuri blade; it just lacks the arc-shaped point.

Unokubi zukuri—This style has the same cross-section as a shinogi zukuri near the tang. Then it has a scalloped section in the mid-part where it has a shallow diamond cross-section. The tip has a shallow wedge section.

Kanmuri-otoshi—This is the same as the unokubi shape shown except that it has the arc-shaped section at the tip. Notice how much better this makes the blade look by giving a logical finish.

Moroha—This has a shallow diamond cross-section.

Katakiri ba—This has a shallow cross-section like a hira zukuri, but it has a bevel near the edge on one side.

There were even more unusual shapes than these, but they are so incredibly ugly that I don't want to draw them; it would hurt my eyes. Luckily for me, they are extremely rare. I do not think they are very functional, and I believe they were done just to be different, near the end of the Samurai system when functionality was no longer so important.

I have only seen tanto and wakazashi done in these unusual shapes, never a katana. Any of these are rare. I personally believe these shapes were ordered by rich merchants, who sat around in geisha houses and amazed their friends with their weird wakazashi and tanto, sort of like early Weatherby rifles. Rich merchants were not noted in old Japan for their good taste.

The Japanese had various types of polearm blades, which used the same manufacturing technology as sword

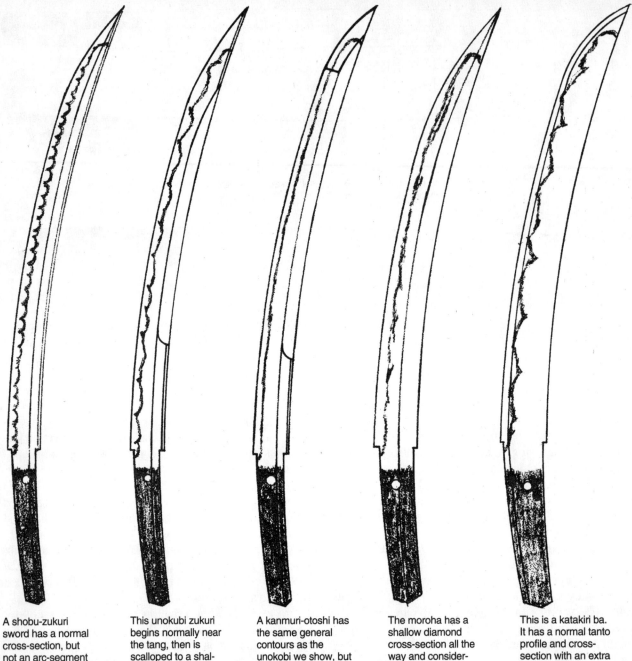

A shobu-zukuri sword has a normal cross-section, but not an arc-segment point.

This unokubi zukuri begins normally near the tang, then is scalloped to a shallow diamond cross-section and a wedge-section tip.

A kanmuri-otoshi has the same general contours as the unokobi we show, but with a better arc-segment tip.

The moroha has a shallow diamond cross-section all the way and considerable curvature to a slim point.

This is a katakiri ba. It has a normal tanto profile and cross-section with an extra bevel on one side.

blades, including hardened edges. The first type of these blades was a spear point, called *yari*. Both the complete spear with shaft and blade alone seem to be called yari. They are three-sided, and all three edges are hardened, even though it is primarily a stabbing weapon. Most yari blades are 4 to 6 inches long. Occasionally, you will see a very large one, but I believe these were for show, carried by Samurai in processions, and are not really functional. Yari have a long slender tapered nakago which fits down in the shaft and also have a hole for a peg just like sword blades. We show a yari blade. There were also yari blades that had side arms on; they are quite rare.

The second type of polearm blade we show is called a *naginata* and is the only Japanese blade that swells as it goes towards the point. They are usually wakazashi length and were sometimes reshaped to use as wakazashi. The dashed lines in the sketch show how one would be reshaped. They originally had long nakago to fit the shaft. If they were reshaped to use as wakazashi, then the nakago would be cut to normal length as shown by the lines. The amount of swell changed at different times, sometimes being fairly straight and other times being very pronounced. They were extremely thick for their size. I personally find naginata very awkward looking. Supposedly,

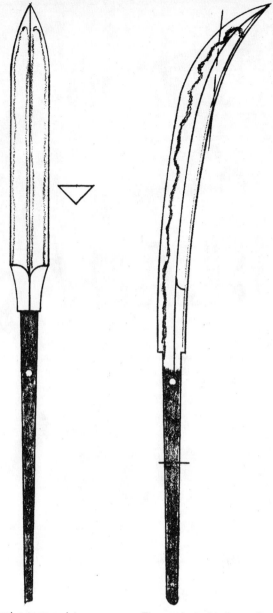

The yari, a spear point, normally has three hardened edges and is 4 to 6 inches long.

The naginata blade swells toward the point and was the chosen wall defense weapon of samurai women.

tang sticking out. I believe this was because it was very difficult for a G.I. to bring back a complete polearm with shaft from Japan after WWII.

Arrowheads were made using the same technology as the blades described and with long tangs. They were made in a variety of shapes other than a normal broadhead. Some were Y-shaped to use for cutting, some were heavy to be used to make holes in the sides of boats, and some were an unusual hollow shape to make a sound for signalling.

Some Japanese blades may have carvings. The first type are grooves which may be to lighten the sword, or to decorate it. If they are to lighten, they usually consist of a single deep groove between the shinogi and the mune on each side of the blade. This gives a cross-section similar to an "I" beam in that area and lightens the blade without substantially weakening it. Katana and wakazashi may have decorative carvings on the blade, but I think they detract from the appearance of the blade, rather than adding to it, and they also cause stress concentrations that weaken the blade. The large grooves are functional and at least look right because they are functional. Hira-zukuri tanto frequently have shallow grooves which relieve the blank surface of the blade and do not look too bad or introduce stress concentrations. Our sketched low shinogi blade shows grooves in dotted lines.

High-quality Japanese swords have a complex, subtle and beautiful shape, and their study is rewarding. It is absolutely necessary to study shape if you want to acquire high-quality swords and if you want to be able to tell where, when and by whom a sword was made.

If you wish to study Japanese swords more intensively, I recommend that you read the following two books: *The Japanese Sword* by Kazan Sato and *The Craft of the Japanese Sword* by L&H Kapp and Yoshindo Yoshihara. They are published by Kodansha International, can be ordered from any bookseller and are currently in print.

I also recommend that you join the Japanese Sword Society of the U.S. They publish a newsletter bi-monthly and a bulletin once a year. This group is your window to the world of Japanese swords. The newsletter contains articles, book reviews, notices of sword shows, addresses of sword study groups, etc. I recommend you write and ask for membership details. •

the Samurai stopped cavalry charges by cutting off the horses' legs with naginata. Samurai women fought with naginatas. Apparently, when a Samurai household or castle was attacked, it was a case of all hands to the pumps.

A third type of polearm blade is called a *nagamaki*. It is always considered to have a blade of katana length with the shobu-zukuri shape and a long tang. They are also reshaped to be used as katana. It is also a cutting weapon, but was probably used as a stabbing weapon at times because of the shobu-zukuri shape.

Complete polearms with shafts are quite rare. You usually see only the blades in their scabbards with the bare

THE LATE ALLAN H. PRESSLEY

In November, 1993, seized by an unshakable depression, Allan Pressley took his own life.

He would have published a good deal more of interest to readers of DBI Books, but his voice is gone and will be missed. There are still some short articles to be published, we're please to note.

Ken Warner

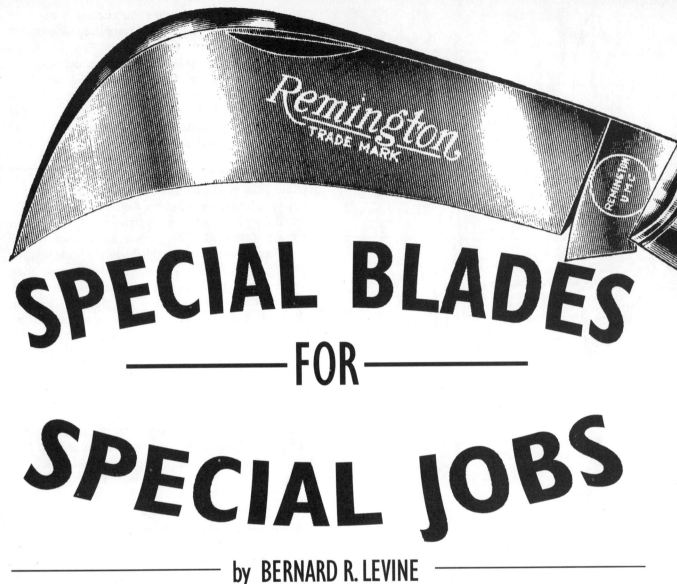

SPECIAL BLADES
— FOR —
SPECIAL JOBS

by BERNARD R. LEVINE

MOST MODERN FOLDING knives have just one blade, usually a locking blade. It is the only blade in the knife, so it must perform all sorts of cutting tasks. No matter how well designed, though, it cannot perform all of these tasks equally well.

Knives with two or more blades can be more flexible, offering a choice of more specialized blade types. Of course, multiple-bladed folding knives usually pay a penalty both in handling comfort—the backs of the closed blades stick out of the handle—and in bulk.

At its simplest, a two-blade knife can have a large blade for long cuts and rough work, along with a small blade for short cuts and delicate work. Alternately, some two-blade knives, such as the trapper-pattern jackknife or the electrician's knife, can have two long blades of different shapes or edge profiles. Indeed, one of these two blades need not be a cutting blade at all. It can be a screwdriver, a nail file, a leather punch, or some other tool.

Multi-blade knives, such as premium stock knives, Scout knives and Swiss Army knives, can incorporate a large assortment of specialized blades and tools. Several knives currently in production have twenty or more distinct gadgets. I have seen functional antique multi-blades with as many as forty-two blades, and I have seen many display knives with 100 blades or more. The all-time record was set by the Joseph Rodgers Year Knife, which at the time of its retirement had more than 1950 blades in its cross-shaped frame.

In the more usual multi-blade folding knife, some "blades" are more properly considered tools. These tools can include: can opener, cap lifter, corkscrew, screwdriver, leather punch, gimlet, letter opener, marlinspike, nail file, metal file, saw, scissors, spatula, button hook, hoof pick, dog stripping comb, weed digger, cigar punch, pipe tamper, pliers, wrench, ruler, pencil, glass cutter, fish scaler, key blank, spoon, and fork—not to

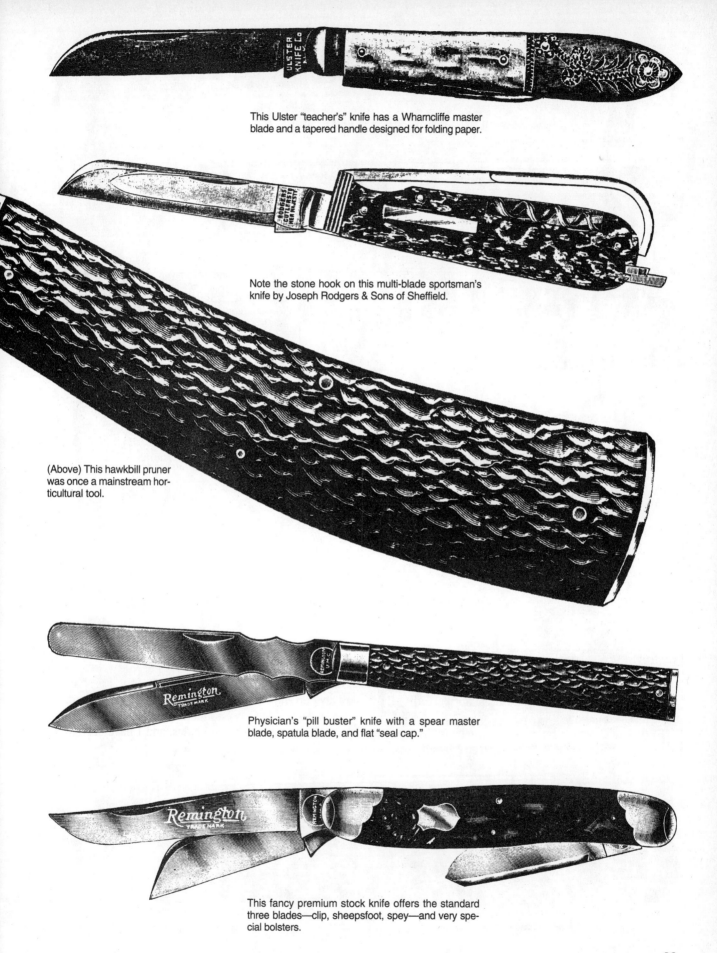

This Ulster "teacher's" knife has a Wharncliffe master blade and a tapered handle designed for folding paper.

Note the stone hook on this multi-blade sportsman's knife by Joseph Rodgers & Sons of Sheffield.

(Above) This hawkbill pruner was once a mainstream horticultural tool.

Physician's "pill buster" knife with a spear master blade, spatula blade, and flat "seal cap."

This fancy premium stock knife offers the standard three blades—clip, sheepsfoot, spey—and very special bolsters.

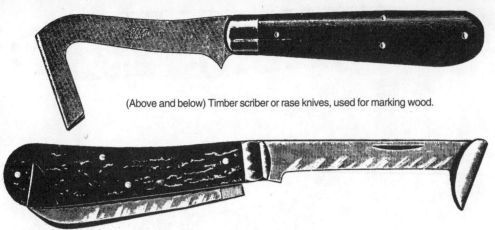

(Above and below) Timber scriber or rase knives, used for marking wood.

TRAPPERS' KNIVES

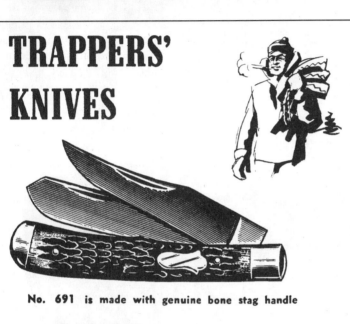

No. 691 is made with genuine bone stag handle

No. 692 is made with yellow composition handle.

(Left) Trapper jackknives have a clip blade and a long spey blade, for skinning. These are by Western Cutlery. (Courtesy Harvey Platts)

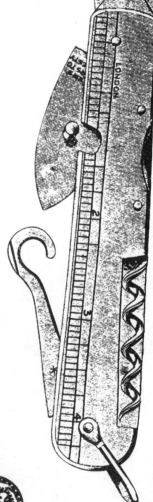

Pearl-handled English silver fruit knife with seed-pick blade.

(Above) English multi-blade with ruler handles, British-style tin opener, and button hook.

Angler's knife with combination fish scaler/hook disgorger/caplifter blade—and a long-clip cutting blade, of course.

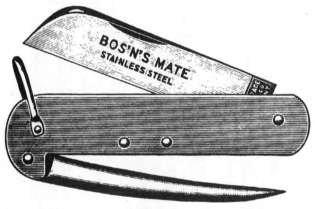

Some sailor knives, like this Schrade, have a marlinspike along with the rope blade.

Western States' folding hunter with a hatchet blade.

mention toothpicks and tweezers concealed within the handles.

There are always cutting blades. And even basic main blades come in a variety of shapes. Most generic is the symmetrical spear blade. There is also a variety of clip blades, which all offer slimmer points than the spear blades.

The sheepsfoot blade (and its smaller British cousin, the lambsfoot) are characterized by a straight cutting edge. This edge is useful in precise whittling and also in clean cuts where the blade is placed on the item being cut (such as rope) to be then struck with a blunt implement (such as a belaying pin). The name comes from the profile of this blade—it is like a sheep's foot—and also (I believe) from the use of this blade by English farmers in treating foot rot in sheep.

The Wharncliffe blade was introduced by Joseph Rodgers & Sons of Sheffield in the early 19th century. It combines the straight edge of the sheepsfoot blade with a keener more delicate point. Originally, there was a specific Wharncliffe handle shape as well.

The razor-style blade could be sharpened for shaving, much like its namesake. The notch at the end of the blade also facilitated one-hand opening.

One common blade that frequently baffles the uninitiated is the hawkbill blade. This flat, hook-shaped blade was originally developed for agricultural use, pruning and certain types of harvesting. In the previous century, the hawkbill was adopted for cutting and fitting oilcloth. More recently, it has been widely used for cutting and fitting linoleum, wall-to-wall carpet, and sometimes even sheetrock. Some Australian and New Zealand sheep ranchers use small hawkbill blades for castrating lambs.

These days, electricians often use the hawkbill blade for stripping insulation from heavy-gauge cable, though the more familiar wire stripping blade is a modified screwdriver. This blade design dates back to before the First World War.

Two other flat, hooked blades are sometimes still seen today, although neither has been made in many years. One type is a short blade with a keen point and file-like serrations on the inside of the curve. This blade is a champagne wire cutter. It became obsolete when champagne bottlers began to incorporate twist-off loops in the wire that retained their corks.

The other unusual blade is also small. Its distinguishing feature is a step or lip inside the curve. This blade is a type of shotshell extractor, for use when a shell swells and sticks in the chamber. The more usual type of extractor incorporated into some folding knives (especially in Italy) is a dovetail-shaped cut-out in the cross-guard, or sometimes in a pivoting H-shaped blade. There are usually two cut-outs, one for 12-gauge, the other for 16 or 20.

Two other blades that could be considered "hooked" are different from the others in that they are not flat. One is the rase or timber-scriber blade. The usual rase blade is shaped like the figure "7." It is sharpened only

on the very tip, where the steel is rolled over to form a U-shaped profile, like a carpenter's gouge. This blade was designed for making permanent markings upon wood, primarily wooden barrels and shipping crates. Unlike paper labels or painted markings, carved ownership or destination markings could not accidentally wash away.

The other three-dimensional hooked blade is the stone hook, often found wrapped around the outside of a fancy horseman's multi-blade knife. Removing a stone caught in a horse's hoof was just as vital as fixing a flat tire, and of particular importance to the horse.

The spey blade is the most frequently misunderstood blade of all. The traditional cattle knife and premium stock knife both normally have spey blades, but many modern stock knives replace that shape with a more versatile pen blade. This is because only a small proportion of modern-day cattle and stock knives are actually used by working stockmen.

The spey blade was designed for castrating young male animals (calves, piglets, foals, lambs). It is ground thin and keen to cut flesh cleanly, which makes this blade easily broken if abused. Its tip is clipped off to minimize collateral damage to surrounding tissue. The keen edge and safe tip of the spey blade also make it suitable for skinning, which is why long versions of this blade are included in trapper-pattern folding knives.

Skinning is the most delicate part of game preparation. By contrast, the roughest part is splitting the breastbone and pelvis of an animal, preparatory to dressing and disjointing the carcass. The hatchet or cleaver blades incorporated in some folding hunters, and the stout saber-ground main blades in many others, are designed for this function. Folding knife blades don't work well for chopping. Instead, these bone-cutting blades are used much like a rope blade: Placed upon the bone to be broken or the joint to be divided, and then struck with a stick.

The spey blade has several close cousins which are rarely seen today. The smallest and most delicate is the corn blade. Its resemblance to a surgical scalpel is no coincidence. This blade was designed for do-it-yourself podiatry and no doubt led to many cases of blood poisoning following dirty corn surgery.

Not much larger, and almost as delicate, is the horticultural budding blade. Budding is a form of grafting used on roses and young fruit trees. A severed bud is inserted under the bark of the stock plant wherever one wishes an additional branch to grow. For pecan trees, a special knife

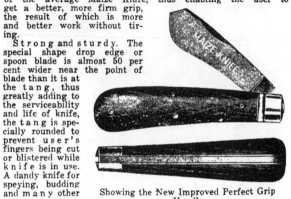

As a primary tool, maize knives got a lot of attention from Hibbard, Spencer and Bartlett.

Australian castrating knives, with spey and hawkbill blades, could be bought monogrammed!

(Left) A fleam with multiple blades for bleeding animals—the blade was struck smartly to set a quick clean wound.

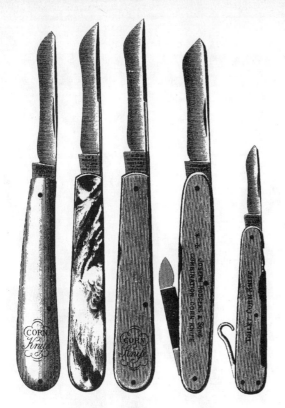

Corn knives of typical pattern, meant to slice calluses.

The cotton sampler, used to cut open bales. It has been sold as a skinning blade.

Rope knives for sailors usually had sheepsfoot-style rope cutting blades. These are J. Russell & Co. New England whalers' knives.

A Joseph Rodgers jackknife with a razor-style blade— the notch up front could be used to open it.

with two widely spaced budding blades is used for "patch budding." More generic horticultural grafting knives have straight-edged blades similar in profile to a sheepsfoot.

Next up the size ladder is the maize or corn-topping knife. It has a large curved wooden handle, like a pruner, but a short relatively delicate blade. The "corn" for which this knife was designed was not our common ear corn, but rather grain sorghum. Before World War II, this important feed grain crop was "topped" or harvested by hand with this style of folding knife.

The largest of the spey-like blades is the cotton sampler. This blade was used by cotton buyers to examine samples from individual bales. Since there are a lot more hunters in the world than cotton buyers, some enterprising cutlery firms tended to market this blade shape as a skinner, for which I suppose it would work reasonably well.

Cotton sampler pocketknife blades are no longer made, and neither are fleam blades. A fleam does not look like a spey blade, or like any other blade for that matter, but it too was used for operating on livestock. When bleeding was believed to be therapeutic, the fleam was used upon cattle and horses much the way the lancet was used upon humans. Unlike people, however, animals were too smart to volunteer for this procedure, so surprise was of the essence. The point of the fleam blade was placed gently upon the part of the animal to be bled, and then the back of the blade was struck smartly with a stick, driving home the point. Note the similarity of this method to the use of both the rope blade and the hatchet blade.

A small blade like a miniature fleam, sometimes seen in fancy pen knives, is in fact a gum lancet. It was used for emergency bleeding of inflamed gums, when no other treatment was available. Other types of dental, surgical and veterinary blades were occasionally included in pocketknives, as well.

Fork and spoon blades do not need much explanation, nor do can opener and bottle opener blades, although the British spear-point style tin opener does sometimes baffle Americans. More mystifying to many, however, are the fruit knife blades. Originally made of sterling silver, or even solid gold, and more recently wrought from silverplate or stainless steel, the fruit knife was once an essential adjunct to genteel picnicking and snacking. Not only was it uncouth for a lady to tear into an apple, pear or orange with her teeth, the experience could also prove to be very unpleasant if a worm or other pest happened to reside therein.

The solution to this problem was the fruit knife. Precious metals were used because they were ostentatious, and also because they would not tarnish readily, nor discolor or taint the fruit. Some late 18th-century silver fruit knives came with matching folding forks. Later versions often incorporated a seed-pick blade, along with the silver or plated cutting blade. ●

The KNIVES Of CORSICA

by RAYMOND CARANTA

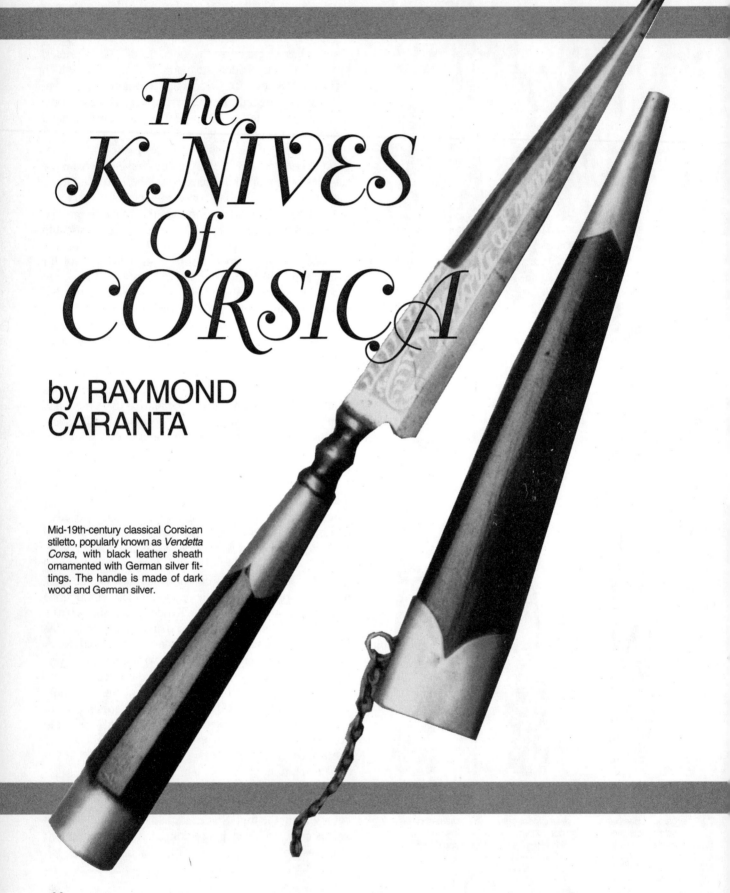

Mid-19th-century classical Corsican stiletto, popularly known as *Vendetta Corsa*, with black leather sheath ornamented with German silver fittings. The handle is made of dark wood and German silver.

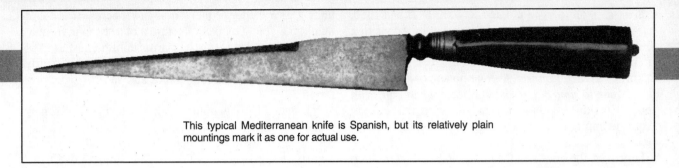

This typical Mediterranean knife is Spanish, but its relatively plain mountings mark it as one for actual use.

IT MUST BE said, before all, that Corsica is a wonderful island in the Mediterranean, about one hundred miles from the Southern French coastline. With a population of about 250,000 scattered over 3300 square miles, the place—properly known as the *Ile de Beauté*—is a true paradise for the modern hunter, fisherman or tourist.

In Corsica, as soon as you leave the beach you are in the mountains, with typical villages, brown pigs that look like boars idling alone under the sun along torturous narrow roads, and, above all, everywhere, the impenetrable *maquis*—the thick bush where all those who were *caduti in disgrazia* (who "fell into misfortune," an elegant term for qualifying those who are shunning the law) along the centuries found safety and quiet, provided they had a good dog, a sturdy knife, dry powder and a trusty double gun.

In Corsica, even now, at this turn of the third millennium, nobody is kidding with honor. There are only two towns (Bastia: 45,000 inhabitants; and Ajaccio: 54,000, the place where Napoleon was born) on the island—everybody knows everybody.

Nowadays, thanks to the steamship and the airliner, people can easily move to the continent. But back in the olden times, they had only, when touched on points of honor, to choose among the three Ss, as they used to say in dialect: *schioppetto, stiletto, strada* (shotgun, dagger, flight), and then to go *alla campagna* (to the countryside) in order to avoid *mala morte* (violent death).

During the last century, hundreds of former shepherds, fishermen, farmers, and even townsmen lived *alla campagna* for years, after having killed—often for futile offenses grossly exaggerated by the promiscuity of the village life—a neighbour, a competitor or even a good friend who had the misfortune to say something wrong.

Those living *alla campagna* were called bandits of honor, and as long as they respected the code—which mostly prohibited stealing, racketeering and insulting women—they could be well thought of in their rural environment and were certain to find, at night, a barn for sleeping, some wine, meat, cheese and ammunition. It was common, in that time, to leave the doors unlocked and, at the family table, to provide an additional empty dish, called "the bandit's plate." The most famous bandits traveled with guides, usually shepherds. Less celebrated types had a partner or a dog trained to snarl (not to bark, of course) when there were *gendarmes* in the area.

Such a life could last for years, and the longevity record of this kind was unquestionably Antoine Bonelli's. He was better known as *Bellacoscia* (Legs). Born in 1828, he became a bandit in 1848 and surrendered in 1892, forty-four years later, after having invented the phrase "Green Palace" to describe his rustic habitat under the stars.

After the guide, partner or dog, the next precious items were the shotgun and the knife. And it is the knives we're here to discuss.

Traditional Corsican daggers are normally the so-called "Mediterranean style" also found in Spain and Southern Italy. Such knives invariably have triangular blades with a single sharp edge, sometimes ornamented on the back, and a tapered handle, thinner near the hilt, with either four or six flats and a pommel. Some handles can be fluted.

After the visit of Prosper Mérimée to Corsica in 1839, the island became fashionable among Romantic people,

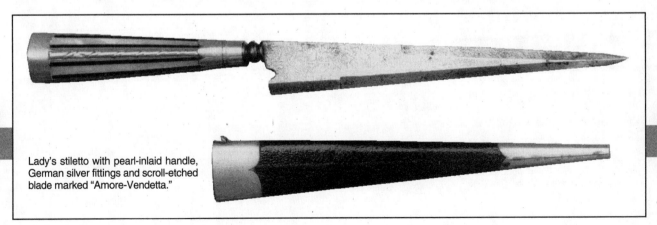

Lady's stiletto with pearl-inlaid handle, German silver fittings and scroll-etched blade marked "Amore-Vendetta."

with its 4319 murders committed between 1821 and 1850, and very nice Corsican knives were made for the visiting gentry. Such blades often bear mottos like *Amore-Vendetta* (Love-Vengeance), *Morte al Nemico* (Death to the Enemy), *Vendica l'onore* (Avenge honor) or *Abia confidenza quando sono con te* (Be confident when I am with you). The knives made for ladies were particularly exquisite and now command high prices among collectors.

However, the guests in the Green Palace had nothing to do with delicate blade engravings and ornate pearl inlays. As a matter of fact, among shepherds, as a rite of manhood, young men cut the throat of a sheep in front of the family and held it in their arms until the last drop of blood had hit the ground. These people needed sturdy sharp blades, while steel handles and sheaths were preferred.

It is one of these genuine bandit stilettos I was given by Ange-Pierre, a Corsican friend from Prunelli-di-Casacconi, a small mountain village 16 miles south of Bastia, the Northern Corsican capital. Today, Prunelli-di-Casacconi is only a picturesque village on a small road between

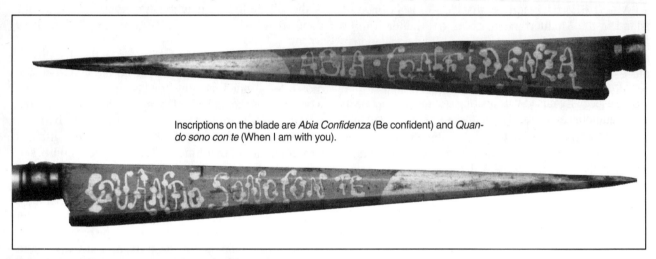

Inscriptions on the blade are *Abia Confidenza* (Be confident) and *Quando sono con te* (When I am with you).

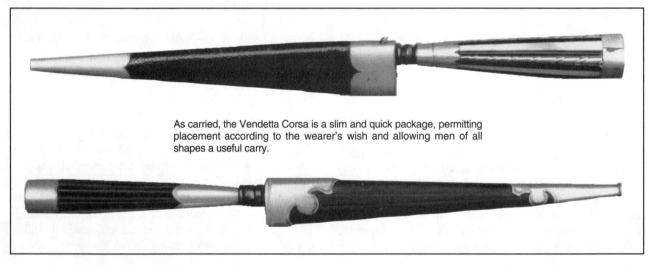

As carried, the Vendetta Corsa is a slim and quick package, permitting placement according to the wearer's wish and allowing men of all shapes a useful carry.

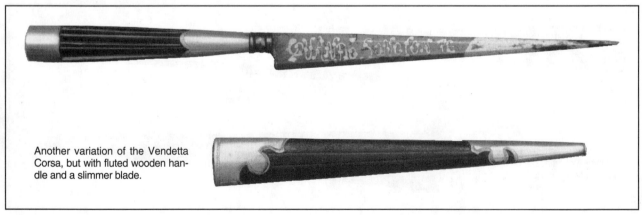

Another variation of the Vendetta Corsa, but with fluted wooden handle and a slimmer blade.

Casamozza and Ponte Leccia, but during the Restoration period, in the 1820s, it was famous as the place of one of the bloodiest vendettas in Corsican history.

Once, the French government, indignant with the repetitive murders committed in the face of powerless *gendarmes* and *voltigeurs*, permanently set a guillotine on the main square, ready to take the heads of those killers.

This spectacular drama started in 1814, when two innocent sheep entered a vineyard without permission and ate some leaves. Such a grave insult obviously required a ruthless vengeance, and the Agostini brothers immediately took their flintlock shotguns and began to shoot the Filippis. The latter were not long returning the fire. Even widows were not spared. Killings went so fast that just a few years later nobody in a position to remember who was the owner of what remained alive.

The Agostinis were so terrible even a gendarmerie force especially raised was unable to catch them. The sinister guillotine soon became considered as a normal village implement. So, in 1821, the government sent the army, with a permanent garrison in the village, and twenty-one Agostini relatives were jailed in Bastia.

Along the years, twenty-seven Filippis were killed during the vendetta, and when only a single male remained alive, the grandmother blessed him and allowed his depar-

Ange-Pierre, himself, shooting in the dusk with his Beretta 92 fitted with laser sight—a very different sort of tool to carry in the belt.

ture to Venezuela, where he founded a new family to keep the name living. Thus, many years later, the Filippi name returned to Prunelli-di-Casacconi, and they now occupy their family mansion in peace, everything being forgotten, 180 years later. It is a knife carried by his ancestors that Ange-Pierre recently gave me in a gesture of friendship.

It is entirely made of steel, including the sheath, and nickel-plated, with the exception of the rust-blackened blade. The nickel plating is scaled off, and the end of the sheath has been distorted probably when dropped. The handle has two wide side flutes and five circular grooves above the hilt.

The knife is 9.5 inches long, with a 6-inch blade and a 3.5-inch handle. It weighs approximately 3 ounces naked and 4.3 ounces with the sheath, which is decorated with a long scroll and crude dotted lines on the inner side, the outer one being polished by years of use.

Obviously, this is not a fancy knife like the nice pieces illustrated elsewhere here, but it is nevertheless an interesting vestige of a time when the sense of honor was so extreme in Corsica that a village population could be wiped out over two sheep surreptitiously grazing a vineyard under the dazzling Mediterranean sun. ●

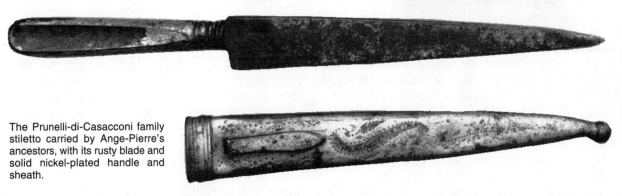

The Prunelli-di-Casacconi family stiletto carried by Ange-Pierre's ancestors, with its rusty blade and solid nickel-plated handle and sheath.

Finally. . . One Good Pocketknife

by JIM FORAL

I CAN FONDLE, admire and appreciate mastodon ivory handles, delicate scrimshawing and engraving, pretty Damascus blades, and the other well-executed embellishments applied to custom knives as much and as long as the next person. Like most men, I am an appreciator of beauty and craftsmanship in any form, and have the profoundest respect for the talent of the artisan capable of crafting these items. I recognize the tremendous interest in and attention to the knife as an art form, but I have resisted being smitten.

As a personal matter, my interest in knives has a pure-ly practical and utilitarian viewpoint. My knives are in the same classification as the wrench, the pliers, and the Phillips screwdriver. Knives are tools to be used to get a job done. Aside from general dimensions, I only insist that my knife be sharp, inconspicuous and handy. I buy my pocketknives off the rack, and I put them to work.

I haven't had the best of luck with knives, I'll admit. My first folder, a small twin-bladed hand-me-down of inexpensive grade, sported garish blue speckled celluloid handles. It was given to me by my father. Its quality and proportions notwithstanding, this knife was briefly the

This Buck #311 is Number Two. The first is keeping a pair of gloves company in Nebraska's Sandhills.

source of no small measure of pride, judged by the standards of a kid.

"Don't cut yourself and don't take it to school" was the extent of his instructions. Apparently my dad thought that, at age eight or so, I was mature enough to possess a knife. When it slipped out of my shirt pocket and plunked irretrievably into the depths of a Minnesota lake two days later, he might have had cause for a different opinion. That loss, thirty-five years ago, taught me that, under all conditions, a pants pocket is the only safe place to store a pocketknife.

While still pre-pubescent, I received as a Christmas gift, a Cub Scout jackknife. It was a good one. Camillus made it.

This was meant to be a versatile knife, and it had one logically shaped, basically boy-proof cutting blade. The knife also featured the indispensable screwdriver/can and bottle opener blade, which for me proved to be useful in the days before pop was sold in aluminum cans. Boys with fertile imaginations may have discovered other uses for this multiple-purpose blade, as well.

Then there was the awl. Its purpose, as I recall, was for

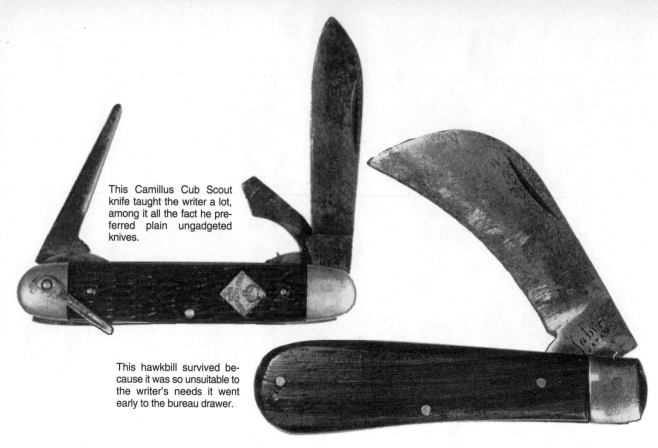

This Camillus Cub Scout knife taught the writer a lot, among it all the fact he preferred plain ungadgeted knives.

This hawkbill survived because it was so unsuitable to the writer's needs it went early to the bureau drawer.

piercing small holes in leather. I can't look at this knife today without recalling one of the most terrifying episodes of my formative years.

While punching an unneeded extra hole in my belt, I miscalculated the path of the awl's swing and drove it squarely into the fleshiest part of my thumb. Only the bone prevented complete penetration. I spent the next two weeks walking around with my hand in my pocket, lest Mom or Dad take the knife away from such an irresponsible child. I was lucky, and my wound healed without parental detection. The scar remains to this day.

Owning the Camillus was educational from a couple of standpoints. First and foremost, I taught myself the basics of safe knife handling. In addition, I learned that a knife should, above all, be a knife. Although a combination of features may entice a boy, any appeal to me has worn away over the years.

For reasons that still mystify me, I still have this pocketknife. It went into retirement before I had a chance to lose it. Big kids, after all, don't flash Cub Scout knives. I've told my own boy that he could have it when he gets old enough.

There was a long parade of pocketknives in my youth and young adulthood. Many I have forgotten. Some were too big or too small. Most were bad decisions, and the fact that they got lost or carelessly misplaced with regularity never bothered me too much. The necessities of a teen-age budget, coupled with the short life expectancy of my knives, dictated that my pockets were normally occupied by the cheaper grade of knife.

As many do, I entered adolescence with a know-it-all attitude. During these years, I fell for flashy knives with trick blades.

At age thirteen or thereabouts, my eye was caught by a Sabre folding knife with a single formidable pruner blade. Just what the attraction may have been, I don't recall, and I'm a bit fuzzy on what my expectations were, but the Sabre turned out a dismal failure. The shape of the blade made it a poor excuse for a whittler and impossible to sharpen. Moreover, the knife's bulk didn't ride the pocket properly. I didn't carry it long enough to lose it. My pruning knife was unceremoniously tossed into a cigar box and remains there to this day. The dumb thing provided a serious lesson in knife selection.

In my view, a pocketknife should be reasonably substantial. It needs to possess enough mass so that it could be controlled by the hand, rather than the fingers, yet not be a handful. Also, it should have enough bulk that it makes its presence known in a pants pocket, but not be a pocketful.

My dad and I had opposing views concerning tool selection. He preferred hand tools on a half-scale. He used a puny 12-ounce hammer, while I swung a 16- or 20-ouncer. Five-inch pliers got him by, when I felt comfortable only with a pair of at least 8 inches.

So it was with knives. He always bought pocketknives with 1½- to 2-inch blades and was quite content with them. I was given a couple of these after they had been worn out and never could get used to them. They got lost

Skull collector Graham is a mighty talker—talked his Dad into using his pocketknife to decapitate a road-killed deer.

in a hurry. My own knives tended to be proportionately bigger. Privately, I never saw much of a need for a blade longer than 3 inches, or much of an excuse to own one half as short.

When I shot the Sixth Army Rifle and Pistol Championships at Fort Ord in 1974, I was given a souvenir knife/manicurist tool, nicely inscribed for the occasion. In stainless steel, it included a nail file, small screwdriver and a miniature scissors. Under the circumstances, most folks would expect this gadget to be American-made, but the root of the blade bears the imprint "Japan." Its dinky 1 1/2-inch cutting blade proved worthless for anything besides opening letters. It did a creditable job of keeping fingernails in trim, but for more serious business had no particular merit. Besides, its 2 1/2-inch length and flat shape made it indistinguishable from the stub of carpenter's pencil I habitually carry in my front pocket.

I was between knives at the time, so this little tool kept the key ring and change company in my pocket for a few weeks. Its utter worthlessness as a knife notwithstanding, I was too proud of this keepsake to risk losing it. I stuck it in a drawer and replaced it with a longer bladed specimen since lost and forgotten.

I have found almost as many knives as I have lost. In the deer hills of Eastern Wyoming, I stumbled across an ancient Western sheath knife. This one had probably doubtlessly found its way under some now-long-gone gut pile years before. With fine sandpaper, I cleaned it up and kept it in my tackle box for years. I haven't seen it for

awhile, and suspect that it could be found on a creekbank near here, rusting away once more.

"Japan" was the only marking on a small Buck-looking jackknife, a parking lot pickup. Well-made, it would hold an edge as well as anything I've ever owned, but the 1 1/4-inch blade was just too short for me, and I gave it to a pal who now uses it to open his mail.

My first really good knife made its way into my pocket about ten years ago, a birthday gift from my wife and infant daughter. While on a mission to locate a strap hinge or something at the neighborhood hardware store, I was abruptly sidetracked by a display case full of Buck folding knives. My bride noticed my interest in the display and, since a birthday was near, invited me to pick one out.

The Buck name, like Winchester or Colt, has been a benchmark of quality in knives for years. I didn't feel that I could go wrong.

After a few minutes of back and forth, I chose based upon what I had learned from the shortcomings of knives past. From the lot of them, I picked the Buck #311. It offered no more and no less than two blades. Their shape and length seemed to fill my general-purpose requirements. I considered the #311's heft to be neither lightweight nor unduly cumbersome, the perfect compromise between too big and too small. Generally, birthday presents aren't especially memorable; this one is an exception.

The #311 is a combination of a pointed clip blade and spey blade. Both are 2 3/4 inches long, made of high carbon stainless steel. Holsters and liners are stainless, too, and the handles are black composition. The sleekly profiled folding knife has an overall length of 4 inches.

The #311 was introduced as the "Muskrat" in 1972. From 1975 on, it was listed in trade literature as the "Trapper." It disappeared from the catalog only recently. Fred Wilson at Buck Knives' headquarters told me that since the #311 was discontinued in 1990, input from pocketknife customers and dealers has been in the form of loud and steady insistence that the knife be brought back, so I'm not alone.

The Buck was a constant companion and saw some sort of use daily. Mostly, I use it to open bills, letters, boxes and parcels. Oftentimes, I put it to work cutting hose, rope or twine; trimming toenails; or accomplishing one of the countless other needs a man has for a knife. It has sliced its share of apples and has carved a pumpkin or two. It won't take the place of a pair of scissors, but the spey blade does a clean job of cutting out pictures from a magazine or notices from a newspaper. There is a part of me that is perpetually thirteen, so the Buck and I whittle now and again.

It has filled the bill as an outdoorsman's knife, and I have yet to discover any reasonable task that is beyond its capacity. Besides removing the hides from squirrels and rabbits galore, it has opened up a number of deer and a couple of antelope, and has caped more than a few of them. Once I used it to skin a runty Montana black bear I

Squirrels to black bear, the slim Buck trapper has done 'em all.

bumped into rather unexpectedly. We have cleaned, scaled and filleted fish together, and removed the shell from at least one snapping turtle.

On one memorable occasion, the Buck came this close to joining its predecessors in the lost-and-found department of knifedom. On an October outing for squirrels, I stopped and sat in the woods to field-dress a half-limit of bushytails. From the earth between my legs, a swarm of ground-dwelling yellow jackets emerged. Dropping squirrel and knife, I made a hasty departure, stung a half-dozen times. When the dust settled, I snuck back to retrieve the knife and my rifle. I didn't have the time or the courage to reclaim the squirrels.

I lost this knife four or five years ago. About midday during the opener of a Nebraska firearms deer season, I spotted a small bunch of prairie mule deer bedded on the crest of a hill. From a sitting position, I took a 200-yard poke at the biggest of the bucks. The group bounded off, trailed by the buck, obviously favoring a hind leg.

Opening the action of the Ruger No. 1, I ejected the empty and reached into my front pocket for another cartridge. In my haste, I dropped the shell on the sandy soil. Chambering the 375 H&H handload anyway, I closed the breech just in time to take a hurried shot at the neck of the departing deer as it limped out of view. The fired case was now stuck in the chamber, wedged so tightly the ejector had torn through the case rim. I tried to pry the shell out with the Buck, but failed.

With all my thoughts on getting after the venison, I laid the knife down and dug out the jointed cleaning rod I habitually carry in my day pack. (Doesn't everybody?) With the rifle back in commission, I went off on the trail of the wounded buck, but left the knife and a pair of gloves. A good part of the next day was devoted to the retrieval of my favorite knife. Each of the countless grassy mounds that comprise the Nebraska Sandhills looks pretty much like the one to the north or the south of it, and I was never able to relocate the scene. I eventually caught up with that deer, but my Buck knife is still out there somewhere.

When I got home, I couldn't find another #311 locally. A mail-order dealer in outdoor gear was willing to place a special order, but the wait would be up to three weeks.

In the meantime, I armed myself with a flimsy advertising knife, emblazoned with the logo of the outfit that generously provided it. The wimpy 2-inch blade retreated into a plastic case when not in use. Its only virtue was that it was better than no knife at all. By the time the new #311 arrived, the disposable knife was a wreck from routine usage.

When this current #311 meets its inevitable fate, I have resigned myself it may well be the last of its species. I am doubly careful where I leave it. Also, I tend to be acutely aware of any holes developing in the pockets of my jeans. Having managed to hang on to this one for five years, a personal record, I have thoroughly enjoyed being its owner. If I continue to keep a close eye on it, perhaps it won't go the route of its many predecessors. ●

TRENDS

It was not possible to ignore function when subdividing the hundreds and hundreds of photos you're used to seeing in these pages. So, some places, we group some sorts of hunters and such together.

Mainly, though, we're going with the small-medium-large breakdown. There are a lot of field-grade looks here, too, and it seems more and more knives are showing up from overseas makers.

As usual, all these are handmade or benchmade by hand in small series with few exceptions. And, as for some time, what "handmade" means varies widely.

And what is a *trend*?

You're the one to figure that out from the pictures we present. It should be easy because these are the only pages in the world that show you this many examples of new work this close together, pre-sorted, you might say.

There are maybe 450 photos in this section, something over 250 in the rest of the book. They're chosen because they seemed to one guy at one place the best photos of the good stuff.

Enjoy them, please.

Ken Warner

No Plowshares Yet 54
Small Knives 58
Backwoods Cutlery 63
The Folding Knife 66
Field-Grade Knives 77
The Overseas Contribution 84
Big Knives 92
Medium Knives .102
Really Small Is Still Big 115
More Automatics Than Ever 119
Investment-Grade Knives 122
The Elegant Knife 125
Miscellany 132

NO PLOWSHARES YET

THE YEAR'S CROP of swords—handmade and not—offers no new trend at all. The trend has been toward grace and richness and sophistication and wildly fluctuating prices, and there's no change.

The overseas manufactories are indulging themselves in riots of color and glitz—one overdressed model after another. They're *very* handsome and, make no mistake, would have been eagerly acquired, at least for parade use, in all the centuries since the Romans left the British Isles.

We tend to forget that our ancestors painted and dyed and shined *everything*. The stern gray medieval legions of current fiction, all grim brown and polished iron, with touches of dull gray, never existed except at the end of long and unsuccessful campaigns.

There was no such thing as too gaudy. Gaudy was the whole idea. A merchant who could have offered fluorescent orange would have owned Europe.

There were, of course, such things as parade swords. Caesar had one, and so did that desert monarch we remember only because he hunted the lion, and a wide range of European notables from William the Conqueror to Bonnie Prince Charlie never left home without one. And as the masters went, so went the minions.

Your cheerful reporter here has even owned a pretty classy "real" parade sword, this one from the Phillipines. The Moros were among the last of the sword-bearing societies. They bore those swords on many bloody occasions, right in amongst American troops who didn't like it much, though armed with repeating rifles.

Anyway, mine had about forty little-finger-sized plates of mother-of-pearl set into a mildly massive hilt. It must have been a bright spot, indeed, even amongst red, yellow and purple silks, when the tropical sun played upon it.

And there are a lot of bright spots now on the market. You can see them here, in fact.

Ken Warner

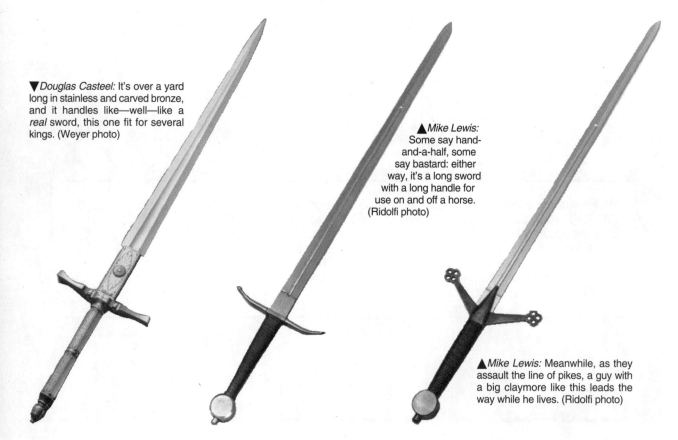

▼*Douglas Casteel:* It's over a yard long in stainless and carved bronze, and it handles like—well—like a *real* sword, this one fit for several kings. (Weyer photo)

▲*Mike Lewis:* Some say hand-and-a-half, some say bastard: either way, it's a long sword with a long handle for use on and off a horse. (Ridolfi photo)

▲*Mike Lewis:* Meanwhile, as they assault the line of pikes, a guy with a big claymore like this leads the way while he lives. (Ridolfi photo)

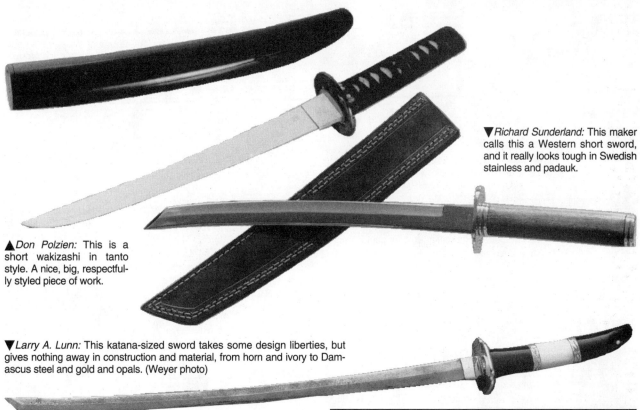

▼*Richard Sunderland:* This maker calls this a Western short sword, and it really looks tough in Swedish stainless and padauk.

▲*Don Polzien:* This is a short wakizashi in tanto style. A nice, big, respectfully styled piece of work.

▼*Larry A. Lunn:* This katana-sized sword takes some design liberties, but gives nothing away in construction and material, from horn and ivory to Damascus steel and gold and opals. (Weyer photo)

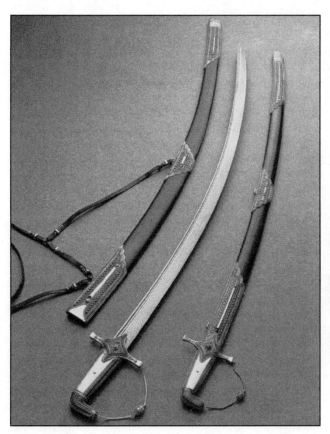

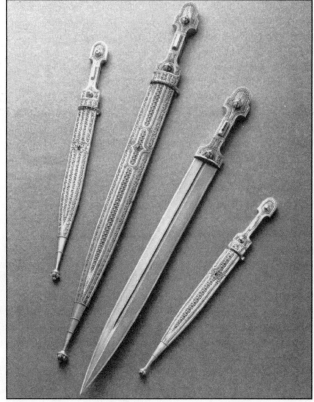

◄▲*Zaza Revishvili:* Sabers and kindjals, en suite and separately, done up in the grandest tradition of the Czars and their Cossacks. Unimpeachable original styling and presentation—the Sword Cold War is over. (Weyer photo)

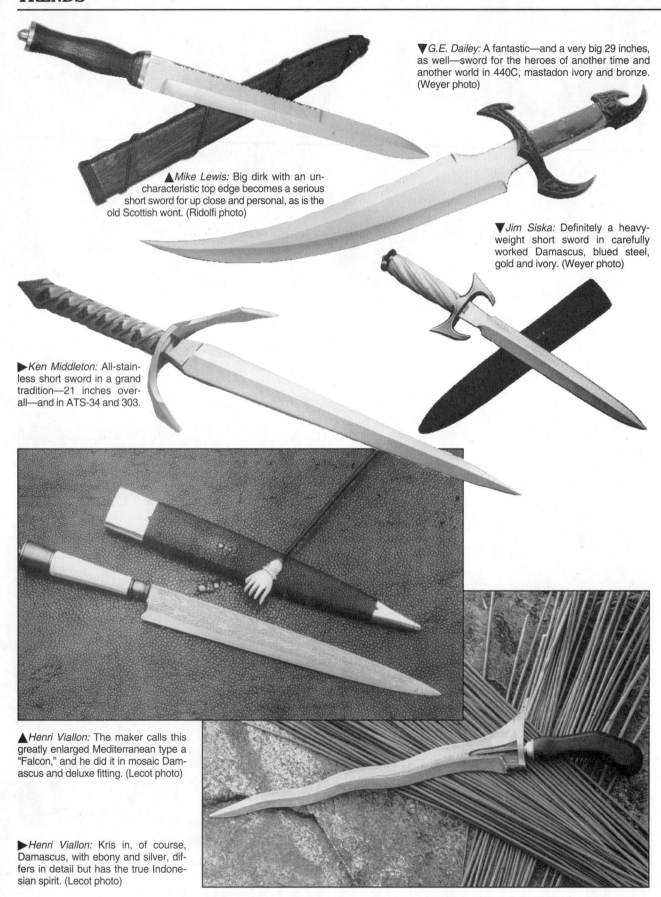

▼*G.E. Dailey:* A fantastic—and a very big 29 inches, as well—sword for the heroes of another time and another world in 440C, mastadon ivory and bronze. (Weyer photo)

▲*Mike Lewis:* Big dirk with an un-characteristic top edge becomes a serious short sword for up close and personal, as is the old Scottish wont. (Ridolfi photo)

▼*Jim Siska:* Definitely a heavy-weight short sword in carefully worked Damascus, blued steel, gold and ivory. (Weyer photo)

▶*Ken Middleton:* All-stain-less short sword in a grand tradition—21 inches over-all—and in ATS-34 and 303.

▲*Henri Viallon:* The maker calls this greatly enlarged Mediterranean type a "Falcon," and he did it in mosaic Dam-ascus and deluxe fitting. (Lecot photo)

▶*Henri Viallon:* Kris in, of course, Damascus, with ebony and silver, dif-fers in detail but has the true Indone-sian spirit. (Lecot photo)

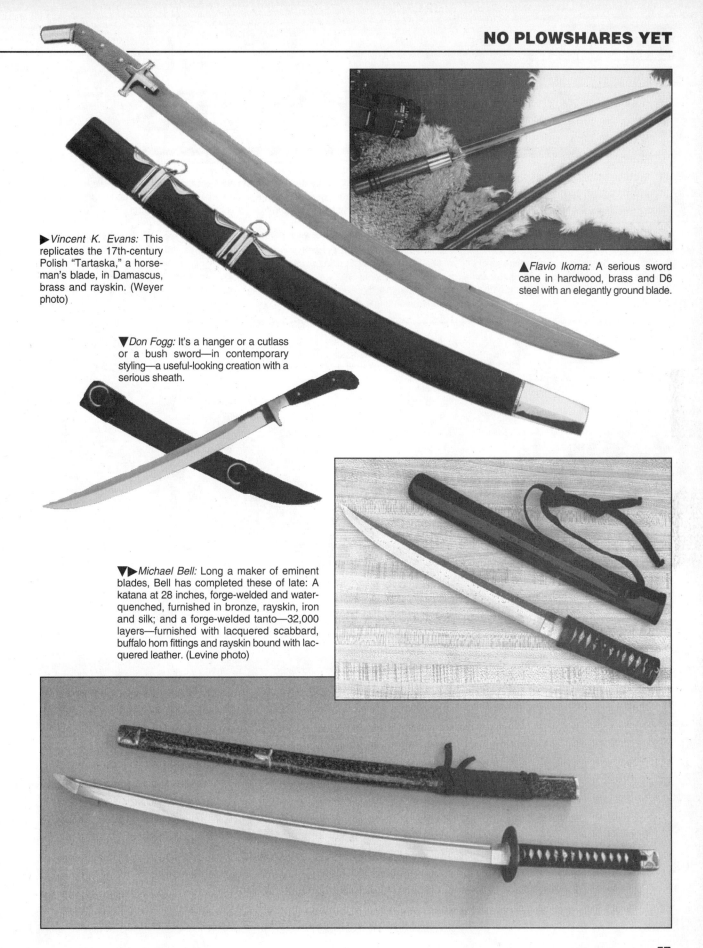

▶*Vincent K. Evans:* This replicates the 17th-century Polish "Tartaska," a horseman's blade, in Damascus, brass and rayskin. (Weyer photo)

▲*Flavio Ikoma:* A serious sword cane in hardwood, brass and D6 steel with an elegantly ground blade.

▼*Don Fogg:* It's a hanger or a cutlass or a bush sword—in contemporary styling—a useful-looking creation with a serious sheath.

▼▶*Michael Bell:* Long a maker of eminent blades, Bell has completed these of late: A katana at 28 inches, forge-welded and water-quenched, furnished in bronze, rayskin, iron and silk; and a forge-welded tanto—32,000 layers—furnished with lacquered scabbard, buffalo horn fittings and rayskin bound with lacquered leather. (Levine photo)

SMALL KNIVES

As WE HAVE REPEATEDLY said, there is more to the small knife than not being big. Whatever the benefits of bulk, the small guy has to do without.

There are all sorts of sports analogies that might apply here. A good big man, for instance, can beat a good little man—every time. In cutlery, however, if a little guy can get it done pretty well, he (or she) might be the choice.

A clever small knife is hardly any burden at all, and it's likely to be quick. A small sheathed knife is inconspicuous, too. And the sheathing can be versatile and flexible.

There are danglers and swingers, little sheaths hanging from harness hardware; there are necklace knives; and pocket sheaths. A lot of small knives live in Kydex sheaths.

And what, exactly, is small? Well, there is no exactly, of course, but the blade has to be under—maybe well under—4 inches, maybe down below 3 inches. The length overall is under 6 inches, for sure—that's ⅛-inch less than a dollar bill.

And the type? Well, there aren't many camp knives and Bowies, but there are small knives of virtually any purpose—service, sport, emergency or defense. See for yourself—here they are, including a Bowie.

Ken Warner

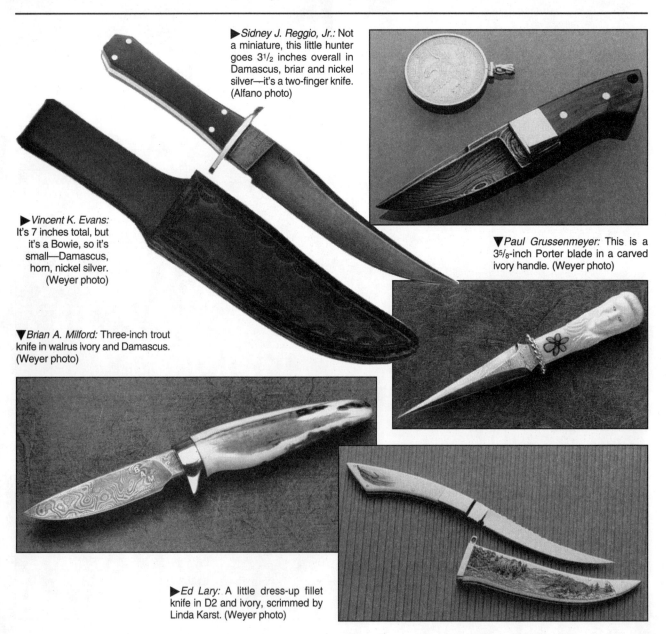

▶*Sidney J. Reggio, Jr.:* Not a miniature, this little hunter goes 3½ inches overall in Damascus, briar and nickel silver—it's a two-finger knife. (Alfano photo)

▶*Vincent K. Evans:* It's 7 inches total, but it's a Bowie, so it's small—Damascus, horn, nickel silver. (Weyer photo)

▼*Paul Grussenmeyer:* This is a 3⅝-inch Porter blade in a carved ivory handle. (Weyer photo)

▼*Brian A. Milford:* Three-inch trout knife in walrus ivory and Damascus. (Weyer photo)

▶*Ed Lary:* A little dress-up fillet knife in D2 and ivory, scrimmed by Linda Karst. (Weyer photo)

◀ *Steve Smart:* Bird and trout with 2¼-inch ATS-34 blade and tortoise shell scales. (LeBlanc photo)

▼ *Ernie Self:* A nice caper-skinner pair in ATS-34 and stag. (Box photo)

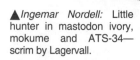

▲ *Ingemar Nordell:* Little hunter in mastodon ivory, mokume and ATS-34— scrim by Lagervall.

▲ *Ron Gaston:* Stylish 3-inch hunter with hand-rubbed ATS-34 and stag. (Weyer photo)

▶ *Walt Neering and Mike Repke:* Short trail-point—quite sturdy—in 440C, brass and stag. (Weyer photo)

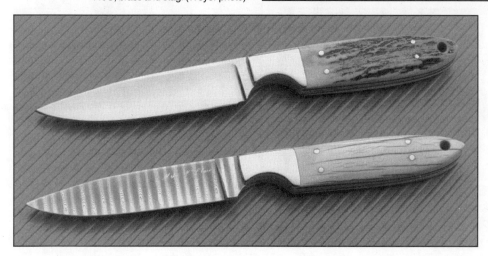

◀ *Michael McClure:* A pair of slim and light boot knives in 440C and Damascus. (Weyer photo)

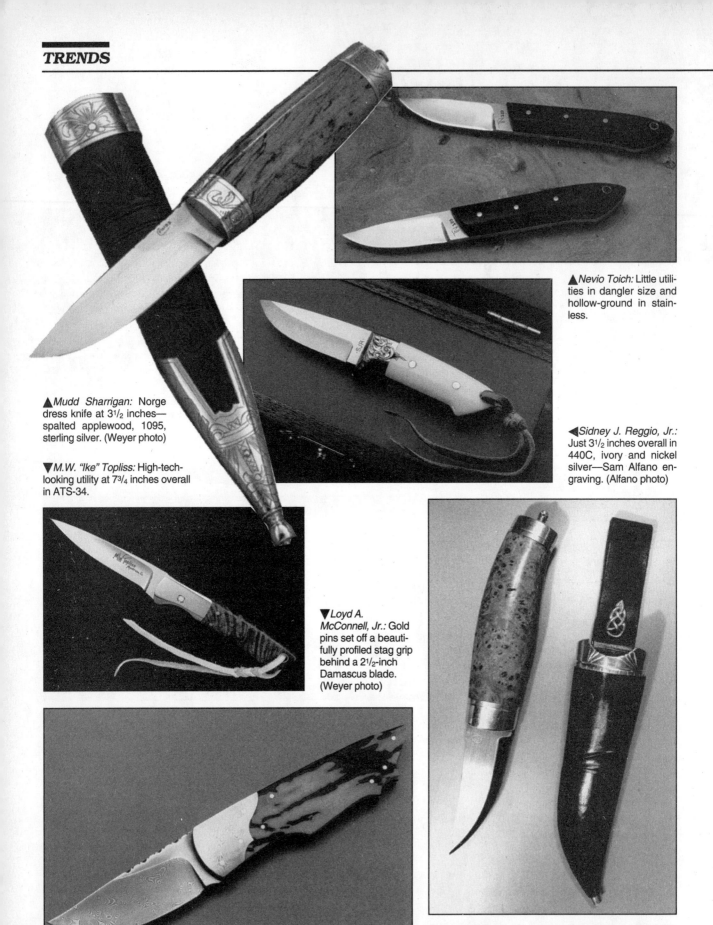

▲*Nevio Toich:* Little utilities in dangler size and hollow-ground in stainless.

▲*Mudd Sharrigan:* Norge dress knife at 3¹/₂ inches—spalted applewood, 1095, sterling silver. (Weyer photo)

▼*M.W. "Ike" Topliss:* High-tech-looking utility at 7³/₄ inches overall in ATS-34.

◄*Sidney J. Reggio, Jr.:* Just 3¹/₂ inches overall in 440C, ivory and nickel silver—Sam Alfano engraving. (Alfano photo)

▼*Loyd A. McConnell, Jr.:* Gold pins set off a beautifully profiled stag grip behind a 2¹/₂-inch Damascus blade. (Weyer photo)

▲*Harald Sellevold:* Laminated Scandinavian blade with burl ash and handle mounted in silver.

▲*Anthony B. Schaller:* Small utility hunters in ATS-34 and 440C—the large one is 6 inches long.

▲*Chuck Ward:* Almost a regular knife, this semi-skinner *looks* small in Damascus, cocobolo and brass.

▲*Mickey L. Ames:* The coke-bottle grip is moridillo; the blade is the maker's Damascus; it's 6 inches overall. (Weyer photo)

▶*Larry Page:* A 3¹/₄-inch utility sports blade in ATS-34 and cocobolo handle—nice clean knife. (Weyer photo)

▶*Robert Branton:* A near-standard, very clean semi-skinner with 3¹/₄-inch ATS-34 blade and big grip. (Weyer photo)

◀*Keith Batts:* Controllable skinner with drop-point has 2¹/₂-inch blade and 5-inch ironwood grip. (Weyer photo)

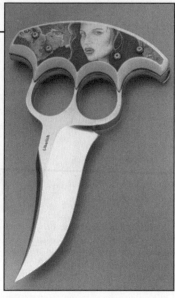

◀*Steve Likarich:* Called "Fatal Beauty," it's 6 1/4 inches overall, scrimmed on ivory by Darrel Morris. (Weyer photo)

▲*Mike Yurco:* Only 4 inches long, this one is stag and stainless in a clipped leather sheath. (Weyer photo)

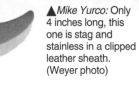

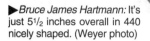

▶*Bruce James Hartmann:* It's just 5 1/2 inches overall in 440 nicely shaped. (Weyer photo)

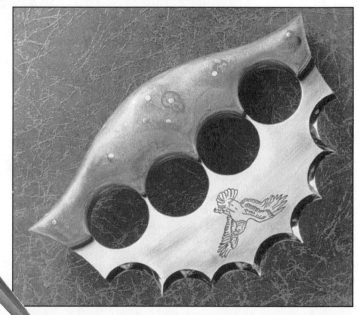

▲*John Zembko III:* Knuckle knife is sharpened on all edges and has birdseye maple grip. (Landis photo)

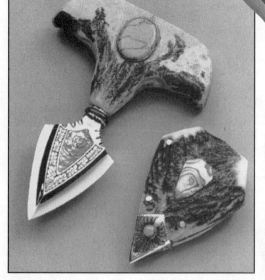

▲*Nobuhiko (Hank) Ishihara:* Just 4 1/2 inches overall in moose antler, turquoise and Swedish steel. (Weyer photo)

▶*Gary (Wolf) Rua:* Old-timey push dagger with 5-inch triangular blade forged in 1095; furniture is brass.

BACKWOODS CUTLERY

MOST CURRENT KNIFE buyers want the best and latest and shiniest—new tech all the way. And there's sense to that because fit and finish have always been gauges of knife quality.

But a minority like their handmade knives to *look* handmade, whatever that means. And another minority want them to look as if a talented blacksmith made them in some place like Washington, Arkansas, about 1832, or perhaps somewhere above the Schuykill in 1740 or so.

Part of this minority, of course, owns a lot of backwoods stuff—they are what are called "buckskinners." Such folks rush back 150 or 200 or 250 years every chance they get—and they have to look right when they get there. In fact, there are rules—Jockey shorts and stainless steel are no-nos, for instance.

Of course, for the essential business of a knife, a century or so of design detail doesn't make a lot of difference. If he can find a spreading chestnut tree, a modern smith can set up with his anvil in a stump next to a stone chimney with a leather bellows blower and make good knives, darned good knives.

It all depends, given steel with about a point of carbon and not too many other alloying elements, on the ability and intent of the smith. If the edge is true and clean, the rest of it is style.

This is America, so the backwoods style has evolved for some. That is, they don't look homemade, just handmade.

So, there's a market for the backwoods look. And all around you here you see how it's met.

Ken Warner

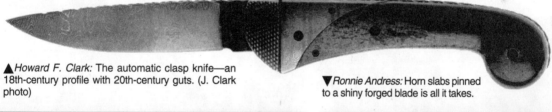

▲*Howard F. Clark:* The automatic clasp knife—an 18th-century profile with 20th-century guts. (J. Clark photo)

▼*Ronnie Andress:* Horn slabs pinned to a shiny forged blade is all it takes.

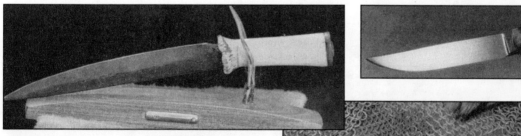

▲*Mario Eiras Garcia:* There are other backwoods than those in North America, and that is where this rifle knife in 5160 and bone is from.

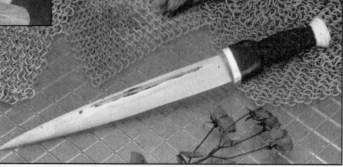

▲*Robert Alderman:* Frontier American with a New Orleans look—a backwoods hunter.

▲*Chuck Patrick:* Rifle knife of the 18th century in near-dirk pattern of forged L6—all local handle material. (Long photo)

◄*Ed Small:* A rifle knife in forged steel and bone with an Indian-style sheath.

►*Joseph F. Keeslar:* In the big Iron Mistress mode, these are famous patterns first forged in the backwoods. (Weyer photo)

▲*Mudd Sharrigan:* This is, the maker says, a Viking woman's clasp knife in brass and 1095, embellished by the maker. (Weyer photo)

▲*Donald E. Weiler:* A forged rasp and a piece of ironwood—not unusual at all 150 years ago.

▲*E. Jay Hendrickson:* Perhaps the fullest sort of 20th-century expression of the talents of the 18th- and early 19th-century smith. (Weyer photo)

▲▼*Joseph F. Keeslar:* Highly finished backwoods patterns in belt knives—crown stag, copper and forged 5160. (Weyer photo)

▼*Daryle Hughes:* A piece of antler and a slim, forged 5160 blade are essential; the spacer is for dress-up.

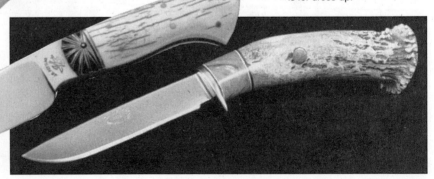

▶*Timothy F. Potier:* A sophisticated rendition of a cross between a Meigs ax and a tomahawk—very stylish. (Weyer photo)

◀*Dan Summers:* Tomahawks and belt axes were frontier commodities. This one has a walnut handle. (Weyer photo)

▲*P.J. Tomes:* William Scagel chose the 20th-century backwoods to live in, so these forged Scagel replicas make backwoods sense today. (Weyer photo)

▲*Don R. Broughton:* D-guard Bowies went off to war in the thousands and looked just like this, except mostly *lots* cruder. (Weyer photo)

◀*Ken Largin:* This is an 8½-inch Scagel-style Bowie, but in the sensible 440C steel. (Weyer photo)

▼*Aubrey G. Barnes:* This is how the old-timers would have made them given modern tools and pay scales. (Weyer photo)

▲*Billy Watson:* This is a copy of a mid-18th-century folder found in Ohio. It's all steel and antler. (Long photo)

THE FOLDING KNIFE

THE BIG ONES are here to stay, and so are the medium sizes, it looks like. And, miniatures aside, there are starting to be small ones, too. There were handmade 2½-inch swell-center balloon pens with two blades at this year's Guild Show—little tiny gents' knives of the type once sold by the thousands in all 48 states.

The new folding knife—the handmade all-out folder—started as a real gee-whiz item, a lockblade hunter. "If Buck can do it, so can I," said the prototypical knifemaker, and we were off to the races, albeit with what we know today were some pretty clunky knives.

It is now fair to say that modern individual craftsmen have taken the folding knife well beyond where it was, visually and technically,

in its so-called Golden Age. To the collector of the old products of Sheffield, to those who specialize in mint specimens of the high-end folders of the past, and some friends of mine, that's heresy. I can't help it, though. I've looked at as many of all of them as I could—a lot of knives—and that's where I come down.

No, the modern guys don't do them by the dozens as piecework. No, they can't be run off in job lots and sold to working stiffs. No, they don't make 2,043 patterns. But what they do make tops the old guys, and in stainless steel to boot, not to mention the quality of engraving, the impeccable materials and the general artistic quality of today's top end.

And, besides, they build a lot of stout

knives for other purposes, too. The latest hand-crafted locks and unlocks, the slick new authomtics, the seemingly all-purpose liner-lock designs. There are whole schools of self-defense thinking based on rather quick legal folding knives, and folders are finding new places in the more exotic forms of military endeavor.

So the prospect is that the knives you see here will be replaced by even better knives. And those better designs will be put into production by the factories. That's already going on and will continue.

It's pretty exciting, this standing around watching cultural and industrial history happening. Take a peek right here.

Ken Warner

◀*Howard F. Clark:* Textures like rushing waters; shape like Old Home Week.

▼▶*Rick Eaton:* Clever layout lengthens the look of this 5-inch blade; embellished by maker. (Weyer photos)

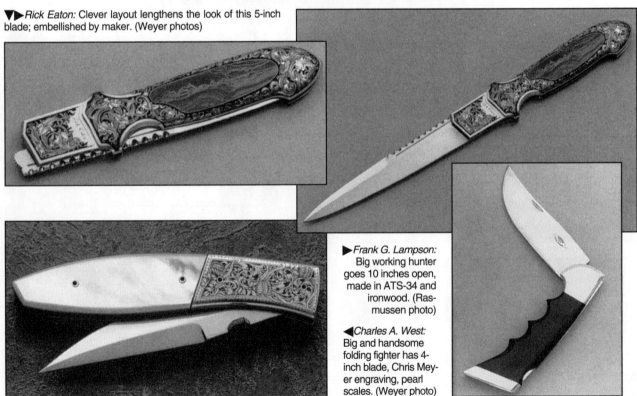

▶*Frank G. Lampson:* Big working hunter goes 10 inches open, made in ATS-34 and ironwood. (Rasmussen photo)

◀*Charles A. West:* Big and handsome folding fighter has 4-inch blade, Chris Meyer engraving, pearl scales. (Weyer photo)

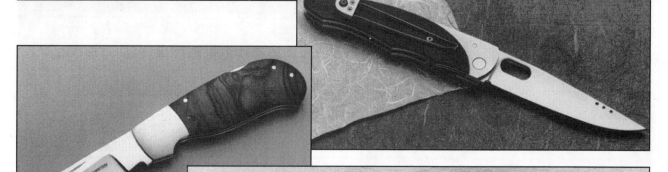

THE FOLDING KNIFE

◀*Jason L. Williams:* Big S-shaped creation goes 12 inches overall in mastodon ivory and a lot of Damascus steel. (Weyer photo)

▼*H.J. Viele:* Not much like most, except it folds in the middle; there's G10 and ATS-34 and a ton of slick. (Weyer photo)

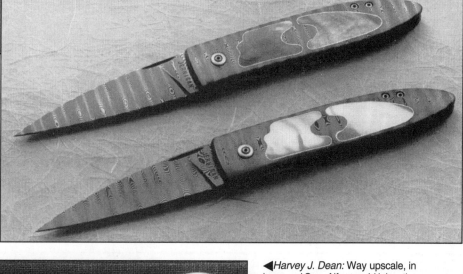

▲*R.C. (Joe) Knipstein:* This blade has five surfaces just on this side; very handsome cotton sampler/ skinner shape in ATS-34 and desert ironwood. (Weyer photo)

▶*Steve Jernigan:* The liner-lock is called a side-plate lock here; they're 6½ inches long overall, in stainless Damascus and mollusk hide. (Weyer photo)

◀*Harvey J. Dean:* Way upscale, in ivory and Sam Alfano gold inlay, the ladder-pattern blade is 2½ inches long. (Box photo)

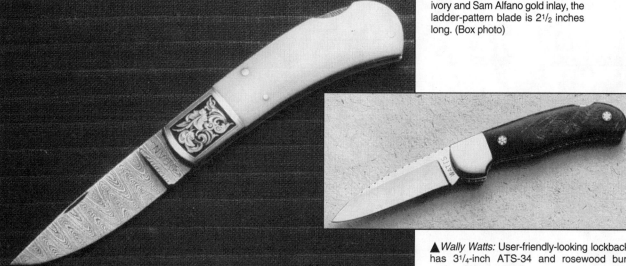

▲*Wally Watts:* User-friendly-looking lockback has 3¼-inch ATS-34 and rosewood burl scales. (Weyer photo)

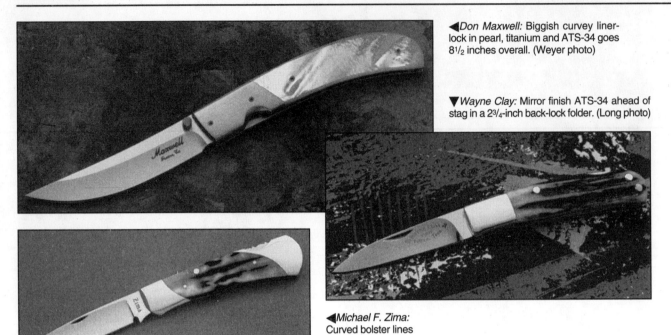

◄*Don Maxwell:* Biggish curvey liner-lock in pearl, titanium and ATS-34 goes 8½ inches overall. (Weyer photo)

▼*Wayne Clay:* Mirror finish ATS-34 ahead of stag in a 2¾-inch back-lock folder. (Long photo)

◄*Michael F. Zima:* Curved bolster lines and stag dress up a small knife.

▼*Rex Robinson:* Fluted mastodon ivory and worked mokume at 8 inches overall. (Weyer photo)

THE FOLDING KNIFE
Lockblades

▼*R.C. (Joe) Knipstein:* A diamond cross-section and a fencing grip angle—an interesting knife. (Weyer photo)

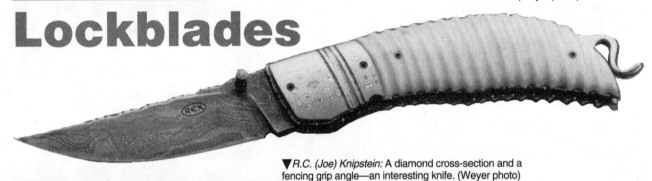

▼*Leon Treiber:* Dark fossil walrus ivory and vine pattern-filed CPMT 440V blade at 6³⁄₈ inches overall. (Weyer photo)

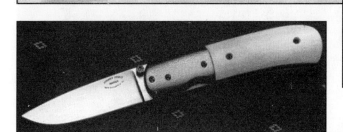

◀*Alan W. Patterson:* File-worked liners, Barlow-sized bolsters and a *san-mai* laminated blade. (Weyer photo)

▼*John W. Smith:* New maker started with this pearl and 440C gents'-size locker. (Long photo)

▲*Johnny Stout:* Shimmering bolster is titanium; the rest is ivory and ATS-34. (Box photo)

▲*A.W. Dippold:* This is a tail-lock folder in twist and mosaic Damascus and oosic—7½ inches overall. (Weyer photo)

THE FOLDING KNIFE
Lockblades

◀*Mike Watts:* Nice old-time hunter pattern in ATS-34, fossil bone and nickel silver. (Weyer photo)

▶*Ralph Dewey Harris:* Strong grind, neat inlay and his own engraving in a 6¾-inch (overall) liner-locker. (Weyer photo)

▶*John C. Howser:* Delicious grinds on a big bullet trapper in brown jig bone and stainless steel—5³/₈ inches closed.

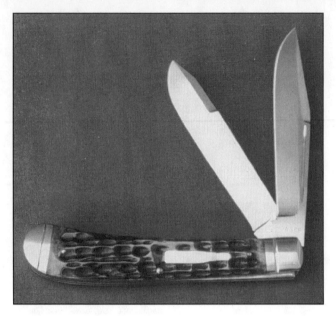

◀*Clifton Polk:* Four sizes, from 2⁵/₈-inch closed to 5 inches, cased in Arkansas-shaped box—choice of steels and finish. (Weyer photo)

THE FOLDING KNIFE
Slip-Locks

▼*Eugene W. Shadley:* Two-blade pen at 2¹/₂ inches closed in black lip pearl, ATS-34 and 416—very cleanly cut. (Weyer photo)

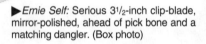

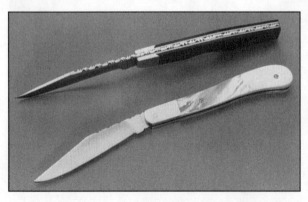

▶*Ernie Self:* Serious 3¹/₂-inch clip-blade, mirror-polished, ahead of pick bone and a matching dangler. (Box photo)

▼*Richard Plinkett:* Elegant Slim Jims in pearl or horn and filework—blades of O1 steel, too. (Weyer photo)

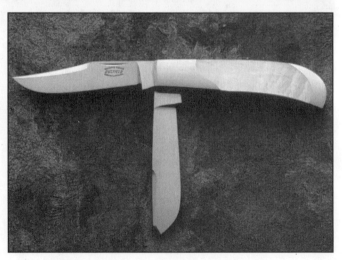

▶*John Busfield:* This trapper has 2³/₄-inch blades of ATS-34, all dressed up with gold pearl and handsomely curved bolsters. (Weyer photo)

▶*Tony Bose:* Dogleg or peanut jack, 3¾ inches closed, in hand-rubbed ATS-34 and amber stag and gold pins and shield. (Hanlon photo)

▲*Barry L. Davis:* Doubled up in two sizes—Damascus, mokume, black or white pearl, filework—big one is 8 inches open. (Weyer photo)

▼*Eugene W. Shadley:* Stockman at 3⅝ inches in ATS-34 and jig bone—awful good-looking work. (Weyer photo)

THE FOLDING KNIFE
Slip-Locks

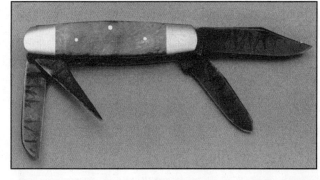

▲*Rick Hinderer:* Four-blade deluxe Cattleman in mokume, black lip pearl and Damascus *san-mai* laminated blades—3¾ inches closed. (Weyer photo)

▲*Philip W. Booth:* Brawny bolstered jackknife in 1095 steel, brass, nickel silver and ebony. Blade is 4 inches.

▶*Warren Osborne:* One interframe, one integral bolster, stag and red bone, 6¼ inches overall, and about as slick as it gets. (Weyer photo)

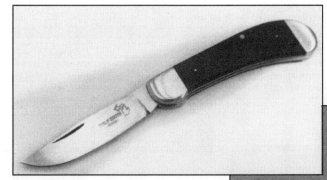

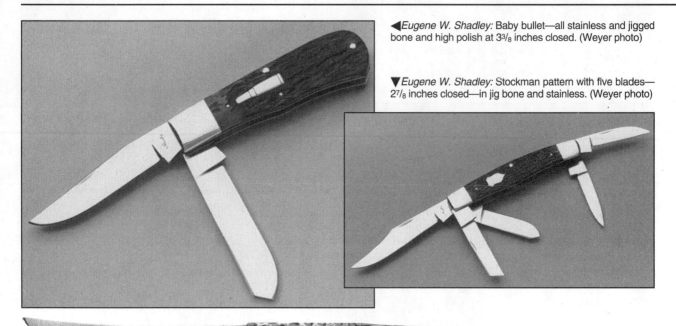

◄*Eugene W. Shadley:* Baby bullet—all stainless and jigged bone and high polish at 3³/₈ inches closed. (Weyer photo)

▼*Eugene W. Shadley:* Stockman pattern with five blades—2⁷/₈ inches closed—in jig bone and stainless. (Weyer photo)

THE FOLDING KNIFE
Slip-Locks

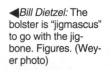

◄*Bill Dietzel:* The bolster is "jigmascus" to go with the jigbone. Figures. (Weyer photo)

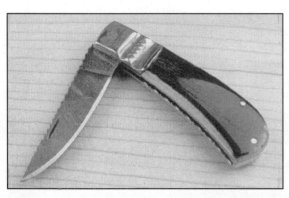

▲*Dale Strickland:* Damascus jack-knife—2¹/₂ inches closed—with mokume bolsters and mastodon scales.

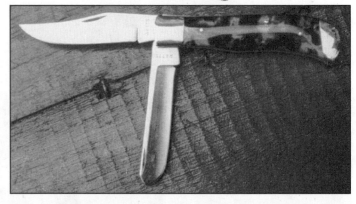

▲*Wally Watts:* Deluxe tortoiseshell small trapper is a real eye catcher.

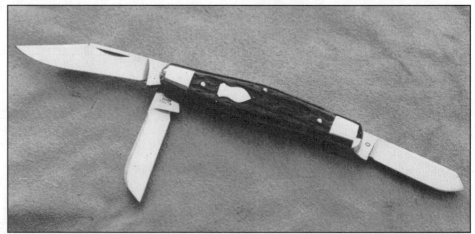

►*Tony Bose:* Swell-center stock-man at 3¹/₄ inches closed—ATS-34 and brown bone. (Hanlon photo)

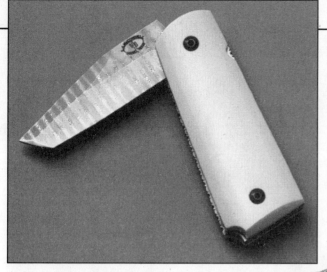

▲*Loyd A. McConnell, Jr.:* The 45 Auto pistol grip knife in all-out American tanto grind. (Weyer photo)

▲*Alan T. Bloomer:* Little button-locked single-blade, with opening stud.

◄*Bob Garbe:* Appleseed folder, all in George Werth Damascus, with 1³/₄-inch blade, under 5 inches open. (Weyer photo)

THE FOLDING KNIFE
Butter Beans, Etc.

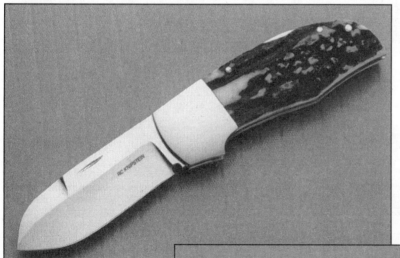

▲*Don Fogg:* Not very big, these Butter Beans offer Damascus blades and bolsters, gold accents, buckeye and redwood burl scales.

▲*R.C. (Joe) Knipstein:* A 21st-century locking sunfish with the old stabber-style spear-point. (Weyer photo)

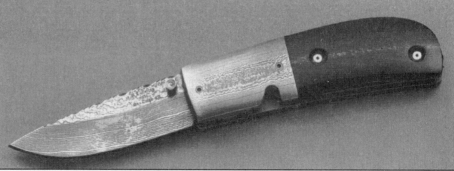

►*Roy Helton:* Big-bolstered in Meier Damascus and handled in buffalo horn. (Weyer photo)

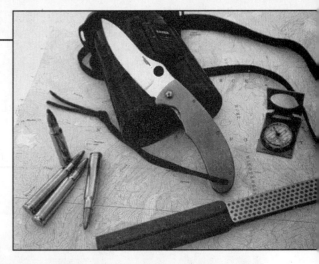

◀*Roy Helton:* Variations, with Buck's permission, on the Crosslock theme—8¼ inches long, open. (Weyer photo)

▶*Phil Boguszewski:* Tim Wegner design as a tough all-arounder in ATS-34 and titanium.

▲*Michael L. Irie:* Special version of the Woods, Irie Woods-patent folder in stainless, engraved by Gil Randolph. (Weyer photo)

THE FOLDING KNIFE

Fighters

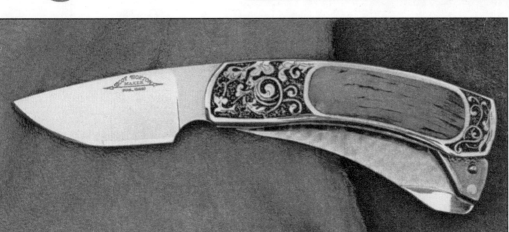

▲*Keith E. Coleman:* A combat folder, liner-locked, with 4-inch stainless Damascus blade in titanium frame.

◀*Scot Horton:* Another swinging grip folder with interframe, engraving and inlays.

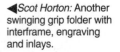

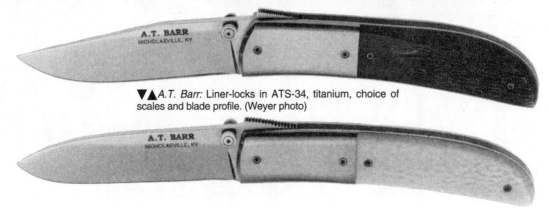

▼▲*A.T. Barr:* Liner-locks in ATS-34, titanium, choice of scales and blade profile. (Weyer photo)

▼*Bill Wolf:* Big liner-lock, inlaid with charolite, 8³/₄ inches overall. (Weyer photo)

▲*Ernest R. Emerson:* Pearl and titanium and stainless Damascus to make the ideal pocket piece. (Weyer photo)

▶*John A. Kubasek:* At 7¹/₄ inches overall, this has a machined titanium grip; blade is Werth Damascus. (Weyer photo)

THE FOLDING KNIFE
Fighters

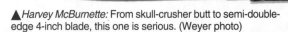

▲*Harvey McBurnette:* From skull-crusher butt to semi-double-edge 4-inch blade, this one is serious. (Weyer photo)

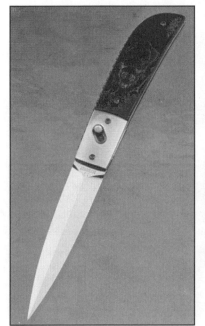

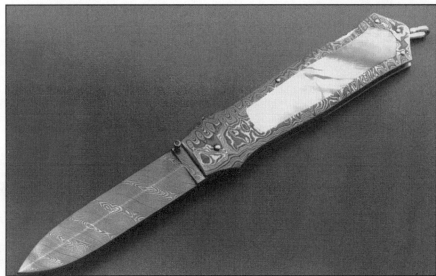

◀*Jack Davenport:* Called the Panther, this goes 12¹/₄ inches overall in Swedish steel and horn with Susan Davenport scrim. (Weyer photo)

▲*Barry L. Davis:* Folding dagger, 8¹/₂ inches overall, in the classic mode of the working smith. (Weyer photo)

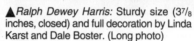

▲*Ralph Dewey Harris:* Sturdy size (3⅞ inches, closed) and full decoration by Linda Karst and Dale Boster. (Long photo)

▲*Elvan Allred:* Family effort—the embellishment is by Scott Allred—produces a 1990s-looking upscale slip-lock inlaid with blue coral. (Weyer photo)

▶*Kent Draper:* Pink mother of pearl, ATS-34 and his own engraving make a distinctive Wharncliffe folder. (Weyer photo)

THE FOLDING KNIFE

Investment Styles

▲*W.D. Pease:* A mokume shield, pearl and Chris Meyer engraving for a San Francisco touch. (Weyer photo)

▲*Robert Blasingame:* Creative inside-out frame, inset with rosewood, engraved and inlaid by Jimmie Nixon.

▶*Tim Herman:* Intricate intermingling of engraving patterns in a neat folder with Wharncliffe blade. (Weyer photo)

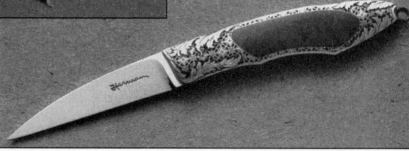

TRENDS

FIELD-GRADE KNIVES

THE TOUGH-LOOKING, boondocks-ready knife didn't take any steps back this year. More and more, fellows who normally do their stuff bright and shiny have taken to providing an option—the same knives in fatigue uniform, so to speak.

And there are guys who do it the other way around —*their* basic knife style is bead-blasted steel, dull Micarta, hard-duty sheaths. And, for those who want something a little brighter, such fellows will doll one up.

The look—that military sort of readiness—is probably riveted in a tactical need to be inconspicuous in use. It's also somewhat easier, even cheaper, to achieve, although the maker who expects sandblasting to hide mistakes is kidding himself. In hunter patterns and utility knives, field grade doesn't mean sand-blasted or dull; these wind up in medi-um polish, plain wood, often guardless—nice, plain knives.

There's no hot new thing in field grades. When these guys use titanium, it's to lose ounces, not get anodized colors. The ideal, one supposes, in the field-grade pattern is to have the best there is, unadorned and only enough—nothing extra.

Field grade emphatically does not mean low-priced, especially in the more exotic tactical kinds of knives. In the hunter/utility business, though, there are a lot of economy models.

There's no field-grade *pattern*. It seemed unlikely that we'd see multi-blade pocket folders in dull finishes, but now they're around.

Ken Warner

▶*Frank Vought, Jr.:* One of the fathers of field-grade finish does 'em by the dozens, this one a man-sized Outfitter neck knife.

▲*Mike Franklin:* The very spirit of the field-grade idea in Franklin's full line of Hawg knives.

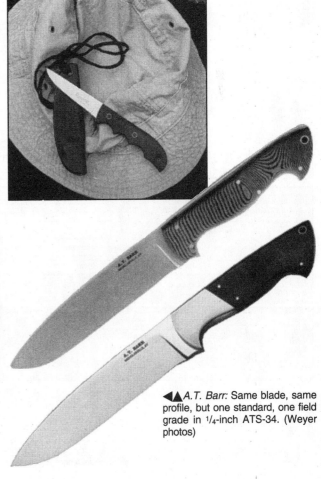

◀▲*A.T. Barr:* Same blade, same profile, but one standard, one field grade in 1/4-inch ATS-34. (Weyer photos)

▼*Wayne Watanabe:* Rayskin and cord wrap is Japanese field grade; ATS-34 is, too.

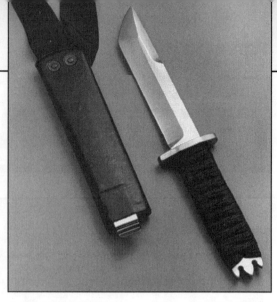

▲*Phill Hartsfield:* Cord-wrapped A2 tool steel in a design called KHAN at 12 inches overall—has two sheaths. (Weyer photo)

▼*Barry M. and Phillip G. Jones:* Six-inch dagger in flat-ground D2 has canvas Micarta—11 inches overall.

FIELD-GRADE KNIVES
Fighters

◀*Robert Rippy:* Camp knife based on SEAL experience has full-tang ATS-34 blade and Micarta handle. (Lum photo)

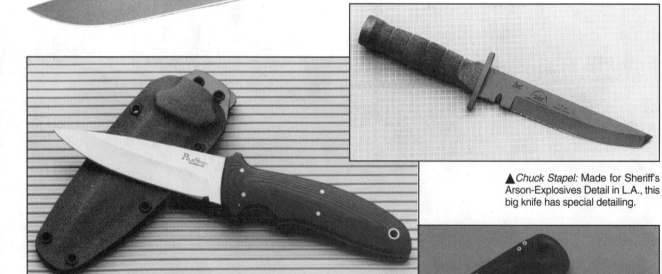

▲*Chuck Stapel:* Made for Sheriff's Arson-Explosives Detail in L.A., this big knife has special detailing.

▲*Al Polkowski:* At 4¹/₄ inches, the ATS-34 blade is set up with G10 grips and a Kydex sheath. (Weyer photo)

▶*Kevin L. Hoffman:* Survival dagger has screw-on scales over a hollow handle with Kydex sheath.

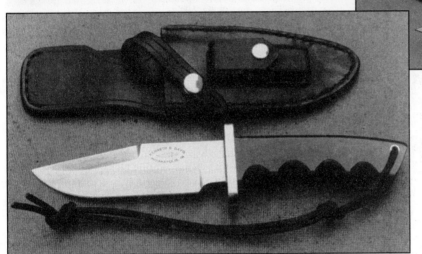

◀*Robert Rippy:* Cord-wrapped stripped-down "Special Ops Bowie" is 12 inches long and 3/16-inch thick in 440C. (Box photo)

▲*Ed Halligan:* Tough-styled 6 1/2-inch fighter design is a prize-winner in ATS-34 and Micarta. (Weyer photo)

FIELD-GRADE KNIVES
Fighters

▲*Ken Davis:* Heavy chute knife at 5 inches in 1/4-inch D2 has Micarta handle.

▲*Jerry Busse:* Big working blade in all-purpose leaf shape goes 13 1/4 inches overall. (Weyer photo)

▲*Ben Voss:* Slick 5 1/2-inch full-tang design called The Baron offers ATS-34 and canvas Micarta.

▶*Mike Franklin:* The short Hawgs look like this; so do the long Hawgs, only bigger.

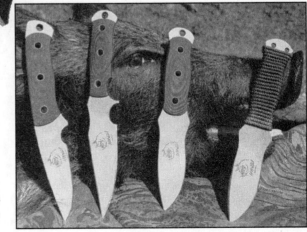

▲*Pat Crawford:* High-tech in G10, titanium and ATS-34, these 4-inch blades are flat on right side.

◄*Robert Terzuola:* Field-grade folder and the Century Star Fighter— both have 4-inch blades and liner-lock mechanisms. (Weyer photo)

◄*Harold J. "Kit" Carson:* These are combat folders at 3 and 4 inches. No non-sense anywhere. (Weyer photo)

FIELD-GRADE KNIVES
Folders

◄*A.T. Barr:* Chisel-ground .170-inch ATS-34 blade is 3½ inches long and bolstered in titanium. Scales are G10. (Weyer photo)

◄*Ernest R. Emerson:* Heavy no-nonsense grind from the guy who popularized this one—plus the usu-al goodies. (Weyer photo)

▶*Ed Halligan:* That's 7075 T-6 alu-minum, with titanium spring and clip, and 3¾-inch ATS-34 blade. (Weyer photo)

◀*Allen Elishewitz:* Smoothed-out folder goes 9 inches overall and aims at the all-around utility role. (Weyer photo)

▶*Allen Elishewitz:* Titanium and carbon fiber around a 4-inch ATS-34 blade, called the Omega. (Weyer photo)

▲*Mike Franklin:* There's a HAWG folder, of course— a heavy-duty liner-lock.

FIELD-GRADE KNIVES
Folders

▲▼*Scott Sawby:* Little guys (3-inch bead-blasted blades) in Micarta and stainless. (Weyer photo)

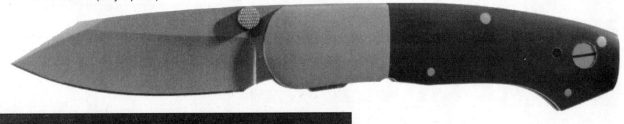

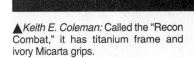

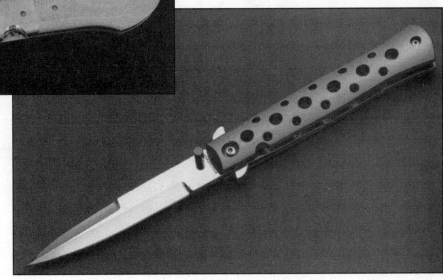

▲*Keith E. Coleman:* Called the "Recon Combat," it has titanium frame and ivory Micarta grips.

▶*Phil Boguszewski:* Smooth sidelock stiletto in titanium and 440C goes 8³/₄ inches overall. (Weyer photo)

▶*Daniel L. Cannady:* ATS-34 and walnut Pakkawood and two rivets are all it takes in the right shape. (Weyer photo)

▶*Charley L. Webb, Jr.:* Field grade can mean ironwood and 1/4-inch ATS-34 and plenty of weight.

▲*Tom McLuin:* It's 3/16-inch 01 tool steel (like the old days) and has moose antler slabs, 9 3/8 inches overall.

FIELD-GRADE KNIVES
Hunters

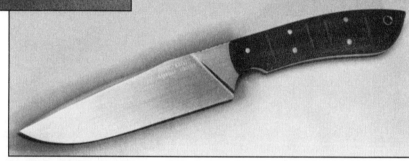

▲*Barry M. and Phillip G. Jones:* Biggish plain fighter is flat-ground ATS-34 and canvas Micarta—10 5/8 inches overall.

◀*Ken Davis:* Big all-purpose design, 1/4-inch thick, takes stag to the field.

▼*Terry L. Kranning:* Budget hunters—6 inches overall—offer nice materials, pins, filework.

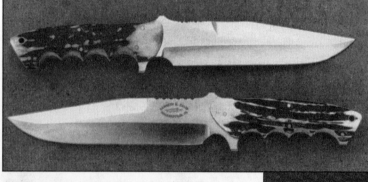

▲*David Ellis:* Utility/boot knife in 1095 steel has 5-inch blade and bocote handle. (Weyer photo)

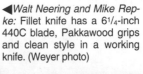

▲*Ken Largin:* Straightforward drop-points, 7¹/₂ inches overall, with wood handles. (Weyer photo)

▲*Roy Blum:* Hunter/utilities in wood and stag and Micarta, made in ATS-34 or D2. (Weyer photo)

FIELD-GRADE KNIVES
Hunters

▶*Chuck Stapel:* This is the new Stapel mark on using knives—another world for field grade.

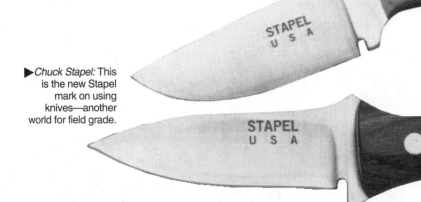

◀*Walt Neering and Mike Repke:* Fillet knife has a 6¹/₄-inch 440C blade, Pakkawood grips and clean style in a working knife. (Weyer photo)

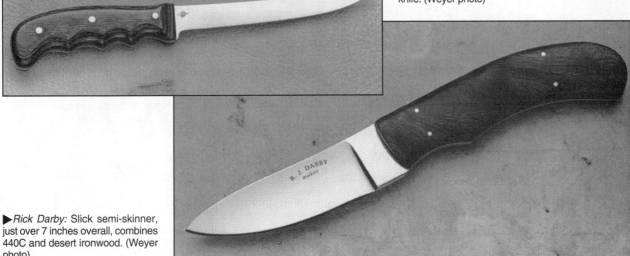

▶*Rick Darby:* Slick semi-skinner, just over 7 inches overall, combines 440C and desert ironwood. (Weyer photo)

THE OVERSEAS CONTRIBUTION

HERE'S WHERE WE show what they've got, those people who make their knives outside the USA. And they have plenty to show. And more of them show up every year.

One doesn't have to be very far from the U.S. to make very different-looking knives. Only a morning's drive will do it. Canadians make very different knives. Some of those march to a Francophone drum. The knifemakers of Quebec retain a Continental sense of design and make some classy knives.

And not very many Canadian craftsmen do

the ordinary drop-point full-tang sort of thing. Of course, one shouldn't expect them to—that's what's done *below* the border.

Elsewhere—and elsewhere reaches from Down Under to the Fjords of Norway and the old cities of Muscovy—the styles range from ethnic to eclectic. South Africans are working toward a sort of heavy-duty look in almost all their knives, while in Scandinavia they march in several directions.

One cannot tell about the Japenese. They are still big-time in *commercial* knifemaking,

of course. Now, we begin to know more names of individual Japanese craftsmen working in Japan.

It boils down to the fact that knifemakers overseas manage nearly complete diversity with fewer workers than here in the Great Melting Pot. The distinguishing characteristic—at least of the overseas knives we show right here—is that they don't look typically American.

That's a good thing.

Ken Warner

▼*Yasutaka Wada:* A 6¹/₂-inch stoutly ground dagger blade mounted in carved wood, 11¹/₂ inches overall. (Weyer photo)

▼*Arpad Bojtos:* The Rain Forest in ATS-34, ivory and gold complete with an archer and a jaguar. (Weyer photo)

▲*Arpad Bojtos:* Wildly sculpted short knives in ATS-34. On one Hercules kills a lion; on the other, a gazelle awaits the leopard. (Weyer photo)

◄*Jean-Yves Bourbeau:* Carved Kasanda wood and an unusual blade pattern add up to a fighter called Flame, 11 inches overall. (Weyer photo)

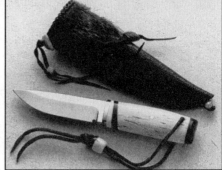

▲*Michel Blum:* Robust puukko, bone-handled and 8¹/₄ inches long, has crocodile-beaver fur sheath. (Weyer photo)

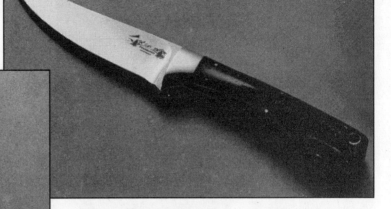

▼▶*Andrew Frankland:* Two small ones—the caper is 3¹/₂ inches of ATS-34 and has a buffalo horn handle; the other, the "Ferret," has a 2¹/₂-inch D2 sheepsfoot blade and blackwood for a grip. (Mumford photos)

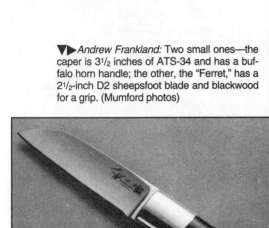

◀▲*Henri Viallon:* Damascus blades and ivory handles notwithstanding, these are interpretations of old French country knives. (Lecot photos)

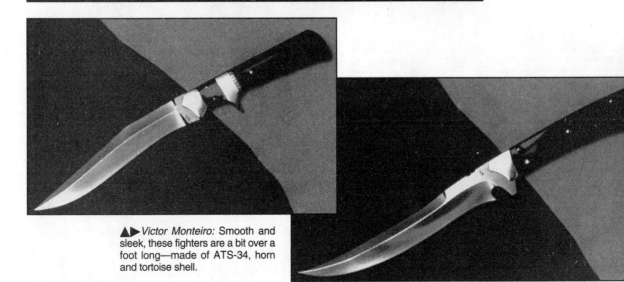

▲▶*Victor Monteiro:* Smooth and sleek, these fighters are a bit over a foot long—made of ATS-34, horn and tortoise shell.

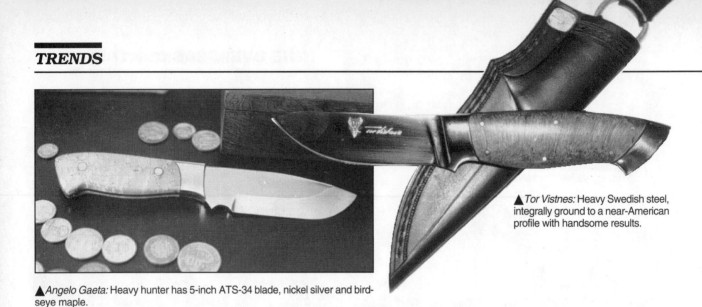

▲ *Tor Vistnes:* Heavy Swedish steel, integrally ground to a near-American profile with handsome results.

▲ *Angelo Gaeta:* Heavy hunter has 5-inch ATS-34 blade, nickel silver and bird-seye maple.

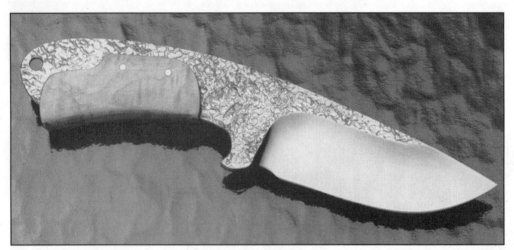

◄ *Akihisa Kawasaki:* This big (9¼ inches) hunter shape—chisel-ground—offers texture and a saddle-mount hand-grip of wood. (Weyer photo)

▼ *Mario Eiras Garcia:* A fighter in 5160 and bone with very personal shape and four different edges.

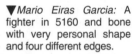

▲ *Luiz Villa:* Small, sturdy-looking designs for the hunter, each purpose-built.

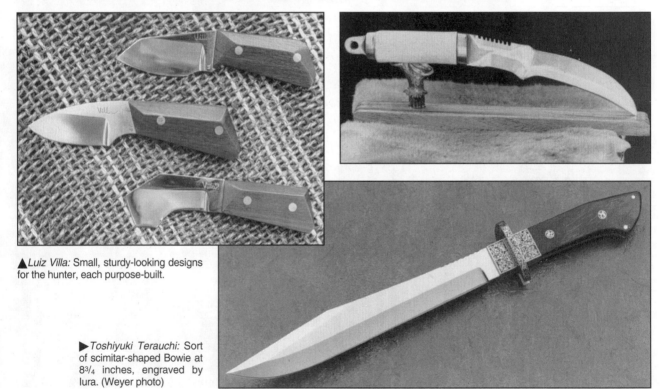

► *Toshiyuki Terauchi:* Sort of scimitar-shaped Bowie at 8¾ inches, engraved by Iura. (Weyer photo)

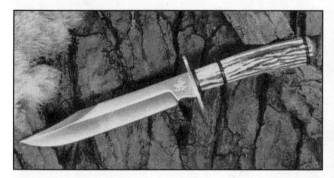

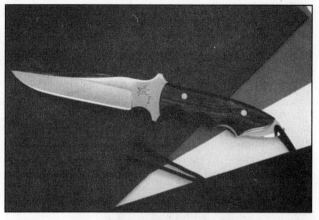

▲▼▶*Paulo Richardo P. Lala:* Big fighters and Bowies in D6 steel, hardwood, stag and Micarta.

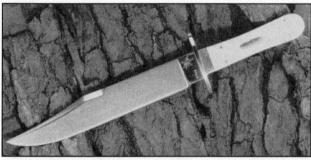

▶*Bruce James Hartmann:* Large, but delicate, this dagger in stainless steel goes over 15 inches overall. (Weyer photo)

▲▶*T. Michinaka:* Classic Western dagger patterns in classic trim on ATS-34 blades, engraved by Simon M. Lytton.

Marc Bjorn Carlsson: Lemonwood handle and D2 blade, with gold and silver touches, make a trailing-point hunter. (Hansen photo)

Wolfgang Loerchner: Imagination in a Persian fighter, 15 inches overall. (Weyer photo)

Uwe H. Hoffman: Dagger in D2 at 6½ inches with red Micarta handle and spiraled pins.

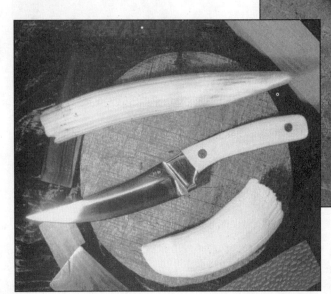

Nobuhiko (Hank) Ishihara: Six inches of complex embellishment, including horn and silver. (Weyer photo)

Mick R. Wardell: Plain, not fancy, in a North African shape—6-inch blade of D2, Micarta handle.

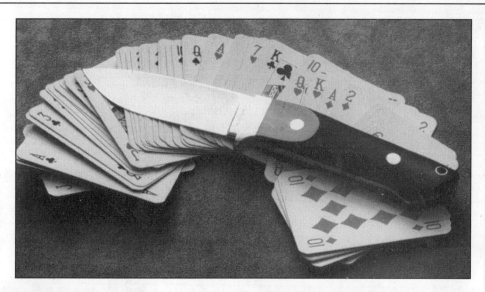

Ettore Bertuzzi: An admirer of classic design, this maker has produced a Loveless/Kressler model in ironwood and D2; a Lake model in D2, silver and lapis; two D'Holders in ATS-34 and stacked handles, neither marked; and a Loveless drop-point, also unmarked.

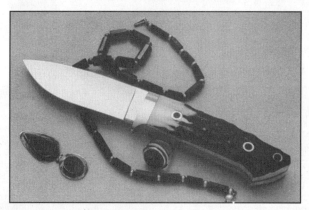

◄*Gerard Doursin:* Integral Damascus hunter—very straightforward, very robust.

Corrie Schoeman: Two liner-lock folders cleanly profiled and fitted with high-tech fasteners.

Nobuhiko (Hank) Ishihara: Elaboration with touches of fantasy in a dagger with something to look at in every square inch. (Weyer photo)

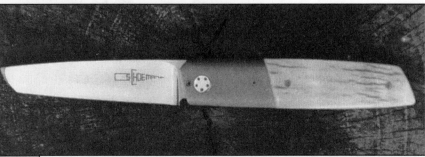

Franco Bonassi: Immaculate small hunter and liner-lock folder offer stainless blades, stag, ivory, and titanium trimmings.

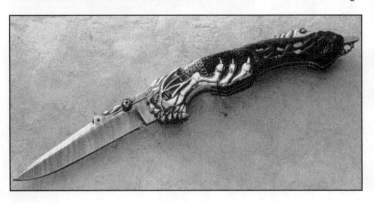

Laurent Doussot: Fantastic 7-inch folder called "Leviathan" brings snakewood and sterling silver and Zowada Damascus to the party. (Weyer photo)

◀▼*Tom Bache-Wiig:* Not quite Norse patterns in sturdy hunters with contoured grips, nice pin-work.

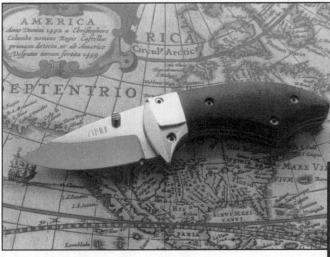

▲*Marc Bjorn Carlsson:* A liner-lock all his own cleanly sculpted in ATS-34, briar, silver and tita-nium. (Hansen photo)

▲▶*Aad Van Rijswijk:* Clean pro-files and full embellishment in a folder and a pair of heavy hunters—the new Netherlands look.

▲*Keidoh Sugihara:* This is a traditional Japanese fold-er pattern, done here in the maker's Damascus and ironwood. (Weyer photo)

BIG KNIVES

WE MADE THE CASE last year: when you need 'em, there ain't nothing like inches. Ounces, we said, we can do without, most times, but inches can make a difference.

As a lifelong student of outdoors literature, I am quite aware of the attitudes of some toward any knife over 4 inches or so.

"If you need that much knife, carry an ax," they say.

They're perfectly correct—indeed, in terms of the old-timer's books, they are even better, they are *politically* correct. However, correct isn't quite the same thing as *right*. What's right is that if you carry an

ax, a small knife is fine. What's also right is: How often do you carry an ax? Or even a hatchet?

Personally, I own about a dozen working axes and hatchets. I like them; I even work with them; I keep them sharp. And I avoid carrying any of them any farther than I have to. And I bet you're the same.

So a largish knife makes sense, maybe anytime you're out of sight of the pickup. Long ago, I carried an 8-inch Western knife in Florida, especially to build turkey blinds (out of palmetto fans) in a hurry. There's a big knife—actually several—I carry around the

property to trim out deer trails so I may walk as easily as the deer.

There are all kinds of more pressing reasons for a big knife. We've talked about them here a lot, even built a cabin with one, one time. And then there are the more lurid possibilities us and Rambo know about.

Regardless of all that, there are a lot of people out there who want big knives, and there are a lot of people in here who make them for those people.

Look around—you can see for yourself.

Ken Warner

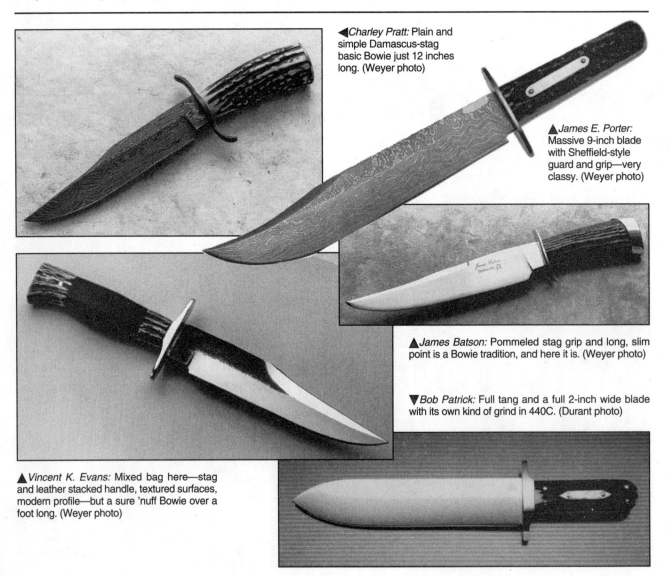

◀*Charley Pratt:* Plain and simple Damascus-stag basic Bowie just 12 inches long. (Weyer photo)

▲*James E. Porter:* Massive 9-inch blade with Sheffield-style guard and grip—very classy. (Weyer photo)

▲*James Batson:* Pommeled stag grip and long, slim point is a Bowie tradition, and here it is. (Weyer photo)

▼*Bob Patrick:* Full tang and a full 2-inch wide blade with its own kind of grind in 440C. (Durant photo)

▲*Vincent K. Evans:* Mixed bag here—stag and leather stacked handle, textured surfaces, modern profile—but a sure 'nuff Bowie over a foot long. (Weyer photo)

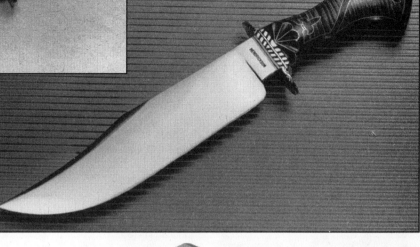

▲*James Batson:* Antiqued in San Francisco style, this Bowie's forged in 5160. (Weyer photo)

▶*E. Jay Hendrickson:* Classic curvey Bowie with the typical ABS grip—first-class work all through. (Weyer photo)

◀*William J. Tyc:* Cleaned-up Sheffieldian pattern over 15 inches long, fiercely pointed. (Weyer photo)

BIG KNIVES
The Bowies

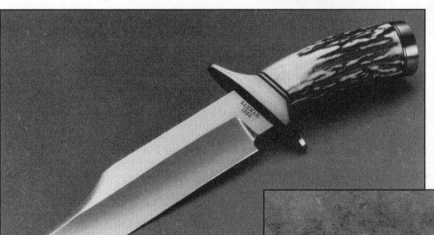

▲*Loyd A. McConnell, Jr.:* Bear-spirited big knife—gold bear paws by Meyer and such—over 15 inches long. (Weyer photo)

▲*Mike Sakmar:* All modern conveniences here—8-inch ATS-34 blade, comfy shaped guard, good looks. (Weyer photo)

▶*Kelly S. Kennedy:* Brawny is the word: The blade is 10$\frac{1}{2}$ inches long and *big*; the rest is ivory and forged fittings. (Weyer photo)

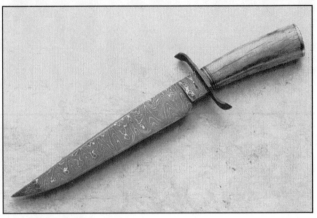

▲*Timothy F. Potier:* Called the *Bayou Bowie*, it goes 16½ inches in blackwood and 5160. (Weyer photo)

▲*David Anders:* A quick-looking knife, it as a 10-inch blade, silver inlays and an oosic handle. (Weyer photo)

▼*Robert E. Barber:* A 440C blade, star pins, alternate ivory slabs; it's called a BlueRidge Bowie. (Armontrout photo)

BIG KNIVES
The Bowies

▲▶*Harvey J. Dean:* Deluxe D-guards in engraved (by Theis) sterling silver are grace notes in these *big* knives, one in walrus ivory, the other black walnut. (Weyer photos)

◀*Kim Thomas:* A touch of *hirschfänger* from Germany in this Bowie-with-clamshell—at 13 inches overall. (Weyer photo)

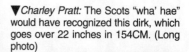

BIG KNIVES

◄*Don Polzien:* All-out tanto in 1065 steel, silk, rayskin, bronze, silver, horn and lacquer. (Weyer photo)

▼*Charley Pratt:* The Scots "wha' hae" would have recognized this dirk, which goes over 22 inches in 154CM. (Long photo)

▲*Don Fogg:* Wenge and steel colored and textured in the forge, 13½ inches long. (Weyer photo)

BIG KNIVES
The Ethnics

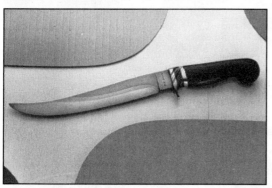

▲*Michael K. Manabe:* Mostly Persian lines and triple-temper like Persians never saw. (Weyer photo)

▲*John Greco:* Another wakisazhi-length tanto in A2, in a rosewood storage sheath carved by Sherry Lott. (Weyer photo)

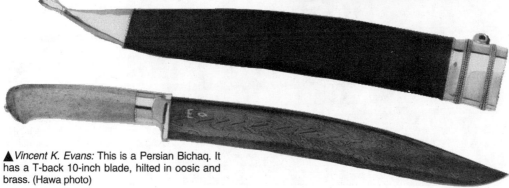

▲*Vincent K. Evans:* This is a Persian Bichaq. It has a T-back 10-inch blade, hilted in oosic and brass. (Hawa photo)

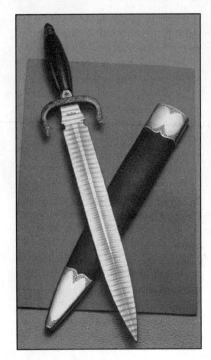

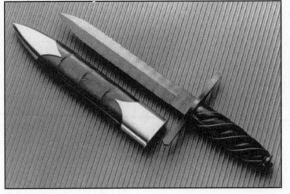

▲*Timothy F. Potier:* Straight-up quillon dagger, 12 inches overall, in Damascus and spiraled blackwood. (Weyer photo)

▶*Todd M. Kopp:* A band of gold nuggets in the bolster and blued steel all over. (Weyer photo)

◀*Tom Black:* Seriously large, this one goes 24 inches overall—a lot of stainless Damascus. (Weyer photo)

BIG KNIVES
The Daggers

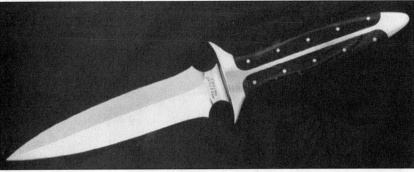

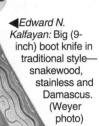

◀*Edward N. Kalfayan:* Big (9-inch) boot knife in traditional style—snakewood, stainless and Damascus. (Weyer photo)

▲*Edmund Davidson:* You could call it a double integral, for fitting the wood crossways is more than twice the work. Looks nice, though.

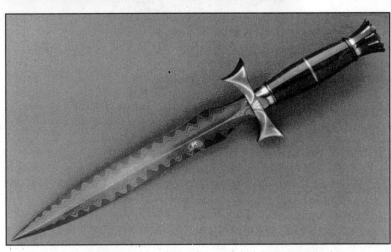

◀*Bertie Rietveld:* Big ladder-Damascus blade, stone grips, color and gold inlays by Winkler—an impressive, colorful knife.

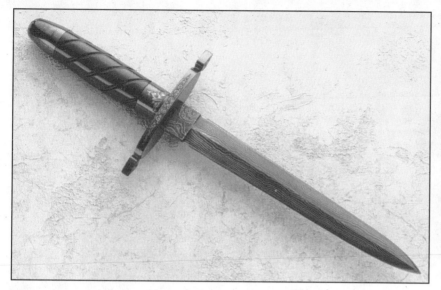

▲*Marvin Solomon:* Medieval short dagger style in buffalo, Damascus, blued steel; Billy Bates engraving. (Weyer photo)

▶*Kirby C. Bailey:* Elephant ivory and ATS-34 at 10¼ inches with its own box of padauk. (Weyer photo)

The Daggers

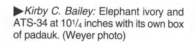

◀*Ed Small:* Fanciful forge play produces a tendrilic guard for a triple-drawn blade.

◀*Chuck Patrick:* Slim Scots dagger/dirk in walnut root, ivory, silver and 1095. (Long photo)

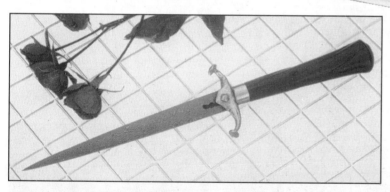

▲*Randy Lee:* It's 11 inches overall, engraved by Bruce Shaw—a clean forthright dagger.

▶*Dennis E. Friedly:* Dressy dagger in stainless Damascus (Thomas), ironwood and gold. (Weyer photo)

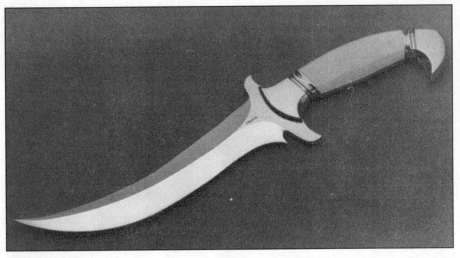

▲*Steve Likarich:* Maker calls this the "Big Bent Sharp Thing." It's ATS-34 and ivory, 13½ inches long. (Weyer photo)

▶*Edward N. Kalfayan:* A kris elaborated into a medieval look in ivory and gold and stainless steel. (Weyer photo)

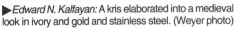

BIG KNIVES
The Fanciful

◀*Don Pavack:* Once you have a *blesbok* horn, the rest is simple; it's 13 inches long overall. (Weyer photo)

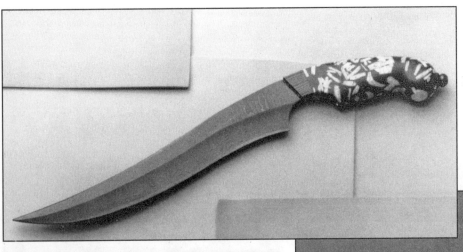

◀*Douglas Casteel:* This dark Damascus 10-inch blade has a Chinese writing stone handle, and that brings up several questions. (Weyer photo)

▼*Mike Sakmar:* The curved fighter as sculpture in ATS-34 and ivory—somebody has to do it.

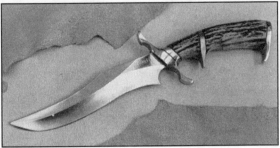

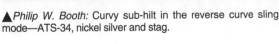

▲*Philip W. Booth:* Curvy sub-hilt in the reverse curve sling mode—ATS-34, nickel silver and stag.

◄*Edward N. Kalfayan:* A halfway house of styles—modern sculpture in the grip, Damascas USA up front. (Weyer photo)

▼*Charles F. Ochs:* Delicate wavy-blade dagger, forged from 52100 bearing steel, with horn handle. (Weyer photo)

BIG KNIVES

The Fanciful

►*Don Hume:* Lost wax castings in copper for the leafy look; blade is 440C. (Weyer photo)

◄►*Bruce James Hartmann:* Winged dagger in 440 shown with its wood model. (Weyer photo)

▼*Paul P. Sheehan:* "Desperado" is its name, but it isn't flashy, just solid 440C. (Weyer photo)

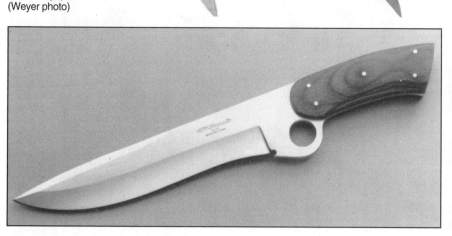

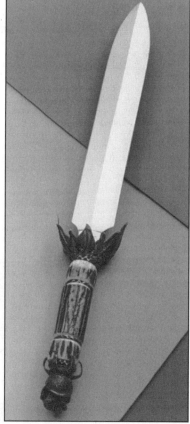

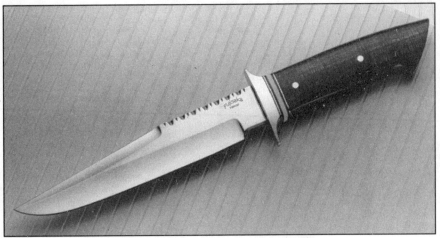

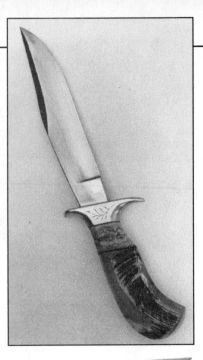

▲*Stanley Fujisaka:* Fighter from Hawaii in koa wood and 440C at 13½ inches overall. (Weyer photo)

▶*Ed A. Fowler:* A large clip-point companion knife in sheephorn and 52100 steel.

BIG KNIVES
The Workers

▲*Philip C. Wilson:* The large fillet knife in ATS-34 and stacked oosic and ironwood. (Kelley photo)

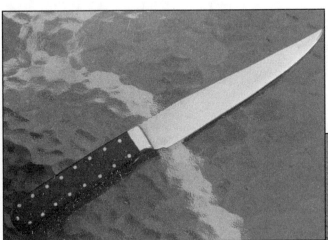

▲*Jim Fister:* Long single-edged slim blade for the cutting problem at hand.

▲*Gary (Wolf) Rua:* Forged from 1095, with pewter bolsters and purpleheart grips, it's an old-time gent's belt knife. (Dailey photo)

▶*Anthony B. Schaller:* Nearly a Big Bear, it's double hollow-ground 440C and green canvas Micarta. (Weyer photo)

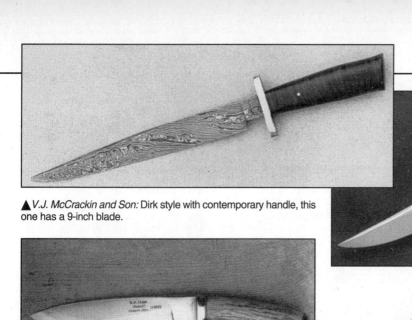

▲ *V.J. McCrackin and Son:* Dirk style with contemporary handle, this one has a 9-inch blade.

▲ *Mark Rochmans:* Long and slim and curly maple—over 15 inches as you see it. (Weyer photo)

▲ *Richard D. liams:* Forged 52100 bearing steel in a good-looking antler-handled camp knife.

▶ *Tim Hancock:* Called the "Black Fighter" in ebony and Damascus. (Bittner photo)

BIG KNIVES

The Workers

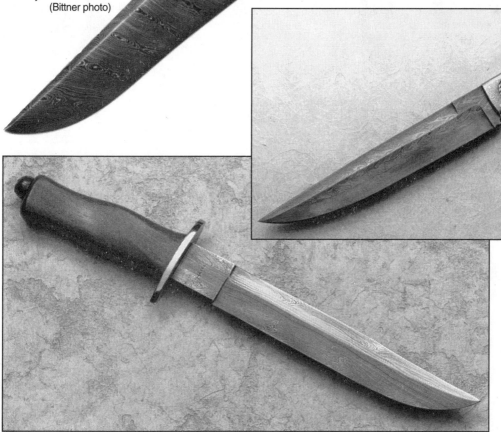

▲ *Ralph J. Selvidio:* Slim and beefy at the same time ain't easy, but here it is at over 15 inches. (Weyer photo)

◀ *Wally Hayes:* Pink ivory and a lengthwise Damascus pattern in a big 15-inch knife. (Weyer photo)

MEDIUM KNIVES

WHATEVER THE SHAPE, the materials, the design intent, the fabrication methods—the most important thing about a medium knife is its size. That sounds really dumb, but it's so: A clear majority of people who buy knives want them to be 7 inches to 11 inches or so, overall.

Your standard hunter; the 6-inch utilities; all manner of skinners and personal defense knives; best-sellers (for decades) in commer-cial knives—that's how big they are. Take a ruler to the next show and see.

Within that size range, which could in-clude a 7- or 8-inch fillet knife or a pretty beefy chute knife, or a dandy Green River skinner, you can find something that works at your job. That something will be a little or a lot smaller than the KaBar military knife.

Nope. No big classic camp knives and Bowies, but lots of such *shapes*. Boot knives, even big boot knives, but no all-out fighters. Lots of concealment and gents' belt knives. Nothing very medieval, but some. Solid users, mostly.

Except for the extra-pretty ones. There seem to be a lot of upgraded medium-sized knives about. And some pretty jazzy ones, too.

We show some of all of them here. Medi-um knives are easy to find.

Ken Warner

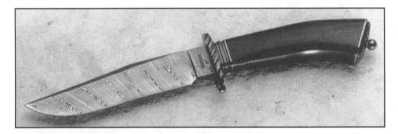

▶*Tim Hancock:* Full-dress fighter-styled knife about right for comfortable carry. (Weyer photo)

▼*J.D. Smith:* Turkish twist Dam-ascus at 6½ inches, set up Sheffield-shaped with dark stag. (Weyer photo)

▲*Harvey J. Dean:* It's "The Huckleberry," in 1095 steel, a repro of a 90-year-old Rodgers knife. (Box photo)

▼*Mark Lubrich:* Nice-sized big hunter—camp-knife style—in stacked stag and leather.

▼*William Behnke:* Aggres-sive-looking, this is 11 inch-es overall; stag is sambar. (Weyer photo)

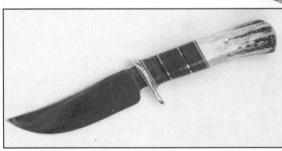

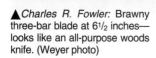

▼*Mickey L. Ames:* Sharp-pointed 10½-inch (overall) curved Bowie in 320-layer Damascus and moridillo. (Weyer photo)

▲*Charles R. Fowler:* Brawny three-bar blade at 6½ inches—looks like an all-purpose woods knife. (Weyer photo)

MEDIUM KNIVES
Bowie Styles

◄*John M. Cross:* At 5 inches, this straight Damascus hunter is the right shape. (Weyer photo)

▼*Jim Walker:* A 5-inch low-point fighter, very slim in the blade. (Weyer photo)

▼*Jim Brown:* Camp knife for use at short range—moose antler and nickel silver. (Weyer photo)

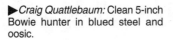

►*Craig Quattlebaum:* Clean 5-inch Bowie hunter in blued steel and oosic.

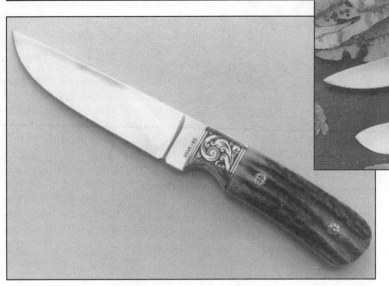

▲*Joel Humphreys:* A pair—caper and skinner—in glorious stag. (Long photo)

◄*Rade Hawkins:* Straight hunter with dropped point, shaped bolster and stag scales.

▼*Rade Hawkins:* Full tang semi-skinner with bone slabs and a place for a forefinger.

MEDIUM KNIVES
Contemporary Styles

▲*Barry Gallagher:* Really interesting special grind, with a sort of tanto point. (Studio 7 photo)

▲*A.T. Barr:* It's 3/16-inch ATS-34, deeply hollow-ground, with stabilized maple burl. (Weyer photo)

►*Ralph Freer:* Spalted maple on a quick 5-inch fighter in ATS-34.

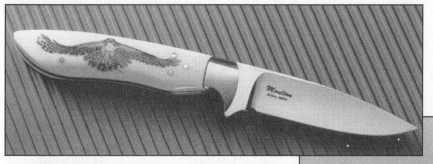

◀*Dusty Moulton:* Ivory and ATS-34 and a very handsome falcon. (Weyer photo)

▼*Thomas S. Hetmanski:* Tough-looking knife called the "Master Hunter" offers five finger grooves in Micarta and ATS-34. (Weyer photo)

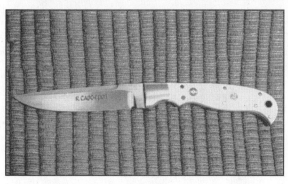

▲*Randy Capdepon:* Slim personal knife in ATS-34 and ivory, about 9 inches long.

MEDIUM KNIVES
Contemporary Styles

◀*M.W. "Ike" Topliss:* Nearly 8 inches of complex shape offers specific grips; ATS-34 and Micarta.

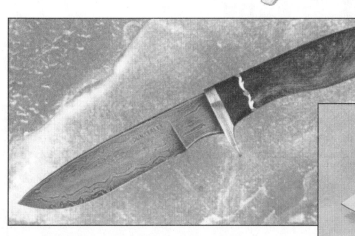

▲*Rick Dunkerley:* A hunter you can choke up on in Damascus and some splendid filework.

▶*James Darby:* Not a pair, but close—skinner with a forefinger pad, full-bellied hunter—in 440C and stag. (Weyer photo)

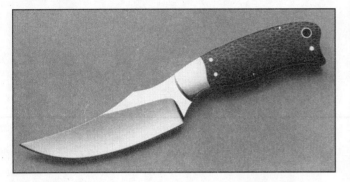

◀*Brian Barron:* Intricate interesting curves of the blade and bolsters make a slick shape. Grip is black palm. (Weyer photo)

▲*Karlis A. Povisils:* Drop-point skinner matches pool-and-eye Damascus and Thuya burl patterns; guard is amber. (Weyer photo)

▼*Chris Perry:* Sturdy short hunter—about 8 inches overall—in ATS-34 and maple burl. (Weyer photo)

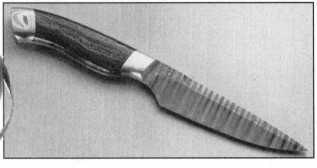

MEDIUM KNIVES

▲*Melvin S. Nishiuchi:* Lavish use of mokume and stainless Damascus steel with Australian tiger wood in a 9½-inch personal knife. (Weyer photo)

Contemporary Styles

◀*Don Hethcoat:* Called the "Canary Islander" by the maker, it's his own Damascus with stacked stag and oosic. (Weyer photo)

▶*Devin Thomas:* Dramatic blade pattern melds nicely with the maker's mokume and with fossil ivory. (Bittner photo)

▲*Jed Darby:* Fighters at 7¹/₂ and 8¹/₈ inches in 440C and pinned Micarta—simpled right down, they are. (Weyer photo)

▶*Ernie Self:* Solid-looking all-purpose hunter at 8³/₈-inch overall in ATS-34 and pinned stag slabs. (Box photo)

MEDIUM KNIVES
Simply Built

▼*Phill Hartsfield:* Called "The Hunt," it goes 8³/₄ inches in the typical Hartsfield finish in A2 steel and Wenge wood. (Weyer photo)

◀*Don Davis:* Bag grip with finger grooves on an 8-inch trout-and-bird design in 440C. (Weyer photo)

▼*George Cousino:* Plain vanilla with nice edge-and-point presentation made in stainless steel and hardwood.

▲*Ken Davis:* Personal defense shapes at 8 inches or so; stainless steel bead-blasted, D2 acid-etched; pinned on scales.

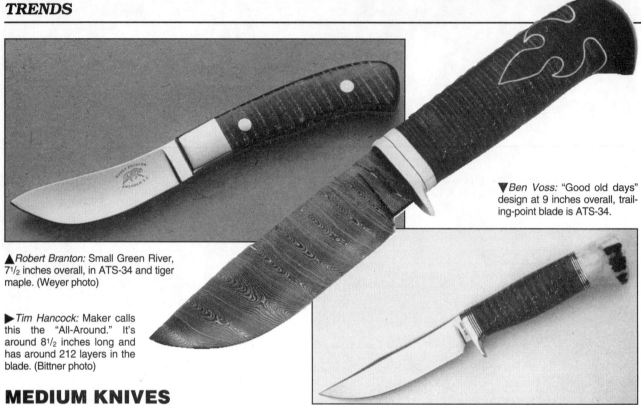

▼*Ben Voss:* "Good old days" design at 9 inches overall, trailing-point blade is ATS-34.

▲*Robert Branton:* Small Green River, 7½ inches overall, in ATS-34 and tiger maple. (Weyer photo)

▶*Tim Hancock:* Maker calls this the "All-Around." It's around 8½ inches long and has around 212 layers in the blade. (Bittner photo)

MEDIUM KNIVES
Old-Time Styles

▶*Louise Cook:* Forged 5160 and hand-peened pins in curly maple makes a spear-pointed carry knife. (Weyer photo)

◀*Cody Wescott:* The very spirit of old time—a handmade Marble's Woodcraft in ATS-34, hollow-ground.

▶*Charles (Dickie) Robinson:* A skinner in 5160, 9 inches long, fitted in ironwood and brass. (Weyer photo)

▶*E. Jay Hendrickson:* About as fancy as old-timey gets—composite handle, wire inlay, turquoise stones, forged 5160 in a hunter's pair. (Weyer photo)

◀*E. Jay Hendrickson:* A caper/skinner pair, hand-forged and handled in maple, furnished with a wood-lined twin sheath. (Weyer photo)

◀*Ed A. Fowler:* Here's a Woodcraft as interpreted in his own 52100 and sheephorn by a great Marble's fan.

MEDIUM KNIVES
Old-Time Styles

◀*Alton Lawrence:* Smallish straight hunter reminiscent of the Randall Model 7. (Weyer photo)

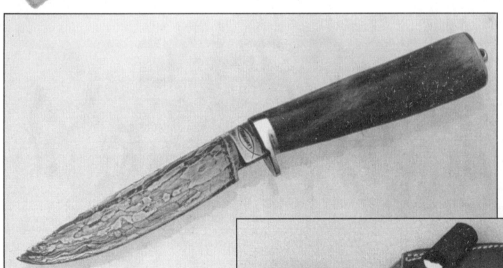

▶*Art Tycer:* Virtually a standard size and shape—a 5-inch 440C blade and polished stag.

▶*Leonard J. Wood:* Five-inch double-edge blade mounted in blue wildwood and sterling silver. (Weyer photo)

▲*J.D. Smith:* Integral Damascus daggers about 10 inches long, one with mokume panels. (Weyer photo)

◀*Jim Fister:* Ten inches of slim-twist Damascus with a pearl coffin-shaped handle.

MEDIUM KNIVES

Dagger Styles

▲*D'Alton Holder:* San Francisco profile in stainless and gold and applied ivory slabs. (Weyer photo)

▼*Mike Schirmer:* Little single-edge, 7³/₄ inches overall, with fossil ivory, embellished by Tim Adlam. (Weyer photo)

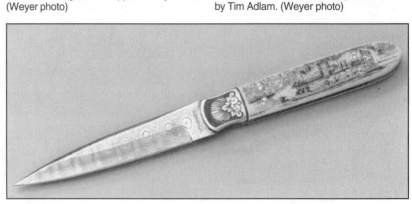

▲*Loyd A. McConnell, Jr.:* Ladder-pattern nickel Damascus and spiraled pearl suit this 9⁷/₈-inch dagger. (Weyer photo)

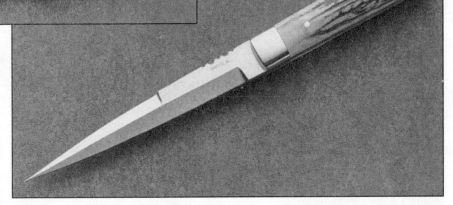

◀ *Jeff L. Chaffee:* American tantos at 9½ and 11½ inches in ATS-34 and stag. (Weyer phto)

▼ *Jeff L. Chaffee:* Modern stiletto at 11 inches overall, ground from 440C. (Weyer photo)

◀ *Dwight L. Towell:* Big push dagger in stainless steel with blackwood insert, inlaid in gold and pearl by the maker.

MEDIUM KNIVES

Dagger Styles

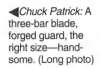

◀ *Chuck Patrick:* A three-bar blade, forged guard, the right size—handsome. (Long photo)

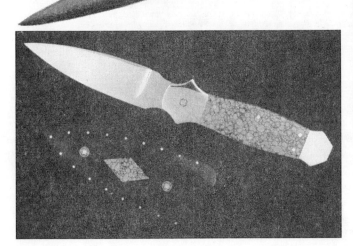

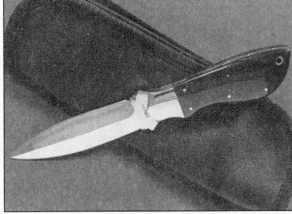

▲ *Gerald E. Corbit:* Buffalo horn and brass and 440C to make a 10½-inch boot knife.

◀ *M.W. "Ike" Topliss:* Bright single-edged 4-inch blade set off with reconstructed turquoise grip.

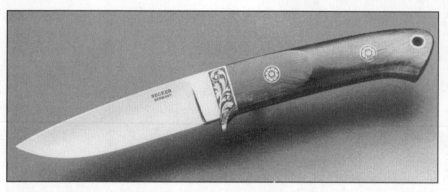

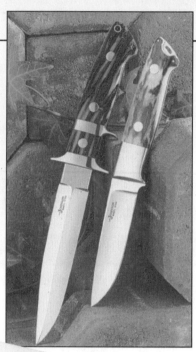

▲*Franz Becker:* The classic drop-point hunter ("drop hunter" in the jargon) in hardwood and stainless and nice engraving. (Strauss photo)

▶*Steven R. Johnson:* The sub-hilt boot and the drop hunter, immaculately presented in stag and ATS-34. (Weyer photo)

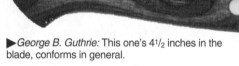

▶*George B. Guthrie:* This one's 4½ inches in the blade, conforms in general.

MEDIUM KNIVES

California Classic Styles

▶*Chuck Ward:* A little pointier 4½-inch A2 blade than usual with nice rosewood and nickel silver.

▲*Robert Nelson Parker:* Semi-skinner and drop hunter in ATS-34 and Micarta—the classic prescription. (Weyer photo)

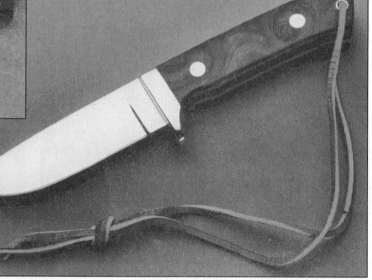

▶*Kevin Sjostrand:* Simplified grind and detail, but in the main line—ATS-34 and ironwood. (Weyer photo)

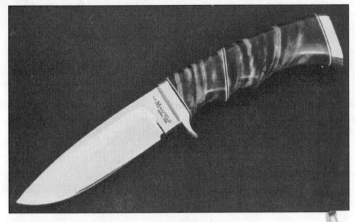

Lynn Maxfield: He calls it the Badger, made it at 4 inches in 154CM—a drop hunter with some difference.

▲*George B. Guthrie:* Short semi-drop hunter in stainless and stag—with its own ricasso.

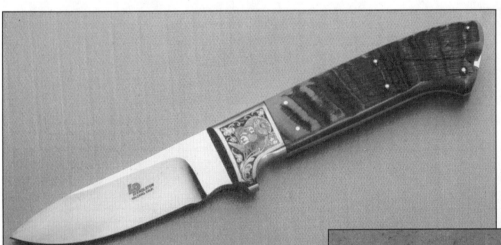

◄*Lloyd Pendleton:* Another sub-hilt boot, still hewed to the line, in ATS-34 and mother of pearl. (Weyer photo)

MEDIUM KNIVES

California Classic Styles

◄*Lloyd Pendleton:* All-out classic, but with European touches—a semi-skinner with sheephorn, Terry Wallace engraving, gold, and thonghole at the butt. (Weyer photo)

▼*Robert Nelson Parker:* Long (5½ inches) drop hunter in ATS-34 and Micarta, somewhat narrow. (Weyer photo)

▲*John H. Holland:* Uncharacteristic spear-point, but the ebony Micarta is right. Engraved by Barry Snell. (Weyer photo)

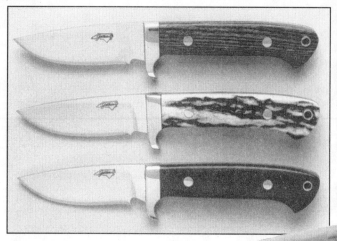

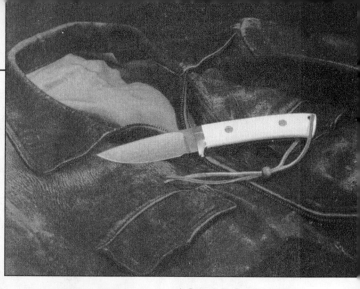

▲*George B. Guthrie:* Three of them—all drop hunters—and your choice of grip.

▲*Steven E. Serafen:* All-out in drop-hunter detail—stainless and ivory.

◀*Ben R. Ogletree, Jr.:* Fossil ivory and fancy pins in a high-ground drop hunter. (Weyer photo)

MEDIUM KNIVES

California Classic Styles

◀*Steve Smart:* Short straight hunter with slim longish grip in blackwood. (LeBlanc photo)

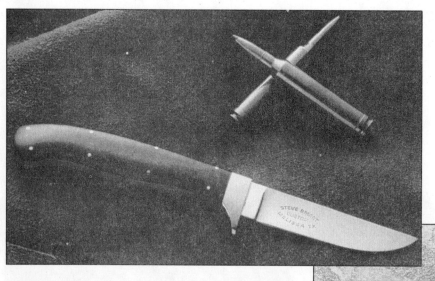

▼*W.J. "Jerry" McDonald:* Handsome clip-point, flat-ground, in ATS-34, all nicely fitted. (Weyer photo)

▲*Ben R. Ogletree, Jr.:* Classic grip, uncharacteristic choil, saber ground—in ATS-34 and Micarta. (Weyer photo)

REALLY SMALL IS STILL BIG

PROBABLY THE FIRST notable cutlery miniatures this writer ever saw were miniature swords. Toledo in Spain was a main source for these, done up in letter-opener size. Dixie Gun Works (and others, no doubt) sold them in U.S. Army and U.S. Navy patterns. There were many other patterns.

There were also crude little things around, mostly as souvenirs. I saw them in the Great Smokies, in Garmisch-partenkirchen in Germany, even Oslo in Norway and Chicago in Illinois. They were little knives about as long as a finger, sometimes with a keychain and always with printing like "Remember The Windy City."

One supposes all that stuff is still out there. Somewhere around here there's a Colonial knife marked "Souvenir of Pipestem Park." I can see—twenty miles away—that park's lookout tower from my place. I guess that explains it.

This world of miniature knives, the one you're looking at, is different. Among other differences, you and your family could stay the summer at Pipestem's wonderful lodge for the price of one of the more elaborate miniatures now being made.

There's a new art called *micro-scrimshaw*, and you can see examples here. Amazing. And there is a new source for tiny knives. There's a fellow in Illinois who makes full sets of kitchen cutlery for scale-model dollhouses.

And miniature swords are no longer letter-opener size, unless you are a very small person who gets very small letters. There's a katana here that's a little longer than your forefinger, but not much. There are folders here about as long, when closed, as one phalange of that forefinger. Wonderful stuff. All of them.

Ken Warner

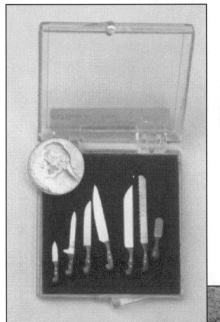

▲*J. Getzan:* These tiny kitchen knives are intended for display in scale-model dollhouses and are sold in—that's right—dollhouse stores.

▶*Tim Scholl:* These are 3 inches long, in Damascus, Micarta, snakewood, brass—a camp knife and a Bowie. (Weyer photo)

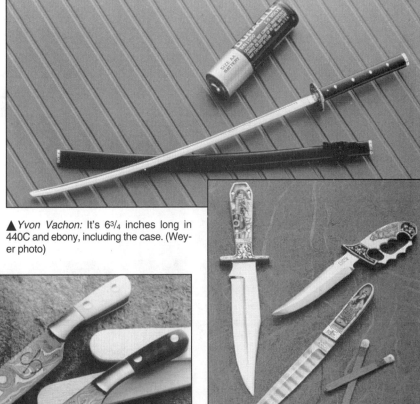

▲*Yvon Vachon:* It's 6³/₄ inches long in 440C and ebony, including the case. (Weyer photo)

▲*Michael Tamboli:* These are 3¹/₂, 3³/₄ and 4³/₄ inches long, engraved by Pat Holder; the bear scrimmed by Lou McClaren; the others by Bob Hergert. (Weyer photo)

▲*Dale Ballew:* Walnut and 440C hand saw at 4 inches overall on a full-size claw-hammer. (Long photo)

▶*Yvon Vachon:* Daggers, a folder, a hunter, all at paperclip scale, trimmed in mammoth ivory, horn, even .925 silver. (Weyer photo)

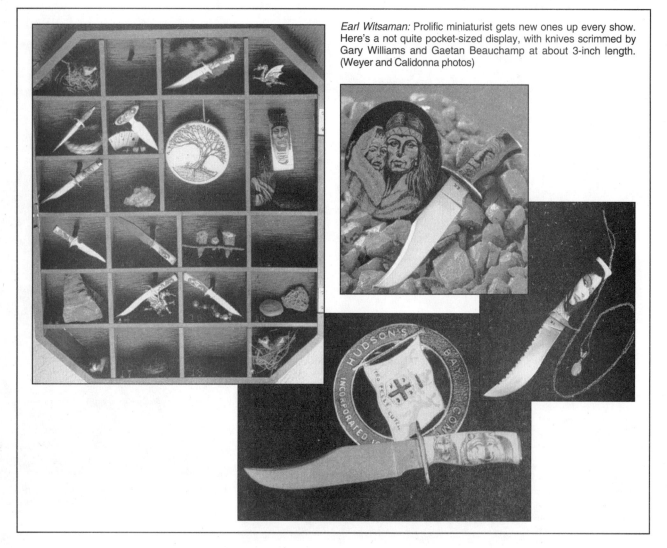

Earl Witsaman: Prolific miniaturist gets new ones up every show. Here's a not quite pocket-sized display, with knives scrimmed by Gary Williams and Gaetan Beauchamp at about 3-inch length. (Weyer and Calidonna photos)

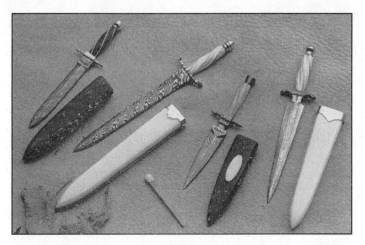

▲*Harry L. Stalter:* A whole collection of Damascus daggers, all with twist handles and lengths up to 4 inches. (Weyer photo)

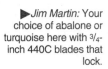

▶*Jim Martin:* Your choice of abalone or turquoise here with ³/₄-inch 440C blades that lock.

◀*Dale Strickland:* Stainless Damascus from Devin Thomas, buffalo horn for sheath and grip—3 inches overall.

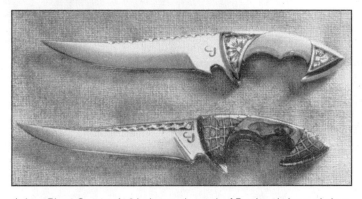

▲*Jean-Pierre Ganster:* At 2 inches each, a pair of Persians in ivory, abalone, gold and mosaic Damascus.

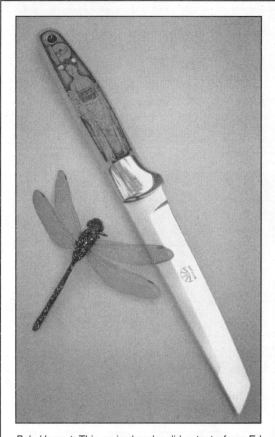

Bob Hergert: This scrimshander did a tanto from Ed Schempp, a hunter from Dusty Moulton, a Bowie from Michael Tamboli.

▼▶*Dale Ballew:* Two-man cross-cut saws, the one on the axehead is 4¹/₂ inches, the other goes 6 inches. They're 440C. (Long photos)

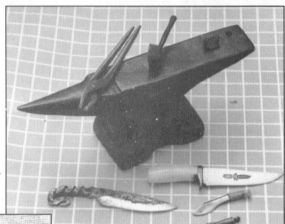

▲*Charles W. Carey, Jr.:* Miniature knives at a variety of scales, and those aren't very big blacksmith tools, either. (Long photo)

▲*Jean-Pierre Ganster:* About 2 inches of stainless Damascus Bowie with gold blade back and guard and horn grip.

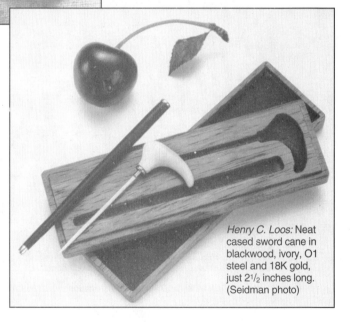

Henry C. Loos: Neat cased sword cane in blackwood, ivory, O1 steel and 18K gold, just 2¹/₂ inches long. (Seidman photo)

▲*Barry Lee Hands:* Micro-engraving by Hands on miniatures, the elegant pearl folder by Mike Mercer.

MORE AUTOMATICS THAN EVER

WELL, THERE JUST doesn't seem to be a point in discussing law and the switchblade knife anymore, not here. They used to say about Oklahomans and public drinking that Sooners would vote Dry as long as they could stagger to the polls. Knifemakers—some knifemakers—are apparently going to make automatics as long as collectors or whomever show up with money.

Technically, this is kind of a bonanza, because there are some very intersting mechanisms going "click!" And for the makers, there's a different bonanza—automatics sell fast at upscale prices.

It's too soon to start comparisons. The knives are not *that* out in the open. And they really can be pretty expensive, since most are either elaborate or embellished. There do seem to be several basic kinds.

They still make automatics that masquerade as ordinary lockblades, top lock and all. They are switchblade lockblades. And there are automatics with hidden buttons and studs. Some lock open and lock closed. There are the right-out-front automatics, too, most of them versions of the "SEAL" or Black Knife discussed at length here two years ago. And the lockwork of that knife is in use everywhere, even or perhaps especially, in Germany, where an automatic is available on that plan. And get this: A manually opening version *of the same knife* will be sold in the U.S.!

You won't find all the automatics we've seen displayed here. A number of them are elegant enough or pricey enough to be shown in those categories.

Ken Warner

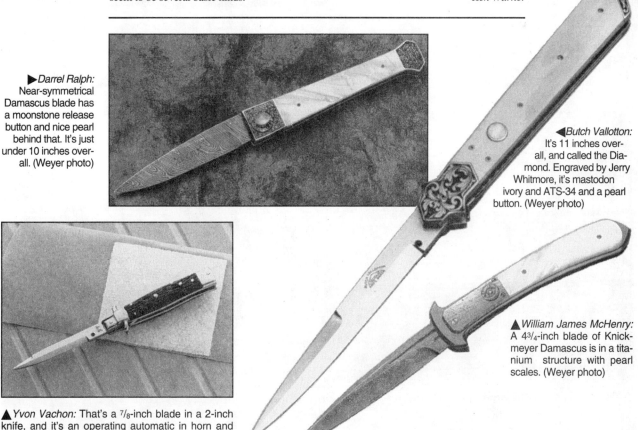

▶*Darrel Ralph:* Near-symmetrical Damascus blade has a moonstone release button and nice pearl behind that. It's just under 10 inches overall. (Weyer photo)

◀*Butch Vallotton:* It's 11 inches overall, and called the Diamond. Engraved by Jerry Whitmore, it's mastodon ivory and ATS-34 and a pearl button. (Weyer photo)

▲*William James McHenry:* A 4³/₄-inch blade of Knickmeyer Damascus is in a titanium structure with pearl scales. (Weyer photo)

▲*Yvon Vachon:* That's a ⁷/₈-inch blade in a 2-inch knife, and it's an operating automatic in horn and 440C. (Weyer photo)

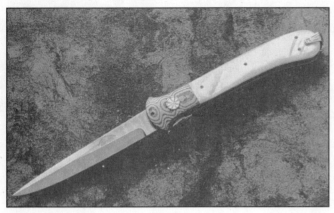

▲*Butch Vallotton:* Something a little slicker in pearl and stainless Damascus with all-titanium innards at 9¼ inches overall. (Weyer photo)

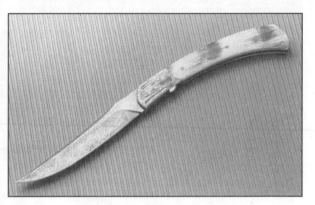

▲*William James McHenry:* A really big one—14 inches long as you see it—in Meier and Clark steels called "Victoria's Secret." (Weyer photo)

▼*R. Bill Saindon:* The pearl is quilted; the furniture on blade Damascus; it's 9½ inches long.

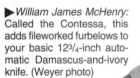

▶*William James McHenry:* Called the Contessa, this adds fileworked furbelows to your basic 12¾-inch automatic Damascus-and-ivory knife. (Weyer photo)

▼*Jason L. Williams:* Somewhat brawny fighter has both Knickmeyer and Meier Damascus steel. You can't see the abalone and pearl inlays, but they're there. (Weyer photo)

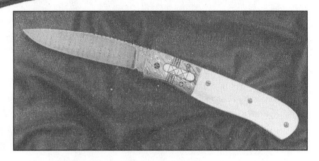

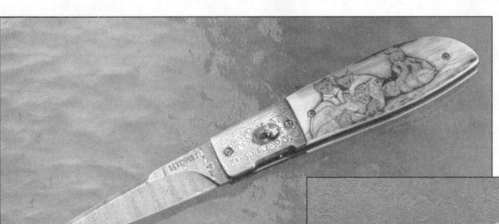

▼*C.M. Dake:* This is your basic "double-action" lockback in severe and comfortable style—ATS-34 and mastodon ivory and 9 inches overall. (Weyer photo)

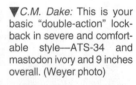

▲*Jack Davenport:* Upgraded with mokume and scrimshaw, this Damascus dagger is just 8½ inches long as you see it. (Weyer photo)

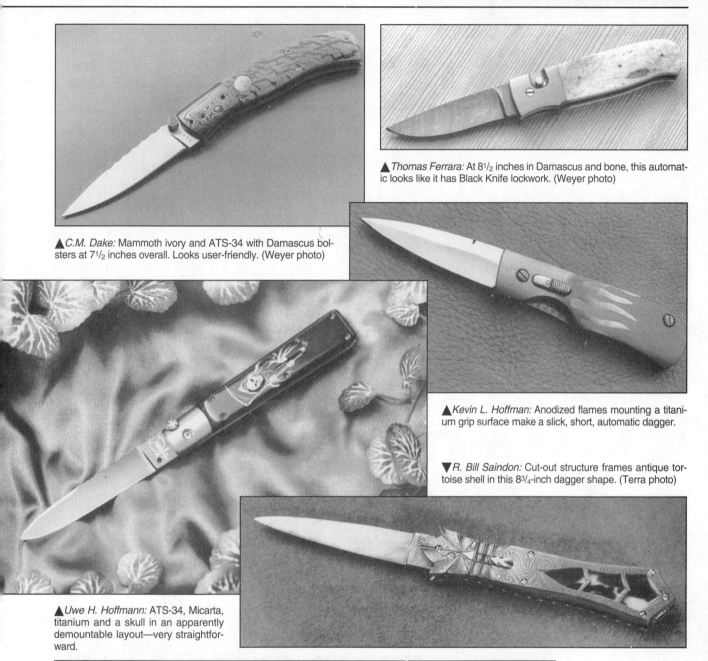

▲*C.M. Dake:* Mammoth ivory and ATS-34 with Damascus bolsters at 7¹/₂ inches overall. Looks user-friendly. (Weyer photo)

▲*Thomas Ferrara:* At 8¹/₂ inches in Damascus and bone, this automatic looks like it has Black Knife lockwork. (Weyer photo)

▲*Kevin L. Hoffman:* Anodized flames mounting a titanium grip surface make a slick, short, automatic dagger.

▼*R. Bill Saindon:* Cut-out structure frames antique tortoise shell in this 8³/₄-inch dagger shape. (Terra photo)

▲*Uwe H. Hoffmann:* ATS-34, Micarta, titanium and a skull in an apparently demountable layout—very straightforward.

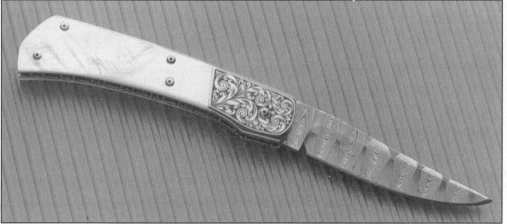

◄*C.E. "Gene" Johnson:* This scale-release automatic offers pearl and Damascus and Billy Bates engraving. (Weyer photo)

INVESTMENT-GRADE KNIVES

"INVESTMENT-GRADE" IS not just a synonym for "high-priced knife." Yes, there is an overlap—some high-priced knives have aspects that make them later more saleable than other high-priced knives, and some investment-grade knives are toward the bottom of the list—but, in general, "investment grade" means tasteful, luxurious, best-grade knives which, at least, won't depreciate markedly. It helps a *great* deal if they are artistically sound as well.

There are a fortunate few who carry the best folding knives ever made, $5,000 and $12,000 creations, as you and I carry our Schrade Old-Timers and Case 9-dots. They also drive $200,000 autos, wear $25,000

watches and pay $750 for a pair of pants and $200 for a T-shirt. Those such who carry knives insist the cutlery match the rest of the ensemble. And I can't blame them—I always switch to a $50 pocketknife when I put on the clean 501 jeans.

Moneyed people aren't the only market. Your basic doctor-lawyer-stockbroker guys are probably the mainstream. And they tend to own collections, not single knives to carry. Of course, you can carry a heavyweight group of genuine investment-grade knives in a very slim attache case.

So, if you wondered, that's who winds up with these enormously elegant creations, most of them. It's probably worth noting that until

there were knifemakers who could make stuff this well, there weren't many such customers around.

As for the knives themselves, there's no change. They remain among the planet's best-made artifacts, regardless of shape or size. They're very impressive—if you know what you're looking at. That's true of all sorts of artifacts, of course. Study the watch market if you want a parallel—what's a Movado, anyway?

Folders, daggers, hunter patterns, little gents' knives—they're all here. From an elegant point of view, this is as good as it got here lately.

Ken Warner

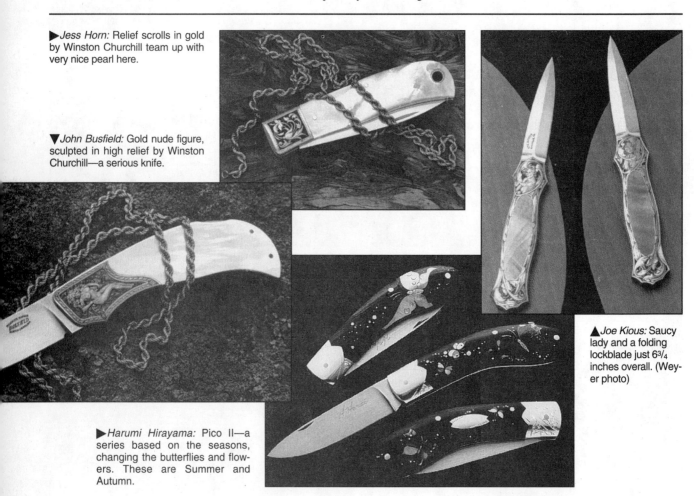

▶*Jess Horn:* Relief scrolls in gold by Winston Churchill team up with very nice pearl here.

▼*John Busfield:* Gold nude figure, sculpted in high relief by Winston Churchill—a serious knife.

▲*Joe Kious:* Saucy lady and a folding lockblade just 6³/₄ inches overall. (Weyer photo)

▶*Harumi Hirayama:* Pico II—a series based on the seasons, changing the butterflies and flowers. These are Summer and Autumn.

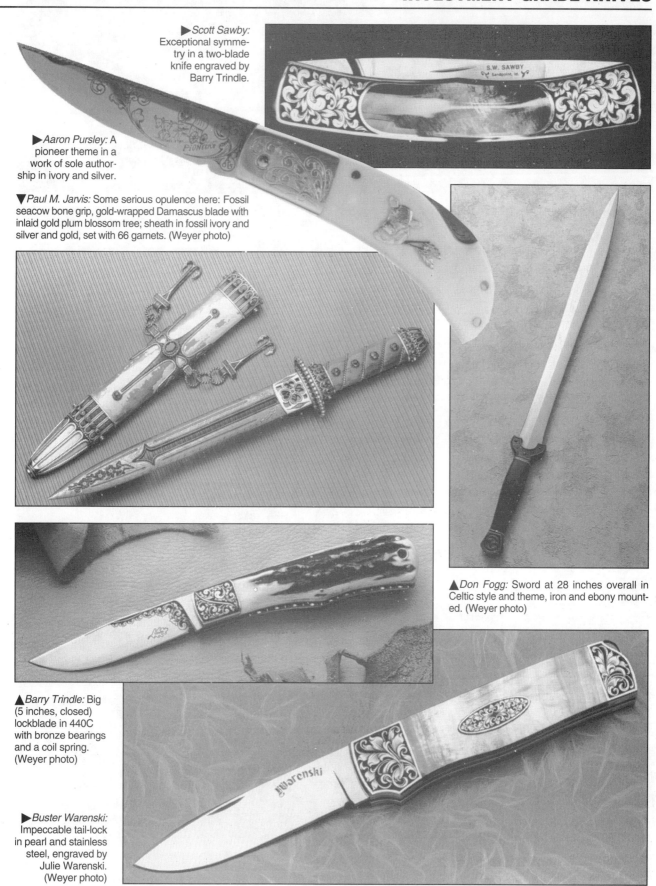

▶*Scott Sawby:* Exceptional symmetry in a two-blade knife engraved by Barry Trindle.

▶*Aaron Pursley:* A pioneer theme in a work of sole authorship in ivory and silver.

▼*Paul M. Jarvis:* Some serious opulence here: Fossil seacow bone grip, gold-wrapped Damascus blade with inlaid gold plum blossom tree; sheath in fossil ivory and silver and gold, set with 66 garnets. (Weyer photo)

▲*Don Fogg:* Sword at 28 inches overall in Celtic style and theme, iron and ebony mounted. (Weyer photo)

▲*Barry Trindle:* Big (5 inches, closed) lockblade in 440C with bronze bearings and a coil spring. (Weyer photo)

▶*Buster Warenski:* Impeccable tail-lock in pearl and stainless steel, engraved by Julie Warenski. (Weyer photo)

▲*Jim Martin:* Interframe offers Burmese jade, 440C and a Gil Rudolph leopard.

▲*Darrel Ralph:* One of ten, called General Patton, it locks open and closed, is 10 inches open, and has star Damascus blade and gold inlays.

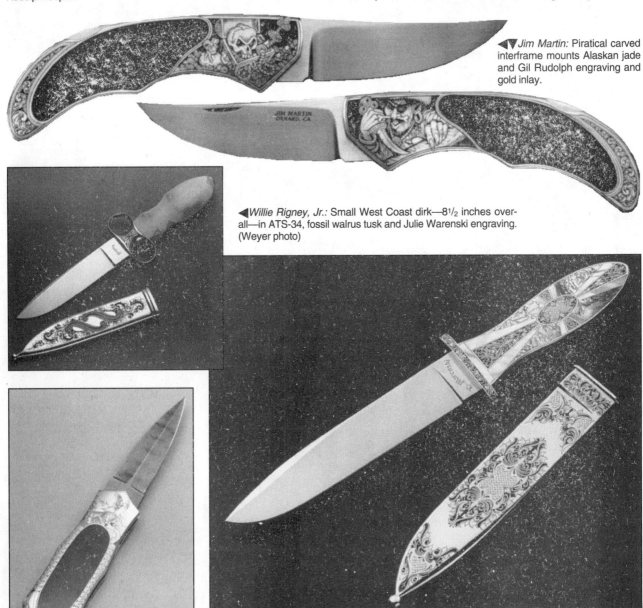

◄▼*Jim Martin:* Piratical carved interframe mounts Alaskan jade and Gil Rudolph engraving and gold inlay.

◄*Willie Rigney, Jr.:* Small West Coast dirk—8¹/₂ inches over-all—in ATS-34, fossil walrus tusk and Julie Warenski engraving. (Weyer photo)

◄*Judy Gottage:* A Robert Finkelstein design, engraved by Chris Meyer, is more interesting than average. (Weyer photo)

▲*Buster Warenski:* Startling inlay pattern is all shell and nickel silver; size is 11 inches; extensive engraving by Julie Warenski. (Weyer photo)

THE ELEGANT KNIFE

ELEGANT IS ELEGANT. You just have to know, as Louis Armstrong said about jazz and J.P. Morgan said about money and steam yachts.

To a little extent, elegance is in the eye of the beholder. An honest judge, however, will admit elegance in knives he hates—if they really have class.

There do seem to be more such graceful, tasteful pieces about. They are sometimes not even high-priced. When an elegant piece gets a dose of opulence as well—gold, fine ivory, really superior engraving, special furnishings—then we can get pricey, indeed.

Mainly, though, it's a question of line and defined space and beautiful materials. That is so of dresses and dinnerware and home furnishings, and performance styles, and it is so of knives.

You see some of them here, and, yes, a lot of them are knives by guys who made elegant knives last year. They're the guys who know, like Louis Armstrong and J.P. Morgan.

K.W. Warner

▼*H.J. Viele:* G10 and ATS-34 is all it takes if you have complete control of line. (Weyer photo)

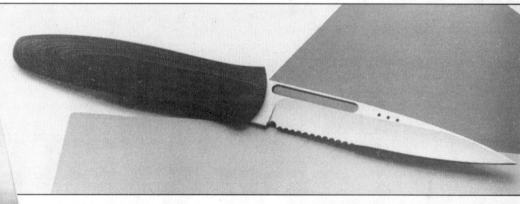

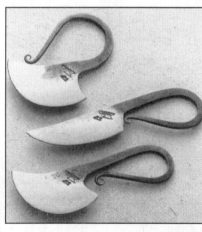

▲*Chris Marks:* Three like this together, with not a single mis-lick, is pure elegance in the craft alone. (Weyer photo)

▶*Don Polzien:* Elegant tanto in silk and rayskin and gold lacquer—with temper line, too.

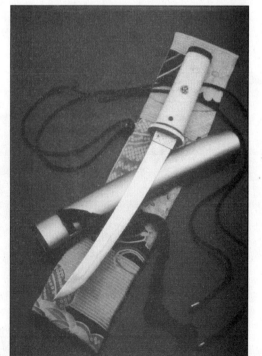

▲*William R. "Bill" Herndon:* It doesn't look over a foot long, but it is—in 1095 steel and ironwood and Peter Frankson gold inlay. (Weyer photo)

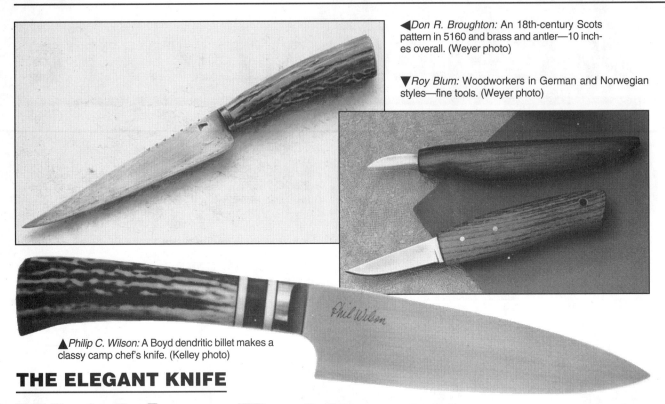

◀Don R. Broughton: An 18th-century Scots pattern in 5160 and brass and antler—10 inches overall. (Weyer photo)

▼Roy Blum: Woodworkers in German and Norwegian styles—fine tools. (Weyer photo)

▲Philip C. Wilson: A Boyd dendritic billet makes a classy camp chef's knife. (Kelley photo)

THE ELEGANT KNIFE
Working Patterns

▶Tim Hancock: Immaculate skinner in ebony—elegance from clean line. (Bittner photo)

▲Jerry L. Snell: Big butcher knife in Damascus and stag—impeccable. (Weyer photo)

◀Steve Leland: A hunter with Persian lines in ivory, ATS-34 and Sornberger engraving. (Weyer photo)

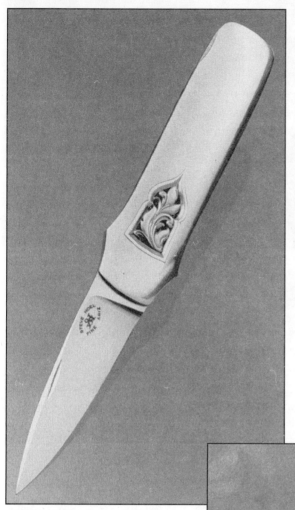

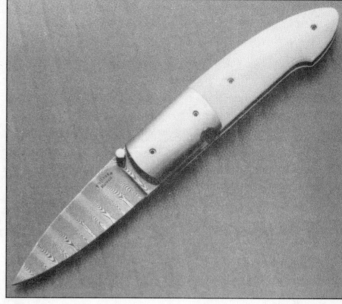

▲*Stanley Fujisaka:* Ivory, stainless Damascus, titanium liners and bolster, and exactly chosen proportions of each. (Weyer photo)

THE ELEGANT KNIFE
Folders

▼*Fred Carter:* Pierced Moschetti scroll and line set in a just-right profile—a smallish folder. (Weyer photo)

▲*Steve Hoel:* All-stainless folder with pierced Mitch Moschetti engraving; 6 inches overall. (Weyer photo)

▼*Jim Minnick:* Mastodon ivory and O1 steel, with steel furniture and gold inlay by Joyce Minnick. (Weyer photo)

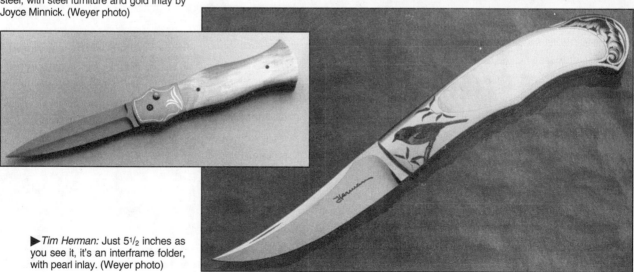

▶*Tim Herman:* Just 5¹/₂ inches as you see it, it's an interframe folder, with pearl inlay. (Weyer photo)

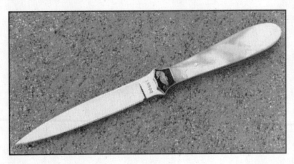

▲*James F. Downs:* Small single-edge dagger—smooth in mother-of-pearl and 440C, nicely embellished by Leo McCombs. (Ross photo)

▶*Jim Ence:* Fossil walrus, 440C, gold and nickel pins and fittings in a first-class tribute to San Francisco history. (Weyer photo)

▶*Mark C. Sentz:* Broad-bladed forged copper dagger, sweetly proportioned in curly maple and wire inlays. (Weyer photo)

THE ELEGANT KNIFE

Daggers and Such

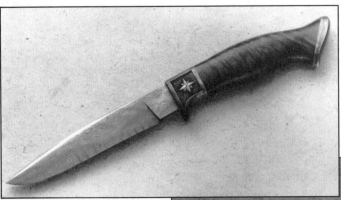

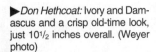

▲*David Ellis:* Small blade for a small hippo tooth handle and mokume fittings. (Weyer photo)

▲*Don Fogg and Murad Sayen:* Teamed up in bronze and walnut and Damascus at 10½ inches overall. (Weyer photo)

▶*Don Hethcoat:* Ivory and Damascus and a crisp old-time look, just 10½ inches overall. (Weyer photo)

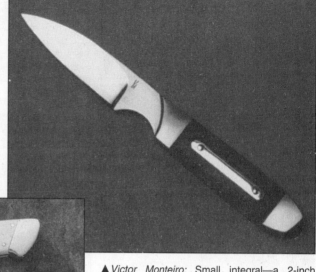

▲*James Ray Cook:* Happy confluence of mastodon ivory, copper and the maker's Damascus at 10¾ inches overall. (Weyer photo)

▲*Victor Monteiro:* Small integral—a 2-inch blade—cleanly ground and fitted with domed pins.

◄*Larry A. Lunn:* Matching a pair this cleanly is not easy—they're just over a foot long in ivory and 440C. (Weyer photo)

THE ELEGANT KNIFE

Daggers and Such

◄*Tim Zowada:* Just blackwood and a spacer and handsomely forged bolster and blade. It ain't big, but it is neat. (Weyer photo)

▼*Anthony B. Schaller:* Practically a model for a short fighter, but so clean in 440C and 416 and red and black Micarta. (Weyer photo)

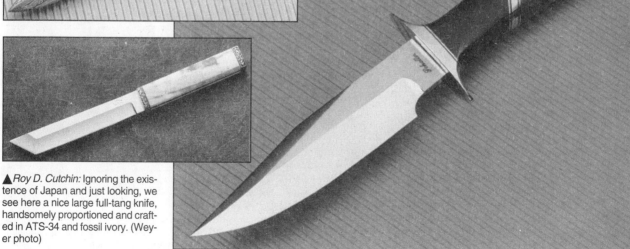

▲*Roy D. Cutchin:* Ignoring the existence of Japan and just looking, we see here a nice large full-tang knife, handsomely proportioned and crafted in ATS-34 and fossil ivory. (Weyer photo)

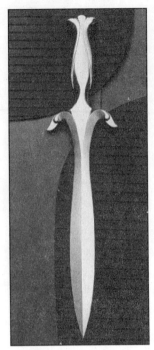

C. Robbin Hudson: Walnut and W2 and brass make up an impeccable modern Bowie. (Weyer photo)

Joe A. Yeates: It isn't easy to be over 16 inches long and still slick, but here it is in polished stag and 440C. (Weyer photo)

Wolfgang Loerchner: Just one piece of ⅝-inch 440C, now considerably altered, finished with both satin and mirror polishes. (Weyer photo)

THE ELEGANT KNIFE
Big Knives

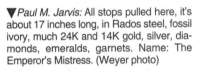

Jay Harmon: The medium Bowie, hafted in Guatemalan jade, has ATS-34 blade and impressive good looks. (Weyer photo)

Paul M. Jarvis: All stops pulled here, it's about 17 inches long, in Rados steel, fossil ivory, much 24K and 14K gold, silver, diamonds, emeralds, garnets. Name: The Emperor's Mistress. (Weyer photo)

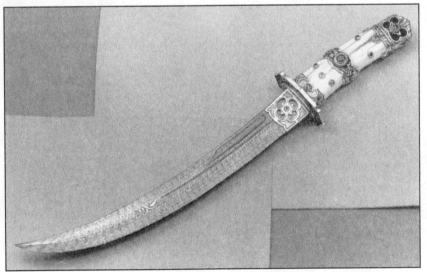

J.D. Smith: Carved blackwood, copper, bronze and six-bar Damascus steel—over 16 inches long. (Weyer photo)

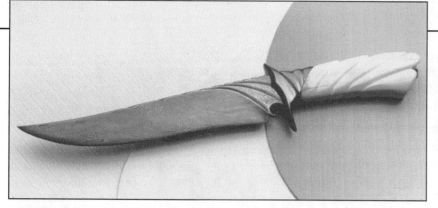

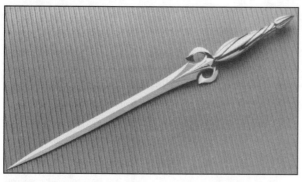

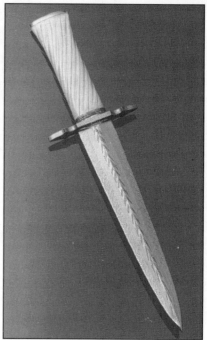

▲*David Broadwell:* A Robertson design, John M. Smith steel, fossil ivory—very integrated. (Weyer photo)

▶*J.D. Smith:* Silver-copper mokume, fossil ivory, six-bar Damascus—14¹/₂ inches of careful texture. (Weyer photo)

▲*Wolfgang Loerchner:* Start with another bar of 440C 15 inches long and you get this—but guard and grip are not integral. (Weyer photo)

▼*Michael K. Manabe:* Ebony, German silver, forged steel—triple tempered and slick at 12 inches overall. (Weyer photo)

THE ELEGANT KNIFE
Big Knives

▶*Wolfgang Loerchner:* Derivative San Franciso detail—interframe handle, pearl panel, silver shield—in a lady-length dagger just 8¹/₂ inches long. (Weyer photo)

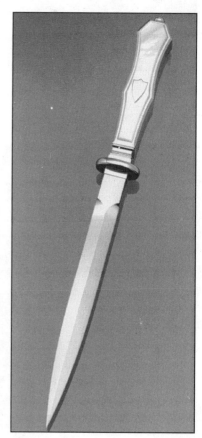

▲*Timothy F. Potier:* An elegant camp knife? Of course. This is L6 and blackwood and *very* careful work. (Weyer photo)

TRENDS

MISCELLANY

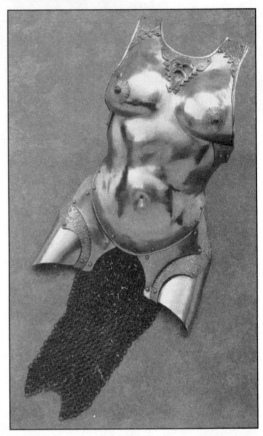

▲*V.J. McCrackin:* A 30th wedding anniversary present for Vera McCrackin in 1095 and nickel.

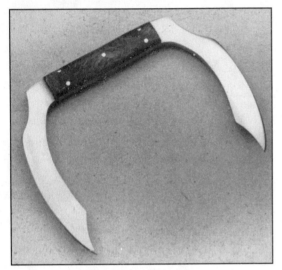

◄*Tim Scholl:* This push dagger is designed to surround the problem. In 5160 and burl walnut. (Weyer photo)

▶*Robb Martin:* This is, of course, battle dress for a Valkyrie in 18-gauge mild steel, copper furniture and steel mail. (Weyer photo)

▼*Mudd Sharrigan:* The Lobster Country is made with brass state-law lobster measures; the blade is 4 inches. (Weyer photo)

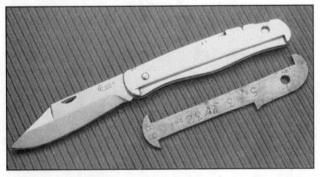

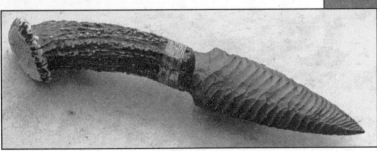

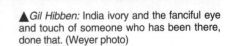

▲*Gil Hibben:* India ivory and the fanciful eye and touch of someone who has been there, done that. (Weyer photo)

◄*Errett Callahan:* Handsomely flaked, this 5½-inch obsidian blade looks as serious as a heartbeat. (Weyer photo)

STATE
OF
THE ART

We have said before that here we deal with facts—"this is a leopard scrimmed on ivory"—and subjective facts—"this is an elegant knife." The latter means the writer is pretty sure the knife shown is extra-classy in one way or another.

As we get to them, we try to shed sufficient light on small technical matters to help the reader see them, too. Textures, surfaces and new shapes, sometimes new materials, can be revealed easily in photos and captions.

So that's what we do here. We're looking at *parts* of knives or the knifemaking process to see how they affect the knives. We have done that for sixteen years, and there are still new things to see.

So that's the other thing we do—we keep track of technical stuff. We don't *chart it*, mind you, but mostly if it's new we showed it here. It's the State of the Art, this year.

Ken Warner

Interesting Knives 134
Study of Steel and
    Shape and Stuff 140

Embellishment .148
Leatherwork 160

INTERESTING KNIVES

THE KNIVES YOU see on these six pages interest me. That's all they have in common, apart from their basic nature and the fact that none seems to fit elsewhere.

They're not *miscellaneous*, you can see, nor are they special objects of study. We have folders and straight knives, straight-off working pieces and some for the fantasy-minded, weapons and tools, big and little—all interesting.

Neither is it a question of preference. Some of these, speaking personally, are butt-ugly, but I have learned not to hold that against man, woman, child or knife. Some, I hasten to add, I find special, really special.

We just had to tell you all that in case you were wondering.

Ken Warner

▲*Christoph Deringer:* Finely designed and executed up-and-down integral handle and a graceful carver blade.

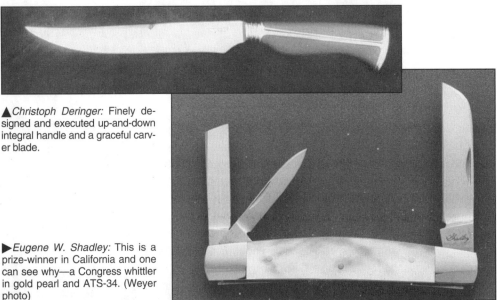

▲*Steve Likarich:* Ever seen fluted Micarta with silver wire before? Called Black Ice, the three-sided spike is 5¹/₂ inches long. (Weyer photo)

▶*Eugene W. Shadley:* This is a prize-winner in California and one can see why—a Congress whittler in gold pearl and ATS-34. (Weyer photo)

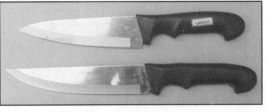

◀*Factory Stuff:* Picked up at a flea market with two different Japanese factory names, these help explain good-looking—the bottom knife is a handsome profile, the other definitely not.

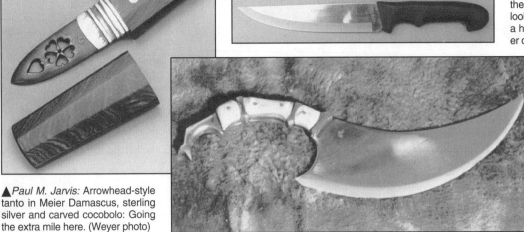

▲*Paul M. Jarvis:* Arrowhead-style tanto in Meier Damascus, sterling silver and carved cocobolo: Going the extra mile here. (Weyer photo)

◀*Mario Eiras Garcia:* Its maker calls this a "large combat knife." Handle is sectioned bone, and it's forged, of course.

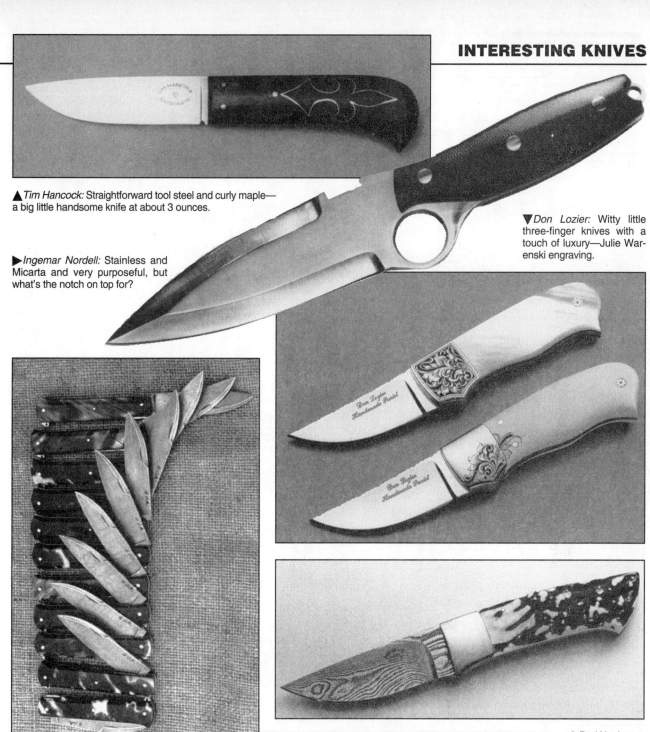

▲ *Tim Hancock:* Straightforward tool steel and curly maple—a big little handsome knife at about 3 ounces.

▶ *Ingemar Nordell:* Stainless and Micarta and very purposeful, but what's the notch on top for?

▼ *Don Lozier:* Witty little three-finger knives with a touch of luxury—Julie Warenski engraving.

▲ *Henri Viallon:* A nice batch of Damascus-and-turtle folders patterned after an old French (naturally) knife. A lot of handmade knives here.

▲ *Bud Nealy:* The maker never sold this one, No. 1425, because somebody stole it at a New York knife show. (Weyer photo)

▶ *Samuel Wragg:* An antique folding dirk owned by Bill Dirnberger—a mid-19th-century serious knife with a 10³/₄-inch blade. (Weyer photo)

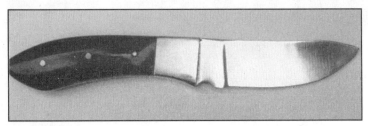

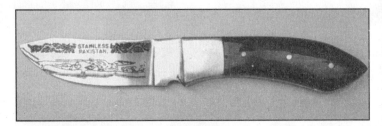

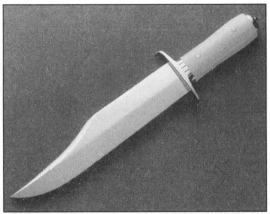

▲*Bob Luchak:* Tough 5-inch spear-point hunter with a chopping edge on top—laminated horn grip.

▲▼*Anon. Pakistani:* On the plain side, it's an OK-looking semi-skinner; turn it over and the blade etch spoils the effect. Just $5 is the full retail.

▲*Joe A. Yeates:* This Texas maker turns out this Iron Mistress pattern in three sizes—the smallest is a nice-size deer hunters' knife. (Weyer photo)

▲▶*William J. Tyc:* The sincerest form of flattery here, both large and small, in D.E. Henry- and William F. Moran-pattern Bowies. (Weyer photos)

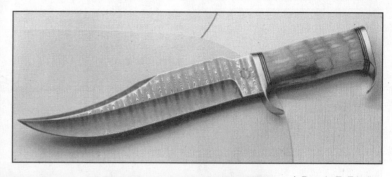

▲*Dennis E. Friedly:* The famous Elmer Keith design taken seriously and made as a Bowie in Damascus and fossil ivory. (Weyer photo)

▲*Gil Hibben:* This is Serial No.1; so will there be thousands and thousands of them? (Weyer photo)

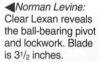

◀*Norman Levine:* Clear Lexan reveals the ball-bearing pivot and lockwork. Blade is 3¹/₂ inches.

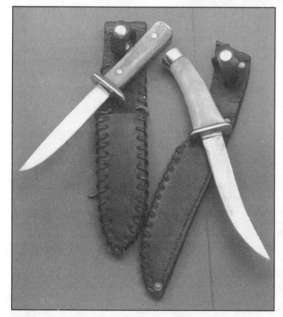

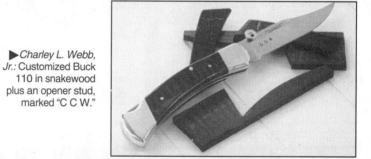

▶*Charley L. Webb, Jr.:* Customized Buck 110 in snakewood plus an opener stud, marked "C C W."

▲*Leo Leoffler:* The knifemaker has passed on; the knives remain—the blades were made of files, the handle of one is shin bone from a special horse, the other antler from a first deer. (Weyer photo)

▶*Charley L. Webb, Jr.:* Jambiya shape makes sense—this knife is marked "Riyadh, KSA" which is the capital of Saudi Arabia.

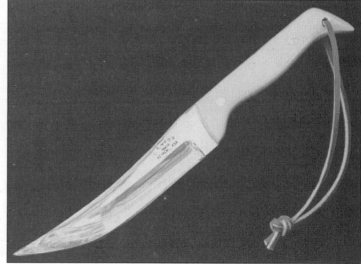

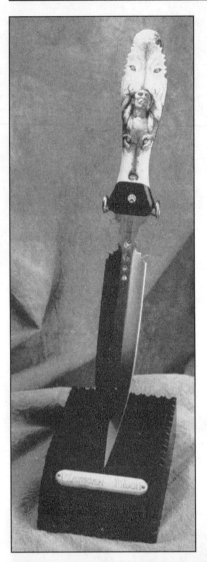

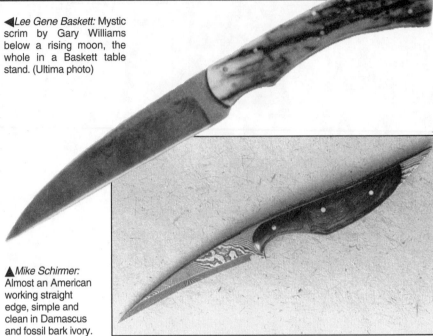

Lee Gene Baskett: Mystic scrim by Gary Williams below a rising moon, the whole in a Baskett table stand. (Ultima photo)

Mike Schirmer: Almost an American working straight edge, simple and clean in Damascus and fossil bark ivory.

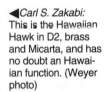

J.W. Townsend: Slick 3½-inch personal knife with a slim point and a slight sickle edge—neat. (Weyer photo)

Carl S. Zakabi: This is the Hawaiian Hawk in D2, brass and Micarta, and has no doubt an Hawaiian function. (Weyer photo)

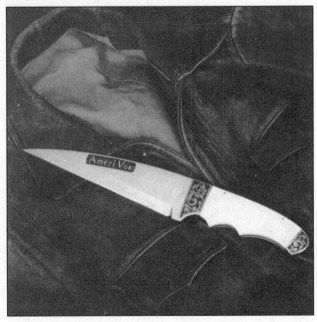

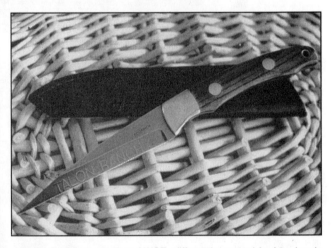

Mike Schirmer: Another AWSE, differently ground in A2, deeply etched to *raise* the "Talon Ranch" legend.

Steven E. Serafen: Six-inch straight edge, dual finger placement grip, marked "Ameri-Vox"—not your usual belt knife.

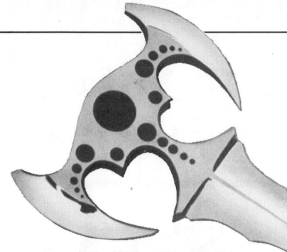

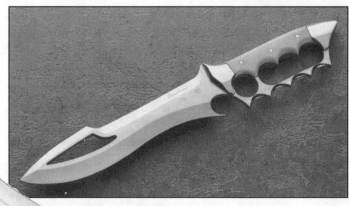

▶*Ken Middleton:* This one's 11³/₄ inches long of half-inch 440C—it's an integral.

▲*Gaetan Beauchamp:* Fanciful fighter with a sub-hilted D-guard, knuckle points and a lance tip—nasty-looking. (Weyer photo)

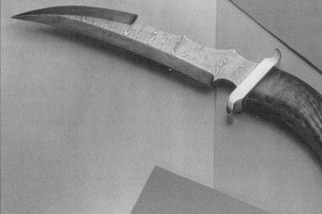

◀*Harlan M. Willson:* An Engnath ground-to-order blade and a wild handle carving by Willson makes the Night Child. (Weyer photo)

▼*Al Eaton:* This is the Star Warrior; it's 22¹/₂ inches long, but details of some function remain a secret. (Weyer photo)

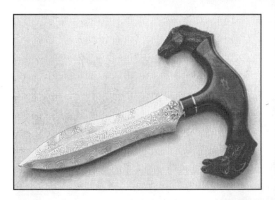

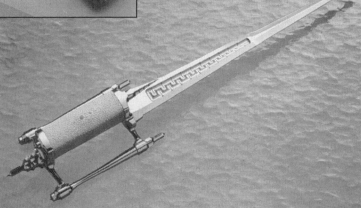

▲*Joseph E. Knuth:* Giant push dagger, 10¹/₄ inches long in cocobolo, bronze, ebony and Damascus. Horse heads by Joseph Sczlasky. (Weyer photo)

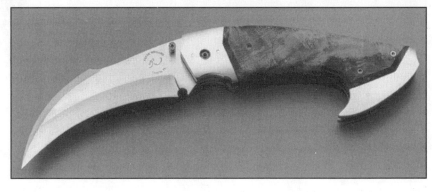

▶*J. Reese Weiland, Jr.:* Called the Rastor, it goes 10¹/₂ inches open in stainless, stabilized burls and titanium. (Weyer photo)

STUDY OF STEEL AND SHAPE AND STUFF

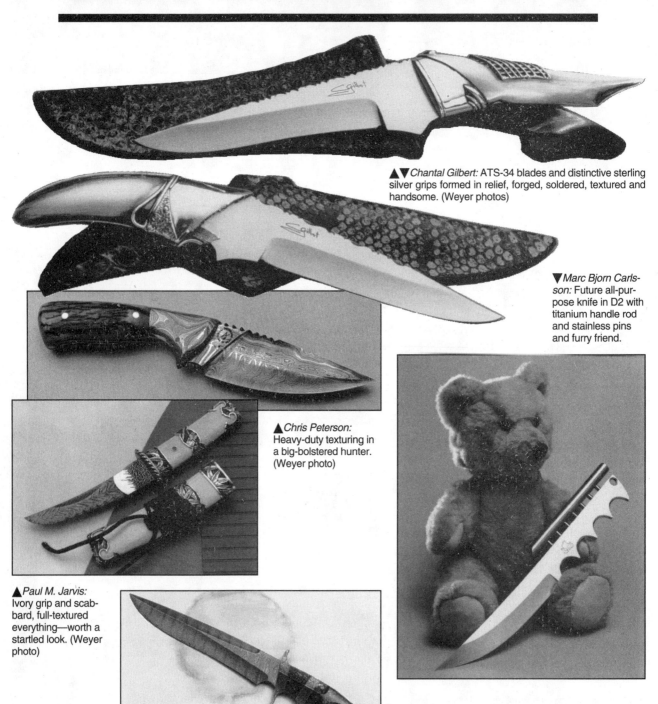

▲▼*Chantal Gilbert:* ATS-34 blades and distinctive sterling silver grips formed in relief, forged, soldered, textured and handsome. (Weyer photos)

▼*Marc Bjorn Carlsson:* Future all-purpose knife in D2 with titanium handle rod and stainless pins and furry friend.

▲*Chris Peterson:* Heavy-duty texturing in a big-bolstered hunter. (Weyer photo)

▲*Paul M. Jarvis:* Ivory grip and scabbard, full-textured everything—worth a startled look. (Weyer photo)

◄*David Broadwell:* Exotic sculpting of lapis lazuli stone provides great faceting in a sub-hilt fighter. (Impress photo)

▲*Ingemar Nordell:* Unaccustomed boldness from Scandinavia in ATS-34 and fossil ivory.

▲*Gerard Doursin:* Stiletto-turned handle and quillons, three-sided blade, all Damascus.

▲*Don Lozier:* You don't hardly see deep double hollow grinds like these now—very pretty. (Weyer photo)

▲*Gerry Gerus:* Heavy textures in a short trailing-point hunter—ATS-34 and horn.

►*Mike Sakmar:* A 4-inch hunter with wildwood grip—an integral in A2 steel.

▼*Fred G. Millard:* Leaf-shaped O1 blade, unusually ground—1/4-inch stock and ebony insert.

▼*William G. Chapo:* This is a 3¹/₂x7¹/₂ ax head on a 17-inch shaft—a big ax. (Weyer photo)

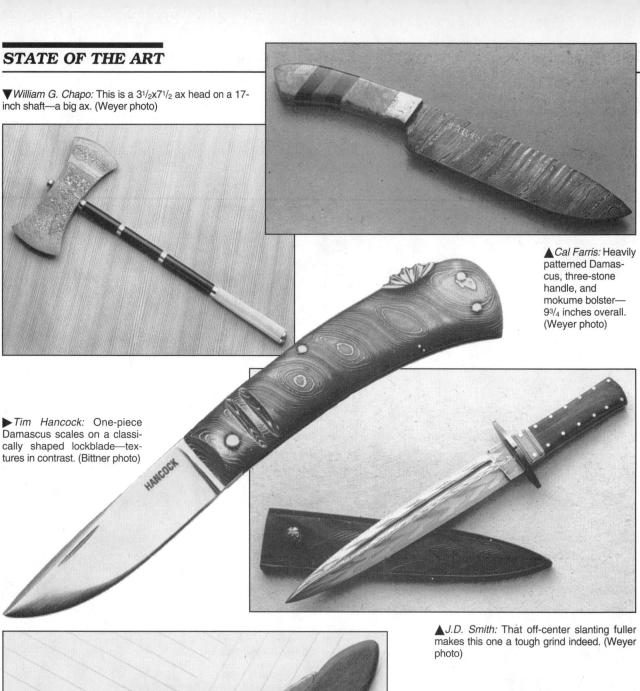

▲*Cal Farris:* Heavily patterned Damascus, three-stone handle, and mokume bolster—9³/₄ inches overall. (Weyer photo)

▶*Tim Hancock:* One-piece Damascus scales on a classically shaped lockblade—textures in contrast. (Bittner photo)

▲*J.D. Smith:* That off-center slanting fuller makes this one a tough grind indeed. (Weyer photo)

▼*Ralph Freer:* Star-pattern nickel Damascus in an 11-inch knife, scrolled by Norvell Foster.

▲*Marvin Meshejian:* Timing-chain Damascus, pierced back—yep, the edge is the straight side. (Weyer photo)

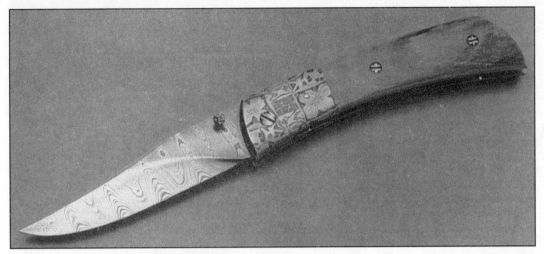

◀*Jason L. Williams:* Knickmeyer Damascus in mosaic and ladder patterns, some fossil ivory—all it takes. (Weyer photo)

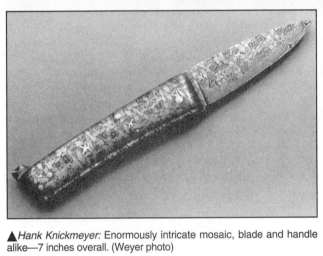

▲*Hank Knickmeyer:* Enormously intricate mosaic, blade and handle alike—7 inches overall. (Weyer photo)

▲*William James McHenry:* All Damascus structure for a big automatic—note the faces on the release. (Weyer photo)

▶*Bob Garbe:* All kinds of mosaic Damascus trim fore 'n' aft on this Appleseed folder only 4¹/₂ inches long. (Weyer photo)

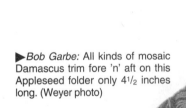

▲*R. Bill Saindon:* A wave breaks and bubbles bubble in this picture-frame folder body. (Weyer photo)

◀*Marvin Meshejian:* Finger knives in choice of convex or concave edges. (Weyer photo)

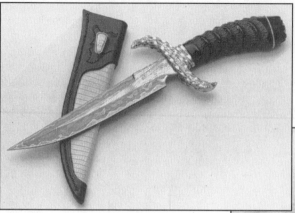

▲*Keith Kilby:* First polish; then etch, but not all of it. This is a 15-inch Bowie. (Weyer photo)

▲*Ed Halligan:* Bird-wing Damascus blade at 8 inches; massive worked sterling silver guard; reedbuck horn; a prize-winning knife. (Weyer photo)

▶*Joe Flournoy:* Some very serious manipulation here in camouflage Damascus which almost hides the Sheffield shape. (Weyer photo)

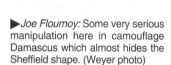

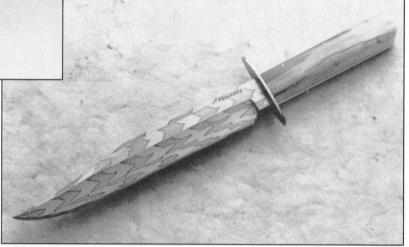

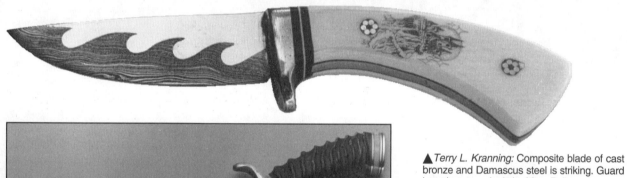

▲*Terry L. Kranning:* Composite blade of cast bronze and Damascus steel is striking. Guard is mokume; scrim is by Mary Bailey.

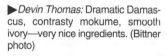

▲*Joseph G. Cordova:* Mash a Harley Davidson chain just right and you get this blade. Maker calls the knife Marco Polo. (Weyer photo)

▶*Devin Thomas:* Dramatic Damascus, contrasty mokume, smooth ivory—very nice ingredients. (Bittner photo)

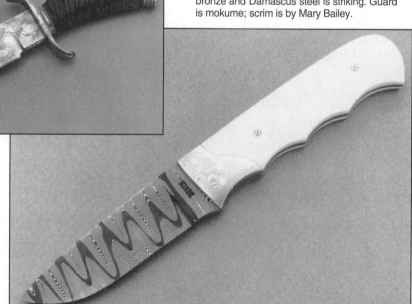

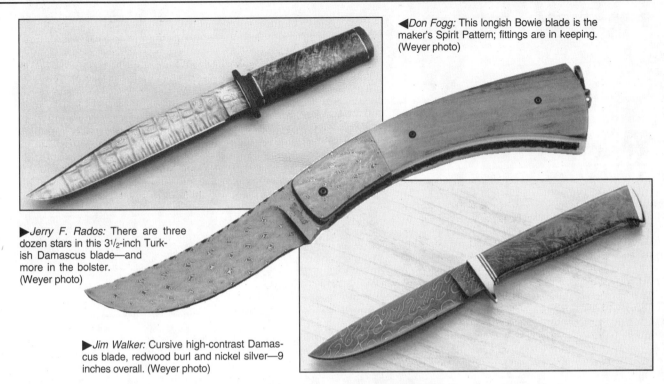

Don Fogg: This longish Bowie blade is the maker's Spirit Pattern; fittings are in keeping. (Weyer photo)

▶*Jerry F. Rados:* There are three dozen stars in this 3¹/₂-inch Turkish Damascus blade—and more in the bolster. (Weyer photo)

▶*Jim Walker:* Cursive high-contrast Damascus blade, redwood burl and nickel silver—9 inches overall. (Weyer photo)

◀*Steve R. Brooks:* Different patterns, different shapes; imagine the patterns switched—wouldn't look as good. (Weyer photo)

▼*Robert Blasingame:* Chain saw chain—no brand stated—gets a stretched-out pattern here.

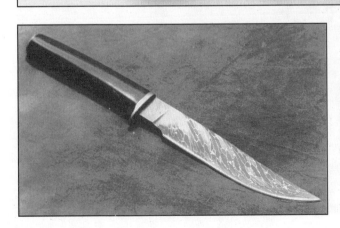

◀*Ronnie Andress:* Plain old cable Damascus done right, mounted in blackwood and more Damascus.

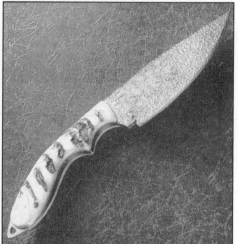

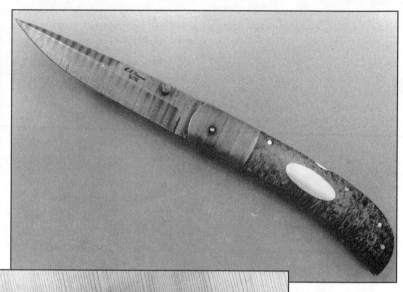

▲*John Zembko III:* Blade is D2, 4 inches long; detail is hand-carved; the knife is blued. (Landis photo)

▲*Eldon G. Peterson:* Smooth grayed stainless Damascus and black ash burl in a big ($4\frac{1}{2}$-inch blade) easy-opener fighter.

▶*James E. Porter:* A whole lot of pattern going on—grooved horn, layered guard, watershed blade—and the fabulous brass back besides. (Weyer photo)

◀*Don Maxwell:* First in the Gold Nugget series. The 14K gold is not cast; each will be individual. (Weyer photo)

▼*Don Hethcoat:* A topographic Damascus handle pattern behind a ladder-pattern blade; it's a tail-locker. (Weyer photo)

▲*Don Fogg:* Forged high carbon blade, left textured; forge-colored steel fittings; textured Wenge grip—very smithy. (Weyer photo)

Bog Iron Knives

WE CAN READ of the beginnings of the Iron Age in Northern Europe. At the base of it—trade iron excepted—we often find bog ore mentioned.

Indeed, bog ore workings seem to have been a prime target for archaeologists anywhere north of the Rhine. And we know a lot as a result.

Back then, it did not matter that better iron and better steel would be along. Implements of bog iron were a long way ahead of bronze and copper.

A fellow in Holland named Thijs van de Manakker is recreating the torturous bog iron process these days. The chunks of ore come—naturally—from bogs. The process remains primitive—a one-man show.

In the end, iron is concentrated into "blooms," and the blooms forged into useful articles, especially knives. With a great deal of labor—and a lot of ore—there can be swords, and if the smith has the skill and knowledge, such swords can be steel.

Smith van de Manakker is thus far just showing us the beginnings. They are fascinating.

Ken Warner

(Above) The chunk on which the knives lean is bog ore from Stiphout, a village near Eindhoven in the Netherlands. Above the knives is part of a fired, unforged bloom.

(Left) Here van de Manakker strikes a hot bloom at an outdoor demonstration.

(Below) These bog ore knives are differently smithed. The lower blade is forged straight from the bloom; the upper blade was doubled and forged three times.

Van de Manakker does knife art like this when not hammering out bog iron knives.

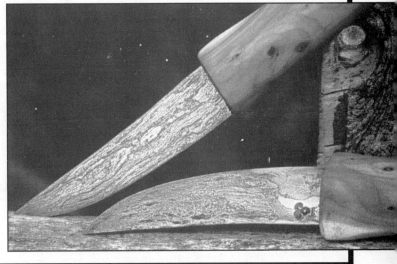

EMBELLISHMENT

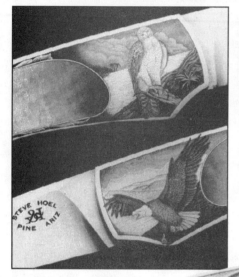

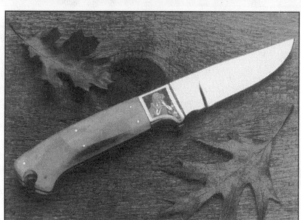

Terry Wallace: Mammoth on the bolster of a Lloyd Pendleton knife with—you're right—mammoth ivory scales.

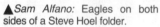

Sam Alfano: Eagles on both sides of a Steve Hoel folder.

Terry Theis: African game on both sides of a Henry Heitler folder.

Jim Ence: Droll fore 'n' aft treatment of a raccoon in the bolster of a small stag hunter. (Weyer photo)

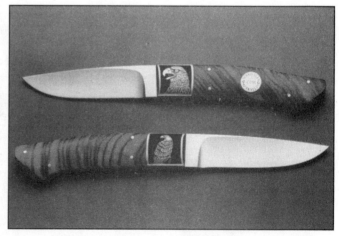

Jim Sornberger: Just twenty of this 20th anniversary knife will be made; the inlay is 18K. (Weyer photo)

▼▶*Chris Meyer:* Full coverage of a Kious folder with sheephorn grip. (Weyer photos)

▼*Chris Meyer:* Leopard stalks across a Charles A. West folder. (Weyer photo)

EMEBELLISHMENT
Engraving

▲▶*Bruce Shaw:* Deep relief of a horseback Indian in robust style on a Tom Black knife and a trophy deer on a J.E. Parker knife

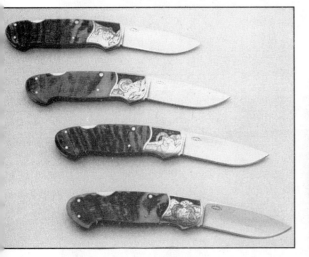

▲*Simon M. Lytton:* Grand slam of sheephorn on Kious folder handles matched by the bolster treatment.

▲*Judy Beaver:* Porpoises frolicking on a Fujisaka folder's titanium bolsters. (Weyer photo)

▶*Scott Pilkington, Jr.:* Simple dramatic bolster treatment on a small Wayne Clay belt knife. (Long photo)

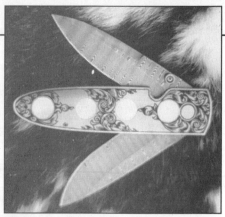

▲*Billy Bates:* Bilaterally symmetrical engraving suits the Kit Carson crosslock folder.

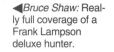

◀*Bruce Shaw:* Really full coverage of a Frank Lampson deluxe hunter.

EMBELLISHMENT

Engraving

◀*Jeff Crowell:* This Slim Cannady fighter's bolster is dramatically scrolled. (Weyer photo)

▼*Julie Warenski:* Gold inlay and scroll on the 416 stainless bolsters of a Lloyd Pendleton.

▲*John Dickson:* Personal style in scrollwork on a Ron Gaston boot knife. (Weyer photo)

▶*Chris Meyer:* Flowing scroll in and out of the interframe section of a Chuck Stewart knife.

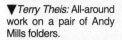

▼*Billy Bates:* Bolster work on a W.D. Pease gent's knife.

▼*Terry Theis:* All-around work on a pair of Andy Mills folders.

▲*Ki Hagberg:* Full coverage on all surfaces of a German Gerus & Hagberg short hunter.

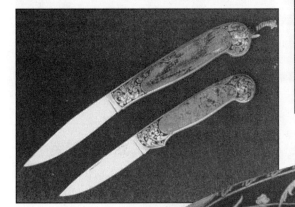

EMBELLISHMENT

Engraving

▶*Jim Blair:* Flush gold inlays in an Eldon Peterson folder—the insert is blued steel.

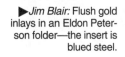

▶*Julie Warenski:* All-out gold inlay and pin engraving on a pair of Don Lozier hunters. (Weyer photo)

▼*Bruce Shaw:* Full-house treatments of five Fujisaka folders.

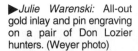

▲*Jere Davidson:* Full treatment of a Eldon G. Peterson small folder includes gold inlay.

◄*Sandra Brady:* Bald eagle in ivory on a Rardon boot knife. (Weyer photo)

▲*Bob Hergert:* It's a 1933 Stutz on a Lile knife. (Kelley photo)

◄*Rick B. Fields:* Blackfeet encamped beneath the Grand Tetons on a Centofante folder.

EMBELLISHMENT
Scrimshaw

▲*Rick B. Fields:* Rising trout on the fossil ivory scales of a Barry Davis knife.

▲*Rick B. Fields:* Dawn or sunset in the Boundary Waters canoe country scrimmed on a Centofante folder.

►*Faustina L. Mead:* Angulated dancing whooping crane in the buffalo horn grip of a Dennis Mead tanto.

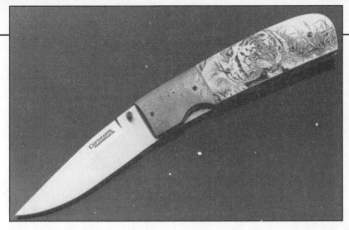

▲*Sandra Brady:* This tiger stalks the ivory jungle of a Centofante folder. (Weyer photo)

▼*Gary Williams:* A cougar, maybe up a tree, on the ivory of a Corbit folder.

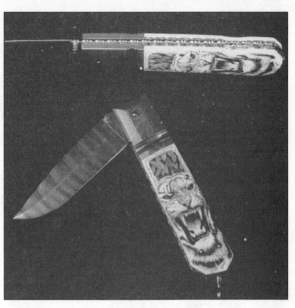

▲*Gary Williams:* A snarling tiger on a Brad Davis folder. (Caldonna photo)

▼*Linda Karst:* Contemplative feline sits up on a Tommy Lee knife.

Scrimshaw

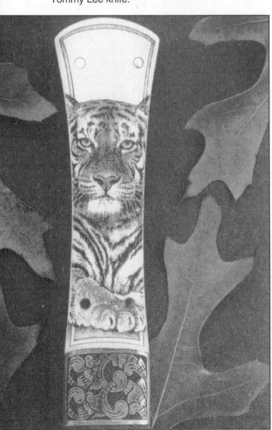

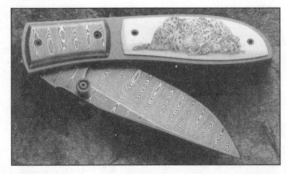

▲*Rick B. Fields:* A lynx and dinner on a folder by Barry Davis.

▶*Charles V. Rece:* A lion at rest on a Joel Humphreys skinner.

▲*Stephen Stuart:* A nicely folded leopard on a Carson folder. (Weyer photo)

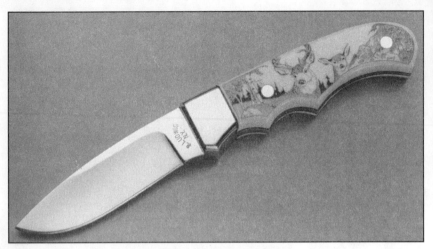

▲Sandra Brady: Whitetails up in big country on a Rich Ludwig drop-point. (Weyer photo)

▲▼Faustina L. Mead: Two sides of an Emery Bowie show grizzlies.

EMBELLISHMENT
Scrimshaw

◄Charles V. Rece: Wolf threads through aspens on a Joel Humphreys skinner.

▼Rick B. Fields: Reversed wolf on blue mammoth ivory of a Jack Davenport folder.

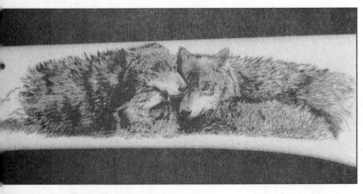

▲Faustina L. Mead: Wolf family on ivory on a big Reese Weiland knife.

▲Faustina L. Mead: Wolves on a Weiland tanto's ivory handle.

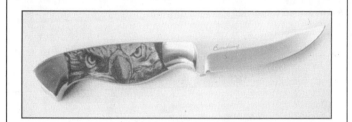

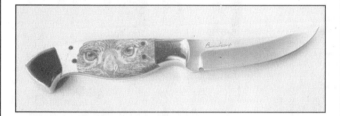

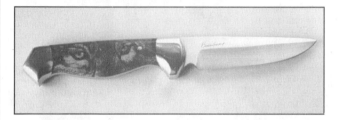

Gaetan Beauchamp: The eyes of prey and a big cat on matching knives—scrimmed by the maker.

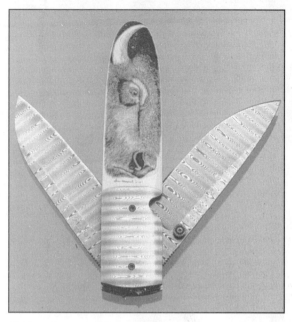

▲*Susan Davenport:* A bison's eye gleams in an elegant layout on a Kit Carson folder. (Weyer photo)

EMBELLISHMENT
Scrimshaw

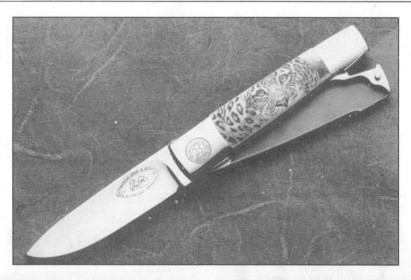

Gary Williams: A wolf, a puma, and a leopard stare from a Wood, Irie & Co. folder and two Corbits.

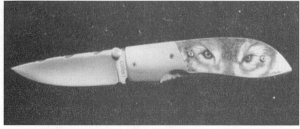

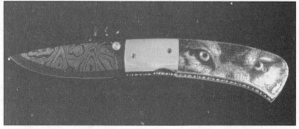

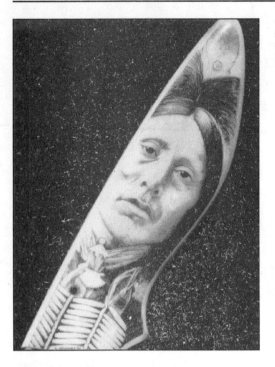

◀*Charles Hargraves, Sr.:* Clear-eyed warrior calmly observes from a Rodney Rogers knife.

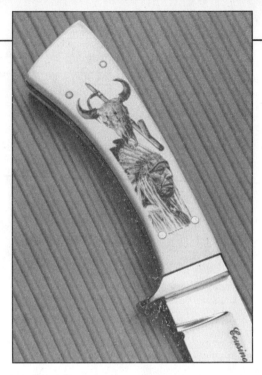

▶*Gary Kiracofe:* Native American motifs on a Cousino knife. (Weyer photo)

EMBELLISHMENT
Scrimshaw

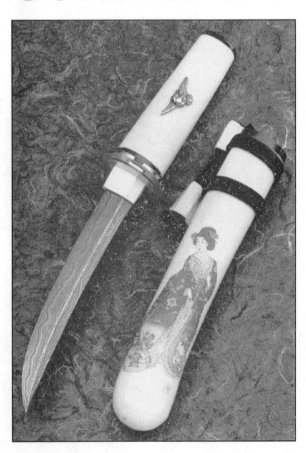

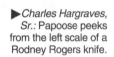

▲*John Gemma:* Emaciation in horse and man on an Al Gentile knife. (Weyer photo)

▶*Charles Hargraves, Sr.:* Papoose peeks from the left scale of a Rodney Rogers knife.

◀*Dennis K. Holland:* Nice lady on the alternative ivory scabbard of a Don Polzien tanto. (Weyer photo)

▶*Jean Yves Bourbeau:* Water buffalo horn holds a profile—scrimmed by the knifemaker. (Weyer photo)

◀*Toniutti Nelida:* Scrim of a male nude is signed but illegible.

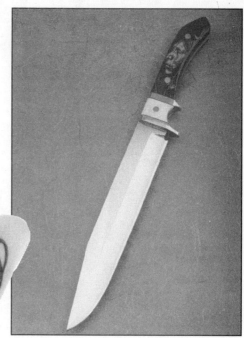

EMBELLISHMENT
Scrimshaw

◀*Gary Kiracofe:* Smiling hunter and his prey on a Dennis Friedly Bowie. (Weyer photo)

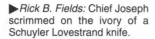

▲*Petria Mitchell:* High plains warrior on ivory in a Saindon knife.

▶*Rick B. Fields:* Chief Joseph scrimmed on the ivory of a Schuyler Lovestrand knife.

▶*Gary (Wolf) Rua:* Maker file-worked pearl of this ladies' knife in Damascus. (Dailey photo)

▼*Todd Kinnikin:* Sculptured ebony grip surmounts a shooting star mosaic blade—all by the maker. (Weyer photo)

▶*Sherry Lott:* Full coverage in a dragonish motif on a tanto-style knife by John Greco. (Weyer photo)

EMBELLISHMENT
Carving & Etching

▶*Paul G. Grussenmeyer:* Fossil walrus dolphin with cast wave-form guard in sterling silver atop a James Porter blade. (Weyer photo)

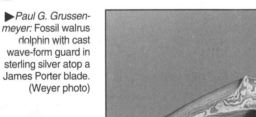

◀*Ken Steigerwalt:* Bolster carved in flutes; pearl checkered and fluted; all by the maker.

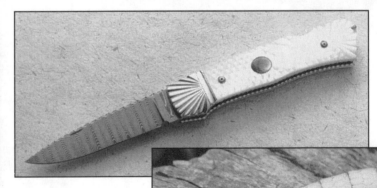

▲*Howard F. Clark:* Clever layout in ivory of a female torso as automatic folder handle. (J. Clark photo)

▶*Tom Bullard:* Texas ivory—armadillo—provides a natural carved look to this gut-hook skinner.

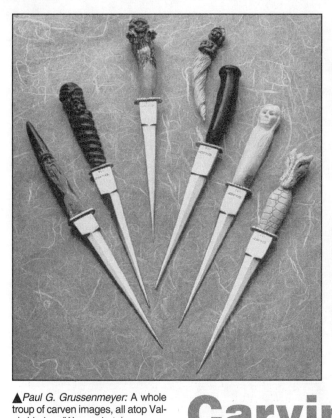

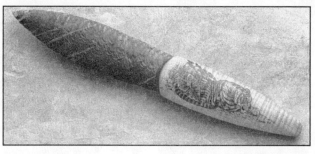

▲*Denise Kondrla:* Tiger burned into curly maple on an Errett Callahan obsidian knife. (Weyer photo)

▼*Jim Turecek:* Modest maiden, lightly carved in pearl, inlaid in ebony by the maker. (Weyer photo)

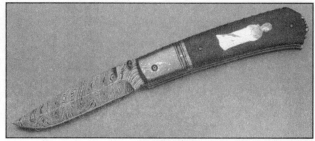

▲*Paul G. Grussenmeyer:* A whole troup of carven images, all atop Valois blades. (Weyer photo)

Carving & Etching

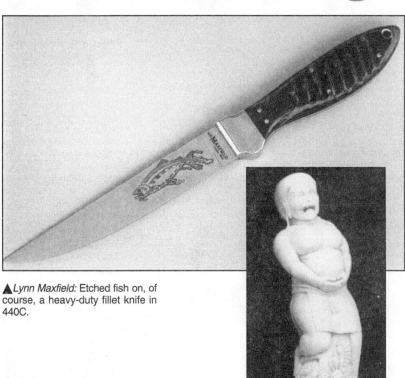

▲*Lynn Maxfield:* Etched fish on, of course, a heavy-duty fillet knife in 440C.

▶*Henri Viallon:* Kris handle in ivory represents Raksasa, who chases demons. (Lecot photo)

▲*Don Hume:* Big fighter blade handled with a lost wax casting in oxidized bronze of squid tentacles. (Weyer photo)

LEATHERWORK

▶*Kenny Rowe:* Professional basketweave sheath for a Thayer camp knife hangs on a swivel.

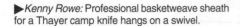

▼*Chris Kravitt:* Tree Stump's tooled sheath has iguana overlay and holds a Coombs knife.

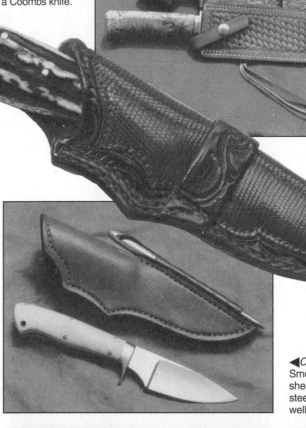

▼*Sonja Lee:* Fully tooled sheath for Randy's 5½-inch fighter. (Weyer photo)

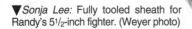

◀*C.A. Pennington:* Smooth hunter pouch sheath carries a smooth steel or marlinspike as well.

▲*Bud Nealy:* Patented "MCS" Kydex sheath works a lot of ways. (Weyer photo)

▶*Johnny Stout:* Texas Trophy Set and a really stout holstering set-up. (Lum photo)

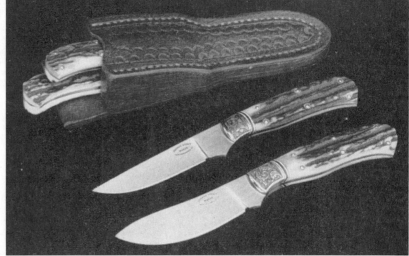

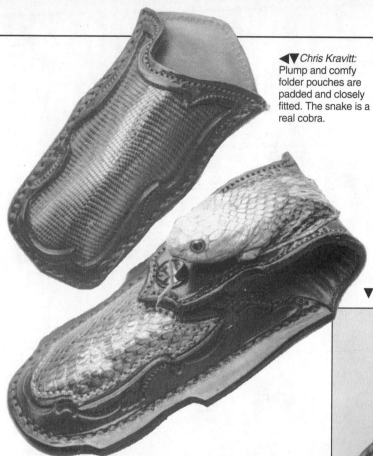

◀▼*Chris Kravitt:* Plump and comfy folder pouches are padded and closely fitted. The snake is a real cobra.

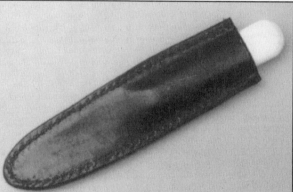

▲*Robert G. Schrap:* Reproduction Cooper sheaths in authentic detail.

▼*Dave Graves:* Pocket sheath for a small kitchen knife—to order.

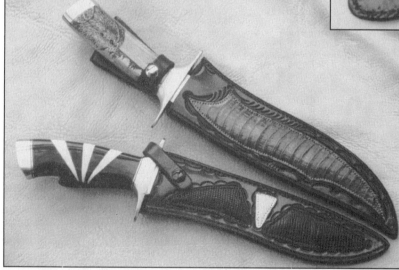

▲*Chris Kravitt:* Big Sakmar knives in snake and lizard—overlaid fitted sheaths.

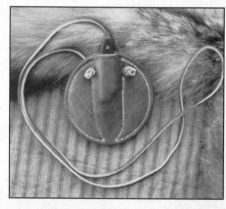

▲*Congdon Blade Leather:* Round neck sheath for a very small knife.

▶*Dave Graves:* Custom sheath for a Vorpal sword, the Blackjack version.

▶*Tim Hancock:* Very protective pouch for a long dagger with frogskin overlay. (Bittner photo)

▼*Karen Shook:* A correct sheath for an 18th-century Daniel Winkler-pattern Bowie. (Weyer photo)

◀*Kelly S. Kennedy:* Slim blade cover and fully floral carved—very simple. (Weyer photo)

▶*Chris Kravitt:* Big pouch for cross-draw, overlaid with ring lizard skin.

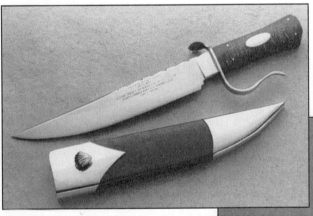

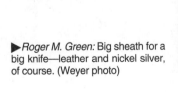

▲*E. Jay Hendrickson:* Basswood and leather and nickel silver, fit to tote the 8th ABS Board Knife of the Year. (Weyer photo)

▶*Roger M. Green:* Big sheath for a big knife—leather and nickel silver, of course. (Weyer photo)

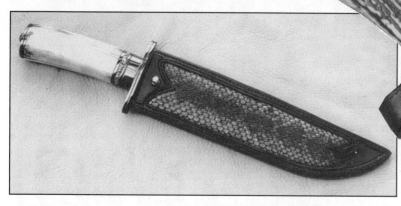

▼*Kenny Rowe:* Pin-loc sheath for a Neely knife with inlaid timber rattler skin.

▼*Liz McGowan:* Left-side cross-draw sheath with diamondback inlay. (Wirlack photo)

▲*Chris Kravitt:* Cowhide and rattlesnake skin around a Friedley Bowie.

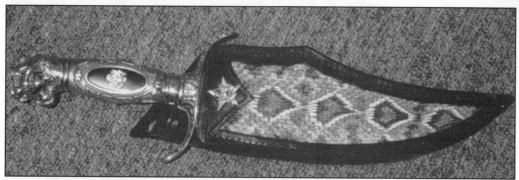

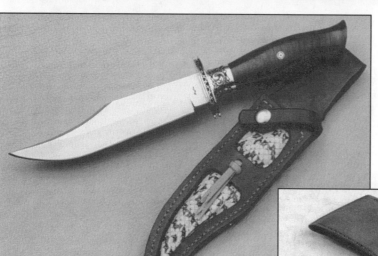

▲*Barney Foley:* No hardware sheath for a Corbet Sigman hunter—full basketweave.

▲*Ed Hughes:* Interframe-style Bowie sheath, lined with rattlesnake. (Weyer photo)

▶*Tom McLuin:* Heavy knife, pouch sheath—and rattlesnake inlay.

▲*Roger M. Green:* Classic knife, classic sheath—black leather and nickel silver throat and tip. (Weyer photo)

▲*Mike Schirmer:* Full pouch, with a lot of tooling—a comfortable home for a 4-inch hunter.

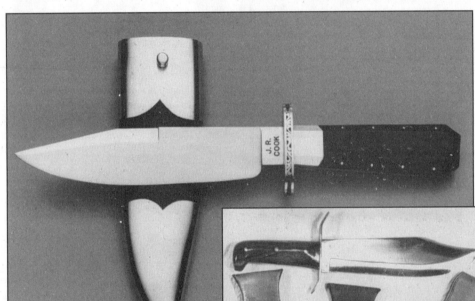

▶*James Ray Cook:* High-style sheath for a Saline River Bowie. (Weyer photo)

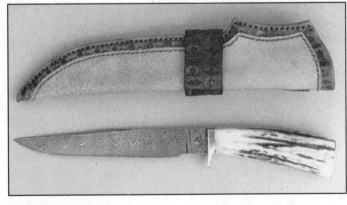

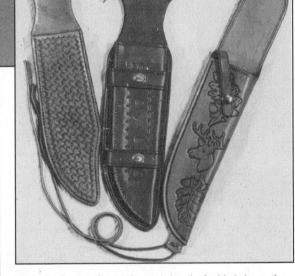

▲*Harold Cooper:* Straightforward sheaths for big knives—three separate plans here.

▲*Jim Fister:* Slim pouch overlaid in pigskin—frontier style for a slim fighter.

FACTORY TRENDS

Commercial cutlery tends toward the tried and true. The market needs millions of knives every year, and the market uses them up. So much of the market is replacement.

There are, however, counter-trends. That is, the marketing guys in the knife business want new stuff to talk about. And those—at least, quite a few of them—are what you see here in our "New Knives In Production" pages.

And we remark on the passing parade as well, when the commercial market displays a new direction.

Ken Warner

New Knives in Production 166
Sabatier Again 178

NEW KNIVES IN PRODUCTION

Muela: An 18th-century clasp knife in the grand old Iberian tradition.

▼*Tool Logic:* The Credit Card Companion is about as thick as four typical plastic cards and really does hold all this stuff.

▲*Buck:* A 20th-century double liner-lock, built of all the new stuff. This is the Hunter model.

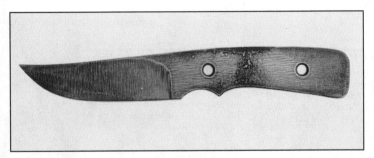

Reproduction Blades: This year's cast blades—tempered to RC 60—in Dendtric (as cast) D2 are offered as spearhead, rifle knife and ready-to-finish hunter.

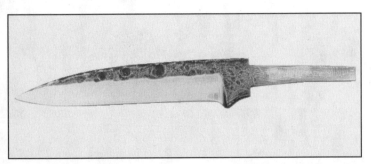

◀*Marking Methods, Inc.:* A big kit for electro-etching blade marks looks like this ready to go.

▼*Edgecraft Corp.:* Diamond hone set interchanges two grooved pads and works for all sort of edges, they say.

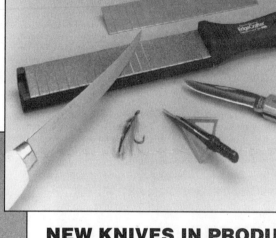

NEW KNIVES IN PRODUCTION
Neat Stuff

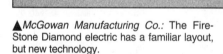

▲*McGowan Manufacturing Co.:* The Fire-Stone Diamond electric has a familiar layout, but new technology.

▶*Muela:* More Siglo XVIII (18th-century) designs—the real old-time feel.

▶*Diamond Machining Technology, Inc.:* Key-chain-sized dimond hone, self-sheathing.

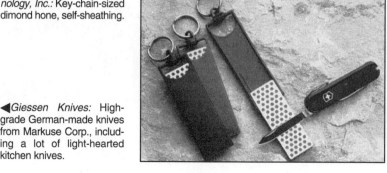

◀*Giessen Knives:* High-grade German-made knives from Markuse Corp., including a lot of light-hearted kitchen knives.

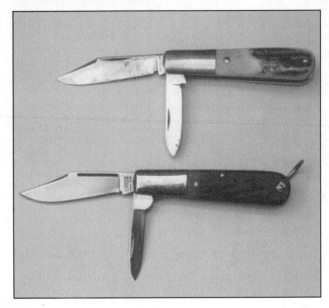

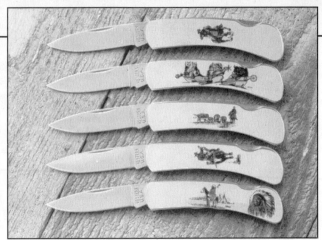

▲*Camillus:* Five kinds of Model 510s—all in Western themes.

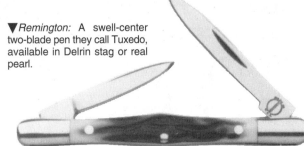

▼*Remington:* A swell-center two-blade pen they call Tuxedo, available in Delrin stag or real pearl.

▲*Camillus and Colonial:* This pair of Barlows "borrowed" to use worked out fine. The Colonial (actually marked Old Cutler) in stag is under $30; the Delrin Camillus under $20. Remarkable values.

NEW KNIVES IN PRODUCTION

Traditional Folding Knives

▶*Schrade:* The Golden Claw and the Golden Bear, variations on an old and useful and profitable theme.

▼*Ranger:* Another Colonial—a flat, large, cheap, useful jackknife with an inner lock.

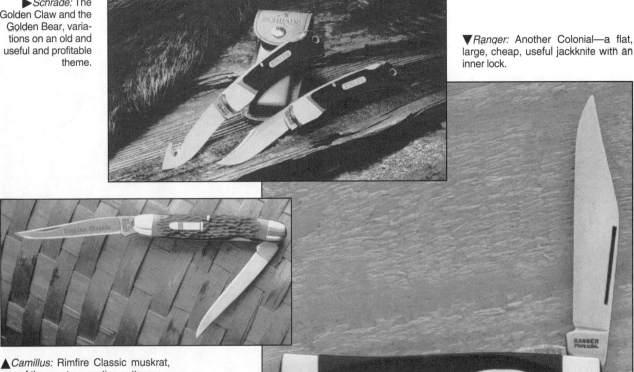

▲*Camillus:* Rimfire Classic muskrat, one of the great serpentine patterns.

◄*Colonial Knife:* In the tradition, this one appears to have all the good stuff.

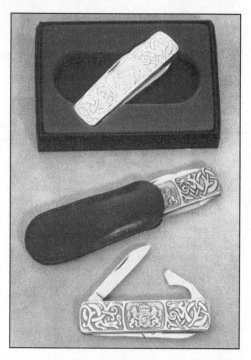

▼*Remington:* European vent hook on a nice upland knife in Delrin stag.

▶*EKA:* Swedish-quality pocket cutlery from Nichols, leather pouched and boxed.

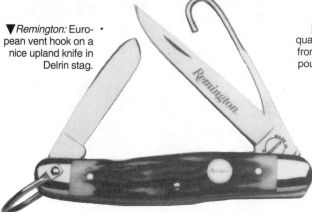

NEW KNIVES IN PRODUCTION

Traditional Folding Knives

◄*EKA:* Brush-finished stainless steel in a variety of Swedish-made shapes. The big one is assembled by welding.

▼*Colonial Knife:* The Swiss-style fruit sampler does well in the Heartland and in produce production areas.

▼*Colonial Knife:* Another Swiss-styled multi-tool knife, made in the USA. There are eight blades showing here.

◀▲*Kopromed:* Polish-made sports cutlery in the grand Mittel Europa tradition—a magnum skinner and a safari style here.

▼*Damascus USA:* The Gayden-styled Green River in stainless Damascus and wildwoods; 9½ inches overall. (Weyer photo)

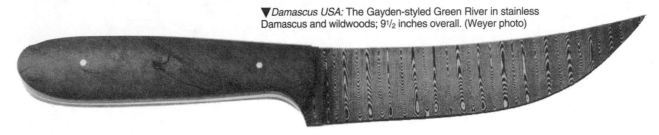

NEW KNIVES IN PRODUCTION
Outdoors Belt Knives

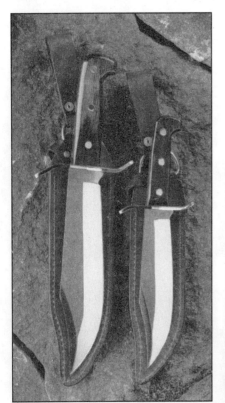

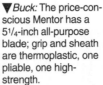

▶*Muela:* C.A.S. Iberia, Inc., is presenting some big no-nonsense Bowies—the big spear-point is very Bowie-looking.

▼*Buck:* The price-conscious Mentor has a 5¼-inch all-purpose blade; grip and sheath are thermoplastic, one pliable, one high-strength.

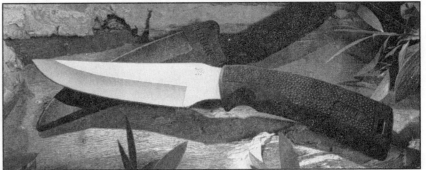

▲*Camillus/Western:* The long-time staple Model 49 Bowie has a little brother, the Model 47.

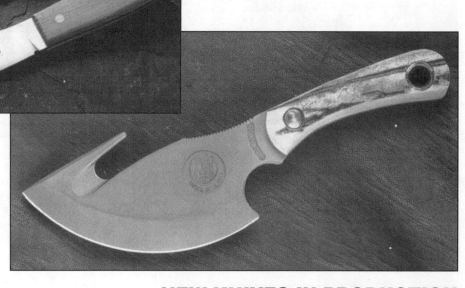

◄*Cold Steel, Inc.:* These are Red River Knives, hunters in the 19th-century professional style.

►*Knives Of Alaska:* Moose Tool, designed for doing most of what there is to make meat out of something big.

NEW KNIVES IN PRODUCTION

Outdoors Belt Knives

►*Helle Knives:* From Nichols Co., these Norwegian blades are called Pan, Ton and Turi. Rather neat.

▼*Schrade:* Old Timer Trail Boss gets some serious size to it—10³/₄ inches overall.

▼*Outdoor Edge Cutlery Corp.:* Big and little, they both work. Those little serrations are good cut-starters.

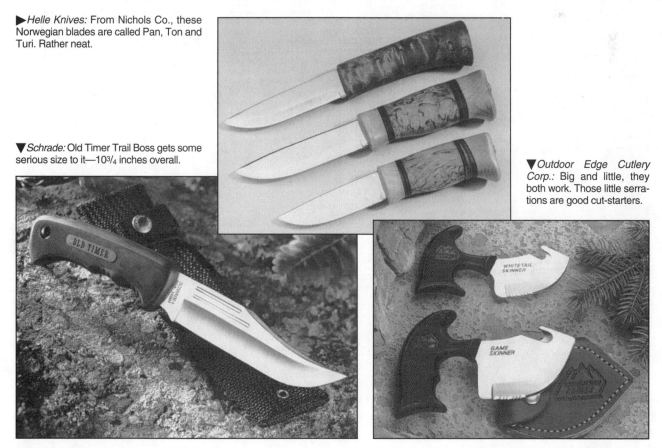

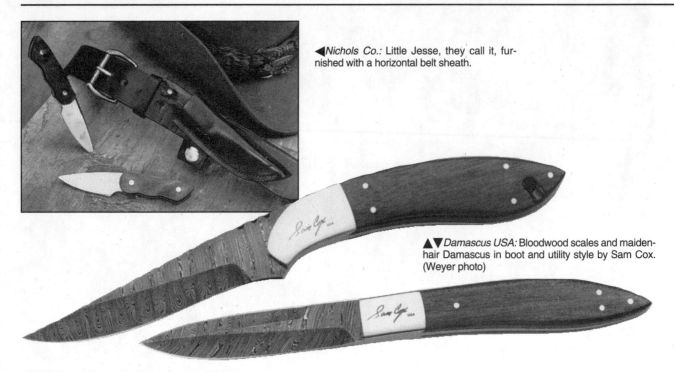

◀*Nichols Co.:* Little Jesse, they call it, furnished with a horizontal belt sheath.

▲▼*Damascus USA:* Bloodwood scales and maidenhair Damascus in boot and utility style by Sam Cox. (Weyer photo)

NEW KNIVES IN PRODUCTION

Outdoors Belt Knives

▶*Roselli Knives:* Short Finnish working tools—the Hunter, Grandad, Carpenter, Granny. Neat; not cheap—from Nichols Co.

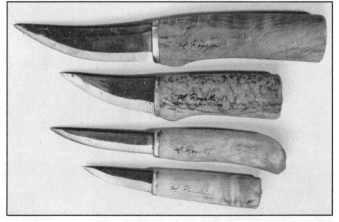

▲▶*Muela:* They make the good Spanish stuff in small and medium sizes, too. From C.A.S. Iberia, Inc.

▲*Cold Steel, Inc.:* These are extra-large Voyagers, set up with 5-inch blades.

▼*Schrade:* The Cliphanger—it's a 4½-inch Viper with a clip strap.

▲*Buck Knives:* Protege lockblades having 3-inch blades with a Cordura sheath and handles you can hang onto.

NEW KNIVES IN PRODUCTION
Outdoors Folders

▲*Normark Corp.* Solid folding fillet knife, stainless and plastic.

▲*Schrade:* The Outback is a drop-point stout fella, 5¼ inches closed. Sheath is nylon.

▶*Colonial Knife:* Scalloped Life-Knife is 4 inches closed in red Zytel.

▼*Cold Steel, Inc.:* Named Culloden, here's a seriously tough-loooking knife. The clans would have loved the serrations.

▲*Cold Steel, Inc.:* This one's the Bush Ranger, a serious Bowie shape and a no-nonsense look.

▲*Remington:* A boot knife in the Western tradition; indeed, probably on the Western tooling.

NEW KNIVES IN PRODUCTION
Tactical Shapes

▼*Ontario Knife Co.:* Part of a big military output, this is an early World War II style.

◄*Frost Cutlery Co.:* When the Galactic Warrior comes calling, he may have one of these along.

▼*Ontario Knife Co.:* This is the SpecPlus machete, a useful-looking tool that can chop, saw, slice and dig.

▲*Frost Cutlery Co.:* These are the Wild Cat and the Road Warrior, and people just love them and most knives like them.

▶*Buck Knives:* Not one but two Nighthawks, one not so dark. Blade is 6½ inches; shape is superb.

Tactical Shapes

◀*SOG:* This is really a picture of Blade-Tech's jump-proof Kydex sheath for the SOG Seal 2000, an issue knife.

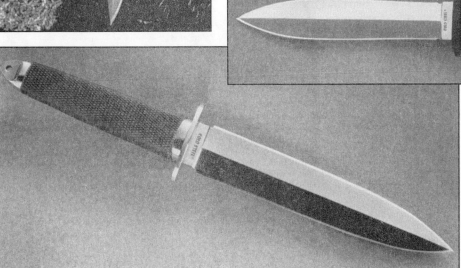

◀▲*Cold Steel, Inc.:* The wire-wrapped one is called Tai Pan; the others are Peace Keeper I and II. Neat-looking.

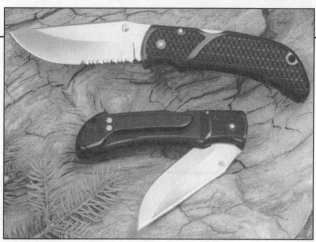

▲*Benchmade Knife Co., Inc.:* Model 970, the Ernest Emerson design with the super chisel blade.

▶*Outdoor Edge Cutlery Corp.:* This is the Field-Lite, thumb stud, pocket clip, serrations and all.

▼*Benchmade Knife Co., Inc.:* With ATS-34 blades and big hole action, these are go-getting liner-locks.

NEW KNIVES IN PRODUCTION
Tactical Shapes

Spyderco, Inc.: All kinds of profiles in amongst the Clip-Its and the un-Clip-Its, but they *all* open quick.

▲*Ontario Knife Co.:* Some righteous-looking survival piece here, but it's different from the World War II one.

►*Cold Steel, Inc.:* Variations on the Voyager theme. These are the medium size.

NEW KNIVES IN PRODUCTION

Tactical Shapes

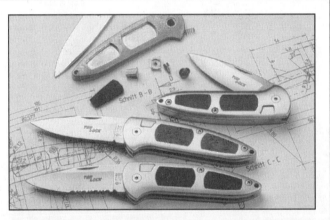

Boker: Dietmar Pohl is the new hot ticket at Boker in Solingen. He's shepherding new and juicy designs to market. The first is the TopLock—a switch-blade in Germahy, a lockblade here—all dismountable and very good feeling. The belt knives are getting better, too.

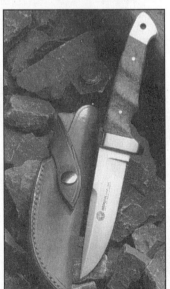

FACTORY TRENDS

SABATIER AGAIN

YEP. I STOPPED by this store in South Carolina again. Last time, in 1988 or so, the tab went about $200, including some nice French cooking pots and a couple of big knives.

Things have changed a lot. The French pots are up the road in their own store, and there are now *a lot* of French-made knives on display. And you can still spend $114 for a ham slicer.

Darned handsome, most of these knives. There are traditional patterns in carbon steel and in stainless steel. There are new approaches in choice of steel. And when I say *lots*, I mean there are several thousand knives—a dozen to three dozen or more of each of 60 or 80 patterns—right there where you can reach them.

So it was fun. The French are apparently ever-willing to perform a number of variations—a given paring knife, for instance, could be found at four lengths. And there are a bunch of different ways to build knives.

They forge them with bolsters; they apply bolsters; they go without bolsters; they do integral bolsters *and* pommels. They rivet wood; they rivet fancy wood; they fabricate high-in plastic; they injection-mould plastic. Very busy, the French cutlers are.

Specifically, we are discussing the Sabatier factory outlet store at Exit 33 of I-95 South in Point South, South Carolina. It's been there for a decade or more.

This by-the-highway store offers kitchen cutlery goods from several, perhaps most, French manufacturers. But this little sketch is not meant to discuss them.

We're here to announce a triumph. Your intrepid reporter went in, looked at them all and liked them a lot. He then plunked down $7.50 for a plain-pipe-rack paring knife and walked out with head held high. This is going to be a tough record to beat.

Ken Warner

DIRECTORY

The only reason a maker or a source in the United States is not listed somewhere in this section is that we didn't hear of him or it, or something went wrong. This is intended to be a complete directory for knife owners. If you know of someone who should be in this Directory and isn't, please write and tell us. If you are that someone, please write. We'll definitely appreciate it.

This is not a catalog, so there will be incomplete entries, though not many. And with probably 1,000 or more entries, it will have omissions. Very often, that will be the result of error on the part of the omitted. We tried to give everyone a chance.

The Directory is divided into different lists. The biggest is a compilation of short profiles of custom knifemakers, followed by a state-by-state list of those same knifemakers, and membership lists of professional knifemaker associations. In the knife photo index, we list all the photos of handmade knives in this edition, as well as the last five editions.

Then we list specialty cutlers; general cutlers; importers and foreign cutlers; sources for knifemaking supplies; mail-order houses that specialize in knives; knife services, which include scrimshanders, engravers, leatherworkers and several other categories. Finally, we list major organizations and publications. Those seem the most useful categories. We hope they work for you.

Ken Warner

Custom Knifemakers 180
Knifemakers State-By-State 269
Knifemakers Membership Lists 277
Knife Photo Index
    Knives '96 281
    Knives '91-'95 283
Specialty Cutlers 290

General Cutlers 291
Importers & Foreign Cutlers 291
Knifemaking Supplies 293
Mail-Order Sales 295
Knife Services 297
Organizations & Publications 304

custom knifemakers

a

ABBOTT, WILLIAM M., Box 102A, RR #2, Chandlerville, IL 62627/217-458-2325
Specialties: High-grade edged weapons. **Patterns:** Locking folders, Bowies, working straight knives, kitchen cutlery, minis. **Technical:** Grinds D2, ATS-34, 440C and commercial Damascus. Heat-treats; Rockwell tests. Prefers natural handle materials. **Prices:** $100 to $1,000. **Remarks:** Part-time maker; first knife sold in 1984. **Mark:** Name.

A CUT ABOVE (See Hartsfield, Phill)

ADAMS, LES, 6413 NW 200 St., Hialeah, FL 33015/305-625-1699
Specialties: Working straight knives of his design. **Patterns:** Fighters, hunters and filet knives. **Technical:** Grinds ATS-34, 440C and D2. Offers scrimshawed handles. **Prices:** $100 to $200; some to $290. **Remarks:** Part-time maker first knife sold in 1989. **Mark:** First initial, last name, Custom Knives.

ADAMS, WILLIAM D., 9318 Cole Creek Dr., Houston, TX 77040/713-855-5643; FAX: 713-855-5638
Specialties: Working knives of his design. **Patterns:** Hunters, kitchen knives and utility/camp knives. **Technical:** Grinds 1095, 440C and 440V. Uses stabilized wood and other stabilized materials. **Prices:** $100 to $150. **Remarks:** Part-time maker; first knife sold in 1994. Doing business as William D. Adams & Associates. **Mark:** First and middle initials above last name.

AIDA, YOSHIHITO, 26-7, Narimasu 2-chome, Itabashi-ku, Tokyo 175, JAPAN/81-3-3939-0052; FAX: 81-3-3939-0058
Specialties: High-tech working straight knives and folders of his design. **Patterns:** Bowies, lockbacks, hunters, fighters, fishing knives, boots. **Technical:** Grinds CV-134, ATS-34; buys Damascus; works in traditional Japanese fashion for some handles and sheaths. **Prices:** $300 to $700; some higher. **Remarks:** Full-time maker; first knife sold in 1978. **Mark:** Initial logo and Riverside West.

ALASKA KNIFE & SERVICE CO. (See Trujillo, Thomas A.)

ALASKAN MAID (See Kubaiko, Hank)

ALBERICCI, EMILIO, 19, via Masone, 24100, Bergamo, ITALY/01139-35-215120
Specialties: Folders and Bowies. **Patterns:** Collector knives. **Technical:** Uses stock removal with extreme lavoration accuracy; offers exotic and high-tech materials. **Prices:** Not currently selling. **Remarks:** Part-time maker. **Mark:** None.

ALDEN JR., KENNETH E., P.O. Box 1995, Ramona, CA 92065/619-789-4870; FAX: 619-788-6894
Specialties: Traditional working and using straight knives of his design and in standard patterns. **Patterns:** Bowies, fighters and hunters. **Technical:** Forges 5160 and 1095; grinds 440C. Makes own Damascus; offers filework and tooled, carved and stamped leather sheaths. **Prices:** $300 to $1,500; some to $3,000. **Remarks:** Full-time maker. Doing business as Alden Trading Co. **Mark:** Last name; first inital, last name; Lionmaker.

ALDEN TRADING CO. (See Alden Jr., Kenneth E.)

ALDERMAN, ROBERT, 3388 Jewel Lake Rd., Sagle, ID 83860/208-263-5996
Specialties: Classic and traditional working straight knives in standard patterns or to customer specs and his design; period pieces. **Patterns:** Bowies, fighters, hunters and utility/camp knives. **Technical:** Casts, forges and grinds 10 84; forges and grinds L6 and 0-1. Prefers an old appearance. **Prices:** $100 to $350; some to $700. **Remarks:** Full-time maker; first knife sold in 1975. Doing business as Trackers Forge. **Mark:** Deer track.

ALEXANDER, DARREL, Box 381, Ten Sleep, WY 82442/307-366-2699
Specialties: Traditional working straight knives. **Patterns:** Hunters, boots and fishing knives. **Technical:** Grinds D2, 440C, ATS-34 and 154CM. **Prices:** $75 to $120; some to $250. **Remarks:** Full-time maker; first knife sold in 1983. **Mark:** Name, city, state.

ALLEN, JOE, RR #3, Box 182, Princeton, IN 47670/812-385-8010
Specialties: Hunting and outdoor knives. **Patterns:** Bowies, working hunters, daggers and skinners. **Technical:** Grinds 440C and ATS-34. **Prices:** $125 to $300. **Remarks:** Part-time maker; first knife sold in 1976. **Mark:** Cable Joe Knives.

ALLEN, MIKE "WHISKERS", 12745 Fontenot Acres Rd., Malakoff, TX 75148/903-489-1026
Specialties: Working and collector-quality lockbacks and automatic folders to customer specs. **Patterns:** Hunters, tantos, Bowies, swords and miniatures. **Technical:** Forges Damascus to shape; grinds 440C and ATS-34. Engraves. **Prices:** $125 and up. **Remarks:** Full-time maker; first knife sold in 1984. **Mark:** Whiskers and serial number.

ALLRED AND SONS (See Allred, Elvan)

ALLRED, ELVAN, 2403 Lansing Blvd., Wichita Falls, TX 76309/817-691-9563
Specialties: Fancy, high-art straight knives and folders of his design. **Patterns:** Fighters, hunters and locking folders. **Technical:** Grinds ATS-34, 440C and D2. Most knives are engraved; many have custom-fitted cases or sheaths. **Prices:** $250 to $750; some to $1,500. **Remarks:** Full-time maker; first knife sold in 1992. Doing business as Allred and Sons. **Mark:** First initial, last name, city, state.

ALSTAR (See Amoureux, A.W.)

ALVERSON, TIM (R.V.), 1158 Maple St., Klamath Falls, OR 97601/503-884-9119
Specialties: Fancy working knives to customer specs; other types on request. **Patterns:** Bowies, daggers, folders and miniatures. **Technical:** Grinds 440C, ATS-34; buys some Damascus. **Prices:** $175 and up. **Remarks:** Full-time maker; first knife sold in 1981. **Mark:** Rosebud or R.V.A.

AMERI, MAURO, Via Trensasco, 13a/8, 16138 Genova, ITALY/010-8363035
Specialties: Working and using knives of his design. **Patterns:** Hunters, Bowies and utility/camp knives. **Technical:** Grinds 440C, ATS-34, 154CM and Damascus by C. Peterson. Handles in wood or Micarta; offers sheaths. **Prices:** $200 to $1,200. **Remarks:** Spare-time maker; first knife sold in 1982. **Mark:** Last name, city.

AMES FORGE (See Ames, Mickey L.)

AMES, MICKEY L., P.O. Box 62, 528 Spruce, Lebo, KS 66856/316-256-6222
Specialties: Traditional working and using straight knives of his design and to customer specs. **Patterns:** Bowies, hunters and utility/camp knives. **Technical:** Forges 5160, 1084 and makes own Damascus. Filework; silver wire inlay. **Prices:** $100 and up. **Remarks:** Part-time maker; first knife sold in 1990. Doing business as Ames Forge. **Mark:** Last name.

AMOR JR., MIGUEL, 1711 White Water Rd., Lancaster, PA 17603/717-394-7590
Specialties: Working and fancy straight knives in standard patterns; some to customer specs. **Patterns:** Bowies, hunters, fighters and tantos. **Technical:** Grinds 440C, ATS-34, carbon steel and commercial Damascus; forges some in high carbon steels. **Prices:** $125 to $500; some to $1,500 and higher. **Remarks:** Part-time maker; first knife sold in 1983. **Mark:** Last name. On collectors' pieces: last name, city, state.

AMOUREUX, A.W., 3210 Woodland Pk. Dr., Anchorage, AK 99517/907-248-4442

Specialties: Heavy-duty working straight knives. **Patterns:** Bowies, fighters, camp knives and hunters for Alaska use. **Technical:** Grinds 440C, ATS-34 and 154CM. **Prices:** $80 to $2,000. **Remarks:** Part-time maker; first knife sold in 1974. **Mark:** ALSTAR.

ANDERS, DAVID, Rt. 1, Box 157, Center Ridge, AR 72027/501-893-2294
Specialties: Working straight knives of his design. **Patterns:** Bowies, fighters and hunters. **Technical:** Forges 5160, 1080 and Damascus. **Prices:** $175 to $2,500. **Remarks:** Part-time maker; first knife sold in 1988. Doing business as Dutton Mountain Forge. **Mark:** Last name/MS.

ANDERSEN, HENRIK LEFOLII, Jagtvej 8, Groenholt, 3480 Fredensborg, DENMARK/4228-3026
Specialties: Hunters and matched pairs for the serious hunter. **Patterns:** Working folders for bowhunters. **Technical:** Grinds A2; uses materials native to Scandinavia. **Prices:** Start at $250. **Remarks:** Part-time maker; first knife sold in 1985. **Mark:** Initials with arrow.

ANDERSON, CHARLES B., P.O. Box 209, Lampe, MO 65681/417-779-3926
Specialties: High-tech working straight knives of his design. **Patterns:** Hunting, kitchen and fishing knives. **Technical:** Grinds 01, D2, 154CM and 440C. **Prices:** $95 to $500; exceptional knives to $1,000. **Remarks:** Full-time maker; first knife sold in 1980. **Mark:** Full name.

ANDERSON, EDWIN, c/o Glen Cove Sport Shop, 189 Forest Ave., Glen Cove, NY 11542/516-676-7120
Specialties: Hunters, fighters, boot knives and folders. **Patterns:** Standard patterns or customer designs. **Technical:** Grinds Stellite 6K, ATS-34, and 440C. Offers integral patterns. **Prices:** $200 to $500; some to $1,500. **Remarks:** Full-time gunsmith, part-time knifemaker; first knife sold in 1977. **Mark:** Name over state.

ANDERSON, GARY D., RD 2, Box 2399C, Spring Grove, PA 17362-9802/717-229-2665
Specialties: Art-quality blades, folders and working knives. **Patterns:** Traditional and classic designs; customer patterns welcome. **Technical:** Forged Damascus and carbon steels. Offers silver inlay, mokume, filework, checkering. **Prices:** $250 to $750; some higher. **Remarks:** Full-time maker; first knife sold in 1985. **Mark:** GAND,MS.

ANDERSON, MEL, 1718 Lee Lane, Cedaredge, CO 81413/970-865-6465; FAX: 970-856-6465
Specialties: Full-size, miniature and one-of-a-kind straight knives and folders of his design, to customer specs and in standard patterns. **Patterns:** Bowies, daggers, fighters, hunters and pressure folders. **Technical:** Grinds 440C, 5160, D2, 1095 and Damascus; offers antler, ivory and wood carved handles. **Prices:** $125 and up. **Remarks:** Full-time maker; first knife sold in 1987. **Mark:** Scratchy Hand.

ANDERSON, MICHAEL D., 2227 Spanish Trail, Arlington, TX 76013/817-274-3398
Specialties: Working and using straight knives of his design. **Patterns:** Hunters, Bowies, utility/camp knives and some fighters. **Technical:** Grinds D2, 01. All knives are individually ground using true North American Indian flaking styles. **Prices:** $175 to $350; some to $800. **Remarks:** Part-time maker; first knife sold in 1985. Doing business as Flint Steel Knives. **Mark:** Stylized initials.

ANDERSON, VIRGIL W., 16318 SE Taggart, Portland, OR 97236/503-761-4053
Specialties: Working straight knives of his design; fancy knives. **Patterns:** Bowies, boots, hunters and push knives. **Technical:** Grinds D2, 154CM and F8 Silvanite. **Prices:** $100 to $250; some to $500. **Remarks:** Part-time maker; first knife sold in 1984. **Mark:** Last name.

ANDRESS, RONNIE, 415 Audubon Dr. N., Satsuma, AL 36572/334-675-7604
Specialties: Working straight knives in standard patterns. **Patterns:** Boots, Bowies, hunters, friction folders and camp knives. **Technical:** Forges 1095, 5160, 01 and his own Damascus. Offers filework and inlays. **Prices:** $125 to $500. **Remarks:** Full-time maker; first knife sold in 1983. Doing business as Andress Knives. **Mark:** Last name.

ANDREWS, DON, N. 5155 Ezy St., Coeur D'Alene, ID 83814/208-765-8844
Specialties: Plain and fancy folders and straight knives. **Technical:** Grinds D2, 440C, ATS-34; does lost wax casting for guards and pommels. **Prices:** Moderate to upscale. **Remarks:** Full-time maker; first knife sold in 1983. **Mark:** Name.

ANGEL SWORD (See Watson, Daniel)

ANKROM, W.E., 14 Marquette Dr., Cody, WY 82414/307-587-3017
Specialties: Straight working knives and folders of his design. **Patterns:** Hunters, fighters, boots; lockbacks, liner locks and interchangeables. **Technical:** Grinds ATS-34 and commercial Damascus. **Prices:** $175 to $995. **Remarks:** Full-time maker; first knife sold in 1975. **Mark:** Name, city, state.

ANTHONY, THOMAS (See Trujillo, Thomas A.)

ANTONIO JR., WILLIAM J., 14540 Stirrup Lane, Golts, MD 21635/410-755-6789
Specialties: Fancy working straight knives of his design. **Patterns:** Hunting, survival and fishing knives. **Technical:** Grinds D2, 440C and 154CM; offers stainless Damascus. **Prices:** $125 to $395; some to $900. **Remarks:** Part-time maker; first knife sold in 1978. **Mark:** Last name, city, state.

ANVIL HEAD FORGE (See Leone, Nick)

ANZA KNIVES (See Davis, Charlie)

APPLETON, RAY, Box 321, Byers, CO 80103/303-822-5866
Specialties: One-of-a-kind folding knives. **Patterns:** Unique multi-locks and high-tech patterns. **Technical:** All parts machined or ground; likes D2. **Prices:** Start at $500. **Remarks:** Spare-time maker; first knife sold in 1986. **Mark:** Initials connected in arrowhead, date.

ARC MOUNTAIN FORGE (See Dearing, John)

ARMORBANE (See Pagnard, Philip E.)

ARNOLD, JOE, 47 Patience Cres., London, Ont., CANADA N6E 2K7/519-686-2623; FAX: 519-649-6553
Specialties: Traditional working and using straight knives of his design and to customer specs. **Patterns:** Fighters, hunters and Bowies. **Technical:** Grinds 440C, ATS-34 and 5160. **Prices:** $75 to $500; some to $2,500. **Remarks:** Part-time maker; first knife sold in 1988. **Mark:** Last name, country.

ARROW FORGE (See Harless, Walt)

ARROWOOD, DALE, 556 Lassetter Rd., Sharpsburg, GA 30277/404-253-9672
Specialties: Fancy and traditional straight knives of his design and to customer specs. **Patterns:** Bowies, fighters and hunters. **Technical:** Grinds ATS-34 and 440C; forges high-carbon steel. Engraves and scrimshands. **Prices:** $125 to $200; some to $245. **Remarks:** Part-time maker; first knife sold in 1989. **Mark:** Anvil with an arrow through it; Old English "Arrowood Knives."

ASHBY, DOUGLAS, 10123 Deermont, Dallas, TX 75243/214-238-7531
Specialties: Traditional and fancy straight knives of his design or to customer specs. **Patterns:** Hunters, fighters, utility/camp knives. **Technical:** Grinds 440C, ATS-34 and commercial Damascus. **Prices:** $75 to $200; some to $500. **Remarks:** Part-time maker; first knife sold in 1990. **Mark:** Name, city.

ASHLEY FORGE (See Bartrug, Hugh E.)

directory

ASHWORTH, BOYD, 3135 Barrett Ct., Powder Springs, GA 30073/ 404-943-4963
Specialties: Fancy straight knives and folders; working/using knives of his design and to customer specs. **Patterns:** Fighters, hunters and locking folders. **Technical:** Grinds 440C and ATS-34; forges and grinds Damascus. Scrimshaws; offers leatherwork. **Prices:** $100 to $350; some to $1,000. **Remarks:** Part-time maker; first knife sold in 1993. **Mark:** Last name.

ATHENS FORGE (See Fannin, David A.)

ATHERN FORGE (See Sanders, A.A.)

ATKINSON, DICK, General Delivery, Wausau, FL 32463/904-638-8524
Specialties: Working straight knives and folders of his design; some fancy. **Patterns:** Hunters, fighters, boots; locking folders in interframes. **Technical:** Grinds A2, 440C and 154CM. Likes filework. **Prices:** $85 to $300; some exceptional knives. **Remarks:** Full-time maker; first knife sold in 1977. **Mark:** Name, city, state.

AYARRAGARAY, CRISTIAN L., Buenos Aires 250, (3100) Parana-Entre Rios, ARGENTINA/043-231753
Specialties: Traditional working straight knives of his design. **Patterns:** Fishing and hunting knives. **Technical:** Grinds and forges carbon steel. Uses native Argentine woods and deer antler. **Prices:** $150 to $250; some to $400. **Remarks:** Full-time maker; first knife sold in 1980. **Mark:** Last name, signature.

b

BABCOCK, RAYMOND G., Rt. 1, Box 328A, Vincent, OH 45784/614-678-2688
Specialties: Fancy working straight knives and some folders of his design or to customer specs. **Patterns:** Hunters and Bowies. **Technical:** Grinds L6. **Prices:** $65 to $350. **Remarks:** Full-time maker; first knife sold in 1973. **Mark:** First initial and last name.

BACHE-WIIG, TOM, N-5966 Eivindvik, NORWAY/4757784290; FAX: 4757784122
Specialties: High-art and working knives of his design. **Patterns:** Hunters, utility knives, hatchets, axes and art knives. **Technical:** Grinds Uddeholm Elmax, powder metallurgy tool stainless steel. Handles made of rear burls of Nordic woods stabilized with vacuum/high-pressure technique. **Prices:** $430 to $900; some to $2,300. **Remarks:** Part-time maker; first knife sold 1988. **Mark:** Etched name and eagle head.

BAGWELL, BILL, P.O. Box 265, Marietta, TX/903-835-8441
Specialties: Traditional working and using knives of his design. **Patterns:** Bowies, fighters, utility/camp knives. **Technical:** Forges 1065. Makes own Damascus. Heat-treats. **Prices:** $225 to $1,200; some to $3,000. **Remarks:** Full-time maker; first knife sold in 1968. **Mark:** Name in script or block letters.

BAILEY, JOSEPH D., 3213 Jonesboro Dr., Nashville, TN 37214/615-889-3172
Specialties: Working and using straight knives, Bowies and hunters; collector pieces. **Patterns:** Bowies, hunters, fillet knives and personal knives. **Technical:** 440C, ATS-34, Damascus and wire Damascus. Scrimshaw available through Mary Bailey. **Prices:** $65 to $175; some to $500. **Remarks:** Part-time maker; first knife sold in 1988. **Mark:** First and middle initials, last name—Custom Made.

BAILEY, KIRBY C., 13097 F.M. 2790 W., Lytle, TX 78052/210-772-3376
Specialties: Automatic folders and miniatures. **Patterns:** Hunting folders and double-bladed lockbacks; uses all his own patterns. **Technical:** Grinds ATS-34, 440C and 01 tool steel. Offers filework on liners, backlocks and blades. Handles made with natural materials. Scrimshaws, engraves and heat-treats. **Prices:** $150 to $650. **Remarks:** Full-time

maker; first knife sold 1959. Doing business as Hand Made Knives. **Mark:** Initials with serial number.

BAKER, RAY, P.O. Box 303, Sapulpa, OK 74067/918-224-8013
Specialties: High-tech working straight knives. **Patterns:** Hunters, fighters, Bowies, skinners and boots of his design and to customer specs. **Technical:** Grinds 440C, 1095 spring steel or customer request. Custom-made scabbards for any knife. **Prices:** $40 to $300, some to $1,000. **Remarks:** Full-time maker; first first knife sold in 1981. **Mark:** First initial, last name.

BAKER, VANCE, 574 Co. Rd. 675, Riceville, TN 37370/615-745-9157
Specialties: Traditional working straight knives of his design and to customer specs. Prefers drop-point hunters and small Bowies. **Patterns:** Hunters, utility and kitchen knives. **Technical:** Forges Damascus, cable, L6 and 5160. **Prices:** $75 to $175; some to $400. **Remarks:** Part-time maker, first knife sold in 1985. **Mark:** Initials connected.

BAKER, WILD BILL, Box 361, Boiceville, NY 12412/914-657-8646
Specialties: Primitive knives, buckskinners. **Patterns:** Skinners, camp knives and Bowies. **Technical:** Works with L6, files and rasps. **Prices:** $100 to $350. **Remarks:** Part-time maker; first knife sold in 1989. **Mark:** Oak leaf.

BALBACH, MARKUS, Friedrichstrasse 2, 35789 Laubus-Eschbach/Ts., GERMANY/06475-8911; FAX: 06475-8911
Specialties: High-art knives and working/using knives of his design and to customer specs. Straight knives and folders. **Patterns:** Hunters and daggers. **Technical:** Forges and grinds Damascus steel. **Prices:** $250 to $600; some to $2,000. **Remarks:** Full-time maker; first knife sold in 1984. Doing business as Damastschmiede M. Balbach. **Mark:** Initials stamped inside the handle.

BALDWIN, PHILLIP, P.O. Box 563, Snohomish, WA 98290/206-334-5569
Specialties: Elegant table cutlery; exotics. **Patterns:** Contemporary and eclectic. Likes the challenge of axes and such. **Technical:** Forges W2, W1 and his own Damascus. **Prices:** From $300 to $2,500; some higher. **Remarks:** Full-time maker; first knife sold in 1973. **Mark:** Last initial marked with chisel.

BALDY MOUNTAIN FORGE (See Dunkerley, Rick)

BALL, ROBERT, 809 W. 7th Ave., Port Angeles, WA 98362/360-457-0315
Specialties: Classic straight knives; working/using knives of all designs. **Patterns:** Bowies, hunters and filets. **Technical:** Grinds ATS-34 and 440C. Uses local Olympic hardwoods, stabilized woods, horn and antler. **Prices:** $225 to $1,700. **Remarks:** Part-time maker; first knife sold in 1990. Doing business as Olympic Knives. **Mark:** First initial, last name.

BALLEW, DALE, P.O. Box 1277, Bowling Green, VA 22427/804-633-5701
Specialties: Miniatures only to customer specs. **Patterns:** Bowies, daggers and fighters. **Technical:** Files 440C stainless; uses ivory, abalone, exotic woods and some precious stones. **Prices:** $100 to $800. **Remarks:** Part-time maker; first knife sold in 1988. **Mark:** Initials and last name.

BAM FORGE (See Milford, Brian A.)

BANDIT BLADES (See Roberts, George A.)

BANKS, DAVID L., 99 Blackfoot Ave. #3, Riverton, WY 82501/307-856-3154
Specialties: Heavy-duty working straight knives. **Patterns:** Hunters, Bowies and camp knives. **Technical:** Forges 5160 and 52100. Handles made of horn, antlers and exotic wood. Hand-stitched harness leather sheaths. **Prices:** $200 to $500; some higher. **Remarks:** Part-time maker. **Mark:** Initials connected.

BARBEE, JIM, Box 1173, Ft. Stockton, TX 79753/915-336-2882
Specialties: Texas-type hunter's knives. **Patterns:** Solid using patterns. **Technical:** Grinds 440C; likes stag, Micarta and ivory. **Prices:** $125 to $200; some to $500. **Remarks:** Full-time maker and heat-treater. First knife sold in the '60s. **Mark:** Name, city.

BARBER, ROBERT E., 1828 Franklin Dr., Charlottesville, VA 22901/804-295-4036
Specialties: Working straight knives and trapper pocketknives, some fancy with filework. **Patterns:** Hunters, skinners, combat knives/fighters and Bowies. **Technical:** Grinds ATS-34, 440C, D2 and A2. **Prices:** $35 to $800. **Remarks:** Part-time maker; first knife sold in 1984. **Mark:** Initials within rebel hat logo.

BARDSLEY, NORMAN P., 197 Cottage St., Pawtucket, RI 02860/401-725-9132
Specialties: Working and fantasy knives. **Patterns:** Fighters, tantos, boots in renaissance and fantasy fashion; upscale display and presentation pieces. **Technical:** Grinds 440C, ATS-34, 01 and Damascus. Uses exotic hides for sheaths. **Prices:** $100 to $15,000. **Remarks:** Full-time maker. **Mark:** Last name in script with logo.

BARE KNIVES (See Stevens, Barry B.)

BAREFOOT, JOE W., 117 Oakbrook Dr., Liberty, SC 29657
Specialties: Working straight knives of his design; mirror finishes. **Patterns:** Hunters, fighters and boots; tantos and survival knives. **Technical:** Grinds D2, 440C and ATS-34. Uses ivory and stag on customer request only. **Prices:** $50 to $160; some to $500. **Remarks:** Part-time maker; first knife sold in 1980. **Mark:** Bare footprint.

BARKER, ROBERT G., 262 Laurie Dr., Athens, GA 30605/706-546-4525
Specialties: Traditional working/using straight knives of his design. **Patterns:** Bowies, hunters and utility knives. **Technical:** Forges to shape high-carbon 5160, cable and chain. Differentially heat-treats. **Prices:** $200 to $500; some to $1,000. **Remarks:** Spare-time maker; first knife sold in 1987. **Mark:** Last name.

BARLOW, KEN, 3800 Rohner St., Fortuna, CA 95540/707-725-3106
Specialties: Working straight knives and folders, some fancy. **Patterns:** Hunters, Bowies, skinners and locking folders. **Technical:** Grinds ATS-34, 440C and D2. Heat-treats, engraves and scrimshaws. Prefers mirror finishes and hollow-grinds. **Prices:** $100 to $250; some higher. **Remarks:** Part-time maker; first knife sold in 1980. **Mark:** Stylized initials.

BARNES, AUBREY G., 10404 Bailey Rd., Hagerstown, MD 21742/301-791-1647
Specialties: Classic working and using knives of his design, to customer specs and in standard patterns. **Patterns:** Bowies, hunters and utility knives. **Technical:** Forges 5160, 9260 and 1085. Silver-wire inlays. **Prices:** $190 to $900; some to $2,500. **Remarks:** Full-time maker; first knife sold in 1992. Doing business as Falling Waters Forge. **Mark:** First and middle initials, last name.

BARNES, GARY L., 305 Church St., Box 138, New Windsor, MD 21776/410-635-6243
Specialties: High-art, high-tech working knives of his design; titanium and stainless folders. **Patterns:** Folders only. **Technical:** Mostly forges his own Damascus; uses exotic handle materials; creates unique locking mechanisms. Most knives are embellished. **Prices:** $300 to $1,500; some to $8,000. **Remarks:** Full-time maker. First knife sold in 1976. Believes in sole authorship. **Mark:** Name or an ornate last initial with a dagger.

BARNES, JACK, P.O. Box 1315, Whitefish, MT 59937-1315/406-862-6078

BARNES, JIM, 2909 Forest Trail, San Angelo, TX 76904/915-944-2239
Specialties: Traditional and working straight, folders and automatic knives of all designs. **Patterns:** Automatics, hunters and locking folders. **Technical:** Grinds ATS-34, 440C and D2; heat-treats. All folders have filework. Offers hand-tooled sheaths with basket weave. Engraves some knife bolsters. **Prices:** $95 to $350; some to $1000. **Remarks:** Full-time maker; first knife sold in 1984. Doing business as Jim Barnes Custom Knives. **Mark:** Logo with name, city and state.

BARNETT, VAN, P.O. Box 1012, New Haven, WV 25265/304-882-3481
Specialties: Investor-grade one-of-a-kind daggers and fighters. **Patterns:** Folders, miniatures and hunters. **Technical:** Grinds 440C, D2, Damascus and ATS-34. **Prices:** Start at $200. **Remarks:** Full-time maker; first knife sold in 1981. **Mark:** Barnett Blades or first initial, last name.

BARR, A.T., P.O. Box 828, Nicholasville, KY 40340-0828/606-885-1042
Specialties: Working and collector-grade straight knives and folders. **Patterns:** Hunters, camp/survival knives and liner lock folders. **Technical:** Flat-grinds ATS-34; hand-rubbed satin or bead blasted finish. **Prices:** Start at $125. **Remarks:** Part-time maker; first knife sold in 1979. **Mark:** Full name, city and state.

BARR CUSTOM KNIVES (See Quarton, Barr)

BARRETT, CECIL TERRY, 2514 Linda Lane, Colorado Springs, CO 80909/719-473-8325
Specialties: Working and using straight knives and folders of his design, to customer specs and in standard patterns. **Patterns:** Bowies, hunters, kitchen knives, locking folders and slip-joint folders. **Technical:** Grinds 440C, D2 and ATs-34. Wood and leather sheaths. **Prices:** $65 to $500; some to $750. **Remarks:** Full-time maker. **Mark:** Stamped middle name.

BARRETT, R.W., 3214 Montrose Dr., Huntsville, AL 35805/205-539-3439
Specialties: Traditional and fancy straight knives. Makes standard patterns and one-of-a-kinds. **Patterns:** Hunters, fighters, skinners and art knives. **Technical:** Grinds 440C, ATS-34 and 01. Scrimshaws and offers photography. Prices: $150 to $250; some to $500. **Remarks:** Spare-time maker; first knife sold in 1989. **Mark:** First and middle initials, last name, city, state.

BARRETT-SMYTHE (See Howard, Durvyn M.)

BARRON, BRIAN, 123 12th Ave., San Metro, CA 94402/415-341-2683
Specialties: Traditional straight knives. **Patterns:** Daggers, hunters and swords. **Technical:** Grinds 440C, ATS-34 and 1095. Sculpts bolsters using an S-curve. **Prices:** $130 to $270; some to $1500. **Remarks:** Part-time maker; first knife sold in 1993. **Mark:** Diamond Drag "pantagraph."

BARRON, DAVID, P.O. Box 133, Etowah, NC 28729/704-692-4007
Specialties: Fancy working straight knives of his design. **Patterns:** Hunters, Bowies and using knives. **Technical:** Grinds 01, 440C and 154CM. Scrimshaws. **Prices:** $100 to $225; some to $750. **Remarks:** Full-time maker; first knife sold in 1968. **Mark:** Last name, serial number.

BARRY, JAMES J., P.O. Box 1571, West Palm Beach, FL 33402/407-832-4197
Specialties: High-art working straight knives of his design. **Patterns:** Hunters, daggers and fishing knives. **Technical:** Grinds 440C only. Prefers exotic materials for handles. Most knives embellished with filework, carving and scrimshaw. Many pieces designed to stand unassisted. **Prices:** $100 to $500; some to $5,000. **Remarks:** Part-time maker; first knife sold in 1975. Believes in sole authorship. **Mark:** Branded initials.

BARTLOW, JOHN, 111 Orchard Rd., Box 568, Norris, TN 37828/615-494-9421

directory

BARTRUG—BEHNKE

Specialties: Working straight knives, some fancy. **Patterns:** Working hunters, skinners, capers, bird and trout knives, saltwater fillets. **Technical:** Grinds 440C and ATS-34; uses Tim Zowada and Jerry Rados Damascus. **Prices:** $150 to $1,500. **Remarks:** Part-time maker, first knife sold in 1979. Field-tests knives. **Mark:** Last name.

BARTRUG, HUGH E., 505 Rhodes St., Elizabeth, PA 15037/412-384-3476
Specialties: Inlaid straight knives and exotic folders; high-art knives and period pieces. **Patterns:** Hunters, Bowies and daggers; traditional patterns. **Technical:** Diffuses mokume. Forges 100 percent nickel, wrought iron, mosiac Damascus, shokeedo and 01 tool steel; grinds. **Prices:** $210 to $2,500; some to $5,000. **Remarks:** Full-time maker; first knife sold in 1980. **Mark:** Ashley Forge or name.

BASKETT, LEE GENE, 427 Sutzer Ck. Rd., Eastview, KY 42732/502-862-5019
Specialties: Fancy working knives and fantasy pieces, often set up in desk stands. **Patterns:** Fighters, Bowies and survival knives; locking folders, butterflies and traditional styles. **Technical:** Grinds 01, 440C; buys Damascus. Filework provided on most knives. **Prices:** Start at $95. **Remarks:** Part-time maker; first knife sold in 1980. **Mark:** Last name.

BATSON, JAMES, 176 Brentwood Lane, Madison, AL 35758/205-971-6860
Specialties: Forged Damascus blades and fittings in collectible period pieces. **Patterns:** Integral art knives, Bowies, folders, American-styled blades and miniatures. **Technical:** Forges 52100, 5160 and his Damascus. Believes in sole authorship. **Prices:** $150 to $1,800; some to $4,500. **Remarks:** Full-time maker; first knife sold in 1978. **Mark:** Name, bladesmith with horse's head.

BATSON, RICHARD G., 6591 Waterford Rd., Rixeyville, VA 22737/703-937-5932
Specialties: Military, utility and fighting knives in working and presentation grade. **Patterns:** Daggers, combat and utility knives. **Technical:** Grinds 01. Etches and scrimshaws; offers polished, Parkerized finishes. **Prices:** $175 to $350; some to $900. **Remarks:** Full-time maker. First knife sold in 1958. **Mark:** Bat in circle, hand-signed and serial numbered.

BATTS, KEITH, Rt. 1, Box 266E, Hooks, TX 75561/903-832-1140
Specialties: Working straight knives of his design or to customer specs. **Patterns:** Bowies, hunters, skinners, camp knives and others. **Technical:** Forges 5160 and his Damascus; offers filework. **Prices:** $125 to $475. **Remarks:** Part-time maker; first knife sold in 1988. **Mark:** Last name.

BAUCHOP, PETER, Germiston, SOUTH AFRICA. C/O Beck's Cutlery Specialties, 748-F E. Chatham St., Cary, NC 27511/919-460-0203
Specialties: Working straight knives and period pieces. **Patterns:** Fighters, swords and survival knives. **Technical:** Grinds 01, D2, G3, 440C and ATS-34. Scrimshaws. **Prices:** $100 to $350; some to $1,500. **Remarks:** Full-time maker; first knife sold in 1980. **Mark:** Bow and axe (BOW-CHOP).

BAUCHOP, ROBERT, P.O. Box 9821, Elsburg 1407, SOUTH AFRICA/011-824-1300; FAX: 011-824-2662
Specialties: Fantasy knives; working and using knives of his design and to customer specs. **Patterns:** Hunters, swords, utility/camp knives, diver's knives and large swords. **Technical:** Grinds Sandvick 12C27, D2, 440C. Uses South African hardwoods—red ivory, wild olive, african blackwood, etc.—on handles. **Prices:** $200 to $800; some to $2,000. **Remarks:** Full-time maker; first knife sold in 1986. Doing business as Robert Bauchop Handmade Knives. **Mark:** Viking helmet with Bauchop (bow and chopper) crest.

BAYOU CUSTOM CUTLERY (See Dake, C.M.)

BEAM, JOHN R., 1310 Foothills Rd., Kalispell, MT 59901/406-755-2593
Specialties: Classic, high art and working straight knives of his design. **Patterns:** Bowies and hunters. **Technical:** Grinds 440C, Damascus and scrap. **Prices:** $175 to $600; some to $3,000. **Remarks:** Part-time maker; first knife sold in 1996. Doing business as Beam's Knives. **Mark:** Beam Knives.

BEAR KNIVES (See Goode, Bear)

BEAR RUN KNIFE (See Thill, Jim)

BEAR'S CUTLERY (See Jensen, Jr., Carl A.)

BEATTY, GORDON H., 121 Petty Rd., Seneca, SC 29678/803-882-6278
Specialties: Working straight knives, some fancy. **Patterns:** Traditional patterns, mini-skinners and letter openers. **Technical:** Grinds 440C, D2 and ATS-34; makes knives one at a time. **Prices:** $45 to $200; some to $450. **Remarks:** Part-time maker; first knife sold in 1982. **Mark:** Name.

BEAUCHAMP, GAETAN, 125, de la Riviere, Stoneham, PQ. CANADA/418-848-1914; FAX: 418-848-1035
Specialties: Working knives and folders of his design and to customer specs. **Patterns:** Hunters, fighters, fantasy knives. **Technical:** Grinds ATS-34, 440C, Damascus. Scrimshaws on ivory; specializes in buffalo horn and black backgrounds. Offers a variety of handle materials. **Prices:** Start at $125. **Remarks:** Part-time maker; first knife sold in 1992. **Mark:** Signature and year etched on blade.

BEAVER, D. "BUTCH" AND JUDY, 48835 N. 25 Ave. Phoenix, AZ 85027/602-465-7831; FAX: 602-465-7077
Specialties: Straight knives, daggers and "see-thru" titanium art folders. **Patterns:** No models or standard designs; prefer custom orders. **Technical:** Grind 440C and ATS-34. Most knives are embellished. **Prices:** $135 to $800; some much higher. **Remarks:** Full-time makers. First D. Beaver knife sold in 1979; first J. Beaver knife sold in 1984. **Mark:** Name, city, state with desert scene.

BEAVER, JUDY (See Beaver, D. "Butch" and Judy)

BECKER, FRANZ, AM Kreuzberg 2, 84533 Marktl/Inn, GERMANY/08678-8020
Specialties: Stainless steel knives in working sizes. **Patterns:** Semi- and full-integral knives; interframe folders. **Technical:** Grinds stainless steels; likes natural handle materials. **Prices:** $200 to $2,000. **Mark:** Name, country.

BECKETT, NORMAN L., 1501 N. Chaco Ave., Farmington, NM 87401/505-325-4468
Specialties: Fancy, traditional and working straight knives of his design. **Patterns:** Bowies, fighters and hunters. **Technical:** Grinds ATS-34, 440C and Damascus. File works blades; hollow and flat grinds. Prefers mirror finishes. Uses exotic handle material and stabilized woods. Hand-tooled or inlaid sheaths. **Prices:** $150 to $750; some to $1,500. **Remarks:** Full-time maker; first knife sold in 1993. Doing business as Norm Beckett Knives. **Mark:** First and last name, maker, city and state.

BEERS, RAY, 8 Manorbrook Rd., Monkton, MD 21111 (summer)/410-472-2229, 813-696-3036; FAX: 410-472-9136
Specialties: Working straight knives, some fancy. **Patterns:** All fighters and tantos are popular. **Technical:** Grinds all steels; many patterns have a palm hunter handle. **Prices:** $100 to $5,000. **Remarks:** Full-time maker; first knife sold in 1976. **Mark:** Initials connected.

BEERS, RAY, 2501 Lakefront Dr., Lake Wales, FL 33853 (winter)/813-696-3036; FAX: 813-696-9421

BEHNKE, WILLIAM, P.O. Box 174, Lake City, MI 49651/616-839-3342
Specialties: Hunters, belt knives and folders. **Patterns:** Traditional

styling in moderate-sized straight and folding knives. **Technical:** Forges his own Damascus, cable, saw chain and 5160; likes brass and natural materials. **Prices:** $100 to $1,500. **Remarks:** Part-time maker. **Mark:** Name.

BELL, DONALD, 2 Division St., Bedford, Nova Scotia, B4A 1Y8 CANADA/902-835-2623
Specialties: Fancy knives; working/using straight knives and folders of his design. **Patterns:** Hunters, locking folders, jewelry knives. **Technical:** Grinds Damascus and ATS-34; forges and grinds 01. **Prices:** $150 to $650; some to $1,200. **Remarks:** Spare-time maker; first knife sold in 1993. **Mark:** Bell symbol with first initial inside.

BELL, MICHAEL, Rt. 1, Box 1220, Coquille, OR 97423/503-396-3605
Specialties: Full line of traditional Japanese swords. **Patterns:** Tantos and Katanas in various styles. **Technical:** Uses own special steel; all blades forge-welded. **Prices:** $750 to $10,000. **Remarks:** Full-time maker; first knife sold in 1972. Served apprenticeship with Japanese swordmaker. Doing business as Dragonfly Forge. **Mark:** Kuni Mitsu or Dragonfly.

BENJAMIN JR., GEORGE, 3001 Foxy Lane, Kissimmee, FL 34746/407-846-7259
Specialties: Fighters in various styles to include Persian, Moro and military. **Patterns:** Daggers, skinners and one-of-a-kind grinds. **Technical:** Forges 01, D2, A2, 5160 and Damascus. Favors Pakkawood, Micarta, and mirror or Parkerized finishes. Makes unique para-military leather sheaths. **Prices:** $150 to $600; some to $1,200. **Remarks:** Doing business as The Leather Box. **Mark:** Southern Pride Knives.

BENNETT, PETER, P.O. Box 143, Engadine N.S.W. 2233, AUSTRALIA/02-520-4975 (home), 02-528-8219 (work)
Specialties: Fancy and embellished working and using straight knives to customer specs and in standard patterns. **Patterns:** Fighters, hunters, bird/trout and filet knives. **Technical:** Grinds 440C, ATS-34 and Damascus. Uses rare Australian desert timbers for handles. **Prices:** $90 to $500; some to $1,500. **Remarks:** Full-time maker; first knife sold in 1985. **Mark:** First and middle initials, last name; country.

BENSON, DON, 2505 Jackson St. #112, Escalon, CA 95320/209-838-7921
Specialties: Working straight knives of his design. **Patterns:** Axes, Bowies, tantos and hunters. **Technical:** Grinds 440C. **Prices:** $100 to $150; some to $400. **Remarks:** Spare-time maker; first knife sold in 1980. **Mark:** Name.

BER, DAVE, 2230 Miller Rd., San Juan Island, WA 98250/206-378-7230
Specialties: Working straight knives for the sportsman; camp knives. Welcomes customer designs. **Patterns:** Hunters, Bowies, kitchen and fishing knives. **Technical:** Forges and grinds saw blade steel, welded wire Damascus, 01, L6 and 440C. **Prices:** $100 to $200; some to $500. **Remarks:** Full-time maker; first knife sold in 1985. Doing business as Cloudy Mt. Iron Works. **Mark:** Name.

BERTUZZI, ETTORE, Via Partigiani 3, 24068 Seriate (Bergamo) ITALY/035-294262; FAX: 035-294262
Specialties: Classic straight knives and folders of his design, to customer specs and in standard patterns. **Patterns:** Bowies, hunters and locking folders. **Technical:** Grinds ATS-34, D2 and 01. **Prices:** $200 to $300. **Remarks:** Part-time maker; first knife sold in 1993. **Mark:** Name and year etched on ricasso in script.

BESEDICK, FRANK E., 29 Tyler Ave., Charleroi, PA 15022/412-483-2734
Specialties: Traditional working and using straight knives of his design. **Patterns:** Hunters, utility/camp knives and miniatures; buckskinner blades and tomahawks. **Technical:** Forges and grinds 5160, 01 and Damascus. Offers filework and scrimshaw. **Prices:** $75 to $300; some to $750. **Remarks:** Part-time maker; first knife sold in 1990. **Mark:** Name or initials.

BEUKES, TINUS, 83 Henry St., Risiville, Vereeniging 1939, Republic of South Africa/016-232053
Specialties: Working straight knives. **Patterns:** Hunters, skinners and kitchen knives. **Technical:** Grinds D2, 440C and Damascus. **Prices:** $80 to $180. **Remarks:** Part-time maker; first knife sold in 1993. **Mark:** Full name, city, logo.

BEVERLY II, LARRY H., P.O. Box 741, Spotsylvania, VA 22553/703-898-3951
Specialties: Working straight knives, slip-joints, liner locks and miniatures. Welcomes customer designs. **Patterns:** Bowies, hunters, guardless fighters. **Technical:** Grinds 440C, A2 and 01. **Prices:** $65 to $400. **Remarks:** Part-time maker; first knife sold in 1986. **Mark:** Initials or last name in script.

BEZUIDENHOUT, BUZZ, 30 Surlingham Ave., Malvern, Queensburgh, Natal 4093, SOUTH AFRICA/031-444098; 031-3631259
Specialties: Traditional working and using straight knives of his design and to customer specs. **Patterns:** Boots, hunters, kitchen knives and utility/camp knives. **Technical:** Grinds 12C27, 440C and ATS-34. Uses local hardwoods, horn—kudu, impala, buffalo—giraffe bone and ivory for handles. **Prices:** $150 to $200; some to $1,500. **Remarks:** Spare-time maker; first knife sold in 1988. **Mark:** First name with a bee emblem.

BIGHORN KNIFEWORKS (See Padilla, Gary)

BILLY'S BLACKSMITH SHOP (See Watson, Billy)

BILLY'S BLADES (See Ellis, William Dean)

BLACK, EARL, 3466 South 700 East, Salt Lake City, UT 84106/801-466-8395
Specialties: High-art straight knives and folders; period pieces. **Patterns:** Boots, Bowies and daggers; lockers and gents. **Technical:** Grinds 440C and 154CM. Buys some Damascus. Scrimshaws and engraves. **Prices:** $200 to $1,800; some to $2,500 and higher. **Remarks:** Full-time maker; first knife sold in 1980. **Mark:** Name, city, state.

BLACK, SCOTT, 570 Malcom Rd., Covington, GA 30209
Specialties: Working/using folders of his design. **Patterns:** Daggers, hunters, utility/camp knives and friction folders. **Technical:** Forges pattern welded, cable, 1095, 01 and 5160. **Prices:** $100 to $500. **Remarks:** Part-time maker; first knife sold in 1992. Doing business as Copperhead Forge. **Mark:** Hot mark on blade, copperhead snake.

BLACK, TOM, 921 Grecian NW, Albuquerque, NM 87107/505-344-2549
Specialties: Working knives to fancy straight knives of his design. **Patterns:** Drop-point skinners, folders, using knives, Bowies and daggers. **Technical:** Grinds 440C, 154CM, ATS-34, A2, D2 and Damascus. Engraves and scrimshaws. **Prices:** $125 to $1,250; some over $7,500. **Remarks:** Full-time maker; first knife sold in 1971. **Mark:** Name, city, state.

BLACK, T.J., 1507 Wayne St., Alexandria, LA 71301/318-443-6100
Specialties: Straight knives of his design or to customer specs. **Patterns:** Hunters, Bowies, skinners, utility knives and some collector pieces. **Technical:** Grinds 440C and ATS-34. Prefers natural handle materials. **Prices:** $75 to $1,000. **Remarks:** Part-time maker; first knife sold in 1987. **Mark:** First and middle initials, last name, city, state.

BLACK FOREST BLADES (See Neering, Walt and Repke, Mike)

BLACK OAK BLADES (See Sjostrand, Kevin)

BLACKTON, ANDREW E., 12521 Fifth Isle, Bayonet Point, FL 34667/813-869-1406
Specialties: Straight and folding knives, some fancy. **Patterns:** Hunters, Bowies and daggers. **Technical:** Grinds D2, 440C and

154CM.Offers some embellishment. **Prices:** $125 to $450; some to $2,000. **Remarks:** Full-time maker. **Mark:** Michigan state outline with knife across it and "Blackton the Great Lakes Knifemaker."

BLADE RIGGER (See Piorek, James S.)

BLANCHARD, G.R., 3025 Las Vegas Blvd. #120, Las Vegas, NV 89109/702-733-8333; FAX: 702-732-0333.
Specialties: Fancy and high art straight knives of his design. **Patterns:** Boots, daggers and locking folders. **Technical:** Grinds 440C and ATS-34, 01 blueable. Engraves all knives. **Prices:** $600 to $15,000; some to $18,000 or more. **Remarks:** Full-time maker; first knife sold in 1989. **Mark:** First and middle initials, last name in banner.

BLASINGAME, ROBERT, 2906 Swanson Lane, Kilgore, TX 75662/903-983-3546
Specialties: Classic working and using straight knives and folders of his design and to customer specs. **Patterns:** Bowies, daggers, fighters and hunters; one-of-a-kind historic reproductions. **Technical:** Hand-forges P.W. Damascus, cable Damascus and chain Damascus. **Prices:** $150 to $1,000; some to $2,000. **Remarks:** Full-time maker; first knife sold in 1968. **Mark:** Large knives—last name over anvil; folders—initials.

BLAUM, ROY, 319 N. Columbia St., Covington, LA 70433/504-893-1060
Specialties: Working straight knives and folders of his design; lightweight easy-open folders. **Patterns:** Hunters, boots, fishing and wood-carving/whittling knives. **Technical:** Grinds A2, D2, 01, 154CM and ATS-34. Offers leatherwork. **Prices:** $75 to $200; some to $500. **Remarks:** Full-time maker; first knife sold in 1976. **Mark:** Signature engraved.

BLOMBERG, GREGG, Rt. 1, Box 1762, Lopez, WA 98261/206-468-2103
Specialties: Edged tools for carvers and sculptors. **Patterns:** Crooked knives; straight utilities; adzes. **Technical:** Forges and grinds W2, D2, 1095 and ATS-34. **Prices:** Straight knives average $160. **Remarks:** Full-time maker; first knife sold in 1978. Doing business as Kestrel Tool. **Mark:** Kestrel with flying falcon logo.

BLOOMER, ALAN T., RR 1, Box 108, Maquon, IL 61458/309-875-3583
Specialties: Working and using straight knives and folders of his design. **Patterns:** Lock-back folders and Damascus straight knives and folders. **Technical:** Grinds 440C, D2 and A2. Does own leatherwork. **Prices:** $85 to $450. **Remarks:** Part-time maker; first knife sold in 1986. **Mark:** Last name stamp.

BLUM, CHUCK, 743 S. Brea Blvd. #10, Brea, CA 92621/714-529-0484
Specialties: Art and investment daggers and Bowies. **Technical:** Flat-grinds; hollow-grinds 440C, ATS-34 on working knives. **Prices:** $125 to $8,500. **Remarks:** Part-time maker; first knife sold in 1985. **Mark:** First and middle initials and last name with sailboat logo.

BLUM, KENNETH, Rt. 6, Box 6033, Brenham, TX 77833/409-836-9577
Specialties: Traditional working straight knives of his design. **Patterns:** Camp knives, Hunters and Bowies. **Technical:** Forges 5160; grinds 440C and D2. Uses exotic woods and Micarta for handles. **Prices:** $150 to $300. **Remarks:** Part-time maker; first knife sold in 1978. **Mark:** Last name on ricasso.

BLUM, MICHEL, 1044, Chemin de St. Joseph, 83300 Draguignan, FRANCE/94 47 01 74
Specialties: Fantasy and working straight knives and folders to customer specs. **Patterns:** Hunters and fighters. **Technical:** Grinds D2 and commercial Damascus. **Remarks:** Full-time maker; first knife sold in 1988.

BLUM, RONALD A., 201 Masters Ct., #4, Walnut Creek, CA 94598/510-934-3381

Specialites: Miniatures only—collectible one-of-a-kind straight knives. **Patterns:** Miniature swords, fantasy and historical replicas, some battle axes. **Technical:** Files and forges 1050, 440C and commercial Damascus. **Prices:** $125 to $275; some to $400. **Remarks:** Part-time maker; first knife sold in 1988. **Mark:** None.

BLUM, ROY, 319 N. Columbia St., Covington, CA 70433

BOARDMAN, GUY, 39 Mountain Ridge R., New Germany, 3619 SOUTH AFRICA/031-726-921
Specialties: American and South African styles. **Patterns:** Bowies, American and South African hunters, plus more. **Technical:** Grinds Bohler steels, some ATS-34. **Prices:** $100 to $600. **Remarks:** Part-time maker; first knife sold in 1986. **Mark:** Name, city, country.

BOB-SKY KNIVES (See Hajovsky, Robert J.)

BOCHMAN, BRUCE, 183 Howard Place, Grants Pass, OR 97526/503-471-1985
Specialties: Working straight knives in standard patterns. **Patterns:** Bowies, hunters, fishing and bird knives. **Technical:** 440C; mirror or satin finish. **Prices:** $140 to $250; some to $750. **Remarks:** Part-time maker; first knife sold in 1977. **Mark:** Custom blades by B. Bochman.

BODEN, HARRY, Via Gellia Mill, Bonsall, Matlock, Derbyshire DE4 2AJ, ENGLAND/0629-825176
Specialties: Traditional working straight knives and folders of his design. **Patterns:** Hunters, locking folders and utility/camp knives. **Technical:** Grinds Sandvik 12C27, D2 and 01. **Prices:** £70 to £150; some to £300. **Remarks:** Full-time maker; first knife sold in 1986. **Mark:** Full name.

BODOLAY, ANTAL, R.17, #31, Cerrado, Belo horizonte, MG-31760-190, BRAZIL/031-4941885
Specialties: Working folders and fixed blades of his design or to customer specs; some art daggers and period pieces. **Patterns:** Daggers, hunters, locking folders, utility knives and Khukris. **Technical:** Grinds D6, high carbon steels and 420 stainless. Forges files on request. **Prices:** $30 to $350. **Remarks:** Full-time maker; first knife sold in 1975. **Mark:** Last name in script.

BOGACHEV, ANATOLY (See Fisk, Jerry)

BOGUSZEWSKI, PHIL, P.O. Box 99329, Tacoma, WA 98499/206-581-7096
Specialties: Working folders—some fancy—mostly of his design. **Patterns:** Folders, slip-joints and lockers; also makes anodized titanium frame folders. **Technical:** Grinds 440C; offers filework. **Prices:** $300 to $1,500. **Remarks:** Full-time maker; first knife sold in 1979. **Mark:** Name, city and state.

BOHRMANN, BRUCE, 29 Portland St., Yarmouth, ME 04096/207-846-3385
Specialties: Straight using sport knives. **Patterns:** Hunters, fishing, camp and steak knives. **Technical:** Grinds 154CM; likes wood handles. **Prices:** $350 to $450. **Remarks:** Full-time maker; first knife sold in 1976. **Mark:** Name, city and state.

BOJTOS, ÁRPÁD, Dobsinskeho 10, Lucenec, Slovakia, 98403

BOLTON, CHARLES B., P.O. Box 6, Jonesburg, MO 63351/314-488-5785
Specialties: Working straight knives in standard patterns. **Patterns:** Hunters, skinners, boots and fighters. **Technical:** Grinds 440C and ATS-34. **Prices:** $100 to $300; some to $600. **Remarks:** Full-time maker; first knife sold in 1973. **Mark:** Last name.

BONASSI, FRANCO, Via Superiore 14, Pordenone 33170 ITALY/434-550821
Specialties: Fancy and working one-of-a-kind straight knives of his design. **Patterns:** Hunters, skinners, boots, fighters and titanium liner

locks. **Technical:** Grinds 440C, ATS-34, 154CM and commercial Damascus. Uses only titanium foreguards and pommels. **Prices:** $250 to $400; some to $800. **Remarks:** Spare-time maker; first knife sold in 1988. **Mark:** FRANK.

BOOCO, GORDON, 175 Ash St., P.O. Box 174, Hayden, CO 81639/303-276-3195
Specialties: Fancy working straight knives of his design and to customer specs. **Patterns:** Hunters and Bowies. **Technical:** Grinds 440C, D2 and A2. Heat-treats. **Prices:** $150 to $350; some $600 and higher. **Remarks:** Part-time maker; first knife sold in 1984. **Mark:** Last name with push dagger artwork.

BOOTH, PHILIP W., 301 S. Jeffery Ave., Ithaca, MI 48847/517-875-2844
Specialties: Working and traditional straight knives and folders; some fancy. **Patterns:** Fighters, hunters, pocket and personal knives. **Technical:** Grinds 440C, ATS-34, 1095 and commercial Damascus. Uses only natural materials. **Prices:** $100 to $500. **Remarks:** Part-time maker; first knife sold in 1991. **Mark:** Last name or name with city and map logo.

BORGER, WOLF, Benzstrasse 8, 76670 Graben-Neudorf, GERMANY/07255-8314; FAx: 07255-6921
Specialties: High-tech working and using straight knives and folders, many with corkscrews or other tools, of his design. **Patterns:** Hunters, Bowies and folders with various locking systems. **Technical:** Grinds 440C, ATS-34 and CPM. Uses stainless Damascus. **Prices:** $250 to $900; some to $1,500. **Remarks:** Full-time maker; first knife sold in 1975. **Mark:** Howling wolf and name; first name on Damascus blades.

BOSCOLI, MELQUISEDEC RICCI (See Ikoma, Flavio and Boscoli, Melquisedec Ricci)

BOSE, TONY, RR #1, Box 340, Shelburn, IN 47879/812-397-5114
Specialties: Traditional working and using knives in standard patterns; multi-blade folders. **Patterns:** Multi-blade slip-joints. **Technical:** Grinds commercial Damascus, ATS-34 and D2. **Prices:** $225 to $800. **Remarks:** Full-time maker; first knife sold in 1975. **Mark:** First initial, last name, city and state.

BOURBEAU, JEAN YVES, 15 Remillard, Notre Dame, Ilc Perrot, Quebec CANADA

BOUSE, D. MICHAEL, 1010 Victoria Pl., Waldorf, MD 20602/301-932-4135

BOWEN, TILTON, Rt. 1, Box 225A, Baker, WV 26801/304-897-6159
Specialties: Straight, stout working knives. **Patterns:** Hunters, fighters and boots; also offers buckskinner and throwing knives. **Technical:** Grinds D2 and 4140. **Prices:** $60 to $275. **Remarks:** Full-time maker; first knife sold in 1982-1983. Sells wholesale to dealers. **Mark:** Initials and BOWEN BLADES, WV.

BOYD, FRANCIS, 1811 Prince St., Berkeley, CA 94703/510-841-7210
Specialties: Folders and kitchen knives; Japanese swords. **Patterns:** Push-button sturdy locking folders; San Francisco-style chef's knives. **Technical:** Forges and grinds; mostly uses high-carbon steels. **Prices:** Moderate to heavy. **Remarks:** Designer. **Mark:** Name.

BOYE, DAVID, P.O. Box 1238, Dolan Springs, AZ 86441/602-767-4273
Specialties: Handsome working knives for field and kitchen. Forerunner in the use of dendritic steel for blades. **Patterns:** Chef's knives, small and large hunters, folding "pocket tool" and Boye Basics. **Technical:** Casts blades in stainless 440C; etches blade surfaces with animals, plant motifs. **Prices:** From $59 to $395. **Remarks:** Full-time maker; author of *Step-by-Step Knifemaking*; sells at craft shows. **Mark:** Name.

BRACK, DOUGLAS D., 103 Camino Ruiz #16, Camirillo, CA 93012/805-987-0490

Specialties: Working straight knives of his design. **Patterns:** Heavy-duty skinners, fighters and boots. **Technical:** Grinds 440C, ATS-34 and 5160; forges cable. **Prices:** $90 to $180; some to $300. **Remarks:** Part-time maker; first knife sold in 1984. **Mark:** "tat."

BRADBURN, GARY, 1714 Park Place, Wichita, KS 67203/316-269-4273
Specialties: Straight knives and miniatures of his design and to customer specs. **Patterns:** Bowies, fighters, hunters. **Technical:** Forges 5160 and his Damascus; forges and grinds vascowear. **Prices:** $50 to $350; some to $800. **Remarks:** Part-time maker; first knife sold 1991. **Mark:** Last name or last initial inside a shamrock.

BRADLEY, DENNIS, 2410 Bradley Acres Rd., Blairsville, GA 30512/706-745-4364
Specialties: Working straight knives and folders, some high-art. **Patterns:** Hunters, boots and daggers; slip-joints and two-blades. **Technical:** Grinds ATS-34, D2, 440C and commercial Damascus. **Prices:** $100 to $500; some to $2,000. **Remarks:** Part-time maker; first knife sold in 1973. **Mark:** BRADLEY KNIVES in double heart logo.

BRADLEY, JOHN, P.O. Box 37, Pomona Park, FL 32181/904-649-4739
Specialties: Fixed-blade using knives. **Patterns:** Skinners, camp knives, fillet knives and Bowies. **Technical:** All knives forged and heat-treated by hand. Uses 52100, 1095 and own Damascus. **Prices:** $50 to $500; some higher. **Remarks:** Full-time maker; first knife sold in 1988. **Mark:** Last name.

BRANDSEY, EDWARD P., 1207 Portage Lane, Woodstock, IL 60098/815-337-6010
Specialties: Working straight knives; period pieces and art knives. **Patterns:** Hunters, fighters, Bowies and daggers, some buckskinner styles. **Technical:** Grinds ATS-34, 440C and 01. **Prices:** $125 to $250; some to $2,500. **Remarks:** Part-time maker; first knife sold in 1973. **Mark:** Initials connected.

BRANNAN, RALPH, RR1, Box 343, West Frankfort, IL 62896/618-627-2450
Specialties: Working straight knives of his design. **Patterns:** Traditional using skinners, hunters and utility knives. **Technical:** Grinds 1095, 440C and commercial Damascus. Offers filework. **Prices:** $75 to $150; some to $250. **Remarks:** Part-time maker; first knife sold in 1976. **Mark:** Initials.

BRANTON, ROBERT, 4976 Seewee Rd., Awendaw, SC 29429/803-928-3624
Specialties: Working straight knives of his design or to customer specs; throwing knives. **Patterns:** Hunters, fighters and some miniatures. **Technical:** Grinds ATS-34, A2 and 1050; forges 5160, 01. Offers hollow- or convex-grinds. **Prices:** $25 to $400. **Remarks:** Part-time maker; first knife sold in 1985. Doing business as Lowcountry Throwing Knives. **Mark:** Last name; or first and last name, city, state.

BRAY JR., W. LOWELL, 6931 Manor Beach Rd., New Port Richey, FL 34652
Specialties: Traditional working and using straight knives of his design. **Patterns:** Hunters, kitchen knives and utility knives. **Technical:** Grinds 440C; forges high carbon. **Prices:** $50 to $300. **Remarks:** Spare-time maker; first knife sold in 1992. **Mark:** Last name on stock removal blades; interlocking initials on forged blades.

BRAYTON, JIM, 713 Park St., Burkburnett, TX 76354/817-569-4726
Specialties: Working knives and period pieces, some fancy. **Patterns:** Bowies, hunters, fighters. **Technical:** Grinds ATS-34, delivers it at 60 Rc. **Prices:** $55 to $500; some higher. **Remarks:** Full-time maker; first knife sold in 1970. **Mark:** Initials or name.

BRAZOS FORGE (See Crawford, Larry)

BRDLIK, DAN E., 166 Campbell St. S., Prescott, WI 54021/715-262-5296

Specialties: Linerlock folders. **Patterns:** Fighters, boots, folders and Bowies; utilitarian fighter designs. **Technical:** Grinds 440C and Damascus. **Prices:** $65 to $250; some to $500. **Remarks:** Full-time maker; first knife sold in 1983. **Mark:** First name and middle initial over stylized toothpick.

BREITER, THOMAS, Rose Lane 1B, Topanga, CA 90290/310-455-2554; FAX: 310-305-1003
Specialties: Fantasy high-art knives of his design and to customer specs; dolphin knife. **Patterns:** Hunters, kitchen knives and fantasy knives. **Technical:** Grinds ATS-34, 440C and 5160. Custom makes sheaths; prefers natural handle materials. **Prices:** $80 to $500. **Remarks:** Full-time maker; first knife sold in 1987. **Mark:** Stylized initials and serial number.

BREND, WALTER J., Rt. 7, Box 224, Walterboro, SC 29488/803-538-8256; FAX: 803-538-8416
Specialties: Art and working knives. **Patterns:** Combat knives, survival knives, liner locks and Bowies. **Technical:** ATS-34. **Prices:** $425 to $1,100; some to $3,500. **Remarks:** Full-time maker; first knife sold in 1980. **Mark:** Confederate flag.

BRENNAN, JUDSON, P.O. Box 1165, Delta Junction, AK 99737/907-895-5153
Specialties: Period pieces. **Patterns:** All kinds of Bowies, rifle knives, daggers. **Technical:** Forges miscellaneous steels. **Prices:** Upscale, good value. **Remarks:** Muzzle-loading gunsmith; first knife sold in 1978. **Mark:** Name.

BRESHEARS, CLINT, 1261 Keats, Manhattan Beach, CA 90266/310-372-0739
Specialties: Working straight knives and folders. **Patterns:** Hunters, Bowies and survival knives. Folders are mostly hunters. **Technical:** Grinds 440C, 154CM and ATS-34; prefers mirror finishes. **Prices:** $125 to $175; some to $300. **Remarks:** Part-time maker; first knife sold in 1978. **Mark:** First name.

BREUER, LONNIE, P.O. Box 877384, Wasilla, AK 99687-7384
Specialties: Fancy working straight knives. **Patterns:** Hunters, camp knives and axes, folders and Bowies. **Technical:** Grinds 440C, AEB-L and D2; likes wire inlay, scrimshaw, decorative filing. **Prices:** $60 to $150; some to $300. **Remarks:** Part-time maker; first knife sold in 1977. **Mark:** Signature.

BRIAR KNIVES (See Ralph, Darrel)

BRIDGES, JUSTIN W., Box 974, Fish Hatchery Rd., Dubois, WY 82513/307-455-2769
Specialties: Working and using straight knives and folders in standard patterns. **Patterns:** Hunters, gent's knives and locking folders. **Technical:** Grinds 440C, 154 CM and buys Damascus. **Prices:** $250 to $1,000; some to $3,000. **Remarks:** Full-time maker; first knife sold in 1988. Doing business as Wind River Knives. **Mark:** WRK connected; sometimes a circle with name, city and state.

BRIDWELL, RICHARD A., Rt. 2, Milford Ch. Rd., Taylors, SC 29687/803-895-1715
Specialties: Working straight knives and folders. **Patterns:** Boot and fishing knives, fighters and hunters. **Technical:** Grinds stainless steels and D2. **Prices:** $85 to $165; some to $600. **Remarks:** Part-time maker; first knife sold in 1974. **Mark:** Last name logo.

BRIGHTWELL, MARK, 21104 Creekside Dr., Leander, TX 78641/512-267-4110
Specialties: Fancy and plain folders of his design. **Patterns:** Fighters, hunters and gents, some traditional. **Technical:** Hollow- or flat- grinds ATS-34, D2, commercial Damascus; elaborate filework; heat-treats. Extensive choice of natural handle materials; no synthetics. **Prices:** $200 to $700. **Remarks:** Full-time maker. **Mark:** Last name.

BRIGNARDELLO, E.D., Rt. 2, Box 152A, Beecher, IL 60401/708-946-6609

Specialties: Working straight knives; some display pieces. **Patterns:** Hunters, fighters, boots and Bowies; some push knives. **Technical:** Grinds 440C, 154CM and ATS-34; likes mirror finishes. **Prices:** $130 to $250; some to $500. **Remarks:** Part-time maker; first knife sold in 1978. **Mark:** Name and city.

BRITTON, TIM, Rt. 1, Box 141, Kinston, NC 28501/919-523-8631
Specialties: Small and simple working knives, sgian dubhs and toggle lock folders to customer specs. **Technical:** Forges and grinds stainless steel. **Prices:** Upscale. **Remarks:** Veteran knifemaker. **Mark:** Etched signature.

BROADWELL, DAVID, P.O. Box 4314, Wichita Falls, TX 76308/817-692-1727
Specialties: One-of-a-kind pieces, especially fighters. **Patterns:** Daggers, sub-hilted fighters, Bowies, some hunters and folders of his design. **Technical:** Grinds 440C, Damascus; all hand-finished. Some embellishment. **Prices:** $200 to $2,500; some higher. **Remarks:** Full-time maker; first knife sold in 1982. **Mark:** Name, city and state.

BROCK, KENNETH L., P.O. Box 375, 207 N. Skinner Rd., Allenspark, CO 80510/303-747-2547
Specialties: Full-tang working straight knives, folders and button-lock folders. **Patterns:** Hunters, survival knives, miniatures and minis. **Technical:** Flat-grinds D2; makes own sheaths. **Prices:** $50 to $500. **Remarks:** Part-time maker; first knife sold in 1978. **Mark:** Last name, city, state and serial number.

BRONK'S CUSTOM KNIVES (See Brunckhorst, C. Lyle)

BROOKER, DENNIS, Rt. 1, Box 12A, Derby, IA 50068/515-533-2103
Specialties: Fancy straight knives and folders of his design. **Patterns:** Hunters, folders and boots. **Technical:** Forges and grinds. Full-time engraver and designer; instruction available. **Prices:** Moderate to upscale. **Remarks:** Part-time maker. Takes no orders; sells only completed work. **Mark:** Name.

BROOKS, MICHAEL, 1903 B 16th St., Lubbock, TX 79401/406-762-6413
Specialties: Working straight knives of his design or to customer specs. **Patterns:** Tantos, swords, Bowies, hunters, skinners and boots. **Technical:** Grinds 440C, D2 and ATS-34; offers wide variety of handle materials. **Prices:** $40 to $800. **Remarks:** Part-time maker; first knife sold in 1985. Does business as The Weapons Shop. **Mark:** Initials.

BROOKS, STEVE R., Box 105, Big Timber, MT 59011/406-932-5114
Specialties: Working straight knives and folders; period pieces. **Patterns:** Hunters, Bowies and camp knives; folding lockers; axes, tomahawks and buckskinner knives; swords and stilettos. **Technical:** Forges 01 and his own Damascus. Some knives come embellished. **Prices:** $100 to $350; some to $1,000. **Remarks:** Full-time maker; first knife sold in 1982. **Mark:** Lazy initials.

BROOME, THOMAS A., 1212 E. Aliak Ave., Kenai, AK 99611-8205
Specialties: Traditional working straight knives and folders. **Patterns:** Full range of straight knives and a few folders. **Technical:** Grinds D2, 440C, 440V, ATS-34 and BG42. **Prices:** $75 to $175; some to $2,000. **Remarks:** Full-time maker; first knife sold in 1979. Doing business as Thom's Custom Knives. **Mark:** Full name, city, state in logo.

BROTHERS, ROBERT L., 989 Philpott Rd., Colville, WA 99114/509-684-8922
Specialties: Traditional working and using straight knives and folders of his design and to customer specs. **Patterns:** Bowies, fighters and hunters. **Technical:** Grinds D2; forges Damascus. Makes own Damascus from saw steel wire rope and chain; part-time goldsmith and stonesetter. **Prices:** $100 to $400; some higher. **Remarks:** Part-time maker; first knife sold in 1986. **Mark:** Initials and year made.

BROUGHTON, DON R., 4690 Edwardsville-Galena Rd., Floyd Knobs, IN 47119/812-923-9222

Specialties: Traditional knives of his design; period pieces. **Patterns:** Bowies, hunters, utility/camp knives and 18th century-style knives. **Technical:** Forges 1095, 5160, 52100 and own Damascus. Uses antique finish. **Prices:** $150 to $750; some to $1,500. **Remarks:** Part-time maker; first knife sold in 1987. **Mark:** Tomahawk head, M.S.

BROWER, MAX, 2016 Story St., Boone, IA 50036/515-432-2938
Patterns: Bowies, hunters and boots. **Technical:** Grinds 440C. **Prices:** $125 and up. **Remarks:** Spare-time maker; first knife sold in 1981. **Mark:** Last name.

BROWN, DAVID B., 3209 N. 60th St., Omaha, NE 68104/402-345-8302
Specialties: Working straight knives and folders; some fancy. **Patterns:** Hunters, tantos and Bowies; lockers and butterflies. **Technical:** Forges and grinds W2, 440C and his own Damascus. Etches. **Prices:** $85 to $750; some to $2,000. **Remarks:** Spare-time maker; first knife sold in 1979. **Mark:** First and middle initials, last name.

BROWN, HAROLD E., 3654 NW Hwy. 72, Arcadia, FL 33821/813-494-7514
Specialties: Fancy and exotic working knives. **Patterns:** Hunters, folders and fillet knives. **Technical:** Grinds D2, 440C and ATS-34. Embellishment available. **Prices:** $100 to $750; some to $1,000. **Remarks:** Full-time maker; first knife sold in 1976. **Mark:** Name and city with logo.

BROWN, JIM, 1097 Fernleigh Cove, Little Rock, AR 72210

BROWN, PETER, 10 Island View St., Emerald Beach 2456, AUSTRALIA/02-809-0265
Specialties: Heavy-duty working knives. **Patterns:** Swords, fighters, tantos, hunting and fishing knives. **Technical:** Grinds 440C, 420 and ATS-34; makes his own Damascus steel. Heat-treats; scrimshaws. **Prices:** $135 to $500; some to $800. **Remarks:** Spare-time maker; first knife sold in 1978. **Mark:** Interlacing initials.

BROWN, ROB E., P.O. Box 15107, Emerald Hill, 6011 Port Elizabeth, SOUTH AFRICA/27-41-361086; FAX: 27-41-411731
Specialties: Contemporary-designed straight knives and period pieces. **Patterns:** Utility knives, hunters, boots, fighters and daggers. **Technical:** Grinds 440C, D2, ATS-34 and commercial Damascus. Knives mostly mirror finished; African handle materials. **Prices:** $150 to $1,500. **Remarks:** Full-time maker; first knife sold in 1985. **Mark:** Name and country.

BROWN, TED, 7621 Firestone Blvd., Suite 104, Downey, CA 90241/213-869-9945
Specialties: Working straight knives in standard patterns. **Patterns:** Hunters, Bowies, fishing knives. **Technical:** Grinds stainless steel; some integral work. **Prices:** $100 to $350; some to $500. **Remarks:** Part-time maker; first knife sold in 1982. **Mark:** Name, address in snake logo.

BROWN, TOM, Suite 106, 5710-K High Point Rd., Greensboro, NC 27407/919-656-4955
Specialties: Classic and working straight knives of his design and in standard patterns. **Patterns:** Daggers, double edge fighters, hunters and folders. **Technical:** Grinds ATS-34 and 440C; scratch D2. No jigs or fixtures. **Prices:** $165 to $550. **Remarks:** Part-time maker; first knife sold in 1991. **Mark:** Brown Knives.

BROWNE, RICK, 980 West 13th St., Upland, CA 91786/714-985-1728
Specialties: High-tech working straight knives of his design. **Patterns:** Hunters, fighters and daggers. No heavy-duty knives. **Technical:** Grinds D2, 440C and ATS-34. **Prices:** $80 to $500; some to $1,500. **Remarks:** Part-time maker; first knife sold in 1975. **Mark:** Name, city, state.

BROZ KNIVES (See Meloy, Sean)

BRUMAGEN, JERRY (See Fannin, David A. and Brumagen, Jerry)

BRUNCKHORST, C. LYLE, 1450 Prospect Ave., Suite 222, Helena, MT 59601
Specialties: Working straight knives and folders, some fancy. **Patterns:** Head knives, fillet knives, Bowies and backpack folders. **Technical:** ATS-34. Offers carved antler handles and scrimmed ivory. **Prices:** $85 to $3,500. **Remarks:** Full-time maker; first knife sold in 1976. Doing business as Bronk's Custom Knives. **Mark:** Bucking horse logo or BRONK.

BUCHMAN, BILL, 63312 South Rd., Bend, OR 97701/503-382-8851
Specialties: Working straight knives. **Patterns:** Hunters, Bowies, fighters, kitchen cutlery, carving sets and boots. Makes some saddlemaker knives. **Technical:** Forges 440C and Sandvik 15N20. Prefers 440C for saltwater. **Prices:** $95 to $400. **Remarks:** Part-time maker; first knife sold in 1982. **Mark:** Initials or last name.

BUCHNER, BILL, P.O. Box 73, Idleyld Park, OR 97447/503-498-2247
Specialties: Working straight knives, kitchen knives and high-art knives of his design. **Technical:** Uses W1, L6 and his own Damascus. Invented "spectrum metal" for letter openers, folder handles and jewelry. Likes sculpturing and carving in Damascus. **Prices:** $40 to $3,000; some higher. **Remarks:** Full-time maker; first knife sold in 1978. **Mark:** Signature.

BUCHOLZ, MARK A., 9197 West Parkview Terrace Loop, Eagle River, AK 99577/907-694-1037
Specialties: Working straight knives in standard patterns, some fancy. **Patterns:** Hunters, fighters and liner locks. **Technical:** Grinds 440C and ATS-34. **Prices:** $250 to $475; some to $2,500. **Remarks:** Part-time maker; first knife sold in 1976. **Mark:** Name, city and state in buffalo skull logo.

BUCKBEE, DONALD M., 42683 Jonathan Place, Clinton Township, MI 48038/313-228-2673
Specialties: Working straight knives, some fancy, in standard patterns; concentrating on kitchen knives. **Patterns:** Kitchen knives, hunters, Bowies. **Technical:** Grinds D2, 440C, ATS-34. Makes ultra-lights in hunter patterns. **Prices:** $100 to $250; some to $350. **Remarks:** Part-time maker; first knife sold in 1984. **Mark:** Antlered bee—a buck bee.

BUCKNER, JIMMIE H., P.O. Box 162, Putney, GA 31782/912-436-4182
Specialties: High-tech working straight knives and locking folders of his design or to customer specs. **Patterns:** Hunters, fighters and camp knives. **Technical:** Forges 01, 1095 and his Damascus; heat-treats. **Prices:** $100 to $300; some to $900. **Remarks:** Full-time maker; first knife sold in 1980. **Mark:** Last name over spade.

BUEBENDORF, ROBERT E., 108 Lazybrooke Rd., Monroe, CT 06468/203-452-1769
Specialties: Traditional and fancy straight knives of his design. **Patterns:** Hand-makes and embellishes belt buckle knives. **Technical:** Forges and grinds 440C, 01, W2, 1095, his own Damascus and 154CM. **Prices:** $200 to $500. **Remarks:** Full-time maker; first knife sold in 1978. **Mark:** First and middle initials, last name and MAKER.

BUGDEN, JOHN, Rt. #6, Box 7, Murray, KY 42071/502-753-0305
Specialties: Working straight knives; period pieces. **Patterns:** Hunters, boots and survival knives. **Technical:** Grinds 01, 440C; buys Damascus. Offers filework. **Prices:** $125 to $500. **Remarks:** Full-time maker; first knife sold in 1975. **Mark:** Initials.

BULLARD, BILL, Rt. 5, Box 35, Andalusia, AL 36420/205-222-9003
Specialties: Traditional working and using straight knives and folders of his design. **Patterns:** Hunters, slip-joint folders and utility/camp knives. **Technical:** Forges Damascus, cable and carbon steels. Offers filework. **Prices:** $100 to $500; some to $1,500. **Remarks:** Part-time maker; first knife sold in 1974. Doing business as Five Runs Forge. **Mark:** Last name stamped on ricasso.

BULLARD, RANDALL, 7 Mesa Dr., Canyon, TX 79015/806-655-0590
Specialties: Working/using straight knives and folders of his design or

to customer specs. **Patterns:** Hunters, locking folders and slip-joint folders. **Technical:** Grinds 01, ATS-34 and 440C. Does file work. **Prices:** $125 to $300; some to $500. **Remarks:** Part-time maker; first knife sold in 1993. Doing business as Bullard Custom Knives. **Mark:** First and middle initials, last name, maker, city and state.

BULLARD, TOM, Rt. 1, Box 127-B, Comfort, TX 78013/210-995-2003 **Specialties:** Traditional, classic, working and using straight knives and folders to customer specs. **Patterns:** Hunters, locking folders and utility knives. **Technical:** Grinds 01, 1095, ATS-34 and 440C; forges and grinds leaf springs. Heat-treats. Offers filework on blades, tangs, liners and guards. Armadillo tail handle material. **Prices:** $150 to $500. **Remarks:** Full-time maker; first knife sold in 1966. **Mark:** Full name, maker, city and state in football.

BURDEN, JAMES, 405 Kelly St., Burkburnett, TX 76354

BURGER, FRED, P.O. Munster 4278, Kwa-Zulu Natal SOUTH AFRICA/03930-92316 **Specialties:** Straight knives of his design. **Patterns:** Bowies, fighters and gentlemen's sword canes. **Technical:** Grinds ATS-34 and 440C. **Prices:** $200 to $400; some to $1,000. **Remarks:** Full-time maker; first knife sold in 1987. **Mark:** Last name in an oval pierced by a dagger.

BURGER, PON, 12 Glenwood Ave., Woodlands, Bulawayo, AFRICA/48628 **Specialties:** High-art knives—sets of two or four. **Patterns:** Fighters, locking folders of traditional styles, buckles. **Technical:** Uses 440C. African themes scrimshawed on handles. **Prices:** $750—two knives; $1,500—four knives. **Remarks:** Full-time maker; first knife sold in 1973. Doing business as Burger Products. **Mark:** Last name.

BURGER PRODUCTS (See Burger, Pon)

BURNS, DAVE, 2825 SW 5 St., Boynton Beach, FL 33435/407-734-8806 **Specialties:** Working straight knives of his design or to customer specs. **Patterns:** Hunters, boots, Bowies and survival knives. **Technical:** Forges and grinds 01, L6 and 1095. **Prices:** $65 to $200; some to $325. **Remarks:** Full-time maker; first knife sold in 1980. **Mark:** Last name and serial number.

BURROWS, STEPHEN R., 3532 Michigan, Kansas City, MO 64109/816-921-1573 **Specialties:** Fantasy straight knives of his design, to customer specs and in standard patterns; period pieces. **Patterns:** Daggers and fighters. **Technical:** Forges 5160 and 1090 high-carbon steel, 01 and his Damascus. Offers casting and lost wax bronzing of crossguards and pommels. **Prices:** $100 to $200; some to $1,000. **Remarks:** Full-time maker; first knife sold in 1983. Doing business as Gypsy Silk. **Mark:** Etched name.

BUSFIELD, JOHN, 153 Devonshire Circle, Roanoke Rapids, NC 27870/919-537-3949; FAX: 919-537-8704 **Specialties:** Investor-grade folders; high-grade working straight knives. **Patterns:** Original price-style and trailing-point interframe and sculpted-frame folders, drop-point hunters and semi-skinners. **Technical:** Grinds 154CM and ATS-34. Offers interframes, gold frames and inlays; uses jade, agate and lapis. **Prices:** $650 to $2,000. **Remarks:** Full-time maker; first knife sold in 1979. **Mark:** Last name and address.

BUSSE, JERRY, 11651 Co. Rd. 12, Wauseon, OH 43567/419-923-6471 **Specialties:** Working straight knives. **Patterns:** Heavy combat knives and camp knives. **Technical:** Grinds D2, A2, ATS-34 and 440C; hollow-grinds most blades. **Prices:** $1,100 to $3,500. **Remarks:** Full-time maker; first knife sold in 1983. **Mark:** Last name in logo.

BUZZARD'S KNOB FORGE (See Hurst, Jeff)

"BY GEORGE" (See Englebretson, George)

BYBEE, BARRY J., 795 Lock Rd. E., Cadiz, KY 42211-8615 **Specialties:** Working straight knives of his design. **Patterns:** Hunters, fighters, boot knives, tantos and Bowies. **Technical:** Grinds ATS-34, 440C. Likes stag and Micarta for handle materials. **Prices:** $125 to $200; some to $1,000. **Remarks:** Part-time maker; first knife sold in 1968. **Mark:** Arrowhead logo with name, city and state.

BYRD, DON E., Rt. 3, Box 223-A, Roanoke, TX 76262/817-430-1986 **Specialties:** Classic and working straight knives in standard patterns. **Patterns:** Fighters, hunters and utility knives. **Technical:** Grinds ATS-34, D2 and 440C. **Prices:** $125 to $275; some to $500. **Remarks:** Part-time maker; first knife sold in 1983. **Mark:** Last name.

BYWATER HOMESTEAD (See Williams, David)

C

CABLE JOE KNIVES (See Allen, Joe)

CACTUS CUSTOM KNIVES (See McConnell, Jr., Loyd A.)

CADILLAC BLACKSMITHING (See Pogreba, Larry)

CAFFREY, EDWARD J., 2608 Central Ave. West, Great Falls, MT 59404/406-727-9102 **Specialties:** Working/using knives, some collector pieces; will accept customer designs. **Patterns:** Hunters, skinners, fighters, camp knives and friction folders. **Technical:** Forges 5160, 52100, his Damascus, cable and chain Damascus. Offers a special effect steel using various steels and nickel forge welding. **Prices:** $125 and up. **Remarks:** Part-time maker; first knife sold in 1989. **Mark:** Last name or engraved initials.

CALDWELL, BILL, 255 Rebecca, West Monroe, LA 71292/318-323-3025 **Specialties:** Straight knives and folders with machined bolsters and liners. **Patterns:** Fighters, Bowies, survival knives, tomahawks, razors and push knives. **Technical:** Owns and operates a very large, well-equipped blacksmith and bladesmith shop extant with six large forges and eight power hammers. **Prices:** $400 to $3,500; some to $10,000. **Remarks:** Full-time maker and self-styled blacksmith; first knife sold in 1962. **Mark:** Wild Bill & Sons.

CALLAHAN, ERRETT, 2 Fredonia, Lynchburg, VA 24503 **Specialties:** Obsidian knives. **Patterns:** Modern styles and Stone Age replicas. **Technical:** Flakes and knaps to order. **Prices:** $100 to $2,100. **Remarks:** Full-time maker; first flint blades sold in 1974. **Mark:** Blade—engraved name; handle—signed edition, year and unit number.

CALLAHAN, F. TERRY, P.O. Box 880, Boerne, TX 78006/210-981-8274; FAX: 210-981-8274 **Specialties:** Custom hand-forged edged knives, collectible and functional. **Patterns:** Bowies, folders, daggers, hunters, camp knives and swords. **Technical:** Forges 5160, 1095 and his own Damascus. Offers filework and handmade sheaths. **Prices:** $125 to $2,000. **Remarks:** First knife sold in 1990. **Mark:** Initials inside a keystone symbol.

CAMP, JEFF, 9987 Hwy. 146-W, Ruston, LA 71270/318-255-7796 **Specialties:** Fancy working and using straight knives of his design and to customer specs. **Patterns:** Bowies, hunters, utility/camp knives and folders. **Technical:** Forges 5168, L6 and his Damascus. Offers filework; makes mokume. **Prices:** $260 to $1,000. **Remarks:** Part-time maker; first knife sold in 1991. **Mark:** Initials in script and JS.

CAMPBELL, DICK, 20000 Silver Ranch Rd., Conifer, CO 80433/303-697-0150 **Specialties:** Fancy working straight knives and folders; period pieces. **Patterns:** Bowies, fighters, miniatures and titanium folders. **Technical:** Grinds 440C; uses titanium. Prefers natural materials. **Prices:** $130 to $750; some to $1,200. **Remarks:** Part-time maker; first knife sold in 1975. **Mark:** Name.

CANDRELLA, JOE, 1219 Barness Dr., Warminster, PA 18974/215-675-0143
Specialties: Working straight knives, some fancy. **Patterns:** Daggers, boots, Bowies. **Technical:** Grinds 440C and 154CM. **Prices:** $100 to $200; some to $1,000. **Remarks:** Part-time maker; first knife sold in 1985. Does business as Franjo. **Mark:** FRANJO with knife as J.

CANNADY, DANIEL L., Box 301, Allendale, SC 29810/803-584-2813
Specialties: Working straight knives and folders in standard patterns. **Patterns:** Drop-point hunters, Bowies, skinners, fishing knives with concave grind, steak knives and kitchen cutlery. **Technical:** Grinds D2, 440C and ATS-34. **Prices:** $65 to $150; some to $325. **Remarks:** Full-time maker; first knife sold in 1980. **Mark:** Last name.

CANNON, RAYMOND W., 894 Mattox Ct., Homer, AK 99603/907-235-7779
Specialties: Fancy working knives, folders and swords of his design or to customer specs; many one-of-a-kind pieces. **Patterns:** Bowies, daggers and skinners. **Technical:** Forges and grinds 01, A6, 52100, 5160, his combinations for his own Damascus. **Prices:** Start at $180. **Remarks:** First knife sold in 1984. **Mark:** Last name, state.

CANTER, RONALD E., 96 Bon Air Circle, Jackson, TN 38305/901-668-1780
Specialties: Traditional working knives to customer specs. **Patterns:** Beavertail skinners, Bowies, hand axes and folding lockers. **Technical:** Grinds A1, 440C and 154CM. **Prices:** $65 to $250; some $500 and higher. **Remarks:** Spare-time maker; first knife sold in 1973. **Mark:** Three last initials intertwined.

CAREY JR., CHARLES W., 1003 Minter Rd., Griffin, GA 30223/404-227-6854
Specialties: Working and using knives of his design and to customer specs; period pieces. **Patterns:** Fighters, hunters, utility/camp knives and forged-to-shape miniatures. **Technical:** Forges 5160, old files and cable. Offers filework; ages some of his knives. **Prices:** $35 to $400. **Remarks:** Part-time maker; first knife sold in 1991. **Mark:** Knife logo.

CARGILL, BOB, Rt. 1, Box 501-B, Oldfort, TN 37362/615-338-8418; FAX: 615-338-2086
Specialties: Unique multi-blade folders of his design. **Patterns:** Adaptations of traditional pocketknives in many styles. **Technical:** Grinds 1095, 440, ATS-34 and Damascus. **Prices:** Start at $500; some to $10,000. **Remarks:** Full-time maker; first knife sold in 1974. **Mark:** Cargill Knives.

CARISOLO (See Maestri, Peter A.)

CARLISLE, FRANK, 5930 Hereford, Detroit, MI 48224/313-882-8349
Specialties: Fancy/embellished and fantasy folders of his design. **Patterns:** Hunters, locking folders and swords. **Technical:** Grinds Damascus and stainless. **Prices:** $80 to $300. **Remarks:** Full-time maker; first knife sold in 1993. Doing business as Carlisle Cutlery. **Mark:** Last name.

CARLSSON, MARC BJORN, Sct. Hansgade 31, 4000 Roskilde, DENMARK/+45 42 35 97 24
Specialties: High-tech aluminum-handled knives. **Patterns:** Skinners, tantos, folders and art knives. **Technical:** Grinds D2 and ATS-34. **Prices:** $110 to $600; some higher. **Remarks:** Professional jeweler and knifemaker. **Mark:** First name in runic letters within Viking ship.

CAROLINA CUSTOM KNIVES (See Daniel, Travis E.; McNabb, Tommy)

CARSON, HAROLD J. "KIT", 1076 Brizendine Lane, Vine Grove, KY 40175/502-877-6300; FAX: 502-877-6338
Specialties: Military fixed blades and folders; art pieces. **Patterns:** Fighters, D handles, daggers, combat folders and Grosslock styles. **Technical:** Grinds 440C, ATS-34, D2, 01 and Damascus. **Prices:** $250 to $750; some to $5,000. **Remarks:** Full-time maker; first knife sold in 1973. **Mark:** Name stamped or engraved.

CARTER, FRED, 5219 Deer Creek Rd., Wichita Falls, TX 76302/817-723-4020
Specialties: High-art investor-class straight knives; some working hunters and fighters. **Patterns:** Classic daggers, Bowies; interframe, stainless and blued steel folders with gold inlay. **Technical:** Grinds a variety of steels. Uses no glue or solder. Engraves and inlays. **Prices:** Generally upscale. **Remarks:** Full-time maker. Won the W.W. Cronk award in 1988, 1989. **Mark:** Signature in oval logo.

CASHEN, KEVIN R., 5615 Tyler St., Hubbardston, MI 48845/517-981-6780
Specialties: Traditional working straight knives of his design or to customer specs. **Patterns:** Hunters, skinners, Bowies, fighters, tantos and utilty/camp knives. **Technical:** Forges 1095, 5160 and his own 1095/L6 Damascus, mokume and cable; does Japanese temper lines. **Prices:** $80 to $500; some to $1,000. **Remarks:** Full-time maker; first knife sold in 1985. **Mark:** Old English initials and journeyman stamp.

CASTEEL, DIANNA, P.O. Box 63, Monteagle, TN 37356/615-924-2797
Specialties: Small, delicate daggers and miniatures; most knives one-of-a-kinds. **Patterns:** Daggers, boot knives, fighters and miniatures. **Technical:** Grinds 440C; makes her own Damascus. **Prices:** Start at $350; miniatures start at $250. **Remarks:** Full-time maker. **Mark:** Di in script.

CASTEEL, DOUGLAS, P.O. Box 63, Monteagle, TN 37356/615-924-2797
Specialties: One-of-a-kind collector-class period pieces. **Patterns:** Daggers, Bowies, swords and folders. **Technical:** Grinds 440C; makes his own Damascus. Offers gold and silver castings. **Prices:** Upscale. **Remarks:** Full-time maker; first knife sold in 1982. **Mark:** Last name.

CASTLE KNIVES (See Courtois, Bryan)

CELLUM, TOM S., 9 Cude Cemetary Rd., Willis, TX 77378/409-856-5937
Specialties: Working straight knives in standard patterns. **Patterns:** Bowies, camp knives, hunters. **Technical:** Forges W2, 01, 5165; makes own Damascus; prefers natural handle materials. **Prices:** Start at $100. **Remarks:** Full-time maker; first knife sold in 1982. **Mark:** Name, J.S.

CENTOFANTE, FRANK and TONY, P.O. Box 928, Madisonville, TN 37354-0928/615-442-5767
Specialties: Fancy working folders. **Patterns:** Lockers and liner locks. **Technical:** Grinds ATS-34; hand-rubbed satin finish on blades. **Prices:** $300 to $900. **Remarks:** Full-time maker; first knife sold in 1968. Son Tony is co-worker. **Mark:** Name, city, state.

CENTOFANTE, TONY (See Centofante, Frank and Tony)

CHAFFEE, JEFF L., Washington St., P.O. Box 1, Morris, IN 47033/812-934-6350
Specialties: Traditional working and using straight knives of his design or to customer specs. **Patterns:** Hunters, Bowies, fighters and kitchen knives. **Technical:** Grinds commercial Damascus, 440C, ATS-34, D2 and 01. Prefers natural handle materials. **Prices:** $25 to $250. **Remarks:** Part-time maker; first knife sold in 1988. **Mark:** First and middle initials and last name or last name only.

CHAMBERLAIN, CHARLES R., 2370 Meadowcreek Rd., Christiansburg, VA 24073/703-381-5137

CHAMBERLAIN, JOHN B., 1621 Angela St., Wenatchee, WA 98801/509-663-6720
Specialties: Fancy working and using straight knives mainly to customer specs, though starting to make some standard patterns. **Patterns:** Hunters, Bowies and daggers. **Technical:** Grinds D2, ATS-34, M2, M4 and L6. **Prices:** $60 to $190; some to $2,500. **Remarks:** Full-time maker; first knife sold in 1943. **Mark:** Name, city, state.

CHAMBERLAIN, JON A., 15 S. Lombard, E. Wenatchee, WA 98802/509-884-6591
Specialties: Working knives to customer specs; exotics on special order. **Patterns:** Over 75 patterns in stock. **Technical:** Prefers ATS-34 and L6; also works 440C, M-2, commercial Damascus, stellite and tool steels. **Prices:** $30 and up. **Remarks:** New maker. **Mark:** Name in oval with city and state enclosing.

CHAMBERLIN, JOHN A., 11535 Our Rd., Anchorage, AK 99516/907-346-1524; FAX: 907-562-4583
Specialties: Art and working knives. **Patterns:** Daggers and hunters; some folders. **Technical:** Grinds ATS-34, 440C, A2, D2 and Damascus. Uses Alaskan handle materials such as oosic, jade, whale jawbone, fossil ivory. **Prices:** Start at $100. **Remarks:** Full-time maker; first knife sold in 1984. **Mark:** Name over English shield and dagger.

CHAMBLIN, JOEL, 296 New Hebron Church Rd., Concord, GA 30206/706-495-9055
Specialties: Folders. **Patterns:** Fighters, hunters, locking folders and miniatures. **Technical:** Grinds ATS-34 and commercial Damascus. Offers filework. **Prices:** Start at $125. **Remarks:** Full-time maker; first knife sold in 1989. **Mark:** First and last name, city and state.

CHAMPAGNE, PAUL, 48 Brightman Rd., Mechanicville, NY 12118/518-664-4179
Specialties: Rugged, ornate straight knives in the Japanese tradition. **Patterns:** Katanas, wakizashi's, tantos and some European daggers. **Technical:** Forges and hand-finishes carbon steels and his own Damascus. Makes Tamahagane for use in traditional blades; uses traditional heat-treating techniques. **Prices:** Start at $750. **Remarks:** First knife sold in 1988. Doing business as Twilight Forge. **Mark:** Three diamonds over a stylized crown; also NOBUHIRA in Kanji.

CHAMPION, ROBERT, P.O. Box 19427, Amarillo, TX 79114/806-359-0446
Specialties: Traditional working straight knives and folders. **Patterns:** Hunters, locking and slip-joint folders; some sub-hilt fighters. **Technical:** Grinds A2, 440C, D2. **Prices:** $100 to $600. **Remarks:** Part-time maker; first knife sold in 1979. **Mark:** Last name with dagger logo, city and state.

CHAPMAN, MIKE, 907 Old Mill Ln., Houston, TX 77073/713-821-6609
Specialties: Using knives, mostly hunters. **Patterns:** Fixed blades—full and narrow tang in traditional styles; lock-back and spring-back folders—boots, fighters, camp knives, Bowies and double-edged knives. **Technical:** Grinds 440C, A2, D2, 01, ATS-34. Filework available on all styles. Heat-treats and tempers. Makes own leather sheaths, plain or tooled. **Prices:** Begin at $85. **Remarks:** Part-time maker; first knife sold in 1975. **Mark:** Cherokee Knives.

CHAPO, WILLIAM G., 45 Wildridge Rd., Wilton, CT 06897/203-544-9424
Specialties: Classic straight knives and folders of his design and to customer specs; period pieces. **Patterns:** Boots, Bowies and locking folders. **Technical:** Forges stainless Damascus. Offers filework. **Prices:** $350 to $950; some to $2,200. **Remarks:** Full-time maker; first knife sold in 1989. **Mark:** First and middle initials, last name, city, state.

CHARD, GORDON R., 104 S. Holiday Lane, Iola, KS 66749/316-365-2311
Specialties: High-tech locking folders. **Patterns:** Titanium sidelock folders, push-button locking folders, interframe lockbacks and some art knives. **Technical:** Flat- and hollow-grinds mostly ATS-34, some Damascus; hand-finishes blades. **Prices:** $300 to $2,000. **Remarks:** Part-time maker; first knife sold in 1983. **Mark:** Name, city and state in wheat logo.

CHASE, JOHN E., P.O. Drawer H, Aledo, TX 76008/817-441-8331
Specialties: Straight high-tech working knives in standard patterns or to customer specs. **Patterns:** Hunters, fighters, daggers and Bowies. **Technical:** Grinds D2, 440C; offers mostly satin finishes. **Prices:** Start at $150. **Remarks:** Part-time maker; first knife sold in 1974. **Mark:** Last name in logo.

CHASTAIN, WADE, Rt. 2, Box 137-A, Horse Shoe, NC 28742/704-891-4803
Specialties: Fancy fantasy and high-art straight knives of his design; period pieces. Known for unique mounts. **Patterns:** Bowies, daggers and fighters. **Technical:** Grinds 440C, ATS-34 and 01. Engraves; offers jeweling. **Prices:** $400 to $1,200; some to $2,000. **Remarks:** Full-time maker; first knife sold in 1984. Doing business as The Iron Master. **Mark:** Engraved last name.

CHEATHAM, BILL, 2930 W. Marlette, Phoenix, AZ 85017/602-242-1497
Specialties: Working straight knives and folders. **Patterns:** Hunters, fighters, boots and axes; locking folders. **Technical:** Grinds 440C. **Prices:** $150 to $350; exceptional knives to $600. **Remarks:** Full-time maker; first knife sold in 1976. **Mark:** Name, city, state.

CHELQUIST, CLIFF, P.O. Box 91, Arroyo Grande, CA 93421/805-489-8095
Specialties: Highly polished sportsman's knives. **Patterns:** Bird knives to Bowies. **Technical:** Grinds D2 and ATS-34. **Prices:** $75 to $150; some to $400. **Remarks:** Spare-time maker; first knife sold in 1983. **Mark:** Last initial.

CHEROKEE KNIVES (See Chapman, Mike)

CHURCHMAN, T.W., 8201 Lamount Dr., Amarillo, TX 79110/806-355-8507
Specialties: Fancy and traditional straight knives of his design and to customer specs. **Patterns:** Daggers, fighters and bird/trout knives. **Technical:** Grinds 440C and D2. Offers fancy filework, lined sheaths, exotic and stabilized woods, and twisted silver wire on fluted handles. **Prices:** $100 to $300; some to $1,500. **Remarks:** Part-time maker; first knife sold in 1981. Doing business as Custom Knives Churchman Made. **Mark:** Last name with dagger.

CISCO (See Syslo, Chuck)

CLAIBORNE, RON, 2918 Ellistown Rd., Knox, TN 37924/615-524-2054
Specialties: Working and using straight knives; period pieces. **Patterns:** Hunters, Bowies and daggers. **Technical:** Forges his own Damascus; grinds 440C, 01, W2 and 1095. Prefers bone and natural handle materials; some exotic woods. **Prices:** $125 to $300; some to $900. **Remarks:** Part-time maker; first knife sold in 1979. Doing business as Thunder Mountain Forge Claiborne Knives. **Mark:** Last name.

CLARK, DAVE, P.O. Box 1867, Andrews, NC 28901/704-321-2230
Specialties: High-tech working and using straight knives and folders to customer specs; knives for law enforcement officers and fire fighters. **Patterns:** Daggers, swords and locking folders. **Technical:** Grinds 440C, D2 and ATS-34. **Prices:** $75 to $500; some to $750. **Remarks:** Full-time maker; first knife sold in 1988. **Mark:** Name or Dave's Daggers.

CLARK, D.E. (LUCKY), 126 Woodland St., Mineral Point, PA 15942/814-322-4725
Specialties: Working straight knives and folders to customer specs. **Patterns:** Customer designs. **Technical:** Grinds D2, 440C, 154CM. **Prices:** $100 to $200; some higher. **Remarks:** Part-time maker; first knife sold in 1975. **Mark:** Name on one side; "Lucky" on other.

CLARK, HOWARD F., RR 1, Box 74, Runnells, IA 50237/515-966-2126
Specialties: Traditional working straight knives and folders of his design or to customer specs. **Patterns:** Hunters, Bowies and utility/camp knives. **Technical:** Forges 1086, 02, L6, 52100 and his own all tool steel Damascus. Bar stock and forged blade blanks also available. **Prices:** $100 to $2,000; some higher. **Remarks:** Full-time maker; first knife sold in 1979. Doing business as Morgan Valley Forge. **Mark:** Initials connected inside anvil, M.S.

CLARK, ROGER, Rt. 1, Box 538, Rockdale, TX 76567/512-446-3388 **Specialties:** Traditional working and using straight knives of his design or to customer specs. **Patterns:** Hunters, Bowies and camp knives; primitive styles for blackpowder hunters. **Technical:** Forges 5160, 1084, 01 and Damascus. Sheaths are extra. **Prices:** $100 to $450. **Remarks:** Full-time maker; first knife sold in 1989. **Mark:** First initial, last name.

CLAY, J.D., 5050 Hall Rd., Greenup, KY 41144/606-473-6769 **Specialties:** Fancy working straight knives and folders; field- and collector-grade working knives. **Patterns:** Practical hunters and locking folders. **Technical:** Grinds 01 and ATS-34; some 440C. **Prices:** $65 to $300; some to $400. **Remarks:** Full-time maker; first knife sold in 1972. **Mark:** Name on blade or in small medallion in handle.

CLAY, WAYNE, Box 474B, Pelham, TN 37366/615-467-3472; FAX: 615-467-3076 **Specialties:** Working straight knives and folders in standard patterns. **Patterns:** Hunters, fighters and kitchen knives; gents and hunter patterns. **Technical:** Grinds 154CM and ATS-34. **Prices:** $125 to $250; some to $1,000. **Remarks:** Full-time maker; first knife sold in 1978. **Mark:** Name.

CLOUDY MT. IRON WORKS (See Ber, Dave)

COATS, ELDON, P.O. Box 201, Bonanza, OR 97623/503-545-6960 **Specialties:** Plain to fancy working knives of his design or to customer specs. Will work with collectors. **Patterns:** Hunters, skinners, fighters, survival knives, Bowies, boots, fillet knives, axes and miniatures. **Technical:** Flat-grinds mostly by hand 440C, D2, 5160. Uses exotic hardwoods, Micarta and ivory for handles. Bead blasts; uses commercial heat-treater. Makes own sheaths. Scrimshaws and engraves. **Prices:** $50 to $250; miniatures start at $35; collector pieces to $1,200. **Remarks:** Full-time maker; first knife sold in 1987. **Mark:** Name, with dagger in "T."

COBB, LOWELL D., 823 Julia St., Daytona Beach, FL 32114/904-252-3514 **Specialties:** Working straight knives of his design or to customer specs. **Patterns:** Fighters, hunters, skinners, fillet knives and Bowies. **Technical:** Grinds 440C; embellishments available. **Prices:** $100 to $500. **Remarks:** Part-time maker; first knife sold in 1986. **Mark:** Name.

COFER, RON, 2861 Woodruff Dr., Duluth, GA 30136/404-476-5117 **Specialties:** Fancy working and using straight knives of his design. **Patterns:** Hunters, Bowies and fighters. **Technical:** Grinds 440C and ATS-34. Heat-treats. Some knives have carved stag handles or scrimshaw. Makes leather sheath for each knife and walnut and deer antler display stands for art knives. **Prices:** $125 to $250; some to $600. **Remarks:** Spare-time maker; first knife sold in 1991. **Mark:** Name and serial number.

COFFMAN, DANNY, 505 Angel Dr. S., Jacksonville, AL 36265/205-435-5848 **Specialties:** Straight knives and folders of his design. **Patterns:** Hunters, locking and slip-joint folders. **Technical:** Grinds Damascus, 440C and D2. Offers filework and engraving. **Prices:** $100 to $400; some to $800. **Remarks:** Spare-time maker; first knife sold in 1992. Doing business as Customs by Coffman. **Mark:** Last name stamped or engraved.

COHEN, N.J. (NORM), 2408 Sugarcone Rd., Baltimore, MD 21209/410-484-3841 **Specialties:** Working class knives. **Patterns:** Hunters, skinners, bird knives, push daggers, boots, kitchen and practical customer designs. **Technical:** Stock removal 440C, ATS-34. Uses Micarta, Corian. Some woods in handles. **Prices:** $50 to $250. **Remarks:** Part-time maker; first knife sold in 1982. **Mark:** Etched initials or NJC MAKER.

COHEN, TERRY A., P.O. Box 406, Laytonville, CA 95454 **Specialties:** Working straight knives and folders. **Patterns:** Bowies to

boot knives and locking folders; mini-boot knives. **Technical:** Grinds stainless; hand rubs; tries for good balance. **Prices:** $85 to $150; some to $325. **Remarks:** Part-time maker; first knife sold in 1983. **Mark:** TERRY KNIVES, city and state.

COIL, JIMMIE J., 2936 Asbury Pl., Owensboro, KY 42302/502-684-7827 **Specialties:** Traditional working and using straight knives of his design. **Patterns:** Hunters, Bowies and fighters. **Technical:** Grinds 440C, ATS-34 and D2. Blades are flat-ground with brush finish; most have tapered tang. Offers filework. **Prices:** $65 to $250; some to $750. **Remarks:** Spare-time maker; first knife sold in 1974. **Mark:** Name.

COLD SPRINGS FORGE (See Solomon, Marvin)

COLE, WELBORN I., 3284 Inman Dr. NE, Atlanta, GA 30319/404-261-3977 **Specialties:** Traditional straight knives of his design. **Patterns:** Hunters. **Technical:** Grinds 440C, ATS-34 and D2. Good wood scales. **Prices:** NA. **Remarks:** Full-time maker; first knife sold in 1983. **Mark:** Script initials.

COLEMAN, KEITH E., 13 Jardin Rd., Los Lunas, NM 87031/505-864-0024 **Specialties:** Affordable collector-grade straight knives and folders; some fancy. **Patterns:** Fighters, tantos, combat folders, gents folders and boots. **Technical:** Grinds ATS-34 and Damascus. Prefers specialty woods; offers filework. **Prices:** $150 to $700; some to $1,500. **Remarks:** Full-time maker; first knife sold in 1980. **Mark:** Name, city and state.

COLLETT, JERRY D., P.O. Box 296, Charlotte, TX 78011/210-277-1468 **Specialties:** Traditional-style folders. **Patterns:** Mainly slip-joint folders. **Technical:** 440C, ATS-34, D2 anbd 01. Extensive filework offered as standard. **Prices:** $175 to $500. **Remarks:** Full-time maker; first knife sold in 1989. **Mark:** Initials or last name.

COLLINS, A.J., 9651 Elon Ave., Arleta, CA 91331/818-762-7728 **Specialties:** Working dress knives of his design. **Patterns:** Street survival knives, swords, axes. **Technical:** Grinds 01, 440C, 154CM. **Prices:** Start at $100. **Remarks:** Full-time maker; first knife sold in 1972. Doing business as Kustom Krafted Knives—KKK. **Mark:** Name.

COLLINS, HAROLD, 503 First St., West Union, OH 45693/513-544-2982 **Specialties:** Traditional using straight knives and folders of his design or to customer specs. **Patterns:** Hunters, Bowies and locking folders. **Technical:** Forges and grinds 440C, ATS-34, D2, 01 and 5160. Flat-grinds standard; filework available. **Prices:** $75 to $300. **Remarks:** Full-time maker; first knife sold in 1989. **Mark:** First initial, last name, Maker.

COLLINS, LYNN M., 138 Berkley Dr., Elyria, OH 44035/216-366-7101 **Specialties:** Working straight knives. **Patterns:** Field knives, boots and fighters. **Technical:** Grinds D2, 154CM and 440C. **Prices:** Start at $150. **Remarks:** Spare-time maker; first knife sold in 1980. **Mark:** Initials, asterisks.

COMPTON, WILLIAM E., 106 N. Sequoia Ct., Sterling, VA 20164/703-430-2129 **Specialties:** Working straight knives of his design or to customer specs; some fancy knives. **Patterns:** Hunters, camp knives, Bowies and some kitchen knives. **Technical:** Grinds ATS-34, 440C, D2 and 01. **Prices:** $65 to $300; some to $700. **Remarks:** Part-time maker; first knife sold in 1994. Doing business as Comptons Custom Knives. **Mark:** Last name, left side of blade.

CONKEY, TOM, 9122 Keyser Rd., Nokesville, VA 22123/703-791-3867 **Specialties:** Classic straight knives and folders of his design and to customer specs. **Patterns:** Boots, hunters and locking folders. **Technical:** Grinds ATS-34, 01 and commercial Damascus. Lockbacks have jew-

eled scales and locking bars with dovetailed bolsters. Folders utilize unique 2-piece bushing of his design and manufacture. Sheaths are handmade. Presentation boxes made upon request. **Prices:** $100 to $500. **Remarks:** Part-time maker; first knife sold in 1991. Collaborates with Dan Thomas. **Mark:** Last name with "handcrafted" underneath.

CONKLIN, GEORGE L., Box 902, Ft. Benton, MT 59442/406-622-3268; FAX: 406-622-5670
Specialties: Designer and manufacturer of the "Brisket Breaker". **Patterns:** Hunters, utility/camp knives and hatchets. **Technical:** Grinds 440C, ATS-34, D2, 1095, 154CM and 5160. Offers some forging and heat-treats for others. Offers some jeweling. **Prices:** $65 to $200, some to $1,000. **Remarks:** Full-time maker. Doing business as Rocky Mountain Knives. **Mark:** Last name in script.

CONKLIN MEADOWS FORGE (See Little, Gary M.)

CONLEY, BOB, 1013 Creasy Rd., Jonesboro, TN 37659/615-753-3302
Specialties: Working straight knives and folders. **Patterns:** Lockers, two-blades, gents, hunters, traditional styles, straight hunters. **Technical:** Grinds 440C, 154CM and ATS-34. Engraves. **Prices:** $250 to $450; some to $600. **Remarks:** Full-time maker; first knife sold in 1979. **Mark:** Full name, city, state.

CONN JR., C.T., 206 Highland Ave., Attalla, AL 35954/205-538-7688
Specialties: Working folders, some fancy. **Patterns:** Full range of folding knives. **Technical:** Grinds 02, 440C and 154CM. **Prices:** $125 to $300; some to $600. **Remarks:** Part-time maker; first knife sold in 1982. **Mark:** Name.

CONNELL, STEVE, 4204 Denniston Circle, Adamsville, AL 35005/205-674-0440
Specialties: Working and using straight knives, some one-of-a-kind. **Patterns:** Hunters, fighters, Bowies and daggers. **Technical:** Uses 440C, ATS-34, Damascus. Satin finishes. **Prices:** $75 to $500; some to $600. **Remarks:** Part-time maker; first knife sold in 1987. **Mark:** Last name in block lettering.

CONNOLLY, JAMES, P.O. Box 182, Palermo, CA 95968/916-534-5303
Specialties: Classic working and using knives of his design. **Patterns:** Boots, Bowies and daggers. **Technical:** Grinds ATS-34; forges 5160; forges and grinds 01. Engraving by George Sherwood. **Prices:** $100 to $500; some to $1,500. **Remarks:** Full-time maker; first knife sold in 1980. Doing business as Gold Rush Designs. **Mark:** First initial, last name, Handmade.

CONNOR, MICHAEL, Box 502, Winters, TX 79567/915-754-5602
Specialties: High-art straight knives and folders. **Patterns:** Hunters to camp knives to traditional locking folders. **Technical:** Forges 5160, 01 and his own Damascus. **Prices:** $275 to $3,000. **Remarks:** Part-time maker; first knife sold in 1974. **Mark:** Last name, M.S.

CONTI, JEFFREY D., 4629 Feigley Rd. W., Port Orchard, WA 98366/206-405-0075
Specialties: Working straight knives. **Patterns:** Fighters and survival knives; hunters, camp knives and fishing knives. **Technical:** Grinds D2, 154CM and 01. Engraves. **Prices:** Start at $80. **Remarks:** Part-time maker; first knife sold in 1980. **Mark:** Initials, year, steel type, name and number of knife.

COOGAN, ROBERT, 1560 Craft Center Dr., Smithville, TN 37166/615-597-6801
Specialties: One-of-a-kind knives. **Patterns:** Unique items like ooloo-style Appalachian herb knives. **Technical:** Forges; his Damascus is made from nickel steel and W1. **Prices:** Start at $100. **Remarks:** Part-time maker; first knife sold in 1979. **Mark:** Initials.

COOK, JAMES RAY, Rt. 5, Box 218B, Nashville, AR 71852/501-845-5173
Specialties: Working straight knives and folders of his design or to customer specs. **Patterns:** Bowies, hunters and camp knives. **Technical:**

Forges 5160, 01 and Damascus from 01 and 1018. **Prices:** $195 to $2,500. **Remarks:** Part-time maker; first knife sold in 1986. **Mark:** First and middle initials, last name.

COOK, LOUISE, 475 Robinson Ln., Ozark, IL 62972/618-777-2932
Specialties: Working and using straight knives of her design and to customer specs; period pieces. **Patterns:** Bowies, hunters and utility/camp knives. **Technical:** Forges 5160. Filework; pin work; silver wire inlay. **Prices:** Start at $50/inch. **Remarks:** Part-time maker; first knife sold in 1990. Doing business as Panther Creek Forge. **Mark:** First name and journeyman stamp on one side; panther head on the other.

COOK, MIKE, Rt. 1, Box 104, Ozark, IL 62972/618-777-2932
Specialties: Traditional working and using straight knives of his design and to customer specs. **Patterns:** Bowies, hunters and utility/camp knives. **Technical:** Forges 5160. Filework; pin work. **Prices:** Start at $50/inch. **Remarks:** Spare-time maker; first knife sold in 1991. **Mark:** First initial, last name and journeyman stamp on one side; panther head on the other.

COOK, MIKE A., 10927 Shilton Rd., Portland, MI 48875/517-647-2518

COOMBS JR., LAMONT, RFD #1, Box 1412, Bucksport, ME 04416/207-469-3057
Specialties: Classic fancy and embellished straight knives; traditional working and using straight knives. Knives of his design and to customer specs. **Patterns:** Hunters and utility/camp knives. **Technical:** Hollow-grinds ATS-34, 440C and 01; heat-treats. Offers three styles of filework. Handle embellishment available. **Prices:** With sheaths—$65 to $300; some to $1,500. **Remarks:** Part-time maker; first knife sold in 1988. **Mark:** First and middle initials, last name, Handmade with scroll.

COPELAND, GEORGE "STEVE", Star Rt., Box #36, Alpine, TN 38543/615-823-5214
Specialties: Traditional and fancy working straight knives and folders. **Patterns:** Wide range includes tomahawks, butterfly folders, camp knives, slip-joint folders. **Technical:** Grinds variety of steels. **Prices:** $60 to $350; some $1,000 and higher. **Remarks:** Part-time maker; first knife sold in 1979. **Mark:** Four-leaf clover, initials.

COPPERHEAD FORGE (See Black, Scott)

CORBIN KNIVES (See Newcomb, Corbin)

CORBIT, GERALD E. AND PHILIP E., 1701 St. John Rd., Elizabethtown, KY 42701/502-765-7728
Specialties: Fancy and working/using straight knives and folders of all designs. **Patterns:** Daggers, hunters and locking folders. **Technical:** Grinds 440C, ATS-34 and commercial Damascus. Heat treats; offers scrimshaw, engraving and filework on blades and liners. Finishes include polished, satin and bead blasted. **Prices:** $75 to $250; some to $1,000. **Remarks:** Part-time makers; first knife sold in 1991. Doing business as Corbit Custom Knives. **Mark:** Last name.

CORBIT, PHILIP E. (See Corbit, Gerald E. and Philip E.)

CORBY, HAROLD, 218 Brandonwood Dr., Johnson City, TN 37604/615-926-9781
Specialties: Large fighters and Bowies; self-protection knives; art knives. **Patterns:** Sub-hilt fighters and hunters. **Technical:** Grinds 154CM, ATS-34 and 440C. **Prices:** $200 to $6,000. **Remarks:** Full-time maker; first knife sold in 1969. Doing business as Knives by Corby. **Mark:** Last name.

CORDOVA, JOSEPH G., P.O. Box 977, Peralta, NM 87042/505-869-3912
Specialties: One-of-a-kind designs, some to customer specs. **Patterns:** Fighter called the 'Gladiator,' hunters, boots and cutlery. **Technical:** Forges 1095, 5160; grinds ATS-34, 440C and 154CM. **Prices:** Moderate to upscale. **Remarks:** Full-time maker; first knife sold in 1953. **Mark:** Cordova made.

CORKEN KNIVES (See Johnson, Kenneth R.)

CORRADO, JIM, 2915 Cavitt Creek Rd., Glide, OR 97443/503-496-3951; FAX: 503-496-3595
Specialties: High-tech, high-art folding knives. **Patterns:** Makes early European single and multi-blade designs. **Technical:** Forges mostly L6 and his own Damascus. Uses natural handle material; stag, pearl, ivory, and imitation tortoise shell. **Prices:** Start at $250. **Remarks:** Full-time maker; first knife sold in 1974. **Mark:** Name, date and state with shield logo.

CORWIN, DON, 5064 Eber Rd., Monclova, OH 43542/419-877-5210
Specialties: Traditional-style knives to customer specs; miniatures. **Patterns:** One- to five-blade folders, slip-joints and lockers. **Technical:** Grinds 440C, ATS-34, 154CM and Damascus; makes own mokume. **Prices:** $200 to $600. **Remarks:** Part-time maker; first knife sold in 1987. **Mark:** Last name in arrowhead logo and year.

COSBY, E. BLANTON, 2954 Pierpont Ave., Columbus, GA 31904/706-323-0327
Specialties: Traditional working and using straight knives and folders of his design or to customer specs. **Patterns:** Hunters, Bowies, boots and switchblades. Has made a 23-inch hollow-ground machete with handguard. **Technical:** Grinds 440C, 12C27 and commercial Damascus. **Prices:** $125 to $350; some to $550. **Remarks:** Full-time maker; first knife sold in 1988. **Mark:** Engraved initials and year.

COSGROVE, CHARLES G., 2112 Briarwood Dr., Amarillo, TX 79124/806-352-0334
Specialties: Traditional fixed or locking blade working knives. **Patterns:** Hunters, Bowies and locking folders. **Technical:** Stock removal using 440C, ATS-34 and D2; heat-treats. Makes heavy, hand-stitched sheaths. **Prices:** $250 to $2,500. **Remarks:** Full-time maker; first knife sold in 1968. No longer accepting customer designs. **Mark:** First initial, last name, or full name over city and state.

COSTA, SCOTT, Rt. 2, Box 503, Spicewood, TX 78669/210-693-3431
Specialties: Working straight knives. **Patterns:** Hunters, skinners, fillet knives, axes, diver's knives, custom boxed steak knives, carving sets and bar knives. **Technical:** Grinds D2, ATS-34, 440 and Damascus. Heat-treats. **Prices:** $150 to $1,000; some to $2,000. **Remarks:** Full-time maker; first knife sold in 1985. **Mark:** Initials connected.

CÔTÉ, YVES, 1A-788 Philippe, Ste-Foy (Quebec), CANADA G1V 2R1/418-683-3285
Specialties: Classic and fancy knives and miniatures. **Patterns:** Bowies, daggers and swords. **Technical:** Grinds ATS-34 and Damascus. Full-time scrimshander and carver. **Prices:** $50 to $700. **Remarks:** Full-time maker; first knife sold in 1991. **Mark:** First name.

COTTRILL, JAMES I., 1776 Ransburg Ave., Columbus, OH 43223/614-274-0020
Specialties: Working straight knives of his design. **Patterns:** Caters to the boating and hunting crowd. **Technical:** Grinds 01, D2 and 440C. Likes filework. **Prices:** $95 to $250; some to $500. **Remarks:** Full-time maker; first knife sold in 1977. **Mark:** Name, city, state, in oval logo.

COUGHLIN, MICHAEL M., 52 Brittania Dr., Danbury, CT 06810/203-791-8580
Specialties: Edged weapons and fighters. **Patterns:** Bowies, fighters, tomahawks, utility/camp knives, concealment knives, duty knives for police/fire rescue. **Technical:** Grinds 01, D2, ATS-34 and Damascus. Offers filework; Bowies have aged blue/gray finish. **Prices:** $75 to $400; some to $600. **Remarks:** Part-time maker; first knife sold in 1985. **Mark:** Last name and year.

COURTNEY, ELDON, 2718 Bullinger, Wichita, KS 67204/316-838-4053
Specialties: Working straight knives of his design. **Patterns:** Hunters, fighters and one-of-a-kinds. **Technical:** Grinds and tempers L6, 440C and spring steel. **Prices:** $100 to $500; some to $1,500. **Remarks:** Full-time maker; first knife sold in 1977. **Mark:** Full name, city and state.

COURTOIS, BRYAN, 3 Lawn Avenue, Saco, ME 04072
Specialties: Working straight knives; prefers customer designs, no standard patterns. **Patterns:** Functional hunters; everyday knives. **Technical:** Grinds S7, 01, 440C or customer request. Hollow-grinds with a variety of finishes. Specializes in granite handles and custom skeleton knives. **Prices:** Start at $75. **Remarks:** Part-time maker; first knife sold in 1988. Doing business as Castle Knives. **Mark:** A rook chess piece machined into blade using electrical discharge process.

COUSINO, GEORGE, 7818 Norfolk, Onsted, MI 49265/517-467-4911
Specialties: Working straight knives. **Patterns:** Hunters, Bowies, buckskinners and daggers. **Technical:** Grinds D2, 440C. **Prices:** $85 to $125; some to $600. **Remarks:** Part-time maker; first knife sold in 1981. **Mark:** Last name.

COVER, RAYMOND A., Rt. 1, Box 194, Mineral Point, MO 63660/314-749-3783
Specialties: High-tech working straight knives and folders in standard patterns. **Patterns:** Bowies and boots; two-bladed folders. **Technical:** Grinds D2, 440C and 154CM. **Prices:** $135 to $250; some to $400. **Remarks:** Part-time maker; first knife sold in 1974. **Mark:** Name.

COWLES, DON, 1026 Lawndale Dr., Royal Oak, MI 48067/810-541-4619
Specialties: Traditional and working/using straight knives of his design. **Patterns:** Hunters, kitchen knives and utility/camp knives. **Technical:** Grinds 01, 440C and ATS-34. Scrimshaws; pearl inlays in some handles. **Prices:** $75 to $400; some to $750. **Remarks:** Part-time maker; first knife sold in 1994. **Mark:** Full name, city and state with oak leaf.

COX CALL (See Cox, Sam)

COX, COLIN J., 1609 Votaw Rd., Apopka, FL 32703/407-889-7887
Specialties: Working straight knives and folders of his design; period pieces. **Patterns:** Hunters, fighters and survival knives. Folders, two-blades, gents and hunters. **Technical:** Grinds D2, 440C, 154CM and ATS-34. **Prices:** $125 to $750; some to $4,000. **Remarks:** Full-time maker; first knife sold in 1981. **Mark:** Full name, city and state.

COX, SAM, 1756 Love Springs Rd., Gaffney, SC 29341/803-489-1892; FAX: 803-489-0403
Specialties: Classic high-art working straight knives of his design. Duck knives copyrighted. **Patterns:** Hunters, fighters and boots. **Technical:** Grinds 440C, ATS-34 and Damascus. **Prices:** $165 to $550. **Remarks:** Full-time maker; first knife sold in 1983. **Mark:** Cox Call and name.

C.P. KNIFEMAKER (See Pienaar, Conrad)

CRAFT III, JOHN M., Lockett Springs Ranch, P.O. Box 682, Williams, AZ 86046/602-635-2190
Specialties: High-art straight knives to customer specs; period pieces. **Patterns:** Daggers, swords and utility/camp knives. **Technical:** Forges his own Damascus; 440C and ATS-34 by stock removal. **Prices:** $95 to $450; some to $2,500. **Remarks:** Full-time maker; first knife sold in 1985. **Mark:** Runic M in pommel or near butt.

CRAFT, RICHARD C., 3045 Longwood Dr., Jackson, MS 39212/601-373-4046
Specialties: Fancy working knives. **Patterns:** Offers chopping knife and block for kitchen, bird knives and steak knives with presentation case. **Technical:** Grinds 01, L6 and 440C. Cases made of cherry or mahogany. **Prices:** $65 to $275; some to $600. **Remarks:** Full-time maker; first knife sold in 1985. **Mark:** Last name.

CRAIG, ROGER L., 1327 Lane, Topeka, KS 66604/913-233-3845
Specialties: Fantasy and working/using knives of his design. **Patterns:** Fighters, hunters and locking folders. **Technical:** Grinds 01 tool steel and 5160. Offers filework and cowhide sheaths colored to match the knives. **Prices:** $80 to $175; some to $450. **Remarks:** Part-time maker; first knife sold in 1991. Doing business as Craig Knives. **Mark:** Last name, sometimes with a coyote.

CRAIN, JACK W., 400 Walden Rd., Weatherford, TX 76087 **Specialties:** Fantasy and period knives; combat and survival knives. **Patterns:** One-of-a-kind art or fantasy daggers, swords and Bowies; survival knives. **Technical:** Forges Damascus; grinds stainless steel. Carves. **Prices:** $350 to $2,500; some to $20,000. **Remarks:** Full-time maker; first knife sold in 1969. Designer and maker of the knives seen in the films *Demolition Man, Predator I and II, Commando, Die Hard I and II, Road House, Ford Fairlane* and *Action Jackson* and television shows *War of the Worlds, Air Wolf, Kung Fu: The Legend Cont.* and *Tales of the Crypt.* **Mark:** Annual change of registered trademark—stylized crane.

CRAWFORD, LARRY, 1610 Hutto Rd., Georgetown, TX 78626-7310/713-341-5234 **Specialties:** Fancy folding knives in standard patterns. **Patterns:** Locking and slip-joint folders. **Technical:** Forges 1095 and his own Damascus. Prefers exotic woods for handles; makes own mokume. **Prices:** $300 to $500; some to $1,200. **Remarks:** Part-time maker; first knife sold in 1983. Doing business as Brazos Forges. **Mark:** Last name.

CRAWFORD, PAT, 205 N. Center, West Memphis, AR 72301/501-735-4632 **Specialties:** High-tech working straight knives—self-defense and combat types—and folders. **Patterns:** Folding patent locks, interframes, fighters and boots. **Technical:** Grinds 440C, ATS-34, D2 and 154CM. **Prices:** $125 to $2,000. **Remarks:** Full-time maker; first knife sold in 1973. **Mark:** Last name.

CRAWLEY, BRUCE R., 16 Binbrook Dr., Croydon 3136, Victoria, AUSTRALIA **Specialties:** Folders. **Patterns:** Hunters, lockback folders and Bowies. **Technical:** Grinds 440C, ATS34 and commercial Damascus. Offers filework and mirror polish. **Prices:** $160 to $850. **Remarks:** Part-time maker; first knife sold in 1990. **Mark:** Initials.

CREATION YVON VACHON (See Vachon, Yvon)

CRENSHAW, AL, Rt. 1 Box 717, Eufaula, OK 74432/918-452-2128 **Specialties:** Folders of his design and in standard patterns. **Patterns:** Hunters, locking folders and slip-joint folders. **Technical:** Grinds 440C, D2 and ATS-34. Does filework on backsprings and blades; offers scrimshaw on some handles. **Prices:** $175 to $300. **Remarks:** Full-time maker; first knife sold in 1981. Doing business as A. Crenshaw Knives. **Mark:** First initial, last name, Lake Efaula, state stamped; first initial last name in rainbow; Lake Efaula across bottom with Okla. in middle.

CRISP, HAROLD, 3885 Bow St. NE, Cleveland, TN 37312/615-476-8240 **Specialties:** Fancy working straight knives and folders. **Patterns:** Hunters to Bowies, tomahawks to miniatures. Locking folders, interframes and traditional-style knives. **Technical:** Grinds 01, D2 and 440C; forges. **Prices:** $85 to $250; some to $800. **Remarks:** Part-time maker; first knife sold in 1972. **Mark:** Initials or name.

CROCKFORD, JACK, 1859 Harts Mill Rd., Chamblee, GA 30341/404-457-4680 **Specialties:** Lockback folders. **Patterns:** Hunters, fishing and camp knives, traditional folders. **Technical:** Grinds A2, D2, ATS-34 and 440C. Engraves and scrimshands. **Prices:** Start at $175. **Remarks:** Part-time maker; first knife sold in 1975. **Mark:** Name.

CROSS, JOHN M., Rt. 1, Box 351, Bryceville, FL 32009/904-266-9092 **Specialties:** Traditional working and using straight knives of his design or to customer specs. **Patterns:** Hunters, Bowies, utility/camp knives. **Technical:** Forges his own Damascus, 01 and 1095. Prefers natural handle materials, especially buffalo bone. **Prices:** $150 to $350; some up to $750. **Remarks:** Full-time maker; first knife sold in 1985. **Mark:** A cross.

CROSS, ROBERT, RMB 200B, Manilla Rd., Tamworth 2340 NSW, AUSTRALIA/067-618385

CROWDER, ROBERT, Box 1374, Thompson Falls, MT 59873/406-827-4754 **Specialties:** Traditional working knives to customer specs. **Patterns:** Hunters, Bowies, fighters and fillets. **Technical:** Grinds ATS-34, 154CM, 440C, Vascowear and commercial Damascus. **Prices:** $160 to $250; some to $2,500. **Remarks:** Part-time maker; first knife sold in 1985. **Mark:** Name, city and state in logo.

CROWELL, JAMES L., H.C. 74, Box 368, Mtn. View, AR 72560/501-269-4215 **Specialties:** Fancy period pieces and working knives to customer specs. **Patterns:** Hunters to daggers, war hammers to tantos; locking folders and slip-joints. **Technical:** Forges W2, 01 and his own Damascus. **Prices:** $250 to $1,500; some to $4,000. **Remarks:** Full-time maker; first knife sold in 1980. **Mark:** A shooting star.

CULPEPPER, JOHN, 2102 Spencer Ave., Monroe, LA 71201/318-323-3636 **Specialties:** Working straight knives. **Patterns:** Hunters, Bowies and camp knives in heavy-duty patterns. **Technical:** Grinds 01, D2 and 440C; hollow- grinds. **Prices:** $75 to $200; some to $300. **Remarks:** Part-time maker; first knife sold in 1970. Doing business as Pepper Knives. **Mark:** Pepper.

CULVER, STEVE, 1604 Willow, Valley Falls, KS 66088/913-945-3553 **Specialties:** Period pieces and working straight knives. **Patterns:** Hunters, Bowies, daggers. **Technical:** Forges his own Damascus, 01 and 5160. Fancy filework available. **Prices:** $100 to $500; some to $1000. **Remarks:** Full-time maker; first knife sold in 1989. **Mark:** Last name, J.S.

CUMMING, R.J., American Embassy Tunis, U.S. Dept. of State, Washington D.C., 20521-6360/Int'l. direct dial 216-1-741-314 **Specialties:** Custom designs. **Patterns:** Hunters, fighters, Bowies and one-of-a-kind straight knives. Diver's tool knife. **Technical:** Grinds D2, 440C and 154CM. **Prices:** $175 to $550; some to $2,000. **Remarks:** Part-time maker; first knife sold in 1978. **Mark:** Last name.

CUSTOM CUTLERY (See Boeckman, R. Von)

CUTCHIN, ROY D., 960 Hwy. 169 South, Seale, AL 36875/334-855-3080 **Specialties:** Working straight knives and folders of his design, to customer specs and in standard patterns. **Patterns:** Hunters, boots, fighters and locking liner folders. **Technical:** Grinds ATS-34 and Damascus. **Prices:** $125 to $450; some to $700. **Remarks:** Part-time maker. **Mark:** First initial, last name, city and state.

CUTE, THOMAS, RD 4, Rt. 90, Cortland, NY 13045/607-749-4055 **Specialties:** Working straight knives to customer specs. **Patterns:** Hunters, Bowies and fighters. **Technical:** Grinds 01, 440C and ATS-34. **Prices:** $100 to $1,000. **Remarks:** Full-time maker; first knife sold in 1974. **Mark:** Full name.

CYPRESS BEND CUSTOM KNIVES (See Ellerbe, W.B.)

d

DACONCEICAO, JOHN M., 159 Homestead Ave., Rehoboth, MA 02769/508-252-9686 **Specialties:** One-of-a-kind straight knives of his design and to customer specs. **Patterns:** Boots and fighters. **Technical:** Grinds 01, 1095 and commercial Damascus. All knives come with leather sheath; cross-draw and shoulder harnesses available. **Prices:** $90 to $200; some to $500. **Remarks:** Part-time maker; first knife sold in 1993. **Mark:** JMD Blades.

DAHL, CHRIS W., Rt. 4, Box 558, Lake Geneva, WI 53147/414-248-2464 **Specialties:** Period pieces and high-art display knives. **Patterns:** Daggers, fighters and hunters. **Technical:** Grinds 440C and stainless steel

Damascus. Works exclusively with gemstone handles on all daggers. **Prices:** $500 to $5,000; some to $10,000. **Remarks:** Full-time maker. **Mark:** Full name—maker.

DAILEY, G.E., 577 Lincoln St., Seekonk, MA 02771/508-336-5088 **Specialties:** Big working knives and period pieces. **Patterns:** Bowies and swords. **Technical:** Grinds 01 and 440C. **Prices:** $125 to $2,000. **Remarks:** Part-time maker. First knife sold in 1982. Likes broadswords. **Mark:** Signature or initials.

DAKE, C.M., 19759 Chef Menteur Hwy., New Orleans, LA 70129-9602/504-254-0357 **Specialties:** Fancy working folders. **Patterns:** Front-lock lockbacks, button-lock folders. **Technical:** Grinds ATS-34 and 440C. **Prices:** $200 to $850; some higher. **Remarks:** Full-time maker; first knife sold in 1988. Doing business as Bayou Custom Cutlery. **Mark:** Last name.

DAMLOVAC, SAVA, 10292 Bradbury Dr., Indianapolis, IN 42631/317-839-4952 **Specialties:** Working knives, fantasy and period pieces of his design. **Patterns:** Bowies and hunters. **Technical:** Uses Damascus, 440C, ATS-34 and other steels. Offers filework; uses exotic woods and fossilized ivory for handles. **Prices:** $75 to $1000; some higher. **Remarks:** Full-time maker; first knife sold in 1993. **Mark:** First name on top of bowie knife inside a shield with city and state on outside of shield.

D'ANDREA, JOHN, 77 Pinecrest Terrace, Wayne, NJ 07470/201-839-4559 **Specialties:** Fancy working straight knives and folders with filework and distinctive leatherwork. **Patterns:** Hunters, fighters, daggers, folders and an occasional sword. **Technical:** Grinds ATS-34, 154CM, 440C and D2. **Prices:** $180 to $600; some to $1,000. **Remarks:** Part-time maker; first knife sold in 1986. **Mark:** First name, last initial imposed on Samurai sword.

D'ANGELO, LAURENCE, 14703 NE 17th Ave., Vancouver, WA 98686/206-576-0724 **Specialties:** Straight knives of his design. **Patterns:** Bowies, hunters and locking folders. **Technical:** Grinds D2, ATS-34 and 440C. Handmakes all sheaths. **Prices:** $100 to $200. **Remarks:** Full-time maker; first knife sold in 1987. **Mark:** Football logo—first and middle initials, last name, city, state, Maker.

DANIEL, TRAVIS E., 4015 Brownsboro Rd., Winston-Salem, NC 27106/919-759-0640 **Specialties:** Traditional working straight knives of his design or to customer specs. **Patterns:** Hunters, fighters and utility/camp knives. **Technical:** Forges and grinds ATS-34 and his own Damascus. **Prices:** $90 to $1,250; some to $2,000. **Remarks:** Full-time maker; first knife sold in 1976. **Mark:** Carolina Custom Knives.

DANIELS, ALEX, 1416 County Rd. 415, Town Creek, AL 35672/205-685-0943 **Specialties:** Working and using straight knives and folders; period pieces. **Patterns:** Hunters, reproduction Bowies, fishing knives, locking folders and traditional slip-joints. **Technical:** Grinds 440C and ATS-34. **Prices:** $150 to $1,000. **Remarks:** Full-time maker; first knife sold in 1963. **Mark:** First and middle initials, last name, city and state.

DARBY, JED, 7878 E. Co. Rd. 50 N., Greensburg, IN 47240/812-663-2696 **Specialties:** Traditional working/using straight knives of his design and to customer specs. **Patterns:** Bowies, hunters and utility/camp knives. **Technical:** Grinds 440C, ATS-34 and D2. Prefers natural handle materials. **Prices:** $45 to $275; some to $400. **Remarks:** Full-time maker; first knife sold in 1992. Doing business as Darby Knives. **Mark:** Last name.

DARBY, RICK, 4026 Shelbourne, Youngstown, OH 44511/216-793-3805 **Specialties:** Working straight knives. **Patterns:** Boots, fighters and hunters with mirror finish. **Technical:** Grinds 440C and CPM-440V. **Prices:** $90 to $300. **Remarks:** Part-time maker; first knife sold in 1974. **Mark:** First and middle initials, last name.

DAUBERMANN, DESMOND P., Private Bag TO12, Tlokweng, Gaborone, Botswana SOUTH AFRICA **Specialties:** Straight working knives to customer specs and in standard patterns. **Patterns:** Hunters and skinners to Bowies. **Technical:** Hollow-grinds K110 N690 and Bohler steel and forges his Damascus. Handle materials include natural woods, buffalo horn and ivory. Offers presentation cases in stinkwood or oak. **Prices:** $250 to $750. **Remarks:** part-time maker; first knife sol in 1991. **Mark:** Last name and city with dog in oval logo, or initials.

DAVENPORT, JACK, 36842 W. Center Ave., Dade City, FL 33525/904-521-4088 **Specialties:** Titanium linerlock, button release and lockback folders; some straight knives. **Patterns:** Double-ground fighters and skinners. **Technical:** Grinds ATS-34, 52100 and Damascus; handmade titanium screws. Scrimshaws. **Prices:** $250 to $2,500. **Remarks:** Part-time maker; first knife sold in 1986. **Mark:** Last name.

DAVIDSON, EDMUND, Rt. 1, Box 319, Goshen, VA 24439/703-997-5651 **Specialties:** Working straight knives; many integral patterns. **Patterns:** Heavy-duty skinners and camp knives. **Technical:** Grinds A2, ATS-34, S7, 440C, CPM-T-440V. **Prices:** $75 to $1,500. **Remarks:** Full-time maker; first knife sold in 1986. **Mark:** Name in deerhead or motorcycle logo.

DAVIS, BARRY L., 4262 U.S. 20, Castleton, NY 12033/518-477-5036 **Specialties:** Collector-quality and Damascus interframe folders. **Patterns:** Traditional gentlemen's folders. **Technical:** Makes Damascus; uses only natural handle materials. **Prices:** $1,000 to $2,500; some to $6,000. **Remarks:** Part-time maker; first knife sold in 1980. **Mark:** Initials.

DAVIS, CHARLIE, P.O. Box 710806, Santee, CA 92072/619-561-9445 **Specialties:** Fancy and embellished working straight knives of his design. **Patterns:** Hunters, camp and utility knives. **Technical:** Grinds high-carbon files. **Prices:** $20 to $80; some to $150. **Remarks:** Full-time maker; first knife sold in 1980. **Mark:** ANZA U.S.A.

DAVIS, DIXIE, Rt. 3, Clinton, SC 29325/803-833-4964 **Specialties:** Working straight knives; fantasy pieces. **Patterns:** Hunters, fighters and boots. **Technical:** Grinds 440C, 154CM and ATS-34 with mirror finish. **Prices:** $85 to $140; some to $200. **Remarks:** Part-time maker; first knife sold in 1981. **Mark:** First name.

DAVIS, DON, 8415 Coyote Run, Loveland, CO 80537-9665/970-669-9016 **Specialties:** Working straight knives in standard patterns or to customer specs. **Patterns:** Hunters, utility knives, skinners and survival knives. **Technical:** Grinds 440C, ATS-34. **Prices:** $75 to $250. **Remarks:** Full-time maker; first knife sold in 1985. **Mark:** Signature, city and state.

DAVIS, JESSE W., Rt. 1, Box 133C, Sarah, MS 38665/601-382-7332 **Specialties:** Working straight knives and folders in standard patterns and to customer specs. **Patterns:** Tantos, Bowies, locking folders and hunters. **Technical:** Grinds D2, 440C and commercial Damascus. **Prices:** $125 to $300. **Remarks:** Part-time maker; first knife sold in 1977. **Mark:** Name or initials.

DAVIS, KEN, 31 S. Butler Ave. #4, Indianapolis, IN 46219/317-359-2320 days and weekends **Specialties:** Classic working and using straight knives of his design and to customer specs. **Patterns:** Fighters, utility/camp knives, skinners, Bowies, chute knives. **Technical:** Hollow-grinds 440C, ATS-34 and D2; enjoys filework. **Prices:** $75 to $350; some to $500. **Remarks:** Full-time maker; first knife sold in 1985. **Mark:** Name, city in an oval, knife logo in center.

DAVIS, K.M. "TWIG", P.O. Box 267, Monroe, WA 98272/206-794-7274
Specialties: Fancy working straight knives. **Patterns:** Hunters, boots, fishing knives, Bowies and daggers. **Technical:** Grinds ATS-34, D2, 440C. **Prices:** $150 to $450; some to $600. **Remarks:** Part-time maker; first knife sold in 1979. **Mark:** Twig.

DAVIS, LLOYD A., Rt.1 Box 114B, Jim Falls, WI 54748/715-382-5188
Specialties: Traditional working knives and classic straight knives of his design. **Patterns:** Bowies, hunters and swords. **Technical:** Forges 1095, 5160 and L6. Makes own Damascus 1020-5160/L6 or 1095/L6/A203-E. Heat-treats; does file work. Makes hand-stiched tooled leather sheath. **Prices:** $75 to $300; some to $1500. **Remarks:** Full- to Part-time maker; first knife sold in 1992. **Mark:** Year, first and middle initials, last name; year on script L.

DAVIS, TERRY, Box 111, Sumpter, OR 97877/503-894-2307
Specialties: Traditional and contemporary folders. **Patterns:** Multi-blade folders, whittlers and interframe multiblades; sunfish patterns. **Technical:** Flat-grinds ATS-34. **Prices:** $400 to $700; some higher. **Remarks:** Full-time maker; first knife sold in 1985. **Mark:** Name in logo.

DAVIS, VERNON M., 1226 LaClede, Waco, TX 76705/817-799-7671
Specialties: Presentation-grade straight knives. **Patterns:** Bowies, daggers, boots, fighers, hunters and utility knives. **Technical:** Hollow-grinds 440C, ATS-34 and D2. Grinds an aesthetic grind line near choil. **Prices:** $125 to $550; some to $5,000. **Remarks:** Part-time maker; first knife sold in 1980. **Mark:** Last name and city inside outline of state.

DAVIS, W.C., 2010 S. Madison, Raymore, MO 64083/816-331-4491
Specialties: Fancy working straight knives and folders. **Patterns:** Folding lockers and slip-joints; straight hunters, fighters and Bowies. **Technical:** Grinds 440C, A2, ATS-34. **Prices:** $80 to $200; some to $1,000. **Remarks:** Full-time maker; first knife sold in 1972. **Mark:** Name.

DAWSON, BARRY, 10A Town Plaza, Suite 303, Durango, CO 81301
Specialties: Samurai swords, combat knives, collector daggers, folding knives and hunting knives. **Patterns:** Offers over 60 different models. **Technical:** Grinds 440C; heat-treats. **Prices:** $75 to $1,500; some to $5,000. **Remarks:** Full-time maker; first knife sold in 1975. **Mark:** Last name, USA in print or last name in script.

DAYNIA FORGE (See Saindon, R. Bill)

DE CARVALHO, HENRIQUE M. (See Neto Jr., Nelson and de Carvalho, Henrique M.)

DEAN, HARVEY J., Rt. 2, Box 137, Rockdale, TX 76567/512-446-3111
Specialties: Collectible, functional knives. **Patterns:** Bowies, hunters, folders, daggers, swords, battle axes, camp and combat knives. **Technical:** Forges 1095, 01 and his Damascus. **Prices:** $195 to $4,000. **Remarks:** Full-time maker; first knife sold in 1981. **Mark:** Last name and MS.

DEARING, JOHN, 1569 Flucom Rd., DeSoto, MO 63020/314-586-1772
Specialties: Traditional working and using straight knives of his design; period pieces and fancy/embellished straight knives. **Patterns:** Hunters, Bowies, fighters, skinners, utility/camp knives and buckskinner blades. **Technical:** Forges and grinds 5160, 154CM and his own Damascus. Prefers natural handle materials. **Prices:** $85 to $350. **Remarks:** Part-time maker; first knife sold in 1985. Doing business as Arc Mountain Forge. **Mark:** Initials stylized into a deer hoofprint.

DeBRAGA, JOSE C., 1519 Du Grand Bourg, Val Belair, Queb. G3J 1K4, CANADA/418-847-7855
Specialties: Art knives, fantasy pieces and working knives of his design or to customer specs. **Patterns:** Knives with sculptured or carved handles, from miniatures to full-size working knives. **Technical:** Grinds and hand-files 440C and ATS-34. A variety of steels and handle materials available. Offers lost wax casting. **Prices:** Start at $300. **Remarks:** Full-time maker; wax modeler, sculptor and knifemaker; first knife sold in 1984. **Mark:** Initials in stylized script and serial number.

DEER (See Laughlin, Don)

DEER CREEK FORGE (See Quarton, Barr)

DEFEO, ROBERT A., 403 Lost Trail Dr., Henderson, NV 89014/702-434-3717
Specialties: Working straight knives and period pieces. **Patterns:** Hunters, fighters, daggers and Bowies. **Technical:** Grinds D2, 440C and ATS-34. **Prices:** $150 to $500; some higher. **Remarks:** Part-time maker; first knife sold in 1982. **Mark:** Last name.

DEFREEST, WILLIAM G., P.O. Box 573, Barnwell, SC 29812/803-259-7883
Specialties: Working straight knives and folders. **Patterns:** Fighters, hunters and boots; locking folders and slip-joints. **Technical:** Grinds 440C, 154CM and ATS-34; clean lines and mirror finishes. **Prices:** $100 to $700. **Remarks:** Full-time maker; first knife sold in 1974. **Mark:** GORDON.

DeGRAEVE, RICHARD, 329 Valencia St., Sebastian, FL 32958/407-589-9005
Specialties: Working straight knives of his design or to customer specs. **Patterns:** Hunters and skinners with or without gut hooks, fillets, fighters, folders, skeleton knives, mini and art knives. **Technical:** Forges and grinds 440C, ATS-34, 01, high carbon steels; scrimshaws; enjoys filework. **Prices:** $55 to $400. **Remarks:** Full-time maker; first knife sold in 1985. **Mark:** Rich

DELLANA (See Warren, Dellana)

DeLONG, DICK, 17561 E. Ohio Circle, Aurora, CO 80017/303-745-2652
Specialties: Fancy working knives and fantasy pieces. **Patterns:** Hunters and small skinners. **Technical:** Grinds and files 01, D2, 440C and Damascus. Offers cocobolo and osage orange for handles. **Prices:** Start at $50. **Remarks:** Part-time maker. **Mark:** Last name; some unmarked.

DEMPSEY, GORDON S., P.O. Box 7497, N. Kenai, AK 99635/907-776-8425
Specialties: Working straight knives and folders. **Patterns:** Hunters, ooloos, harpoons. **Technical:** Forges 01. **Prices:** $80 to $250. **Remarks:** Part-time maker; first knife sold in 1974. **Mark:** Name, city and state.

DENNEHY, DAN, P.O. Box 2F, Del Norte, CO 81132/719-657-2545
Specialties: Working knives, fighting and military knives, throwing knives. **Patterns:** Full range of straight knives, tomahawks, buckle knives. **Technical:** Forges and grinds A2, 01 and D2. **Prices:** $50 to $110. **Remarks:** Full-time maker; first knife sold in 1942. **Mark:** First name and last initial, city, state and shamrock.

DENT, DOUGLAS M., 1208 Chestnut St., S. Charleston, WV 25309/304-768-3308
Specialties: Straight and folding sportsman's knives. **Patterns:** Hunters, boots and Bowies, interframe folders. **Technical:** Forges and grinds D2, 440C, 154CM and plain tool steels. **Prices:** $70 to $300; exceptional knives to $800. **Remarks:** Part-time maker; first knife sold in 1969. **Mark:** Last name.

DERINGER, CHRISTOPH, 207 St. Joseph, Pike River, Que. CANADA J0J 1P0/514-248-7426
Specialties: Traditional working and using straight knives of his design and to customer specs. **Patterns:** Boots, hunters, kitchen knives and utility/camp knives. **Technical:** Forges 5760, 01 and Damascus. Offers a variety of filework. **Prices:** $100 to $250; some to $750. **Remarks:** Part-time maker; first knife sold in 1989. **Mark:** Last name stamped/engraved.

DETMER, PHILLIP, 14140 Bluff Rd., Breese, IL 62230/618-526-4834 **Specialties:** Working knives. **Patterns:** Bowies, daggers and hunters. **Technical:** Grinds ATS-34 and D2. **Prices:** $60 to $400. **Remarks:** Part-time maker; first knife sold in 1977. **Mark:** Last name with dagger.

DeYONG, CLARENCE, 4140 Cripple Creek Way, Kennesaw, GA 30144-2165/404-928-8051 **Specialties:** Working and using straight knives of his design and to customer specs. **Patterns:** Hunters, fighters and boots. **Technical:** Grinds 440C, D2, ATS-34. Son Brian does scrimshaw, filework. **Prices:** $75 to $150; some to $400. **Remarks:** Part-time maker; first knife sold in 1981. **Mark:** Last name and serial number.

D'HOLDER (See Holder, D'Alton)

DICKISON, SCOTT S., 39 Bay View Ave., Portsmouth, RI 02871/401-683-7439 **Specialties:** Working and using straight knives and locking folders of his design. **Patterns:** Trout knives, fishing and hunting knives. **Technical:** Forges and grinds commercial Damascus and D2, 01. Uses natural handle materials. **Prices:** $200 to $600; some higher. **Remarks:** Part-time maker; first knife sold in 1989. **Mark:** Stylized initials.

DIETZEL, BILL, P.O. Box 1613, Middleburg, FL 32068/904-282-1091 **Specialties:** Forged straight knives and folders. **Patterns:** His interpretations. **Technical:** Forges his Damascus and other steels. **Prices:** Middle ranges. **Remarks:** Likes natural materials; uses titanium in folder liners. **Mark:** Name.

DIGANGI, JOSEPH M., Box 225, Santa Cruz, NM 87567/505-753-6414 **Specialties:** Kitchen and table cutlery. **Patterns:** French chef's knives, carving sets, steak knife sets, some camp knives and hunters. Holds patents and trademarks for "System II" kitchen cutlery set. **Technical:** Grinds 440C; buys Damascus. **Prices:** $150 to $450; some to $1,000. **Remarks:** Full-time maker; first knife sold in 1983. **Mark:** Last name.

DILL, DAVE, 7404 NW 30th St., Bethany, OK 73008/405-789-0750 **Specialties:** Folders of his design. **Patterns:** Various patterns. **Technical:** Hand-grinds 440C, ATS-34 and D2. Engraves and does filework on all folders. **Prices:** $275 to $600. **Remarks:** Part-time maker; first knife sold in 1987. **Mark:** First initial, last name.

DILL, ROBERT, 1812 Van Buren, Loveland, CO 80538/303-667-5144; FAX: 303-667-5144 **Specialties:** Fancy and working knives of his design. **Patterns:** Hunters, Bowies and fighters. **Technical:** Grinds 440C and D2. Handles carved by Jim Anderson. **Prices:** $100 to $800. **Remarks:** Full-time maker; first knife sold in 1984. **Mark:** Logo stamped into blade.

DILLON, EARL E., 8908 Stanwin Ave., Arleta, CA 91331 **Specialties:** Fancy straight knives and folders. **Patterns:** Contemporary interpretations. **Technical:** Grinds 440C and AEB. **Prices:** $250 to $350; some over $500. **Remarks:** Part-time maker; first knife sold in 1984. Collaborates with Chuck Stapel. **Mark:** STAPEL-DILLON.

DILLUVIO, FRANK J., 13611 Joyce, Warren, MI 48093/810-775-1216 **Specialties:** Traditional working straight knives, some high-tech. **Patterns:** Hunters, Bowies, fishing knives, sub-hilts and miniatures. **Technical:** Grinds D2, 440C, CPM; works for precision fits—no solder. **Prices:** $95 to $450; some to $800. **Remarks:** Part-time maker; first knife sold in 1984. **Mark:** Name and state.

DINGMAN, SCOTT, 4298 Parkers Lake Rd., NE, Bemidji, MN 56601/218-751-6908 **Specialties:** Fancy working knives of his design. **Patterns:** Hunters, daggers, boots and camp knives. **Technical:** Forges 01, L6 and wire Damascus. Provides lost wax casting and hard cast bronze. Prefers exotic woods and high mirror finishes. **Prices:** $150 to $225; some to $500. **Remarks:** Full-time maker; first knife sold in 1983. **Mark:** Last name.

DION, GREG, 3032 S. Jackson St., Oxnard, CA 93033/805-483-1781 (evenings) **Specialties:** Working straight knives, some fancy. Welcomes special orders. **Patterns:** Hunters, fighters, camp knives, Bowies and tantos. **Technical:** Grinds ATS-34, 154CM and 440C. **Prices:** $85 to $300; some to $600. **Remarks:** Part-time maker; first knife sold in 1985. **Mark:** Name.

DIPPOLD, A.W., RFD 3, Box 162A, Perryville, MO 63775/314-547-1119 **Specialties:** Working knives and embellished folders; one-of-a-kind mosaics. **Patterns:** Hunters, boots, fighters and folders. **Technical:** Forges and grinds own Damascus/Mosaic and carbon steels. Offers filework. **Prices:** $100 to $1,000; some higher. **Remarks:** Full-time maker; first knife sold in 1980. **Mark:** Last name in logo and mosaic blades/weeping heart.

DIXON JR., IRA E., P.O. Box 2581, Ventura, CA 93002-2581 **Specialties:** Traditional working straight knives of his design. **Patterns:** Fighters, hunters, boot knives, utility knives. **Technical:** Forges and grinds 440C, ATS34 and 5160. **Prices:** $140 to $350. **Remarks:** Part-time maker; first knife sold in 1993. **Mark:** First name, Handmade.

DOC HAGEN (See Hagen, Phillip L.)

DOG KNIVES (See Dugger, Dave)

DOLAN, ROBERT L., 220—B Naalae Road, Kula, HI 96790/808-878-6406 **Specialties:** Working straight knives in standard patterns, his designs or to customer specs. **Patterns:** Fixed blades and potter's tools, ceramic saws. **Technical:** Grinds 01, D2, 440C and ATS-34. Heat-treats and engraves. **Prices:** Start at $75. **Remarks:** Full-time tool and knifemaker; first knife sold in 1985. **Mark:** Last name, USA.

DOMINY, CHUCK, P.O. Box 593, Colleyville, TX 76034/817-498-4527 **Specialties:** Traditional working and using straight knives of his design. **Patterns:** Hunters and utility/camp knives. **Technical:** Grinds 440C; heat-treats. **Prices:** $60 to $200; some to $600. **Remarks:** Full-time mkaer; first knife sold in 1976. **Mark:** Last name.

DONOVAN, PATRICK, 1770 Hudson Dr., San Jose, CA 95124/408-267-9825 **Specialties:** Working straight knives and folders; period pieces. **Patterns:** Hunters, boots and daggers; lockers and slip-joints. **Technical:** Grinds 440C. Embellishes. **Prices:** $75 to $475; some to $1,200. **Remarks:** Full-time maker; first knife sold in 1980. **Mark:** First name.

DOOLITTLE, MIKE, 13 Denise Ct., Novato, CA 94947/415-897-3246 **Specialties:** Working straight knives in standard patterns. **Patterns:** Hunters and fishing knives. **Technical:** Grinds 440C, 154CM and ATS-34. **Prices:** $125 to $200; some to $750. **Remarks:** Part-time maker; first knife sold in 1981. **Mark:** Name, city and state.

DOUGLAS, DALE, 361 Mike Cooper Rd., Ponchatoula, LA 70454/504-345-6169 **Specialties:** Working straight knives and folders. **Patterns:** Locking folders and slip-joints; hunters, boots and camp knives. **Technical:** Grinds D2, 440C and 154CM. **Prices:** $75 to $150; some to $350. **Remarks:** Spare-time maker; first knife sold in 1980. **Mark:** Name.

DOUGLAS, JOHN J., Rt. 1, Box 379, Lynch Station, VA 24571/804-369-7196 **Specialties:** Fancy and traditional straight knives and folders of his design and to customer specs. **Patterns:** Locking folders, swords and sgian dubhs. **Technical:** Grinds 440C stainless, ATS-34 stainless and customer's choice. Offers newly designed non-pivot unilock folders. Prefers highly polished finish. **Prices:** $160 to $1,400. **Remarks:** Full-time maker; first knife sold in 1975. Doing business as Douglas Keltic. **Mark:** Stylized initial. Folders are numbered; customs are dated.

DOUGLAS KELTIC (See Douglas, John J.)

DOURSIN, GERARD, Chemin des Croutoules, F 84210 Pernes les Fontaines, FRANCE
Specialties: Period pieces. **Patterns:** Liner locks and daggers. **Technical:** Forges mosaic Damascus. **Prices:** $600 to $4,000. **Remarks:** First knife sold in 1983. **Mark:** First initial, last name and I stop the lion.

DOUSSOT, LAURENT, 4673 Cartier, Montreal, Quebec, CANADA H2H 1W9/514-523-3531; FAX: 514-722-1641
Specialties: Art knives; folders with "apparant lock bar,"; miniatures. **Patterns:** Utility knives, fighters and working straight knives and folders of his design or to customer specs. **Technical:** Grinds and hand files ATS-34, 01, commercial Damascus. Variety of handle materials offered from ivory to anodized titanium. **Prices:** Start at $300; miniatures start at $100. **Remarks:** Part-time maker; first knife sold in 1992. **Mark:** Engraves logo with initials.

DOVE KNIVES (See Rollert, Steve)

DOWELL, T.M., 139 NW St. Helen's Pl., Bend, OR 97701/503-382-8924
Specialties: Integral construction in hunting knives and period pieces. Famous "Funny" folders. **Patterns:** Hunters to sword canes, Price-style daggers to axes. **Technical:** Forges 1060, 5160 and 1095. Grinds BG42, D2, 440C and 154CM. Makes his own bright Damascus. **Prices:** $185 to $1,050. **Remarks:** Full-time maker; first knife sold in 1967. **Mark:** Initials logo.

DOWNIE, JAMES T., RR #1, Port Franks, Ont. NOM 2LO, CANADA/519-243-2290
Specialties: Serviceable straight knives and folders; period pieces. **Patterns:** Hunters, Bowies, camp knives and miniatures. **Technical:** Grinds D2, 440C and ATS-34. **Prices:** $100 to $500; some higher. **Remarks:** Part-time maker; first knife sold in 1978. **Mark:** Signature of first and middle initials, last name.

DOWNING, LARRY, Route 1, Box 387, Bremen, KY 42325/502-525-3523; FAX: 502-525-3372
Specialties: Working straight knives and folders. **Patterns:** From mini-knives to daggers, folding lockers to interframes. **Technical:** Forges and grinds 154CM, ATS-34 and his own Damascus. **Prices:** $150 to $750; some higher. **Remarks:** Part-time maker; first knife sold in 1979. **Mark:** Name in arrowhead.

DOWNING, TOM, 129 S. Bank St., Cortland, OH 44410/216-637-0623
Specialties: Working straight knives; period pieces. **Patterns:** Hunters, fighters and tantos. **Technical:** Grinds 440C, ATS-34 and CPM440V. Prefers natural handle materials. **Prices:** $100 to $400; some to $1,500. **Remarks:** Part-time maker; first knife sold in 1979. **Mark:** First and middle initials, last name.

DOWNS, JAMES F., 35 Sunset Rd., Londonderry, OH 45647/614-887-2099
Specialties: Working straight knives of his design or to customer specs. **Patterns:** Hunting and utility knives, some boots. **Technical:** Grinds 440C. Prefers stag, jigged bone, Micarta and stabilized woods. **Prices:** $68 to $900. **Remarks:** Part-time maker; first knife sold in 1981. **Mark:** Last name.

DOZIER, ROBERT LEE, P.O. Box 1941, Springdale, AR 72765/501-756-0023
Specialties: Using knives. **Patterns:** Some fine collector-grade knives. **Technical:** Uses D2. Prefers Micarta handle material. **Prices:** $75 to $300. **Remarks:** Full-time maker; first knife sold in 1961. **Mark:** State, made, last name in a circle.

DRAGONFLY FORGE (See Bell, Michael)

DRAGON STEEL (See Lewis, Mike)

DRAPER, AUDRA (SHARP), 923 E. Jackson, Riverton, WY 82501/307-856-6807; 307-857-2082
Specialties: Using and individual straight knives. **Patterns:** Hunters and camp knives. **Technical:** Forges 5160 and 52100; heat-treats and freeze-treats upon request. Prefers natural wood and horn handle material; makes hand-stiched, waxed, harness leather sheaths. **Prices:** $100 and up. **Remarks:** Part-time maker; first knife sold in 1995. **Mark:** First name.

DRAPER, BART, 8021 W. Coolidge St., Phoenix, AZ 85033/602-846-0801
Specialties: Classic knives, traditional working knives, fantasy and high-art knives and period pieces. All straight knives of his design and to customer specs. **Patterns:** Boots, Bowies, daggers, fighters, hunters, kitchen knives and utility knives. **Technical:** Grinds ATS-34, 440C and CPM T 440V. Heat-treats. **Prices:** $175 to $725; some to $3,500. **Remarks:** Part-time maker; first knife sold in 1966. **Mark:** First initial, last name and state.

DRAPER, KENT, 23461 Highway 36, Cheshire, OR 97419/503-998-2448
Specialties: Art knives, historical and period pieces of his design. **Patterns:** Hunters, combat fighters, folding knives and swords. **Technical:** Grinds 440C and ATS-34. Heat-treats, engraves and inlays. **Prices:** $100 to $5,000; some esoteric pieces to $10,000. **Remarks:** First knife sold in 1973. **Mark:** First initial, last name, state.

DRISCOLL, MARK, 4115 Avoyer Pl., La Mesa, CA 91941/619-670-0645; FAX: 619-562-2341
Specialties: Straight high art, period pieces and working/using knives of his design or to customer specs; some fancy. **Patterns:** Boots, Bowies, fighters and hunters. **Technical:** Forges 52100, 5160 and his own Damascus; casts own mokume. Uses exotic hardwoods, ivory and horn; scrimshaws. **Prices:** $150 to $550; some to $1,500. **Remarks:** Part-time maker; first knife sold in 1986. Doing business as Mountain Man Knives. **Mark:** Double M.

DRISKILL, BERYL, P.O. Box 187, Braggadocio, MO 63826/314-757-6262
Specialties: Fancy working knives. **Patterns:** Hunting knives, fighters, Bowies, boots, daggers and lockback folders. **Technical:** Grinds 440C, ATS-34, 154CM. **Prices:** $150 to $350; some to $4,000. **Remarks:** Part-time maker; first knife sold in 1984. **Mark:** Name.

DR KNIVES (See Raymond, Donald)

DROST, JASON D., Rt.2 Box 49, French Creek, WV 26218/304-472-7901
Specialties: Working/using straight knives of his design. **Patterns:** Hunters and utility/camp knives. **Technical:** Grinds 154 CM and D2. **Prices:** $75 to $200. **Remarks:** Spare-time maker; first knife sold in 1995. **Mark:** First and middle initials, last name, maker, city and state.

DROST, MICHAEL B., Rt. 2, Box 49, French Creek, WV 26218/304-472-7901
Specialties: Working/using straight knives and folders of all designs. **Patterns:** Hunters, locking folders and utility/camp knives. **Technical:** Grinds ATS-34, D2 and CPM T440V. Offers dove-tailed bolsters and spacers, filework and scrimshaw. **Prices:** $125 to $400; some to $740. **Remarks:** Full-time maker; first knife sold in 1990. Doing business as Drost Custom Knives. **Mark:** Name, city and state.

DUBE, PAUL, P.O. Box 216, Chaska, MN 55318/612-566-9097
Specialties: Traditional working and using straight knives, high-art knives and period pieces of his design and to customer specs. **Patterns:** Fighters, Bowies, daggers, utility knives. **Technical:** Forges A2, 1050, 1095, S5, ATS-34; stock removal 01, S7 and Vascowear. **Prices:** $80 to $1,500; some to $6,000. **Remarks:** Full-time maker; first knife sold in 1988. Doing business as Troll Hammer Forge. **Mark:** Varies.

DUBLIN, DENNIS, 708 Stanley St., Box 986, Enderby, BC VOE 1V0, CANADA/604-838-6753

Specialties: Working straight knives and folders, plain or fancy. **Patterns:** Hunters and Bowies, locking hunters, combination knives/axes. **Technical:** Forges and grinds high carbon steels. **Prices:** $100 to $400; some higher. **Remarks:** Full-time maker; first knife sold in 1970. **Mark:** Name.

DUFF, BILL, P.O. Box 694, Virginia City, NV 89440/702-847-0566
Specialties: Working straight knives and folders. **Patterns:** Hunters and Bowies; locking folders and interframes. **Technical:** Grinds D2, 440C and 154CM. **Prices:** $175 to $3,500. **Remarks:** Part-time maker; first knife sold in 1976. **Mark:** Name, city, state and date.

DUFOUR, ARTHUR J., 8120 De Armoun Rd., Anchorage, AK 99516/907-345-1701
Specialties: Working straight knives from standard patterns. **Patterns:** Hunters, Bowies, camp and fishing knives—grinded thin and pointed. **Technical:** Grinds 440C, ATS-34, AEB-L. Tempers 57-58R; hollow-grinds. **Prices:** $135; some to $250. **Remarks:** Part-time maker; first knife sold in 1970. **Mark:** Prospector logo.

DUGGER, DAVE, 2504 West 51, Westwood, KS 66205/913-831-2382
Specialties: Working straight knives; fantasy pieces. **Patterns:** Hunters, boots and daggers in one-of-a-kind styles. **Technical:** Grinds D2, 440C and 154CM. **Prices:** $75 to $350; some to $1,200. **Remarks:** Part-time maker; first knife sold in 1979. Not currently accepting orders. Doing business as Dog Knives. **Mark:** DOG.

DUNGY HANDCRAFTED (See Dungy, Lawrence)

DUNGY, LAWRENCE, 8 Southmont Dr., Little Rock, AR 72209/501-568-2769
Specialties: Working straight knives and folders. **Patterns:** Bowies, skinners, hunters, boots, bird and trout knives. **Technical:** Grinds stainless and plain steels. **Prices:** $65 to $800. **Remarks:** Part-time maker; first knife sold in 1983. **Mark:** Dungy Handcrafted.

DUNKERLEY, RICK, Baldy Mtn. Ranch, Lincoln, MT 59639/406-362-4942
Specialties: Hand-forged working knives. **Patterns:** Hunters, skinners, camp knives, fighters and Bowies. **Technical:** Forges 5160 and 52100; makes his Damascus, cable Damascus and chain Damascus. Natural handle materials. **Prices:** Start at $150. **Remarks:** Full-time maker; first knife sold in 1984. **Mark:** Last name.

DUNN, CHARLES K., 17740 GA Hwy. 116, Shiloh, GA 31826/706-846-2666
Specialties: Fancy and working straight knives and folders of his design and to customer specs. **Patterns:** Bowies, hunters and locking folders. **Technical:** Grinds 440C and ATS34. Engraves; filework offered. **Prices:** $75 to $300. **Remarks:** Part-time maker; first knife sold in 1988. **Mark:** First initial, last name, city, state.

DUNN, MELVIN T., 5830 NW Carlson Rd., Rossville, KS 66533/913-584-6856
Specialties: Traditional working straight knives and folders. **Patterns:** Locking folders, straight hunters, fishing and kitchen knives. **Technical:** Grinds D2, 440V, 440C and 154CM; likes latest materials; heat-treats. **Prices:** $60 to $500. **Remarks:** Full-time maker; first knife sold in 1972. **Mark:** Name in script.

DUNN, STEVE, 376 Biggerstaff Rd., Smiths Grove, KY 42171/502-563-9830
Specialties: Working and using straight knives of his design; period pieces. **Patterns:** Bowies, fighters and utility/camp knives. **Technical:** Forges his Damascus, 01, 5160, L6 and 1095. **Prices:** Moderate to upscale. **Remarks:** Spare-time maker; first knife sold in 1990. **Mark:** Last name and MS.

DURAN, JERRY T., P.O. Box 80692, Albuquerque, NM 87198-0692/505-255-4255
Specialties: Working straight knives, folders and art knives. **Patterns:** Hunters, skinners, bird and trout knives, fighters. **Technical:** Grinds

440C, ATS-34. Prefers natural handle materials. **Prices:** $125 to $500; some higher. **Remarks:** Paret-time maker; influenced by Joeseph G. Cordova. **Mark:** Initials in elk rack logo.

DURIO, FRED, 289 Gulino St., Opelousas, LA 70570/318-948-4831
Specialties: Working straight knives; period pieces. **Patterns:** Bowies, camp knives, small hunters, fancy period pieces, miniatures. **Technical:** Forges and grinds W2, 5160, 1095 and 01. Makes own Damascus and forge-welds cable Damascus. Offers filework and tapered tangs; prefers exotic and natural materials. **Prices:** $100 to $350; some to $1,000. **Remarks:** Part-time maker; first knife sold in 1986. **Mark:** Last name and J.S.

DUTCH CREEK FORGE & FOUNDRY (See Knickmeyer, Hank)

DUTTON MOUNTAIN FORGE (See Anders, David)

DUVALL, FRED, 10715 Hwy. 190, Benton, AR 72015/501-778-9360
Specialties: Working straight knives and folders. **Patterns:** Locking folders, slip joints, hunters, fighters and Bowies. **Technical:** Grinds D2 and CPM 440V; forges 5160. **Prices:** $100 to $400; some to $800. **Remarks:** Part-time maker; first knife sold in 1973. **Mark:** Last name.

DUVALL, LARRY E., Rt. 3, Gallatin, MO 64640/816-663-2742
Specialties: Fancy working straight knives and folders. **Patterns:** Hunters to swords, minis to Bowies; locking folders. **Technical:** Grinds D2, 440C and 154CM. **Prices:** $150 to $350; some to $2,000. **Remarks:** Part-time maker; first knife sold in 1980. **Mark:** Name and address in logo.

DYESS, EDDIE, 1005 Hamilton, Roswell, NM 88201/505-623-5599
Specialties: Working and using straight knives in standard patterns. **Patterns:** Hunters and fighters. **Technical:** Grinds 440C, 154CM and D2 on request. **Prices:** $85 to $135; some to $250. **Remarks:** Spare-time maker; first knife sold in 1980. **Mark:** Last name.

DYRNOE, PER, Sydskraenten 10, Tulstrup, DK 3400 Hilleroed, DEN-MARK/+45 42287041
Specialties: Hand-crafted knives with zirconia ceramic blades. **Patterns:** Hunters, skinners, Norwegian-style tolleknives, most in animal-like ergonomic shapes. **Technical:** Handles of exotic hardwood, horn, fossile ivory, etc. Norwegian-style sheaths. **Prices:** Start at $500. **Remarks:** Part-time maker in cooperation with Hans J. Henriksen; first knife sold in 1993. **Mark:** Initial logo.

E&E EMPORIUM (See Edwards, Lynn)

EAKER, ALLEN, 416 Clinton Ave., Dept KI, Paris, IL 61944/217-466-5160

EASLER, PAULA, P.O. Box 301-1025, Cross Anchor Rd., Woodruff, SC 29388/803-476-7830; FAx: 803-476-3940
Specialties: Traditional fancy and embellished straight knives of her design. **Patterns:** Miniatures only—hunters, fighters, tantos, razors and mini-replicas. **Technical:** Grinds ATS-34, commercial Damascus. Stainless steel pins and bolsters. Heat-treats blades, many have file-worked tapered tangs; hand-rubbed satin finish standard; natural handle materials and gems. **Prices:** $85 to $400; some to $1,000. **Remarks:** Spare-time maker; first knife sold in 1989. **Mark:** First initial, last name in block letters.

EASLER JR., RUSSELL O., P.O. Box 301, Woodruff, SC 29388/803-476-7830; FAX: 803-476-3940
Specialties: Working straight knives and folders. **Patterns:** Hunters, tantos and boots; locking folders and interframes. **Technical:** Grinds 440C, 154CM and ATS-34. **Prices:** $85 to $250; some to $600. **Remarks:** Part-time maker; first knife sold in 1973. **Mark:** Name or name with bear logo.

EATON, AL, P.O. Box 43, Clayton, CA 94517/510-672-5351 **Specialties:** One-of-a-kind high-art knives and fantasy knives of his design, full size and miniature. **Patterns:** Hunters, fighters, daggers. **Technical:** Grinds 440C, 154CM and ATS-34; ivory and metal carving. **Prices:** $125 to $3,000; some to $5,000. **Remarks:** Full-time maker; first knife sold in 1977. **Mark:** Full name, city and state.

EATON, RICK, 5560 Forbestown Rd., Forbestown, CA 95941/916-675-1632 **Specialties:** Straight and folding art daggers. **Patterns:** Bowies, daggers, fighters and hunters. **Technical:** Grinds 154CM, ATS-34, 440C and other maker's Damascus. Offers high-quality hand engraving, Bulino and gold inlay. **Prices:** $250 to $4,000; some higher. **Remarks:** Full-time maker; first knife sold in 1982. **Mark:** Full name and address.

ECK, LARRY A., P.O. Box 665, Terrebonne, OR 97760/503-548-7599 **Specialties:** Traditional working and using straight knives of his design, to customer specs and in standard patterns. **Patterns:** Boots, Bowies, fighters, hunters, fillets and tantos. **Technical:** Grinds ATS-34, D2, 440C and commercial Damascus. Prefers natural handle materials. Offers mirror and hand-rubbed finishes. **Prices:** $145 to $350; some to $750. **Remarks:** Part-time maker; first knife sold in 1991. **Mark:** First and middle initials, last name and state in logo.

EDGE, TOMMY, P.O. Box 156, Cash, AR 72421/501-477-5210

EDGEWISE KNIVES (See Lott, David)

EDWARDS, FAIN E., 209 E. Mtn. Ave., Jacksonville, AL 36265/205-435-4994; FAX: 205-435-8499 **Specialties:** Classic and traditional knives, working/using knives and period pieces. **Patterns:** Bowies, daggers, hunters, kitchen knives, locking and slip-joint folders, swords and utility/camp knives. **Technical:** Forges Damascus and 5160. **Prices:** $500 to $2,500; some to $6,000. **Remarks:** Full-time maker; first knife sold in 1976. **Mark:** First and middle initials, last name, city and state with two bleeding hearts.

EDWARDS, LYNN, Rt. 2, Box 614, W. Columbia, TX 77486/409-345-4080; FAX: 409-345-3472 **Specialties:** Traditional working and using straight knives of his design and to customer specs. **Patterns:** Bowies, hunters and utility/camp knives. **Technical:** Forges 5168 and 01; forges and grinds D2. Triple-hardens on request; offers silver wire inlay, stone inlays and spacers, filework. **Prices:** $100 to $395; some to $800. **Remarks:** Part-time maker; first knife sold in 1988. Doing business as E&E Emporium. **Mark:** Last name in script.

EK, GARY WHITNEY, 1580 NE 125th St., North Miami, FL 33161/305-891-2283 **Specialties:** Working straight knives of his design and to customer specs; period pieces. **Patterns:** Bowies, fighters and special-effect knives and swords. **Technical:** Grinds D2, Sandvik 13 c 26; forges and grinds 43-40 Ni Crm Moly. Offers custom refinishing and sharpening. **Prices:** $150 to $450; some to $1,200. **Remarks:** Full-time maker; first knife sold in 1971. **Mark:** Name or EKNIVES, city.

EKNIVES WORKS (See Ek, Gary Whitney)

EKLUND, ROLF, Soltappan, S-195 95 Rosersberg, SWEDEN/46-076036005 **Specialties:** Fishing and hunting knives of his design. **Patterns:** Swedish fishing and hunting knives. **Technical:** Forges his own laminated blades. Offers black oak handles he dived for from 17th century wreck. Traditional Swedish cowhide sheaths provided. **Prices:** $150 to $600. **Remarks:** Spare-time maker. **Mark:** Initials.

ELDRIDGE, ALLAN, 1424 Kansas Lane, Gallatin, TN 37066/615-452-6027 **Specialties:** Fancy classic straight knives in standard patterns. **Patterns:** Hunters, Bowies, fighters and miniatures. **Technical:** Grinds 01 and Damascus. Engraves, silver-wire inlays, pearl inlays, scrimshaws

and offers filework. **Prices:** $50 to $500; some to $1,200. **Remarks:** Spare-time maker; first knife sold in 1965. **Mark:** Initials.

ELISHEWITZ, ALLEN, 300 Mill St., San Marcos, TX 78666/512-754-8658 **Specialties:** Collectible high-tech working straight knives and folders of his design. **Patterns:** Fighters, combat knives, skinners and utility/camp knives. **Technical:** Grinds ATS-34, D2, A2 and Vascowear. All designs drafted and field-tested. **Prices:** $200 to $500; some to $1,000. **Remarks:** Full-time maker; first knife sold in 1989. **Mark:** Initials in a box with a dragon head.

ELKINS, R. VAN, P.O. Box 156, Bonita, LA 71223/318-823-2124 **Specialties:** High-art Bowies, fighters, folders and period daggers; all one-of-a-kind pieces. **Patterns:** Welcomes customer designs. **Technical:** Forges his own Damascus in several patterns, 01 and 5160. **Prices:** $250 to $2,800. **Remarks:** First knife sold in 1984. **Mark:** Last name.

THE ELK RACK (See Peele, Bryan)

ELLEFSON, JOEL, P.O. Box 1016, 310 S. 1st St., Manhattan, MT 59741/406-284-3111 **Specialties:** Working straight knives, fancy daggers and one-of-a-kinds. **Patterns:** Hunters, daggers and some folders. **Technical:** Grinds A2, 440C and ATS-34. Makes own mokume in bronze, brass, silver and shibuishi; makes brass/steel blades. **Prices:** $75 to $500; some to $2,000. **Remarks:** Part-time maker; first knife sold in 1978. **Mark:** Stylized last initial.

ELLENBERG, WILLIAM C., 10 Asbury Ave., Melrose Park, PA 19027/215-635-1313 **Specialties:** Traditional working and using straight knives of his design. **Patterns:** Bowies, hunters and utility/camp knives. **Technical:** Flat-grinds 440C and ATS-34. Offers hardwood or Micarta handles. Stitches leather sheaths with stainless steel wire. **Prices:** $150 to $250; some to $450. **Remarks:** Spare-time maker; first knife sold in 1990. **Mark:** None.

ELLERBE, W.B., 3871 Osceola Rd., Geneva, FL 32732/407-349-5818 **Specialties:** Period and primitive knives and sheaths. **Patterns:** Bowies to patch knives, some tomahawks. **Technical:** Grinds Sheffield 01 and files. **Prices:** Start at $35. **Remarks:** Full-time maker; first knife sold in 1971. Doing business as Cypress Bend Custom Knives. **Mark:** Last name or initials.

ELLIOTT, J.P., 4507 Kanawha Ave., Charleston, WV 25304/304-925-5045 **Specialties:** Classic and traditional straight knives and folders of his design and to customer specs. **Patterns:** Hunters, locking folders and Bowies. **Technical:** Grinds ATS-34, 154CM, 01, D2 and T-440-V. All guards silver-soldered; bolsters are pinned on straight knives, spot-welded on folders. **Prices:** $80 to $265; some to $1,000. **Remarks:** Full-time maker; first knife sold in 1972. **Mark:** First and middle initials, last name, knifemaker, city, state.

ELLIOTT, MARCUS, Pen Dinas, Wyddfydd Rd., Great Orme, Llandudno, Gwynedd, GREAT BRITAIN LL30 2QL/01492-872747 **Specialties:** Fancy working knives. **Patterns:** Boots and small hunters. **Technical:** Grinds 01, 440C and ATS-34. **Prices:** $160 to $250. **Remarks:** Spare-time maker; first knife sold in 1981. Makes only a few knives each year. **Mark:** Last name.

ELLIS, DAVID, 3505 Camino Del Rio S. #334, San Diego, CA 92108/619-285-1305 days; 619-632-7302 evenings **Specialties:** Fighters and Bowies. **Patterns:** Utility knives. **Technical:** Forges and grinds 5160, 01, 1095; now working with pattern-welded Damascus. Most knives have hand-rubbed finish and single and double temper lines. All knives are double or triple hardened and triple drawn. Prefers natural handle materials. **Prices:** $250 to $450; some to $1,500. **Remarks:** Part-time maker; first knife sold in 1988. **Mark:** Last name.

ELLIS, WILLIAM DEAN, 8875 N. Barton, Fresno, CA 93720/209-299-0303
Specialties: Classic and fancy knives of his design. **Patterns:** Boots, fighters and utility knives. **Technical:** Grinds ATS34, D2 and Damascus. Offers tapered tangs and six patterns of filework; tooled multi-colored sheaths. **Prices:** $180 to $350; some to $1,300. **Remarks:** Part-time maker; first knife sold in 1991. Doing business as Billy's Blades. **Mark:** "B" in a five-point star next to "Billy", city and state within a rounded-corner rectangle.

EMBRETSEN, KAJ, P.O. Box 54, S-82821 Edsbyn, SWEDEN/46-271-20883; FAX: 46-271-22961
Specialties: Straight knives. **Patterns:** Traditional Swedish and modern hunters; folders. **Technical:** Forges Damascus. Uses only his blades; natural materials. **Prices:** Upscale. **Remarks:** Full-time maker. **Mark:** Name.

EMERSON, ERNEST R., 4142 W. 173nd St., Torrance, CA 90504/310-542-3050
Specialties: High-tech folders and combat fighters. **Patterns:** Fighters, linerlock combat folders and SPECWAR combat knives. **Technical:** Grinds ATS-34 and D2. Makes folders with titanium fittings, liners and locks. Chisel grind specialist. **Prices:** $275 to $475; some to $3,000. **Remarks:** Full-time maker; first knife sold in 1983. **Mark:** Last name or Viper.

ENCE, JIM, 145 S. 200 East, Richfield, UT 84701/801-896-6206
Specialties: High-art period pieces. **Patterns:** Daggers, art folders, fancy boot knives, fighters, Bowies and occasional hunters. **Technical:** Grinds 440C; makes his own and buys Damascus. **Prices:** $300 to $5,000; some higher. **Remarks:** Full-time maker; first knife sold in 1977. **Mark:** Name, city, state.

ENDERS, ROBERT, 3028 White Rd., Cement City, MI 49233/517-529-9667
Specialties: Pocketknives and working straight knives. **Patterns:** Traditional folders with natural materials. **Technical:** Grinds D2, 01, 440C and ATS-34. **Prices:** $125 to $300; some to $1,200. **Remarks:** Full-time maker; first knife sold in 1981. **Mark:** Name in state map logo.

ENGLAND, VIRGIL, 629 W. 15th Ave., Anchorage, AK 99501/907-274-9494
Specialties: Edged weapons and equipage, one-of-a-kind only. **Patterns:** Axes, swords, lances and body armor. **Technical:** Forges and grinds as pieces dictate. Offers stainless and Damascus. **Prices:** Upscale. **Remarks:** A veteran knifemaker. No commissions. **Mark:** Stylized initials.

ENGLE, WILLIAM, 16608 Oak Ridge Rd., Boonville, MO 65233/816-882-6277
Specialties: Traditional working and using straight knives of his design. **Patterns:** Hunters, Bowies and fighters. **Technical:** Grinds 440C, ATS-34 and 154 CM. **Prices:** $250 to $500; some higher. **Remarks:** Part-time maker; first knife sold in 1982. All knives come with certificate of authenticity. **Mark:** Last name in block lettering.

ENGLEBRETSON, GEORGE, 1209 NW 49th St., Oklahoma City, OK 73118/405-840-4784
Specialties: Working straight knives and period pieces. **Patterns:** Hunters, Bowies, fishing knives and axes. **Technical:** Grinds A2, D2, 440C, ATS-34 and C-350. **Prices:** Start at $100. **Remarks:** Full-time maker; first knife sold in 1967. **Mark:** "By George," name and city.

ENGLISH, JIM, 14586 Olive Vista Dr., Jamul, CA 91935/619-669-0833
Specialties: Traditional working straight knives to customer specs. **Patterns:** Hunters, Bowies, fighters, tantos, daggers, boot and utility/camp knives. **Technical:** Grinds 440C, ATS-34, commercial Damascus and customer choice. **Prices:** $130 to $350. **Remarks:** Part-time maker; first knife sold in 1985. In addition to custom line, also does business as Mountain Home Knives. **Mark:** Double A, Double J logo.

ENGNATH, BOB, 1217 B. Crescent Dr., Glendale, CA 91205/818-241-3629

Specialties: Replica antique tantos; complete knives and swords. **Patterns:** Traditional Japanese knives; some miniatures. Kit blades also offered. **Technical:** Makes soft-back/hard-edge blades with temper lines. **Prices:** $125 to $350; some to $600. **Remarks:** Full-time maker/grinder; first knife sold in 1972. **Mark:** KODAN in Japanese script.

ENNIS, RAY W., 509 S. 3rd St., Grand Forks, ND 58201/701-775-8216/800-468-4867
Specialties: Working straight knives and folders of his design or to customer specs. **Patterns:** Hunters, fighters and locking folders. **Technical:** Grinds ATS-34, D2 and 01. **Prices:** $100 to $500; some to $1,500. **Remarks:** Full-time maker; first knife sold in 1973. **Mark:** Initials connected.

ENOS III, THOMAS M., 12302 State Rd. 535, Orlando, FL 32836/407-239-6205
Specialties: Heavy-duty working straight knives to customer specs; unusual designs. **Patterns:** Machetes, saltwater sport knives, carvers. **Technical:** Grinds 440C, D2, 154CM. **Prices:** $75 to $1,000. **Remarks:** Full-time maker; first knife sold in 1972. **Mark:** Name in knife logo and date, type of steel and serial number.

ERIKSEN, JAMES THORLIEF, 3830 Dividend Dr., Garland, TX 75042/214-494-3667; FAX: 214-235-4932
Specialties: Heavy-duty working and using straight knives and folders utilizing traditional, Viking original and customer specification patterns. Some high-tech and fancy/embellished knives available. **Patterns:** Bowies, hunters, skinners, boot and belt knives, utility/camp knives, fighters, daggers, locking folders, slip-joint folders and kitchen knives. **Technical:** Hollow-grinds 440C, D2, ASP-23, ATS-34, 154CM, Vascowear. **Prices:** $150 to $300; some to $600. **Remarks:** Full-time maker; first knife sold in 1985. Doing business as Viking Knives. **Mark:** VIKING or VIKING USA for export.

ERICKSON, CURT, 449 Washington Blvd., Ogden, UT 84404/801-782-1184
Specialties: Daggers and large knives of integral construction. **Patterns:** Period pieces; Bowies and hunting knives. **Technical:** Grinds 440C and commercial Damascus steel; sculpts and carves components. **Prices:** $240 to $1,500; some to $3,000. **Remarks:** Full-time maker; first knife sold in 1982. **Mark:** Name, state.

ERICKSON, L.M., P.O. Box 132, Liberty, UT 84310/801-745-2026
Specialties: Straight knives; period pieces. **Patterns:** Bowies, fighters, boots and hunters. **Technical:** Grinds 440C, 154CM and commercial Damascus. **Prices:** $200 to $900; some to $1,900. **Remarks:** Full-time maker; first knife sold in 1981. **Mark:** Name, city, state.

ERICKSON, WALTER E., 23883 Ada St., Warren, MI 48091/313-759-1105
Specialties: Unusual survival knives and high-tech working knives. **Patterns:** Butterflies, hunters, tantos. **Technical:** Grinds ATS-34 or customer choice. **Prices:** $150 to $500; some to $1,500. **Remarks:** Full-time maker; first knife sold in 1981. **Mark:** ERIC or last name.

ESAKI, SHUSUKE, Bl Fukoku Seimei Building, 2-4 Komatubara Cho Xitaku, Osaka City, 530 JAPAN/06-313-2525; FAX: 06-313-2626
Specialties: Classic and high-art knives of his design. **Patterns:** Bowies, daggers and fighters. **Technical:** Grinds ATS-34, Damascus and 440C. **Prices:** $200 to $3,000. **Remarks:** Spare-time maker; first knife sold in 1097. **Mark:** NA.

ESSEGIAN, RICHARD, 7387 E. Tulare St., Fresno, CA 93727/309-255-5950
Specialties: Fancy working knives of his design; art knives. **Patterns:** Bowies and some small hunters. **Technical:** Grinds A2, D2, 440C and 154CM. Engraves and inlays. **Prices:** Start at $600. **Remarks:** Part-time maker; first knife sold in 1986. **Mark:** Last name, city and state.

ETZLER, JOHN, 11200 N. Island, Grafton, OH 44044/216-748-3980
Specialties: Fancy and working straight knives and folders of his

directory

design and to customer specs. **Patterns:** Fighters, hunters, swords and utility knives. **Technical:** Forges and grinds nickel Damascus and tool steel; grinds stainless steels. Prefers exotic, natural materials. **Prices:** $175 to $300; some to $6,000. **Remarks:** Full-time maker; first knife sold in 1992. **Mark:** Name or initials.

EVANS, GRACE (See Evans, Vincent K. and Grace)

EVANS, VINCENT K. and GRACE, HCR 1, Box 5221, Keaau, HI 96749/808-966-4831
Specialties: Working straight knives; period pieces; swords. **Patterns:** Scottish and central Asian patterns, Bowies and clip-point using knives. **Technical:** Forges 5160 and his own Damascus. **Prices:** $50 to $400; some to $3,000. **Remarks:** Full-time maker; first knife sold in 1983. **Mark:** Bronze-filled double last initial with fish logo.

EWING, JOHN H., 3276 Dutch Valley Rd., Clinton, TN 37716/615-457-5757
Specialties: Working straight knives. **Patterns:** Hunters. **Technical:** Grinds 440C and 01; prefers forging. **Prices:** $150 to $1,000. **Remarks:** Part-time maker; first knife sold in 1985. **Mark:** First initial, last name, Handmade.

EXOTIC BLADES (See Hesser, David)

f

FALCON CREST FORGE (See Fowler, Charles R.)

FALLING WATERS FORGE (See Barnes, Aubrey G.)

FANNIN, DAVID A. and BRUMAGEN, JERRY, 2050 Idle Hour Center #191, Lexington, KY 40502
Specialties: High-tech classic straight knives; period pieces; traditional working knives. **Patterns:** Hunters, fighters and swords. **Technical:** Draws wire from Damascus billets for wire Damascus. High-density, migrationless and hand-smelted Sagami school Damascus steel. Offers Hamon tempering; makes mokume. **Prices:** $200 to $1,200. **Remarks:** Full-time maker; first knife sold in 1985. Doing business as Athens Forge. **Mark:** None.

FARID, 8 Sidney Close, Tunbridge Wells, Kent, ENGLAND TN2 5QQ/01892-520345
Specialties: Working/using knives. **Patterns:** Hunters, Bowies, fighters, combat and special forces knives. **Technical:** Grinds 01 and 440C. Offers satin finish; paracord and wood handles. **Prices:** $150 to $1000. **Remarks:** Full-time maker; first knife sold in 1991. **Mark:** First name.

FARRIS, CAL, Box 41, Altoona, FL 32702/904-669-9427

FASSIO, MELVIN G., 4585 Twin Cr. Rd., Bonner, MT 59823/406-244-5208
Specialties: Working folders to customer specs. **Patterns:** Locking folders, hunters and traditional-style knives. **Technical:** Grinds 440C. **Prices:** $60 to $100; some to $200. **Remarks:** Part-time maker; first knife sold in 1975. **Mark:** Name and city, dove logo.

FAUCHEAUX, HOWARD J., P.O. Box 206, Loreauville, LA 70552/318-229-6467
Specialties: Working straight knives and folders; period pieces. Also a hatchet with caping knife in the handle. **Patterns:** Traditional locking folders, hunters, fighters and Bowies. **Technical:** Forges W2, 1095 and his own Damascus; stock removal D2. **Prices:** $200 and up. **Remarks:** Full-time maker; first knife sold in 1969. **Mark:** Last name.

FAULKNER, ALLAN, Rt. 11, Box 161, Jasper, AL 35501/205-387-0083
Specialties: Working and fancy straight knives; kitchen cutlery. **Patterns:** Pocketknives, traditional folders, miniatures, hunters, fighters and

Bowies. **Technical:** Grinds D2, 440C and 154CM; prefers natural handle materials. **Prices:** $150 to $350; some to $1,500. **Remarks:** Part-time maker, first knife sold in 1978. **Mark:** Last name.

FECAS, STEPHEN J., 1312 Shadow Lane, Anderson, SC 29625/803-287-4834
Specialties: Working straight knives in standard patterns; some period pieces. **Patterns:** Hunters to claws, folding slip-joints to buckskinners. **Technical:** Grinds D2, 440C and 154CM; most knives hand-finished to 600 grit. **Prices:** $140 to $400; some to $750. **Remarks:** Part-time maker; first knife sold in 1977. **Mark:** Last name.

FELFIDEL, RALPH, 15 Budlong Ave., Warrich, RI 02888

FERDINAND, DON, 229 Flounce Rock Dr., Prospect, OR 97536/503-560-3355
Specialties: Working knives and period pieces; all tool steel Damascus. **Patterns:** Bowies, push knives and fishing knives. **Technical:** Forges high-carbon alloy steels—L6, D2; makes his own Damascus. **Prices:** $100 to $500. **Remarks:** Full-time maker since 1980. Does business as Wyvern. **Mark:** Initials connected.

FERGUSON, JIM, P.O. Box 40247, Downey, CA 90239/310-862-7461
Specialties: One-of-a-kind straight knives. **Patterns:** Bowies, daggers, fighters and push blades. **Technical:** Forges nickel and 1095 (twisted nickel) Damascus; grinds. **Prices:** $100 to $3,000. **Remarks:** Part-time maker; first knife sold in 1987. Doing business as Twisted Nickel Knives. **Mark:** Name.

FERGUSON, JIM, P.O. Box 764, San Angelo, TX 76902/915-651-6656
Specialties: Straight working knives and folders. **Patterns:** Working belt knives, hunters, Bowies and some folders. **Technical:** Grinds ATS-34, D2 and Vascowear. Flat-grinds hunting knives. **Prices:** $200 to $600; some to $1,000. **Remarks:** Full-time maker; first knife sold in 1987. **Mark:** First and middle initials, last name.

FERGUSON, LEE, Rt. 2, Box 109, Hindsville, AR 72738/501-443-0084
Specialties: Straight working knives and folders, some fancy. **Patterns:** Hunters, daggers, swords, locking folders and slip-joints. **Technical:** Grinds D2, 440C and ATS-34; heat-treats. **Prices:** $50 to $600; some to $4,000. **Remarks:** Part-time maker; first knife sold in 1977. **Mark:** Last name.

FERRARA, THOMAS, 122 Madison Dr., Naples, FL 33942/813-597-3363; FAX: 813-597-3363
Specialties: High-art, traditional and working straight knives and folders of all designs. **Patterns:** Boots, Bowies, Daggers, Fighters and hunters. **Technical:** Grinds 440C, D2 and ATS-34; heat-treats. **Prices:** $100 to $700; some to $1,300. **Remarks:** Part-time maker; first knife sold in 1983. **Mark:** Last name.

FIELDER, WILLIAM V., 8406 Knowland Circle, Richmond, VA 23229 23229/804-750-1198
Specialties: Fancy working straight knives and folders of his design. **Patterns:** Hunters, boots and daggers; locking folders, interframes and traditional-style knives. **Technical:** Forges W2, 01 and his own Damascus; likes wire inlay. **Prices:** $25 to $500; some to $1,000. **Remarks:** Full-time maker; first knife sold in 1982. **Mark:** Last name, J.S.

FIKES, JIMMY L., P.O. Box 3457, Jasper, AL 35502/205-387-9302; FAX: 205-221-1980
Specialties: High-art working knives; artifact knives; using knives with cord-wrapped handles; swords and combat weapons. **Patterns:** Axes to buckskinners, camp knives to miniatures, tantos to tomahawks; springless folders. **Technical:** Forges W2, 01 and his own Damascus. **Prices:** $135 to $3,000; exceptional knives to $7,000. **Remarks:** Full-time maker. **Mark:** Stylized initials.

FINE CUSTOM KNIVES (See Nielson, Jeff V.)

FIORINI, BILL, P.O. Box 131, LaCrescent, MN 55947

Specialties: Fancy working knives and lockbacks. **Patterns:** Hunters, boots, Japanese-style knives and kitchen/utility knives. **Technical:** Forges own Damascus. **Prices:** Full range. **Remarks:** Full-time metalsmith researching pattern materials. **Mark:** W over F with Japanese lettering.

FIRE FORGED KNIVES (See Lockett, Lowell C.)

FIREPOINT KNIVES (See Renner, Terry Lee)

FISCHER, CLYDE E., HCR 40, Box 133, Nixon, TX 78140-9400/512-582-1353
Specialties: Working knives for serious and professional hunters. **Patterns:** Heavy-duty hunters and survival blades; camp knives and buckskinner knives. **Technical:** Forges and grinds L6, 01 and his own Damascus. **Prices:** $100 to $250; some to $800. **Remarks:** Full-time maker; first knife sold in 1957. **Mark:** Fish.

FISHER, JAY, 104 S. Main St., P.O. Box 267, Magdalena, NM 87825
Specialties: High-art, ancient and exact working and using straight knives of his design. **Patterns:** Hunters, daggers and high-art sculptures. **Technical:** Grinds 440C, ATS-34 and D2. Prolific maker of stone-handled knives. **Prices:** $145 to $20,000; some higher. **Remarks:** Full-time maker; first knife sold in 1984. **Mark:** Very fine—JaFisher—Quality Custom Knives.

FISHER, THEO (TED), 8115 Modoc Lane, Montague, CA 96064/916-459-3804
Specialties: Moderately-priced working knives in carbon steel. **Patterns:** Hunters, fighters, kitchen and buckskinner knives. Damascus miniatures. **Technical:** Grinds ATS-34, L6 and 440C. **Prices:** $65 to $165; exceptional knives to $300. **Remarks:** Full-time maker; first knife sold in 1981. **Mark:** Name in banner logo.

FISK, JERRY, Rt. 1, Box 41, Lockesburg, AR 71846/501-289-3240
Specialties: Edged weapons, collectible and functional. **Patterns:** Bowies, daggers, swords, hunters, camp knives and others. **Technical:** Forges carbon steels and his own pattern welded steels. **Prices:** $200 to $10,000. **Remarks:** Full-time maker; first knife sold in 1980. **Mark:** Name, MS.

FISTER, JIM, 5067 Fisherville Rd., Simpsonville, KY 40067/502-834-7841
Specialties: Bowies and hunters. **Patterns:** Period pieces, buckskinners, fighters, daggers and folders. **Technical:** Forges 01, 5160, 52100, his own wire and regular and exotic Damascus. **Prices:** $100 to $900; some to $1,500. **Remarks:** Part-time maker; first knife sold in 1982. **Mark:** Last name.

FITZGERALD, DENNIS M., 4219 Alverado Dr., Fort Wayne, IN 46816-2847/219-447-1081
Specialties: Straight working knives. **Patterns:** Skinners, fighters, camp and utility knives; period pieces. **Technical:** Forges W2, 01, billet and cable-wire Damascus. Likes integral guards, bolsters and pommels. **Prices:** $100 to $500. **Remarks:** Part-time maker; first knife sold in 1985. Doing business as The Ringing Circle. **Mark:** Name and circle logo.

FIVE RUNS FORGE (See Bullard, Bill)

FLECHTNER, CHRIS, 224 St. Camille St., Fitchburg, MA 01420/508-342-4371

FLINT STEEL KNIVES (See Anderson, Michael D.)

FLOOD, JAMES (NOAH), 18 Kelly Rd., Chaska, MN 55318/612-448-3379
Specialties: High-art straight knives and period pieces of his design and to customer specs. **Patterns:** Bowies, daggers and fighters. **Technical:** Forges high-carbon steels; grinds 01 and Vascowear. **Prices:** $100 to $600; some to $1,500. **Remarks:** Full-time maker; first knife sold in 1989. Doing business as Troll Hammer Forge. **Mark:** Etched signature.

FLOURNOY, JOE, 5750 Lisbon Rd., El Dorado, AR 71730/501-863-7208
Specialties: Large Bowies and camp knives. **Patterns:** Hunters, Bowies, folders and daggers. **Technical:** Forges only high-carbon steel, steel cable and his own Damascus. **Prices:** $250 to $4,000. **Remarks:** First knife sold in 1977. **Mark:** Last name and MS in script.

FLYNN, BRUCE, 8139 W. County Rd. 650 S, Knightstown, IN 46148-9348/317-779-4034
Specialties: Workign straight knives and folders. **Patterns:** Fighters, Bowies, daggers, skinners and hunters. **Technical:** Grinds 440C, 154CM and D2. **Prices:** Moderate. **Remarks:** Full-time maker. **Mark:** First and middle initials, last name.

FOGARIZZU, BOITEDDU, via Crispi, 6, 07016 Pattada, ITALY
Specialties: Traditional italian straight knives and folders. **Patterns:** Collectible folders. **Technical:** Forges and grinds 12C27, ATS-34 and his Damascus. **Prices:** $200 to $3,000. **Remarks:** Full-time maker; first knife sold in 1958. **Mark:** Full name and registered logo.

FOGG, DON, Rt. 6, Box 107, Alma Station Rd., Jasper, AL 35501-8813/205-483-0822
Specialties: Straight knives. **Patterns:** Bowies, stout hunters, daggers. **Technical:** Forges carbon steels, *san mai* and Damascus; all natural materials. **Prices:** $150 to $5,000. **Remarks:** Full-time maker; first knife sold in 1976. Doing business as Kemal. **Mark:** 24K gold cherry blossom.

FORD, ALLEN, 3927 Plumcrest Rd., Smyrna, GA 30080/404-432-5061
Specialties: Art knives of his design. **Patterns:** Bowies, daggers and hunters. **Technical:** Hand finishes every knife. Scrimshaws. **Mark:** First initial, last name in script.

FORSTALL, AL, 971 Walnut St., Sudell, LA 70460/504-643-6217
Specialties: Traditional working and using straight knives of his design. **Patterns:** Fighters, hunters and utility/camp knives. **Technical:** Grinds ATS-34, 440C and commercial Damascus. **Prices:** $60 to $250. **Remarks:** Spare-time maker; first knife sold in 1991. **Mark:** The number 4 with "stall" around it.

FORTHOFER, PETE, 5535 Hwy. 93S, Whitefish, MT 59937/406-862-2674
Specialties: Interframes with checkered wood inlays; working straight knives. **Patterns:** Interframe folders and traditional-style knives; hunters, fighters and Bowies. **Technical:** Grinds D2, 440C, 154CM and ATS-34. **Prices:** $250 to $1,000; some to $1,500. **Remarks:** Part-time maker; full-time gunsmith. First knife sold in 1979. **Mark:** Name and logo.

FOSTER, AL, HC 73, Box 117, Dogpatch, AR 72648/501-446-5137
Specialties: Working straight knives and folders. **Patterns:** Bowies, hunters, lockback and slip-joint folders, fishing knives; trailing-points and impala horn handles. **Technical:** Grinds D2, 440C, ATS-34 and commercial Damascus. **Prices:** $65 to $250; some to $500. **Remarks:** Full-time maker; first knife sold in 1981. **Mark:** Scorpion logo and name.

FOSTER, R.L. (BOB), 745 Glendare Blvd., Mansfield, OH 44907

FOWLER, CHARLES R., Rt. 2, Box 1446 A, Ft. McCoy, FL 32134/904-467-3215
Specialties: Fancy high-art straight knives and traditional working straight knives of his design. **Patterns:** Boots, Bowies, daggers, fighters, hunters and utility knives. **Technical:** Forges L6, W2 and 5160. **Prices:** $300 to $1,200. **Remarks:** Part-time maker; first knife sold in 1986. Doing business as Falcon Crest Forge. **Mark:** Circle with falcon bust, name, bladesmith.

FOWLER FORGE KNIFEWORKS (See Fowler, Jerry)

FOWLER, ED A., Willow Bow Ranch, P.O. Box 1519, Riverton, WY 82501/307-856-9815

Specialties: Heavy-duty working and using straight knives. **Patterns:** Hunters, camp, bird and trout knives, Bowies. **Technical:** Forges 52100 and wire Damascus; multiple-quench heat-treats. Engraves all knives. All handles are domestic sheephorn, processed and aged for a minimum of four years. Makes heavy-duty, hand-stitched, waxed, harness leather pouch-type sheaths. **Prices:** $450 to $950; some over $1,500. **Remarks:** Full-time maker; first knife sold in 1962. **Mark:** Initials connected.

FOWLER, JERRY, 610 FM 1660 N., Hutto, TX 78634/512-846-2860
Specialties: Using straight knives of his design. **Patterns:** A variety of hunting and camp knives, combat knives. Custom designs considered. **Technical:** Forges 5160, his own Damascus and cable Damascus. Makes sheaths. Prefers natural handle materials. **Prices:** Start at $150. **Remarks:** Part-time maker; first knife sold in 1986. Doing business as Fowler Forge Knifeworks. **Mark:** First initial, last name, date and J.S.

FOX, JACK L., 7085 Canelo Hills Dr., Citrus Heights, CA 95610/916-723-8647
Specialties: Traditional working/using straight knives of all designs. **Patterns:** Hunters, utility/camp knives and bird/fish knives. **Technical:** Grinds ATS-34, 440C and D2. **Prices:** $125 to $225; some to $350. **Remarks:** Spare-time maker; first knife sold in 1985. Doing business as Fox Knives. **Mark:** Stylized fox head.

FOX, PAUL, Rt. 3, Box 208-F Rockbarn Rd., Claremont, NC 28610/704-459-2000 evenings; 404-327-5516 days
Specialties: Unusual one-of-a-kinds of all-bolted construction; mostly folders. **Patterns:** High-tech folding fighters; straight daggers and fighters. **Technical:** Grinds 01, 154CM and commercial Damascus. **Prices:** $200 to $6,000. **Remarks:** Full-time maker; first knife sold in 1977. **Mark:** Signature.

FOX, WENDELL, 4080 S. 39th, Springfield, OR 97478/503-747-2126
Specialties: Classic and traditional straight knives and folders of his design and to customer specs. **Patterns:** Hunters, locking folders, slip-joint folders and utility/camp knives. **Technical:** Forges high-carbon steel, cable, 52100 and his own timbers steel. All carbon cable blades are differentially tempered; all sheaths are wet-moulded. **Prices:** $200 to $500. **Remarks:** Full-time maker; first knife sold in 1952. **Mark:** Name or initials.

FOX VALLEY FORGE (See Werth, George W.)

FOXWOOD FORGE (See Kilby, Keith)

FRALEY, DEREK, 430 South Ct., Dixon, CA 95620/916-678-0393
Specialties: Traditional working/using straight knives and folders of his design and in standard patterns. **Patterns:** Fighters, hunters, utility/camp knives. **Technical:** Grinds ATS-34. Offers hand-stitched sheaths. **Prices:** $100 to $400. **Remarks:** Part-time maker; first knife sold in 1990. **Mark:** First and middle initials, last name over buffalo.

FRANCE, DAN, Box 218, Cawood, KY 40815/606-573-6104
Specialties: Traditional working and using straight knives of his design. **Patterns:** Hunters, Bowies and utility/camp knives. **Technical:** Forges and grinds 01, 5160 and L6. **Prices:** $35 to $125; some to $350. **Remarks:** Spare-time maker; first knife sold in 1985. **Mark:** First name.

FRANJO (See Candrella, Joe)

FRANK'S PLACE (See Niro, Frank)

FRANK, HEINRICH H., Box 984, Whitefish, MT 59937/406-862-2681
Specialties: High-art investor-class folders, handmade and engraved. **Patterns:** Folding daggers, hunter-size folders and gents. **Technical:** Grinds 07 and 01. **Prices:** $4,800 to $16,000. **Remarks:** Full-time maker; first knife sold in 1965. **Mark:** Name, address and date.

FRANKLAND, ANDREW, P.O. Box 256, Wilderness 6560, SOUTH AFRICA/0027-441-877-0260; FAX: 0027-441-745203

Specialties: Classic working and using straight knives and folders of his design and to customer specs. **Patterns:** Daggers, fighters, hunters and utility/camp knives. **Technical:** Grinds 440C, D2 and ATS-34. All double-edge knives have broad spine. **Prices:** $250 to $400; some to $1,500. **Remarks:** Part-time maker; first knife sold in 1979. **Mark:** Last name surrounded by mountain, lake, forest scene.

FRANKLIN, MIKE, 9878 Big Run Rd., Aberdeen, OH 45101/513-549-2598
Specialties: Small, lightweight hunters and boots; double-action locking folders. **Patterns:** Straight and folding knives; some period pieces. **Technical:** Grinds A2, 440C and ATS-34. **Prices:** $350 to $800. **Remarks:** Full-time maker; first knife sold in 1973. **Mark:** Last name.

FRANKS, JOEL, 6610 Quaker, Lubbock, TX 79413/806-792-7112
Specialties: Working straight knives and folders in standard patterns or to customer specs. **Patterns:** Belt knives, hunters, gut hook skinners, folders and utility knives. **Technical:** Grinds 440C, 440A and L6. Makes trophy and commemorative cases and racks to accompany his knives. Repairs and refinishes old knives. **Prices:** $35 to $300. **Remarks:** Part-time maker; first knife sold in 1973. **Mark:** Initials connected.

FRASER, GRANT, RR2 Foresters Falls, Ont., CANADA K0J 1V0/613-582-3582
Specialties: Fancy and working straight knives of his design and to customer specs. **Patterns:** Bowies, daggers and hunters. **Technical:** Forges and grinds 01 and 5160; grinds ATS-34. **Prices:** $125 to $255; some to $1,200. **Remarks:** Full-time maker; first knife sold in 1983. **Mark:** Initial tang stamp.

FRAZIER, RON, 2107 Urbine Rd., Powhatan, VA 23139/804-794-8561
Specialties: Classy working knives of his design; some high-art straight knives. **Patterns:** Wide assortment of straight knives, including miniatures and push knives. **Technical:** Grinds 440C; offers satin, mirror or sand finishes. **Prices:** $85 to $700; some to $3,000. **Remarks:** Full-time maker; first knife sold in 1976. **Mark:** Name in arch logo.

FRED, REED WYLE, 3233 W Street #2, Sacramento, CA 95817/916-739-8481
Specialties: Working/using straight knives of his design. **Patterns:** Hunters, kitchen and utility/camp knives. **Technical:** Forges any 10 series, old files and carbon steels. Offers initialing upon request; prefers manzzinith for handles or leather. **Prices:** $20 to $125; some to $300. **Remarks:** Part-time maker; first knife sold in 1994. Doing business as R.W. Fred Knifemaker. **Mark:** Engraved first and last initials.

FREEMAN, ART F., 3176 Kathy Way, Loomis, CA 95650-8776
Specialties: Fantasy and high-art knives. **Patterns:** Hunters to Bowies, fighters to swords. **Technical:** Uses 440C, ATS-34, D2 and nickel/1095 Damascus. Customer requests. **Prices:** Start at $500. **Remarks:** Full-time maker; first knife sold in 1979. **Mark:** First initial, last name in script.

FREEMAN, JOHN, 160 Concession St., Cambridge, Ont. N1R 2H7 CANADA/519-740-2767; FAX: 519-740-2785
Specialties: Working straight knives. **Patterns:** Hunters, skinners, utilities, backpackers. **Technical:** Grinds A2, 440C and ATS-34. **Prices:** Start at $125. **Remarks:** Full-time maker; first knife sold in 1985. **Mark:** Full name, city, state, Handmade.

FREER, RALPH, P.O. Box 3482, Seal Beach, CA 90740/310-493-4925; FAX: 310-799-8844
Specialties: Hunters, fighters, Bowies and art pieces. **Patterns:** All his design. **Technical:** ATS-34, 440C, 5160, Damascus, 1060, 1095 and 01. **Prices:** $200 to $1,500. Offers custom filework. Works with natural materials, exotic woods and horn. Flawless mirror-polished or hand-rubbed satin finishes. **Remarks:** Full-time maker; first knife sold in 1991. Doing business as Freer Custom Knives. **Mark:** Last name.

FREILING, ALBERT J., 3700 Niner Rd., Finksburg, MD 21048/301-795-2880
Specialties: Working straight knives and folders; some period pieces.

Patterns: Boots, Bowies, survival knives and tomahawks in 4130 and 440C; some locking folders and interframes; ball-bearing folders. **Technical:** Grinds 01, 440C and 154CM. **Prices:** $100 to $300; some to $500. **Remarks:** Part-time maker; first knife sold in 1966. **Mark:** Initials connected.

FRESE, WILLIAM R., 5374 Fernbeach, St. Louis, MO 63128/314-849-3272
Specialties: Unusual blade designs coupled with exotic handles. **Patterns:** Hunters, skinners and utility knives. **Technical:** Grinds D2, 440C and 01. Offers filework and scrimshaw. **Prices:** $50 to $150; miniatures range $25 to $35. **Remarks:** Part-time maker; first knife sold in 1985. Offers display stands. **Mark:** Last name.

FREY JR., W. FREDERICK, 305 Walnut St., Milton, PA 17847/717-742-9576
Specialties: Working straight knives and folders, some fancy. **Patterns:** Wide range—boot knives to tomahawks. **Technical:** Grinds A2, 01 and D2; hand finishes only. **Prices:** $55 to $170; some to $600. **Remarks:** Spare-time maker; first knife sold in 1983. **Mark:** Last name in script.

FRIEDLY, DENNIS E., 12 Cottontail Ln., Cody, WY 82414/307-527-6811
Specialties: Fancy working straight knives and daggers. **Patterns:** Hunters, fighters, short swords, minis and miniatures; new line of full-tang hunters/boots. **Technical:** Grinds 440C, ATS-34 and commercial Damascus; prefers hidden tangs. **Prices:** $135 to $900; some to $2,500. **Remarks:** Full-time maker; first knife sold in 1972. **Mark:** Name, city and state.

FRIZZELL, TED, Rt. 2, Box 326, West Fork, AR 72774/501-839-3381
Specialties: Heavy chopping and breaking tools. **Patterns:** Large hatchets to camp knives. **Technical:** Grinds 5160 almost exclusively—1/4" to 1/2" bars—some 01 and A2 on request. All hatchets come with 8-oz. leather head covers. **Prices:** $55 to $150; some to $500. **Remarks:** Full-time maker; first knife sold in 1984. Doing business as Mineral Mountain Hatchet Works. **Mark:** A circle with line in the middle; MM and HW within the circle.

FRONEFIELD, MIKE, P.O. Box 10268, Truckee, CA 95737/916-587-3003
Specialties: Working straight knives in standard patterns. **Patterns:** Fly knives to remove fly hooks from fish; utility knives; some swords. **Technical:** Forges and grinds cable Damascus, 440C and L6. Scrimshaws and engraves. Makes own sheaths. **Prices:** $50 to $150; some to $500. **Remarks:** Part-time maker; first knife sold in 1986. Doing business as Truckee Knifeworks. **Mark:** Name.

FRUHMANN, LUDWID, Stegerwaldstr 8, 84489 Burghausen, GERMANY

FUEGEN, LARRY, RR 1, Box 279, Wiscasset, ME 04578/207-882-6391
Specialties: High-art folders and classic and working straight knives. **Patterns:** Forged scroll folders, lockback folders and classic straight knives. **Technical:** Forges 5160, 1095 and his own Damascus. Works in exotic leather; offers elaborate filework and carving; likes natural handle materials. **Prices:** $400 to $5,200. **Remarks:** Full-time maker; first knife sold in 1975. **Mark:** Initials connected.

FUJIKAMA, SHUN, 1157 Sawa Kaizuka, Osaka, JAPAN

FUJISAKA, STANLEY, 45-004 Holowai St., Kaneohe, HI 96744/808-247-0017
Specialties: Fancy working straight knives and folders. **Patterns:** Hunters, boots, personal knives, daggers, collectible art knives. **Technical:** Grinds 440C, 154CM and ATS-34; clean lines, inlays. **Prices:** $150 to $1,200; some to $3,000. **Remarks:** Full-time maker; first knife sold in 1984. **Mark:** Name, city and state.

FUKUTA, TAK, 38-Umeagae-cho, Seki-City, Gifu-Pref, JAPAN/0575-22-0264
Specialties: Bench-made fancy straight knives and folders. **Patterns:** Sheffield-type folders, Bowies and fighters. **Technical:** Grinds commercial Damascus. **Prices:** Start at $300. **Remarks:** Full-time maker. **Mark:** Name in knife logo.

FULLCO, INC. (See Fuller, Bruce A.)

FULLER, BRUCE A., 1305 Airhart Dr., Baytown, TX 77520/713-427-1848
Specialties: One-of-a-kind working/using straight knives to customer specs. **Patterns:** Bowies, hunters and utility/camp knives. **Technical:** Forges 5160, 01 and his own Damascus. Prefers El Solo Mesquite and natural materials. **Prices:** Start at $150 with sheath and case. **Remarks:** Part-time maker; first knife sold in 1991. **Mark:** Fullco, J.S.

FULLER, JACK A., 7103 Stretch Ct., New Market, MD 21774/301-831-9749
Specialties: Straight working knives of his design and to customer specs. **Patterns:** Fighters, camp knives, hunters and art knives. **Technical:** Forges 5160, 01, W2 and his own Damascus. Offers leatherwork; scrimshands. **Prices:** $300 to $750; some to $2,000. **Remarks:** Full-time maker; first knife sold in 1979. **Mark:** Fuller's Forge, MS.

FULLER, JOHN W., 6156 Ridge Way, Douglasville, GA 30135/404-942-1155
Specialties: Fancy working straight knives and folders in standard patterns. **Patterns:** Straight and folding hunters, gents, fighters. **Technical:** Grinds ATS-34, 440C and commercial Damascus. **Prices:** $75 to $300. **Remarks:** Part-time maker; first knife sold in 1978. **Mark:** Name, city, state.

FULLER'S FORGE (See Fuller, Jack A.)

FULTON, MICKEY, P.O. Box 1062, Willows, CA 95988/916-934-5780
Specialties: Working straight knives of his design. **Patterns:** Hunters, Bowies, kitchen and fishing knives, steak knife sets. **Technical:** Hand-filed, sanded, buffed ATS-34, 440C and A2. Uses natural handle materials. All knives mirror-finished. **Prices:** $65 to $600; some to $2,000. **Remarks:** Full-time maker; first knife sold in 1979. **Mark:** Signature.

g

GADDY, GARY LEE, 205 Ridgewood Lane, Washington, NC 27889/919-946-4359
Specialties: Working/using straight knives of his design; period pieces. **Patterns:** Bowies, hunters, utility/camp knives. **Technical:** Grinds ATS-34, D2 and 01. Offers filework. **Prices:** $100 to $225; some to $400. **Remarks:** Spare-time maker; first knife sold in 1991. **Mark:** Etched name and quarter moon logo.

GAETA, ANGELO, R. Saldanha Marinho, 1295, Centro, Jau, SP-17201-310, BRAZIL/0146-224543; FAX: 0146-224543
Specialties: Straight using knives to customer specs. **Patterns:** Hunters, kitchen and utility knives. **Technical:** Grinds D6, ATS-34 and 440C stainless. Titanium nitride golden finish upon request. **Prices:** $60 to $170. **Remarks:** Full-time maker; first knife sold in 1992. **Mark:** First initial, last name.

GAETA, ROBERTO, Rua Shikazu Myai 80, 05351 Sao Paulo, S.P., BRAZIL/11-268-4626; Av. Francisco Morato, 3680, 05520, Sao Paulo, S.P., BRAZIL (shop)
Specialties: Wide range of using knives. **Patterns:** Brazilian and North American hunting and fighting knives. **Technical:** Grinds stainless steel; likes natural handle materials. **Prices:** $100 to $250; some to $500. **Remarks:** Full-time maker; first knife sold in 1979. **Mark:** BOB'G.

GAINEY, HAL, 904 Bucklevel Rd., Greenwood, SC 29649/803-223-0225

directory

Specialties: Traditional working and using straight knives and folders. **Patterns:** Hunters, slip-joint folders and utility/camp knives. **Technical:** Hollow-grinds ATS-34 and D2; makes sheaths. **Prices:** $95 to $145; some to $500. **Remarks:** Part-time maker; first knife sold in 1975. **Mark:** Eagle head and last name or last initial.

GALLAGHER, BARRY, 714 8th Ave. N., Lewistown, MT 59457/406-538-7056
Specialties: Traditional working/using straight knives and folders of his design and to customer specs. **Patterns:** Bowies, fighters, hunters, folders, fillets and hatchets. **Technical:** Grinds ATS-34, 440C and D2; forges carbon steel and Damascus. Scrimshaws and engraves. **Prices:** $100 to $600; some to $1,500. **Remarks:** Full-time maker; first knife sold in 1993. Doing business as Gallagher Custom Knives. **Mark:** First initial, last name, city, state in football shape with "custom" in center.

GAMBLE, FRANK, P.O. Box 3687, Redwood City, CA 94064/415-368-1430
Specialties: Fantasy and high-art straight knives and folders of his design. **Patterns:** Daggers, fighters, hunters and special locking folders. **Technical:** Grinds 440C and ATS-34; forges Damascus/cable Damascus. Inlays; offers jeweling. **Prices:** $150 to $10,000. **Remarks:** Full-time maker; first knife sold in 1976. **Mark:** First initial, last name.

GAMBLE, ROGER, 2801 65 Way N., St. Petersburg, FL 33710/813-384-1470
Specialties: Traditional working/using straight knives and folders of his design. **Patterns:** Hunters and slip-joints. **Technical:** Grinds ATS-34 and Damascus. **Prices:** $50 to $150; some to $500. **Remarks:** Part-time maker; first knife sold in 1982. Doing business as Gamble Knives. **Mark:** First name in a fan of cards over last name.

GAME TRAIL KNIVES (See Watson, Bert)

GAND (See Anderson, Gary D.)

GANSTER, JEAN-PIERRE, 18, Rue du Vieil Hopital, F-67000 Strasbourg, FRANCE/(0033)88 32 65 61; FAX: 0033 88 32 52 79
Specialties: Fancy and high-art miniatures of his design and to customer specs. **Patterns:** Bowies, daggers, fighters, hunters, locking folders and miniatures. **Technical:** Forges and grinds stainless Damascus, ATS-34, gold and silver. **Prices:** $100 to $380; some to $2,500. **Remarks:** Part-time maker; first knife sold in 1972. **Mark:** Stylized first initials.

GARBE, BOB, 33176 Klein, Fraser, MI 48026/810-293-3664
Specialties: Folders and straight knives. **Patterns:** Hunters, locking folders and slip-joint folders. **Technical:** Grinds 440C and ATS-34. Offers filework. **Prices:** $85 to $800. **Remarks:** Full-time maker; first knife sold in 1991. **Mark:** Last name.

GARCIA, MARIO EIRAS, R. Edmundo Scanapieco, 300, Caxingui, Sao Paulo, SP-05516-070, BRAZIL/011-2124528
Specialties: Fantasy knives of his design; one-of-a-kind only. **Patterns:** Fighters, daggers, boots and two-bladed knives. **Technical:** Forges car leaf springs. Uses only natural handle material. **Prices:** $100 to $200. **Remarks:** Part-time maker; first knife sold in 1976. **Mark:** Two B's, one opposite the other.

GARCIA JR., RAUL, P.O. Box #693, Aberdeen, MD 21001/410-272-4842; FAX: 410-272-6340
Specialties: Classic working and using knives of his design. **Patterns:** Fighters, Bowies and hunters. **Technical:** Hand forges 5160, L6 and W2; differentially head-treats. Makes wood-lined leather sheaths. **Prices:** $150 to $500; some to $1,000. **Remarks:** Part-time maker; first knife sold in 1992. **Mark:** Last name.

GARDNER, ROB, 3828 W. Delhi Ct., Ann Arbor, MI 48103/313-996-0704
Specialties: High-art working and using knives of his design and to customer specs. **Patterns:** Daggers, hunters and ethnic-patterned knives. **Technical:** Forges Damascus, L6 and 10-series steels. Engraves and

inlays. Handles and fittings may be carved. **Prices:** $175 to $500; some to $2,500. **Remarks:** Spare-time maker; first knife sold in 1987. **Mark:** Engraved initials.

GARNER, BERNARD, 207-2515 Trout Lake Rd., North Bay, Ontario P1B 844 CANADA/705-840-5352
Specialties: Mostly folders of his design. **Patterns:** Skinners, fighters and locking folders. **Technical:** Grinds 440C, ATS-34 and O1. Uses anodized titanium; flat grinds; hand finishes to 2000+ grit. **Prices:** $400 to $600. **Remarks:** Part-time maker; first knife sold in 1989. **Mark:** Initials or signature.

GARNER JR., WILLIAM O., 2803 East DeSoto St., Pensacola, FL 32503/904-438-2009
Specialties: Working straight knives, some fancy. **Patterns:** Hunters, Bowies, fighters, double-edged daggers, folders and fishing knives. **Technical:** Grinds 440C, 154CM and ATS-34, D2 and 01 steels. **Prices:** $85 to $500. **Remarks:** Full-time maker; first knife sold in 1985. **Mark:** First and last name in oval logo or last name.

GARTMAN, M.D., Rt. 4, Box 423G, Gatesville, TX 76528/817-865-6090
Specialties: Working straight knives and folders in standard patterns. **Patterns:** A variety of folders, some Bowies and miniatures. **Technical:** Uses ATS-34; likes unusual natural handles such as swordfish bill. **Prices:** $125 to $235. **Remarks:** Part-time maker; first knife sold in 1982. **Mark:** Last name.

GASTON, BERT, P.O. Box 9047, North Little Rock, AR 72119/501-372-4747; 800-264-0747
Specialties: Traditional working and using straight knives of his design. **Patterns:** Hunters, Bowies and fighters. **Technical:** Forges his Damascus, 5168 and L6. Only uses natural handle materials. **Prices:** $200 to $500; some to $1,500. **Remarks:** Part-time maker; first knife sold in 1989. **Mark:** Stylized last initial and M.S.

GASTON, RON, 330 Gaston Dr., Woodruff, SC 29388/803-433-0807; FAX: 803-433-9958
Specialties: Working period pieces. **Patterns:** Hunters, fighters, tantos, boots and a variety of other straight knives; single-blade slip-joint folders. **Technical:** Grinds ATS-34. Hand-rubbed satin finish is standard. **Prices:** $100 to $350; some to $1,000. **Remarks:** Full-time maker; first knife sold in 1980. **Mark:** Name.

GAUDETTE, LINDEN L., 5 Hitchcock Rd., Wilbraham, MA 01095/413-596-4896
Specialties: Traditional working knives in standard patterns. **Patterns:** Broad-bladed hunters, Bowies and camp knives; wood carver knives; locking folders. **Technical:** Grinds ATS-34, 440C and 154CM. **Prices:** $150 to $400; some higher. **Remarks:** Full-time maker; first knife sold in 1975. **Mark:** Last name in Gothic logo; used to be initials in circle.

GAULT, CLAY, Rt. 1, Box 287, Lexington, TX 78947/512-273-2873
Specialties: Straight and folding hunting knives. **Patterns:** Classic drop-points; traditional folding styles. **Technical:** Grinds BX-NSM 174 steel, custom rolled from billets to his specifications. **Prices:** $250 to $375; some higher. **Remarks:** Full-time maker; first knife sold in 1970. **Mark:** Name or name with cattle brand.

G-E KNIVES (See Van Den Elsen, Gert)

GEISLER, GARY R., P.O. Box 294, Clarksville, OH 45113/513-289-2469
Specialties: Traditional working straight knives. **Patterns:** English-style Bowies, drop-point hunters, and a few daggers. **Technical:** Flat-grinds A2, 440C, 01 and ATS-34. Prefers mirror finishes. **Prices:** $50 to $250; some higher. **Remarks:** Part-time maker; first knife sold in 1982. **Mark:** First and middle initials, last name and Maker in script.

GENGE, ROY E., P.O. Box 57, Eastlake, CO 80614/303-451-7991
Specialties: High-tech working knives. **Patterns:** Bowies, hatchets,

hunters, survival knives, buckskinners, kukris and others. **Technical:** Forges and grinds L6, S7, W1, W2, 01, Vascowear, 154CM, ATS-34 and commercial Damascus. **Prices:** $50 to $500; embellished knives are higher. **Remarks:** Part-time maker; first knife sold in 1968. **Mark:** Name, city, state.

GENOVESE, RICK, 781 Richard St., Clarkdale, AZ 86324/602-634-2558
Specialties: Fancy and embellished folders of his design. **Patterns:** Locking folders. **Technical:** Grinds ATS-34 and J. Rados Damascus. All folders are interframes with inlays such as jade, lapis, dinosaur bone, charoite, etc. **Prices:** $800 to $1,500; some to $10,000. **Remarks:** Full-time maker; first knife sold in 1976. **Mark:** Last name.

GENSKE, JAY, 262 1/2 Elm St., Fon du Lac, WI 54935/414-921-6505
Specialties: Working/using knives and period pieces of his design and to customer specs. **Patterns:** Bowies, fighters, hunters. **Technical:** Grinds ATS-34 and 440C; forges and grinds Damascus and cable. Offers custom-tooled sheaths, scabbards and hand carved handles. **Prices:** $85 to $300; some to $1,000. **Remarks:** Full-time maker; first knife sold in 1985. Doing business as Genske Knives. **Mark:** Stamped or engraved last name.

GENTILE, AL, 101 Ticonderoga Dr., Warwick, RI 02889/401-737-4534

GEORGE, HARRY, 3137 Old Camp Long Rd., Aiken, SC 29801/803-649-1963
Specialties: Working straight knives of his design or to customer specs. **Patterns:** Hunters, skinners and utility knives. **Technical:** Grinds ATS-34. Prefers natural handle materials, hollow-grinds and mirror finishes. **Prices:** Start at $65. **Remarks:** Part-time maker; first knife sold in 1985. Trained under George Herron. Member SCAK. **Mark:** Name, city and state.

GEORGE, TOM, P.O. Box 1298, Magalia, CA 95954/916-873-3306
Specialties: Large Bowies and display knives. **Patterns:** Hunters, Bowies, daggers and buckskinners. **Technical:** Uses D2, 440C, ATS-34 and 154CM. **Prices:** $175 to $4,500. **Remarks:** Part-time maker; first knife sold in 1981. Accepting orders on past Glories series and broken-back jacks only. **Mark:** Name.

GEPNER, DON, 2615 E. Tecumseh, Norman, OK 73071/405-364-2750
Specialties: Traditional working and using straight knives of his design. **Patterns:** Bowies and daggers. **Technical:** Forges his Damascus, 1095 and 5160. **Prices:** $100 to $400; some to $1,000. **Remarks:** Spare-time maker; first knife sold in 1991. Has been forging since 1954; first edged weapon made at 9 years old. **Mark:** Last initial.

GERUS, GERRY, P.O. Box 2295, G.P.O. Cairns, Qld. 4870 AUSTRALIA/070-341451
Specialties: Fancy working and using straight knives of his design. **Patterns:** Hunters, Bowies and fighters. **Technical:** Uses 440C, ATS-34 and commercial Damascus. **Prices:** $275 to $600; some to $1,200. **Remarks:** Part-time maker; first knife sold in 1988. **Mark:** Last name; or last name, Hand Made, city, country.

GEVEDON, HANNERS (HANK), 1410 John Cash Rd., Crab Orchard, KY 40419-9770
Specialties: Traditional working and using straight knives. **Patterns:** Hunters, swords, utility and camp knives. **Technical:** Forges and grinds his own Damascus, 5160 and L6. Cast aluminum handles. **Prices:** $50 to $250; some to $400. **Remarks:** Part-time maker; first knife sold in 1983. **Mark:** Initials and LBF tang stamp.

G.H. KNIVES (See Hielscher, Guy)

GIBSON, JIM, RR1, Box 177F, Bunnell, FL 32110/904-437-4383

GILBERT, CHANTAL, 1421 Cb du South, St. Romuald, Quebec G6W 2MX CANADA

GILBREATH, RANDALL, Rt. 5, Box 823B, Dora, AL 35062/205-648-3902

Specialties: Damascus. **Patterns:** Folders and fixed blades. **Technical:** Forges Damascus and stainless steel. **Prices:** $100 to $1,500. **Remarks:** Part-time maker; first knife sold in 1979. **Mark:** Name in ribbon.

GILJEVIC, BRANKO, 35 Hayley Cresent, Queanbeyan 2620, N.S.W., AUSTRALIA/06-2977613
Specialties: Classic working straight knives and folders of his design. **Patterns:** Hunters, Bowies, skinners and locking folders. **Technical:** Grinds 440C and D2. Offers acid etching, scrimshaw and leather carving. **Prices:** $150 to $500. **Remarks:** Part-time maker; first knife sold in 1987. Doing business as Sambar Custom Knives. **Mark:** Name, serial number and sambar head logo in handle.

GILLIS, C.R. "REX", 3000 Central Ave., Great Falls, MT 59401/406-771-1082
Specialties: Working/using straight knives of all designs. **Patterns:** Fighters and hunters. **Technical:** Grinds ATS-34 and 440C. Heat-treats. Offers hand-sewn leather sheaths. **Prices:** $100 to $500. **Remarks:** Full-time maker; first knife sold in 1983. Doing business as Steel Talon Cutlery. **Mark:** Eagle head and claws with a Bowie.

GILPIN, DAVID, 902 Falling Star Ln., Alabaster, AL 35007/205-664-4777
Specialties: Classic, fancy and traditional knives of his design. **Patterns:** Japanese style swords. **Technical:** Grinds 440C, forges and grinds Damascus stainless, 1010, 1095 and 1084. Offers metal casting, electoplate and inlay. **Prices:** $500 to $5000; some to $12,000. **Remarks:**Full-time maker; first knife sold in 1994. **Mark:** First name in Japanese/Chinese characters.

GLASER, KEN, Rt. #1, Box 148, Purdy, MO 65734/417-442-3371
Specialties: Working straight knives in standard patterns. **Patterns:** Hunters, bird and trout knives, boots. **Technical:** Hollow-grinds 01, D2 and 440C. **Prices:** $75 to $125; some to $250. **Remarks:** Part-time maker; first knife sold in 1983. **Mark:** Initials.

GLOVER, RON, 6775 Socialville-Foster Rd., Mason, OH 45040/513-398-7857
Specialties: High-tech working straight knives and folders. **Patterns:** Hunters to Bowies; some interchangeable blade models; unique locking mechanisms. **Technical:** Grinds 440C, 154CM; buys Damascus. **Prices:** $70 to $500; some to $800. **Remarks:** Part-time maker; first knife sold in 1981. **Mark:** Name in script.

GODDARD, WAYNE, 473 Durham Ave., Eugene, OR 97404/503-689-8098
Patterns: Fixed blades and folders. **Technical:** Works exclusively with wire Damascus and his own pattern-welded material. **Prices:** $250 to $4,000. **Remarks:** Full-time maker; first knife sold in 1963. Three-year backlog on orders. **Mark:** Blocked initials on forged blades; regular capital initials on stock removal.

GOERS, BRUCE, 3423 Royal Ct. S., Lakeland, FL 33813/813-647-3093, 800-392-7496
Specialties: Fancy working and using straight knives of his design and to customer specs. **Patterns:** Hunters, fighters, Bowies and fantasy knives. **Technical:** Grinds ATS-34, some Damascus. **Prices:** $195 to $600; some to $1,300. **Remarks:** Full-time maker; first knife sold in 1990. Doing business as Vulture Cutlery. **Mark:** Buzzard with initials.

GOERTZ, PAUL S., 201 Union Ave. SE, #207, Renton, WA 98059/206-228-9501
Specialties: Working straight knives of his design and to customer specs. **Patterns:** Hunters, skinners, camp, bird and fish knives, camp axes, some Bowies, fighters and boots. **Technical:** Grinds ATS-34, D2 and 440C. **Prices:** $75 to $500; some to $900. **Remarks:** Full-time maker; first knife sold in 1985. **Mark:** Signature.

GOFOURTH, JIM, 3776 Aliso Cyn. Rd., Santa Paula, CA 93060/805-659-3814

Specialties: Period pieces and working knives. **Patterns:** Bowies, locking folders, patent lockers and others. **Technical:** Grinds A2 and 154CM. **Prices:** Moderate. **Remarks:** Spare-time maker. **Mark:** Initials interconnected.

GOGUEN, SCOTT, 166 Goguen Rd., Newport, NC 28570/919-393-6013
Specialties: Classic and traditional straight knives; working/using knives of all designs. **Patterns:** Boots, Bowies, fighters, hunters, kitchen knives, utility/camp knives, fillets. **Technical:** Grinds ATS-34; forges 1095 and 01. Offers clay tempering and cord wrapped handles. **Prices:** $65 to $500. **Remarks:** Spare-time maker; first knife sold in 1988. **Mark:** Last name.

GOLD HILL KNIFE WORKS (See Scarrow, Wil)

GOLDBERG, DAVID, 1120 Blyth Ct., Blue Bell, PA 19422/215-654-7117
Specialties: Japanese style designs. **Patterns:** Kozuka to dai-sho. **Technical:** Forges his own Damascus; hand-rubbed finish. Uses traditional materials, carves fittings, handles and scabbards. **Remarks:** Full-time maker; first knife sold in 1987. **Mark:** Last name in English and Japanese.

GOLDENBERG, T.S., P.O. Box 238, Fairview, NC 28730
Specialties: Working straight knives and period pieces to customer specs. **Patterns:** Hunters, boots and Bowies. **Technical:** Grinds A2, 01 and 440C. **Prices:** $75 to $500; some to $700. **Remarks:** Part-time maker; first knife sold in 1975. **Mark:** Surname in mountain; some with TEDDYHAWK.

GOLDING, ROBIN, P.O. Box 267, Lathrop, CA 95330/209-982-0839
Specialties: Working straight knives of his design. **Patterns:** Survival knives, Bowie extractions, camp knives, diver's knives and skinners. **Technical:** Grinds 440C, 154CM and ATS-34. **Prices:** $75 to $250; some to $600. **Remarks:** Full-time maker; first knife sold in 1985. Up to 1-year waiting period on orders. **Mark:** Last name, USA.

GOLD RUSH DESIGNS (See Connolly, James)

GOLTZ, WARREN L., 802 4th Ave. E., Ada, MN 56510/218-784-7721
Specialties: Fancy working knives in standard patterns. **Patterns:** Hunters, Bowies and camp knives. **Technical:** Grinds 440C and ATS-34. **Prices:** $120 to $595; some to $950. **Remarks:** Part-time maker; first knife sold in 1984. **Mark:** Last name.

GONZALEZ, LEONARDO WILLIAMS, Ituzaingo 473, Maldonado, CP 20000, URUGUAY/(598.42)21617
Specialties: Classic high-art and fantasy straight knives; traditional working and using knives of his design, in standard patterns or to customer specs. **Patterns:** Hunters, Bowies, daggers, fighters, boots, swords and utility/camp knives. **Technical:** Forges and grinds 440C, 1095 and carbon steel. **Prices:** $100 to $900. **Remarks:** Full-time maker; first knife sold in 1985. **Mark:** Willy, whale, R.O.U.

GOO, TAI, 3225 N. Winstel Blvd., Tucson, AZ 85716/602-325-8095
Specialties: High-art, neo-primitive and fantasy knives; some working knives. **Patterns:** Fighters, daggers, Bowies, buckskinners, edged fetishes and sculptures. **Technical:** Forges and grinds A6, 440C and his own Damascus with iron meteorites. **Prices:** $150 to $500; some to $10,000. **Remarks:** Full-time maker; first knife sold in 1978. **Mark:** Chiseled signature; mark in spacer and tang.

GOODE, BEAR, P.O. Box 6474, Navajo Dam, NM 87419/505-632-8184
Specialties: Working/using straight knives of his design and in standard patterns. **Patterns:** Bowies, hunters and utility/camp knives. **Technical:** Grinds 440C, ATS-34, 154-CM; forges and grinds 1095, 5160 and other steels on request; uses Damascus. **Prices:** $45 to $125; some to $350. **Remarks:** Part-time maker; first knife sold in 1993. Doing business as Bear Knives. **Mark:** First name, or first name and year, or first name and last initial.

GORDON (See Defreest, William G.)

GORENFLO, JAMES T., 9145 Sullivan Rd., Baton Rouge, LA 70818/504-261-5868
Specialties: Traditional working and using straight knives of his design. **Patterns:** Bowies, hunters and utility/camp knives. **Technical:** Forges 5160, 1095 and 52100. **Prices:** $125 to $300. **Remarks:** Spare-time maker; first knife sold in 1992. **Mark:** Last name or initials.

GOTTAGE, DANTE, 21700 Evergreen, St. Clair Shores, MI 48082-1935/810-293-6615
Specialties: Working knives of his design or to customer specs. **Patterns:** Large and small skinners, fighters, Bowies, fillet knives and miniatures. **Technical:** Grinds 01, 440C and 154CM. **Prices:** $100 to $400; some to $500. **Remarks:** Part-time maker; first knife sold in 1975. **Mark:** Full name in script letters.

GOTTAGE, JUDY, 21700 Evergreen, St. Clair Shores, MI 48082-1935/810-293-6615; FAX: 313-293-7540
Specialties: Interframe folders of her design or to customer specs. **Patterns:** From 5 to 9 inches overall length. **Technical:** 440C, 154CM, ATS-34, Damascus. Heat-treats. **Prices:** $300 to $3,000. **Remarks:** Full-time maker; first knife sold in 1980. **Mark:** Full name or first name.

GOTTSCHALK, GREGORY J., 12 First St. (Ft. Pitt), Carnegie, PA 15106/412-279-6692
Specialties: Fancy working straight knives and folders to customer specs. **Patterns:** Hunters to tantos, locking folders to minis. **Technical:** Grinds 440C, 154CM, ATS-34. Now making own Damascus. Most knives have mirror finishes. **Prices:** Start at $75. **Remarks:** Part-time maker; first knife sold in 1977. **Mark:** Full name in crescent.

GOUKER, GARY B., P.O. Box 955, Sitka, AK 99835/907-747-3476
Specialties: Hunting knives for hard use. **Patterns:** Skinners, semi-skinners, and such. **Technical:** Likes natural materials, inlays, stainless steel. **Prices:** Moderate. **Remarks:** New Alaskan maker. **Mark:** Name.

GRAFFEO, ANTHONY I., 100 Riess Place, Chalmette, LA 70043/504-277-1428
Specialties: Traditional working and using straight knives of his design, to customer specs and in standard patterns. **Patterns:** Hunters, utility/camp knives and fishing knives. **Technical:** Hollow- and flat-grinds ATS-34, 440C and 154CM. Handle materials include Pakkawood, Micarta and sambar stag. **Prices:** $65 to $100; some to $250. **Remarks:** Part-time maker; first knife sold in 1991. Doing business as Knives by: Graf. **Mark:** First and middle initials, last name city, state, Maker.

GREBE, GORDON S., P.O. Box 296, Anchor Point, AK 99556-0296/907-235-8242
Specialties: Working straight knives and folders, some fancy. **Patterns:** Tantos, Bowies, boot fighter sets, locking folders. **Technical:** Grinds stainless steels; likes 1/4-inch stock and glass-bead finishes. **Prices:** $75 to $250; some to $2,000. **Remarks:** Full-time maker; first knife sold in 1968. **Mark:** Initials in lightning logo.

GRECO, JOHN, 4099 14th St., Bay St. Louis, MS 39520
Specialties: One-of-a-kind limited edition knives. **Patterns:** Fighters, daggers, camp knives. **Technical:** Forges and stock removes carbon steel. **Prices:** Moderate. **Remarks:** Full-time maker; first knife sold in 1986. **Mark:** Last name.

GREEN, BILL, 706 Bradfield, Garland, TX 75042/214-272-4748
Specialties: High-art and working straight knives and folders of his design and to customer specs. **Patterns:** Bowies, hunters, kitchen knives and locking folders. **Technical:** Grinds ATS34, D2 and 440V. Hand-tooled custom sheaths. **Prices:** $70 to $350; some to $750. **Remarks:** Part-time maker; first knife sold in 1990. **Mark:** Last name.

GREEN, ROGER M., 3412 Co. Rd. 1022, Joshua, TX 76058/817-641-5057

Specialties: 19th century period pieces. **Patterns:** Investor-grade Sheffield Bowies and dirks. **Technical:** Grinds 440C and D2; prefers flat-grinds; offers checkererd ivory. **Prices:** $550 to $2,500. **Remarks:** Full-time maker; first knife sold in 1984. **Mark:** First and middle initials, last name.

GREEN, WILLIAM (BILL), 46 Warren Rd., View Bank, Vic. 3084, AUSTRALIA/03-9459-1529
Specialties: Traditional high-tech straight knives and folders. **Patterns:** Japanese-influenced designs, hunters, Bowies, folders and miniatures. **Technical:** Forges 01, D2 and his own Damascus. Offers lost wax castings for bolsters and pommels. Likes natural handle materials, gems, silver and gold. **Prices:** $400 to $750; some to $1,200. **Remarks:** Full-time maker. **Mark:** Initials.

GREENE, DAVID, 570 Malcom Rd., Covington, GA 30209/404-784-0657

GREENFIELD, G.O., POB 295, Everett, WA 98206/206-259-1672
Specialties: High-tech and working straight knives and folders of his design and to customer specs. **Patterns:** Boots, daggers and hunters. **Technical:** Grinds ATS34, D2 and 440V. Makes sheaths for each knife. **Prices:** $100 to $800; some to $10,000. **Remarks:** Full-time maker; first knife sold in 1978. **Mark:** Springfield®, serial number.

GREGORY, MICHAEL, 211 Calhoun Rd., Belton, SC 29627/803-338-8898
Specialties: Working straight knives and folders. **Patterns:** Hunters, tantos, locking folders and slip-joints, boots and fighters. **Technical:** Grinds 440C, 154CM and ATS-34; mirror finishes. **Prices:** $95 to $200; some to $1,000. **Remarks:** Part-time maker; first knife sold in 1980. **Mark:** Name, city in logo.

GREINER, RICHARD, 1073 E. County Rd. 32, Green Springs, OH 44836

GREISS, JOCKL, obere Muhlstr. 5, 73252 Gutenberg, GERMANY/07026-3224
Specialties: Classic and working/using straight knives of his design. **Patterns:** Bowies, daggers and hunters. **Technical:** Uses stainless Damascus, D2 and ATS-34. All knives are one-of-a-kind made by hand; no machines are used. **Prices:** $500 to $1500; some to $3000. **Remarks:** Full-time maker; first knife sold in 1984. **Mark:** An X with a long vertical line through it.

GRENIER, ROGER, 497 Chemin Paquette, Saint Jovite, P. Que. J0T 2H0, CANADA/819-425-8893
Specialties: Working straight knives. **Patterns:** Heavy-duty Bowies, fighters, hunters, swords and miniatures. **Technical:** Grinds 01, D2 and 440C. **Prices:** $70 to $225; some to $800. **Remarks:** Full-time maker; first knife sold in 1981. **Mark:** Last name on blade.

GREY, PIET, P.O. Box 1493, Silverton 0127, REPUBLIC OF SOUTH AFRICA/012-803-8206
Specialties: Fancy working and using straight knives of his design. **Patterns:** Fighters, hunters and utility/camp knives. **Technical:** Grinds ATS-34 and AEB-L; forges and grinds Damascus. Solderless fitting of guards. Engraves and scrimshaws. **Prices:** $125 to $750; some to $1,500. **Remarks:** Full-time maker; first knife sold in 1970. **Mark:** Last name.

GRIFFIN JR., HOWARD A., 14299 SW 31st Ct., Davie, FL 33330/305-474-5406
Specialties: Working straight knives and folders. **Patterns:** Hunters, Bowies, locking folders with his own push-button lock design. **Technical:** Grinds 440C. **Prices:** $100 to $200; some to $500. **Remarks:** Part-time maker; first knife sold in 1983. **Mark:** Initials.

GRIFFIN, MARK (See Griffin, Rendon and Mark)

GRIFFIN, RENDON and MARK, 9706 Cedardale, Houston, TX 77055/713-468-0436

Specialties: Working folders of their designs. **Patterns:** Standard lockers and slip-joints. **Technical:** Grind and forge 440C, 154CM and their Damascus. **Prices:** $185 to $300; some to $800. **Remarks:** Part-time makers; Rendon's first knife sold in 1966; Mark's in 1974. **Mark:** Last name logo.

GRIFFIN, THOMAS J., 591 Quevli Ave., Windom, MN 56101/507-831-1089
Specialties: Period pieces and fantasy straight knives of his design. **Patterns:** Daggers and swords. **Technical:** Forges 1095, 52100 and L6. Most blades are his own Damascus; turned fittings and wire wrapped grips. **Prices:** $250 to $600; some to $1500. **Remarks:** Full-time maker; first knife sold in 1991. Doing business as Griffin Knives. **Mark:** Last name etched.

GRIGSBY, BEN, The Bluff Dweller House, P.O. Box 2096, 318 E. Main, Mt. View, AR 72560/501-269-3337
Specialties: Period pieces in steel or flint. **Patterns:** Arkansas toothpicks, Bowies and flint blades of late archaic period. **Technical:** Grinds 01, D2, 440C and knappes flint of Ozark Hills. **Prices:** $150 to $500; some to $1,500. **Remarks:** Full-time maker; first knife sold in 1976. Doing business as Ben Grigsby Edged Tools and Weapons. **Mark:** Initials with cache river arrowhead logo.

GRINDERE OF HANDIECRAFTE CUTELLERIE (See Lozier, Don)

GRINDSTONE, THE (See Grospitch, Ernie)

GROSPITCH, ERNIE, 18440 Amityville St., Orlando, FL 32820/407-568-5438
Specialties: Working knives of his design and in standard patterns. **Patterns:** Bowies, hunters and kitchen knives. **Technical:** Grinds ATS-34, 440V and 440C. Offers dovetailed bolsters and brass space between blade and bolster. Hand-stitched sheaths. **Prices:** $140 to $180; some to $300. **Remarks:** Part-time maker; first knife sold in 1989. Doing business as The Grindstone. **Mark:** First and last name, city, state.

GROSS, W.W., 325 Sherbrook Dr., High Point, NC 27260
Specialties: Working knives. **Patterns:** Hunters, boots, fighters. **Technical:** Grinds. **Prices:** Moderate. **Remarks:** Full-time maker. **Mark:** Name.

GROSSMAN, STEWART, 24 Water St. #419, Clinton, MA 01510/508-365-2291; 800-my sword
Specialties: Miniatures and full-size knives and swords. **Patterns:** One-of-a-kind miniatures—jewelry, replicas—and wire-wrapped figures. Full-size art, fantasy and combat knives, daggers and modular systems. **Technical:** Forges and grinds most metals and Damascus. Uses gems, crystals, electronics and motorized mechanisms. **Prices:** $20 to $300; some to $4,500 and higher. **Remarks:** Full-time maker; first knife sold in 1985. **Mark:** G1.

GRUBB, RICHARD E., 2759 Maplewood Dr., Columbus, OH 43231/614-882-1530
Specialties: Miniatures to Bowies. **Patterns:** Bowies, drop-point hunters, fighters, tantos and miniatures. **Technical:** Grinds 440C; likes filework; offers exotic woods, stag and Micarta, wire wrap. **Prices:** $50 to $500. **Remarks:** Part-time maker; first knife sold in 1989. **Mark:** Name.

GRUSSENMEYER, PAUL, 101 S. White Horse Pike, Lindenwold, NJ 08021-2304/609-435-1859; FAX: 609-435-3786

GUESS, RAYMOND L., 7214 Salineville Rd. NE, Mechanicstown, OH 44651/216-738-2793
Specialties: Working straight knives and folders of his design or to customer specs. **Patterns:** Hunters, Bowies, fillet knives, steak and paring knife sets. **Technical:** Grinds 440C. Offers silver inlay work and mirror finishes. **Prices:** $45 to $400; some to $700. **Remarks:** Spare-time maker; first knife sold in 1985. **Mark:** First initial, last name.

GUIGNARD, GIB, Box 3477, Quartzsite, AZ 85359/520-927-4831
Specialties: Traditional working/using straight knives of his design and in standard patterns. **Patterns:** Bowies, hunters, kitchen knives and utility/camp knives. **Technical:** Forges 5160 and 1095; grinds 440C. Heat-treats; offers turquoise inlays in handles. **Prices:** $50 to $275; some to $400. **Remarks:** Part-time maker; first knife sold in 1989. Doing business as Cactus Forge. **Mark:** Last name and GT.

THE GUN ROOM (See Shostle, Ben)

GURGANUS, CAROL, Star Rt., Box 50-A, Colerain, NC 27924/919-356-4831
Specialties: Working and using straight knives. **Patterns:** Fighters, hunters and kitchen knives. **Technical:** Grinds D2, ATS-34 and Damascus steel. Uses stag, sheephorn and exotic wood handles. **Prices:** $100 to $300. **Remarks:** Full-time maker; first knife sold in 1992. **Mark:** Female symbol, last name, city, state.

GURGANUS, MELVIN H., Star Rt., Box 50-A, Colerain, NC 27924/919-356-4831
Specialties: High-tech working folders. **Patterns:** Leaf-lock and back-lock designs, bolstered and interframe. **Technical:** D2 and 440C; makes mokume. Wife Carol scrimshaws. Heat-treats, carves and offers lost wax casting. **Prices:** $300 to $3,000. **Remarks:** Full-time maker; first knife sold in 1983. **Mark:** First initial, last name and Maker.

GUTEKUNST, RALPH, 117 SW 14th St., Richmond, IN 47374/317-966-3225
Specialties: Traditional straight knives of his design and to customer specs; period pieces. **Patterns:** Daggers, fighters and hunters. **Technical:** Forges 1084, 5160 and his own Damascus and cable. **Prices:** $35 to $300; some to $1,000. **Remarks:** Full-time maker; first knife sold in 1989. **Mark:** Rampant wolf inside shield.

GUTH, KENNETH, 8 S. Michigan, 32nd Floor, Chicago, IL 60603/312-346-1760
Specialties: One-of-a-kind ornate straight knives and folders. **Patterns:** Flemish, Japanese and African-styled knives. Also makes a few forged Damascus miniature knives with fossil ivory handles and 18K gold fittings and rivets. **Technical:** Forges and grinds high carbon and 440C. Offers brass and steel laminations, goldsmithing. **Prices:** Upscale. **Remarks:** Full-time goldsmith and knifemaker. **Mark:** Last name.

GUTHRIE, GEORGE B., 1912 Puett Chapel Rd., Bassemer City, NC 28016/704-629-3031
Specialties: Working knives of his design or to customer specs. **Patterns:** Hunters, boots, fighters, locking folders and slip-joints in traditional styles. **Technical:** Grinds D2, 440C and 154CM. **Prices:** $85 to $300; some to $450. **Remarks:** Part-time maker; first knife sold in 1978. **Mark:** Name in state.

GWOZDZ, BOB, 71 Starr Ln., Attleboro, MA 02703/508-226-7475
Specialties: Fancy working straight knives. **Patterns:** Fighters, tantos and hunters. **Technical:** Grinds 440C. **Prices:** $150 to $400; some $500 and higher. **Remarks:** Part-time maker; first knife sold in 1983. Now attending law school. Will accept phone orders during summer months only. **Mark:** Name and serial number.

GYPSY SILK KNIVES (See Burrows, Stephen R.)

h

H&K ENTERPRISE (See Hunter, Hyrum and Kellie)

HAGEN, PHILIP L., P.O. Box 58, Pelican Rapids, MN 56572/218-863-8503
Specialties: High-tech working straight knives and folders. **Patterns:** Defense-related straight knives; wide variety of folders. **Technical:** Forges and grinds 440C and his own Damascus; Uddeholm UHB. **Prices:** $100 to $800; some to $3,000. **Remarks:** Part-time maker, first knife sold in 1975. **Mark:** DOC HAGEN in shield, knife, banner logo; or DOC.

HAGGERTY, GEORGE S., P.O. Box 88, Jacksonville, VT 05342/802-368-7437
Specialties: Working straight knives and folders. **Patterns:** Hunters, claws, camp and fishing knives, locking folders and backpackers. **Technical:** Forges and grinds W2, 440C and 154CM. **Prices:** $85 to $300. **Remarks:** Part-time maker; first knife sold in 1981. **Mark:** Initials or last name.

HAGUE, GEOFF, The Malt House, Hollow Ln., Wilton, Marlborough, Wiltshire, SN8 3SR, ENGLAND/01672-870212
Specialties: Working knives to his design or to customer specs. **Patterns:** Hunters, skinners and fillet knives. **Technical:** Grinds ATS-34, 440C, D2 and others. **Prices:** $120 to $400. **Remarks:** Full-time maker; first knife sold in 1992. **Mark:** Last name.

HAGWOOD, KELLIE, 9231 Ridgetown, San Antonio, TX 78250/210-521-8710
Specialties: Working straight knives and folders of his design or to customer specs. **Patterns:** Folders, fighters, Bowies, hunters and swords. **Technical:** Grinds 440C, ATS-34, D2 and Damascus; heat-treats. Makes leather sheaths. **Prices:** Start at $200. **Remarks:** Full-time maker; first knife sold in 1969. Exclusive maker for Texas Parks and Wildlife. Doing business as Longhorn Knife Works. **Mark:** Name, city and state in script.

HAJOVSKY, ROBERT J., P.O. Box 77, Scotland, TX 76379/817-541-2219
Specialties: Working straight knives; sub-hilted fighters. **Patterns:** Variety of straight knives. **Technical:** Grinds ATS-34 and others on request. **Prices:** $150 to $700. **Remarks:** Part-time maker; first knife sold in 1973. **Mark:** Bob-Sky Knives and name, city, state.

HALLIGAN & SON (See Halligan, Ed and Shawn)

HALLIGAN, ED and SHAWN, 14 Meadow Way, Sharpsburg, GA 30277/404-251-7720; FAX: 404-251-7720
Specialties: Working straight knives and folders, some fancy. **Patterns:** Linerlocks, hunters, skinners, boots, fighters and swords. **Technical:** Grind 440C and ATS-34; forge 5160; make cable and pattern Damascus. **Prices:** $125 to $1,200. **Remarks:** Full-time makers; first knife sold in 1985. **Mark:** Halligan & Son, city, state and USA.

HALLIGAN, SHAWN (See Halligan, Ed and Shawn)

HAMLET JR., JOHNNY, 300 Billington, Clute, TX 77531/409-265-6929
Specialties: Working straight knives and folders. **Patterns:** Hunters, fighters, fillet and kitchen knives, locking folders. Likes upswept knives and trailing-points. **Technical:** Grinds 440C, D2, ATS-34. Makes sheaths. **Prices:** $55 to $225; some $500. **Remarks:** Part-time maker; first knife sold in 1988. **Mark:** Hamlet's Handmades in script.

HAMMERSMITH (See Smith, J.D.)

HAMMOND, JIM, P.O. Box 486, Arab, AL 35016/205-586-4151
Specialties: High-tech fighters and folders. **Patterns:** Proven-design fighters. **Technical:** Grinds 440C and ATS-34. **Prices:** $200 to $975; some to $8,500. **Remarks:** Full-time maker; first knife sold in 1977. **Mark:** Full name, city, state in shield logo.

HANCOCK, RONALD E., P.O. Box 402, Lecanto, FL 34460/904-628-4595
Specialties: Working knives, period pieces, bucksinners, early folder patterns, daggers, patch knives, skinners and small axes. **Patterns:** Frontlocks, backlocks, interframes and stag folders. **Technical:** Forges and grinds A2, ATS-34 and 01. **Prices:** $100 to $800. **Remarks:** First knife sold in 1973. **Mark:** Last name.

HANCOCK, TIM, 10805 N. 83rd St., Scottsdale, AZ 85260/602-998-8849

Specialties: High-art and working straight knives and folders of his design and to customer specs. **Patterns:** Fighters, hunters, daggers, tantos, swords and locking folders. **Technical:** Forges Damascus and 52100; grinds ATS-34. Makes Damascus. Silver-wire inlays; offers carved fittings. **Prices:** $175 to $350; some to $5,000. **Remarks:** Full-time maker; first knife sold in 1988. **Mark:** Last name or heart.

HAND, BILL, P.O. Box 773, 1103 W. 7th St., Spearman, TX 79081/806-659-2967
Specialties: Traditional working and using straight knives of his design or to customer specs. **Patterns:** Hunters, Bowies and fighters. **Technical:** Forges 5160 and Damascus. **Prices:** Start at $125. **Remarks:** Spare-time maker; first knife sold in 1988. Current delivery time six to eight weeks. **Mark:** Stylized initials.

HAND M.D., JAMES E., No. 1 Mocking Bird Ln., Gloster, MS 39638/601-225-4197
Specialties: All types of straight knives. **Patterns:** Hunters, fighters, boots and collector knives. **Technical:** Grinds ATS-34 and commercial Damascus. All knives are handmade. **Prices:** $125 to $850; some to $1,200. **Remarks:** Part-time maker; first knife sold in 1985. **Mark:** Name and city.

HAND MADE KNIVES (See Bailey, Kirby C.)

HANDMADE KNIVES BY MARK LUBRICH (See Lubrich, Mark)

HANGAS & SONS (See Ruana Knife Works)

HANSEN, ROBERT W., 35701 University Ave. N.W., Cambridge, MN 55008/612-689-3242
Specialties: Working straight knives and folders. **Patterns:** From hunters to minis, camp knives to miniatures; folding lockers and slip-joints in original styles. **Technical:** Grinds 01, 440C and 154CM; likes filework. **Prices:** $75 to $175; some to $550. **Remarks:** Part-time maker; first knife sold in 1983. **Mark:** Fish with last initial inside.

HANSON, TRAVIS, 651 Rangeline Rd., Mosinees, WI 54455/715-693-3940
Specialties: Straight knives of his design and in standard patterns. **Patterns:** Hunters and miniatures. **Technical:** Grinds D2, 440C and Damascus. Offers scrimshaw and filework. **Prices:** $50 to $300; some to $550. **Remarks:** First knife sold in 1993. **Mark:** Name in script.

HARA, KOUJI, 292-2, Oosugi, Seki-City, Gifu-Pref., 501-32, JAPAN/81-575-24-7569; FAX: 81-575-24-7569
Specialties: High tech and working straight knives of his design; some folders. **Patterns:** Hunters, locking folders and utility/camp knives. **Technical:** Grinds Cowry X, Cowry Y and ATS-34. Prefers high mirror polish; pearl handle inlay. **Prices:** $80 to $500; some to $1,000. **Remarks:** Full-time maker; first knife sold in 1980. Doing business as Knife House "Hara". **Mark:** First initial, last name in fish.

HARDIN, ROBERT K. "FUZZY", 814 Pamela Dr., Dalton, GA 30720/404-226-3624
Specialties: Working straight knives; high-art knives of his design. **Patterns:** Bowies, skinners, Japanese short swords and using belt knives. **Technical:** Grinds 01, D2 and 154CM. Uses precious gems and ivories; engraves. **Prices:** $100 to $5,000; one has gone for $80,000. **Remarks:** Part-time maker; first knife sold in 1948. **Mark:** Name.

HARDY, SCOTT, 639 Myrtle Ave., Placerville, CA 95667/916-622-5780
Specialties: Traditional working and using straight knives of his design. **Patterns:** Bowies, hunters and utility knives. **Technical:** Forges 01 and W2. Offers mirror finish; differentially tempers. **Prices:** $65 to $350; some to $1,000. **Remarks:** Part-time maker; first knife sold in 1982. **Mark:** First initial, last name and Handmade with bird logo.

HARKINS, J.A., P.O. Box 218, Conner, MT 59827/406-821-4724
Specialties: One-of-a-kind modern art knives of his design. **Patterns:** Folders, fighters and swords. **Technical:** Grinds ATS-34 and Ferguson Damascus. Engraves; offers gem work. **Prices:** Start at $450. **Remarks:** Full-time maker and engraver; first knife sold in 1988. **Mark:** First and middle initials, last name.

HARLESS, WALT, P.O. Box 845, Stoneville, NC 27048-0845/910-573-9768
Specialties: Traditional working straight knives. **Patterns:** Hunters, utility, combat and specialty knives; one-of-a-kind historical interpretations. **Technical:** Grinds ATS-34 and 440C. **Prices:** $75 to $350; some to $1,000. **Remarks:** Full-time maker; first knife sold in 1978. Doing business as Arrow Forge. **Mark:** A with arrow; name, city and state.

HARLEY, LARRY W., 348 Deerfield Dr., Bristol, TN 37620/615-878-5368 (shop); 703-466-6771 (home)
Specialties: Working knives; period pieces. **Patterns:** Full range of straight knives, tomahawks, razors, buckskinners and hog spears. **Technical:** Forges and grinds ATS-34, D2, 440, 01, L6 and his own Damascus. **Prices:** $65 to $6,500. **Remarks:** Full-time maker; first knife sold in 1983. Guides (knife only) wild boar hunts. Doing business as Lonesome Pine. **Mark:** Name, city and state in pine logo.

HARMON, JAY, 462 Victoria Rd., Woodstock, GA 30188/404-928-2734
Specialties: Working straight knives and folders of his design or to customer specs; collector-grade pieces. **Patterns:** Bowies, daggers, fighters, boots, hunters and folders. **Technical:** Grinds 440C, 440V, ATS-34, D2 1095 and Damascus; heat-treats. **Prices:** Start at $185. **Remarks:** Part-time maker; first knife sold in 1984. **Mark:** Last name.

HARMON, JOE, 8014 Fisher Dr., Jonesboro, GA 30236/770-471-0024
Specialties: High-tech and working folders of his design. **Patterns:** Liner lock and traditional folders. **Technical:** Grinds 12C27 Sandvik, ATS-34 and A2. Offers heat-treating, anodized-titanium and inlays; prefers natural handle materials. **Prices:** $125 and up. **Remarks:** Part-time maker; first knife sold in 1988. **Mark:** First name, middle initial, last name, city, state.

HARRIS, JAY, 991 Johnson St., Redwood City, CA 94061/415-366-6077
Specialties: Traditional high-tech straight knives and folders of his design. **Patterns:** Daggers, fighters and locking folders. **Technical:** Uses 440C, ATS-34 and CPM. **Prices:** $250 to $850. **Remarks:** Spare-time maker; first knife sold in 1980.

HARRIS, RALPH DEWEY, 2607 Bell Shoals Rd., Brandon, FL 33511/813-681-5293
Specialties: Collectible and working interframe locking folders. **Patterns:** Straight and folding hunters, fighters and pocketknives; backlocks, sidelocks, leverlocks and buttonlocks. **Technical:** Grinds 440C, ATS-34 and some commercial Damascus. Uses jeweled and color anodized titanium and 416SS for frames. **Prices:** $150 to $800; some to $1,000. **Remarks:** Full-time maker; first knife sold in 1978. **Mark:** Last name, or name and city.

HARSEY, WILLIAM H., 82710 N. Howe Ln., Creswell, OR 97426/503-895-4941
Specialties: High-tech kitchen and outdoor knives. **Patterns:** Folding hunters, trout and bird folders; straight hunters, camp knives and axes. **Technical:** Grinds; etches. **Prices:** $125 to $300; some to $1,500. Folders start at $350. **Remarks:** Full-time maker; first knife sold in 1979. **Mark:** Full name, state, U.S.A.

HARTMAN, ARLAN (LANNY), 340 Ruddiman, N. Muskegon, MI 49445/616-744-3635
Specialties: Working straight knives and folders. **Patterns:** Drop-point hunters, coil spring lockers, slip-joints. **Technical:** Flat-grinds D2, 440C and ATS-34. **Prices:** $150 to $250; some to $2,000. **Remarks:** Part-time maker; first knife sold in 1982. **Mark:** Last name.

HARTMANN, BRUCE JAMES, 961 Waterloo, Port Elgin, Ontario NOH 2C0, CANADA

HARTSFIELD, PHILL, P.O. Box 1637, Newport Beach, CA 92659-0637/714-722-9792; 714-636-7633
Specialties: Heavy-duty working and using straight knives. **Patterns:** Fighters, swords and survival knives, most in Japanese profile. **Technical:** Grinds A2 and M2. Believes in sole authorship. **Prices:** $350 to $20,000. **Remarks:** Full-time maker; first knife sold about 1966. Doing business as A Cut Above. **Mark:** Initials, chiseled character plus register mark.

HARVEST MOON FORGE (See Rua, Gary [Wolf])

HARVEY MOUNTAIN KNIVES (See Wahlers, Herman F.)

HARVEY, MAX, 14 Bass Rd., Bull Creek, Perth, 6155, WESTERN AUSTRALIA/09-332-7585
Specialties: Daggers, Bowies, fighters and fantasy knives. **Patterns:** Hunters, Bowies, tantos and skinners. **Technical:** Hollow- and flat-grinds 440C, ATS-34, 154CM and Damascus. Offers gem work. **Prices:** $250 to $4,000. **Remarks:** Part-time maker; first knife sold in 1981. **Mark:** First and middle initials, last name.

HATCH, KEN, P.O. Box 82, Jensen, UT 84035/801-789-8219
Specialties: Working knives; period pieces. **Patterns:** Buckskinners, tomahawks, period Bowies. **Technical:** Forges and grinds 1095, 01, W2, ATS-34. Prefers natural handle materials. **Prices:** $60 to $250. **Remarks:** Part-time maker; first knife sold in 1977. **Mark:** Name or dragonfly stamp.

HAWK, JACK L., Rt. 1, Box 771, Ceres, VA 24318/703-624-3878, 703-624-3282
Specialties: Fancy and embellished working and using straight knives of his design or to customer specs. **Patterns:** Hunters, Bowies and daggers. **Technical:** Hollow-grinds 440C, ATS-34 and D2; likes bone and ivory handles. **Prices:** $75 to $1,200. **Remarks:** Full-time maker; first knife sold in 1982. **Mark:** Full name and initials.

HAWK, JOE, Rt. 1, Box 196, Ceres, VA 24318/703-624-3282
Specialties: Fancy working knives of his design or to customer specs. **Patterns:** Hunters, combat knives, Bowies and fighters. **Technical:** Grinds mostly ATS-34, 154CM and 440C. Scrimshaws, carves, engraves and silver inlays. **Prices:** $150 to $2,100. **Remarks:** Full-time maker; first knife sold in 1958. **Mark:** Name with tomahawk logo.

HAWK, JOEY K., Rt. 1, Box 196, Ceres, VA 24318/703-624-3282
Specialties: Working straight knives, some fancy. Welcomes customer designs. **Patterns:** Hunters, fighters, daggers, Bowies and miniatures. **Technical:** Grinds 440C or customer preference. Offers some knives with jeweling. **Prices:** $100 to $250; some to $500. **Remarks:** Part-time maker; first knife sold in 1983. **Mark:** First and middle initials, last name stamped.

HAWKINS, RADE, P.O. Box 400, Red Oak, GA 30272/404-964-1177; FAX: 404-306-2877
Specialties: Exotic steels, custom designs, one-of-a-kind knives. **Patterns:** All styles. **Technical:** Grinds CPM 10V, CPM 440V, Vascomax C-350, Stelite K6 and Damascus. **Prices:** Start at $190. **Remarks:** Full-time maker; first knife sold in 1972. **Mark:** Full name, city and state, some last name only.

HAYES, DOLORES, P.O. Box 41405, Los Angeles, CA 90041/213-258-9923
Specialties: High-art working and using straight knives of her design. **Patterns:** Art knives and miniatures. **Technical:** Grinds 440C, stainless AEB, commercial Damascus and ATS-34. **Prices:** $50 to $500; some to $2,000. **Remarks:** Spare-time maker; first knife sold in 1978. **Mark:** Last name.

HAYES, WALLY, 1024 Queen St., Orleans, Ont., CANADA K4A-3N2/613-824-9520
Specialties: Classic and fancy straight knives and folders. **Patterns:** Daggers, Bowies, fighters, tantos. **Technical:** Forges own Damascus and 01; engraves. **Prices:** $250 to $1,500; some to $4,500. **Mark:** Last name.

HAYNES, CHAP, RR #4, Tatamagouche, NS B0K 1V0, CANADA
Specialties: Ergonomic handles fitted to grips; forged carbon tools. **Patterns:** Hunters, Bowies, tomahawks, swords, miniatures. **Technical:** Forges W2, his own Damascus, and meteorite and nickel composites. **Prices:** $200 to $450; some to $1,500. **Remarks:** Part-time maker; first knife sold in 1985. **Mark:** Smith at anvil logo with HAYNES GREAT BLADES.

HAYS, MARK, 1034 Terry Way, Carrollton, TX 75006/214-242-5197
Specialties: Traditional working and using straight knives and folders in standard patterns. **Patterns:** Bowies, hunters and slip-joint folders. **Technical:** Grinds 440C. Custom sheaths by John Simon. **Prices:** $125 to $650. **Remarks:** Part-time maker; first knife sold in 1984. **Mark:** Name.

HEASMAN, H.G., 28, St. Mary's Rd., Llandudno, N. Wales U.K., LL302UB/(UK)0492-876351
Specialties: Miniatures only. **Patterns:** Bowies, daggers and swords. **Technical:** Files from stock high-carbon and stainless steel. **Prices:** $400 to $600. **Remarks:** Part-time maker; first knife sold in 1975. Doing business as Reduced Reality. **Mark:** NA.

HEDRICK, DON, 131 Beechwood Hills, Newport News, VA 23602/804-877-8100
Specialties: Working straight knives; period pieces and fantasy knives. **Patterns:** Hunters, boots, Bowies and miniatures. **Technical:** Grinds 440C and commercial Damascus. **Prices:** $150 to $550; some to $1,200. **Remarks:** Part-time maker; first knife sold in 1982. **Mark:** First initial, last name in oval logo.

HEGWALD, J.L., 1106 Charles, Humboldt, KS 66748/316-473-3523
Specialties: Working straight knives, some fancy. **Patterns:** Makes Bowies, miniatures. **Technical:** Forges or grinds 01, L6, 440C; mixes materials in handles. **Prices:** $35 to $200; some higher. **Remarks:** Part-time maker; first knife sold in 1983. **Mark:** First and middle initials.

HEGWOOD, JOEL, Rt. 4, Box 229, Summerville, GA 30747/404-397-8187
Specialties: High-tech working knives of his design. **Patterns:** Hunters, boots and survival knives; locking folders, slip-joints and interframes. **Technical:** Grinds A2, 01 and D2; uses 7075 aluminum in lightweight folder frames. **Prices:** $65 to $125; some to $200. **Remarks:** Part-time maker; first knife sold in 1979. **Mark:** Last name.

HEHN, RICHARD KARL, Lehnmuehler Str. 1, D-6531 Doerrebach GERMANY/06724 3152
Specialties: High-tech working knives. **Patterns:** Hunters, fighters, Bowies and locking folders. **Technical:** Forges and grinds 440C, CPM and his own stainless Damascus; high-tech polishing for all steels; clean grinds; deluxe natural handles. **Prices:** $350 to $4,000; some to $9,000. **Remarks:** Full-time maker; first knife sold in 1963. **Mark:** Runic last initial in logo.

HEITLER, HENRY, P.O. Box 15025, Tampa, FL 33684-5025/813-933-1645
Specialties: Traditional working and using straight knives of his design and to customer specs. **Patterns:** Fighters, hunters, utility/camp knives and fillet knives. **Technical:** Flat-grinds ATS-34; offers tapered tangs. **Prices:** $120 to $350; some to $600. **Remarks:** Part-time maker; first knife sold in 1990. **Mark:** First initial, last name, city, state circling double Hs.

HELTON, ROY, 11535 Phantom Ln., San Diego, CA 92126/619-578-3399
Specialties: Locking folders and straight knives in utility, fancy and interframe styles. **Patterns:** Hunters, boots, fighters, daggers and some art pieces. **Technical:** Grinds ATS-34, others on request. Likes filework; uses mostly natural handle materials. **Prices:** $100 to $525; some higher. **Remarks:** Part-time maker; first knife sold in 1975. **Mark:** Lion logo with name, city and state.

HEMBROOK, RON, P.O. Box 153, Neosho, WI 53059/414-625-3607 **Specialties:** Period pieces, art knives and working straight knives; enjoys customer designs. **Patterns:** Hunters, push daggers, miniatures, fighters and Bowies. **Technical:** Grinds 01, 440C, D2 and ATS-34; uses Damascus; laser-engraves handles. **Prices:** $95 to $325; some to $750. **Remarks:** Part-time maker; first knife sold in 1980. **Mark:** Last name and serial number.

HEMPHILL, JESSE, 896 Big Hill Rd., Berea, KY 40403 **Specialties:** Period pieces, folders and scagel reproductions. **Patterns:** Hawks, Bowies sets, fighters and utility knives. **Technical:** Forges his own Damascus, D2, 5160 and 52100. **Prices:** $50 to $300; some to $500. **Remarks:** Full-time maker; first knife sold in 1986. **Mark:** Initials or a turtle.

HENDRICKS, SAMUEL J., 2162 Van Buren Rd., Maurertown, VA 22644/703-436-3305 **Specialties:** Integral hunters and skinners of thin design. **Patterns:** Boots, hunters and locking folders. **Technical:** Grinds ATS-34, 440C and D2. Integral liners and bolsters of N-S and 7075 T6 aircraft aluminimum. Does leatherwork. **Prices:** $50 to $250; some to $500. **Remarks:** Full-time maker; first knife sold in 1992. **Mark:** First and middle initials, last name, city and state in football-style logo.

HENDRICKSON, E. JAY, 4204 Ballenger Creek Pike, Frederick, MD 21701/301-663-6923 **Specialties:** Classic collectors and working straight knives of his design. **Patterns:** Bowies, Kukri's, camp, hunters, and fighters in the Moran styles. **Technical:** Forges W2, 01, 1095, 5160; makes Damascus; does a lot of wire inlay. **Prices:** $300 to $4,000. **Remarks:** Full-time maker; first knife sold in 1975. **Mark:** Last name, M.S.

HENDRIX, WAYNE, Rt.1, Box 111P, Allendale, SC 29810/803-584-3825

HENNON, ROBERT, 940 Vincent Lane, Ft. Walton Beach, FL 32547/904-862-9734

HENRIKSEN, HANS J., Birkegaardsvej 24, DK 3200 Helsinge, DENMARK/FAX: 45 4879 4899 **Specialties:** Zirconia ceramic blades. **Patterns:** Customer designs. **Technical:** Slip-cast zirconia-water mix in plaster mould; offers hidden or full tang. **Prices:** White blades start at $10/cm; colored +50 percent. **Remarks:** Part-time maker; first ceramic blade sold in 1989. **Mark:** Initial logo.

HENRY & SON, PETER, 332 Nine Mile Ride, Wokingham, Berkshire RG11 3NJ, ENGLAND/01734-734475 **Specialties:** Period pieces to customer specs only. **Patterns:** Period pieces only—Scottish dirks, Sgian Dubhs and Bowies, moden hunters. **Technical:** Grinds 01 and Damascus. **Prices:** $67 to $247; Damascus knives cased $975 to $1800. **Remarks:** Full-time maker; first knife sold in 1974. **Mark:** P. Henry & Son.

HENSLEY, WAYNE, P.O. Box 904, Conyers, GA 30207/404-483-8938 **Specialties:** Period pieces and fancy working knives. **Patterns:** Boots to Bowies, locking folders to miniatures. Large variety of straight knives. **Technical:** Grinds D2, 440C, 154CM and commerical Damascus. **Prices:** $50 to $150; some to $800. **Remarks:** Part-time maker; first knife sold in 1974. **Mark:** Last name.

HERBST, PETER, Komotauer Strasse 26, 91207 Lauf a.d. Pegn., GERMANY/09123-13315; FAX: 09123-13379 **Specialties:** Working/using knives. **Patterns:** Personal and sporting knives. **Technical:** Grinds stainless; prefers natural material. **Remarks:** Full-time maker.

HERMAN, TIM, 7721 Foster, Overland Park, KS 66204/913-649-3860; FAX: 913-649-0603 **Specialties:** Investment-grade folders of his design; interframes and bolster frames. **Patterns:** Boots, Bowies, daggers and push knives;

high-quality folders and interframes. **Technical:** Grinds ATS-34 and A.J. Hubbard Damascus. Engraves and gold inlays with pearl, jade, lapis and Australian opal. **Prices:** $1,000 to $15,000. **Remarks:** Full-time maker; first knife sold in 1978. **Mark:** Etched signature.

HERMES, DANA E., 39594 Kona Ct., Fremont, CA 94538/415-490-0393 **Specialties:** Fancy and embellished classic straight knives of his design. **Patterns:** Hunters and Bowies. **Technical:** Grinds 440C and D2. **Prices:** $200 to $600; some to $1,000. **Remarks:** Spare-time maker; first knife sold in 1985. **Mark:** Last name.

HERNDON, WM. R. "BILL", 32520 Michigan St., Acton, CA 93510/805-269-5860; FAX: 805-269-4568 **Specialties:** Straight knives, plain and fancy. **Technical:** Carbon steel (white and blued), Damascus, stainless steels. **Prices:** $120 and up. **Remarks:** Part-time maker; first knife sold in 1981. **Mark:** Signature and/or helm.

HERRON, GEORGE, 474 Antonio Way, Springfield, SC 29146/803-258-3914 **Specialties:** High-tech working and using straight knives; some folders. **Patterns:** Hunters, fighters, boots in personal styles. **Technical:** Grinds 154CM, ATS-34. **Prices:** $75 to $500; some to $750. **Remarks:** Full-time maker; first knife sold in 1963. About a seven- to eight-year (or more) backlog; will not quote a delivery date. **Mark:** Last name in script.

HESSER, DAVID, P.O. Box 1079, Dripping Springs, TX 78620/512-894-0100 **Specialties:** High-art daggers and fantasy knives of his design; court weapons of the Renaissance. **Patterns:** Daggers, swords, axes, miniatures and sheath knives. **Technical:** Forges 1065, 1095, 01, D2 and recycled tool steel. Offers custom lapidary work and stone-setting, stone handles and custom hardwood scabbards. **Prices:** $95 to $500; some to $6,000. **Remarks:** Full-time maker; first knife sold in 1989. Doing business as Exotic Blades. **Mark:** Last name, year.

HETHCOAT, DON, Box 1764, Clovis, NM 88101/505-762-5721 **Specialties:** Working straight knives and folders. **Patterns:** Hunters, axes, fishing knives, Bowies, boots and locking folders. **Technical:** Grinds ATS-34 and 440C. Forges some 5168 on Bowies; uses his own Damascus. **Prices:** $100 to $2,000. **Remarks:** Part-time maker; first knife sold in 1969. **Mark:** Last name and zip code on stock removal; last name on forged 5168 and Damascus.

HETMANSKI, THOMAS S., 1107 William St., Trenton, NJ 08610/609-989-9371 **Specialties:** Working knives, replicas, military-style knives and miniatures. **Patterns:** Hunters, boots, miniatures and some folders. **Technical:** Grinds A2, 440C, ATS-34 and commercial Damascus. **Prices:** $150 to $400; some higher. **Remarks:** Part-time maker; first knife sold in 1982. **Mark:** Initials in monogram.

HIBBEN, DARYL, P.O. Box 172, 1331 Dawkins Rd., LaGrange, KY 40031-0172/502-222-0983 **Specialties:** Working straight knives, some fancy to customer specs. **Patterns:** Hunters, fighters, Bowies, short sword, art and fantasy. **Technical:** Grinds 440C, ATS-34, 154CM, Damascus; prefers hollow-grinds. **Prices:** $175 to $3,000. **Remarks:** Full-time maker; first knife sold in 1979. **Mark:** Block letters.

HIBBEN, GIL, P.O. Box 13, LaGrange, KY 40031/502-222-1397 **Specialties:** Working knives and fantasy pieces to customer specs. **Patterns:** Full range of straight knives, including swords, axes and miniatures; some locking folders. **Technical:** Grinds D2, 440C and 154CM. **Prices:** $300 to $2,000; some to $10,000. **Remarks:** Full-time maker; first knife sold in 1957. Maker and designer of *Rambo III* knife; made swords for movie *Marked for Death* and throwing knife for movie *Under Seige*; made belt buckle knife and knives for movie *Perfect Weapon*; made knives featured in movie *Star Trek the Next Generation*; designer for United Cutlery. **Mark:** Hibben Knives, city and state, or signature.

directory

HIBBEN, JOLEEN, P.O. Box 172, LaGrange, KY 40031/502-222-0983 **Specialties:** Miniature straight knives of her design; period pieces. **Patterns:** Hunters, axes and fantasy knives. **Technical:** Grinds Damascus, 1095 tool steel and stainless 440C or ATS-34. Uses wood, ivory, bone, feathers and claws on/for handles. **Prices:** $60 to $200. **Remarks:** Spare-time maker; first knife sold in 1991. **Mark:** Initials or first name.

HIBBEN, WESTLEY G., 14101 Sunview Dr., Anchorage, AK 99515 **Specialties:** Working straight knives of his design or to customer specs. **Patterns:** Hunters, fighters, daggers, combat knives and some fantasy pieces. **Technical:** Grinds 440C mostly. Filework available. **Prices:** $200 to $400; some to $3,000. **Remarks:** Part-time maker; first knife sold in 1988. **Mark:** Signature.

HIELSCHER, GUY, HC34, P.O. Box 992, Alliance, NE 69301/308-762-4318 **Specialties:** Traditional and working straight knives of his design, to customer specs and in standard pattersn. **Patterns:** Bowies, fighters, skinners, daggers and hunters. **Technical:** Forges his own Damascus from 0-1 and 1018 steel. **Prices:** $150 to $225; some to $850. **Remarks:** Part-time maker; first knife sold in 1988. Doing business as G.H. Knives. **Mark:** Initials in arrowhead.

HIGH, TOM, 5474 S. 112.8 Rd., Alamosa, CO 81101/719-589-2108 **Specialties:** Hunters, some fancy. **Patterns:** Drop-points in several shapes; some semi-skinners. Knives designed by and for top outfitters and guides. **Technical:** Grinds ATS-34; likes hollow-grinds, mirror finishes; prefers scrimmable handles. **Prices:** $100 to $5,000. **Remarks:** Full-time maker; first knife sold in 1965. Three-year backlog on all ordered knives. **Mark:** Initials connected; arrow through last name on fancy knives.

HILKER, THOMAS N., 500 Holmestead Rd., Williams, OR 97544/503-846-6461 **Specialties:** Traditional working straight knives and folders. **Patterns:** Folding skinner in two sizes, Bowies, fork and knife sets, camp knives and interchangeables. **Technical:** Grinds D2, 440C and ATS-34. Heat-treats. **Prices:** $50 to $350; some to $400. Doing business as Thunderbolt Artisans. Only limited production models available; not currently taking orders. **Remarks:** Full-time maker; first knife sold in 1983. **Mark:** Last name.

HILL, HOWARD E., 111 Mission Lane, Polson, MT 59860/406-883-3405 **Specialties:** All types of straight knives and folders in personal designs. **Patterns:** Bowies, daggers, skinners and lockback folders. **Technical:** Grinds 440C; uses micro and satin finish. **Prices:** $150 to $1,000. **Remarks:** Full-time maker; first knife sold in 1981. **Mark:** Persuader.

HILL, RICK, 20 Nassau, Collinsville, IL 62234/618-288-4370 **Specialties:** Working knives and period pieces to customer specs. **Patterns:** Hunters, locking folders, fighters and daggers. **Technical:** Grinds D2, 440C and 154CM; forges his own Damascus. **Prices:** $75 to $500; some to $3,000. **Remarks:** Part-time maker; first knife sold in 1983. **Mark:** Full name in hill shape logo.

HILL, STEVEN E., 7814 Toucan Dr., Orlando, FL 32822/407-277-3549 **Specialties:** Bowies and liner-lock folders; some exotic mechanisms. **Patterns:** Bowies, California daggers, fighters, hunters, and liner-lock folders. **Technical:** Grinds D2, 440C and Damascus; ATS-34 on request. Likes filework, exotic woods and hand-rubbed finishes. **Prices:** $160 to $1,000; some higher. **Remarks:** Full-time maker; first knife sold in 1978. **Mark:** First initial, last name and handmade.

HINDERER, RICK, 5423 Kister Rd., Wooster, OH 44691/216-263-0962 **Specialties:** Working knives to one-of-a-kind Damascus straight knives and folders. **Patterns:** All. **Technical:** Grinds ATS-34 and D2; forges 01, W2 and his own nickel Damascus steel. **Prices:** $50 to $3,200. **Remarks:** Part-time maker; first knife sold in 1988. Doing business as Mustang Forge. **Mark:** Initials or first initial, last name.

HINK III, LES, 1599 Aptos Lane, Stockton, CA 95206/209-547-1292 **Specialties:** Working straight knives and traditional folders in standard patterns or to customer specs. **Patterns:** Hunting and utility/camp knives; others on request. **Technical:** Grinds carbon and stainless steels. **Prices:** $80 to $200; some higher. **Remarks:** Part-time maker; first knife sold in 1980. **Mark:** Last name, or last name 3.

HINSON and SON, R., 2419 Edgewood Rd., Columbus, GA 31906/706-327-6801 **Specialties:** Working straight knives and folders. **Patterns:** Locking folders, liner locks, combat knives and swords. **Technical:** Grinds 440C and commercial Damascus. **Prices:** $100 to $350; some to $1,500. **Remarks:** Part-time maker; first knife sold in 1983. Son Bob is co-worker. **Mark:** HINSON.

HINTZ, GERALD, 5402 Sahara Ct., Helena, MT 59605

HIRAM KNIVES (See Price, Joel Hiram)

HIRAYAMA, HARUMI, 4-5-13, Kitamachi, Warabi City, Saitama Pref., JAPAN/048-443-2248 **Specialties:** High-tech working knives of her design. **Patterns:** Locking folders, interframes, straight gents and slipjoints. **Technical:** Grinds 440C or equivalent; uses natural handle materials and gold. **Prices:** Start at $700. **Remarks:** Part-time maker; first knife sold in 1985. **Mark:** First initial, last name.

HITCHMOUGH, HOWARD, 3 Highland Lodge, Fox Hill, London SE 19 2UJ, ENGLAND/0181-653-6166 **Specialties:** High class folding knives. **Patterns:** Locking folders, pocket knives, linerlocks, hunters and boots. **Technical:** Uses ATS-34, stainless Damascus and titanium. Prefers hand-rubbed finishes and natural handle materials. **Prices:** $250 to $1,500; some to $4,000. **Remarks:** Full-time maker; first knife sold in 1967. **Mark:** Last name, country.

HOCKENSMITH, DAN, P.O. Box E, Drake, CO 80515/970-669-5404 **Specialties:** Traditional working and using straight knives of his design. **Patterns:** Hunters, Bowies, folders and utility/camp knives. **Technical:** Uses his Damascus, 5160, carbon steel and wire cable. **Prices:** $150 to $600; some to $1,000. **Remarks:** Full-time maker; first knife sold in 1987. **Mark:** Stylized initials.

HODGE, J.B., 1100 Woodmont Ave. SE, Huntsville, AL 35801/205-536-8388 **Specialties:** Fancy working folders. **Patterns:** Slipjoints. **Technical:** Grinds 154CM and ATS-34. **Prices:** Start at $175. **Remarks:** Part-time maker; first knife sold in 1978. Not currently taking orders. **Mark:** Name, city and state.

HODGE III, JOHN, 422 S. 15th St., Palatka, FL 32177/904-328-3897 **Specialties:** Fancy straight knives and folders. **Patterns:** Various. **Technical:** Pattern-welded Damascus—"Southern-style". **Prices:** To $1,000. **Remarks:** Part-time maker; first knife sold in 1981. **Mark:** JH3 logo.

HODGSON, RICHARD J., 9081 Tahoe Lane, Boulder, CO 80301/303-666-9460 **Specialties:** Straight knives and folders in standard patterns. **Patterns:** High-tech knives in various patterns. **Technical:** Grinds 440C, AEB-L and CPM. **Prices:** $850 to $2,200. **Remarks:** Part-time maker. **Mark:** None.

HOEL, STEVE, P.O. Box 283, Pine, AZ 85544/602-476-4278 **Specialties:** Investor-class folders, straight knives and period pieces of his design. **Patterns:** Folding interframes—lockers and slip-joints; straight Bowies, boots and daggers. **Technical:** Grinds 154CM, ATS-34 and commercial Damascus. **Prices:** $600 to $1,200; some to $7,500. **Remarks:** Full-time maker. **Mark:** Initial logo with name and address.

HOFFMAN, HAROLD, 7174 Hoffman Rd., San Angelo, TX 76905/915-655-5953

Specialties: Stout using folders. **Patterns:** Spring-back and lock-back folders only. **Technical:** Close tolerance fitting of high-strength parts; practical finishes. **Prices:** Moderate. **Remarks:** Veteran metalworker and knifemaker. **Mark:** Name.

HOFFMAN, KEVIN L., P.O. Box 5107, Winter Park, FL 32793/407-678-3124
Specialties: High-tech working knives. **Patterns:** Fighters, tantos, liner lock folders, claws and survival knives. **Technical:** Grinds ATS-34, 440C and D2. Tantos have polished temper lines and sandblasted finishes. Makes Kydex sheaths. **Prices:** $115 to $600; some to $1500. **Remarks:** Full-time maker; first knife sold in 1981. **Mark:** Initials.

HOFFMANN, UWE H., P.O. Box 60114, Vancouver, BC V5W 4B5 CANADA/604-572-7320 (after 5 p.m.)
Specialties: High-tech working knives, folders and fantasy knives of his design or to customer specs. **Patterns:** Hunters, fishing knives, combat and survival knives, folders and diver's knives. **Technical:** Grinds 440C, ATS-34, D2 and commercial Damascus. **Prices:** $95 to $900; some to $2,000 and higher. **Remarks:** Full-time maker; first knife sold in 1985. **Mark:** Hoffmann Handmade Knives.

HOLDER, D'ALTON, 7148 W. Country Gables Dr., Peoria, AZ 85381/602-878-3064; FAX: 602-879-3964
Specialties: Deluxe working knives and high-art hunters. **Patterns:** Drop-point hunters, fighters, Bowies, miniatures and locking folders. **Technical:** Grinds 440C and 154CM; uses amber and other materials in combination on stick tangs. **Prices:** $150 to $350; some to $1,000. **Remarks:** Full-time maker; first knife sold in 1970. **Mark:** D'HOLDER, city and state.

HOLLAND, DALE J., 4561 247th Place SE, Issaquah, WA 98027/206-391-4665
Specialties: Fancy folders. **Patterns:** Locking folders, patent locks and interframes. **Technical:** Grinds 440C, 154CM and ATS-34. **Prices:** $120 to $350; some to $450. **Remarks:** Part-time maker; first knife sold in 1980. **Mark:** Initials.

HOLLAND, JOHN H., 143 Green Meadow Lane, Calhoun, GA 30701/706-629-9622
Specialties: Traditional and fancy straight knives and folders. **Patterns:** Hunters, locking folders, slip-joints. **Technical:** Grinds 440V, 440C, 01. **Prices:** $200 to $500; some to $1,000. **Remarks:** Spare-time maker; first knife sold in 1988. **Mark:** First and last name, city, state.

HOLLETT, JEFF, 905 Krider Rd., P.O. Box 255, Fate, TX 75132/214-771-2014
Specialties: Classic, traditional, fantasy and working straight knives and folders of his design, to customer specs and in standard patterns; period pieces. **Patterns:** Bowies, fighters and hunters. **Technical:** Grinds ATS-34, 440C and D2. Heat-treats. **Prices:** $100 to $700; some to $1,000. **Remarks:** Full-time maker; first knife sold in 1989. **Mark:** Name, city, state, month and year.

HOLLOWAY, PAUL, 714 Burksdale Rd., Norfolk, VA 23518/804-588-7071
Specialties: Working straight knives and folders to customer specs. **Patterns:** Lockers and slip-joints; fighters and boots; fishing and push knives, from swords to miniatures. **Technical:** Grinds A2, D2, 154CM, 440C and ATS-34. **Prices:** $125 to $400; some to $1,200. **Remarks:** Part-time maker; first knife sold in 1981. **Mark:** Last name, or last name and city in logo.

HOLMES, DOC (See Holmes, Robert)

HOLMES, ROBERT, 4423 Lake Larto Circle, Baton Rouge, LA 70816/504-291-4864
Specialties: Using straight knives and folders of his design or to customer specs. **Patterns:** Bowies, utility hunters, camp knives, skinners, slip-joint and lock-back folders. **Technical:** Forges 1065, 1095 and L6. Makes his own Damascus and cable Damascus. Offers clay tempering.

Prices: $150 to $1,500. **Remarks:** Part-time maker; first knife sold in 1988. **Mark:** DOC HOLMES, or anvil logo with last initial inside.

HOLUM, MORTEN, Bolerskrenten 28, 0691 Oslo, NORWAY/011-47-22-27-69-96
Specialties: Working straight knives. **Patterns:** Traditional Norwegian knives, hunters, fighters, axes. **Technical:** Forges Damascus. Uses his own blades. **Prices:** $200 to $800; some to $1,500. **Remarks:** Part-time maker; first knife sold in 1986. **Mark:** Last name.

HOMER, GLEN, P.O. Box 2702, Bloomfield, NM 87413/505-632-9615
Specialties: Damascus skinners. **Patterns:** Bowies, skinners, camp knives and folders. **Technical:** Forges 5160; will grind stainless on request; makes his own Damascus. **Prices:** $100 to $500. **Remarks:** Part-time maker; first knife sold in 1987. **Mark:** Name or initials.

HOOT'S HANDMADE KNIVES (See Gibson, Jim)

HORN, JESS, 87481 Rhodowood Dr., Florence, OR 97439/503-997-2593; FAX: 503-997-4550
Specialties: Investor-class working folders; period pieces; collectibles. **Patterns:** High-tech design and finish in folders; liner locks, traditional slip-joints and featherweight models. **Technical:** Grinds ATS-34, 154CM. **Prices:** Start at $600. **Remarks:** Full-time maker; first knife sold in 1968. **Mark:** Full name or last name.

HORNBY, GLEN, 1317 Ethel St., Glendale, CA 91207/818-244-1354
Specialties: Fancy working knives. **Patterns:** Hunters, fighters, folders. **Technical:** Grinds ATS-34, 154CM and 440C; likes bighorn sheep handles. **Prices:** $200 to $1,000. **Remarks:** Part-time maker. **Mark:** Script name under sheep horns.

HORTON, SCOT, 604 Parnell Dr., Buhl, ID 83316/208-543-4413
Specialties: Traditional working and using straight knives and folders. **Patterns:** Hunters, Bowies, fighters and skinners. **Technical:** Grinds 440C and ATS-34. Uses Rocky Mountain sheephorn, elk antler and exotic woods. Mirror finish. **Prices:** $200 to $900; some to $2,000. **Remarks:** Full-time maker; first knife sold in 1990. **Mark:** Full name in arch underlined with arrow, city, state.

HOWARD, DURVYN M., 4220 McLain St. S., Hokes Bluff, AL 35903/205-492-5720
Specialties: Collectible upscale folders; multiple patents. **Patterns:** Fine gentlemen's folders. **Technical:** Uses natural and exotic materials, precious metals and gemstones. **Prices:** $5,000 to $20,000. **Remarks:** Full-time maker; now accepting orders—purchase through Barrett-Smythe Gallery, New York, NY, exclusive agent. **Mark:** Last name etched on tang; opposite side marked Barrett-Smythe.

HOWARD, SETH, P.O. Box 65051, Baton Rouge, LA 70896

HOWELL, LEN, 550 Lee Rd. 169, Opelika, AL 36801/205-749-1942
Specialties: Traditional and working knives of his design and to customer specs. **Patterns:** Bowies, hunters and utility/camp knives. **Technical:** Forges cable Damascus, 1085 and 5160. **Prices:** $100 to $175; some to $400. **Remarks:** Full-time maker; first knife sold in 1991. **Mark:** Stamped or engraved last name.

HOWELL, ROBERT L., Box 1617, Kilgore, TX 75663/903-986-4364
Specialties: Straight knives and folders of his design. **Patterns:** Hunters and locking folders. **Technical:** Grinds D2 and ATS-34; forges and grinds Damascus. **Prices:** $75 to $200; some to $2,500. **Remarks:** Part-time maker; first knife sold in 1978. Doing business as Howell Knives. **Mark:** Last name.

HOWELL, TED, 1294 Wilson Rd., Wetumpka, AL 36092/205-569-2281; FAX: 205-569-1764
Specialties: Working/using straight knives and folders of his design; period pieces. **Patterns:** Bowies, fighters, hunters. **Technical:** Forges 5160, 1085 and cable. Offers light engraving and scrimshaw; filework. **Prices:** $75 to $250; some to $450. **Remarks:** Part-time maker; first

knife sold in 1991. Doing business as Howell Co. **Mark:** Last name, Slapout AL.

HOWSER, JOHN C., 54 Bell Ln., Frankfort, KY 40601/502-875-3678
Specialties: Practical working knives. **Patterns:** Hunters, fighters, locking folders, fillet knives, slip-joint folders, liner locks. **Technical:** Grinds D2 and ATS-34; hand-rubbed satin finish; natural materials. **Prices:** $85 to $350; some to $500. **Remarks:** Part-time maker; first knife sold in 1974. **Mark:** Signature or stamp.

HRISOULAS, JIM, 330 S. Decatur Ave., Suite 109, Las Vegas, NV 89107/702-566-8551
Specialties: Working straight knives; period pieces. **Patterns:** Swords, daggers and sgian dubhs. **Technical:** Double-edged differential heat treating. **Prices:** $85 to $175; some to $600 and higher. **Remarks:** Full-time maker; first knife sold in 1973. Author of *The Complete Bladesmith*, *The Pattern Welded Blade* and *The Master Bladesmith*. Doing business as Salamander Armoury. **Mark:** 8R logo and sword and salamander.

HRS CUSTOM KNIVES (See Simmons, H.R.)

HUBBARD, ARTHUR J., 574 Cutlers Farm Road, Monroe, CT 06468/203-268-3998
Specialties: Working knives of his design or to customer specs. **Patterns:** Hunters, fighters, boots, wood carvers; traditional locking folders. **Technical:** Makes precision engineered Damascus in all-stainless steel, Mokume of copper and stainless steel, copper, brass and nickel silver, copper and brass. **Prices:** Start at $100. **Remarks:** Full-time maker; first knife sold in 1976. **Mark:** Name, city and state; first and middle initials, last name, stainless; P.E.D. stainless.

HUDSON, C. ROBBIN, 22280 Frazier Rd., Rock Hall, MD 21661/410-639-7273
Specialties: High-art working knives. **Patterns:** Hunters, Bowies, fighters and kitchen knives. **Technical:** Forges W2, nickle steel, pure nickle steel, composite and mosaic Damascus; makes knives one at a time. **Prices:** $300 to $700; some to $5,000. **Remarks:** Full-time maker; first knife sold in 1970. **Mark:** Last name and MS.

HUDSON, ROBERT, 3802 Black Cricket Ct., Humble, TX 77396/713-454-7207
Specialties: Working straight knives of his design. **Patterns:** Bowies, hunters, skinners, fighters and utility knives. **Technical:** Grinds D2, 440C, 154CM and commercial Damascus. **Prices:** $85 to $350; some to $1,500. **Remarks:** Part-time maker; first knife sold in 1980. **Mark:** Full name, handmade, city and state.

HUDSON, TOMMY, P.O. Box 2046, Monroe, NC 28110/704-283-8556
Specialties: Classic high-art straight knives and folders of his design and to customer specs. **Patterns:** Bowies, hunters and slip-joint folders; high-art golf putters. **Technical:** Grinds 440C, ATS-34. Engraves. **Prices:** $400 to $1,000; some to $2,500. **Remarks:** Part-time maker; first knife sold in 1989. **Mark:** First initial, last name or last name only.

HUEY, STEVE, 27645 Snyder Rd. #38, Junction City, OR 97448/503-689-5010
Specialties: Working straight knives, some one-of-a-kind. **Patterns:** Hunters, fighters, fishing knives and kitchen cutlery. **Technical:** Hollow- or flat-grinds 1095, L6, 440C, D2 and ATS-34. **Prices:** $75 to $600. **Remarks:** Full-time maker; first knife sold in 1981. **Mark:** Last name in rectangle.

HUGHES, DAN, 13743 Persimmon Blvd., West Palm Beach, FL 33411
Specialties: Working straight knives to customer specs. **Patterns:** Hunters, fighters, fillet knives. **Technical:** Grinds 440C and ATS-34. **Prices:** $55 to $175; some to $300. **Remarks:** Part-time maker; first knife sold in 1984. **Mark:** Initials.

HUGHES, DARYLE, 10979 Leonard, Nunica, MI 49448/616-837-6623
Specialties: Working knives. **Patterns:** Buckskinners, hunters, camp knives, kitchen and fishing knives. **Technical:** Forges and grinds W2,

01 and D2. **Prices:** $40 to $100; some to $400. **Remarks:** Part-time maker, first knife sold in 1979. **Mark:** Name and city in logo.

HUGHES, ED, 280½ Holly Lane, Grand Junction, CO 81503/970-243-8547
Specialties: Working and art folders. **Patterns:** Folders. **Technical:** Grinds stainless steels. Engraves. **Prices:** $75 to $250; some to $600. **Remarks:** Full-time maker; first knife sold in 1978. **Mark:** Name or initials.

HUGHES, LAWRENCE, 207 W. Crestway, Plainview, TX 79072/806-293-5406
Specialties: Working and display knives. **Patterns:** Bowies, daggers, hunters, buckskinners. **Technical:** Grinds D2, 440C and 154CM. **Prices:** $125 to $300; some to $2,000. **Remarks:** Full-time maker; first knife sold in 1979. **Mark:** Name with buffalo skull in center.

HULL, MICHAEL J., 1330 Hermits Circle, Cottonwood, AZ 86326/520-634-2871
Specialties: Working knives and period pieces to customer specs. **Patterns:** Hunters, fighters, Bowies, camp and mediterranean knives, etc. **Technical:** Grinds 440C, ATS-34 and D2. **Prices:** $100 to $350; some to $700. **Remarks:** Full-time maker; first knife sold in 1983. **Mark:** Name, city, state.

HULSEY, HOYT, 5699 Pope Ave., Steele, AL 35987/205-538-6765
Specialties: Traditional working straight knives and folders of his design. **Patterns:** Hunters and utility/camp knives. **Technical:** Grinds 440C, ATS-34, 01 and A2. **Prices:** $75 to $150. **Remarks:** Part-time maker; first knife sold in 1989. **Mark:** Full name, city and state.

HUME, DON, 3511 Camino De La Cumbre, Sherman Oaks, CA 91423/818-783-5486
Specialties: Medieval theme, straight blade working and collector designed pieces. **Patterns:** Hunters, daggers and Bowies. **Technical:** Grinds Damascus, 440C, 154CM with exotic handle material. **Prices:** $180 to $1600. **Remarks:** Part-time maker; first knife sold in 1987. **Mark:** Curved first and middle initials and last name; first of a series or one-of-a-kinds also marked with the Fiera Madonna.

HUMENICK, ROY, P.O. Box 55, Rescue, CA 95672
Specialties: Working knives of his design. **Patterns:** Bowies, hunters, fighters and folders. **Technical:** Grinds ATS-34; forges W2 and 5160; makes Damascus. **Prices:** $200 to $600; some to $1,500. **Remarks:** First knife sold in 1984. **Mark:** Name or initials in logo.

HUMPHREYS, JOEL, Rt. 1, Box 179-B, Bowling Green, FL 33834/813-773-0439
Specialties: Traditional working/using straight knives and folders of his design and in standard patterns. **Patterns:** Hunters, locking folders, utility/camp knives. **Technical:** Grinds ATS-34, D2, 440C. All knives have tapered tangs, mitered bolster/handle joints, handles of horn or bone and hand-stitched fitted sheaths. **Prices:** $135 to $225; some to $350. **Remarks:** Part-time maker; first knife sold in 1990. Doing business as Sovereign Knives. **Mark:** First name.

HUNT, ALEX, 1916 Simsbury Ct., Ft. Collins, CO 80524/303-490-1065
Specialties: Fancy working straight knives. **Patterns:** Hunters, fighters and boot knives. **Technical:** Grinds 440C, ATS-34 and commercial Damascus. **Prices:** $75 to $200; some to $300. **Remarks:** Part-time maker; first knife sold in 1989. Apprenticed under Bill Amoureaux in Alaska. **Mark:** First name in knife shape.

HUNTER, HYRUM AND KELLIE, 285 N. 300 W., P.O. Box 179, Aurora, UT 84620/801-529-7244

HURST, JEFF, Rt. 1, Box 22-A, Rutledge, TN 37861/615-828-5729
Specialties: Working straight knives and folders of his design. **Patterns:** Tomahawks, hunters, boots, folders and fighters. **Technical:** Forges W2, 01 and his own Damascus. Makes mokume. **Prices:** $175 to $350; some to $500. **Remarks:** Full-time maker; first knife sold in

1984. Doing business as Buzzard's Knob Forge. **Mark:** Last name; partnered knives are marked with Newman L. Smith, handle artisan, and SH in script.

HURT, WILLIAM R., 9222 Oak Tree Cir., Frederick, MD 21701/301-898-7143
Specialties: Traditional and working/using straight knives. **Patterns:** Bowies, hunters, fighters and utility knives. **Technical:** Forges 5160, 01 and 06; makes own Damascus. Offers silver wire inlay. **Prices:** $200 to $600; some higher. **Remarks:** Full-time maker; first knife sold in 1989. **Mark:** First and middle initials, last name.

HUSIAK, MYRON, P.O. Box 238, Altona 3018, Victoria, AUSTRALIA/03-315-6752
Specialties: Straight knives and folders of his design or to customer specs. **Patterns:** Hunters, fighters, lock-back folders, skinners and boots. **Technical:** Forges and grinds his own Damascus, 440C and ATS-34. **Prices:** $200 to $900. **Remarks:** Part-time maker; first knife sold in 1974. **Mark:** First initial, last name in logo and serial number.

HYDE, JIMMY, 5094 Stagecoach Rd., Ellenwood, GA 30049/404-968-1951; FAX: 404-209-1741
Specialties: Working straight knives of any design; period pieces. **Patterns:** Bowies, hunters and utility knives. **Technical:** Grinds 440C and 5160; forges 01. Makes his own Damascus and cable Damascus. **Prices:** $75 to $200; some to $400. **Remarks:** Part-time maker; first knife sold in 1978. **Mark:** First initial, last name.

i

IIAMS, RICHARD D., P.O. Box 963, Mills, WY 82644/307-265-2435 evenings
Specialties: Using straight knives and folders. **Patterns:** camp knives, drop-point hunters, lock-back folders and skinners. **Technical:** Pattern-welded DAmascus, 52100 and mild steel. Uses filework on folders. **Prices:** $85 to $300; some higher. **Remarks:** Part-time maker; first knife sold in 1981. **Mark:** First and middle initials, last name on blade.

IKOMA, FLAVIO AND BOSCOLI, MELQUISEDEC RICCI, R. Manoel R. Teixeira, 108, Centro, Presidente Prudente, SP-19031-220, BRAZIL/0182-220115
Specialties: Straight knives and folders of all designs. **Patterns:** Fighters, hunters, Bowies, swords, skinners, utility and defense knives. **Technical:** Grinds and forges D6, 440C, high carbon steels and Damascus. **Prices:** $60 to $350; some to $3,300. **Remarks:** Full-time maker; first knife sold in 1991. **Mark:** Eagle beside 1MK and serial number.

IMBODEN II, HOWARD L., 620 Deauville Dr., Dayton, OH 45429/513-439-1536
Specialties: One-of-a-kind art knives with hand-carved wildlife antler handles; ivory. **Technical:** Grinds stainless and other steels; satin, bead-blasted and gun-blued blades. Uses commercial Damascus, obsidian, other maker's blades, cast sterling silver; 14K, 18K and 24K gold guards and animals. Recycles animal parts; carves handles for other knifemakers. Scrimshands and carves. **Prices:** $65 to $25,000. **Remarks:** Full-time maker; first knife sold in 1986. **Mark:** First and last initials, II.

IMEL, BILLY MACE, 1616 Bundy Ave., New Castle, IN 47362/317-529-1651
Specialties: High-art working knives, period pieces and personal cutlery. **Patterns:** Daggers, fighters, hunters; locking folders and slip-joints with interframes. **Technical:** Forges and grinds D2, 440C and 154CM. **Prices:** $200 to $2,000; some to $6,000. **Remarks:** Part-time maker; first knife sold in 1973. **Mark:** Name in monogram.

IRIE, MICHAEL L. (See Wood, Barry B. and Irie, Michael L.)

THE IRON MASTER (See Chastain, Wade)

IRON MOUNTAIN FORGE WORKS (See Small, Ed)

ISHIHARA, HANK (See Ishihara, Nobuhiko)

ISHIHARA, NOBUHIKO, 86-18 Motomachi, Sakura City, Chiba Pref. JAPAN/043-485-3208; FAX: 043-485-3208
Specialties: Fantasy and working straight knives and folders of his design. **Patterns:** Boots, Bowies, daggers, fighters, hunters, locking folders, utility/camp, filet and kitchen knives. **Technical:** Grinds CV134, 440C, ATS-34, D2, CO525, 440V and Damascus. Engraves. **Prices:** $450 to $1,000; some to $10,000. **Remarks:** Full-time maker; first knife sold in 1987. Doing business as Hank Ishihara. **Mark:** Hank.

IVANOV, BLADIMIR (See Shushunov, Sergei)

j

JACKS, JIM, 344 S. Hollenbeck Ave., Covina, CA 91723-2513/818-331-5665
Specialties: Working straight knives in standard patterns. **Patterns:** Bowies, hunters, fighters, fishing and camp knives, miniatures. **Technical:** Grinds Stellite 6K, 440C and 154CM. **Prices:** Start at $100. **Remarks:** Spare-time maker; first knife sold in 1980. **Mark:** Initials in diamond logo.

JACKSON, JIM, 10 Chantry Close, Windsor, Berkshire SL4 5EP, ENGLAND/01-930-4832
Specialties: His designs. **Patterns:** Bowies, hunters, art knives and folders. **Technical:** Forges 01, 5160 and occasionally Damascus. Offers leatherwork. **Prices:** NA. **Remarks:** Part-time maker. **Mark:** Kentucky Dreamer around last initial.

JAGED (See Smith, Gregory H.)

JAMES, PETER, 2549 W. Golf Rd. #290, Hoffman Estates, IL 60194/708-310-9113; FAX: 708-885-1716
Specialties: Working/using straight knives of his design and in standard patterns. **Patterns:** Bowies, daggers and urban companion knives. **Technical:** Grinds 440C and soligen tool. Makes a variety of sheaths for urban companion series. **Prices:** $48 to $250. **Remarks:** Part-time maker; first knife sold in 1986. Doing business as Peter James & Sons. **Mark:** Initials overlapped.

JARVIS, PAUL M., 30 Chalk St., Cambridge, MA 02139/617-491-2900, 617-547-4355
Specialties: High-art knives and period pieces of his design. **Patterns:** Japanese and Mid-Eastern knives. **Technical:** Grinds Myer Damascus, ATS-34, D2 and 01. Specializes in height-relief Japanese-style carving. Works with silver, gold and gems. **Prices:** $200 to $17,000. **Remarks:** Part-time maker; first knife sold in 1978.

JEAN, GERRY, 25B Cliffside Dr., Manchester, CT 06040/203-649-6449
Specialties: Historic replicas. **Patterns:** Survival and camp knives. **Technical:** Grinds A2, 440C and 154CM. Handle slabs applied in unique tongue-and-groove method. **Prices:** $125 to $250; some to $1,000. **Remarks:** Spare-time maker; first knife sold in 1973. **Mark:** Initials and serial number.

JENSEN JR., CARL A., RR #3, Box 74, Blair, NE 68008/402-426-3353
Specialties: Working knives of his design; some customer designs. **Patterns:** Hunters, fighters, boots and Bowies. **Technical:** Grinds A2, D2, 01, 440C and ATS-34; recycles old files, leaf springs; heat-treats. **Prices:** $35 to $350. **Remarks:** Part-time maker; first knife sold in 1980. **Mark:** Bear's Cutlery.

JERNIGAN, STEVE, 3082 Tunnel Rd., Milton, FL 32571/904-994-0802
Specialties: Investor-class folders. **Patterns:** Array of models and sizes in sideplate locking interframes and conventional liner construction. **Technical:** Grinds D2, ATS-34, stainless steel interframes with multiple assymetrical inlays, anodized titanium and all mokume interframes; occasional fancy dagger with "Italian Smalti" glass tiles for unique mosa-

ic handles. **Prices:** $350 to $1,300; some to $4,000. **Remarks:** Full-time maker; first knife sold in 1982. Takes orders for folders only. **Mark:** Last name.

JETTON, CAY, P.O. Box 315, Winnsboro, TX 75494/903-342-3317

JMD BLADES (See DaConceicao, John M.)

JOBIN, JACQUES, 46 St. Dominique, Lauzon, PQ G6V 2M7, CANADA/418-833-0283; FAX: 418-833-8378
Specialties: Fancy and working straight knives and folders; miniatures. **Patterns:** Minis, fantasy knives, fighters and some hunters. **Technical:** ATS-34, some Damascus and titanium. Likes native snakewood. Heat-treats. **Prices:** Start at $150. **Remarks:** Full-time maker; first knife sold in 1986. **Mark:** Signature on blade.

JOHNS, ROB, 1423 S. Second, Enid, OK 73701/405-242-2707
Specialties: Classic and fantasy straight knives of his design or to customer specs; fighters for use at Medieval fairs. **Patterns:** Bowies, daggers and swords. **Technical:** Forges and grinds 440C, D2 and 5160. Handles of nylon, walnut or wire-wrap. **Prices:** $150 to $350; some to $2,500. **Remarks:** Full-time maker; first knife sold in 1980. **Mark:** Medieval Customs, initials.

JOHNSON, C.E. "GENE", 5648 Redwood Ave., Portage, IN 46368/219-762-5461
Specialties: Lock-back folders and springers of his design or to customer specs. **Patterns:** Hunters, Bowies, survival lock-back folders. **Technical:** Grinds D2, 440C, A18, 01, Damascus; likes filework. **Prices:** $100 to $2,000. **Remarks:** Full-time maker; first knife sold in 1975. **Mark:** "Gene," city, state and serial number.

JOHNSON, DAVID L., P.O. Box 222, Talkeetna, AK 99676/907-733-2777
Specialties: Traditional working and using straight knives. **Patterns:** Bowies, fighters and hunters; outdoor knives. **Technical:** Grinds ATS-34, D2 and 440C. **Prices:** $100 to $200; some to $450. **Remarks:** Full-time maker; first knife sold in 1979. **Mark:** Name, city and state in banner.

JOHNSON, DURRELL CARMON, P.O. Box 594, Sparr, FL 32192/904-622-5498
Specialties: Old-fashioned working straight knives and folders of his design or to customer specs. **Patterns:** Bowies, hunters, fighters, daggers, camp knives and Damascus miniatures. **Technical:** Forges 5160, his own Damascus, W2, wrought iron, nickel and horseshoe rasps. Offers filework. **Prices:** $100 to $2,000. **Remarks:** Full-time maker and blacksmith; first knife sold in 1957. **Mark:** Middle name.

JOHNSON, GORDEN W., 5426 Sweetbriar, Houston, TX 77017/713-645-8990
Specialties: Working knives and period pieces. **Patterns:** Hunters, boots and Bowies. **Technical:** Flat-grinds 440C; most knives have narrow tang. **Prices:** $90 to $450. **Remarks:** Full-time maker; first knife sold in 1974. **Mark:** Name, city, state.

JOHNSON, HAROLD "HARRY" C., 1014 Lafayette Rd., Chickamauga, GA 30707
Specialties: Working straight knives. **Patterns:** Mostly hunters, and large Bowies. **Technical:** Grinds popular steels. Offers heat treating, leatherwork, sheaths and cases; keeps large assortment of woods in stock. **Prices:** $125 to $2,000; some higher. **Remarks:** Part-time maker; first knife sold in 1973. **Mark:** First initial, last name, city, state in oval logo.

JOHNSON, KENNETH R., W3565 Lockington, Mindoro, WI 54644/608-857-3035
Specialties: Hunters, clip-points, special orders. **Patterns:** Hunters, utility/camp knives and kitchen knives. **Technical:** Grinds 440C, D2 and 01. Scrimshaw by Corinne Johnson; makes sheaths. **Prices:** $65 to $500. **Remarks:** Full-time maker; first knife sold in 1990. Doing business as Corken Knives. **Mark:** CORKEN.

JOHNSON, R.B., Box 11, Clearwater, MN 55320/612-558-6128
Specialties: Automatic switch blades and lockbacks. **Patterns:** Traditional hunters and locking folders; liner locks with titanium. **Technical:** Grinds 440C, 154CM, 1095 steel and ATS-34; uses no plastic; prefers natural materials; offers mammoth ivory. **Prices:** $140 to $750. **Remarks:** Full-time maker; first knife sold in 1973. Now accepting orders. **Mark:** Signature.

JOHNSON, RUFFIN, 215 LaFonda Dr., Houston, TX 77060/713-448-4407
Specialties: Working straight knives and folders. **Patterns:** Hunters, fighters and locking folders. **Technical:** Grinds 440C and 154CM; hidden tangs and fancy handles. **Prices:** $200 to $400; some to $1,095. **Remarks:** Full-time maker; first knife sold in 1972. **Mark:** Wolf head logo and signature.

JOHNSON, RYAN M., 7320 Foster Hixson Cemetery Rd., Hixson, TN 37343/615-842-9323
Specialties: Working and using straight knives of his design and to customer specs. **Patterns:** Bowies, hunters and utiltiy/camp knives. **Technical:** Forges 5160, Damascus and files. **Prices:** $70 to $400; some to $800. **Remarks:** Full-time maker; first knife sold in 1986. **Mark:** Sledgehammer with halo.

JOHNSON, STEVEN R., 202 E. 200 N., P.O. Box 5, Manti, UT 84642/801-835-7941; FAX: 801-835-8052
Specialties: Investor-class working knives. **Patterns:** Hunters, fighters and boots in clean-lined contemporary patterns. **Technical:** Grinds ATS-34 and 154CM. **Prices:** $450 to $4,500. **Remarks:** Full-time maker; first knife sold in 1972. **Mark:** Name, city, state.

JOHNSON, W.C. "BILL", 1006 Clayton Ct., New Carlisle, OH 45344/513-845-1185
Specialties: Fancy working knives to order. **Patterns:** Hunters, fighters, tantos and push knives. **Technical:** Grinds 440C and ATS-34. **Prices:** $125 to $350; some higher. **Remarks:** Full-time maker; first knife sold in 1979. **Mark:** First and middle initials, last name.

JOKERST, CHARLES, 9312 Spaulding, Omaha, NE 68134/402-571-2536
Specialties: Working knives in standard patterns. **Patterns:** Hunters, fighters and pocketknives. **Technical:** Grinds 440C, ATS-34. **Prices:** $90 to $170. **Remarks:** Spare-time maker, first knife sold in 1984. **Mark:** Early work marked RCJ; current work marked with last name and city.

JONES, BARRY M. and PHILLIP G., 221 North Ave., Danville, VA 24540/804-793-5282
Specialties: Working and using straight knives and folders of their design and to customer specs; combat and self-defense knives. **Patterns:** Bowies, fighters, daggers, swords, hunters and lockback folders. **Technical:** Flat-grinds only 440C, ATS-34 and D2. All blades hand polished. **Prices:** $100 to $500, some higher. **Remarks:** Part-time makers; first knife sold in 1989. **Mark:** Jones Knives, city, state.

JONES, BOB, 6219 Aztec NE, Albuquerque, NM 87110/505-881-4472
Specialties: Fancy working knives of his design. **Patterns:** Mountain-man/buckskinner-type knives; multi-blade folders, locking folders and slip-joints. **Technical:** Grinds A2, 01, 1095 and commercial Damascus; uses no stainless steel. Engraves. **Prices:** $100 to $500; some to $1,500. **Remarks:** Full-time maker; first knife sold in 1960. **Mark:** Initials on fixed blades; initials encircled on folders.

JONES, CHARLES ANTHONY, 36 Broadgate Close, Bellaire Barnstaple, No. Devon E31 4AL, ENGLAND/0271-75328
Specialties: Working straight knives. **Patterns:** Simple hunters, fighters and utility knives. **Technical:** Grinds 440C, 01 and D2; filework offered. Engraves. **Prices:** $100 to $500; engraving higher. **Remarks:** Spare-time maker; first knife sold in 1987. **Mark:** Tony engraved.

JONES, CURTIS J., 39909 176th St. E., Palmdale, CA 93591/805-264-2753

Specialties: Big Bowies, daggers, his own style of hunters. **Patterns:** Bowies, daggers, hunters, swords, boots and miniatures. **Technical:** Grinds A2, 440C and D2. Fitted guards only; does not solder. Heat-treats. Custom sheaths—hand-tooled and stitched. **Prices:** $125 to $1,500; some to $3,000. **Remarks:** Part-time maker; first knife sold in 1975. **Mark:** Stylized initials on either side of three triangles interconnected.

JONES, ENOCH, 310A Moss Ln., Warrenton, VA 22186/703-341-0292
Specialties: Fancy working straight knives. **Patterns:** Hunters, fighters, boots and Bowies. **Technical:** Forges and grinds 01, W2, 440C and Damascus. **Prices:** $100 to $350; some to $1,000. **Remarks:** Part-time maker; first knife sold in 1982. **Mark:** First name.

JONES, JOHN, 23 Sunstone St., Manly, West Brisbane 4179, AUSTRALIA/07-393-3390
Specialties: Straight knives and folders. **Patterns:** Working hunters, folding lockbacks, fancy daggers and miniatures. **Technical:** Grinds 440C, 01 and L6. **Prices:** $180 to $1200; some to $2,000. **Remarks:** Part-time maker; first knife sold in 1986. **Mark:** Jones Custom in script.

JONES, PHILLIP G. (See Jones, Barry M. and Phillip G.)

J.P.M. KNIVES (See McMahon, John P.)

J&S KNIVES (See Kitsmiller, Jerry)

k

KACZOR, TOM, 375 Wharncliffe Rd. N., Upper London, Ont., CANADA N6G 1E4/519-645-7640

KAGAWA, KOICHI, 1556 Horiyamashita Hatano-Shi, Kanagawa, JAPAN
Specialties: Fancy high-tech straight knives and folders to customer specs. **Patterns:** Hunters, locking folders and slip-joints. **Technical:** Uses 440C and ATS-34. **Prices:** $500 to $2,000; some to $20,000. **Remarks:** Part-time maker; first knife sold in 1986. **Mark:** First initial, last name-YOKOHAMA.

KALFAYAN, EDWARD N., 410 Channing, Ferndale, MI 48220/313-548-4882
Specialties: Working straight knives and folders to customer specs. **Patterns:** Bowies, toothpicks, fighters and hunters. **Technical:** Grinds 440C and ATS-34. **Prices:** $75 to $600. **Remarks:** Part-time maker; first knife sold in 1973. **Mark:** Last name.

KALUZA, WERNER, Lochnerstr. 32, 90441 Nurnberg, GERMANY/0911 666047
Specialties: Fancy high-art straight knives of his design. **Patterns:** Boots and ladies knives. **Technical:** Grinds ATS-34, CPM T 440V and Schneider Damascus. Engraving available. **Prices:** NA. **Remarks:** Part-time maker. **Mark:** First initial and last name.

KAMADA, YOSHIKAZU, B1 Fokoku Seimei Building 2-4, Komatu bara-cho kita-ku, Osaka City, 530 JAPAN/06-313-2525; FAX: 06-313-2626
Specialties: High-art working knives of his design. **Patterns:** Hunters, bush fishing knives and Japanese-style desk knives. **Technical:** Grinds D2. **Prices:** $450 to $1,800. **Remarks:** Full-time maker, first knife sold in 1953. Doing business as World Gallery Co., Ltd. **Mark:** Initials; or first initial, last name.

KANDA, MICHIO, 7-32-5 Shinzutumi-cho, Shinnanyo-shi, Yamaguchi 746 JAPAN/0834-62-1910; FAX: 011-81-83462-1910
Specialties: Fantasy knives of his design. **Patterns:** Animal knives. **Technical:** Grinds ATS-34. **Prices:** $300 to $3,000. **Remarks:** Full-time maker; first knife sold in 1985. Doing business as Shusui Kanda. **Mark:** Last name inside M.

KANDA, SHUSUI (See Kanda, Michio)

KAP FORGE (See Povisils, Karlis A.)

KATO, KIYOSHI, 4-6-4 Himonya Meguro-ku, Tokyo, 152 JAPAN
Specialties: Swords, Damascus knives, working knives and paper knives. **Patterns:** Traditional swords, hunters, Bowies and daggers. **Technical:** Forges his own Damascus and carbon steel. Grinds ATS-34. **Prices:** $260 to $700; some to $4,000. **Remarks:** Full-time maker. **Mark:** First initial, last name.

KAUFFMAN, DAVE, P.O. Box 9041, Helena, MT 59604/406-442-9328
Specialties: Fancy working straight knives of his design; also enjoys customer designs. **Patterns:** Lockblade folder interframes. **Technical:** Uses ATS-34, D2, 1095 and 203E Damascus; offers filework; heat-treats and tests. **Prices:** $65 to $500; some to $1,200. **Remarks:** Full-time maker; first knife sold in 1989. **Mark:** First and last name, Helena, MT.

KAUFMAN, SCOTT, 302 Green Meadows Cr., Anderson, SC 29624/803-231-9201
Specialties: Classic and working/using straight knives in standard patterns. **Patterns:** Fighters, hunters and utility/camp knives. **Technical:** Grinds ATS-34, 440C, 01. **Prices:** $100 to $500. **Remarks:** Part-time maker; first knife sold in 1987. **Mark:** Kaufman Knives with Bible in middle.

KAWASAKI, AKIHISA, 11-8-9 Chome Minamiamachi, Suzurandai Kita-Ku, Kobe JAPAN

KAY, J. WALLACE, 332 Slab Bridge Rd., Liberty, SC 29657

KEESLAR, JOSEPH F., RR #1, Box 252, Almo, KY 42020/502-753-7919
Specialties: Classic Bowie reproductions and contemporary Bowies. **Patterns:** Period pieces, combat knives, hunters, daggers. **Technical:** Forges 5160 and his own Damascus. Decorative filework, engraving and custom leather sheaths available. **Prices:** $200 to $3,000. **Remarks:** Full-time maker; first knife sold in 1976. **Mark:** First and middle initlas, last name in hammer, knife and anvil logo.

KEESLAR, STEVEN C., 115 Lane 216, Hamilton, IN 46742/219-488-3161; FAX: 219-488-3149
Specialties: Traditional working/using straight knives of his design and to customer specs. **Patterns:** Bowies, hunters, utility/camp knives. **Technical:** Forges 5160, files, 52100. **Prices:** $100 to $600; some to $1,500. **Remarks:** Part-time maker; first knife sold in 1976. **Mark:** First initial, last name.

KEETON, WILLIAM L., 6095 Rehoboth Rd. SE, Laconia, IN 47135/812-969-2836
Specialties: Plain and fancy working knives. **Patterns:** Hunters and fighters; locking folders and slip-joints. Names patterns after Kentucky Derby winners. **Technical:** Grinds D2, ATS-34, 440C and 154CM; mirror and satin finishes. **Prices:** To $1,500; some to $5,000. **Remarks:** Full-time maker; first knife sold in 1971. **Mark:** Logo of key.

KEHIAYAN, ALFREDO, Cuzco 1455, Ing. Maschwitz, CP 1623 Buenos Aires, ARGENTINA/0488-4-2212
Specialties: Functional straight knives. **Patterns:** Utility knives, skinners, hunters and boots. **Technical:** Forges and grinds SAE 52.100, SAE 6180, SAE 9260, SAE 5160, 440C and ATS-34, titanium with nitride. All blades mirror-polished; makes leather sheaths and wood cases. **Prices:** $150 to $800; some to $3,000. **Remarks:** Full-time maker; first knife sold in 1983. **Mark:** Name.

KEIDEL, GENE W. AND SCOTT J., 4661 105th Ave. SW, Dickinson, ND 58601
Specialties: Fancy/embellished and working/using straight knives of his design. **Patterns:** Bowies, hunters and miniatures. **Technical:** Grind 440C, ATS-34 and 1095. Offer scrimshaw, filework and leather tooling. **Prices:** $95 to $500. **Remarks:** Full-time makers; first knife sold in 1990. Doing business as Keidel Knives. **Mark:** Last name.

KEIDEL, SCOTT J. (See Keidel, Gene W. and Scott J.)

KELGIN KNIVES (See Largin, Ken)

KELLEY, GARY, 17485 SW Pheasant Lane, Aloha, OR 97006/503-649-7867
Specialties: Exotic miniatures, custom belt buckle and primitive knives. **Patterns:** Period and fantasy miniatures. **Technical:** Forges Damascus miniatures; casts precious metals and dendritic steel. **Prices:** $100 to $2,500. **Remarks:** Part-time maker. Knife consultant. Publishes *The Directory of Knifemaking Supplies.* Owns Reproduction Blades Co. **Mark:** Full name or initials.

KELLOGG, BRIAN R., Rt. 1, Box 357, New Market, VA 22844/703-740-4292
Specialties: Fancy and working straight knives of his design and to customer specs. **Patterns:** Fighters, hunters and utility/camp knives. **Technical:** Grinds 440C, D2 and A2. Offers filework and fancy pin and cable pin work. Prefers natural handle materials. **Prices:** $75 to $225; some to $350. **Remarks:** Part-time maker; first knife sold in 1983. **Mark:** Last name.

KELLY, LANCE, 1723 Willow Oak Dr., Edgewater, FL 32132/904-423-4933
Specialties: Investor-class straight knives and folders. **Patterns:** Kelly style in contemporary outlines. **Technical:** Grinds 01, D2 and 440C; engraves; inlays gold and silver. **Prices:** $600 to $3,500. **Remarks:** Full-time engraver and knifemaker; first knife sold in 1975. **Mark:** Last name.

KELSO, JIM, RD 1, Box 5300, Worcester, VT 05682/802-229-4254
Specialties: Fancy high-art straight knives and folders that mix Eastern and Western influences. Only uses own designs, but accepts suggestions for themes. **Patterns:** Daggers, swords and locking folders. **Technical:** Grinds only custom Damascus. Works with top Damascus bladesmiths. **Prices:** $3,000 to $8,000; some to $15,000. **Remarks:** Full-time maker; first knife sold in 1980. **Mark:** Stylized initials.

KEMAL (See Fogg, Don and Sayen, Murad)

KENNEDY JR., BILL, P.O. Box 850431, Yukon, OK 73085/405-354-9150
Specialties: Working straight knives. **Patterns:** Hunters, fighters, minis and fishing knives. **Technical:** Grinds D2, 440C and Damascus. **Prices:** $80 and higher. **Remarks:** Part-time maker; first knife sold in 1980. **Mark:** Last name and year made.

KENNEDY, JERRY, 2104 S.W.8A, Blue Springs, MO 64015/816-229-5468
Specialties: Traditional working and using knives. **Patterns:** Bowies, fighters, hunters and camp knives. **Technical:** Forges W2, 52100 and Damascus. Makes own Damascus with W2 and 203E. **Prices:** $125 to $750; some to $1,500. **Remarks:** Full-time maker; first knife sold in 1990. **Mark:** First initial, last name.

KENNEDY, KELLY S., 9894 A.W. University, Odessa, TX 79764/915-381-6165
Specialties: Traditional working and using straight knives of his design and to customer specs. **Patterns:** Bowies, hunters and utility/camp knives. **Technical:** Forges 5160, W2 and own Damascus. **Prices:** Moderate to upscale. **Remarks:** Full-time maker; first knife sold in 1991. Doing business as Noble House Armourers. **Mark:** Last name in script, J.S., A.B.S.

KENNELLEY, J.C., 326 S. Summit, Arkansas City, KS 67005/316-442-0848
Specialties: Working straight knives; some fantasy pieces. **Patterns:** Hunters, fighters, skinners and fillet knives. **Technical:** Grinds D2 and 440C. **Prices:** $75 to $200; some to $500. **Remarks:** Part-time maker; first knife sold in 1982. **Mark:** Name logo.

KENTUCKY DREAMER (See Jackson, Jim)

KERMIT'S KNIFE WORKS (See Laurent, Kermit)

KERSTEN, MICHAEL, Borkzeile 17, 13583 Berlin, GERMANY
Specialties: Working/using straight knives and folders of his design and to customer specs. **Patterns:** Fighters, locking folders and utility/camp knives. **Technical:** Grinds 01, D2, 440C, 440V and Damascus. Handle materials include brass, hardwood and bone. **Prices:** $250 to $1,000. **Remarks:** Spare-time maker; first knife sold in 1993. **Mark:** Last initial.

KESSLER, RALPH A., P.O. Box 357, 345 Sherwood Rd., Marietta, SC 29661/803-836-7944
Specialties: Traditional-style knives. **Patterns:** Folders, hunters, fighters, Bowies and kitchen knives. **Technical:** Grinds D2, 01, A2 and ATS-34. **Prices:** $100 to $500. **Remarks:** Part-time maker; first knife sold in 1982. **Mark:** Last name or initials with last name.

KESTREL TOOL (See Blomberg, Gregg)

KHALSA, JOT SINGH, 368 Village St., Millis, MA 02054/508-376-8162; FAX: 508-376-8081
Specialties: Liner locks, autos and one-of-a-kind daggers; some with scabbards. **Patterns:** Classic with contemporary flair. Has line of knife jewelry sold through stores and dealers. **Technical:** Grinds ATS-34; forges his Damascus. Engraves; uses unusual natural handle material. Offers embellishment on daggers. **Prices:** Start at $175. **Remarks:** Full-time maker; first knife sold in 1978. **Mark:** An Adi Skakti symbol.

KHARLAMOV, YURI, Oboronnay 46/2, Tula, 300007 RUSSIA
Specialties: Classic, fancy and traditional knives of his design. **Patterns:** Daggers and hunters. **Technical:** Forges only Damascus with nickel. Uses natural handle materials; engraves on metal, carves on nut-tree; silver and pearl inlays. **Prices:** $600 to $2,000; some to $2,800. **Remarks:** Full-time maker; first knife sold in 1988. **Mark:** Initials.

KI, SHIVA, 5222 Ritterman Ave., Baton Rouge, LA 70805/504-356-7274
Specialties: Fancy working straight knives and folders to customer specs. **Patterns:** Emphasis on personal defense knives, martial arts weapons. **Technical:** Forges and grinds; makes own Damascus; prefers natural handle materials. **Prices:** $135 to $850; some to $1,800. **Remarks:** Full-time maker; first knife sold in 1981. **Mark:** Name with logo.

KIEFER, TONY, 112 Chateaugay Dr., Pataskala, OH 43062/614-927-6910
Specialties: Traditional working and using straight knives in standard patterns. **Patterns:** Bowies, fighters and hunters. **Technical:** Grinds 440C and D2; forges D2. Flat-grinds Bowies; hollow-grinds drop-point and trailing-point hunters. **Prices:** $95 to $140; some to $200. **Remarks:** Spare-time maker; first knife sold in 1988. **Mark:** Last name.

KILBY, KEITH, 402 Jackson Trail Rd., Jefferson, GA 30549/706-367-9997
Specialties: Works with all designs. **Patterns:** Mostly Bowies, camp knives and hunters of his design. **Technical:** Forges 52100, 5160, 1095, Damascus and mosaic Damascus. **Prices:** $100 to $3,500. **Remarks:** Part-time maker; first knife sold in 1974. Doing business as Foxwood Forge. **Mark:** Name or fox logo.

KIMSEY, KEVIN, 1246 Woodleigh Rd., Marietta, GA 30060/404-432-0044
Specialties: Classic and working straight knives of his design. **Patterns:** Fighters, hunters and utility knives. **Technical:** Grinds 440C, ATS-34 and D2 carbon. **Prices:** $100 to $300; some to $600. **Remarks:** Part-time maker; first knife sold in 1983. Doing business as Rafter KK Custom Knives. **Mark:** Last name and year.

KINKADE, JACOB, 197 Rd. 154, Carpenter, WY 82054/307-649-2446
Specialties: Working/using knives of his design or to customer specs; some miniature swords, daggers and battle axes. **Patterns:** Hunters,

daggers, boots; some miniatures. **Technical:** Grinds M2 and L6. Prefers natural handle material. **Prices:** Start at $30. **Remarks:** Part-time maker; first knife sold in 1990. **Mark:** Connected initials or none.

KING, BILL, 14830 Shaw Road, Tampa, FL 33625/813-961-3455
Specialties: Slip-joint folders, lockbacks, liner locks and stud openers. **Patterns:** Wide varieties; folders and dive knives. **Technical:** 12C27, ATS-34 and some Damascus; single and double grinds. Offers filework and jewel embellishment; nickel-silver Damacus and mokume bolsters. **Prices:** $135 to $400; some to $550. **Remarks:** Full-time maker; first knife sold in 1976. **Mark:** Name in crown.

KING, FRED, P.O. Box 200342, Cartersville, GA 30120/404-382-8478
Specialties: Fancy and embellished working straight knives and folders. **Patterns:** Hunters, Bowies and fighters. **Technical:** Grinds ATS-34 and D2; forges 5160, L6, 52100, 203E and Damascus. Offers filework. **Prices:** $45 to $2,500. **Remarks:** Spare-time maker; first knife sold in 1984. **Mark:** Kings Edge.

KING JR., HARVEY G., 312 Walnut, Box 184, Eskridge, KS 66423-0184/913-449-2487
Specialties: Traditional working and using straight knives of his design and to customer specs. **Patterns:** Hunters, Bowies and fillet knives **Technical:** Grinds 01, A2 and D2. Prefers natural handle materials; offers leatherwork. **Prices:** $50 to $650. **Remarks:** Part-time maker; first knife sold in 1988. **Mark:** Name and serial number based on steel used, year made and number of knives made that year.

KING, KEMP, 6452 Paradise Point Rd., Flowery Branch, GA 30542/404-967-1887
Specialties: Fancy straight knives and folders in standard patterns or to customer specs. **Patterns:** Hunters, locking and slip-joint folders. **Technical:** Flat-grinds 440C, ATS-34 and D2. Hand-finish is standard. **Prices:** $250 to $750; some to $2,000. **Remarks:** Part-time maker; first knife sold in 1981. **Mark:** First name.

KING, RANDALL, 54 Mt. Carmel Rd. #12, Asheville, NC 28806/704-254-7340
Specialties: Fancy and working straight knives of his design, to customer specs and in standard patterns; movie knives, prop knives and swords. **Patterns:** Fighters, hunters and locking folders. **Technical:** Grinds ATS-34, D2 and 440C. Prefers tapered tangs. Scrimshaws. Sheaths made by Vicky King. **Prices:** $100 to $250; some to $500. **Remarks:** Part-time maker; first knife sold in 1987. **Mark:** First initial, last name, city and state.

KINGS EDGE (See King, Fred)

KINNIKIN, TODD, Eureka Forge, 8356 John McKeever Rd., House Springs, MO 63051/314-938-6248

KIOUS, JOE, 1015 Ridge Pointe Rd., Kerrville, TX 78028/210-367-2277; FAX: 210-367-2286
Specialties: Investment-quality interframe folders. **Patterns:** Hunters, fighters, Bowies and miniatures; traditional folders. **Technical:** Grinds D2, 440C, CPM 440V, 154CM and stainless Damascus. **Prices:** $175 to $1,000; some to $5,000. **Remarks:** Full-time maker; first knife sold in 1969. **Mark:** Last name, city and state.

KITSMILLER, JERRY, 63347 E. Juniper Rd., Montrose, CO 81401/303-249-4290
Specialties: Working straight knives in standard patterns. **Patterns:** Hunters, boots and locking folders. **Technical:** Grinds ATS-34 and 440C only. **Prices:** $75 to $200; some to $300. **Remarks:** Spare-time maker; first knife sold in 1984. **Mark:** J&S Knives.

KLIMASZEWSKI, BERNARD E., 2214 Spicewood Dr., Killeen, TX 76543/817-628-9052
Specialties: Classic working and using straight knives to customer specs. **Patterns:** Hunters, Bowies and fighters. **Technical:** Grinds 440C, 01 and commercial Damascus. Offers filework. **Prices:** $75 to

$1,000; some to $2,500. **Remarks:** Part-time maker; first knife sold in 1989. **Mark:** Stylized initials.

KNEUBUHLER, W.K. (See Votaw, David P.)

KNICKMEYER, HANK, 6300 Crosscreek, Cedar Hill, MO 63016/314-285-3210
Specialties: Complex mosaic Damascus constructions. **Patterns:** Hunters, fighters, swords and folders. **Technical:** Mosaic Damascus with all tool steel Damascus edges. **Prices:** $450 to $1,000; some $1,500 and higher. **Remarks:** Part-time maker; first knife sold in 1989. Doing business as Dutch Creek Forge & Foundry. **Mark:** Initials connected.

KNIFECRAFT (See Wise, Donald)

KNIGHT, JIM (See Brunckhorst, C. Lyle)

KNIP CUSTOM KNIVES (See Knipschield, Terry)

KNIPSCHIELD, TERRY, 808 12th Ave. NE, Rochester, MN 55906/507-288-7829
Specialties: Working straight and some folding knives in standard patterns. **Patterns:** Lockback and slip-joint knives. **Technical:** Grinds ATS-34. **Prices:** $55 to $350; some to $600. **Remarks:** Part-time maker; first knife sold in 1986. Doing business as Knip Custom Knives. **Mark:** KNIP in Old English with shield logo.

KNIPSTEIN, R.C. (JOE), 731 N. Fielder, Arlington, TX 76012/817-265-2021
Specialties: Straight working knives and folders in standard patterns; integral construction. **Patterns:** Hunters, Bowies, folders, fighters, utility knives. **Technical:** Grinds 440C, D2, 154CM and ATS-34. Natural handle materials and full tangs are standard. **Prices:** Start at $125. **Remarks:** Part-time maker; first knife sold in 1989. **Mark:** Name, city and state.

KNIVES BY: GRAF (See Graffeo, Anthony I.)

KNOB HILL FORGE (See Pulliam, Morris C.)

KNOTT, STEVE, 206 Academy St., Clinton, SC 29325/803-833-6348
Specialties: Fantasy working straight knives and folders of his design or to customer specs. **Patterns:** Hunters and slip-joint folders; Bowies, daggers and fighters. **Technical:** Grinds 440C, ATS-34 and commercial Damascus. Offers filework, satin and mirror finishes; will do some bluing. **Prices:** $80 to $500. **Remarks:** Full-time maker; first knife sold in 1988. **Mark:** Last name.

KNUTH, JOSEPH E., 3307 Lookout Dr., Rockford, IL 61109/815-874-9597
Specialties: High-art working straight knives of his design or to customer specs. **Patterns:** Daggers, fighters and swords. **Technical:** Grinds 440C, ATS-34 and D2. **Prices:** $150 to $1,500; some to $15,000. **Remarks:** Full-time maker; first knife sold in 1989. **Mark:** Initials on bolster face.

KODAN (See Engnath, Bob)

KOHLER, J. MARK, 16430 Dawncrest Way, Sugarland, TX 77478
Specialties: Fancy and working straight knives and folders of his design. **Patterns:** Hunters, locking folders, gentleman's embellished folders. **Technical:** Grinds D2, ATS-34 and vascowear or 440V. Enjoys exotic handle materials—tiger coral, cape buffalo, sheephorn. Offers filework and embellished bolsters. **Prices:** $165 to $325. **Remarks:** Part-time maker; first knife sold in 1986. **Mark:** Last name in script, stamped.

KOJETIN, W., 20 Bapaume Rd., Delville, Germiston 1401 SOUTH AFRICA-011 825 6680
Specialties: High-art and working straight knives of all designs. **Pat-**

terns: Daggers, hunters and his own Manhunter Bowie. **Technical:** Grinds D2 and ATS-34; forges and grinds 440B/C. Offers "wrap-around" pava and abalone handles, scrolled wood or ivory, stacked filework and setting of faceted semi-precious stones. **Prices:** $185 to $600; some to $11,000. **Remarks:** Spare-time maker; first knife sold in 1962. **Mark:** Billy K.

KOLITZ, ROBERT, W9342 Canary Rd., Beaver Dam, WI 53916/414-887-1287
Specialties: Working straight knives to customer specs. **Patterns:** Bowies, hunters, bird and trout knives, boots. **Technical:** Grinds 01, 440C; commercial Damascus. **Prices:** $50 to $100; some to $500. **Remarks:** Spare-time maker; first knife sold in 1979. **Mark:** Last initial.

KOPP, TODD M., P.O. Box 3474, Apache Jct., AZ 85217/602-983-6143
Specialties: Classic and traditional straight knives. **Patterns:** Bowies, boots, daggers, fighters and hunters. **Technical:** Grinds M1, ATS-34 and 4160. Some engraving and filework. **Prices:** $125 to $400; some to $800. **Remarks:** Part-time maker; first knife sold in 1989. **Mark:** Name, city and state.

KORMANIK, CHRIS, 6424 Stone Bridge Rd., Carnesville, GA 30521/706-384-4450
Specialties: Working knives and hunters. **Patterns:** Variety, including hunters, fighters and utility knives of his design or to customer specs; folders. **Technical:** Grinds and forges; prefers D2, ATS-34, cable Damascus and 5168. Heat-treats. **Prices:** $80 to $350; some higher. **Remarks:** Part-time maker; first knife sold in 1987. **Mark:** Name.

KOUTSOPOULOS, GEORGE, 41491 Biggs Rd., LaGrange, OH 44050/216-355-5013
Specialties: Heavy-duty working straight knives and folders. **Patterns:** Traditional hunters and skinners; lockbacks. **Technical:** Grinds 440C, 154CM, ATS-34. **Prices:** $75 to $275; some higher. **Remarks:** Spare-time maker; first knife sold in 1976. **Mark:** Initials in diamond logo.

KOVAL, MICHAEL T., 5819 Zarley St., New Albany, OH 43054/614-855-0777
Specialties: Working straight knives of his design; period pieces. **Patterns:** Bowies, boots and daggers. **Technical:** Grinds D2, 440C and 154CM. **Prices:** $95 to $195; some to $495. **Remarks:** Full-time knife-maker supply house; spare-time knifemaker. **Mark:** Last name.

KOVAR, EUGENE, 2626 W. 98th St., Evergreen Park, IL 60642/312-636-3724
Specialties: One-of-a-kind miniature knives only. **Patterns:** Fancy to fantasy miniature knives; knife pendants and tie tacks. **Technical:** Files and grinds nails, nickel silver and sterling silver. **Prices:** $5 to $35; some to $100. **Remarks:** Spare-time maker; first knife sold in 1987. **Mark:** GK connected.

KRAFT, ELMER, 1358 Meadowlark Lane, Big Arm, MT 59910/406-849-5086; FAX: 406-883-3056
Specialties: Traditional working/using straight knives of all designs. **Patterns:** Fighters, hunters, utility/camp knives. **Technical:** Grinds 440C, D2. Custom makes sheaths. **Prices:** $125 to $350; some to $500. **Remarks:** Part-time maker; first knife sold in 1989. **Mark:** Kraft Knives.

KRAFT, STEVE, 315 S.E. 6th, Abilene, KS 67410/913-263-2198
Specialties: Motorcycle chain Damascus with foot peg handle. **Patterns:** Hunters, boot knives and fighters. **Technical:** Forge chain Damascus and stock removal grind ATS-34. **Prices:** $150 to $1,000. **Remarks:** Part-time maker; first knife sold in 1984. **Mark:** Last name.

KRANNING, TERRY L., 1900 West Quinn, #153, Pocatello, ID 83202/208-237-9047
Specialties: Miniature and full-size fantasy and working knives of his design. **Patterns:** Miniatures and some mini straight knives including razors, tomahawks, hunters, Bowies and fighters. **Technical:** Grinds

1095, 440C, commercial Damascus and nickel silver. Uses exotic materials like meteorite. **Prices:** $20 to $100; some to $250. **Remarks:** Part-time maker; first knife sold in 1978. **Mark:** Last initial or full initials in eagle head logo.

KRAPP, DENNY, 1826 Windsor Oak Dr., Apopka, FL 32703/407-880-7115
Specialties: Fantasy and working straight knives of his design. **Patterns:** Hunters, fighters and utility/camp knives. **Technical:** Grinds ATS-34 and 440C. **Prices:** $85 to $300; some to $800. **Remarks:** Spare-time maker; first knife sold in 1988. **Mark:** Last name.

KRAUSE, ROY W., 22412 Corteville, St. Clair Shores, MI 48081/810-296-3995; FAX: 810-296-2663.
Specialties: Military and law enforcement/Japanese-style knives and swords. **Patterns:** Combat and back-up, Bowies, fighters, boot knives, daggers, tantos, wakazashis and katanas. **Technical:** Grinds ATS-34, A2, D2, 1045, 01 and commercial Damascus; differentially hardened Japanese-style blades. **Prices:** Moderate to upscale. **Remarks:** Full-time maker. **Mark:** Last name on traditional knives; initials in Japanese characters on Japanese-style knives.

KREIBICH, DONALD L., 6082 Boyd Ct., San Jose, CA 95123/408-225-8354
Specialties: Working straight knives in standard patterns. **Patterns:** Bowies, boots and daggers; camp and fishing knives. **Technical:** Grinds 440C, 154CM and ATS-34; likes integrals. **Prices:** $100 to $200; some to $500. **Remarks:** Part-time maker; first knife sold in 1980. **Mark:** First and middle initials, last name.

KREMZNER, RAYMOND L., P.O. Box 31, Stevenson, MD 21153/410-653-2657
Specialties: Working straight knives in standard patterns, some fancy. **Patterns:** Hunters, fighters, Bowies and camp knives. **Technical:** Forges 5160, 9260, W2 and his own Damascus. Offers wire inlay. **Prices:** $200 to $700; some higher. **Remarks:** Part-time maker; first knife sold in 1987. **Mark:** Last name, JS.

KRESSLER, D.F., AM Schlossberg 1, D-8063 Odelzhausen, GERMANY/08134-7758; FAX: 08134-7759
Specialties: High-tech working knives. **Patterns:** Hunters, fighters, daggers. **Technical:** Grinds new state-of-the-art steels; prefers natural handle materials. **Prices:** Upscale. **Mark:** Name in logo.

KRETSINGER JR., PHILIP W., 17536 Bakersville Rd., Boonsboro, MD 21713/301-432-6771
Specialties: Fancy and traditional period pieces. **Patterns:** Hunters, Bowies, camp knives, daggers, carvers, fighters. **Technical:** Forges W2, 5160 and his own Damascus. **Prices:** Start at $200. **Remarks:** Full-time knifemaker. **Mark:** Name.

KRUSE, MARTIN, P.O. Box 487, Reseda, CA 91335/818-713-0172
Specialties: Fighters and working straight knives. **Patterns:** Full line of straight knives, swords, fighters, axes, kitchen cutlery. **Technical:** Forges and grinds 01, 1095, 5160 and Damascus; differential tempering. **Prices:** $85 to $700; some to $2,000. **Remarks:** Full-time maker; first knife sold in 1964. **Mark:** Initials.

KUBAIKO, HANK, HC01 Box 6910, Palmer, AK 99645/907-746-4360
Specialties: Working straight knives and folders. **Patterns:** Bowies, fighters, fishing knives, kitchen cutlery, lockers, slip-joints, camp knives, axes and miniatures. **Technical:** Grinds 440C, ATS-34 and D2; will use CPM-T-440V at extra cost. Worked under Joe Cordova. **Prices:** Moderate. **Remarks:** Part-time maker in summer, full-time in winter; first knife sold in 1982. **Mark:** Alaskan Maid and name.

KUBASEK, JOHN A., 74 Northhampton St., Easthampton, MA 01027/413-527-7917
Specialties: Traditional working straight knives and folders of his design or to customer specs. **Patterns:** Hunters, Bowies, titanium liner locks and fighters. **Technical:** Grinds 01, ATS-34 and Damascus. **Prices:**

$100 to $650. **Remarks:** Part-time maker; first knife sold in 1985. **Mark:** Name and address etched.

KUNI MITSU (See Bell, Michael)

KUSTOM KRAFTED KNIVES—KKK (See Collins, A.J.)

L

LABORDE, TERRY, 230 E. Fallbrook St., Unit #11, Fallbrook, CA 92028-3381/619-723-9702
Specialties: Traditional and working straight knives of all designs. **Patterns:** Bowies, daggers and hunters. **Technical:** Forges and grinds CPMT 440V, ATS-34 and ASP-60. Barstock stainless Damascus sold by the inch. Heat-treats stainless steel. Uses stabilized woods for handles. **Prices:** $100 to $3,000; some to $5,000. **Remarks:** Part-time maker; first knife sold in 1990. **Mark:** Dragonfly over water.

LACKOVIC, NIKO, P.O. Box 21782, Port Elizabeth 6000, Republic of SOUTH AFRICA/041-321174; FAX: 041-321174
Specialties: Fancy/embellished, traditional and working/using straight knives of his design. **Patterns:** Boots, Bowies, daggers, fighters, hunters and utility/camp knives. **Technical:** Grinds 440C, D2 (on request) and surgical steel 12C27. Offers hand etching on blades, leather engraving on sheaths, handle engraving and finger guards. **Prices:** $100 to $1,000. **Remarks:** Full-time maker; first knife sold in 1992. **Mark:** Family crest with full name acid etched.

LADD, JIM S., 1120 Helen, Deer Park, TX 77536/713-479-7286
Specialties: Working knives and period pieces. **Patterns:** Hunters, boots and Bowies plus other straight knives. **Technical:** Grinds D2, 440C and 154CM. **Prices:** $125 to $225; some to $550. **Remarks:** Part-time maker; first knife sold in 1965. Doing business as The Tinker. **Mark:** First and middle initials, last name.

LADD, JIMMIE LEE, 1120 Helen, Deer Park, TX 77536/713-479-7186
Specialties: Working straight knives. **Patterns:** Hunters, skinners and utility knives. **Technical:** Grinds 440C and D2. **Prices:** $75 to $225. **Remarks:** First knife sold in 1979. **Mark:** First and middle initials, last name.

LA GRANGE, FANIE, 22 Sturke Rd., Selborne, Bellville 7530, REPUBLIC OF SOUTH AFRICA/27-021-9134199; FAX: 27-021-9134199
Specialties: Fancy high-tech straight knives and folders of his design and to customer specs. **Patterns:** Daggers, hunters and locking folders. **Technical:** Grinds Sandvik 12C27 and ATS-34; forges and grinds Damascus. Engraves, enamels and anodizes bolsters. Uses rare and natural handle materials. **Prices:** $250 to $500; some higher. **Remarks:** Full-time maker; first knife sold in 1987. **Mark:** Name, town, country under Table Mountain.

LA GRANGE KNIFE (See Roghmans, Mark)

LAINSON, TONY, 114 Park Ave., Council Bluffs, IA 51503/712-322-5222
Specialties: Working straight knives, locking folders, straight razors, Bowies and tantos. **Technical:** Grinds ATS-34 and 440C. Prefers mirror finishes; handle materials include Micarta, Pakkawood and bone. **Prices:** $45 to $280; some to $450. **Remarks:** Part-time maker; first knife sold in 1987; not currently taking orders. **Mark:** Name and state.

LAKE, RON, 3360 Bendix Ave., Eugene, OR 97401/503-484-2683
Specialties: High-tech working knives; inventor of the modern interframe folder. **Patterns:** Hunters, boots, etc.; locking folders. **Technical:** Grinds 154CM and ATS-34. Patented interframe with special lock release tab. **Prices:** $2,200 to $3,000; some higher. **Remarks:** Full-time maker; first knife sold in 1966. **Mark:** Last name.

LALA, PAULO RICARDO P. AND LALA, ROBERTO P., R. Daniel Martins, 636, Centro, Presidente Prudente, SP-19031-260, BRAZIL/0182-210125

Specialties: Straight knives and folders of all designs to customer specs. **Patterns:** Bowies, daggers, fighters, hunters and utility knives. **Technical:** Grinds and forges D6, 440C, high carbon steels and Damascus. **Prices:** $60 to $400; some higher. **Remarks:** Full-time makers; first knife sold in 1991. **Mark:** Sword carved on top of anvil under last name and serial number.

LALA, ROBERTO P. (See Lala, Paulo Ricardo P. and Lala, Roberto P.)

LAMBERT, JARRELL D., RR1, Box 67, Granado, TX 77962/512-771-3744
Specialties: Traditional working and using straight knives of his design and to customer specs. **Patterns:** Bowies, hunters and utility/camp knives. **Technical:** Grinds ATS-34; forges W2 and his own Damascus. Makes own sheaths. **Prices:** $80 to $600; some to $1,000. **Remarks:** Part-time maker; first knife sold in 1982. **Mark:** Etched first and middle initials, last name; or stamped last name.

LAMBERT, RONALD S., 24 Vermont St., Johnston, RI 02919/401-831-5427
Specialties: Traditional working and using straight knives of his design. **Patterns:** Boots, bowies and hunters. **Technical:** Grinds 01 and 440C; forges 1070. Offers exotic wood handles; sheaths have exotic skin overlay. **Prices:** $100 to $500; some to $850. **Remarks:** Part-time maker; first knife sold in 1991. Doing business as RL Custom Knives. **Mark:** Initials; each knife is numbered.

LAMPREY, MIKE, 32 Pathfield, Great Torrington, Devon EX38 7BX ENGLAND/01805 622651
Specialties: High-tech working/using straight knives and folders of his design. **Patterns:** Fighters, locking folders, utility/camp knives. **Technical:** Grinds ATS-34, 12C27 and 440C. Offers hand-rubbed finish on blades, bead blast and anodizing on titanium and occasional engraving on bolsters, guards, etc. **Prices:** $250 to $600; some to $1,000. **Remarks:** Part-time maker; first knife sold in 1982. **Mark:** Signature.

LAMPSON, FRANK G., 2052 I Rd., Fruita, CO 81521/970-858-7292
Specialties: Working folders; one-of-a-kinds. **Patterns:** Folders, hunters, utility knives, fillet knives and Bowies. **Technical:** Grinds ATS-34, 440C and 154CM. **Prices:** $100 to $750; some to $3,500; Catalogs $2. **Remarks:** Full-time maker; first knife sold in 1971. **Mark:** Name in fish logo.

LANCASTER, C.G., P.O. Box 99, Orkney, Transvaal, SOUTH AFRICA/018-32327
Specialties: High-tech working and using knives of his design and to customer specs. **Patterns:** Hunters, locking folders and utility/camp knives. **Technical:** Grinds Sandvik 12C27, 440C and D2. Offers anodized titanium bolsters. **Prices:** $450 to $750; some to $1,500. **Remarks:** Part-time maker; first knife sold in 1990. **Mark:** Etched logo.

LANCE, BILL, P.O. Box 4427, Eagle River, AK 99577/907-694-1487
Specialties: Ooloos and working straight knives; limited issue sets. **Patterns:** Several ooloo patterns, drop-point skinners. **Technical:** Uses ATS-34, Vascomax 350; ivory, horn and high-class wood handles. **Prices:** $85 to $300; art sets to $3,000. **Remarks:** First knife sold in 1981. **Mark:** Last name over a lance.

LANDERS, JOHN, 758 Welcome Rd., Newnan, GA 30263/404-253-5719
Specialties: High-art working straight knives and folders of his design. **Patterns:** Hunters, fighters and slip-joint folders. **Technical:** Grinds 440C, ATS-34, 154CM and commercial Damascus. **Prices:** $85 to $250; some to $500. **Remarks:** Part-time maker; first knife sold in 1989. **Mark:** Last name.

LANDRUM, LEONARD "LEN", 979 Gumpond-Beall Rd., Lumberton, MS 39455/601-796-4380
Specialties: Traditional working and using straight knives of his design and to customer specs. **Patterns:** Boots, Bowies, daggers, fighters, hunters, kitchen knives and utility/camp knives. **Technical:** Forges

52100, 5160 and pattern-welded steel; heat-treats. **Prices:** $100 to $500; some to $1,000. **Remarks:** Part-time maker; first knife sold in 1987. **Mark:** Handmade by Landrum.

LANE, BEN, 4802 Massie St., North Little Rock, AR 72218/501-753-8238
Specialties: Fancy straight knives of his design and to customer specs; period pieces. **Patterns:** Bowies, hunters, utility/camp knives. **Technical:** Grinds D2 and 154CM; forges and grinds 1095. Offers intricate handle work including inlays and spacers. **Prices:** $120 to $450; some to $5,000. **Remarks:** Part-time maker; first knife sold in 1989. **Mark:** Full name, city, state.

LANE, ED, 440 N. Topping, Kansas City, MO 64123/816-241-3217
Specialties: Fancy working knives to customer specs. **Patterns:** Buck-skinners, hunters, fighters, tantos, fishing knives and lightweight folders under the "Kascey" line. **Technical:** Grinds 440C, 154CM, ATS-34 and commercial Damascus. Offers titanium nitride on blades. **Prices:** $65 to $350; some to $1,000. **Remarks:** Full-time maker; first knife sold in 1982. **Mark:** Signature.

LANG, KURT, 4908 S. Wildwood Dr., McHenry, IL 60050/708-516-4649
Specialties: High-art working knives. **Patterns:** Bowies, utilitarian-type knives with rough finishes. **Technical:** Forges welded steel in European and Japanese styles. **Prices:** Moderate to upscale. **Remarks:** Part-time maker. **Mark:** "Crazy Eye" logo.

LANGE, DONALD G., Rt. 1, Box 66, Pelican Rapids, MN 56572
Specialties: High-quality Damascus hunters; welcomes customer designs. **Patterns:** Hunters, fighters and Bowies. **Technical:** Forges 5160, W2, L6 and his own Damascus. **Prices:** Moderate. **Remarks:** Full-time maker; first knife sold in 1969. **Mark:** Last name, M.S.

LANGLEY, GENE H., 1022 N. Price Rd., Florence, SC 29506/803-669-3150
Specialties: Working knives in standard patterns. **Patterns:** Hunters, boots, fighters, locking folders and slip-joints. **Technical:** Grinds 440C, 154CM and ATS-34. **Prices:** $125 to $450; some to $1000. **Remarks:** Full-time maker; first knife sold in 1979. **Mark:** Name or name, city and state.

LANGLEY, MICK, 960 Bluebird Place, Qualicum Beach, B.C. CANADA V9K 1M7/604-752-5856
Specialties: Working knives; period pieces. **Patterns:** Fighters, tantos, boots, Bowies and folders. **Technical:** Forges W2, 5160 and his own Damascus. **Prices:** $250 to $2,000; some to $3,500. **Remarks:** Full-time maker; first knife sold in 1977. **Mark:** Last name, M.S.

LANGSTON, BENNIE E., 3233 Ridgecrest, Memphis, TN 38127/901-357-4559
Specialties: Traditional working straight knives and folders of his design. **Patterns:** Hunters, daggers and locking folders. **Technical:** Grinds 440C. Filework; mirror-finishes. **Prices:** $50 to $100; some to $200. **Remarks:** Part-time maker; first knife sold in 1970. **Mark:** Last name and outline of state.

LANKTON, SCOTT, 8065 Jackson Rd. R-11, Ann Arbor, MI 48103/313-426-3735
Specialties: Pattern welded swords, krisses and Viking period pieces. **Patterns:** One-of-a-kind. **Technical:** Forges W2, L6 Nickel and other steels. **Prices:** $600 to $12,000. **Remarks:** Part-time bladesmith, full-time smith; first knife sold in 1976. **Mark:** Last name logo.

LAPEN, CHARLES, Box 529, W. Brookfield, MA 01585
Specialties: Fancy working straight knives. **Patterns:** camp knives, Japanese-style swords and wood working tools, hunters, Bowies and fudal European knives. **Technical:** Forges 1075, 9260 and his own Damascus. Favors narrow and Japanese tangs. **Prices:** $200 to $400; some to $2,000. **Remarks:** Full-time maker; first knife sold in 1972. **Mark:** Last name.

LAPLANTE, BRETT, 2821 Hickory Bend, Garland, TX 75044/214-414-1712
Specialties: Working straight knives and folders to customer specs. **Patterns:** Survival knives, Bowies, skinners, hunters. **Technical:** Grinds D2 and 440C. Heat-treats. **Prices:** $125 to $2500. **Remarks:** Part-time maker; first knife sold in 1987. **Mark:** Last name in Canadian maple leaf logo.

LARGIN, KEN, 67 Arlington Dr., Batesville, IN 47006/812-934-5938
Specialties: Working knives in standard patterns. **Patterns:** Hunters, folders, miniatures and butterfly knives. **Technical:** Grinds 440-C, ATS-34; buys Damascus; offers filework. **Prices:** $99 to $250; some to $500. **Remarks:** Full-time maker; first knife sold in 1980. Doing business as KELGIN Knives. **Mark:** KELGIN or name.

LARY, ED, 651 Rangeline Rd., Mosinee, WI 54455/715-693-3940
Specialties: Entry level to embellished investment grade. **Patterns:** Hunters, interframe folders, fighters and one-of-a-kind. **Technical:** Grinds D2, 440C, ATS34 and Damascus; prefers natural handle material. Does fancy filework, scrimshaws, engraves and does matching fabricated sheaths. **Prices:** Moderate to upscale. **Remarks:** First knife sold in 1974. **Mark:** Name in script and serial numbered.

LAUGHLIN, DON, 190 Laughlin Dr., Vidor, TX 77662/409-769-3390
Specialties: Working knives of his design. **Patterns:** Hunters, fighters, Bowies, locking folders and two-blades. **Technical:** Grinds D2, 440C and 154CM. **Prices:** $75 to $200; some to $350. **Remarks:** Full-time maker; first knife sold in 1973. **Mark:** DEER or full name.

LAURENT, KERMIT, 1812 Acadia Dr., LaPlace, LA 70068/504-652-5629
Specialties: Traditional and working straight knives and folders of his design. **Patterns:** Bowies, hunters and utility knives. **Technical:** Forges 1095 and pattern-welded Damascus; grinds 440C. Specializes in altering cable patterns. Uses stabilized handle materials, especially select exotic woods. **Prices:** $75 to $200; some to $1,000. **Remarks:** Full-time maker; first knife sold in 1982. Doing business as Kermit's Knife Works. **Mark:** First name.

LAWLESS, CHARLES, 611 Haynes Rd. N.E., Arab, AL 35016/205-586-4862
Specialties: Classic and traditional straight knives of his design or to customer specs. **Patterns:** Bowies, fighters and hunters. **Technical:** Forges 5160, 01 and 1095. Uses tapered tangs, dovetailed bolsters and mortised handle frames. Mostly natural materials. **Prices:** $50 to $400; some to $1200. **Remarks:** Part-time maker; first knife sold in 1991. Doing business as Lawless Blades. **Mark:** Full name, bladesmith, city and state.

LAWRENCE, ALTON, Rt. 1, Box 488, De Queen, AR 71832/501-642-7643
Specialties: Classic straight knives to customer specs. **Patterns:** Bowies, hunters, folders and utility/camp knives. **Technical:** Forges 5160, 1095, 1084, Damascus and railroad spikes. **Prices:** $100 and up. **Remarks:** Part-time maker; first knife sold in 1988. **Mark:** Last name inside fish symbol.

LAY, L.J., 602 Mimosa Dr., Burkburnett, TX 76354/817-569-1329
Specialties: Working straight knives in standard patterns; some period pieces. **Patterns:** Drop-point hunters, Bowies and fighters. **Technical:** Grinds ATS-34 to mirror finish; likes Micarta handles. **Prices:** Moderate. **Remarks:** Full-time maker; first knife sold in 1985. **Mark:** Name or name with ram head and city.

LAY, R.J. (BOB), R.R.2 Braeside Rd., Vanderhoof, B.C. V0J 3A0 CANADA/604-567-3856
Specialties: Traditional and working/using straight knives of his design. **Patterns:** Bowies, fighters and hunters. **Technical:** Grinds 440C and ATS-34; forges and grinds tool steels. Uses exotic handle and spacer material. File cut; prefers narrow tang. Sheaths available. **Prices:** $150 to $450; some to $1100. (Can.) **Remarks:** Part-time maker; first knife

sold in 1976. Doing business as Lay's Custom Knives. **Mark:** Signature acid etched.

LAZO, ROBERT T., 11850 SW 181 St., Miami, FL 33177/305-232-1569
Specialties: Traditional working and using straight knives and folders in standard patterns. **Patterns:** Utility/camp knives, locking folders, fillet knives and some miniatures. **Technical:** Grinds 440C, ATS-34 and 01. All knives come with hand-tooled leather sheaths, some with fancy inlaids. **Prices:** $90 to $250; some to $500. **Remarks:** Spare-time maker; first knife sold in 1990. **Mark:** Engraved or stamped name.

LDA/LAKELL (See C-G Tay, Larry)

LEACH, MIKE J., 5377 W. Grand Blanc Rd., Swartz Creek, MI 48473/810-655-4850
Specialties: Fancy working knives. **Patterns:** Hunters, fighters, Bowies and heavy-duty knives; slip-joint folders and integral straight patterns. **Technical:** Grinds D2, 440C and 154CM; buys Damascus. **Prices:** Start at $150. **Remarks:** Full-time maker; first knife sold in 1952. **Mark:** Last name.

THE LEATHER BOX (See Benjamin, Jr., Geroge)

LEAVITT JR., EARL F., Pleasant Cove Rd., Box 306, E. Boothbay, ME 04544/207-633-3210
Specialties: 1500-1870 working straight knives and fighters; pole arms. **Patterns:** Historically significant knives, classic/modern custom designs. **Technical:** Flat-grinds 01; heat-treats. Filework available. **Prices:** $90 to $350; some to $1,000. **Remarks:** Full-time maker; first knife sold in 1981. Doing business as Old Colony Manufactory. **Mark:** Initials in oval.

LeBATARD, PAUL M., 14700 Old River Rd., Vancleave, MS 39565/601-826-4137
Specialties: Sound working knives, some fancy; lightweight folders. **Patterns:** Hunters, fillets, camp and kitchen knives, combat/survival utility knives, Bowies, toothpicks and one- and two-blade folders. **Technical:** Grinds ATS-34; forges carbon steel; machines folder frames from aircraft aluminum. **Prices:** $50 to $450. **Remarks:** Part-time maker; first knife sold in 1974. Offers knife repair, restoration and sharpening. **Mark:** Last name.

LEBER, HEINZ, Box 446, Hudson's Hope, BC VOC 1V0, CANADA/604-783-5304
Specialties: Working straight knives of his design. **Patterns:** 20 models, from capers to Bowies. **Technical:** Hollow-grinds M2 exclusively; mirror-finishes and full tang only. Likes moose, elk, stone sheep for handles. **Prices:** $135 to $1,000; 20-page color brochure $3. **Remarks:** Full-time maker; first knife sold in 1975. **Mark:** Initials connected.

LeBLANC, JOHN, Rt. 2, Box 22950, Winnsboro, TX 75494/903-629-7745

LECK, DAL, Box 390, Hayden, CO 81639/303-276-3663
Specialties: Classic, traditional and working knives of his design and in standard patterns; period pieces. **Patterns:** Boots, daggers, fighters, hunters and push daggers. **Technical:** Forges 01 and 5160; makes his own Damascus. **Prices:** $175 to $700; some to $1,500. **Remarks:** Part-time maker; first knife sold in 1990. Doing business as The Moonlight Smithy. **Mark:** Stamped initials.

LEDFORD, BRACY R., 3670 N. Sherman Dr., Indianapolis, IN 46218/317-549-1948
Specialties: Art knives and fantasy knives; working knives upon request. **Patterns:** Bowies, locking folders and hunters; coil spring action folders. **Technical:** Files and sandpapers 440C by hand; other steels available upon request; likes exotic handle materials. **Prices:** Folders start at $250; fixed blades $125 to $3,000. **Remarks:** Part-time maker; first knife sold in 1983. **Mark:** First and middle initials, last name, city and state.

LEE, RANDY, P.O. Box 1873, St. Johns, AZ 85936/520-337-2594
Specialties: Traditional working and using straight knives of his design. **Patterns:** Bowies, fighters, hunters, daggers and professional throwing knives. **Technical:** Grinds ATS-34, 440C and D2. Sheaths by Sonja Lee. **Prices:** $175 to $500; some to $800. **Remarks:** Part-time maker; first knife sold in 1979. **Mark:** Full name, city, state.

LEE, TOMMY, 1011 Grassy Pond Rd., Gaffney, SC 29340/803-489-6699
Specialties: Working knives and period pieces. **Patterns:** Daggers, boots, fighters and folders. **Technical:** Forges and grinds 440C, ATS-34 and his own and commercial Damascus. **Prices:** $200 to $500; some to $2,000. **Remarks:** Full-time maker; first knife sold in 1974. **Mark:** Last name in capital block letters.

LEET, LARRY W., 2001 N. Beard, Shawnee, OK 74801/405-273-7487
Specialties: Heavy-duty working knives. **Patterns:** Hunters, tantos, camp knives and Bowies. **Technical:** Grinds stainless steels; likes filework. **Remarks:** Full-time maker; first knife sold in 1970. **Mark:** Stylized initials.

LeFONT, MARK, 3210 Oakley Dr., Hollywood, CA 90068/213-851-5940
Specialties: Classic high-art fantasy straight knives of his design. **Patterns:** Daggers and swords; chain mail armor, helmets, axes and stone knives. **Technical:** Grinds Pamir Damascus, conventional steel and non-metallic materials. **Prices:** $150 to $250; some higher. **Remarks:** Full-time maker; first knife sold in 1983. **Mark:** None.

LELAND, STEVE, P.O. Box 1173, Fairfax, CA 94978
Specialties: Traditional and working straight knives and folders of his design and to customer specs. **Patterns:** Boots, hunters and locking folders. **Technical:** Grinds 01, ATS-34 and 440C. **Prices:** $150 to $300; some to $750. **Remarks:** Part-time maker; first knife sold in 1987. Doing business as Leland Knives. **Mark:** Last name.

LEMAIRE, DENIS, 534 Verendrye St., Boucherville, P.Q. J4B 2Y1 CANADA

LEONE, NICK, 9 Georgetown, Pontoon Beach, IL 62040/618-797-1179
Specialties: Working straight knives and art daggers. **Patterns:** Bowies, skinners, hunters, camp/utility, fighters, daggers and primitive knives. **Technical:** Forges 5160, W2, 01, 1098, 52100 and his own Damascus and cable. **Prices:** $25 to $1000; some to $2500. **Remarks:** Full-time maker; first knife sold in 1987. Doing business as Anvil Head Forge. **Mark:** Last name or anvil head forge.

LEPORE, MICHAEL J., 66 Woodcutters Dr., Bethany, CT 06524/203-393-3823
Specialties: One-of-a-kind designs to customer specs; mostly handmade. **Patterns:** Fancy working straight knives and folders. **Technical:** Forges and grinds W2, W1 and 01; prefers natural handle materials. **Prices:** $750 and up. **Remarks:** Spare-time maker; first knife sold in 1984. **Mark:** Last name.

LETCHER, BILLY, 200 Milkyway, Fort Collins, CO 80525/970-223-9689
Specialties: Traditional working and using straight knives; fancy knives. **Patterns:** Boots, Bowies, daggers, fighters, hunters, letter openers. **Technical:** Grinds 440C, ATS-34 and D2. **Prices:** $70 to $350. **Remarks:** Part-time maker; first knife sold in 1983. **Mark:** Letcher Knives.

LEVENGOOD, BILL, 15011 Otto Rd., Tampa, FL 33624/813-961-5688
Specialties: Working straight knives and folders. **Patterns:** Hunters, Bowies, folders and collector pieces. **Technical:** Grinds ATS-34 and D2. **Prices:** $65 to $1,200. **Remarks:** Part-time maker; first knife sold in 1983. **Mark:** Last name, city, state.

LEVERETT, KEN, P.O. Box 696, Lithia, FL 33547/813-689-8578
Specialties: High-tech and working straight knives and folders of his

design and to customer specs. **Patterns:** Bowies, hunters and locking folders. **Technical:** Grinds ATS-34, Damascus. **Prices:** $100 to $350; some to $1,500. **Remarks:** Part-time maker; first knife sold in 1991. **Mark:** Name, city, state.

LEVINE, BOB, 101 Westwood Dr., Tullahoma, TN 37388/615-454-9943 **Specialties:** Working left- and right-handed folders. **Patterns:** Hunters and folders. **Technical:** Grinds 154CM, ATS-34, AEBL, 440C, D2, 01 and some Damascus; hollow and some flat grinds. Uses sheephorn, fossil ivory and micarta. Provides custom leather sheath with each knife. **Prices:** $105 to $500; some higher. **Remarks:** Full-time maker; first knife sold in 1984. **Mark:** Name and logo.

LEVINE, NORMAN, 34582 Farm Rd., Lake Elsinore, CA 92532/909-244-0993 **Specialties:** Fancy art knives. **Patterns:** Hunters, boots, daggers, locking folders and slip-joints in gents and hunter patterns. **Technical:** Grinds 440C, D2 and Damascus; provides ball bearing pivot in folders. **Prices:** $135 to $5,000. **Remarks:** Full-time maker; first knife sold in 1974. **Mark:** Dragon on shield with name.

LEWIS, K.J., 374 Cook Rd., Lugoff, SC 29078/803-438-4343

LEWIS, MIKE, 111 W. Central Ave., Tracy, CA 95376/209-836-5753; 408-453-1190 **Specialties:** Traditional straight knives. **Patterns:** Swords and daggers. **Technical:** Grinds 440C, ATS-34 and 5160. Frequently uses cast bronze and cast nickel guards and pommels. **Prices:** $100 to $750. **Remarks:** Part-time maker; first knife sold in 1988. **Mark:** Dragon Steel and serial number.

LEWIS, RON, Box S-365, Edgewood, NM 87015/505-281-8343 **Specialties:** Classic straight knives. **Patterns:** Bowies, skinners, buckskinners, art and utility knives. **Technical:** Grinds and forges Damascus, 1084 and ATS-34. **Prices:** Start at $250. **Remarks:** Full-time maker; first knife sold in 1987. **Mark:** Logo with serial number.

LEWIS, TOM R., 1613 Standpipe Rd., Carlsbad, NM 88220/505-885-3616 **Specialties:** Traditional working straight knives. **Patterns:** Outdoor knives, hunting knives and Bowies. **Technical:** Grinds ATS-34 and CPMT 440V; forges 52100. Makes wire, pattern welded and chainsaw Damascus. **Prices:** $75 to $400. **Remarks:** Part-time maker; first knife sold in 1980. Doing business as TRL Handmade Knives. **Mark:** Lewis family crest.

LICATA, STEVEN, 116 Front St., Mineola, NY 11501/516-248-8633; FAX: 914-779-4234 **Specialties:** Fantasy and high-art knives. **Patterns:** Daggers, fighters, axes and swords. **Technical:** Forges 01, 440C and Damascus. **Prices:** $200 to $5,000. **Remarks:** Full-time maker; first knife sold in 1989. **Mark:** Stylized initials.

LIEBENBERG, ANDRE, 8 Hilma Rd., Bordeauxrandburg 2196, SOUTH AFRICA/011-787-2303 **Specialties:** High-art straight knives of his design. **Patterns:** Daggers, fighters and swords. **Technical:** Grinds 440C and 12C27. **Prices:** $250 to $500; some $4,000 and higher. Giraffe bone handles with semi-precious stones. **Remarks:** Spare-time maker; first knife sold in 1990. **Mark:** Initials.

LIEGEY, KENNETH R., 132 Carney Dr., Millwood, WV 25262/304-273-9545 **Specialties:** Traditional working/using straight knives of his design and to customer specs. **Patterns:** Hunters, utility/camp knives, miniatures. **Technical:** Grinds 440C. **Prices:** $75 to $150; some to $300. **Remarks:** Spare-time maker; first knife sold in 1977. **Mark:** First and middle initials, last name.

LIKARICH, STEVE, 26075 Green Acres Rd., Colfax, CA 95713/916-346-8480

Specialties: Fancy working knives; art knives of his design. **Patterns:** Hunters, fighters and art knives of his design. **Technical:** Grinds ATS-34, 154CM and 440C; likes high polishes and filework. **Prices:** $200 to $2,000; some higher. **Remarks:** Full-time maker; first knife sold in 1987. **Mark:** Name.

LILE, MARILYN (JIMMY), 2721 S. Arkansas Ave., Russellville, AR 72801/501-968-2011 **Specialties:** Fancy working knives. **Patterns:** Bowies, full line of straight knives, button-lock folders. **Technical:** Grinds D2 and 440C. **Prices:** $125 to $800; some higher. **Remarks:** Full-time maker; first knife sold in 1944. Creator of the original *First Blood* **and** *Rambo* survival knives. **Mark:** Last name with a dot between the I and L.

LINDSAY, CHRIS A., 1324 N.E. Locksley Dr., Bend, OR 97701/503-389-3875 **Specialties:** Working knives in standard patterns. **Patterns:** Hunters and camp knives. **Technical:** Hollow- and flat-grinds 440C and ATS-34; offers brushed finishes, tapered tangs. **Prices:** $75 to $160; knife kits $60 to $80. **Remarks:** Part-time maker; first knife sold in 1980. **Mark:** Last name, town and state in oval.

LIONMAKER (See Alden, Jr., Kenneth E.)

LISTER JR., WELDON E., 9140 Sailfish Dr., Boerne, TX 78006/210-981-2210 **Specialties:** One-of-a-kind fancy and embellished folders. **Patterns:** Locking and slip-joint folders. **Technical:** Commercial Damascus and 01. All knives embellished. Engraves, inlays, carves and scrimshaws. **Prices:** Upscale. **Remarks:** Spare-time maker; first knife sold in 1991. **Mark:** Last name.

LITTLE, GARY M., HC84 Box 10301, P.O. Box 156, Broadbent, OR 97414/503-572-2656 **Specialties:** Fancy working knives. **Patterns:** Hunters, tantos, Bowies, axes and buckskinners; locking folders and interframes. **Technical:** Forges and grinds 01, L6, 1095; makes his own Damascus; bronze fittings. **Prices:** $85 to $300; some to $2,500. **Remarks:** Full-time maker; first knife sold in 1979. Doing business as Conklin Meadows Forge. **Mark:** Name, city and state.

LITTLE, JIMMY L., P.O. Box 871652, Wasilla, AK 99687/907-373-7831 **Specialties:** Working straight knives; fancy period pieces. **Patterns:** Bowies, bush swords and camp knives. **Technical:** Grinds 440C, 154CM and ATS-34. **Prices:** $100 to $1,000. **Remarks:** Full-time maker; first knife sold in 1984. **Mark:** First and middle initials, last name.

LIVELY, MARIAN (See Lively, Tim and Marian)

LIVELY, TIM AND MARIAN, 15555 N. Oracle #17, Tucson, AZ 85737/520-825-0679 **Specialties:** Traditional and fancy straight knives of their design. **Patterns:** One-of-a-kinds of all sizes. **Technical:** Grinds and forges a variety of steels. **Prices:** $150 to $750; some higher. **Remarks:** Full-time makers; first knife sold in 1974. **Mark:** Last name with broken arrow.

LIVINGSTON, ROBERT C., P.O. Box 6, Murphy, NC 28906/704-837-4155 **Specialties:** Art letter openers to working straight knives. **Patterns:** Minis to machetes. **Technical:** Forges and grinds his Damascus, 5160, 440C, ATS-34, L6, 1086 and most tool steels. Offers silver and gold castings and stonework—precious and semi-precious. Forges own mokume. **Prices:** $50 to $750. **Remarks:** Full-time maker; first knife sold in 1988. Doing business as Mystik Knifeworks. **Mark:** MYSTIK.

LOCKETT, LOWELL C., 116 Mill Creek Ct., Woodstock, GA 30188/770-926-2998 **Specialties:** Traditional and working/using knives of his design. **Patterns:** Bowies, hunters and utility/camp knives. **Technical:** Forges 5130, D2 and high carbon. Makes his own guards; sewn or riveted sheaths. **Prices:** $75 to $250; some to $600. **Remarks:** Full-time mak-

er; first knife sold in 1994. Doing business as Fire Forged Knives. **Mark:** Script initials.

LOCKETT, STERLING, 527 E. Amherst Dr., Burbank, CA 91504/818-846-5799
Specialties: Working straight knives and folders to customer specs. **Patterns:** Hunters and fighters. **Technical:** Grinds. **Prices:** Moderate. **Remarks:** Spare-time maker. **Mark:** Name, city with hearts.

LOERCHNER, WOLFGANG, P.O. Box 255, Bayfield, Ont. N0M 1G0, CANADA/519-565-2196
Specialties: Traditional straight knives, mostly ornate. **Patterns:** Small swords, daggers and stilettos; locking folders and miniatures. **Technical:** Grinds D2, 440C and 154CM; all knives hand-filed and flat-ground. **Prices:** $300 to $5,000; some to $10,000. **Remarks:** Part-time maker; first knife sold in 1983. Often collaborates wtih engraver Martin Butler. Doing business as Wolfe Fine Knives. **Mark:** WOLFE.

LOFLIN, BOB, San Jose, Costa Rica; c/o Levi Strauss, 5979 N. West 151st St., Miami Lakes, FL 33014/011-506-799155
Specialties: Fancy working knives of his design. **Patterns:** Hunters, fighters and camp knives; locking folders. **Technical:** Grinds D2, 440C and ATS-34. **Prices:** $75 to $250; some to $700. **Remarks:** Part-time maker; first knife sold in 1983. **Mark:** Name.

LONE STAR CUSTOM KNIVES (See Richardson, Jr., Percy)

LONESOME PINE (See Harley, Larry W.)

LONEWOLF, J. AGUIRRE, Rt. 1 Box 1322A, Demorest, GA 30535/706-754-4660
Specialties: High-art working and using straight knives of his design. **Patterns:** Bowies, hunters, utility/camp knives and fint steel blades. **Technical:** Forges Damascus and high-carbon steel; grinds stainless steel. Most knives have hand-carved moose antler handles. **Prices:** $55 to $500; some to $2,000. **Remarks:** Full-time maker; first knife sold in 1980. Doing business as Lonewolf Trading Post. **Mark:** Stamp or etch.

LONEWOLF TRADING POST (See Lonewolf, J. Aguirre)

LONG, GLENN A., 3601 Catalina, Palm Beach Gardens, FL 33410/407-622-1553
Specialties: Classic working and using straight knives of his design and to customer specs. **Patterns:** Hunters, Bowies and utility/camp knives. **Technical:** Grinds ATS-34, 440C and D2. **Prices:** $65 to $200; some to $500. **Remarks:** Part-time maker; first knife sold in 1990. **Mark:** Last name inside diamond.

LONGHORN KNIFE WORKS (See Hagwood, Kellie)

LONGWORTH, DAVE, 1811 SR 774, Hamersville, OH 45130/513-876-3637
Specialties: High-tech working knives. **Patterns:** Locking folders, hunters, fighters and elaborate daggers. **Technical:** Grinds 01, ATS-34, 440C; buys Damascus. **Prices:** $125 to $600; some higher. **Remarks:** Part-time maker; first knife sold in 1980. **Mark:** Last name.

LOOS, HENRY C., 210 Ingraham Ln., New Hope, NY 11040/516-354-1943
Specialties: Miniature fancy knives and period pieces of his design. **Patterns:** Bowies, daggers and swords. **Technical:** Grinds 01 and 440C. Uses sterling, 10K, rubies and emeralds. All knives come with handmade hardwood cases. **Prices:** $90 to $195; some to $250. **Remarks:** Spare-time maker; first knife sold in 1990. **Mark:** Script last initial.

LORD (See Sontheimer, G. Douglas)

LORDITCH, CHARLES RICHARD, 7 Tollgate Rd., Johnstown, PA 15906/814-536-0579
Specialties: Using straight knives and folders of his design or to customer specs. **Patterns:** Miniatures to Bowies; slip-joints and lock-back

folders. **Technical:** Forges high carbon steels and cable Damascus. Prefers natural handle materials such as corn cobs and butternuts. **Prices:** $30 to $250. **Remarks:** Full-time maker; first knife sold in 1965. **Mark:** Initials in various scripts.

LOTT, DAVID, P.O. Box 1252, Addison, TX 75001/214-783-1076; FAX: 214-783-2524

LOVE, ED, 3230 Seawolf Dr., Tallahassee, FL 32312/904-385-1403
Specialties: Fancy working knives in standard patterns or to customer specs. **Patterns:** Hunters, Bowies and and one-of-a-kinds. **Technical:** Grinds ATS-34. **Prices:** $90 to $190; some to $500. **Remarks:** Part-time maker; first knife sold in 1980. **Mark:** Name in weeping heart.

LOVELESS, R.W., P.O. Box 7836, Riverside, CA 92503/909-689-7800
Specialties: Working knives, fighters and hunters of his design. **Patterns:** Contemporary hunters, fighters and boots. **Technical:** Grinds 154CM and ATS-34. **Prices:** $850 to $4950. **Remarks:** Full-time maker since 1969. **Mark:** Name in logo.

LOVESTRAND, SCHUYLER, 206 Bent Oak Cir., Harvest, AL 35749/205-430-0828
Specialties: Fancy working straight knives of his design and to customer specs; unusual fossil ivories. **Patterns:** Hunters, fighters, Bowies and fishing knives. **Technical:** Grinds ATS-34. **Prices:** $150 to $1,095; some higher. **Remarks:** Part-time maker; first knife sold in 1982. **Mark:** Name in logo.

LOWCOUNTRY THROWING KNIVES (See Branton, Robert)

LOZIER, DON, 5394 SE 168th Ave., Ocklawaha, FL 32179/904-625-3576
Specialties: Fancy and working straight knives of his design and in standard patterns. **Patterns:** Bowies, hunters, daggers, boot knives, fighters and fillet knives. **Technical:** Grinds ATS-34, 440C and non-commercial Damascus. Most knives file-worked, custom pinned, exhibition grade handle materials. Handcarves and handsews all sheaths. **Prices:** Start at $165. **Remarks:** Full-time maker. Doing business as Don Lozier Handmade Purist Knives. **Mark:** Full name handmade purist in script.

LUBRICH, MARK, P.O. Box 122, Matthews, NC 28106-0122/704-567-7692
Specialties: Traditional working and using straight knives of his design and to customer specs. **Patterns:** Hunters and utility/camp knives. Some folding loackbacks and woodcarving sets. **Technical:** Forges and grinds 01, 5160 and 1095; using some cable; forges 440C stainless, brass and silver inlaid handles. Differentially heat-treats; makes sheaths; hardwood/stag or leather/stag handles. **Prices:** $75 to $225; some to $500. **Remarks:** Part-time maker; first knife sold in 1980. Doing business as Handmade Knives by Mark Lubrich. **Mark:** Etched last name on stock removal; stamped logo on forged blades.

LUCHAK, BOB, 15705 Woodforest Blvd., Channelview, TX 77530/713-452-1779
Specialties: Presentation knives; start of The Survivor series. **Patterns:** Skinners, Bowies, camp axes, steak knife sets and fillet knives. **Technical:** Grinds 440C. Offers electronic etching; filework. **Prices:** $50 to $1,500. **Remarks:** Full-time maker; first knife sold in 1983. Doing business as Teddybear Knives. **Mark:** Full name, city and state with Teddybear logo.

LUCIE, JAMES R., 4191 E. Fruitport Rd., Fruitport, MI 49415/616-865-6390; FAX: 616-865-3170
Specialties: Hand-forges William Scagel-style knives. **Patterns:** Authentic Scagel-style knives and miniatures. **Technical:** Forges 5160. **Prices:** $375 and up. **Remarks:** Full-time maker; first knife sold in 1975. **Mark:** Scagel kris with name.

LUCK, GREGORY, P.O. Box 2255, Greeley, CO 80632/303-686-7223
Specialties: Forged straight knives. **Patterns:** Bowies, fighters, buckskin-

ners and other working straight knives. **Technical:** Forges carbon steel and own cable Damascus; differential tempers; makes distinctive sheaths. **Prices:** $75 to $400; some higher. **Remarks:** Part-time maker; first knife sold in 1988. **Mark:** Three runes or last name and dragon-knot logo.

LUCKETT, BILL, 108 Amantes Ln., Weatherford, TX 76088/817-599-4629
Specialties: Uniquely patterned robust straight knives. **Patterns:** Fighters, Bowies, hunters. **Technical:** Grinds 440C and commercial Damascus; makes heavy knives with deep grinding. **Prices:** $375 to $800; some to $2,000. **Remarks:** Part-time maker; first knife sold in 1975. **Mark:** Last name over Bowie logo.

LUDWIG, RICHARD O., 57-63 65 St., Maspeth, NY 11378

LUI, RONALD M., 4042 Harding Ave., Honolulu, HI 96816/808-734-7746
Specialties: Working straight knives and folders in standard patterns. **Patterns:** Hunters, boots and liner locks. **Technical:** Grinds 440C and ATS-34. **Prices:** $100 to $700. **Remarks:** Spare-time maker; first knife sold in 1988. **Mark:** Initials connected.

LUM, ROBERT W., 901 Travis Ave., Eugene, OR 97404/503-688-2737
Specialties: High-art working knives of his design. **Patterns:** Hunters, fighters, tantos and folders. **Technical:** Grinds 440C, 154CM and ATS-34; plans to forge soon. **Prices:** $175 to $500; some to $800. **Remarks:** Full-time maker; first knife sold in 1976. **Mark:** Chop with last name underneath.

LUNDSTROM, JAN-AKE, Mastmostigen 8, 66010 Dals-Langed, SWEDEN/0531-41259
Specialties: Viking swords, axes and knives in cooperation with handlemakers. **Patterns:** All traditional styles, especially swords and inlaid blades. **Technical:** Forges his own Damascus and laminated steel. **Prices:** $200 to $1,000. **Remarks:** Full-time maker; first knife sold in 1985; collaborates with museums. **Mark:** Runic.

LUNN, LARRY A., 3432 S.R. 580 #312, Safety Harbor, FL 34695/813-796-2386
Specialties: Art knives of his design. **Patterns:** Bowies, daggers, fighters, swords and fancy hunting knives. **Technical:** Forges and grinds Damascus; grinds ATS-34, 440C and carbon tool steel. Prefers natural materials; uses gold/silver. Carves handles and supplies fancy sheaths. **Prices:** Starting at $100. **Remarks:** Part-time maker; first knife sold in 1989. **Mark:** Last name in script and small Samuri helmet in a circle.

LUTES, ROBERT, 24878 U.S. #6 East (RR 1), Nappanee, IN 46550/219-773-4773
Specialties: Straight working knives of his design or to standard patterns. **Patterns:** Hunters, fighters, boots and axes. **Technical:** Grinds 440C and commercial Damascus. **Prices:** $50 to $1,500. **Remarks:** Part-time maker; first knife sold in 1980. **Mark:** Last name.

LUTZ, GREG, 149 Effie Dr., Greenwood, SC 29649/803-229-7340
Specialties: Working and using knives and period pieces of his design and to customer specs. **Patterns:** Fighters, hunters and swords. **Technical:** Forges 1095 and 01; grinds ATS-34. Differentially heat-treats forged blades; uses cryogenic treatment on ATS-34. **Prices:** $50 to $350; some to $1,200. **Remarks:** Full-time maker; first knife sold in 1986. Doing business as Scorpion Forge. **Mark:** First initial, last name.

LYLE III, ERNEST L., 4501 Meadowbrook Ave., Orlando, FL 32808/407-299-7227
Specialties: Fancy period pieces in standard patterns. **Patterns:** Arabian/Persian influenced fighters, military knives, Bowies and Roman short swords; several styles of hunters; minis and miniatures. **Technical:** Grinds D2, 440C and 154CM. Engraves. **Prices:** $250 to $900; some to $2,300. **Remarks:** Full-time maker; first knife sold in 1972. Doesn't accept orders. **Mark:** Last name in capital letters.

LYONS, RANDY, Rt. 3 Box 677A, Lumberton, TX 77656/409-755-3860
Specialties: Working straight knives and folders. **Patterns:** Bowies,

hunters, locking folders and utility/camp knives. **Technical:** Grinds ATS-34, 440C and D2. **Prices:** $60 to $300; some to $600. **Remarks:** Full-time maker; first knife sold in 1989. Doing business as The Lyons Den. **Mark:** First and middle initials, last name, city and state.

LYTTLE, BRIAN, Box 5697, High River, AB T1V 1M7, CANADA/403-558-3638
Specialties: Fancy working straight knives and folders; art knives. **Patterns:** Hunters, Bowies, daggers, stilettos, fighters and miniatures. **Technical:** Forges his own Damascus, cable and motorcycle chain; offers scrimshaw and forged jewelry to Damascus bits and spurs. **Prices:** $350 to $800; some to $5,000. **Remarks:** Full-time maker; first knife sold in 1983. **Mark:** Last name/country.

m

MacBAIN, KENNETH C., 30 Briarwood Ave., Norwood, NJ 07648/201-768-0652
Specialties: Fantasy straight knives and folders, some high-tech. **Patterns:** Swords, knife-rings, push daggers and some miniatures. **Technical:** Forges and grinds A2, W2 and 01. **Prices:** $200 to $500; some to $2,500. **Remarks:** Part-time maker; first knife sold in 1986. **Mark:** Initials.

MACKRILL, STEPHEN, P.O. Box 1580, Pinegowrie 2123, Johannesburg, SOUTH AFRICA/27-11-886-2893; FAX: 27-11-334-3729
Specialties: Fancy and working knives. **Patterns:** Fighters, hunters and utility/camp knives. **Technical:** N690, K110, 12C27. Silver and gold inlay on handles; wooden sheaths. **Prices:** $98 to $700; some to $1,800. **Remarks:** Full-time maker; first knife sold in 1978. **Mark:** First initial, last name.

MACRI, MIKE, Box 222, Churchill, MB R0B 0E0, CANADA/204-675-2195
Specialties: Working straight knives in standard patterns. **Patterns:** Arctic survival knives, tantos, Bowies, camp knives and locking folders. **Technical:** Grinds 440C, ATS-34 and commercial Damascus. Full-tapered tangs and hollow-grinds. **Prices:** $100 to $500; some to $2,000. **Remarks:** Full-time maker; first knife sold in 1982. **Mark:** Last name.

MADRONA KNIVES (See Rice, Adrienne)

MADSEN, JACK, 3311 Northwest Dr., Wichita Falls, TX 76305/817-322-4112
Specialties: Working straight knives in standard patterns. **Patterns:** Bowies, hunters, swords, tomahawks and heavy-duty camp knives. **Technical:** Forges W2, 01 and his own Damascus. **Prices:** $85 to $350; some to $1,000. **Remarks:** Full-time maker; first knife sold in 1975. **Mark:** Name and city.

MAESTRI BROS. (See Maestri, Peter A.)

MAESTRI, PETER A., Rt. 1, Box 111, Spring Green, WI 53588/608-546-4481
Specialties: Working straight knives in standard patterns. **Patterns:** Camp and fishing knives, utility green-river styled. **Technical:** Grinds 440C, 154CM and 440A. **Prices:** $15 to $45; some to $150. **Remarks:** Full-time maker; first knife sold in 1981. Provides professional cutler service to professional cutters. **Mark:** CARISOLO, MAESTRI BROS., or signature.

MAIENKNECHT, STANLEY, 38648 S.R. 800, Sardis, OH 43946

MAISEY, ALAN, P.O. Box 316, Toongabbie 2146, AUSTRALIA/Sydney 636-2183
Specialties: Daggers, especially krisses; period pieces. **Technical:** Offers knives and finished blades in Damascus and Nickel Damascus. **Prices:** $75 to $2,000; some higher. **Remarks:** Part-time maker; pro-

vides complete restoration service for krisses. Trained by a Javanese kris smith. **Mark:** None, triangle in a box, or three peaks.

MALLOY, JOE, P.O. Box 156, 1039 Schwabe St., Freeland, PA 18224/717-636-2781
Specialties: Working knives; customer designs welcome. **Patterns:** Hunters, utility/camp knives, fighters Bowies, tantos and folders. **Technical:** Grinds 154CM, 440C, D2 and A2. **Prices:** $100 to $800. **Remarks:** Part-time maker; first knife sold in 1982. **Mark:** First and middle initials, last name, city and state.

MANABE, MICHAEL K., 6161 El Cajon Blvd. #176, San Diego, CA 92115/619-583-4880
Specialties: Classic and high-art straight knives of his design or to customer specs. **Patterns:** Bowies, fighters, hunters, utility/camp knives; all knives one-of-a-kind. **Technical:** Forges and grinds 52100, 5160 amd 1095. Does multiple quenching for distinctive temper lines. Each blade triple-tempered. **Prices:** Start at $200. **Remarks:** Part-time maker; first knife sold in 1994. **Mark:** First and middle initials, last name.

MANEKER, KENNETH, RR 2, Galiano Island, B.C. V0N 1P0, CANADA/604-539-2084
Specialties: Working straight knives; period pieces. **Patterns:** Camp knives and hunters; French chef knives. **Technical:** Grinds 440C, 154CM and Vascowear. **Prices:** $50 to $200; some to $300. **Remarks:** Part-time maker; first knife sold in 1981. Doing business as Water Mountain Knives. **Mark:** Japanese Kanji of initials, plus glyph.

MARAGNI, DAN, R.D. 1, Box 106, Georgetown, NY 13072/315-662-7490
Specialties: Heavy-duty working knives, some investor class. **Patterns:** Hunters, fighters and camp knives, some Scottish types. **Technical:** Forges W2 and his own Damascus; toughness and edge-holding a high priority. **Prices:** $125 to $500; some to $1,000. **Remarks:** Full-time maker; first knife sold in 1975. **Mark:** Celtic initials in circle.

MARINGER, TOM, 2692 S. Powell St., Springdale, AR 72764/501-751-9220
Specialties: Investor-class high-tech and fantasy straight knives. **Patterns:** Swords, axes, daggers; state-of-the-art fighters. **Technical:** Grinds D2 and 154CM; forges. Makes wire-wrapped handles; Kydex sheaths. **Prices:** $100 to $1,000; some to $12,000. **Remarks:** Full-time maker; first knife sold in 1975. **Mark:** Full name, serial number and year.

MARKS, CHRIS, 1061 Sherwood Dr., Breaux Bridge, LA 70517/318-332-3930
Specialties: Traditional straight knives of his design; period pieces. **Patterns:** Bowies, hunters and utility/camp knives. **Technical:** Forges W2, 5160 and his own Damascus. **Prices:** NA. **Mark:** Name in anvil logo and Master Smith, ABS.

MARLOWE, DONALD, 2554 Oakland Rd., Dover, PA 17315/717-764-6055
Specialties: Working straight knives in standard patterns. **Patterns:** Bowies, fighters, boots and utility knives. **Technical:** Grinds D2 and 440C. **Prices:** $120 to $525. **Remarks:** Spare-time maker; first knife sold in 1977. **Mark:** Last name.

MARSHALL, GLENN, P.O. Box 1099 (305 Hofmann St.), Mason, TX 76856/915-347-6207
Specialties: Working knives and period pieces. **Patterns:** Straight and folding hunters, fighters and camp knives. **Technical:** Forges and grinds 01, D2 and 440C. **Prices:** $90 to $150; some to $450. **Remarks:** Full-time maker; first knife sold in 1932. **Mark:** First initial, last name, city and state with anvil logo.

MARTIN, BRUCE E., Rt. 6, Box 164-B, Prescott, AR 71857/501-887-2023
Specialties: Fancy working straight knives of his design. **Patterns:** Bowies, camp knives, skinners and fighters. **Technical:** Forges 5160, 1095 and his own Damascus. Uses natural handle materials; filework

available. **Prices:** $75 to $350; some to $500. **Remarks:** Full-time maker; first knife sold in 1979. **Mark:** Name in arch.

MARTIN, JIM, 1120 S. Cadiz Ct., Oxnard, CA 93035/805-985-9849
Specialties: Fancy and working/using folders of his design. **Patterns:** Automatics, locking folders and miniatures. **Technical:** Grinds 440C, AEB-L, 304SS and Damascus. **Prices:** $350 to $700; some to $1500. **Remarks:** Full-time maker; first knife sold in 1992. Doing business as Jim Martin Custom Knives.

MARTIN, PETER, 28220 N. Lake Dr., Waterford, WI 53185/414-662-3629
Specialties: Fancy, fantasy and working straight knives and folders of his design and in standard patterns. **Patterns:** Bowies, fighters, hunters, locking folders and liner locks. **Technical:** Grinds ATS-34, 440C, A2 and D2; forges 1095, 5160, W1, 4340 and his own Damascus. Prefers natural handle material; offers filework and carved handles. **Prices:** $100 to $500; some to $2000. **Remarks:** Part-time maker; first knife sold in 1988. Doing business as Martin Custom Products. **Mark:** Martin Knives, city and state.

MARTIN, RANDALL J., 1477 Country Club Rd., Middletown, CT 06457/203-347-1161
Specialties: Practical working knives. **Patterns:** Lockback folders, kitchen and working knives; Japanese styles. **Technical:** Grinds BG42, CPM-M4 and M2; uses unique patterns. **Prices:** Under $150 to $450; some to $1,000. **Remarks:** Part-time maker; first knife sold in 1976. Doing business as Martinsite Knives. **Mark:** First and middle initials, last name.

MARTIN, ROBB, 7 Victoria St., Elmira Ontario N3B 1R9, CANADA

MARTINSITE KNIVES (See Martin, Randall J.)

MARTRILDONNO, PAUL, P.O. Box 1501, Olivebridge, NY 12461/914-657-8580
Specialties: One-of-a-kind fantasy knives. **Patterns:** "Knifelace"—necklace with push dagger, knuckle knives, fantasy tantos, etc. **Technical:** Grinds 440C and 154CM. Reforges commercial Damascus. **Prices:** $400 to $1,500; some to $5,000. **Remarks:** Full-time maker; first knife sold in 1982. Recipient of 1991 N.Y. Foundation for the Arts Fellowship. **Mark:** PAULIE, or signature.

MARZITELLI, PETER, 19929 35A Ave., Langley, BC V3A 2R1, CANADA/604-532-8899
Specialties: High quality straight hunting and art knives. **Patterns:** Hunters, tantos, Bowies, daggers, unility and fancy art knives. Specializes in natural handle materials. **Technical:** Grinds ATS-34, 440C, D2 and 12C27. **Prices:** $100 to $1,000. **Remarks:** Full-time maker; first knife sold in 1984. **Mark:** "Marz".

MASON, BILL, 1114 St. Louis, #33, Excelsior Springs, MO 64024/816-637-7335
Specialties: Combat knives; some folders. **Patterns:** Fighters to match knife types in book *Cold Steel*. **Technical:** Grinds 01, 440C and ATS-34. **Prices:** $115 to $250; some to $350. **Remarks:** Spare-time maker; first knife sold in 1979. **Mark:** Initials connected.

MASSEY, ROGER, RR19, Box 3300, Texarkana, AR 75502/501-779-1018
Specialties: Traditional and working straight knives and folders of his design and to customer specs. **Patterns:** Bowies, hunters and utility knives. **Technical:** Forges 5168, Damascus and 1084. Offers filework and silver wire inlay in handles. **Prices:** $125 to $500; some to $2,000. **Remarks:** Part-time maker; first knife sold in 1991. **Mark:** Last name, J.S.

MATTIS, JAMES K., 811 N. Central Ave., Glendale, CA 91203/818-247-3400, 818-353-4734
Specialties: Working straight knives in standard patterns. **Patterns:** Hunters, kitchen knives and small utility or specialty patterns. **Techni-**

cal: Offers ATS-34, 440C and carbon; hand-rubbed finishes, hardwood handles. **Prices:** $40 to $200; some to $250. **Remarks:** Spare-time maker; first knife sold in 1990. Usually uses blades by Bob Engnath. **Mark:** Last name plus Hebrew word for "life".

MAXFIELD, LYNN, 382 Colonial Ave., Layton, UT 84041/801-544-4176
Specialties: Sporting knives, some fancy. **Patterns:** Hunters, survival and fishing knives; some locking folders. **Technical:** Grinds 440C, ATS-34, D2 and Damascus. **Prices:** $150 to $350; some to $750. **Remarks:** Part-time maker; first knife sold in 1979. **Mark:** Name, city and state.

MAXWELL, DON, 4435 N. Brawley #107, Fresno, CA 93722/209-275-3460
Specialties: Fancy working and using straight knives of his design. **Patterns:** Hunters, fighters, utility/camp knives, liner lock folders and fantasy knives. **Technical:** Grinds 440C, ATS-34, D2 and commercial Damascus. **Prices:** $100 to $500; some to $2,000. **Remarks:** Full-time maker; first knife sold in 1987. **Mark:** Last name, city, state.

MAY, JAMES E., 6513 State Rd. T., Auxvasse, MO 65231/314-386-2910
Specialties: Working straight knives of his design. **Patterns:** Hunters, Bowies, fighters, camp knives, boots and folders. **Technical:** Makes own Damascus. **Prices:** $65 to $350; some to $450. **Remarks:** Full-time maker; first knife sold in 1978. **Mark:** First initial in diamond.

MAYNARD, LARRY JOE, P.O. Box 493, Crab Orchard, WV 25827
Specialties: Fancy and fantasy straight knives. **Patterns:** Big knives; a Bowie with a full false edge; fighting knives. **Technical:** Grinds standard steels. **Prices:** $350 to $500; some to $1,000. **Remarks:** Full-time maker; first knife sold in 1986. **Mark:** Middle and last initials.

MAYNARD, WILLIAM N., 2677 John Smith Rd., Fayetteville, NC 28306/910-425-1615
Specialties: Traditional and working straight knives of all designs. **Patterns:** Bowies, fighters, hunters and utility knives. **Technical:** Grinds 440C, ATS-34 and commercial Damascus. Offers fancy filework; handmade sheaths. **Prices:** $100 to $300; some to $500. **Remarks:** Part-time maker; first knife sold in 1988. **Mark:** Last name.

MAYO JR., TOM, 67-420 Alahaka St., Waialua, HI 96791/808-637-6560
Specialties: Working straight knives and folders. **Patterns:** Hunters and Bowies. **Technical:** Uses ATS-34 and some D2. **Prices:** $125 to $500; some to $1,000. **Remarks:** Part-time maker; first knife sold in 1983. No longer taking orders. **Mark:** Volcano logo with name and state.

MAYSE, MARTIN L., 10323 Townwalk Dr., Hamden, CT 06518

MAYVILLE, OSCAR L., 2130 E. County Rd. 910S., Marengo, IN 47140/812-338-3103
Specialties: Working straight knives; period pieces. **Patterns:** Kitchen cutlery, Bowies, camp knives and hunters. **Technical:** Grinds A2, 01 and 440C. **Prices:** $50 to $350; some to $500. **Remarks:** Full-time maker; first knife sold in 1984. **Mark:** Initials over knife logo.

MAZAKI, YOSHIO, Bl Fukoku Seimei Building 2-4, Komatu bara-cho Kita-ku, Osaka City, 530 JAPAN/06-313-2525; FAX: 06-313-2626
Specialties: Classic and working knives of his design. **Patterns:** Bowies, hunters and utility knives. **Technical:** Grinds ATS-34, Gingami 3 GO and Cowry X. **Prices:** $250 to $1,500. **Remarks:** Part-time maker; first knife sold in 1992. Doing business as World Gallery Co., Ltd. **Mark:** NA.

McBURNETTE, HARVEY, P.O. Box 227, Eagle Nest, NM 87718/505-377-6254; FAX: 505-377-6218
Specialties: Fancy working folders; some to customer specs. **Patterns:** Front-locking folders. **Technical:** Grinds D2, 440C and 154CM; engraves. **Prices:** $450 to $3,000. **Remarks:** Full-time maker; first knife sold in 1972. **Mark:** Last name, city and state.

McCARLEY, JOHN, 562 Union Brige Rd., Union Bridge, MD 21791
Specialties: Working straight knives; period pieces. **Patterns:** Hunters, Bowies, camp knives, miniatures, throwing knives. **Technical:** Forges W2, 01 and his own Damascus. **Prices:** $150 to $300; some to $1,000. **Remarks:** Part-time maker; first knife sold in 1977. **Mark:** Initials in script.

McCARTY, HARRY, 1121 Brough Ave., Hamilton, OH 45015
Specialties: Working straight knives; period pieces. **Patterns:** Bowies, camp knives, daggers and buckskinners. **Technical:** Forges and grinds 01. **Prices:** $75 to $350; some to $600. **Remarks:** Part-time maker; first knife sold in 1977. **Mark:** Stylized initials.

McCARTY, ZOLLAN, 101½ Ave. E, Thomaston, GA 30286/404-647-6869
Specialties: Working knives; period pieces. **Patterns:** Straight knives and folders; Scagel replicas; gut hook hatchets. **Technical:** Forges and grinds 440C, 154CM and ATS-34. **Prices:** $110 to $600. **Remarks:** Full-time maker; first knife sold in 1971. Doing business as Z Custom Knives. **Mark:** First initial, last name.

McCLURE, MICHAEL, 803-17th Ave., Menlo Park, CA 94025/415-323-2596
Specialties: Working/using straight knives of his design and to customer specs. **Patterns:** Bowies, hunters, utility/camp knives. **Technical:** Grinds ATS-34, 440C and D2. Makes sheaths. **Prices:** $150 to $300; some to $500. **Remarks:** Part-time maker; first knife sold in 1991. **Mark:** Last name.

McCOLL, JOHN, 35 Green St., Stonehouse, Lanarkshire, ML9-3LW SCOTLAND/0698-792223
Specialties: Traditional working straight knives and folders of his design. **Patterns:** Hunters, Bowies and locking folders. **Technical:** Forges his Damascus; grinds 440C, D2 and 01. **Prices:** $125 to $175; some to $590. **Remarks:** Full-time maker; first knife sold in 1980. **Mark:** Full name.

McCONNELL, CHARLES R., 158 Genteel Ridge, Wellsburg, WV 26070/304-737-2015
Specialties: Working straight knives. **Patterns:** Hunters, Bowies, daggers, minis and push knives. **Technical:** Grinds 440C and 154CM; likes full tangs. **Prices:** $65 to $325; some to $800. **Remarks:** Part-time maker; first knife sold in 1977. **Mark:** Name.

McCONNELL JR., LOYD A., 1712 Royalty, Odessa, TX 79761/915-363-8344
Specialties: Working straight knives and folders, some fancy. **Patterns:** Hunters, boots, Bowies, locking folders and slip-joints. **Technical:** Grinds A2, 154CM, CPM10V and commercial Damascus. **Prices:** $175 to $900; some to $10,000. **Remarks:** Full-time maker; first knife sold in 1975. Doing business as Cactus Custom Knives. **Mark:** Name, city and state in cactus logo.

McCOUN, MARK, 14212 Pine Dr., DeWitt, VA 23840/804-469-7631
Specialties: Working/using straight knives and folders of his design and in standard patterns. **Patterns:** Fighters, hunters, locking folders and miniatures. **Technical:** Forges 01 and L6; grinds 440C. Performs scrimshaw, acid etching, handmade full integral and heat treating. **Prices:** $75 to $200; some to $1,500. **Remarks:** Part-time maker; first knife sold in 1989. Doing business as McCoun Knives. **Mark:** Name, city and state.

McCRACKIN and SON, V.J., 3720 Hess Rd., House Springs, MO 63051/314-677-6066
Specialties: Working straight knives in standard patterns. **Patterns:** Hunters, Bowies and camp knives. **Technical:** Forges L6, 5160, his own Damascus, cable Damascus. **Prices:** $75 to $400; some to $1,000. **Remarks:** Part-time maker; first knife sold in 1983. Son Kevin helps make the knives. **Mark:** Last name, M.S.

McDEARMONT, DAVE, 1618 Parkside Trail, Lewisville, TX 7567/214-436-4335

Specialties: Collector-grade knives. **Patterns:** Hunters, fighters, boots and folders. **Technical:** Grinds ATS-34; likes full tangs, mirror finishes. **Prices:** $200 to $1,000. **Remarks:** Part-time maker; first knife sold in 1981. **Mark:** Name.

McDONALD, ROBERT J., 2300 NW 81 Ave., Sunrise, FL 33322/305-748-5090
Specialties: Traditional working straight knives to customer specs. **Patterns:** Fighters, swords and folders. **Technical:** Grinds 440C, ATS-34 and forges own Damascus. **Prices:** $150 to $1,000. **Remarks:** Part-time maker; first knife sold in 1988. **Mark:** Electro-etched logo.

McDONALD, W.J. "JERRY", 7173 Wickshire Cove E., Germantach, TN 38138/901-756-9924

McELHANNON, MARCUS, 14003 Kathi Lynn, Sugarland, TX 77478/713-494-1345
Specialties: Working straight knives and folders of his design and to customer specs. **Patterns:** Fighters, hunters and locking folders. **Technical:** Grinds ATS-34, 440C and 440V. **Prices:** $125 to $300; some to $1,500. **Remarks:** Spare-time maker; first knife sold in 1988. **Mark:** First name.

McFALL, KEN, P.O. Box 458, Lakeside, AZ 85929/602-537-2026
Specialties: Fancy working straight knives and some folders. **Patterns:** Daggers, boots, tantos, Bowies; some miniatures. **Technical:** Grinds D2, ATS-34 and 440C. **Prices:** $175 to $900. **Remarks:** Part-time maker; first knife sold in 1984. **Mark:** Name, city and state.

McFARLIN, ERIC E., P.O. Box 2188, Kodiak, AK 99615/907-486-4799
Specialties: Working knives of his design. **Patterns:** Bowies, skinners, camp knives and hunters. **Technical:** Flat and convex grinds 440C, A2 and AEB-L. **Prices:** Start at $150. **Remarks:** Part-time maker; first knife sold in 1989. **Mark:** Name and city in rectanglar logo.

McGILL, JOHN, P.O. Box 302, Blairsville, GA 30512/404-745-4686
Specialties: Working knives. **Patterns:** Traditional patterns; camp knives. **Technical:** Forges L6 and 9260; makes Damascus. **Prices:** $50 to $250; some to $500. **Remarks:** Full-time maker; first knife sold in 1982. **Mark:** XYLO.

McGINNIS, TOM, Rt.2 Box 251, Ozark, MO 65721/417-581-8203

McGOVERN, JIM, 31 Scenic Dr., Oak Ridge, NJ 07438/201-697-4558
Specialties: Working straight knives and folders. **Patterns:** Hunters and boots. **Technical:** Hollow-grinds 440C, ATS-34; prefers full tapered tangs. Offers filework. **Prices:** $125 to $250, some to $750; folders $175 to $450, some to $675. **Remarks:** Full-time maker; first knife sold in 1985. **Mark:** Name.

McGOWAN, FRANK E., 12629 Howard Lodge Dr., Sykesville, MD 21784/410-489-4323
Specialties: Fancy working knives to customer specs. **Patterns:** Survivor knives, fighters, fishing knives and hunters. **Technical:** Grinds and forges 01, 440C, 5160 and ATS-34. **Prices:** $75 to $500; some to $1,000. **Remarks:** Full-time maker; first knife sold in 1986. **Mark:** Last name.

McGRODER, PATRICK J., 5725 Chapin Rd., Madison, OH 44057

McGUANE IV, THOMAS J., 410 South 3rd Ave., Bozeman, MT 59715/406-586-0248

McHENRY, WILLIAM JAMES, Box 67, Wyoming, RI 02898/401-539-8353
Specialties: Fancy high-tech folders of his design. **Patterns:** Locking folders with various mechanisms. **Technical:** Forges and grinds commercial Damascus and his Damascus. Most pieces disassemble and feature top-shelf materials including gold, silver and gems. **Prices:** $1,000 and $3,500. **Remarks:** Full-time maker; first knife sold in 1988. Former goldsmith. **Mark:** Last name or first and last initials.

McINTOSH, DAVID L., P.O. Box 948, Haines, AK 99827/907-766-3393
Specialties: Working straight knives and folders of all designs. **Patterns:** All styles, except swords. **Technical:** Grinds ATS-34 and top name maker Damascus. Engraves; offers tooling on sheaths. Uses fossil ivory. **Prices:** $60 to $800; some to $2,000. **Remarks:** Full-time maker; first knife sold in 1984. **Mark:** Last name, serial number, steel type, city and state.

McKISSACK II, TOMMY, P.O. Box 991, Sonora, TX 76950/915-387-3253
Specialties: Plain to fancy folders. **Patterns:** Swords to folders, traditional to exotic. **Technical:** Grinds and forges D2, ATS-34, Vascowear, own Damascus and mokume. **Prices:** $100 to $1,500; some to $3,500. **Remarks:** Full-time maker; first knife sold in 1980. **Mark:** Name.

McLEOD, JAMES, 941 Thermalito Ave., Oroville, CA 95965/916-533-3539
Specialties: Working knives; Scottish period pieces. **Patterns:** Dirks and sgian dubhs; buckskinners, boots and daggers. **Technical:** Grinds and files A2, 154CM and ATS-34; offers hand-sanded finishes and full or tapered tangs. **Prices:** $200 to $500; some to $2,500. **Remarks:** Spare-time maker; first knife sold in 1983. McLeod clan motto "HOLD FAST." Makes average of 20 knives per year. **Mark:** Name and clan badge.

McLUIN, TOM, 36 Fourth St., Dracut, MA 01826/508-957-4899
Specialties: Fancy and working/using straight knives of his design. **Patterns:** Boots, hunters, miniatures. **Technical:** Grinds D2, ATS-34, 440C. Offers filework, fancy pins, custom-moulded sheaths, some exotic skins. **Prices:** $50 to $250; some to $400. **Remarks:** Full-time maker; first knife sold in 1991. **Mark:** First initial, last name.

McMAHON, JOHN P., 44871 Santa Anita #A, Palm Desert, CA 92260/619-341-4238
Specialties: Classic working and using straight knives of his design or to customer specs. **Patterns:** Hunters, Bowies and fighters. **Technical:** Grinds 5160 spring steel for large knives and 01 tool steel for small ones. Will grind fil one order. Differentially tempers. **Prices:** $45 to $300; some to $1,000. **Remarks:** Full-time maker; first knife sold in 1989. Doing business as J.P.M. Knives. **Mark:** Initials.

McNABB, TOMMY, P.O. Box 327, Bethania, NC 27010/919-759-0640
Specialties: Working and using straight knives of his design. **Patterns:** Hunters, fighters and utility/camp knives. **Technical:** Forges his own Damascus; grinds ATS-34. **Prices:** $100 to $550; some to $2,500. **Remarks:** Full-time maker; first knife sold in 1979. **Mark:** Carolina Custom Knives.

McWILLIAMS, SEAN, 311 Gem Lane, Bayfield, CO 81122/970-884-9854
Specialties: Stainless steel combat-survival and working knives of his own design. **Patterns:** Fighters, sub-hilts, utility and camp knives. **Technical:** Forges CPM T440V and ATS-34 stainless only. Offers high-tech Kydex-Nylon sheaths and carry systems. **Prices:** $300 to $700. Catalog $3 **Remarks:** Full-time maker; first knife sold in 1979. **Mark:** Stylized bear paw.

MECCHI, RICHARD, 4225 Gibraltar St., Las Vegas, NV 89121/702-435-7448; FAX: 702-435-7448
Specialties: Working straight knives, some fancy. **Patterns:** Hunters, daggers, Bowies and fillets. **Technical:** Grinds 440C, ATS-34 and 154CM. Exotic handle materials offered. **Prices:** $125 to $950. **Remarks:** Part-time maker; first knife sold in 1982. **Mark:** First initial, last name.

MEDIEVAL CUSTOMS (See Johns, Rob)

MEIER, DARYL, 75 Forge Rd., Carbondale, IL 62901/618-549-3234
Specialties: One-of-a-kind knives and swords. **Patterns:** Collaborates on blades. **Technical:** Forges his own Damascus, W1 and A203E, 440C, 431, nickel 200 and clad steel. **Prices:** $250 to $450; some to

$6,000. **Remarks:** Full-time smith and researcher since 1974; first knife sold in 1974. **Mark:** Name or circle/arrow symbol or SHAWNEE.

MELOY, SEAN, 7148 Rosemary Lane, Lemon Grove, CA 91945-2105/619-465-7173
Specialties: Traditional working straight knives of his design. **Patterns:** Bowies, fighters and utility/camp knives. **Technical:** Grinds 440C, ATS-34 and D2. **Prices:** $125 to $300. **Remarks:** Part-time maker; first knife sold in 1985. **Mark:** Broz Knives.

MENDENHALL, HARRY E., Ed.D., 1848 Everglades Dr., Milpitas, CA 95035/408-263-0677
Specialties: Working straight knives. **Patterns:** Hunters, boots, buck-skinners and push knives. **Technical:** Grinds 440C, 154CM and ATS-34; engraves and scrimshaws. **Prices:** $150 to $3,000. **Remarks:** Full-time maker; first knife sold in 1970. Does business as Thunderbird. **Mark:** Thunderbird with logo, or signature.

MERCER, MIKE, 149 N. Waynesville Rd., Lebanon, OH 45036/513-932-2837
Specialties: Jeweled gold and ivory daggers; multi-blade folders. **Patterns:** 1 1/4" folders, hunters, axes, replicas. **Technical:** Uses 01 Damascus and mokume. **Prices:** $150 to $1,500. **Remarks:** Full-time maker since 1991. **Mark:** Last name in script.

MERCHANT, TED, 7 Old Garrett Ct., White Hall, MD 21161/410-343-0380
Specialties: Traditional and classic working knives. **Patterns:** Bowies, hunters, camp knives, fighters, daggers and skinners. **Technical:** Forges W2 and 5160; makes own Damascus. Makes handles with wood, stag, horn, silver and gem stone inlay; fancy filework. **Prices:** $125 to $600; some to $1,500. **Remarks:** Full-time maker; first knife sold in 1985. **Mark:** Last name.

MERZ III, ROBERT L., 20219 Prince Creek Dr., Katy, TX 77450/713-492-7337
Specialties: Working straight knives and folders, some fancy, of his design. **Patterns:** Hunters, skinners, fighters and camp knives. **Technical:** Flat-grinds 440C, 154CM, ATS-34, 440V and commercial Damascus. **Prices:** $150 to $450; some to $600. **Remarks:** Part-time maker; first knife sold in 1974. **Mark:** MERZ KNIVES, city and state, or last name in oval.

MESHEJIAN, MARVIN, 33 Elm Dr., E. Northport, NY 11731

MESSER, DAVID T., 134 S. Torrence St., Dayton, OH 45403-2044/513-228-6561
Specialties: Fantasy period pieces, straight and folding, of his design. **Patterns:** Bowies, daggers and swords. **Technical:** Grinds 440C, 01, 06 and commercial Damascus. Likes fancy guards and exotic handle materials. **Prices:** $100 to $225; some to $375. **Remarks:** Spare-time maker; first knife sold in 1991. **Mark:** Name stamp.

METHENY, H.A. "WHITEY", 7750 Waterford Dr., Spotsylvania, VA 22553/703-582-3228
Specialties: Working and using straight knives of his design and to customer specs. **Patterns:** Hunters and kitchen knives. **Technical:** Grinds 440C. Offers filework; tooled custom sheaths. **Prices:** $125 to $200. **Remarks:** Spare-time maker; first knife sold in 1990. **Mark:** Initials or last name.

METTLER, J. BANJO, 129 S. Second St., North Baltimore, OH 45872/419-257-2210
Specialties: Fancy folders of his design. **Patterns:** Locking folders, interframes, "A-5" automatic and "L-3" lockbacks of his design, deer-foot-style lockbacks 1-inch closed. **Technical:** Grinds ATS-34, D2 and 01. **Prices:** Start at $100. **Remarks:** Part-time maker; first knife sold in 1988. **Mark:** Deer foot underlined with profile of knife.

MICHAEL'S HANDMADE KNIVES (See Bouse, D. Michael)

MICK'S CUSTOM KNIVES (See Sears, Mick)

MIDDLETON, KEN, Carmichael, CA 95608/916-489-6070
Specialties: Traditional and fantasy straight knives and folders of his design. **Patterns:** Hunters, Bowies and daggers. **Technical:** Grinds 440C, ATS-34 and D2. Likes natural handle materials. **Prices:** $150 to $800; some to $3,500. **Remarks:** Spare-time maker; first knife sold in 1986. **Mark:** Last name or Middleton Custom.

MILFORD, BRIAN A., RD 2 Box 294, Knox, PA 16232/814-797-2595; FAX: 814-226-4351
Specialties: Traditional and working/using straight knives of his design or to customer specs. **Patterns:** Fighters, hunters and utility/camp knives. **Technical:** Forges Damascus and 52100; grinds 440C. **Prices:** $50 to $300; some to $750. **Remarks:** Part-time maker; first knife sold in 1991. Doing business as BAM Forge. **Mark:** Full name or initials.

MILLARD, FRED G.,, 5317 N. Wayne, Chicago, IL 60640/312-769-5160
Specialties: Working/using straight knives of his design or to customer specs. **Patterns:** Bowies, hunters, utility/camp knives, kitchen/steak knives. **Technical:** Grinds ATS-34, 01 and 440C. Makes sheaths. **Prices:** $90 to $225; some to $650. **Remarks:** Full-time maker; first knife sold in 1993. Doing business as Millard Knives. **Mark:** Mallard duck in flight with serial number.

MILLER, BOB, 236 Ramsey Ln., Ballwin, MO 63021/314-394-4476
Specialties: Mosaic Damascus; collector using straight knives and folders. **Patterns:** Hunters, Bowies, utility/camp knives, daggers. **Technical:** Forges own Damascus, mosaic-Damascus and 52100. **Prices:** $125 to $500. **Remarks:** Part-time maker; first knife sold in 1983. **Mark:** First and middle initials and last name, or initials.

MILLER JR., CHRIS, P.O. Box 15471, Gainesville, FL 32604-5471
Specialties: Fancy working straight knives. **Patterns:** Swords and large knives of all kinds. **Technical:** Grinds D2, 440C and 154CM. **Prices:** $100 to $500. **Remarks:** Full-time maker; first knife sold in 1976. **Mark:** Last initial.

MILLER, HANFORD J., Box 97, Cowdrey, CO 80434/970-723-4708
Specialties: Working knives in Moran style; period pieces. **Patterns:** Bowies, fighters, camp knives and other large straight knives. **Technical:** Forges W2, 1095, 5160 and his own Damascus; differential tempers; offers wire inlay. **Prices:** $300 to $800; some to $2,000. **Remarks:** Full-time maker; first knife sold in 1968. **Mark:** Initials or name within Bowie logo.

MILLER, JAMES P., 9024 Goeller Rd., RR 2, Box 28, Fairbank, IA 50629/319-635-2294
Specialties: All tool steel Damascus; working knives and period pieces. **Patterns:** Hunters, Bowies, camp knives and daggers. **Technical:** Forges and grinds 1095, 52100, 440C and his own Damascus. **Prices:** $100 to $350; some to $1,500. **Remarks:** Full-time maker; first knife sold in 1970. **Mark:** First and middle initials, last name with knife logo.

MILLER, LARRY, P.O. Box 3064, Missoula, MT 59806-3064/406-549-3276
Specialties: Personally designed knives. **Patterns:** Fighters, folders and skinners. **Technical:** Grinds Damascus and 440C, fileart standard. All knives sold with sheath or displayed on walnut base. **Prices:** Damascus $850 to $1,400; 440C $250 to $600; folders $85 to $400. **Remarks:** Professional/artist maker; first knife sold in 1980. **Mark:** Buffalo skull with last name.

MILLER, M.A., 4131 E. 115th Place, Thornton, CO 80233/303-452-7379
Specialties: Using knives for hunting. 3 1/2"-4" Lovless Drop-point. Made to customer specs. **Patterns:** Skinners and camp knives. **Technical:** Grinds 440C, D2, 01 and ATS-34 Damascus miniatures. **Prices:** $225 to $275; miniatures $75. **Remarks:** Part-time maker; first knife sold in 1988. **Mark:** Last name stamped in block letters or first and middle initials, last name, maker, city and state with triangles on either side etched.

MILLER, MICHAEL K., 28510 Santiam Hwy., Sweet Home, OR 97386/503-367-4927
Specialties: Fancy working and using straight knives of his design or made to customer specs. **Patterns:** Hunters, utility, camp knives and kitchen knives. **Technical:** Grinds 440C and AEB-L. Does special filework/tooling, leather work, and makes carved handles. Makes custom sheaths and holsters. **Prices:** $175. **Remarks:** Full-time maker; first knife sold in 1989. **Mark:** M&M Kustom Krafts.

MILLER, R.D., 10526 Estate Lane, Dallas, TX 75238/214-348-3496
Specialties: One-of-a-kind collector-grade knives. **Patterns:** Boots, hunters, Bowies, camp and utility knives, fishing and bird knives, miniatures. **Technical:** Grinds a variety of steels to include 01, D2, 440C, 154CM and 1095. **Prices:** $65 to $300; some to $900. **Remarks:** Full-time maker; first knife sold in 1984. **Mark:** R.D. Custom Knives with date or bow and arrow logo.

MILLER, RICK, RD 3 Box 273, Rockwood, PA 15557

MILLER, ROBERT, P.O. Box 2722, Ormond Beach, FL 32175/904-676-1193
Specialties: Working straight knives, some fancy, of his design or to customer specs. **Patterns:** Large Bowies, hunters, miniatures. **Technical:** Grinds 01, D2 and 440C. Offers inlay and fancy filework; inlayed military insignias. **Prices:** $35 to $750. **Remarks:** Full-time maker; first knife sold in 1986. **Mark:** Holly and date.

MILLER, RONALD T., 12922 127th Ave. N., Largo, FL 34644/813-595-0378 (after 5 p.m.)
Specialties: Working straight knives in standard patterns. **Patterns:** Combat knives, camp knives, kitchen cutlery, fillet knives, locking folders and butterflies. **Technical:** Grinds D2, 440C and ATS-34; offers brass inlays and scrimshaw. **Prices:** $45 to $325; some to $750. **Remarks:** Part-time maker; first knife sold in 1984. **Mark:** Name, city and state in palm tree logo.

MILLER, TED, P.O. Box 6328, Santa Fe, NM 87502/505-984-0338
Specialties: Carved antler display knives of his design. **Patterns:** Hunters, swords and miniatures. **Technical:** Grinds 440C. **Prices:** $110 to $350; some average $900. **Remarks:** Full-time maker; first knife sold in 1971. **Mark:** Initials and serial number.

MILLER, TERRY, 450 S. 1st, Seward, NE 68434/402-643-2499
Specialties: Working knives and collector pieces. **Patterns:** Hunters, fighters and Bowies. **Technical:** Grinds 440C. **Prices:** $90 to $145; some higher. **Remarks:** Part-time maker; first knife sold in 1978. **Mark:** Stylized name in knife logo.

MILLS, ANDY, 414 E. Schubert, Fredericksburg, TX 78624/512-997-8167
Specialties: Working straight knives and folders. **Patterns:** Hunters. **Technical:** Grinds 440C, D2, A2 and 154CM. Offers leatherwork, fabrication, heat-treating. **Prices:** Moderate. **Remarks:** Full-time maker; first knife sold in 1980. **Mark:** Name.

MILLS, LOUIS G., 9450 Waters Rd., Ann Arbor, MI 48103/313-668-1839
Specialties: High-art Japanese-style period pieces. **Patterns:** Traditional tantos, daggers and swords. **Technical:** Makes steel from iron; makes his own Damascus by traditional Japanese techniques. **Prices:** $900 to $2,000; some to $8,000. **Remarks:** Spare-time maker in partnership with Jim Kelso. **Mark:** Yasutomo in Japanese Kanji.

MINDS' EYE METALMASTER (See Smith, D. Noel)

MINERAL MOUNTAIN HATCHET WORKS (See Frizzell, Ted)

MINK, DAN, 4820 17 Ave. N., St. Petersburg, FL 33713/813-323-7398; FAX: 813-787-2670
Specialties: Traditional and working knives of his design. **Patterns:** Bowies, fighters, folders and hunters. **Technical:** Grinds ATS-34, 440C and D2. Blades and tanges embellished with fancy filework. Uses natural and rare handle materials. **Prices:** $125 to $450. **Remarks:** Part-time maker; first knife sold in 1985. **Mark:** Name and star encircled by custom made, city, state.

MINNICK, JIM, 144 North 7th St., Middletown, IN 47356/317-354-4108
Specialties: Traditional working and using straight knives and folders; classic high-art and fancy/embellished knives of his design or to customer specs. **Patterns:** Hunters, Bowies, daggers, fighters, boots, art knives, locking folders and slip-joint folders. **Technical:** Grinds 440C and 154CM. Scrimshaw by wife Joyce. **Prices:** $185 to $225; some to $1,800. **Remarks:** Part-time maker; first knife sold in 1976. **Mark:** Last name.

MISSION KNIVES, INC. (See Schultz, Richard A.)

MITCHELL, WM. DEAN, P.O. Box 183, Forgan, OK 73938
Specialties: Classic and high-art knives in standard patterns. **Patterns:** Bowies, daggers and swords. **Technical:** Forges 1095, 5160; makes pattern, composite and mosiac Damascus; offers filework and elecroplating. Makes wooden display cases. **Prices:** Mid to upper scale. **Remarks:** Part-time maker; first knife sold in 1986. Doing business as Pioneer Forge & Woodshop. **Mark:** Full name or initials, MS.

MITCHELL, JAMES A., P.O. Box 4646, Columbus, GA 31904/404-322-8582
Specialties: Fancy working knives. **Patterns:** Hunters, fighters, Bowies and locking folders. **Technical:** Grinds D2, 440C and commercial Damascus. **Prices:** $100 to $400; some to $900. **Remarks:** Part-time maker; first knife sold in 1976. Sells knives in sets. **Mark:** Signature and city.

MITCHELL, MAX, DEAN AND BEN, 997 V.F.W. Rd., Leesville, LA 71446/318-239-6416
Specialties: Working knives. **Patterns:** Four-way hunter, hatchet and knife sets, Bowies. **Technical:** Grinds 01. Leatherworkers; heavy basket-weave sheaths. **Prices:** $125 to $500. **Remarks:** Part-time makers; first knife sold in 1976. **Mark:** First names in oval logo.

MITCHELL, R.W. "MITCH", 15980 Grand Ave. #T-44, Lake Elsinore, CA 92530-5621/909-678-2231
Specialties: Working straight knives with Indian influence. **Patterns:** Bowies, fighters, hunters with horseshoe guards, etc. **Technical:** Grinds 440C, 01 and ATS-34; prefers natural handle materials; heat-treats. **Prices:** $125 to $650. **Remarks:** Full-time maker; first knife sold in 1988. **Mark:** Mitch with arrow logo.

M.J.R. KNIVES (See Raymond, Mary Jane)

M&M KUSTOM KRAFTS (See Miller, Michael K.)

M&N ARTS LTD. (See Wattelet, Michael A.)

MOMCILOVIC, GUNNAR, Nordlysv, 16, N-30055 Krokstadelva, NORWAY/0111-47-3287-3586

MONK, NATHAN P., 1304 4th Ave. SE, Cullman, AL 35055/205-737-0463
Specialties: Traditional working and using straight knives of his design and to customer specs; fancy knives. **Patterns:** Bowies, daggers, fighters, hunters, utility/camp knives and one-of-a-kinds. **Technical:** Grinds ATS-34, 440C and A2. Engraving by Billy Bates. **Prices:** $50 to $175. **Remarks:** Spare-time maker; first knife sold in 1990. **Mark:** First and middle initials, last name, city, state.

MONTEIRO, VICTOR, 418 Rue Engeland, 1180 Brussels, BELGIUM/322-375-49-07
Specialties: Working and fancy straight knives, folders and integrals of his design. **Patterns:** Bowies, fighters and hunters. **Technical:** Grinds ATS-34, 440C and commercial Damascus. Offers heat-treating, embellishment, filework, scrimshaw. **Prices:** $300 to $1,000, some higher. **Remarks:** Full-time maker; first knife sold in 1989. Doing business as Monteiro Knives S.C. **Mark:** Initials connected.

MONTEIRO KNIVES S.C. (See Monteiro, Victor)

MONTJOY, CLAUDE, RR 2, Box 1280, Clinton, SC 29325/803-697-6160
Specialties: Fancy working knives. **Patterns:** Hunters, boots, fighters, some art knives and folders. **Technical:** Grinds ATS-34 and 440C. Offers inlaid handle scales. **Prices:** $100 to $500. **Remarks:** Part-time maker; first knife sold in 1982. **Mark:** Last name.

THE MOONLIGHT SMITHY (See Leck, Dal)

MOORE, BILL, 879 Pinewood Rd., Leesburg, GA 31763/912-759-6521
Specialties: Working and using folders of his design and to customer specs. **Patterns:** Bowies, hunters and locking folders. **Technical:** Grinds ATS-34, forges 5168 and cable Damascus. Filework. **Prices:** $100 to $400. **Remarks:** Part-time maker; first knife sold in 1988. **Mark:** Moore Knives.

MOORE, JAMES B., 1707 N. Gillis, Ft. Stockton, TX 79735/915-336-2113
Specialties: Classic working straight knives and folders of his design. **Patterns:** Hunters, Bowies, daggers, fighters, boots, utility/camp knives, locking folders and slip-joint folders. **Technical:** Grinds 440C, ATS-34, D2, L6, CPM and commercial Damascus. **Prices:** $85 to $700; exceptional knives to $1,500. **Remarks:** Full-time maker; first knife sold in 1972. **Mark:** Name, city and state.

MORAN JR., WM. F., P.O. Box 68, Braddock Heights, MD 21714/301-371-7543
Specialties: High-art working knives of his design. **Patterns:** Fighters, camp knives, Bowies, daggers, axes, tomahawks, push knives and miniatures. **Technical:** Forges W2, 5160 and his own Damascus; puts silver wire inlay on most handles; uses only natural handle materials. **Prices:** $400 to $7,500; some to $9,000. **Remarks:** Full-time maker. **Mark:** First and middle initials, last name, M.S.

MORETZ, JIM, P.O. Box 2484, Brookshire Rd., Boone, NC 28607/704-262-0948
Specialties: Traditional working and using straight knives and folders. **Patterns:** Hunters, utility/camp knives and slip-joint folders. **Technical:** Forges and grinds. **Prices:** $105 to $275; some to $995. **Remarks:** Full-time maker; first knife sold in 1978. When ordering, please consider Alaska and Western big game hunting seasons. **Mark:** Stylized initials, or name, city, state.

MORGAN, JEFF, 9200 Arnaz Way, Santee, CA 92071/619-448-8430
Specialties: Fancy working straight knives. **Patterns:** Hunters, fighters, boots, miniatures. **Technical:** Grinds D2, 440C and ATS-34; likes exotic handles. **Prices:** $65 to $140; some to $500. **Remarks:** Full-time maker; first knife sold in 1977. **Mark:** Initials connected.

MORGAN, TOM, 14689 Ellett Rd., Beloit, OH 44609/216-537-2023
Specialties: Working straight knives and period pieces. **Patterns:** Hunters, boots and presentation tomahawks. **Technical:** Grinds 01, 440C and 154CM. **Prices:** $45 to $125; some to $225. **Remarks:** Part-time maker; first knife sold in 1977. **Mark:** Last name and type of steel used.

MORGAN VALLEY FORGE (See Clark, Howard F.)

MORLAN, TOM, 30635 S. Palm, Hemet, CA 92343/714-767-0543
Specialties: Fancy working knives to customer specs. **Patterns:** Bowies, tantos, fishing knives and locking folders. **Technical:** Grinds 440C, 154CM and ATS-34. **Prices:** $75 to $250; some to $3,000. **Remarks:** Part-time maker; first knife sold in 1979. **Mark:** Initials connected.

MORRIS, C.H., 828 Meadow Dr., Atmore, AL 36502/205-368-2089
Specialties: Liner lock folders. **Patterns:** Interframe liner locks. **Technical:** Grinds 440C and ATS-34. **Prices:** Start at $350. **Remarks:** Full-time maker; first knife sold in 1973. **Mark:** First and middle initials, last name.

MORRIS, DARRELL PRICE, 92 Union, St. Plymouth, Devon, ENGLAND PL1 3EZ/0752 223546
Specialties: Traditional Japanese knives, Bowies and high-art knives. **Technical:** Nickel Damascus and mokamame. **Prices:** $1,000 to $4,000. **Remarks:** Part-time maker; first knife sold in 1990. **Mark:** Initials and Japanese name—Kuni Shigae.

MORSETH SPORTS EQUIPMENT CO. (See Russell, A.G.)

MOSSER, GARY E., 11827 NE 102nd Place, Kirkland, WA 98033-5170/206-827-2279
Specialties: Working knives. **Patterns:** Hunters, skinners, camp knives, some art knives. **Technical:** Stock removal method; prefers ATS-34. **Prices:** $100 to $250; special orders and art knives are higher. **Remarks:** Part-time maker; first knife sold in 1976. **Mark:** Name.

MOULTON, DUSTY, 11385 W. Ardyce St., Boise, ID 83713/208-323-7911
Specialties: Fancy and working straight knives. **Patterns:** Hunters, fighters, fantasy and miniatures. **Technical:** Grinds exclusively ATS-34. **Prices:** $160 to $600; some to $1,500. **Remarks:** Full-time maker; first knife sold in 1991. **Mark:** Last name.

MOUNT, DON, 387 Medill Place, Horizon City, TX 79927/915-852-2254
Specialties: High-tech working and using straight knives of his design. **Patterns:** Bowies, fighters and utility/camp knives. **Technical:** Uses 440C and ATS-34. **Prices:** $150 to $300; some to $1,000. **Remarks:** Part-time maker; first knife sold in 1985. **Mark:** Name below a woodpecker.

MOUNTAIN HOME KNIVES, P.O. Box 167, Jamul, CA 91935/619-669-0833
Specialties: High-quality working straight knives. **Patterns:** Hunters, fighters, skinners, tantos, utility and fillet knives, Bowies and *san-mai* Damascus Bowies. **Technical:** Hollow-grind 440C by hand. Feature linen Micarta handles, nickel-silver handle bolts and handmade sheaths. **Prices:** $65 to $270. **Remarks:** Company owned by Jim English. **Mark:** Mountain Home Knives.

MOUNTAIN MAN KNIVES (See Driscoll, Mark)

MOYER, RUSS, 277 71st Ave. NW, Havre, MT 59501/406-265-5116
Specialties: Working knives to customer specs. **Patterns:** Hunters, Bowies and survival knives. **Technical:** Forges W2. **Prices:** $150 to $350. **Remarks:** Part-time maker; first knife sold in 1976. **Mark:** Initials in logo.

MULLIN, STEVE, 500 W. Center Valley Rd., Sandpoint, ID 83864/208-263-7492
Specialties: Damascus period pieces and folders. **Patterns:** Full range of folders, hunters and Bowies. **Technical:** Forges and grinds 01, D2, 154CM and his own Damascus. Engraves. **Prices:** $100 to $2,000. **Remarks:** Full-time maker; first knife sold in 1975. Sells line of using knives under Pack River Knife Co. **Mark:** Full name, city and state.

MURPHY, DAVE, P.O. Box 256, Gresham, OR 97030/503-665-8634
Specialties: Working knives of his design; small kitchen knives. **Patterns:** Hunters, fighters and boots. **Technical:** Grinds 440C, ATS-34 and L6; likes narrow tangs, composite handles. **Prices:** $44 to $12,500. **Remarks:** Full-time maker; first knife sold in 1940. **Mark:** Name, city and state with likeness of face on blade.

MUSTANG FORGE (See Hinderer, Rick)

M.W. KNIVES (See Wesolowski, Mike)

MYERS, MEL, 611 Elmwood Drive, Spencer, IA 51301/712-262-3383
Specialties: Working knives. **Patterns:** Hunters and small utilitarian knives. **Technical:** Uses 440C and no power tools except polisher. **Prices:** $75 to $150. **Remarks:** Spare-time maker; first knife sold in 1982. **Mark:** Signature.

MYERS, PAUL, 614 W. Airwood Dr., E. Alton, IL 62024
Specialties: Fancy working straight knives and folders. **Patterns:** Full range of folders, straight hunters and Bowies; tie tacks; knife and fork sets. **Technical:** Grinds D2, 440C, ATS-34 and 154CM. **Prices:** $100 to $350; some to $3,000. **Remarks:** Full-time maker; first knife sold in 1974. **Mark:** Initials with setting sun on front; name and number on back.

MYSTIK KNIFEWORKS (See Livingston, Robert C.)

n

NEALY, BUD, 822 Thomas St., Stroudsburg, PA 18360/717-421-4040; FAX: 717-421-2593.
Specialties: Concealment knives with designer multi-concealment sheath system. **Patterns:** Hunters, boots, combat and collector pieces. **Technical:** Grinds ATS-34; uses Damascus and clad steel. **Prices:** $150 to $1,200. **Remarks:** Full-time maker; first knife sold in 1980. **Mark:** Name, city and state.

NEALEY, IVAN F. (FRANK), Anderson Dam Rd., Box 65, HC #87, Mt. Home, ID 83647/208-587-4060
Specialties: Working straight knives in standard patterns. **Patterns:** Hunters, skinners and utility knives. **Technical:** Grinds D2, 440C and 154CM. **Prices:** $90 to $135; some higher. **Remarks:** Part-time maker; first knife sold in 1975. **Mark:** Name.

NEELEY, VAUGHN, 666 Grand Ave., Mancos, CO 81328/303-533-7982
Specialties: High-tech working straight knives and folders. **Patterns:** High-tech approaches; locking folders and interframes. **Technical:** Grinds 440C, D2 and 154CM. **Prices:** Upscale. **Remarks:** Full-time maker; first knife sold in 1982. **Mark:** Name.

NEELY, GREG, 9605 Radio Rd., Houston, TX 77075-2238/713-991-2677
Specialties: Traditional patterns and his own patterns for work and/or collecting. **Patterns:** Hunters, Bowies and utility/camp knives. **Technical:** Forges Damascus, W2, 5160 and 5168. Selectively tempers. Prefers natural handle materials. **Prices:** $195 to $3,500. **Remarks:** Part-time maker; first knife sold in 1987. **Mark:** Last name or interlocked initials, MS.

NEERING, WALT AND REPKE, MIKE, 4191 N. Euclid Ave., Bay City, MI 48706/517-684-3111
Specialties: Traditional working and using straight knives of their design or to customer specs; classic knives; display knives. **Patterns:** Hunters, Bowies, skinners, fighters boots, axes and swords. **Technical:** Grind 440C. Offer variety of handle materials. **Prices:** $99 to $1,500. **Remarks:** Full-time makers. Doing business as Black Forest Blades. **Mark:** Knife logo.

NELSON, ROGER S., Box 294, Central Village, CT 06332/203-774-6749
Specialties: Working knives. **Patterns:** Hunters, fighters, camp knives, locking folders, butterflies. **Technical:** Grinds D2, 440C and 154CM. **Prices:** $90 to $140; some to $250. **Remarks:** Spare-time maker; first knife sold in 1975. **Mark:** First initial, last name.

NETO JR., NELSON AND DE CARVALHO, HENRIQUE M., Travessa da Imprensa, 13, Centro, Braganca Paulista, SP-12900-000, BRAZIL/011-433-6889; FAX: 011-433-6889
Specialties: Straight knives and folders. **Patterns:** Bowies, katanas, jambyias and others. **Technical:** Forges high carbon steels. **Prices:** $80 to $1,000. **Remarks:** Full-time makers; first knife sold in 1990. **Mark:** H&N

NEWCOMB, CORBIN, 628 Woodland Ave., Moberly, MO 65270/816-263-4639
Specialties: Working straight knives and folders; period pieces. **Pat-**terns: Hunters, axes, Bowies, folders, buckskinner blades and boots. **Technical:** Hollow-grinds D2, 440C and 154CM; prefers natural handle materials. Makes own Damascus; offers cable Damascus. **Prices:** $100 to $500. **Remarks:** Full-time maker; first knife sold in 1982. Doing business as Corbin Knives. **Mark:** First name and serial number.

NEWTON, LARRY, 1758 Pronghorn Ct., Jacksonville, FL 32225/904-221-2340
Specialties: Traditional and working folders of his design. **Patterns:** Front release locking folders and interframes. **Technical:** Grinds 440C, ATS-34 and D2. **Prices:** Starting at $250. **Remarks:** Spare-time maker; first knife sold in 1989. **Mark:** Last name.

NIBARGER, CHARLIE, 4908 E. 15th St., Tulsa, OK 74112/918-749-8042
Specialties: Working straight knives in standard patterns. **Patterns:** Hunters, fighters and utility knives. **Technical:** Grinds 440C, ATS-34 and D2. **Prices:** $90 to $150. **Remarks:** Full-time maker; first knife sold in 1983. **Mark:** Last name.

NICHOLSON, R. KENT, P.O. Box 204, Phoenix, MD 21131/410-323-6925
Specialties: Large using knives. **Patterns:** Bowies and camp knives in the Moran style. **Technical:** Forges W2, 9260, 5160; makes Damascus. **Prices:** $150 to $995. **Remarks:** Part-time maker; first knife sold in 1984. **Mark:** Name.

NIELSON, JEFF V., 610 S. 200 E., P.O. Box 365, Monroe, UT 84754/801-527-4242
Specialties: Classic folders of his design and to customer specs. **Patterns:** Fighters, hunters, locking folders; miniatures. **Technical:** Grinds 440C stainless; forges Damascus. **Prices:** $80 to $500. **Remarks:** Part-time maker; first knife sold in 1991. Doing business as Fine Custom Knives. **Mark:** Name, location.

NIMO FORGE (See Sinyard, Cleston S.)

NIRO, FRANK, Box 552, Mackenzie, BC V0J 2C0, CANADA/604-997-6975
Specialties: Comfortable working straight knives and folders. **Patterns:** Hunters, Bowies, fishing knives, camp and kitchen knives. **Technical:** Grinds 440C, ATS-34 and CPMT 440V. Specializes in "cross cut" 440C and ATS-34. **Prices:** $40 to $450. **Remarks:** Part-time maker; first knife sold in 1983. Doing business as Frank's Place. **Mark:** Name, city, province.

NISHIUCHI, MELVIN S., 6121 Forest Park Dr., Las Vegas, NV 89115/702-438-2327
Specialties: Working straight knives; collector pieces. **Patterns:** Hunters, fighters, utility knives and some fancy personal knives. **Technical:** Grinds ATS-34; prefers exotic wood and/or stone handle materials. **Prices:** $200 to $1,000; some to $2,000. **Remarks:** Part-time maker; first knife sold in 1985. **Mark:** Circle with a line above it.

NOBLE HOUSE ARMOURERS (See Kennedy, Kelly S.)

NOLEN, GEORGE (See Nolen, R.D. and George)

NOLEN, R.D. and GEORGE, 1110 Lakeshore Dr., Estes Park, CO 80517-7113/303-586-5814
Specialties: Working knives; display pieces. **Patterns:** Wide variety of straight knives, butterflies and buckles. **Technical:** Grind D2, 440C and 154CM. Offer filework; make exotic handles. **Prices:** $100 to $800; some higher. **Remarks:** Full-time makers; first knife sold in 1968. **Mark:** NK in oval logo.

NOLFI, TIM, P.O. Box P, Chapel Hill Rd., Dawson, PA 15428/412-529-2439
Specialties: High-art straight knives and folders of his design; working and using knives. **Patterns:** Hunters, Bowies, fighters and some locking folders. **Technical:** Forges and grinds his own Damascus, 01 and 1095.

Also works with wrought iron and 200 nickel. **Prices:** $125 to $1,500; some to $4,000. **Remarks:** Full-time maker; first knife sold in 1988. **Mark:** Nolfi Forge or last name alone.

NORDELL, INGEMAR, Skarpå 2103, 82041 Färila, SWEDEN/0651-23347
Specialties: Classic working and using straight knives. **Patterns:** Hunters, Bowies and fighters. **Technical:** Forges and grinds ATS-34, D2 and Sandvik. **Prices:** $100 to $700. **Remarks:** Part-time maker; first knife sold in 1985. **Mark:** Initials or name.

NORFLEET, ROSS W., 3947 Tanbark Rd., Richmond, VA 23235/804-276-4169
Specialties: Classic, traditional and working/using knives of his design or in standard patterns. **Patterns:** Hunters and kitchen knives. **Technical:** Grinds 440C and ATS-34. Grinds hollow and flat. **Prices:** $75 to $200; some to $400. **Remarks:** Part-time maker; first knife sold in 1993. **Mark:** Name in arch logo.

NORRIS, MIKE, 2115 W. Main St., Albemarle, NC 28001/704-982-8445
Specialties: Interframe folders and liner locks. **Patterns:** Hunters, fighters, and interframe folders. **Technical:** Grinds ATS-34, 440C, D2 and Damascus. **Prices:** $100 to $900; some to $3,000. **Remarks:** Full-time maker; first knife sold in 1982. **Mark:** Full name, maker, city and state.

NORTH, DAVID and PRATER, MIKE, 105 Sharp, Chickamauga, GA 30707/706-931-2396
Specialties: Variety of horn- and stag-handled belt knives. **Patterns:** Standard patterns in large and small narrow-tang construction. **Technical:** Grind 01, D2 and Damascus. **Prices:** $165 to $10,000. **Remarks:** First knife sold in 1980. **Mark:** Names, date, serial number.

NORTH TEXAS TECHNOLOGIES (See Smart, Steve)

NORTHERN KNIFE CO. (See Crosslen, Timothy J.)

NORTON, DENNIS, 5334 Ashland Dr., Ft. Wayne, IN 46835/219-486-3851
Specialties: Traditional working and using straight knives of his design; martial arts weapons. **Patterns:** Bowies, fighters and utility/camp knives. **Technical:** Grinds 440C, D2 and 01. Most knives have filework and exotic hardwood handles. **Prices:** $60 to $300; some to $750. **Remarks:** Part-time maker; first knife sold in 1985. **Mark:** Initials and last name.

NORTON, DON, 3206 Aspen Dr., Farmington, NM 87401/505-327-3604
Specialties: Fancy and plain straight knives. **Patterns:** Hunters, small Bowies, tantos, boot knives, fillets. **Technical:** Prefers 440C, Micarta, exotic woods and other natural handle materials. Hollow-grinds all knives except fillet knives. **Prices:** $85 to $1,000; average is $200. **Remarks:** Full-time maker; first knife sold in 1980. **Mark:** Full name, Hsi Shugi, city, state.

NOWLAND, RICK, RR 1, Box 277, Waltonville, IL 62894/618-279-3170
Specialties: Working straight knives; collector-grade knives of his design. **Patterns:** One-of-a-kind daggers and Bowies, hunters, fighters, folders and miniatures. **Technical:** Forges 01, 5160 and Damascus. Uses some stainless steel. Makes mokume. **Prices:** $75 to $500; some to $1,000. **Remarks:** Part-time maker; first knife sold in 1986. **Mark:** Last name.

NUNN, GREGORY, CVSR Box 2107, Moab, UT 84532/801-259-8607
Specialties: High-art working and using knives of his design; new edition Emperor's Choice knife with purple sheen obsidian handle; new edition knife with handles made from Agatetized Dinosaur Bone—first ever made. **Patterns:** Flaked stone knives. **Technical:** Uses gem-quality agates, jaspers and obsidians for blades. **Prices:** $125 to $600; some to $1,000. **Remarks:** Full-time maker; first knife sold in 1989. **Mark:** Name, knife and edition numbers, year made.

NYMEYER, EARL, 2802 N. Fowler, Hobbs, NM 88240/505-392-2164
Specialties: One-of-a-kind working straight knives of his design. **Patterns:** Hunters and small and large belt knives. **Technical:** Hollow-grinds; offers filework. **Prices:** $75 to $95; some to $195. **Remarks:** Spare-time maker; first knife sold in 1983. **Mark:** Initials or first initial, last name.

OAKTREE FORGE (See Wagner, Dan)

OCHS, CHARLES F., 124 Emerald Lane, Largo, FL 34641/813-536-3827
Specialties: Working knives; period pieces. **Patterns:** Hunters, fighters, Bowies, buckskinners and folders. **Technical:** Forges 52100, 5160 and his own Damascus. **Prices:** $150 to $1,800; some to $2,500. **Remarks:** Full-time maker; first knife sold in 1978. **Mark:** OX Forge.

ODA, KUZAN, 629 W. 15th Ave., Anchorage, AK 99501-5005/907-746-3018
Specialties: High-tech Japanese-style knives; contemporary working knives. **Patterns:** Swords, fighters, hunters and folders. **Technical:** Forges and grinds BG42, 154CM, tamahagane and his own Damascus; offers traditional and authentic Japanese sword-smithing and polishing. **Prices:** $200 to $600; some to $8,000. **Remarks:** Full-time maker; first knife sold in 1957. Waiting list only. **Mark:** First name.

OGG, ROBERT G., 537 Old Dug Mtn. Rd., Paris, AR 72855/501-963-2767
Specialties: Plain and fancy working knives. **Patterns:** Folding slip-joints. **Technical:** Grinds 440C, ATS-34 and high carbon. **Prices:** Start at $120. **Remarks:** Spare-time maker; first knife sold in 1964. **Mark:** Name.

OGLETREE JR., BEN R., 2815 Israel Rd., Livingston, TX 77351/409-327-8315
Specialties: Working/using straight knives of his design. **Patterns:** Hunters, kitchen and utility/camp knives. **Technical:** Grinds ATS-34, W1 and 1075; heat-treats. **Prices:** $200 to $400. **Remarks:** Part-time maker; first knife sold in 1955. **Mark:** Last name, city and state in oval with a tree on either side.

OKAYSU, KAZOU, 12-2 1 Chome Higashi Veno, Taito-Ku, Tokyo 110, JAPAN

OLD COLONY MANUFACTORY (See Leavitt, Jr., Earl F.)

OLD TOWN CUTLERY (See Ree, David)

OLIVER, ANTHONY CRAIG, 1504 Elaine Pl., Ft. Worth, TX 76106/817-625-0825
Specialties: Fancy and embellished traditional straight knives of his design. **Patterns:** Hunters, full-size folders, Bowies, daggers and miniatures in stainless and nickel Damascus with tempered blades. **Technical:** Grinds 440C and ATS-34. **Prices:** $40 to $500. **Remarks:** Part-time maker; first knife sold in 1988. **Mark:** Initials and last name.

OLSON, ROD, 110 3rd Ave. NE, High River AB, CANADA T1V 1L9/403-652-2744; FAX: 403-652-3061
Specialties: Traditional and working/using folders of his design; period pieces. **Patterns:** Locking folders. **Technical:** Grinds ATs-34. Offers filework, sculptured steel frames. **Prices:** $300 to $750. **Remarks:** Part-time maker; first knife sold in 1979. Doing business as Olson Pocket Knives. **Mark:** Last name on blade; country, serial number inside frame.

OLSON, WAYNE C., 11655 W. 35th Ave., Wheat Ridge, CO 80033/303-420-3415
Specialties: High-tech working knives. **Patterns:** Hunters to folding lockers; some integral designs. **Technical:** Grinds 440C, 154CM and ATS-34; likes hand-finishes; precision-fits stainless steel fittings—no

solder, no nickel silver. **Prices:** $275 to $600; some to $3,000. **Remarks:** Full-time maker; first knife sold in 1979. **Mark:** Name, maker.

OLYMPIC KNIVES (See Ball, Robert)

ONION, KENNETH J., 91-990 Oaniani St., Kapolei, HI 96707/808-674-1300
Specialties: Fancy working straight knives and some folders. **Patterns:** Bowies, daggers, fighters, boots, hunters, utility folders, art knives. **Technical:** ATS-34, 440C, Damascus, 5160, D2. **Prices:** $110 to $800. **Remarks:** Part-time maker; first knife sold in 1991. **Mark:** NA.

ORION (See Reed, Del)

OSBORNE, MICHAEL, 585 Timber Ridge Dr., New Braunfels, TX 78132/210-609-0118
Specialties: Traditional and working/using straight knives of his design. **Patterns:** Bowies, fighters and hunters. **Technical:** Forges 5160, 01 and W2. Tempers all blades. **Prices:** $125 to $500; some to $1,000. **Remarks:** Part-time maker; first knife sold in 1988. Doing business as Michael Osbourne, Bladesmith. **Mark:** Stamped last name.

OSBORNE, WARREN, 215 Edgefield, Waxahachie, TX 75165/214-937-0899; FAX: 214-937-9004
Specialties: Working knives; fancy pieces. **Patterns:** Folders; bolstered and interframe miniatures; conventional lockers, frontlockers and backlockers; some slip-joints; some high-art pieces. **Technical:** Grinds D2, 440C and 154CM; offers serrated bolsters. **Prices:** $200 to $800; some to $2,000. Interframes $650 to $1,500. **Remarks:** Full-time maker; first knife sold in 1980. **Mark:** Last name in boomerang logo.

OSTERMAN, DANIEL E., 1644 W. 10th, Junction City, OR 97448/503-998-1503
Specialties: One-third scale copies of period pieces, museum class miniatures. **Patterns:** Antique Bowies. **Technical:** Grinds all cutlery grade steels, engraves, etches, inlays and overlays. **Prices:** Start at $600. **Remarks:** Full-time maker; first miniature knife sold in 1975. **Mark:** Initials.

OUTFITTER (See Vought Jr., Frank)

OUTLAW, ANTHONY L., 4115 Gaines St., Panama City, FL 32404/904-769-7754
Specialties: Traditional working straight knives. **Patterns:** Tantos, Bowies, camp knives, etc. **Technical:** Grinds A2, W2, 01, L6, 1095 and stainless steels to mirror finish. **Prices:** $85 to $175; some to $300. **Remarks:** Part-time maker; first knife sold in 1984. **Mark:** Last name.

OVEREYNDER, T.R., 1800 S. Davis Dr., Arlington, TX 76013/817-277-4812; FAX: 817-860-5485
Specialties: Highly finished collector-grade working knives. **Patterns:** Fighters, Bowies, daggers, locking folders, slip-joints and 90 percent collector-grade interframe folders. **Technical:** Grinds D2, 440C and 154CM. Has been making titanium-frame folders since 1977. **Prices:** $500 to $1,500; some to $7,000. **Remarks:** Part-time maker; first knife sold in 1977. Doing business as TRO Knives. **Mark:** T.R. OVEREYNDER KNIVES, city and state.

OWEN, BILL, P.O. Box 161, Monterey, VA 24465/703-468-2850
Specialties: Working and using straight knives of his design. **Patterns:** Hunters, Bowies and utility/camp knives. **Technical:** Grinds D2; forges various spring steels. Heat-treats and makes sheaths. **Prices:** $75 to $250. **Remarks:** Spare-time maker; first knife sold in 1990. **Mark:** Stylized paw print mosaic pin in handle.

OWENS, JOHN, 6513 E. Lookout Dr., Parker, CO 80134
Specialties: Contemporary working straight knives; period pieces. **Patterns:** Hunters, Bowies and camp knives. **Technical:** Grinds and forges 440C, 154CM, ATS-34 and 01. **Prices:** $125 to $350. **Remarks:** Spare-time maker. **Mark:** Last name.

OX FORGE (See Ochs, Charles F.)

OYSTER, LOWELL R., RR #1, Box 5605, Kenduskeag, ME 04450/207-884-8663
Specialties: Traditional and original designed multi-blade slip-joint folders. **Patterns:** Hunters, minis, camp and fishing knives. **Technical:** Grinds 01; heat-treats. **Prices:** $55 to $450; some to $750. **Remarks:** Full-time maker; first knife sold in 1981. **Mark:** A scallop shell.

p

PACHI, FRANCESCO, Via Albisola 97B, 16163 Genoa, ITALY/010-713050
Specialties: Fancy working knives. **Patterns:** Hunters and skinners. **Technical:** Grinds 440C. **Prices:** $200 to $500. **Remarks:** Part-time maker; first knife sold in 1991. **Mark:** Logo with last name.

PACK RIVER KNIFE CO. (See Mullin, Steve)

PACKARD, BOB, P.O. Box 311, Elverta, CA 95626/916-991-5218
Specialties: Traditional working/using straight knives of his design and to customer specs. **Patterns:** Hunters, fishing knives, utility/camp knives. **Technical:** Grinds ATS-34, 440C; Forges 52100, 5168 and cable Damascus. **Prices:** $75 to $225. **Mark:** Engraved name and year.

PADILLA, GARY, P.O. Box 741, Weimar, CA 95736/916-637-5182
Specialties: Native American influenced working and using straight knives of his design. **Patterns:** Hunters, kitchen knives, utility/camp knives and obsidian ceremonial knives. **Technical:** Grinds 440C, ATS-34, 01 and Damascus. **Prices:** $65 to $195; some to $500. **Remarks:** Part-time maker; first knife sold in 1977. Doing business as Bighorn Knifeworks. **Mark:** Sylized initials or name over company name.

PAGE, LARRY, 165 Rolling Rock Rd., Aiken, SC 29803/803-648-0001
Specialties: Working knives of his design; period pieces. **Patterns:** Hunters, boots and fighters. **Technical:** Grinds 154CM and ATS-34. **Prices:** Start at $85. **Remarks:** Part-time maker; first knife sold in 1983. **Mark:** Name, city and state in oval.

PAGE, REGINALD, 6587 Groveland Hill Rd., Groveland, NY 14462/716-243-1643
Specialties: High-art straight knives and one-of-a-kind folders of his design. **Patterns:** Hunters, locking folders and slip-joint folders. **Technical:** Forges 01, 5160 and his own Damascus. Prefers natural handle materials but will work with Micarta. **Remarks:** Spare-time maker; first knife sold in 1985. **Mark:** First initial, last name.

PANKIEWICZ, PHILIP R., RFD #1, Waterman Rd., Lebanon, CT 06249
Specialties: Working straight knives. **Patterns:** Hunters, daggers, minis and fishing knives. **Technical:** Grinds D2, 440C and 154CM. **Prices:** $60 to $125; some to $250. **Remarks:** Spare-time maker; first knife sold in 1975. **Mark:** First initial in star.

PANTHER CREEK FORGE (See Cook, Louise and Cook, Mike)

PAPP, ROBERT, P.O. Box 29596, Parma, OH 44129/216-888-9299
Specialties: Swords—broad and fantasy; variety of display knives. **Patterns:** Integral-designed hunters, fighters, minis and boots. **Technical:** Grinds D2, 440C, 154CM, ATS-34, CPM 108 and CPM 440C. **Prices:** $95 to $10,000; some higher. **Remarks:** Full-time maker; first knife sold in 1964. **Mark:** Full name, city and state.

PARDUE, MELVIN M., Rt. 1, Box 130, Repton, AL 36475/205-248-2686
Specialties: Fancy straight knives and folders. **Patterns:** Locking and push-button folders, tantos, krisses, liner locks, fighters and boots. **Technical:** Grinds D2, 440C, 154CM and UHB-A-EBL; uses anodized titanium. Likes coffin handles. **Prices:** $140 to $350. **Remarks:** Full-time maker; first knife sold in 1974. **Mark:** Last name.

PARKER, J.E., 1300 E. Main, Clarion, PA 16214/814-226-4837; FAX: 814-226-4351

Specialties: Fancy/embellished, traditional and working straight knives of his design and to customer specs. **Patterns:** Bowies and hunters. **Technical:** Grinds 440C, 440V, ATS-34 and nickel Damascus. Prefers mastadon, oosik, amber and malachite handle material. **Prices:** $90 to $550; some to $750. **Remarks:** Part-time maker; first knife sold in 1991. Doing business as Custom Knife. **Mark:** Name and city with knife stamped in blade.

PARKER, ROBERT NELSON, 5223 Wilhelm Rd. N.W., Rapid City, MI 49676
Specialties: Traditional working and using straight knives of his design. **Patterns:** Hunters, fighters, utility/camp knives; some Bowies. **Technical:** Grinds ATS-34, D2, 440C; hollow and flat grinds, full and hidden tangs. Micarta corian stag handle material; hand-stitched leather sheaths. **Prices:** $150 to $475. **Remarks:** Part-time maker; first knife sold in 1986. **Mark:** First initial, middle and last names, city and state.

PARKS, BLANE C., P.O. Box 2364, Dale City, VA 22193/703-221-4680
Specialties: Knives of his design. **Patterns:** Boots, Bowies, daggers, fighters, hunters, kitchen knives, locking and slip-joint folders, utility/camp knives, letter openers and friction folders. **Technical:** Grinds ATS-34, 440C, D2 and other carbon steels. Offers filework, silver wire inlay and wooden sheaths. **Prices:** $150 and up. **Remarks:** Part-time maker; first knife sold in 1993. Doing business as B.C. Parks Knives. **Mark:** First and middle initials, last name.

PARKS, JOHN, 3539 Galilee Church Rd., Jefferson, GA 30549/706-367-4916
Specialties: Traditional working and using straight knives of his design. **Patterns:** Trout knives, hunters and integral bolsters. **Technical:** Forges 1095 and 5168. **Prices:** $100 to $250; some to $600. **Remarks:** Part-time maker; first knife sold in 1989. **Mark:** Initials in script.

PARLER, THOMAS O'NEIL, 11 Franklin St., Charleston, SC 29401/803-723-9433
Specialties: Period pieces and traditional straight knives of his design. **Patterns:** Bowies, utility/camp knives, Scottish dirks, skean dhu and other Celtic period pieces. **Technical:** Forges 5160, 1095 and W2. Prefers matte or satin finish, brass or German silver buttcaps and bolsters and some Celtic carving on handles. **Prices:** $300 to $1,000; some to $2,000. **Remarks:** Part-time maker; first knife sold in 1995. Doing business as Raven Forge. **Mark:** Last name in runic letters, rune for "protection."

PARRISH III, GORDON A., 940 Lakloey Dr., North Pole, AK 99705/907-488-0357
Specialties: Classic high-art straight knives of his design and to customer specs.; working and using knives. **Patterns:** Bowies and hunters. **Technical:** Grinds tool steel and ATS-34. Uses mostly Alaskan handle materials. **Prices:** $125 to $750. **Remarks:** Spare-time maker; first knife sold in 1980. **Mark:** Last name, state.

PARRISH, ROBERT, 1922 Spartanburg Hwy., Hendersonville, NC 28792-6527/704-692-3466
Specialties: Heavy-duty working knives of his design or to customer specs. **Patterns:** Survival and duty knives; hunters and fighters. **Technical:** Grinds 440C, D2, 01 and commercial Damascus. **Prices:** $200 to $300; some to $6,000. **Remarks:** Full-time maker; first knife sold in 1970. **Mark:** Initials connected, sometimes with city and state.

PARSONS, MICHAEL R., 1600 S. 11th St., Terre Haute, IN 47802-1722/812-234-1679
Specialties: Fancy straight knives. **Patterns:** Railroad spike knives and variety of one-of-a-kinds including files. **Technical:** Forges and hand-files scrap steel. Engraves, carves, wire inlays and offers leatherwork. **Prices:** $150 to $1,500. **Remarks:** Full-time maker; first knife sold in 1965. **Mark:** Mc with key logo.

PATE, LLOYD D., 219 Cottontail Ln., Georgetown, TX 78626/512-863-7805
Specialties: Traditional working straight knives. **Patterns:** Hunters, fighters and Bowies. **Technical:** Hollow-grinds D2, 440C and ATS-34;

likes mirror-finishes. **Prices:** $75 to $350; some to $500. **Remarks:** Part-time maker; first knife sold in 1983. **Mark:** Last name.

PATRICK, BOB, 12642 24A Ave., Crescent Beach, B.C. V4A 8H9 CANADA/604-538-6214
Specialties: Working knives of his design. **Patterns:** Pacific coast hunters, fishers, Bowies, Ravens and pierce-arrow throwing knives. **Technical:** Grinds ATS-34, D2 and 440C. **Prices:** $90 to $2,000. **Remarks:** Full-time maker; first knife sold in 1987. **Mark:** Name in circle logo; British Columbia etched on other side; serial number.

PATRICK, CHUCK, P.O. Box 127, Brasstown, NC 28902/704-837-7627
Specialties: Period pieces. **Patterns:** Hunters, daggers, tomahawks, pre-Civil War folders. **Technical:** Forges all hardware, 5160, his own cable and Damascus, available in fancy pattern and mosaic. **Prices:** $150 to $1,000; some higher. **Remarks:** Full-time maker; first knife sold in 1980. **Mark:** Name and date hand-engraved.

PATTAY, RUDY, 20 Nevada St., Long Beach, NY 11561/516-431-0847
Specialties: Fancy and working straight knives of his design. **Patterns:** Bowies, hunters, utility/camp knives. **Technical:** Hollow-grinds ATS-34, 440C, 01. Offers stainless steel soldered guards; fabricates guard and buttcap on lathe and milling machine. Heat treats. Prefers synthetic handle materials. Offers hand-sewn sheaths. **Prices:** $100 to $350; some to $500. **Remarks:** Part-time maker; first knife sold in 1990. Doing business as Pattay Knives. **Mark:** First initial, last name in sorcerer logo.

PATTERSON, ALAN W., Rt. 3, Box 131, Hayesville, NC 28904/704-389-9103
Specialties: Working straight knives and folders of his design or to customer specs; period pieces. **Patterns:** Forged knives, swords, tomahawks and folders. **Technical:** Damascus, cable and tool steels. Some custom leatherwork; wife offers scrimshaw. **Prices:** $125 to $5,000. **Remarks:** Full-time maker; first knife sold in 1990. **Mark:** Patterson Forge.

PATTERSON, KARL, 8 Madison Ave., Silver Creek, NY 14136/716-934-2578
Specialties: Working and using straight knives of his design or to customer specs. **Patterns:** Hunters, Bowies and utility/camp knives. **Technical:** Grinds 440C, ATS-34 and 01. Prefers Micarta and pakkawood. **Prices:** $55 to $150; some to $350. **Remarks:** Spare-time maker; first knife sold in 1990. **Mark:** First name with a backward K.

PAVACK, DON, P.O. Box 318, Edgerton, WY 82635/307-437-9240; FAX: 307-437-9240
Specialties: Working straight knives. Will work with customer designs. **Patterns:** Hunters and fillet knives; folders. **Technical:** Grinds ATS-34, 440C, 154CM and Damascus steel. Prefers natural handle materials; uses Micarta and diamond wood. **Prices:** $95 to $2,000. **Mark:** Signature and initials.

PEAGLER, RUSS, P.O. Box 1314, Moncks Corner, SC 29461/803-761-1008
Specialties: Traditional working straight knives of his design and to customer specs. **Patterns:** Hunters, fighters, boots. **Technical:** Hollow-grinds 440C, ATS-34 and 01; uses Damascus steel. Prefers bone handles. **Prices:** $85 to $300; some to $500. **Remarks:** Spare-time maker; first knife sold in 1983. **Mark:** Initials.

PEASE, W.D., Rt. 2 Box 37AA, Ewing, KY 41039/606-845-0387
Specialties: Display-quality working straight knives and folders. **Patterns:** Fighters, tantos and boots; locking folders and interframes. **Technical:** Grinds 440C, ATS-34 and commercial Damascus; has own side-release lock system. **Prices:** $300 to $500; some to $1,500. **Remarks:** Full-time maker; first knife sold in 1970. **Mark:** First and middle initials, lst name.

PEELE, BRYAN, 219 Ferry St., P.O. Box 1363, Thompson Falls, MT 59873/406-827-4633

Specialties: Fancy working and using knives of his design. **Patterns:** Hunters, Bowies and fighters. **Technical:** Grinds 440C, ATS-34, D2, 01 and commercial Damascus. **Prices:** $110 to $300; some to $900. **Remarks:** Part-time maker; first knife sold in 1985. **Mark:** The Elk Rack, full name, city, state.

PENDLETON, LLOYD, 24581 Shake Ridge Rd., Volcano, CA 95689/209-296-3353
Specialties: Contemporary working knives in standard patterns. **Patterns:** Hunters, fighters and boots. **Technical:** Grinds 154CM and ATS-34; mirror finishes. **Prices:** $300 to $700; some to $2,000. **Remarks:** Full-time maker; first knife sold in 1973. **Mark:** First initial, last name logo, city and state.

PENDRAY, ALFRED H., Rt. 2, Box 1950, Williston, FL 32696/904-528-6124
Specialties: Working straight knives and folders; period pieces. **Patterns:** Fighters and hunters, axes, camp knives and tomahawks. **Technical:** Forges Wootz steel; makes his own Damascus; makes traditional knives from old files and rasps. **Prices:** $125 to $1,000; some to $3,500. **Remarks:** Part-time maker; first knife sold in 1954. **Mark:** Last intial in horseshoe logo.

PENNINGTON, C.A., 137 Riverlea Estate Dr., Stewarts Gully, Christchurch 9, NEW ZEALAND/03-323 7292; FAX: 03-323-7292
Specialties: Classic working/using straight knives of his design. **Patterns:** Hunters, kitchen knives, utility/camp knives. **Technical:** Grinds D2, 440C, 154CM. **Prices:** $225 to $450; some to $850. **Remarks:** Full-time maker; first knife sold in 1988. **Mark:** Name, country.

PEPIOT, STEPHAN, 73 Cornwall Blvd., Winnipeg, Manitoba, CANADA R3J-1E9/204-888-1499
Specialties: Working straight knives in standard patterns. **Patterns:** Hunters and camp knives. **Technical:** Grinds 440C and industrial hacksaw blades. **Prices:** $75 to $125. **Remarks:** Spare-time maker; first knife sold in 1982. Not currently taking orders. **Mark:** PEP.

PEPPER KNIVES (See Culpepper, John)

PERRY, CHRIS, 1654 W. Birch, Fresno, CA 93711

PERSUADER (See Hill, Howard E.)

PETEAN, FRANCISCO AND MAURICIO, R. Dr. Carlos de Carvalho Rosa, 52, Centro, Birigui, SP-16200-000, BRAZIL/0186-424786
Specialties: Classic knives to customer specs. **Patterns:** Bowies, boots, fighters, hunters and utility knives. **Technical:** Grinds D6, 440C and high carbon steels. Prefers natural handle material. **Prices:** $70 to $500. **Remarks:** Full-time maker; first knife sold in 1985. **Mark:** Last name, hand made.

PETEAN, MAURICIO (See Petean, Francisco and Mauricio)

PETERSEN, DAN L., 3015 SW Clark Ct., Topeka, KS 66604
Specialties: Period pieces and forged integral hilts on hunters and fighters. **Patterns:** Texas style Bowies, boots and hunters in high carbon and Damascus steel. **Technical:** Austempers forged high-carbon blades. **Prices:** $200 to $3,000; some to $3,000. **Remarks:** First knife sold in 1978. **Mark:** Stylized initials, MS.

PETERSON, CHRIS, Box 143, 2175 W. Rockyford, Salina, UT 84654/801-529-7194
Specialties: Working straight knives of his design. **Patterns:** Large fighters, boots, hunters and some display pieces. **Technical:** Forges 01 and meteor. Makes and sells his own Damascus. Engraves, scrimshands and inlays. **Prices:** $150 to $600; some to $1,500. **Remarks:** Full-time maker; first knife sold in 1986. **Mark:** A drop in a circle with a line through it.

PETERSON, ELDON G., 260 Haugen Hts. Rd., Whitefish, MT 59937/406-862-2204; FAX: 406-862-3103

Specialties: Fancy and working folders, any size. **Patterns:** Lockback interframes, integral bolster folders and two-bladers. **Technical:** Grinds 440C and ATS-34. Offers gold inlay work, gem stone inlays and engraving. **Prices:** $285 to $5,000. **Remarks:** Full-time maker; first knife sold in 1974. **Mark:** Name, city and state.

PHILLIPS, RANDY, 759 E. Francis St., Ontario, CA 91761/909-923-4381
Specialties: Hunters, collector-grade liner locks and high art daggers. **Technical:** Grinds D2, 440C and 154CM; embellishes. **Prices:** Start at $200. **Remarks:** Part-time maker; first knife sold in 1981. **Mark:** Name, city and state in eagle head.

PICKENS, SELBERT, Rt. 1, Box 216, Liberty, WV 25124/304-586-2190
Specialties: Using knives. **Patterns:** Standard sporting knives. **Technical:** Stainless steels; stock removal method. **Prices:** Moderate. **Remarks:** Part-time maker. **Mark:** Name.

PIERCE, HAROLD L., 106 Lyndon Lane, Louisville, KY 40222/502-429-5136
Specialties: Working straight knives, some fancy. **Patterns:** Big fighters and Bowies. **Technical:** Grinds D2, 440C, 154CM; likes sub-hilts. **Prices:** $150 to $450; some to $1,200. **Remarks:** Full-time maker; first knife sold in 1982. **Mark:** Last name with knife through the last initial.

PIENAAR, CONRAD, 19A Milner Rd., Bloemfontein 9300, REPUBLIC OF SOUTH AFRICA/051-314180
Specialties: Fancy working and using straight knives and folders of his design, to customer specs and in standard patterns. **Patterns:** Hunters, locking folders, kitchen and utility/camp knives. **Technical:** Grinds 12C27, D2 and ATS-34. Scrimshands; engraving by Armin Winkler. Knives come with wooden box and custom-made leather sheath. **Prices:** $400 to $600. **Remarks:** Part-time maker; first knife sold in 1981. Doing business sa C.P. Knifemaker. **Mark:** Initials and serial number.

PIESNER, DEAN, 30 King St., St. Jacobs, Ont. CANADA N0B 2N0/519-664-3622; FAX: 519-664-1828
Specialties: Classic period pieces of his design and to customer specs. **Patterns:** Bowies, skinners, fighters and swords. **Technical:** Forges 5160, 52100, steel Damascus and nickel-steel Damascus. Silver wire inlays in wood; copper-brass-silver inlays in steel. **Prices:** Start at $125. **Remarks:** Full-time maker; first knife sold in 1990. **Mark:** First initial, last name, JS.

PIONEER FORGE & WOODSHOP (See Mitchell, Wm. Dean)

PIOREK, JAMES S., P.O. Box 5032, Missoula, MT 59806/406-728-0119
Specialties: Custom tailored high-tech using straight knives. **Patterns:** Fighters, hunters, swords and utility/camp knives. **Technical:** Grinds A2; heat treats. Offers kydex-lined leather laminated sheaths, body harness carry systems and exotic handle and sheath materials. **Prices:** $175 to $4,000. **Remarks:** Full-time maker; first knife sold in 1990. Doing business as Blade Rigger. **Mark:** Initials with abstract cutting edge.

PITT, DAVID F., P.O. Box 1564, Pleasanton, CA 94566/415-846-9751
Specialties: Working straight knives. **Patterns:** Knives for deer and elk hunters, including hatchets and cleavers; small gut hook hunters and capers. **Technical:** Grinds A2, 440C and 154CM. **Prices:** $100 to $200; some to $450. **Remarks:** Full-time maker; first knife sold in 1972. **Mark:** Bear Paw with name.

PLINKETT, RICHARD, 29 Kirk Rd., West Cornwall, CT 06796

POAG, JAMES, RR 1, Box 212A, Grayville, IL 62844/618-375-7106
Specialties: Working straight knives and folders; period pieces; of his design or to customer specs. **Patterns:** Bowies and camp knives, lockers and slip-joints. **Technical:** Forges and grinds stainless steels and

others; provides serious leather; offers embellishments; scrimshaws, engraves and does leather work for other makers. **Prices:** $65 to $1,200. **Remarks:** Full-time maker; first knife sold in 1967. **Mark:** Name.

POGREBA, LARRY, Box 861, Lyons, CO 80540/303-823-6691
Specialties: Steel and Damascus lightweight hunters; kitchen knives. **Patterns:** Fighters, hawks and spears. **Technical:** Forges/grinds his own Damascus. **Prices:** $40 to $1000. **Remarks:** Part-time maker; first knife sold in 1976. Doing business as Cadillac Blacksmithing. **Mark:** Initials.

POLK, CLIFTON, 4625 Webber Creek Rd., Van Buren, AR 72956/501-474-3828
Specialties: Fancy working straight knives and folders. **Patterns:** Locking folders, slip-joints, two-blades, straight knives. **Technical:** Offers 440C, D2 ATS-34 and Damascus. **Prices:** $150 to $3,000. **Remarks:** Full-time maker. **Mark:** Last name.

POLKOWSKI, AL, 8 Cathy Ct., Chester, NJ 07930/908-879-6030
Specialties: High-tech straight knives and folders for adventurers and professionals. **Patterns:** Fighters, side-lock folders, boots and concealment knives. **Technical:** Grinds D2 and ATS-34; features satin and bead-blast finishes; Kydex sheaths. **Prices:** Start at $100. **Remarks:** Full-time maker; first knife sold in 1985. **Mark:** Full name, Handmade.

POLZIEN, DON, 1912 Inler Suite-L, Lubbock, TX 79407/806-791-0766
Specialties: Traditional Japanese-style blades; restores antique Japanese swords, scabbards and fittings. **Patterns:** Hunters, fighters, one-of-a-kind art knives. **Technical:** 1045-1050 carbon steels, 440C, D2, ATS-34, standard and cable Damascus. **Prices:** $150 to $2,500. **Remarks:** Full-time maker. First knife sold in 1990. **Mark:** Oriental characters inside square border.

POOLE, MARVIN O., P.O. Box 5234, Anderson, SC 29623/803-225-5970
Specialties: Traditional working/using straight knives and folders of his design and in standard patterns. **Patterns:** Bowies, fighters, hunters, locking folders, bird and trout knives. **Technical:** Grinds 440C, D2, ATS-34. **Prices:** $50 to $150; some to $750. **Remarks:** Part-time maker; first knife sold in 1980. **Mark:** First initial, last name, year, serial number.

POOLE, STEVE L., 200 Flintlock Trail, Stockbridge, GA 30281/404-474-9154
Specialties: Traditional working and using straight knives and folders of his design, to customer specs and in standard patterns. **Patterns:** Bowies, fighters, hunters, utility and locking folders. **Technical:** Grinds ATS-34; buys Damascus. Heat-treats; offers leatherwork. **Prices:** $85 to $350; some to $800. **Remarks:** Spare-time maker; first knife sold in 1991. **Mark:** First and middle initials, last name and serial number.

POPLIN, JAMES L., 103 Oak St., Washington, GA 30673/404-678-2729
Specialties: Contemporary hunters. **Patterns:** Hunters and boots. **Technical:** Hollow-grinds. **Prices:** Reasonable. **Mark:** POP.

POPP SR., STEVE, 6573 Winthrop Dr., Fayetteville, NC 28311/910-822-3151
Specialties: Working straight knives. **Patterns:** Hunters, Bowies and fighters. **Technical:** Forges and grinds his own Damascus, 01, L6 and spring steel. **Prices:** $75 to $600; some to $1,000. **Remarks:** Full-time maker; first knife sold in 1984. **Mark:** Initials and last name.

PORTER, JAMES E., P.O. Box 2583, Bloomington, IN 47402/812-859-4302
Specialties: Working straight knives; period pieces. **Patterns:** Outdoor knives; Bowies and short swords. **Technical:** Forges W2 and 1095; makes pattern-welded Damascus. Prefers Damascus for blades and fittings. **Prices:** $125 to $3,000. **Remarks:** Part-time maker; first knife sold in 1986. **Mark:** First and middle initials, MS.

POSNER, BARRY E., 12501 Chandler Blvd., Suite 104, N. Hollywood, CA 91607/818-752-8005; FAX: 818-752-8006

Specialties: Working/using straight knives. **Patterns:** Hunters, kitchen and utility/camp knives. **Technical:** Grinds ATS-34; forges 1095 and nickel. **Prices:** $100 to $250. **Remarks:** Part-time maker; first knife sold in 1987. Doing business as Posner Knives. **Mark:** First and middle initials, last name.

POSTON, ALVIN, 1197 Bass Rd., Pamplico, SC 29583/803-493-0066
Specialties: Working straight knives. **Patterns:** Hunters, Bowies and fishing knives; some miniatures. **Technical:** Grinds 154CM and ATS-34. **Prices:** Start at $100. **Remarks:** Part-time maker; first knife sold in 1979. **Mark:** Last name.

POTIER, TIMOTHY F., P.O. Box 711, Oberlin, LA 70655/318-639-2229
Specialties: Classic working and using straight knives to customer specs; some collectible. **Patterns:** Hunters, Bowies, utility/camp knives and belt axes. **Technical:** Forges carbon steel and his own Damascus; offers filework. **Prices:** $300 to $1,800; some to $4,000. **Remarks:** Part-time maker; first knife sold in 1981. **Mark:** Last name, MS.

POVISILS, KARLIS A., P.O. Box 747, Mt. Holly, NJ 08060/609-261-2287
Specialties: Fantasy and working/using straight knives of his design and to customer specs. **Patterns:** Fighters, hunters and utility/camp knives. **Technical:** Forges own Damascus, cable and chain. Offers filework; amber spacers and guards. Oosic and fossil ivory handle material. **Prices:** $200 to $800. **Remarks:** Full-time maker; first knife sold in 1990. Doing business as KAP Forge. **Mark:** Interlocked initials within circle, JS on reverse side.

POYTHRESS, JOHN, P.O. Box 585, 206 Freedom St., Swainsboro, GA 30401/912-237-9233; 912-237-9478
Specialties: Traditional working and using straight knives of his design or to customer specs. **Patterns:** Hunters. **Technical:** Uses 440C, ATS-34 and D2. **Prices:** $75 to $250; some to $400. **Remarks:** Spare-time maker; first knife sold in 1983. **Mark:** J.W. Poythress Handcrafted, serial number.

PRATER, MIKE (See North, David and Prater, Mike)

PRATT, CHARLEY, 1953 Fillmans Bottom Rd., Port Washington, OH 43837/614-498-5404
Specialties: Bowies, fighters, daggers and swords; kitchen knives on request. **Patterns:** Hunters, boot knives and miniatures. **Technical:** Grinds 440C, D-2, ATS-34 and commercial Damascus. **Prices:** Starting at $150. **Remarks:** Full-time maker; first knife sold in 1978. **Mark:** Last name.

PREHISTORIC EDGE, THE (See Stafford, Michael)

PRESLEY, VERN, 3803 Alston Lane, Richmond, VA 23294/804-270-4739
Specialties: Traditional working and using straight knives of his design and to customer specs. **Patterns:** Bowies, hunters and utility/camp knives. **Technical:** Grinds ATS-34, 440C and 154CM. **Prices:** $120 to $175; some to $300. **Remarks:** Part-time maker; first knife sold in 1978. **Mark:** Stamped or etched last name.

PRESSBURGER, RAMON, 59 Driftway Rd., Howell, NJ 07731/908-363-0816
Specialties: Traditional working knives to customer specs. **Patterns:** Hunters, skinners and utility/camp knives. **Technical:** Uses ATS-34, D2 and BG 42 and high-carbon steels. **Prices:** $70 to $500. **Remarks:** Full-time maker; first knife sold in 1970. **Mark:** NA.

PRICE, JERRY L., P.O. Box 782, Springdale, AR 72764
Specialties: Working straight knives in standard patterns. **Patterns:** Fighters, boots and Bowies. **Technical:** Grinds A2, 440C and 154CM; matte black oxide finish on fighters. Offers Kydex sheaths. **Prices:** $60 to $200; some to $400. **Remarks:** Full-time maker; first knife sold in 1975. **Mark:** First initial, last name.

PRICE, JOEL HIRAM, RR1, Box 18GG, Interlochen, FL 32148-9709
Specialties: Working straight knives to customer specs. **Patterns:** Vari-

ety of straight knives. **Technical:** Forges and grinds W2, 01, D2 and 440C—customer choice; buys Damascus. All knives have filework. **Prices:** $50 to $250; some $750 and higher. **Remarks:** Full-time maker; first knife sold in 1984. **Mark:** Hiram Knives in script.

PRICE, STEVE, 899 Ida Lane, Kamloops, BC V2B 6V2, CANADA/604-579-8932
Specialties: Working knives and fantasy pieces of his design or to customer specs. **Patterns:** Hunters, axes, tantos, survival knives, locking folders and some miniatures. **Technical:** Grinds D2, 440C and ATS-34; buys Damascus. **Prices:** $90 to $350; some to $1,200. **Remarks:** Full-time maker; first knife sold in 1982. **Mark:** First initial, last name.

PRINCE, JOE R,, 5406 Reidville Rd., Moore, SC 29369/803-576-7479
Specialties: Traditional straight knives and folders of his design. **Patterns:** Boots and locking folders. **Technical:** Grinds ATS-34 and 154CM. **Prices:** $100 to $500. **Remarks:** Part-time maker; first knife sold in 1975. **Mark:** Last name.

PRITCHARD, RON, 613 Crawford Ave., Dixon, IL 61021/815-284-6005
Specialties: Plain and fancy working knives. **Patterns:** Variety of straight knives, locking folders, interframes and miniatures. **Technical:** Grinds 440C, 154CM and commercial Damascus. **Prices:** $100 to $200; some to $1,500. **Remarks:** Part-time maker; first knife sold in 1979. **Mark:** Name and city.

PROVENZANO, JOSEPH D., 3024 Ivy Place, Chalmette, LA 70043/504-279-3154
Specialties: Working straight knives and folders in standard patterns. **Patterns:** Hunters, Bowies, folders, camp and fishing knives. **Technical:** Grinds ATS-34, 440C, 154CM and Damascus. Hollow-grinds hunters. **Prices:** $75 to $300; some to $500. **Remarks:** Part-time maker; first knife sold in 1980. **Mark:** Joe-Pro.

PUGH, JIM, P.O. Box 711, Azle, TX 76020/817-444-2679; FAX: 817-444-5455
Specialties: Fancy/embellished limited editions by request. **Patterns:** 5- to 7-inch Bowies, Wildlife art pieces, hunters, daggers and fighters; some commemoratives. **Technical:** Grinds 440C and ATS-34; casts guards and buttcaps in bronze, synthetic gold, silver and 14K gold. Offers engraving, fancy file etching and leather sheaths for wildlife art pieces. Ivory and coco bolo handle material on limited editions. Designs animal head buttcaps and paws or bear claw guards; sterling silver heads and guards. **Prices:** $500 to $5,500; some to $20,000. **Remarks:** Full-time maker; first knife sold in 1970. **Mark:** Last name.

PULIS, VLADIMIR, Horna ves 4313125, 96701 KREMNICA, Slowak Rep./42-0857-757114
Specialties: Fancy and high art straight knives of his design. **Patterns:** Daggers and hunters. **Technical:** Forges Damask. All work done by hand. **Prices:** $250 to $3,000; some to $10,000. **Remarks:** Part-time maker; first knife sold in 1990. **Mark:** Initials in octagon.

PULLEN, MARTIN, 813 Broken Bow WHH, Granbury, TX 76049/817-573-1784
Specialties: Working straight knives; period pieces. **Patterns:** Fighters, Bowies and daggers; locking folders. **Technical:** Grinds D2, 440C, ATS-34 and 154CM. **Prices:** Start at $150. **Remarks:** Spare-time maker; first knife sold in 1978. **Mark:** Last name.

PULLIAM, MORRIS C., 560 Jeptha Knob Rd., Shelbyville, KY 40065/502-633-2261; FAX: 502-633-5294.
Specialties: Working knives; period pieces. **Patterns:** Hunters, tomahawks, buckskinners, Bowies. Makes slip-joint folders only by request. **Technical:** Forges 01, L6, 1095, 52100, 5160 and nickel-sheet and bar 1000 to 16,000 layer Damascus. **Prices:** $165 to $1,200. **Remarks:** Full-time maker; first knife sold in 1974. Doing business as Knob Hill Forge. **Mark:** Last name or last initial with JS.

PURSLEY, AARON, Box 1037, Big Sandy, MT 59520/406-378-3200
Specialties: Fancy working knives. **Patterns:** Locking folders, straight

hunters and daggers, personal wedding knives and letter openers. **Technical:** Grinds 01 and 440C; engraves. **Prices:** $300 to $600; some to $1,500. **Remarks:** Full-time maker; first knife sold in 1975. **Mark:** Initials connected with year.

PUTNAM, DONALD S., 590 Wolcott Hill Rd., Wethersfield, CT 06109/203-563-9718; FAX: 203-563-9718
Specialties: Working knives for the hunter and fisherman. **Patterns:** His design or to customer specs. **Technical:** Uses stock removal method, 01, W2, D2, ATS-34, 154CM, 440C and CPM REX 20; stainless steel Damascus on request. **Prices:** NA. **Remarks:** Full-time maker; first knife sold in 1985. **Mark:** Last name with a knife outline.

q

QUALITY CUSTOM KNIVES (See Fisher, Jay)

QUARTON, BARR, P.O. Box 4335, McCall, ID 83638/208-634-3641
Specialties: Plain and fancy working knives; period pieces. **Patterns:** Hunters, tantos and swords. **Technical:** Forges and grinds 154CM, ATS-34 and his own Damascus. **Prices:** $180 to $450; some to $4,500. **Remarks:** Full-time maker; first knife sold in 1978. Doing business as Barr Custom Knives and Deer Creek Forge. **Mark:** First name with bear logo.

QUATTLEBAUM, CRAIG, P.O. Box 983, Searcy, AR 72145-0983
Specialties: Traditional working straight knives, fancy Bowies and one-of-a-kind knives of his design or to customer specs. **Patterns:** Hunters, Bowies and fighters; period pieces. **Technical:** Forges 5168, 52100 and own Damascus. **Prices:** $100 to $600. **Remarks:** Part-time maker; first knife sold in 1988. **Mark:** Stylized initials.

r

RACHLIN, LESLIE S., 1200 W. Church St., Elmira, NY 14905/607-733-6889
Specialties: Classic and working/using straight knives and folders of his design. **Patterns:** Hunters, locking folders and utility/camp knives. **Technical:** Grinds 440C and Damascus. **Prices:** $110 to $200; some to $450. **Remarks:** Spare-time maker; first knife sold in 1989. Doing business as Tinkermade Knives. **Mark:** Stamped initials or Tinkermade, city and state.

RADOS, JERRY F., P.O. Box 531, Grant Park, IL 60940/815-472-3350; FAX: 815-472-3944
Specialties: Deluxe period pieces. **Patterns:** Hunters, fighters, locking folders, daggers and camp knives. **Technical:** Forges and grinds his own Damascus which he sells commercially; makes pattern-welded Turkish Damascus. **Prices:** Start at $900. **Remarks:** Full-time maker; first knife sold in 1981. **Mark:** Last name.

RAFTER KK CUSTOM KNIVES (See Kimsey, Kevin)

RAGSDALE, JAMES D., 3002 Arabian Woods Dr., Lithonia, GA 30038/404-482-6739
Specialties: Fancy and embellished working knives of his design or to customer specs. **Patterns:** Hunters, folders and fighters. **Technical:** Grinds 440C, ATS-34 and A2. **Prices:** $100 to $350; some to $800. **Remarks:** Full-time maker; first knife sold in 1984. **Mark:** Initials connected with fish symbol.

RAHN, JOHN, 323 Concordia Cres, Waterloo, Ont., N2K 2M2 CANADA/519-886-7109
Specialties: Fancy and fantasy straight knives of his design. **Patterns:** Boots, daggers and fighters. **Technical:** Flat-grinds 440C, ATS-34 and 420. Hand files; uses natural handle materials including semi-precious and precious stone inlays. Heat-treats. **Prices:** $200 to $1,000; some to $2,000. **Remarks:** Part-time maker; first knife sold in 1990. **Mark:** First initial, last name.

RAINVILLE, RICHARD, 126 Cockle Hill Rd., Salem, CT 06420/203-859-2776
Specialties: Traditional working straight knives. **Patterns:** Outdoor knives, including fishing knives. **Technical:** Grinds 01, L6, 400C, ATS-34, 154CM. Custom fits handles. **Prices:** $85 to $600. **Remarks:** Part-time maker; first knife sold in 1982. **Mark:** Name, city, state in oval logo.

RALPH, DARREL, 7032 E. Livingston Ave., Reynoldsburg, OH 43068/614-577-1040, 614-241-9793 (Pager)
Specialties: Fancy, high-art, high-tech straight knives and folders of his design and to customer specs; unique mechanisms, some disassemble. **Patterns:** Daggers, fighters and swords. **Technical:** Forges tool steels, nickel and high carbon. Uses mokume and Damascus; mosaics and special patterns. Engraves and heat-treats. Prefers pearl, ivory and abolone handle material; uses stones and jewels. **Prices:** $250 to $2,500; some to $10,000. **Remarks:** Full-time maker; first knife sold in 1986. Doing business as Briar Knives. **Mark:** BCM.

RAMBO, J.T., 113 Weber T.R.V., Rock Springs, WY 82901/307-382-6912
Specialties: Working straight knives and folders of his design or to customer specs. **Patterns:** Hunters, Bowies, fighters, skinners, fillets and sword canes. **Technical:** Stock removal method. Grinds 440C and commercial Damascus; uses other steels on request. Prefers natural handle materials. **Prices:** $150 to $1,000; some to $2,500. **Remarks:** First knife sold in 1986. **Mark:** First and middle initials, last name logo.

RAMEY, MARSHALL F., P.O. Box 2589, West Helena, AR 72390/501-572-7436, 501-572-6245
Specialties: Traditional working knives. **Patterns:** Designs military combat knives; makes butterfly folders, camp knives and miniatures. **Technical:** Grinds D2 and 440C. **Prices:** $100 to $500. **Remarks:** Full-time maker; first knife sold in 1978. **Mark:** Name with ram's head.

RANDALL MADE KNIVES, P.O. Box 1988, Orlando, FL 32802/407-855-8075
Specialties: Working straight knives. **Patterns:** Hunters, fighters and Bowies. **Technical:** Forges and grinds 01 and 440B. **Prices:** $65 to $250; some to $450. **Remarks:** Full-time maker; first knife sold in 1937. **Mark:** Randall, city and state in scimitar logo.

RANKL, CHRISTIAN, Possenhofenerstr. 33, 81476 München, GERMANY/089-7594442; FAX: 089-7594442
Specialties: Tail-lock knives. **Patterns:** Fighters, hunters and locking folders. **Technical:** Grinds ATS-34, 4034 and stainless Damascus by F. Schneider. **Prices:** $450 to $950; some to $2,000. **Remarks:** Full-time maker; first knife sold in 1989. **Mark:** Electrochemical etching on blade.

RAPP, STEVEN J., 2269 Bonniebrook Dr. #2, Salt Lake City, UT 84118/801-968-6620
Specialties: Fancy straight hunters; period pieces. **Patterns:** Gold Rush-era cutlery. **Technical:** Grinds 440C and Damascus bars. **Prices:** $500. **Remarks:** Part-time maker; first knife sold in 1981. **Mark:** Name and state.

RAPPAZZO, RICHARD, 142 Dunsbach Ferry Rd., Cohoes, NY 12047/518-783-6843
Specialties: Damascus locking folders and straight knives. **Patterns:** Folders, dirks, fighters and tantos in original and traditional designs. **Technical:** Hand-forges all blades; specializes in Damascus; uses only natural handle materials. **Prices:** $400 to $1,500. **Remarks:** Part-time maker; first knife sold in 1985. **Mark:** Name, date, serial number.

RARDON, A.D., 1589 S.E. Price Dr., Polo, MO 64671/816-354-2330
Specialties: Working knives, miniatures, automatics and folders. **Patterns:** Hunters, buckskinners, Bowies, miniatures and daggers. **Technical:** Grinds 01, D2, 440C and ATS-34. **Prices:** $100 to $1,500; some higher. **Remarks:** Part-time maker; first knife sold in 1954. **Mark:** Name, address in running fox logo.

RARDON, ARCHIE F., Rt. 1, Box 79, Polo, MO 64671/816-354-2330
Specialties: Working knives. **Patterns:** Hunters, Bowies and minia-tures. **Technical:** Grinds 01, D2, 440C, ATS-34, cable and Damascus. **Prices:** $50 to $500. **Remarks:** Part-time maker. **Mark:** Name and address in razor-back hog logo.

RATTLER BRAND KNIVES (See Selvidio, Ralph J.)

RAVEN FORGE (See Parler, Thomas O'Neil)

RAY, ALAN W., P.O. Box 479, Lovelady, TX 75851/409-636-2301
Specialties: Working straight knives and folders of his design. **Patterns:** Hunters, camp knives, folders, steak knives and carving sets. **Technical:** Forges L6 and 5160 for straight knives; grinds D2 and 440C for folders and kitchen cutlery. **Prices:** $200 to $500. **Remarks:** Full-time maker; first knife sold in 1989. **Mark:** Stylized initials.

RAYMOND, DONALD, P.O. Box 1141, Groveton, TX 75845/409-642-1707
Specialties: Traditional working and using straight knives and folders of his design and to customer specs. **Patterns:** Fighters, hunters, kitchen knives and locking folders. **Technical:** Grinds 440C and D2; forges his own Damascus. **Prices:** $150 to $550; some to $850. **Remarks:** Full-time maker; first knife sold in 1988. Doing business as DR Knives. **Mark:** Stylized initials.

RAYMOND, MARY JANE, P.O. Box 1141, Groveton, TX 75845/408-642-1707
Specialties: Traditional working and using straight knives and folders of her design. **Patterns:** Hunters, locking folders and slip-joint folders. **Technical:** Grinds 440C, D2 and Donald Raymond Damascus. Makes sheaths. **Prices:** $150 to $400; some to $600. **Remarks:** Full-time maker; first knife sold in 1989. Doing business as M.J.R. Knives. **Mark:** Initials or name.

RAZAVI-MEHR (See Farid)

R.D. CUSTOM KNIVES (See Miller, R.D.)

RECE, CHARLES V., 1949 E. Main St., Albemarle, NC 28001/704-982-1178; FAX: 704-982-1178
Specialties: Bowies, hunters and presentation knives. **Technical:** Grinds ATS-34, D2 and 440C. Scrimshawed handles are standard. **Prices:** $150 to $400. **Remarks:** Limited-production maker; first knife sold in 1986. Doing business as Uwharrie Rattler Knives and Wildwood Studios. **Mark:** Engraved timber rattler.

REDDIEX, BILL, 27 Galway Ave., Palmerston North, NEW ZEALAND/06-357-0383; FAX: 06-358-2910
Specialties: Collector-grade working straight knives. **Patterns:** Traditional-style Bowies and drop-point hunters. **Technical:** Grinds 440C, D2 and 01; offers variety of grinds and finishes. **Prices:** $130 to $750. **Remarks:** Full-time maker; first knife sold in 1980. **Mark:** Last name around kiwi bird logo.

REDUCED REALITY (See Heasman, H.G.)

REE, DAVID, 816 Main St., Van Buren, AR 72956/501-474-3198
Specialties: Fancy working knives. **Patterns:** Hunters, locking folders and boots. **Technical:** Grinds 01, D2 and 440C; prefers exotic and unusual handle materials. **Prices:** $125 to $400; some to $900. **Remarks:** Full-time maker; first knife sold in 1982. Doing business as Old Town Cutlery. **Mark:** Last name.

REED, DAVE, Box 132, Brimfield, MA 01010/413-245-3661
Specialties: Traditional styles. Makes knives from chains, rasps, gears, etc. **Patterns:** Bush swords, hunters, working minis, camp and utility knives. **Technical:** Forges 1075 and his own Damascus. **Prices:** Start at $50. **Remarks:** Part-time maker; first knife sold in 1970. **Mark:** Initials.

REED, DEL, 13765 SW Parkway, Beaverton, OR 97005
Specialties: Unusual configurations. **Patterns:** Swing-blade knives.

Technical: Grinds stainless steel. **Prices:** $100 to $125. **Remarks:** First knife sold in 1988. **Mark:** ORION.

REEVE, CHRIS, 6147 Corporal Lane, Boise, ID 83704/208-375-0367
Specialties: Strongest working folder on the market; one-piece utility/military fixed blades. **Patterns:** Working and art folders; variety of fixed-blade shapes in one-piece design. Availability of art pieces very limited. **Technical:** Grinds folder blades of ATS-34, mostly titanium handles; A2 for fixed blades. Art knives ATS-34 or Damascus blades, titanium or exotic handle material. **Prices:** $165 to $800; some to $4,000. **Remarks:** Full-time maker; first knife sold in 1982. **Mark:** Initials connected.

REEVES, JAMES GARY, 416 Delta Ct., Gardondale, AL 35071/205-631-4861
Specialties: Working straight knives in his design and standard patterns. **Patterns:** Bowies, fighters and hunters. **Technical:** Grinds ATS-34; forges and grinds 5160. **Prices:** $75 to $450. **Remarks:** Part-time maker; first knife sold in 1987. **Mark:** First and middle initials, last name, city, state.

REEVES, WINFRED M., P.O. Box 300, West Union, SC 29696/803-638-6121
Specialties: Working straight knives; some elaborate pieces. **Patterns:** Hunters, tantos and fishing knives. **Technical:** Grinds D2, 440C and ATS-34. Does not solder joints; does not use buffer unless requested. **Prices:** $75 to $150; some to $300. **Remarks:** Part-time maker; first knife sold in 1975. **Mark:** Last name, Walhalla, state.

REGGIO JR., SIDNEY J., P.O. Box 851, Sun, LA 70463/504-886-5886
Specialties: Miniature classic and fancy straight knives of his design or in standard patterns. **Patterns:** Fighters, hunters and utility/camp knives. **Technical:** Grinds 440C, ATS-34 and commercial Damascus. Engraves; scrimshaws; offers filework. Hollow grinds most blades. Prefers natural handle material. Offers handmade sheaths. **Prices:** $85 to $250; some to $500. **Remarks:** Part-time maker; first knife sold in 1988. Doing business as Sterling Workshop. **Mark:** Initials.

REH, BILL, 7315 Lolo Creek Rd., Lolo, MT 59847/406-273-2582
Specialties: Traditional and working/using straight knives of his design. **Patterns:** Boots, daggers and hunters. **Technical:** Grinds 440C and ATS-34. **Prices:** $150 to $225; some higher. **Remarks:** Spare-time maker; first knife sold in 1982. Doing business as Reh Custom Knives. **Mark:** Last name in sun-ray logo.

REMINGTON, DAVID W., 3608-17998 Syble Rd., Lincoln, AR 72744/501-846-3526
Specialties: Fancy and traditional straight knives of his design and to customer specs. **Patterns:** Bowies, daggers and hunters. **Technical:** Grinds ATS-34, A2 and D2. Makes own twist and random-pattern Damascus. Wholesale D2, A2, stag and ossic sheephorn. Rope and thorn pattern filework; tapered tangs; heat-treats. **Prices:** $65 to $250; some to $1,000. **Remarks:** Part-time maker; first knife sold in 1991. **Mark:** First and last name, Custom.

RENNER, TERRY LEE, P.O. Box 15063, Bradenton, FL 34209/813-798-3989
Specialties: Fancy working straight knives and folders. **Patterns:** Hunters, game sets, fillets and miniatures. **Technical:** Grinds 440C, D2 and 01. Folders have unique integral blade lock, lightest carry weight. Deep-relief carved stag handles. **Prices:** $95 to $450; some higher. **Remarks:** Part-time maker; first knife sold in 1975. Doing business as Firepoint Knives. **Mark:** Initials with star.

REPKE, MIKE (See Neering, Walt and Repke, Mike)

REVERDY, PIERRE, 21 AV Victor Hugo, 26100 Romans, FRANCE/33-75-05-10-15; FAX: 33-75-02-28-40
Specialties: One-of-a-kind knives. **Patterns:** Daggers, Bowies, hunters and other large patterns. **Technical:** Forges his Damascus and "poetique Damascus"; works with his own EDM machine to create any kind of pattern inside the steel with his own touch. **Prices:** $200 to $40,000. **Remarks:** Full-time maker; first knife sold in 1986. **Mark:** Initials connected.

REVISHVILI, ZAZA, 125438 Moscow N29 P.O. Box, RUSSIA

REXROAT, KIRK, 527 Sweetwater Circle, Box 224, Wright, WY 82732/307-464-0166
Specialties: Traditional working/using straight knives and folders of his design and to customer specs. **Patterns:** Bowies, hunters, locking folders, utility/camp knives. **Technical:** Grinds 440C; forges cable and layered Damascus; triple quenches 52100. Offers tapered tangs and dove-tailed guards. **Prices:** $100 to $250; some to $800. **Remarks:** Part-time maker; first knife sold in 1984. Doing business as Rexroat Knives. **Mark:** First initial, last name, city, state.

REYNOLDS, DAVE, Rt. 2, Box 36, Harrisville, WV 26362/304-643-2889
Specialties: Working straight knives of his design. **Patterns:** Bowies, kitchen and utility knives. **Technical:** Grinds and forges L6, 1095 and 440C. Heat-treats. **Prices:** $50 to $85; some to $175. **Remarks:** Full-time maker; first knife sold in 1980. Doing business as Terra-Gladius Knives. **Mark:** None; serial number on special orders only.

REYNOLDS, JOHN C., #2 Andover, HC77, Gillette, WY 82716/307-682-6076
Specialties: Working knives, some fancy. **Patterns:** Hunters, Bowies, tomahawks and buckskinners; some folders. **Technical:** Grinds D2, 440C and commerical Damascus. Scrimshaws. **Prices:** $100 to $320; some to $3,000. **Remarks:** Spare-time maker; first knife sold in 1969. **Mark:** Last name.

RHEA, DAVID, Rt. 1, Box 272, Lynnville, TN 38472/615-363-5993
Specialties: High-art fantasy knives. **Patterns:** Fighters, Bowies, survival knives and locking folders. **Technical:** Grinds D2, 440C, 154CM and Damascus. Embellishes; offers precious stones, metals and ivory. **Prices:** $300 to $2,000 and higher. **Remarks:** Part-time maker; first knife sold in 1982. **Mark:** Last name.

RHO, NESTOR LORENZO, Primera Junta 589, Junin (6000), Buenos Aires, ARGENTINA/(0362) 32247/21717
Specialties: Classic and fancy straight knives of his design. **Patterns:** Bowies, fighters and hunters. **Technical:** Grinds 420C, 440C and 1050. Offers semi-precious stones on handles, acid etching on blades and blade engraving. **Prices:** $60 to $300 some to $1,200. **Remarks:** Full-time maker; first knife sold in 1975. **Mark:** Name.

RHODES, JAMES D., 205 Woodpoint Ave., Hagerstown, MD 21740/301-739-2657
Specialties: Traditional working and using straight knives of his design. **Patterns:** Bowies, fighters, hunters and kitchen knives. **Technical:** Forges 5160, 1085 and 9260; makes own Damascus. Hard edges, soft backs, dead soft tangs. Heat-treats. **Prices:** $150 to $350. **Remarks:** Part-time maker. **Mark:** Last name, JS.

RIAL, DOUGLAS, Rt. 2, Box 117A, Greenfield, TN 38230/901-235-3994
Specialties: Working knives to customer specs; period pieces. **Patterns:** Hunters, fighters, boots, locking folders, slip-joints and miniatures. **Technical:** Grinds D2, 440C and 154CM. **Prices:** $60 to $100; some to $250. **Remarks:** Spare-time maker; first knife sold in 1978. **Mark:** Name and city.

RICE, ADRIENNE, P.O. Box 252, Lopez Island, WA 98261
Specialties: Marine-oriented knives; working straight knives. **Patterns:** Full line of working knives including skinners, fillets, rigging knives and kitchen knives. Occasionally makes fighters, tantos, short swords and primitive knives. **Technical:** Grinds ATS-34, D2 and 01; forges occasionally. **Prices:** $135 to $225. **Remarks:** Full-time maker; first knife sold in 1981. Doing business as Madrona Knives. **Mark:** Initials connected in Madrona logo with date.

RICHARD, RON, 4875 Calaveras Ave., Fremont, CA 94538/510-796-9767
Specialties: High-tech working straight knives of his design. **Patterns:** Bowies, swords and locking folders. **Technical:** Forges and grinds ATS-34, 154CM and 440V. All folders have dead-bolt button locks. **Prices:** $650 to $850; some to $1,400. **Remarks:** Full-time maker; first knife sold in 1968. **Mark:** Full name.

RICHARDSON JR., PERCY, P.O. Box 4, Milam, TX 75959/409-625-3415
Specialties: Traditional and working straight knives and folders in customer specs and standard patterns. **Patterns:** Bowies, daggers, hunters, locking folders, slip-joints and utility/camp knives. **Technical:** Grinds ATS-34, 440C and D2. **Prices:** $125 to $600; some to $1,800. **Remarks:** Full-time maker; first knife sold in 1990. Doing business as Lone Star Custom Knives. **Mark:** Lone Star with stylized last initial.

RICHTER FORGE (See Richter, John C.)

RICHTER, JOHN C., 932 Bowling Green Trail, Chesapeake, VA 23320
Specialties: Hand-forged knives in original patterns. **Patterns:** Hunters, fighters, utility knives and other belt knives, folders, swords. **Technical:** Hand-forges high carbon and his own Damascus; makes mokume gane. **Prices:** $75 to $1,500. **Remarks:** Part-time maker. **Mark:** Richter Forge.

RICHTER, SCOTT, 31 Broadway, Watertown, MA 02172

RICKE, DAVE, 1209 Adams, West Bend, WI 53095/414-334-5739
Specialties: Working knives; period pieces. **Patterns:** Hunters, boots, Bowies; locking folders and slip-joints. **Technical:** Grinds ATS-34, A2, 440C and 154CM. **Prices:** $75 to $260; some to $1,200. **Remarks:** Part-time maker; first knife sold in 1976. **Mark:** Last name.

RIEGER, CHRIS J., Box 142, Winfield, B.C. V0H 2C0, CANADA/604-766-4000

RIETVELD, BERTIE, P.O. Box 53, Magaliesburg 2805, SOUTH AFRICA/27142-771294
Specialties: Damascus fighters, art daggers and button-lock folders. **Technical:** Damascus, titanium, gold inlay and colored stainless steel. **Prices:** $350 to $2,000. **Mark:** Elephant with last name.

RIGNEY JR., WILLIE, 191 Colson Dr., Bronston, KY 42518/606-679-4227
Specialties: High-tech period pieces and fancy working knives. **Patterns:** Fighters, boots, daggers and push knives. **Technical:** Grinds 440C and 154CM; buys Damascus. Most knives are embellished. **Prices:** $150 to $1,500; some to $10,000. **Remarks:** Full-time maker; first knife sold in 1978. **Mark:** First initial, last name.

RIJSWIJK, AAD VAN, Oberonweg 284, 3208 PG Spijkenisse, HOLLAND/(0)1880-40334; FAX: (0)1880-40334
Specialties: High-art interframe folders of his design and in standard patterns. **Patterns:** Hunters and locking folders. **Technical:** ATS-34. Uses semi-precious stones. Handle materials include ivory, mammoth ivory, iron wood. Offers hand-made sheaths. **Prices:** $400 to $1,200; some to $2,000. **Remarks:** Full-time maker; first knife sold in 1993. **Mark:** NA.

RINGING CIRCLE, THE (See Fitzgerald, Dennis M.)

RINKES, SIEGFRIED, Am Sportpl 2, D 91459 Markterlbach, GERMANY

RIPPY, ROBERT, P.O. Box 891613, Houston, TX 77289/713-333-5843
Specialties: Combat, survival and special operations knives. **Patterns:** Hunters, fighters, utility/camp knives. **Technical:** Grinds ATS-34 and crucible S7. Embellishes. **Prices:** $300 to $750; some higher. **Remarks:** Full-time makers; first knife sold in 1980. **Mark:** Stylized last initial.

RIZZI, RUSSELL J., 6 King Arthur's Ct., E. Setauket, NY 11733/516-689-2698
Specialties: Fancy working and using straight knives and folders of his design or to customer specs. **Patterns:** Hunters, locking folders and fighters. **Technical:** Grinds 440C, D2 and commercial Damascus. **Prices:** $150 to $750; some to $2,500. **Remarks:** Part-time maker; first knife sold in 1990. **Mark:** Last name, Long Island, NY.

RL CUSTOM KNIVES (See Lambert, Ronald S.)

ROATH, DEAN, 3050 Winnipeg Dr., Baton Rouge, LA 70819/504-272-5562
Specialties: Classic working straight knives; specifically turkey hunting knives. **Patterns:** Hunters, boating/sailing and trail knives. **Technical:** Grinds 440C and ATS-34. **Prices:** $150 to $400; some to $1,500. **Remarks:** Part-time maker; first knife sold in 1978. **Mark:** Name, city and state.

ROBBINS, HOWARD P., 875 Rams Horn Rd., Moraine Rt., Estes Park, CO 80517/970-586-8755
Specialties: High-tech working knives with clean designs, some fancy. **Patterns:** Folders, hunters and camp knives. **Technical:** Grinds 440C and ATS-34. Heat-treats; likes mirror finishes. Offers leatherwork. **Prices:** $100 to $500; some to $1,000. **Remarks:** Full-time maker; first knife sold in 1982. **Mark:** Name, city and state.

ROBERTS, CHUCK, 5004 W. 92nd Ave. #207, Westminster, CO 80030/303-650-4563
Specialties: California knives. **Patterns:** Bowies, daggers and hunters. **Technical:** Grinds 440C, 5160, Damascus and ATS-34. Handles made of stag, ivory or mother-of-pearl; fittings made of nickel or sterling silver. **Prices:** Start at $350. **Remarks:** Full-time maker. **Mark:** Last initial or last name.

ROBERTS, GEORGE A., 93 Lewes Blvd., Apt. 207B, Whitehorse Yukon Territories Y1A3J4, CANADA/519-294-0267; FAX: 519-294-6391
Specialties: Bowies with special features not offered before. **Patterns:** Bowies, hunters and liner locks. **Technical:** Grinds 440C, Boye Dendritic, 01, mild Damascus and 440V. Liner lock liners are titanium. Etches, engraves and offers fancy filework on blades; scrimshands and carves handles; makes leather sheaths. Uses fossilized mastadon ivory. **Prices:** $80 to $225; some to $500. **Remarks:** Full-time maker; first knife sold in 1986. Doing business as Bandit Blades. **Mark:** Bandit.

ROBERTS, MICHAEL, 605 Oakwood Dr., Clinton, MS 39056/601-924-3154
Specialties: Working and using knives in standard patterns and to customer specs. **Patterns:** Hunters, Bowies and fighters. **Technical:** Forges 5160, 01, 1095 and his own Damascus. Uses only natural handle materials. **Prices:** $145 to $500; some to $1,100. **Remarks:** Part-time maker; first knife sold in 1988. **Mark:** Last name.

ROBINSON, CHARLES (DICKIE), P.O. Box 221, Vega, TX 79092/806-267-2625
Specialties: Classic and working/using knives. **Patterns:** Bowies, daggers, fighters, hunters and camp knives. **Technical:** Forges 01, 5160, 52100 and his own Damascus. **Prices:** $125 to $850; some to $2,500. **Remarks:** Part-time maker; first knife sold in 1988. Doing business as Robinson Knives. **Mark:** Last name, JS.

ROBINSON, REX, 10531 Poe St., Leesburg, FL 34788

ROCHFORD, MICHAEL R., Trollhaugen Ski Area, 2232 100th Ave., Dresser, WI 54009/715-755-3520
Specialties: Working straight knives in standard patterns. **Patterns:** Bowies, fishing and camp knives. **Technical:** Grinds and forges W2, 440C, 154CM and his Damascus. **Prices:** $100 to $500; some to $800. **Remarks:** Part-time maker; first knife sold in 1984. **Mark:** Name.

ROCKY MOUNTAIN KNIVES (See Conklin, George L.)

ROE JR., FRED D., 4005 Granada Dr., Huntsville, AL 35802/205-881-6847
Specialties: Highly finished working knives of his design; period pieces. **Patterns:** Hunters, fighters and survival knives; locking folders; specialty designs like divers' knives. **Technical:** Grinds 154CM, ATS-34 and Damascus. Field-tests all blades. **Prices:** $125 to $250; some to $2,000. **Remarks:** Part-time maker; first knife sold in 1980. **Mark:** Last name.

ROGERS JR., ROBERT P., 3979 South Main St., Acworth, GA 30101/404-974-9982
Specialties: Traditional working knives. **Patterns:** Hunters, 4-inch trailing-points. **Technical:** Grinds D2, 154CM and ATS-34; likes ironwood and ivory Micarta. **Prices:** $65 to $85; some to $125. **Remarks:** Spare-time maker; first knife sold in 1975. **Mark:** Name.

ROGERS, RODNEY, 602 Osceola St., Wildwood, FL 34785/904-748-6114
Specialties: Traditional straight knives and folders. **Patterns:** Hunters, skinners, fighters and tactical knives. **Technical:** Flat-grinds ATS-34 and Damascus. Prefers natural materials. **Prices:** $100 to $1,200. **Remarks:** Full-time maker; first knife sold in 1986. **Mark:** Last name, Handmade.

ROCHMANS, MARK, 607 Virginia Ave., LaGrange, GA 30240/ 706-884-7040
Specialties: Classic and traditional knives of his design. **Patterns:** Bowies, daggers and fighters. **Technical:** Grinds ATS-34, D2 and 440C. **Prices:** $150 to $500. **Remarks:** Part-time maker; first knife sold in 1984. Doing business as LaGrange Knife. **Mark:** Last name and/or LaGrange Knife.

ROHN, FRED, W7615 Clemetson Rd., Coeur d'Alene, ID 83814/208-667-0774
Specialties: Working straight knives, some unusual. **Patterns:** Hunters, fighters, a unique Bowie design and locking folders. **Technical:** Grinds 440C and 154CM; stainless steel pins, bolsters and guards on all knives. **Prices:** $65 to $200; some to $450 and higher. **Remarks:** Part-time maker. **Mark:** Name in logo and serial number.

ROLLERT, STEVE, P.O. Box 65, Keenesburg, CO 80643-0065/303-732-4858
Specialties: Highly finished working knives. **Patterns:** Variety of straight knives; locking folders and slip-joints. **Technical:** Forges and grinds W2, 1095, ATS-34 and his pattern-welded, cable Damascus and nickel Damascus. **Prices:** $300 to $1,000; some to $3,000. **Remarks:** Full-time maker; first knife sold in 1980. Doing business as Dove Knives. **Mark:** Last name in script.

ROSA, PEDRO GULLHERME TELES, R. das Magnolias, 45, CECAP, Presidente Prudente, SP-19065-410, BRAZIL/0182-271769
Specialties: Using straight knives and folders to customer specs; some high art. **Patterns:** Fighters, Bowies and daggers. **Technical:** Grinds and forges D6, 440C, high carbon steels and Damascus. **Prices:** $60 to $400. **Remarks:** Full-time maker; first knife sold in 1991. **Mark:** A hammer over "Hammer."

ROSS, D.L., 22 Earnscleugh Rd., Alexandra, NZ
Specialties: Hunters, working knives. **Patterns:** Plain using knives. **Technical:** Grinds 440C. **Prices:** $80 to $240; some to $400. **Remarks:** Full-time maker; first knife sold in 1988. **Mark:** Last name.

ROSS, STEPHEN, 534 Remington Dr., Evanston, WY 82930/307-789-7104
Specialties: Working straight knives and folders; some fantasy pieces. **Patterns:** Combat and survival knives, hunters, boots and folders. **Technical:** Grinds ATS-34, D2 and 440C. Offers Kydex sheaths, checkering on knife handles, integral guards and variety of grinds. **Prices:** $160 to $3,000. **Remarks:** Part-time maker; first knife sold in 1971. **Mark:** Last name.

ROSS, TIM, 3239 Oliver Rd., RR #17, Thunder Bay, ON P7B 6C2, CANADA/807-935-2667

Specialties: Fancy working knives of his design. **Patterns:** Fishing and hunting knives, Bowies, daggers and miniatures. **Technical:** Uses D2, Stellite 6K and 440C; forges 52100 and Damascus. Makes antler handles and sheaths; has supply of whale teeth and moose antlers for trade. Prefers natural materials only. Wife Katherine scrimshaws. **Prices:** $100 to $350; some to $2,100. **Remarks:** Part-time maker; first knife sold in 1975. **Mark:** Last name stamped on tang.

ROTELLA, RICHARD A., 643—75th St., Niagara Falls, NY 14304
Specialties: Working knives of his design. **Patterns:** Various fishing, hunting and utility knives; folders. **Technical:** Grinds ATS-34. Prefers hand-rubbed finishes. **Prices:** $65 to $450; some to $900. **Remarks:** Spare-time maker; first knife sold in 1977. **Mark:** Name and city in stylized waterfall logo.

ROWE, STEWART G., 8-18 Coreen Court, Karana Downs, Mt. Crosby, Brisbane 4306, AUSTRALIA/07-201-0906
Specialties: Designer knives—reproduction of ancient weaponry, traditional Japanese tantos and edged tools. **Patterns:** Futuristic knives and weapons. **Technical:** Forges W1, W2, D2; creates own Tamahagne steel and composite pattern-welded billets. **Prices:** $300 to $11,000. **Remarks:** Full-time maker; first knife sold in 1981. **Mark:** Kogatana.

RP KNIVES (See Parrish, Robert)

RUA, GARY (WOLF), 541 Osborn St., Fall River, MA 02724
Specialties: Working knives of his design; 18th- and 19th-century period pieces. **Patterns:** Bowies, hunters, fighters, buckskinners and patch knives. **Technical:** Forges 5160, 1095, old files; uses only natural handle materials. **Prices:** $100 to $500; some to $1,000. **Remarks:** Part-time maker. Doing business as Harvest Moon Forge. **Mark:** Last name.

RUANA KNIFE WORKS, Box 520, Bonner, MT 59823/406-258-5368
Specialties: Working knives and period pieces. **Patterns:** Variety of straight knives. **Technical:** Forges 5160 chrome alloy for Bowies and 1095. **Prices:** $60 to $240; some to $300 and higher. **Remarks:** Full-time maker; first knife sold in 1938. **Mark:** Name.

RUBLEY, JAMES A., 5765 N. 500 W., Angola, IN 46703/219-833-1255
Specialties: Working American knives and collectibles for hunters, buckskinners and re-enactment groups from Pre-Revolutionary War through the Civil War. **Patterns:** Anything authentic, barring folders. **Technical:** Iron fittings, natural materials; forges files. **Prices:** $175 to $2,500. **Remarks:** Museum consultant and blacksmith for two decades. Offers classes in beginning, intermediate and advanced traditional knifemaking. **Mark:** Lightning bolt.

RUBY MOUNTAIN KNIVES (See Schirmer, Mike)

RUPERT, BOB, 301 Harshaville Rd., Clinton, PA 15026/412-573-4569
Specialties: Fantasy and traditional straight knives of his design. **Patterns:** Hunters, slip-joint and primitive folders and utility/camp knives. **Technical:** Forges 1095 and 01; grinds 440C. Offers pattern file work, some crown gargoyle carving and hand-sewn sheaths. **Prices:** $75 to $150; some to $500. **Remarks:** Part-time maker; first knife sold in 1980. **Mark:** Last initial etched or stamped.

RUPLE, WILLIAM H., P.O. Box 370, Charlotte, TX 78011/210-277-1371
Specialties: Traditional working and using straight knives and folders in standard patterns. **Patterns:** Hunters, locking folders and slip-joint folders. **Technical:** Grinds 440C, ATS-34 and D2. Offers filework on blade and spring. **Prices:** $100 to $300; some to $500. **Remarks:** Full-time maker; first knife sold in 1988. **Mark:** Last name.

RUSSELL, A.G., 1705 Hwy. 71 N., Springdale, AR 72764/501-751-7341
Specialties: Morseth knives; contemporary working knives. **Patterns:** Hunters and Bowies; personal utility knives in Morseth line, drop-points and boots in Russell line. **Technical:** Laminated blades in Morseth line; modern stainless steel in Russell line; classic shapes. **Prices:** Moderate. **Remarks:** Old name still at work. Doing business as Morseth Sports Equip. Co. **Mark:** Morseth or first and middle initials, last name.

directory

RUSSELL, MICK, 4 Rossini Rd., Pari Park, Port Elizabeth 6070, SOUTH AFRICA
Specialties: Art knives. **Patterns:** Working and collectible bird, trout and hunting knives, defense knives and folders. **Technical:** Grinds D2, 440C, ATS-34 and Damascus. Offers mirror or satin finishes. Uses nickel silver, 303 stainless and titanium fittings and a wide variety of African hardwoods; ivory, buffalo and antelope horn and bone handle materials. **Prices:** $100 and up. **Remarks:** Full-time maker; first knife sold in 1986. **Mark:** Stylized rhino with initials.

RUSSELL, TOM, 6500 New Liberty Rd., Jacksonville, AL 36265/205-492-7866
Specialties: Straight working knives of his design or to customer specs. **Patterns:** Hunters, folders, fighters, skinners, Bowies and utility knives. **Technical:** Grinds D2, 440C and ATS-34; offers filework. **Prices:** $75 to $225. **Remarks:** Part-time maker; first knife sold in 1987. Full-time tool and die maker. **Mark:** Last name with tulip stamp.

RUST, CHARLES C., P.O. Box 374, Palermo, CA 95968/916-533-9389
Specialties: Working knives, some fancy; period pieces. **Patterns:** Hunters, Bowies, buckskinners, sets. **Technical:** All work done by hand; low production. **Prices:** $125 to $2,000; some to $3,500. **Remarks:** Full-time maker; first knife sold in 1972. Not currently taking orders. **Mark:** Rustway in logo.

RUSTWAY (See Rust, Charles C.)

RV KNIVES (See Vunk, Robert)

RYAN, C.O., 902-A Old Wormley Creek Rd., Yorktown, VA 23692/804-898-7797
Specialties: Working/using knives. **Patterns:** Hunters, kitchen knives, locking folders. **Technical:** Grinds 440C and ATS-34. **Prices:** $45 to $130; some to $450. **Remarks:** Part-time maker; first knife sold in 1980. **Mark:** Name.

RYAN, J.C., Rt. 5, Box 183-A, Lexington, VA 24450/703-348-5014

RYBERG, GOTE, Faltgatan 2, S-562 00 Norrahammar, SWEDEN, 4636-61678

RYDER, BEN M., P.O. Box 133, Copperhill, TN 37317/615-496-2750
Specialties: Working/using straight knives of his design and to customer specs. **Patterns:** Fighters, hunters, utility/camp knives. **Technical:** Grinds 440C, ATS-34, D2, commercial Damascus. **Prices:** $75 to $400. **Remarks:** Part-time maker; first knife sold in 1992. **Mark:** Full name in double butterfly logo.

S

SAINDON, R. BILL, 11 Highland View Rd., Claremont, NH 03743/603-542-9418
Specialties: Folders for work or collecting. **Patterns:** Lockbacks and liner locks of his design or to customer specs. **Technical:** Forges high carbon steels and all tool steel Damascus. Prefers natural handle material. **Prices:** $200 to $1,000; some to $2,000. **Remarks:** Full-time maker; first knife sold in 1981. Doing business as Daynia Forge. **Mark:** Sun logo.

SAKMAR, MIKE, 1670 Morley, Rochester, MI 48307/810-852-6775
Specialties: Fancy and working straight knives of his design and to customer specs. **Patterns:** Bowies, fighters, hunters and integrals. **Technical:** Grinds ATS-34, Damascus and high-carbon tool steels. Uses mostly natural handle materials—elephant ivory, walrus, ivory stag, wildwood, oosic, etc. **Prices:** $150 to $2,500; some to $4,000. **Remarks:** Full-time maker; first knife sold in 1990. **Mark:** Last name, year.

SALAMANDER ARMOURY (See Hrisoulas, Jim)

SAKAKIBARA, MASAKI, 20-8 Sakuragaoka, 2-Chome Setagaya-ku, Tokyo 156, JAPAN/03-420-0375

SALLEY, JOHN D., 3965 Frederick-Ginghamsburg Rd., Tipp City, OH 45371/513-698-4588
Specialties: Fancy working knives and art pieces. **Patterns:** Hunters, fighters, daggers and some swords. **Technical:** Grinds ATS-34, 12C27 and W2; buys Damascus. **Prices:** $85 to $1,000; some to $6,000. **Remarks:** Part-time maker; first knife sold in 1979. **Mark:** First initial, last name.

SAMBAR CUSTOM KNIVES (See Giljevic, Branko)

SAMPSON, LYNN, 381 Deakins Rd., Jonesborough, TN 37659/615-348-8373
Specialties: Highly finished working knives, mostly folders. **Patterns:** Locking folders, slip-joints, interframes and two-blades. **Technical:** Grinds D2, 440C and ATS-34; offers extensive filework. **Prices:** Start at $300. **Remarks:** Full-time maker; first knife sold in 1982. **Mark:** Name and city in logo.

SANDERS, A.A., 3850 72 Ave. NE, Norman, OK 73071/405-364-8660
Specialties: Working straight knives and folders. **Patterns:** Hunters, fighters, daggers and Bowies. **Technical:** Forges his own Damascus; offers stock removal with ATS-34, 440C, A2, D2, 01, 5160 and 1095. **Prices:** $85 to $1,500. **Remarks:** Full-time maker; first knife sold in 1985. Formerly known as Athern Forge. **Mark:** Name.

SANDERS, BILL, 335 Bauer Ave., P.O. Box 957, Mancos, CO 81328/303-533-7223
Specialties: Working straight knives, some fancy and some fantasy, of his design. **Patterns:** Hunters, boots, utility knives, using belt knives. **Technical:** Grinds 440C, ATS-34 and commercial Damascus. Provides wide variety of handle materials. **Prices:** $170 to $350; some to $800. **Remarks:** Full-time maker. **Mark:** Name, city and state.

SANDERS, MICHAEL M., P.O. Box 1106, Ponchatoula, LA 70454/504-294-3601
Specialties: Working straight knives and folders, some deluxe. **Patterns:** Hunters, fighters, Bowies, daggers, large folders and deluxe Damascus miniatures. **Technical:** Grinds 01, D2, 440C, ATS-34 and Damascus. **Prices:** $75 to $650; some higher. **Remarks:** Full-time maker; first knife sold in 1967. **Mark:** Name and state.

SANDERSON, RAY, 4403 Uplands Way, Yakima, WA 98908/509-965-0128
Specialties: One-of-a-kind Buck knives; traditonal working straight knives and folders of his design. **Patterns:** Bowies, hunters and fighters. **Technical:** Grinds 440C and ATS-34. **Prices:** $200 to $750. **Remarks:** Part-time maker; first knife sold in 1984. **Mark:** Sanderson Knives in shape of Bowie.

SANDLIN, LARRY, 4580 Sunday Dr., Adamsville, AL 35005/205-674-1816
Specialties: High art straight knives of his design. **Patterns:** Boots, daggers, hunters and fighters. **Technical:** Forges 1095, L6, 01, carbon steel and Damascus. **Prices:** $200 to $1,500; some to $5,000. **Remarks:** Part-time maker; first knife sold in 1990. **Mark:** Chiseled last name in Japanese.

SASSER, JIM, 926 Jackson, Pueblo, CO 81004
Specialties: Working straight knives and folders of his design. **Patterns:** Makes elk hunters' tools, axes, camp knives, a variety of folders and limited editions. **Technical:** Grinds ATS-34. **Prices:** $75 to $300; some to $800. **Remarks:** Full-time maker; first knife sold in 1970. **Mark:** Last name or full name in circle.

SAWBY, SCOTT, 400 W. Center Valley Rd., Sandpoint, ID 83864/208-263-4171
Specialties: Folders, working and fancy. **Patterns:** Locking folders, patent locking systems and interframes. **Technical:** Grinds D2, 440C, 154CM, CPM T440V and ATS-34. **Prices:** $400 to $1,000. **Remarks:** Full-time maker; first knife sold in 1974. **Mark:** Last name, city and state.

SAYEN, MURAD, P.O. Box 127, Bryant Pond, ME 04219/207-665-2224 **Specialties:** Carved handles. **Patterns:** Fighters, boots, Bowies, daggers and fantasy knives. **Technical:** Forges carbon and Damascus steel only. Handles carved and inlaid, some with stones. **Prices:** $750 to $5,000. **Remarks:** Full-time maker; first knife sold in 1977. Doing business as Kemal. **Mark:** Last name with date.

SCARROW, WIL, c/o L&W Mail Service, 16236 Chicago Ave., Bellflower, CA 90706/310-866-6384 **Specialties:** Working straight knives in standard patterns or to customer specs. **Patterns:** Hunters, fisherman's, skinners, swords and Bowies. **Technical:** Forges and grinds W1, W2, 5160, 1095, 440C, AEB-L, ATS-34 and other steels on request; offers some filework. **Prices:** $85 to $750; some higher. **Remarks:** Part-time maker; first knife sold in 1983. Four to six month construction time on custom orders. Doing business as Gold Hill Knife Works. **Mark:** SC with arrow and year made.

SCHALLER, ANTHONY B., 5609 Flint Ct. NW, Albuquerque, NM 87120/505-899-0155 **Specialties:** Traditional working/using straight knives of his design and in standard patterns. **Patterns:** Boots, daggers, hunters. **Technical:** Grinds 440C, ATS-34. Offers filework, mirror finishes and full and narrow tangs. Prefers exotic woods or Micarta for handle materials. **Prices:** $70 to $160; some to $250. **Remarks:** Part-time maker; first knife sold in 1990. **Mark:** Last name.

SCHEID, MAGGIE, 124 Van Stallen St., Rochester, NY 14621-3557 **Specialties:** Simple working straight knives. **Patterns:** Kitchen and utility knives; some miniatures. **Technical:** Forges 5160 high-carbon steel. **Prices:** $100 to $200. **Remarks:** Part-time maker; first knife sold in 1986. **Mark:** Full name.

SCHELL, CLYDE M., 4735 NE Elliott Circle, Corvallis, OR 97330/503-752-0235

SCHEPERS, GEORGE B., Box 83, Chapman, NE 68827/308-986-2444 **Specialties:** Fancy period pieces of his design. **Patterns:** Bowies, swords, tomahawks, locking folders and miniatures. **Technical:** Grinds W1, W2 and his own Damascus; etches. **Prices:** $125 to $600; some higher. **Remarks:** Full-time maker; first knife sold in 1981. **Mark:** Schep.

SCHEURER, ALFREDO E. FAES, Rincon del Sur #15-21-7, Col. Bosque Res. del Sur, C.P. 16010 MEXICO **Specialties:** Fancy and fantasy knives of his design. **Patterns:** Daggers. **Technical:** Grinds stainless steel; casts and grinds silver. Sets stones in silver. **Prices:** $2,000 to $3,000. **Remarks:** Spare-time maker; first knife sold in 1989. **Mark:** Symbol.

SCHIRMER, MIKE, 28 Biltmore Rd., P.O. Box 534, Twin Bridges, MT 59754/406-684-5868 **Specialties:** Working straight knives of his design or to customer specs; mostly hunters and personal knives. **Patterns:** Bowies, hunters, camp, fighters and boot knives. **Technical:** Grinds 01, D2, A2 and Damascus. **Prices:** Starting at $75. **Remarks:** Full-time maker; first knife sold in 1992. Doing business as Ruby Mountain Knives. **Mark:** Last name or signature.

SCHLOMER, JAMES E., 991 Hickory Ct., Kissimmee, FL 34743/407-348-8044 **Specialties:** Working and show straight knives. **Patterns:** Hunters, Bowies and skinners. **Technical:** Stock removal method, 440C and L6. Scrimshaws; carves sambar stag handles. Works on corean and micarta. **Prices:** $75 to $500. **Remarks:** Full-time maker. **Mark:** Name, steel number and serial number.

SCHMIDT, JAMES A., 1167 Eastern Ave., Ballston Lake, NY 12019/518-882-9322 **Specialties:** High-art Damascus folders and collector-quality period pieces—sole authorship. **Patterns:** Schmidt patterns in folders; variety of investor-class straight knives. **Technical:** Forges W2 and his own Damascus; offers elaborate filework and etching; uses exotic handle

materials. **Prices:** $900 to $2,200; some to $5,000. **Remarks:** Full-time maker; first knife sold in 1975. **Mark:** Last name.

SCHMIDT, RICK, P.O. Box 1318, Whitefish, MT 59937/406-862-6471; 406-862-6078 **Specialties:** Traditional working and using straight knives and folders of his design and to customer specs. **Patterns:** Fighters, hunters, cutlery and utility knives. **Technical:** Flat-grinds D2 and ATS-34. Custom leather sheaths. **Prices:** $120 to $250; some to $1,900. **Remarks:** Full-time maker; first knife sold in 1975. **Mark:** Stylized initials.

SCHNEIDER, CRAIG M., 285 County Rd. 1400 N., Seymour, IL 61875/217-687-2651 **Specialties:** Traditional working straight knives of his design or to customer specs. **Patterns:** Hunters, fighters, Bowies and utility/camp knives. **Technical:** Grinds 440C, 440V, ATS-34, D2 and 01; uses various animal horns, antlers, bones, jawbones, gold, silver, precious stones, minerals and fossil ivory for handle materials. **Prices:** $50 to $400; some to $2,500. **Remarks:** Part-time maker; first knife sold in 1985. **Mark:** Stylized initials.

SCHNEIDER, HERMAN J., 10 Sun Hala Dr., Pittsburg, TX 75686-9318/903-856-9802; FAX: 903-856-9803 **Specialties:** Investor-class straight knives and fantasy pieces of his design. **Patterns:** Fully finished hunters, daggers, fighters and push knives. **Technical:** Forges and grinds 154CM, ATS-34 and his Damascus. Exotic materials are a specialty. **Prices:** $800 and up for hunters. **Remarks:** Full-time maker; first knife sold in 1972. **Mark:** First and middle initials, last name.

SCHNEIDER, KARL A., 209 N. Brownleaf Rd., Newark, DE 19713/302-737-0277 **Specialties:** Traditional working and using straight knives of his design. **Patterns:** Hunters, kitchen and fillet knives. **Technical:** Grinds ATS-34, D2 and 154CM. Shapes handles to fit hands; uses Micarta, Pakkawood and exotic woods. Makes hand-stitched leather cases. **Prices:** $75 to $225; some to $400. **Remarks:** Part-time maker; first knife sold in 1984-85. **Mark:** Name, address.

SCHOEMAN, CORRIE, Box 573, Bloemfontein 9300, SOUTH AFRICA/051-332949; FAX: 051-332228 **Specialties:** Working and using knives to his or customer's designs. **Patterns:** Fighters, boots, hunters, locking and liner lock folders. **Technical:** Grinds ATS-34, 12C27 and 440B. Handles made with hardwoods, horn, ivory, warthog tusks or customer request. All knives come with custom-made sheath and/or wooden display case. **Prices:** $150 to $400. **Remarks:** Part-time maker; first knife sold in 1984. **Mark:** Etched name logo in knife shape.

SCHOENFELD, MATTHEW A., RR #1, Galiano Island, B.C. V0N 1P0, CANADA/604-539-2806 **Specialties:** Working knives of his design. **Patterns:** Kitchen cutlery, camp knives, hunters, swords. **Technical:** Grinds 440C buys Damascus. **Prices:** $85 to $500. **Remarks:** Part-time maker; first knife sold in 1978. **Mark:** Signature, Galiano Is. B.C., and date.

SCHOLL, TIM, Rt. 3, Box 158-1A, Angier, NC 27501/919-897-2051 **Specialties:** Fancy and working/using straight knives and folders of his design and to customer specs. **Patterns:** Hunters, friction folders, utility/camp knives. **Technical:** Grinds ATS-34; forges carbon and tool steel and Damascus. Offers filework. **Prices:** $100 to $650; some to $1,500. **Remarks:** Part-time maker; first knife sold in 1990. Doing business as Tim Scholl Custom Knives. **Mark:** Last name or last initial with arrow.

SCHROEN, KARL, 4042 Bones Rd., Sebastopol, CA 95472/707-823-4057; FAX: 707-823-2914 **Specialties:** Using knives made to fit. **Patterns:** Sgian dubhs, carving sets, wood-carving knives, fishing knives, kitchen knives and new cleaver design. **Technical:** Forges A2, ATS-34 and D2. **Prices:** $100 to $800. **Remarks:** Full-time maker; first knife sold in 1968. Author of *The Hand Forged Knife*. **Mark:** Last name.

directory

SCHULTZ, RICHARD A., P.O. Box 1616, San Juan Capistrano, CA 92693/714-661-3879
Specialties: Traditional working and using straight knives of his design, to customer specs and in standard patterns. **Patterns:** Fighters, hunters, Specwar and survival knives. **Technical:** Grinds 440C, ATS-34, tool steels and titanium. **Prices:** $75 to $250; some to $700. **Remarks:** Part-time maker; first knife sold in 1991. Manufactures specialized knives in titanium to U.S. Government Specwar teams as Mission Knives, Inc. **Mark:** First initial, last name, year.

SCHWARZER, JAMES, P.O. Box 4, Pomona Park, FL 32181/904-649-5026; FAX: 904-649-8585
Specialties: Working straight knives of his design. **Patterns:** Capers and small hunters. **Technical:** Forges high-carbon steel and Damascus. **Prices:** $50 to $300. **Remarks:** Twelve-year-old part-time maker; first knife sold in 1989. Sells only at shows. **Mark:** Last name with anvil and first name underneath.

SCHWARZER, STEPHEN, P.O. Box 4, Pomona Park, FL 32181/904-649-5026; FAX: 904-649-8585
Specialties: Mosaic Damascus. **Patterns:** Hunters, fighters, locking folders, axes and buckskinners. **Technical:** Forges W2, 01, Wootz steel and his own Damascus; all knives have carving or filework. **Prices:** $150 to $500; some to $5,000. **Remarks:** Full-time maker; first knife sold in 1976. **Mark:** Name over anvil; folders marked inside liner.

SCOFIELD, EVERETT, 2873 Glass Mill Rd., Chickamauga, GA 30707/706-861-2911
Specialties: Historic and fantasy miniatures. **Patterns:** All patterns. **Technical:** Uses only the finest tool steels and other materials. Uses only natural, precious, and semi-precious materials. **Prices:** $100 to $1,500. **Remarks:** Full-time maker; first knife sold in 1971. Doing business as Three Crowns Cutlery. **Mark:** Three Crowns logo.

SCORDIA, PAOLO, Via del Collettore Secondario 23, 00119 Ostia Antica, ROMA ITALY /06-5650717
Specialties: Plain working knives. **Patterns:** Skinners, hunters, utility and boot knives, fighters, daggers, bush swords, kitchen knives and liner lock folders. **Technical:** Grinds 420C, 440C, ATS-34; uses hardwoods and Micarta for handles, brass and nickel silver for fittings. Makes sheaths. **Prices:** $80 to $500. **Remarks:** Part-time maker; first knife sold in 1988. **Mark:** Initials with sun and moon logo.

SCORPION FORGE (See Lutz, Greg)

SCOTT, AL, HC63 Box 267, Harper, TX 78631/210-864-4216
Specialties: High art straight knives of his design. **Patterns:** Daggers, swords and early European knives. **Technical:** Uses ATS-34, 440C and Damascus. Hand engraves; does file work; cuts filigree in the blade; offers ivory carving and precious metal inlay. **Remarks:** Full-time maker; first knife sold in 1994. Doing business as Al Scott Maker of Fine Blade Art. **Mark:** Name engraved in old English, sometime inlayed in 24K gold.

SCOTT, WINSTON, Rt. 2, Box 62, Huddleston, VA 24104/703-297-6130
Specialties: Working knives. **Patterns:** Hunting and fishing knives. **Technical:** Grinds ATS-34, 440C and 154CM; likes full and narrow tangs, natural materials, sterling silver guards. **Prices:** $100 to $200; some to $400. **Remarks:** Part-time maker; first knife sold in 1984. **Mark:** Last name.

SEA-MOUNT KNIFE WORKS (See Wilson, Philip C.)

SEARS, MICK, 214 N. Vance St., Gastonia, NC 28052/704-867-3464
Specialties: Scots and confederate reproductions; Bowies and fighters. **Patterns:** Bowies, fighters. **Technical:** Grinds 440C and 1095. **Prices:** $50 to $150; some to $300. **Remarks:** Part-time maker; first knife sold in 1975. Doing business as Mick's Custom Knives. **Mark:** First name.

SELENT, CHUCK, P.O. Box 1207, Bonners Ferry, ID 83805-1207/208-267-5807
Specialties: Period, art and fantasy miniatures; exotics; one-of-a-kinds. **Patterns:** Swords, daggers and others. **Technical:** Works in Damascus, meteorite, 440C and tool steel. Offers scrimshaw. Offers his own casting and leatherwork; uses jewelry techniques. Makes display cases for miniatures. **Prices:** $75 to $400. **Remarks:** Part-time maker; first knife sold in 1990. **Mark:** Last name and bear paw print logo scrimshawed on handles or leatherwork.

SELF, ERNIE, HC02 Box 109F, Dripping Springs, TX 78620-9760/512-858-7133
Specialties: Traditional and working straight knives and folders of his design and in standard patterns. **Patterns:** Hunters, locking folders and slip-joints. **Technical:** Grinds 440C, D2, 440V and ATS-34. Offers fancy filework. **Prices:** $125 to $350; some to $500. **Remarks:** Full-time maker; first knife sold in 1982. **Mark:** Initials brand.

SELLEVOLD, HARALD, S.Kleivesmau:2, 5023 Dreggen, NORWAY/55-310682
Specialties: Norwegian styles; collaborates with other Norse craftsmen. **Patterns:** Distinctive ferrules and other mild modifications of traditional patterns; Bowies and friction folders. **Technical:** Buys Damascus blades; blacksmiths his own blades. Semi-gemstones used in handles; gemstone inlay. **Prices:** $100 to $350; some to $1,000. **Remarks:** Full-time maker; first knife sold in 1980. **Mark:** Horseshoe last initial.

SELVIDIO, RALPH J., 15 Budlong Ave., Warwick, RI 02888/401-941-0758; FAX: 401-377-1006
Specialties: Collector-grade folders with unique mechanisms; straight and folding fantasy knives of his design. **Patterns:** Locking folders, swords and fighters. **Technical:** Grinds and forges Damascus and 1095; grinds 01. Handle material is mostly ivory and pearl. Uses exotic skin overlays on cases. **Prices:** $200 to $950; some to $1,500. **Remarks:** Part-time maker; first knife sold in 1986. Doing business as Rattler Brand Knives. **Mark:** RATTLER BRAND.

SENTZ, MARK C., 4084 Baptist Rd., Taneytown, MD 21787/410-756-2018
Specialties: Fancy straight working knives of his design. **Patterns:** Hunters, fighters, utility/camp knives. **Technical:** Forges 1085, 1095, 5160, 5155 and his Damascus. Most knives come with wood-lined leather sheath or wooden presentation sheath. **Prices:** Start at $225. **Remarks:** Full-time maker; first knife sold in 1989. Doing business as M. Charles Sentz Gunsmithing, Inc. **Mark:** Last name.

SENTZ GUNSMITHING, INC., M. CHARLES (See Sentz, Mark C.)

SERAFEN, STEVEN E., P.O. Box 898, Norwich, NY 13815/607-334-3166
Specialties: Traditional working/using straight knives of his design and to customer specs. **Patterns:** Bowies, fighters, hunters. **Technical:** Grinds ATS-34, 440C, high-carbon steel. **Prices:** $175 to $600; some to $1,200. **Remarks:** Part-time maker; first knife sold in 1990. **Mark:** First and middle initial, last name in script.

SERVEN, JIM, P.O. Box 1, Fostoria, MI 48435/517-795-2255
Specialties: Highly finished unique folders. **Patterns:** Fancy working folders, axes, miniatures and razors; some straight knives. **Technical:** Grinds 440C; forges his own Damascus. **Prices:** $150 to $800; some to $1,500. **Remarks:** Full-time maker; first knife sold in 1971. **Mark:** Name in map logo.

SHADLEY, EUGENE W., 645 Norway Dr., Bovey, MN 55709/218-245-3820
Specialties: Classic multi-blade folders. **Patterns:** Stockman, sowbelly, congress, trapper, etc. **Technical:** Grinds ATS-34, 416 frames. **Prices:** $150 to $750; some to $1,000. **Remarks:** Full-time maker; first knife sold in 1985. Doing business as Shadley Knives. **Mark:** Last name.

SHADOWMAKER (See Urstadt, E.W.)

SHARP, MARGIE (See Sharp, Wes and Margie)

SHARP, WES and MARGIE, 1220 N. 18th Ave., Milton, FL 32583/904-994-3779
Specialties: Traditional and working straight knives of their design and to customer specs. **Patterns:** Bowies, hunters and fillet knives. **Technical:** Grind 440C and ATS-34. Offer filework and custom leather work. **Prices:** $75 to $300; some to $500. **Remarks:** Full-time maker; first knife sold in 1985. **Mark:** Last name.

SHARRIGAN, MUDD, RR4 Box 1164, Wiscasset, ME 04578-9330/207-882-9820
Specialties: Classic and using straight knives and folders of his design and to customer specs. **Patterns:** Daggers, fighters, hunters and seaman working knives; traditional Scandinavian styles. **Technical:** Forges 1095, 01 and Rolls Royce steel. Laminates 1095 and mild steel. **Prices:** $50 to $325; some to $1,200. **Remarks:** Full-time maker; first knife sold in 1982. **Mark:** First name and swallow tail carving.

SHAWNEE (See Meier, Daryl)

SHEEHAN, PAUL P., 390 Fairway Oaks Dr., Sedona, AZ 86351/520-284-1403
Specialties: Fancy and presentation-grade working straight knives of his design or to customer specs. **Patterns:** Bowies, kukris, fighters, hunters, daggers, push daggers and fantasy knives. **Technical:** Hollowgrinds 440C and commercial Damascus. Prefers natural materials, big horn sheep, buffalo horn and mammoth. Dovetailed bolsters on all knives; tapered tangs, filework and mirror or satin finish available. **Prices:** $195 to $1,000; some to $2,000. **Remarks:** Part-time maker; first knife sold in 1987. **Mark:** Last name, city, state and Kokopelli symbol.

SHELTON, PAUL S., 17051 County Rd. 8440, Rolla, MO 65401/314-364-3151
Specialties: Fancy working straight knives of his design or to customer specs. **Patterns:** All types from camp knives to miniatures, except folders. **Technical:** Grinds ATS-34 and commercial Damascus. Offers filework, texturing, natural handle materials and exotic leather sheaths. **Prices:** $100 and up. **Remarks:** Part-time maker; first knife sold in 1984. **Mark:** Last name and serial number.

SHERMAN KNIVES (See Williams, Sherman A.)

SHIKAYAMA, TOSHIAKI, 259-2 Suka Yoshikawa Machi, Kitakatsushika, Saitama JAPAN/04-89-81-6605; FAX: 04-89-81-6605
Specialties: Folders in standard patterns. **Patterns:** Locking and slipjoint folders. **Technical:** Grinds ATS. **Prices:** $400 to $2,500; some to $8,000. **Remarks:** Full-time maker; first knife sold in 1952. **Mark:** First initial, last name.

SHINOSKY, ANDY, 2978 Beal St. NW, Warren, OH 44485/216-898-6298
Specialties: Fancy working and using folders. **Patterns:** Gentlemen's knives, folding fighters and boots, interframes. **Technical:** Grinds ATS-34 and commercial Damascus. Prefers natural handle materials, horns, pearls, exotic woods. **Prices:** $350 to $900; some to $1,500. **Remarks:** Part-time maker; first knife sold in 1992. **Mark:** Last name.

SHOEMAKER, CARROLL, 380 Yellowtown Rd., Northup, OH 45658/614-446-6695
Specialties: Working/using straight knives of his design. **Patterns:** Hunters, utility/camp and early American backwoodsmen knives. **Technical:** Grinds ATS-34; forges old files, 01 and 1095. Uses some Damascus; offers scrimshaw and engraving. **Prices:** $100 to $175; some to $350. **Remarks:** Spare-time maker; first knife sold in 1977. **Mark:** Name and city or connected initials.

SHOEMAKER, SCOTT, 316 S. Main St., Miamisburg, OH 45342/513-859-1935
Specialties: Twisted, wire-wrapped handles on swords, fighters and fantasy blades; new line of seven models with quick-draw, multi-carry Kydex sheaths. **Patterns:** Bowies, boots and one-of-a-kinds in his design or to customer specs. **Technical:** Grinds A6 and ATS-34; buys Damascus. Hand satin finish is standard. **Prices:** $100 to $1,500; swords to $8,000. **Remarks:** Part-time maker; first knife sold in 1984. **Mark:** Angel wings with last initial, or last name.

SHOGER, MARK O., 14780 SW Osprey Dr., Suite 345, Beaverton, OR 97007/503-579-2495
Specialties: Working and using straight knives and folders of his design; fancy and embellished knives. **Patterns:** Hunters, Bowies, daggers and locking folders. **Technical:** Forges 01, W2 and his own pattern-welded Damascus. **Remarks:** Spare-time maker. **Mark:** Last name or stamped last initial over anvil.

SHOSTLE, BEN, 1121 Burlington, Muncie, IN 47302/317-282-9073
Specialties: Fancy high-art straight knives of his design. **Patterns:** Bowies, daggers and fighters. **Technical:** Uses 440C, ATS-34 and commercial Damascus. All knives are engraved. **Prices:** $900 to $3,200; some to $4,000. **Remarks:** Full-time maker; first knife sold in 1987. Doing business as The Gun Room (T.G.R.). **Mark:** Last name.

SHOWERS, ROBERT, Rt. 1 Box 552, Longbeach, WA 98631
Specialties: Fantasy and working knives of all designs; some exotic. **Patterns:** Hunters, daggers and survival knives. **Technical:** Forges, stock removal method and wire-feed EDM, 440C, VH-64, 01 and Turkish Damascus. **Prices:** $50 to $2,500; some to $25,000. **Remarks:** Full-time maker; first knife sold in 1983. **Mark:** Etched thumbprint on tang, Kriegtag and year engraved on blade.

SHUFORD, RICK, Rt. 8, Box 256A, Statesville, NC 28677/704-873-0633
Specialties: Fancy working knives to customer specs. **Patterns:** Hunters, buckskinners, camp and fishing knives and miniatures. **Technical:** Forges and grinds 01, D2 and 440C. **Prices:** $125 to $250; some to $450. **Remarks:** Part-time maker; first knife sold in 1981. **Mark:** Last name and three dots.

SHUSHUNOV, SERGEI, P.O. Box 1304, Bath, OH 44210/216-665-4117

SIBRIAN, AARON, 4308 Dean Drive, Ventura, CA 93003/805-642-6950
Specialties: Tough working knives of his design and in standard patterns. **Patterns:** Makes a "Viper utility"—a kukri derivative—and a variety of straight using knives. **Technical:** Grinds 440C and ATS-34. Offers traditional Japanese blades; soft backs, hard edges, temper lines. **Prices:** $60 to $100; some to $250. **Remarks:** Spare-time maker; first knife sold in 1989. **Mark:** Initials in diagonal line.

SIDELINGER, ROBERT, 1365 St. Francis Rd., Bel Air, MD 21014/410-879-0963
Specialties: Folders only of his design. **Patterns:** Drop-points, trailing-points and daggers. **Technical:** Grinds ATS-34 and Damascus. Likes interframes, integral spring locks. Handle inlays made of ivory, horn, wood, coral and pearl. **Prices:** Start at $590. **Remarks:** Part-time maker; first knife sold in 1990. **Mark:** Gothic last initial inside shield.

SIGMAN, CORBET R., Rt. 1, Box 212-A, Liberty, WV 25124/304-586-9131
Specialties: Collectible working straight knives and folders. **Patterns:** Hunters, fighters, boots, camp knives and exotics such as sgian dubhs—distinctly Sigman lines; folders. **Technical:** Grinds D2, 154CM, plain carbon tool steel and ATS-34. **Prices:** $60 to $800; some to $4,000. **Remarks:** Full-time maker; first knife sold in 1970. **Mark:** Name or initials.

SIGMAN, JAMES P., 52474 Johnson Rd., Three Rivers, MI 49093/616-279-2508
Specialties: High-tech working knives of his design. **Patterns:** Daggers, hunters, fighters and folders. **Technical:** Forges and grinds L6, 01, W2 and his Damascus. **Prices:** $150 to $750. **Remarks:** Part-time maker; first knife sold in 1982. **Mark:** First initial, last name or SIG.

SIMMONDS, KURT BARNES, RSD 181, North Castlemaine, Vic. 3450, AUSTRALIA/054-705864
Specialties: Straight knives and folders; fancy period pieces. **Patterns:** Art daggers, traditional Bowies, fancy folders and miniatures. **Technical:** Grinds ATS-34, D2, 440C; offers filework, chisel work and inlays. **Prices:** $185 to $375; some to $2,500. **Remarks:** Full-time maker; first knife sold in 1983. **Mark:** Initials and address in Southern Cross motif.

SIMMONS, H.R., P.O. Box 176, Grantsboro, NC 28529/919-249-0094
Specialties: Working/using straight knives of his design. **Patterns:** Fighters, hunters and utility/camp knives. **Technical:** Forges and grinds Damascus and L6; grinds ATS-34. **Prices:** $150 to $250; some to $400. **Remarks:** Part-time maker; first knife sold in 1987. Doing business as HRS Custom Knives. **Mark:** Initials.

SIMONELLA, GIANLUIGI, 15, via Rosa Brustolo, 33085 Maniago, ITALY/01139-427-730350
Specialties: Traditional and classic working/using knives of his design and to customer specs. **Patterns:** Bowies, fighters, hunters, utility/camp knives. **Technical:** Forges ATS-34, D2, 440C. **Prices:** $250 to $400; some to $1,000. **Remarks:** Full-time maker; first knife sold in 1988. **Mark:** Wilson.

SIMONICH, ROB, P.O. Box 278, Clancy, MT 59634/406-933-8274
Specialties: Working knives in standard patterns. **Patterns:** Hunters, combat knives, Bowies and small fancy knives. **Technical:** Grinds D2, ATS-34 and 440C; forges own cable Damascus. Offers filework on most knives. **Prices:** $75 to $300; some to $1,000. **Remarks:** Spare-time maker; first knife sold in 1984. Not currently taking orders. **Mark:** Last name in buffalo logo.

SIMONS, BILL, 6217 Michael Ln., Lakeland, FL 33811/813-646-3783
Specialties: Working folders. **Patterns:** Locking folders, liner locks, slip-joints in hunters; some straight camp knives. **Technical:** Grinds D2, 440C and ATS-34. **Prices:** Start at $100. **Remarks:** Full-time maker; first knife sold in 1970. **Mark:** Last name.

SIMS, BOB, P.O. Box 772, Meridian, TX 76665/817-435-6240
Specialties: Traditional working straight knives and folders in standard patterns; banana/sheepfoot blade combinations in trapper patterns. **Patterns:** Locking folders, slip-joint folders and hunters. **Technical:** Grinds D2, ATS-34 and 01. Offers filework on some knives. **Prices:** $150 to $275; some to $600. **Remarks:** Part-time maker; first knife sold in 1975. **Mark:** The division sign.

SINYARD, CLESTON S., 27522 Burkhardt Dr., Elberta, AL 36530/334-986-7984
Specialties: Working straight knives and folders of his design. **Patterns:** Hunters, buckskinners, Bowies, daggers, fighters and all-Damascus folders. **Technical:** Makes Damascus from 440C, stainless steels, D2 and regular high-carbon steel; forges "forefinger pad" into hunters and skinners. **Prices:** In Damascus $450 to $1,500; some to $2,500. **Remarks:** Full-time maker; first knife sold in 1980. Doing business as Nimo Forge. **Mark:** Last name, U.S.A. in anvil.

SISEMORE, CHARLES, HC 63, Box 5550, Hodgen, OK 74939/918-651-3321
Specialties: Traditional straight knives of his design. **Patterns:** Bowies, daggers and hunters. **Technical:** Forges 5160 and Damascus. **Prices:** $125 to $450. **Remarks:** Full-time maker; first knife sold in 1986. **Mark:** Last name.

SISKA, JIM, 6 Highland Ave., Westfield, MA 01085/413-568-9787; FAX: 413-568-6341
Specialties: Traditional working straight knives and folders. **Patterns:** Hunters, fighters, Bowies and one-of-a-kinds; folders. **Technical:** Grinds D2 and ATS-34; buys Damascus. Likes exotic woods. **Prices:** $195 to $2,500. **Remarks:** Part-time maker; first knife sold in 1983. **Mark:** Last name in Old English.

SJOSTRAND, KEVIN, 1541 S. Cain St., Visalia, CA 93292/209-625-5254
Specialties: Traditional and working/using straight knives of his design or to customer specs. **Patterns:** Bowies, hunters and utility/camp knives. **Technical:** Grinds ATS-34, 440C and 1095. Prefers high polished blades and full tang. Natural and stabilized hardwoods, micarta and stag handle material. **Prices:** $75 to $300. **Remarks:** Part-time maker; first knife sold in 1992. Doing business as Black Oak Blades. **Mark:** Oak tree, Black Oak Blades, name.

SKELLERN, DR. M.J., P.O. Munster 4278, SOUTH AFRICA/03930-92537; FAX: 03931-76513
Specialties: Fancy high-tech folders of his design. **Patterns:** Locking and slip-joint folders. **Technical:** Grinds ATS-34 and Sandvick 12C27; uses Damascus. Inlays his stainless steel integral handles; offers rare African handle materials. **Prices:** $200 to $500; some to $700. **Remarks:** Part-time maker; first knife sold in 1986. **Mark:** Last name.

SLEE, FRED, 9 John St., Morganville, NJ 07751/908-591-9047
Specialties: Working straight knives, some fancy, to customer specs. **Patterns:** Hunters, fighters, boots, fancy daggers and folders. **Technical:** Grinds D2, 440C and ATS-34. **Prices:** $90 to $450; some to $1,200. **Remarks:** Part-time maker; first knife sold in 1980. **Mark:** Last name in old English.

SLOAN, SHANE, Rt. 1, Box 17, Newcastle, TX 76372/817-846-3290
Specialties: Collector grade straight knives and folders. **Patterns:** Bowies, lockers, slip-joints, fancy folders, fighters and period pieces. **Technical:** Grinds D2 and ATS-34. Uses hand-rubbed satin finish. Prefers rare natural handle materials. **Prices:** $250 to $1,600. **Remarks:** Full-time maker; first knife sold in 1985. **Mark:** Name and city.

SLOBODIAN, SCOTT, 13570 Norma Ct., Pine Grove, CA 95665/209-296-3809; FAX: 209-296-3828
Specialties: Japanese-style knives and swords, period pieces, fantasy pieces and miniatures. **Patterns:** Small kweikens, tantos, wakazashis, katanas, traditional Samurai swords. **Technical:** Flat-grinds 1045, 1060 and commercial Damascus; differentially hardens blades with fireclay. **Prices:** $800 to $3,500; some to $7,500. **Remarks:** Full-time maker; first knife sold in 1987. **Mark:** Blade signed in Japanese characters and various scripts.

SMALL, ED, Rt. 1, Box 178-A, Keyser, WV 26726/304-298-4254
Specialties: Working knives of his design; period pieces. **Patterns:** Hunters, daggers, buckskinners and camp knives; likes one-of-a-kinds. **Technical:** Forges and grinds W2, L6 and his own Damascus. Uses no solder joint at guard or spacing material. **Prices:** $150 to $1,500. **Remarks:** Part-time maker; first knife sold in 1978. Business name is Iron Mountain Forge Works. **Mark:** Script initials connected.

SMALL, JIM, P.O. Box 67, Madison, GA 30650/404-342-4707
Specialties: Fancy working knives of his design or to customer specs. **Patterns:** Bowies, camp and fishing knives, hunters and locking folders. **Technical:** Grinds D2, 440C, 154CM and ATS-34; engraves his knives and other's. **Prices:** $75 to $185; some to $1,000. **Remarks:** Full-time maker; first knife sold in 1970. **Mark:** Last name.

SMART, STEVE, 1 Meadowbrook Cir., Melissa, TX 75454/214-881-0638; FAX: 214-881-0212
Specialties: Working/using straight knives and folders of his design, to customer specs and in standard patterns. **Patterns:** Bowies, hunters, kitchen knives, locking folders, utility/camp, fishing and bird knives. **Technical:** Grinds ATS-34, D2, 440C and 01. Prefers mirror polish or satin finish; hollow-grinds all blades. All knives come with sheath. Offers some filework. **Prices:** $95 to $225; some to $500. **Remarks:** Spare-time maker; first knife sold in 1983. **Mark:** Name, Custom, city and state in oval.

SMIT, GLENN, 627 Cindy Ct., Aberdeen, MD 21001/410-272-2959
Specialties: Working and using straight knives of his design or to customer specs. **Patterns:** Hunters, Bowies, daggers, fighters, utility/camp, kitchen knives and miniatures. **Technical:** Grinds 440C, ATS-34, 01

and A2; reforges commercial Damascus. **Prices:** Miniatures start at $20; full-size knives start at $40. **Remarks:** Spare-time maker; first knife sold in 1986. Doing business as Wolf's Knives. **Mark:** WOLF or first and middle initials, last name.

SMITH, BOBBIE D., 802 W. WHy. 90., Bonifay, FL 32425/904-547-5935
Specialties: Working straight knives and folders. **Patterns:** Bowies, hunters and slip-joints. **Technical:** Grinds 440C and ATS-34; custom sheaths for each knife. **Prices:** $75 to $250. **Remarks:** Part-time maker. **Mark:** NA.

SMITH, D. NOEL, P.O. Box 1363, Canon City, CO 81215-1363/719-275-2574
Specialties: Fantasy and high-art knives of his design. **Patterns:** Daggers, hunters and art knives. **Technical:** Grinds 01, D2 and stainless. Offers ivory and horn-carved handles; acid-etched blades; bronze-sculptured guards, buttcaps and bases. Engraves and scrimshaws. **Prices:** $400 to $3,500; some to $10,000. **Remarks:** Full-time maker; first knife sold in 1990. Doing business as Minds' Eye Metalmaster. **Mark:** Signature, date and number.

SMITH, GREGORY H., 8607 Coddington Ct., Louisville, KY 40299/502-491-7439
Specialties: Traditional working straight knives and fantasy knives to customer specs. **Patterns:** Fighters and modified Bowies; camp knives and swords. **Technical:** Grinds 01, 440C and commercial Damascus bars. **Prices:** $55 to $300. **Remarks:** Part-time maker; first knife sold in 1985. **Mark:** JAGED, plus signature.

SMITH, J.D., 516 Second St., S. Boston, MA 02127/617-269-1699
Specialties: Classic working and using straight knives and folders; period pieces mainly from his design. **Patterns:** Bowies, fighters and locking folders. **Technical:** Forges and grinds ATS-34, his Damascus, 01, 1095 and wootz-pattern hammer steel. **Prices:** $200 to $800; some to $1,500. **Remarks:** Full-time maker; first knife sold in 1987. Doing business as Hammersmith. **Mark:** Last initial alone or in cartouche.

SMITH, JOHN M., RR 6, Box 52A, Centralia, IL 62801/618-249-6444
Specialties: Art knives and some work knives. **Patterns:** Daggers, Bowies, fighters, boots, and folders. **Technical:** Forges Damascus. **Prices:** $700 to $3,000. **Remarks:** Full-time maker; first knife sold in 1980. **Mark:** Etched signature or logo.

SMITH, JOHN W., 1416 Cow Branch Rd., West Liberty, KY 41472/606-743-3599
Specialties: Fancy and working locking folders of his design or to customer specs. **Patterns:** Interframes, traditional and daggers. **Technical:** Grinds ATS-34, 440C and commercial Damascus. Offers gold inlay, engraving with gold inlay, hand-fitted mosaic pearl inlay and filework. Prefers hand-rubbed finish. Pearl and ivory available. **Prices:** $650 to $1,500; some higher. **Remarks:** Full-time maker. **Mark:** Initials engraved inside diamond.

SMITH JR., JAMES B. "RED", Rt. 2, Box 1525, Morven, GA 31638/912-775-2844
Specialties: Folders. **Patterns:** Rotating rear-lock folders. **Technical:** Grinds ATS-34, D2 and Vascomax 350. **Prices:** Start at $350. **Remarks:** Full-time maker; first knife sold in 1985. **Mark:** GA RED in cowboy hat.

SMITH, JOSH, Box 64, Lincoln, MT 59639/406-362-4485
Specialties: Working/using knives. **Patterns:** Hunters and skinners. **Technical:** Stock removal method, 1095; forges 5160. **Prices:** $70 and up. **Remarks:** Part-time maker; first knife sold in 1992. **Mark:** Joshua Smith's Custom Knives, city and state.

SMITH, MICHAEL J., 14802 N. Florida T308, Tampa, FL 33613/813-962-3538
Specialties: Working and using straight knives and folders of his design, to customer specs and in standard patterns; fantasy knives.

Patterns: Daggers, fighters and utility/camp knives. **Technical:** Grinds ATS-34 and Damascus. Uses titanium on folders; silver casting and wire/silk wraps on daggers. **Prices:** $85 to $500; some to $3,000. **Remarks:** Part-time maker; first knife sold in 1989. **Mark:** Name, city, state.

SMITH, NEWMAN L., 676 Glades Rd., Shop #3, Gatlinburg, TN 37738/615-436-3322
Specialties: Collector grade and working knives. **Patterns:** Hunters, slip-joint and lock-back folders, some miniatures. **Technical:** Grinds 01 and ATS-34; makes fancy sheaths. **Prices:** $110 to $450; some to $1,000. **Remarks:** Full-time maker; first knife sold in 1984. Partners part-time to handle Damascus blades by Jeff Hurst; marks these with SH connected. **Mark:** First and middle initials, last name.

SMITH, RALPH L., F21, 100 Stallings Rd., Taylors, SC 29687/803-230-5760
Specialties: Working knives. **Patterns:** Hunters, fighters and folders. **Technical:** Grinds 440C, 154CM and ATS-34. **Prices:** $100 to $225; some to $500. **Remarks:** Part-time maker; first knife sold in 1971. **Mark:** Last name in map logo.

SMITH, RAYMOND L., Box 370, Breesport, NY 14816/607-739-3126
Specialties: Working/using straight knives and folders to customer specs and in standard patterns; period pieces. **Patterns:** Bowies, hunters, slip-joints. **Technical:** Forges 5160, 52100, 1018 Damascus and wire cable Damascus. Filework. **Prices:** $55 to $225; some to $500. **Remarks:** Part-time maker; first knife sold in 1991. **Mark:** Oval with initials.

SMITH, W.M., 802 W. Hwy. 90, Bonifay, FL 32425/904-547-5935

SMOKER, RAY, 113 Church Rd., Searcy, AR 72143/501-796-2712
Specialties: Working/using straight knives of his design. **Patterns:** Fighters, hunters and utility/camp knives. **Technical:** Forges his own Damascus, 01 and 1095; makes sheaths. **Prices:** $100 to $250. **Remarks:** Full-time maker; first knife sold in 1992. **Mark:** Last name and buffalo skull.

SMYTHE, KEN, Box 494, Underberg 4590, SOUTH AFRICA/033-7011542
Specialties: Working and using straight knives of his design and to customer specs. **Patterns:** Fighters and hunters. **Technical:** Grinds 12C27 and 440C. Scrimshands. **Prices:** $150 to $480. **Remarks:** Part-time maker; first knife sold in 1982. **Mark:** Sword lying on Bible.

SNARE, MICHAEL, 3352 E. Mescal St., Phoenix, AZ 85028

SNELL, JERRY L., 235 Woodsong Dr., Fayetteville, GA 30214/404-461-0586
Specialties: Working straight knives of his design and in standard patterns. **Patterns:** Hunters, boots, fighters, daggers and a few folders. **Technical:** Grinds 440C, ATS-34; buys Damascus. **Prices:** $175 to $1,000. **Remarks:** Part-time maker. **Mark:** Last name, or name, city and state.

SOKOL, RICHARD, Box 90057, Indianapolis, IN 46290
Specialties: Fantasy and medieval straight knives of his design. **Patterns:** Medieval knives. **Technical:** Grinds 440C and ATS-34. **Prices:** $70 to $250. **Remarks:** Full-time maker. **Mark:** Engraved runic initials.

SOLOMON, MARVIN, 23750 Cold Springs Rd., Ferndale, AR 72122/501-821-3170
Specialties: Traditional working and using straight knives of his design and to customer specs. **Patterns:** Bowies, hunters and utility/camp knives. **Technical:** Forges 5160, 1095, 01 and random Damascus. **Prices:** $100 to $500. **Remarks:** Part-time maker; first knife sold in 1990. Doing business as Cold Springs Forge. **Mark:** Last name.

SONTHEIMER, G. DOUGLAS, 12604 Bridgeton Dr., Potomac, MD 20854/301-948-2933

directory

SOPPERA—STEIGER

Specialties: Working straight knives of his design. **Patterns:** Fighters, backpackers, claws and straightedges. **Technical:** Grinds. **Price:** $275 to $900; some to $1,500. **Remarks:** Spare-time maker; first knife sold in 1976. **Mark:** LORD.

SOPPERA, ARTHUR, Morgentalstr. 37, P.O. Box 708, CH-8038 Zurich, SWITZERLAND/1-482 86 12
Specialties: High-art, high-tech knives of his design. **Patterns:** Locking folders, daggers and boots. **Technical:** Grinds ATS-34 and commercial Damascus. Folders have button lock and push-button release. Also makes jewelry with integrated small knives. **Prices:** $350 to $900; some $2,000 and higher. **Remarks:** Full-time maker; first knife sold in 1986. **Mark:** Stylized initials, name, country.

SORNBERGER, JIM, 25126 Overland Dr., Volcano CA 95689/209-295-7819
Specialties: Collectible straight knives. **Patterns:** Fighters, daggers, Bowies; locking folders and miniatures; hunters. **Technical:** Grinds 440C, 154CM and ATS-34; engraves, carves and embellishes. **Prices:** $500 to $1,500; some to $3,500. **Remarks:** Full-time maker; first knife sold in 1970. **Mark:** First initial, last name, city and state.

SOUTHERN PRIDE KNIVES (See Benjamin, Jr., George)

SOVEREIGN KNIVES (See Humphreys, Joel)

SPANO, DOMINICK, 2726 Rice Ave., San Angelo, TX 76904/915-944-9630
Specialties: Working/using straight knives of his design and to customer specs. **Patterns:** Boots, hunters, slip-joints and lockbacks. **Technical:** Grinds ATS-34. Heat-treats. Makes sheaths. **Prices:** $145 to $300. **Remarks:** Part-time maker; first knife sold in 1989. Doing business as Spano Knives. **Mark:** Last name in script.

SPENCER, JOHN E., HC63 Box 267, Harper, TX 78631/512-864-4216
Specialties: Working straight knives. **Patterns:** Hunters, fighters and survival knives; locking folders; axes. **Technical:** Grinds 01, D2 and 440C; commercial Damascus. **Prices:** $60 to $300; some to $500. **Remarks:** Full-time maker; first knife sold in 1982. **Mark:** Last name.

SPINALE, RICHARD, 4021 Canterbury Ct., Lorain, OH 44053/216-282-1565
Specialties: High-art working knives of his design. **Patterns:** Hunters, fighters, daggers and locking folders. **Technical:** Grinds 440C, ATS-34 and 07; engraves. Offers gold bolsters and other deluxe treatments. **Prices:** $200 to $1,000; some to $3,000. **Remarks:** Spare-time maker; first knife sold in 1976. **Mark:** Name, address, year and model number.

SPIVEY, JEFFERSON, 9244 W. Wilshire, Yukon, OK 73099/405-721-4442
Specialties: A hatchet and sword of his design. **Patterns:** Horseman's Sabertooth built for the wilderness and similar profiles in several sizes. **Technical:** Grinds chromemoly steel. **Prices:** $300 and up. **Remarks:** First knife sold in 1977. **Mark:** Varies, but includes name and patent number.

SPRAGG, WAYNE E., P.O. Box 508, 1314 3675 East Rd., Ashton, ID 83420
Specialties: Working straight knives, some fancy. **Patterns:** Hunters, skinners, kitchen knives, Bowies and miniatures. **Technical:** Grinds ATS-34, 440C, D2, 01 and commercial Damascus. Likes filework and fancy handlework. All blades heat-treated by Paul Bos. **Prices:** $110 to $400; some higher. **Remarks:** Spare-time maker; first knife sold in 1989. **Mark:** Name, city and state with bucking horse logo.

SPRINGFIELD® (See Greenfield, G.O.)

SPROUSE, TERRY, 1633 Newfound Rd., Asheville, NC 28806/704-683-3400
Specialties: Traditional and working straight knives of his design. **Patterns:** Bowies and hunters. **Technical:** Grinds ATS-34, 440C and D2.

Makes sheaths. **Prices:** $85 to $125; some to $225. **Remarks:** Part-time maker; first knife sold in 1989. **Mark:** NA.

STAFFORD, MICHAEL, 3109 Todd Dr., Madison, WI 53713/608-273-3022
Specialties: Traditional and high-art stone-bladed knives of his design. **Patterns:** Bowies, daggers and fighters. **Technical:** Hand-chips Obsidian, English flint, Danish flint. Laminations and inlays on handles; specializes in stone handles. **Prices:** $80 to $225; some to $350. **Remarks:** Part-time maker; first knife sold in 1987. Doing business as The Prehistoric Edge. **Mark:** Engraved last name.

STAFFORD, RICHARD, 104 Marcia Ct., Warner Robins, GA 31088/912-923-6372
Specialties: High-tech straight knives and some folders. **Patterns:** Hunters in several patterns, fighters, boots, camp knives, combat knives and period pieces. **Technical:** Grinds ATS-34 and 440C; satin finish is standard. **Prices:** Starting at $75. **Remarks:** Part-time maker; first knife sold in 1983. **Mark:** Last name.

STAHL, JOHN, 2049 Windsor Rd., Baldwin, NY 11510/516-223-5007
Specialties: Miniatures. **Patterns:** Bowies, daggers, tantos, push daggers and unique jewelry-type miniatures. **Technical:** Uses stainless steels and commercial Damascus. Offers scrimshaw. **Prices:** $35 to $100. **Mark:** First initial inside last initial.

STALTER, HARRY L., 2509 N. Trivoli Rd., Trivoli, IL 61569/309-362-2306
Specialties: Fancy working knives of his design and in standard patterns; period pieces. **Patterns:** Hunters, fighters and Bowies; fancy daggers, miniatures—fancy swords, daggers, fantasy knives. **Technical:** Stock removal; 440C, D2, 154CM and Damascus. Currently makes 60 styles of miniatures with 440C, Damascus. **Prices:** $110 to $2,000. **Remarks:** Full-time maker; first knife sold in 1980. **Mark:** Last name.

STAPEL, CHUCK, Box 1617, Glendale, CA 91209/213-66-KNIFE; FAX: 213-669-1577
Specialties: Working knives of his design. **Patterns:** Variety of straight knives—tantos, hunters, folders and utility knives. **Technical:** Grinds D2, 440C and AEB-L. **Prices:** $185 to $3,000. **Remarks:** Full-time maker; first knife sold in 1974. **Mark:** Last name or last name, U.S.A.

STAPEL, CRAIG, Box 1617, Glendale, CA 91209/213-668-2669
Specialties: Working knives. **Patterns:** Hunters, tantos and fishing knives. **Technical:** Grinds 440C and AEB-L. **Prices:** $80 to $150. **Remarks:** Spare-time maker; first knife sold in 1981. **Mark:** First and middle initials, last name.

STEEL TALON CUTLERY (See Gillis, C.R. "Rex")

STEELMASTER, P.O. Box 27237, San Diego, CA 92198/619-789-9658
Specialties: Working and using straight knives to customer specs; period pieces. **Patterns:** Bowies, fighters and utility/camp knives. **Technical:** Forges and grinds D2, 01, commercial Damascus and various stainless and corrosion-resistant steels. **Prices:** $120 to $275; some to $450. **Remarks:** Full-time maker; first knife sold in 1976. **Mark:** S.

STEGALL, KEITH, summer: 2101 W. 32nd, Anchorage, AK 99517/907-276-6002; winter: P.O. Box 1035, Barrow, AK 99723
Specialties: Traditional working straight knives. **Patterns:** Most patterns. **Technical:** Grinds 440C and 154CM. **Prices:** $100 to $300. **Remarks:** Spare-time maker; first knife sold in 1987. **Mark:** Name and state with anchor.

STEIGER, MONTE L., Box 186, Genesee, ID 83832/208-285-1769
Specialties: Traditional working/using straight knives of all designs. **Patterns:** Hunters, utility/camp knives. **Technical:** Grinds 1095, 01, 440C. Handles of stacked leather, Micarta or Pakkawood. Each knife comes with right- or left-handed sheath. **Prices:** $70 to $220. **Remarks:** Spare-time maker; first knife sold in 1988. **Mark:** First initial, last name.

STEIGERWALT, KEN, 6 Collister Dr., Box 8, Nescopeck, PA 18635/717-379-2869
Specialties: Fancy classic folders of his design. **Patterns:** Folders—liner locks, button locks and rear locks. **Technical:** Grinds ATS-34, 440C and commercial Damascus. Experiments with unique filework. **Prices:** $200 to $600; some to $1,500. **Remarks:** Full-time maker; first knife sold in 1981. **Mark:** Initials.

STEINAU, JURGEN, Julius-Hart Strasse 44, Berlin 0-1162, GERMANY/372-6452512; FAX: 372-645-2512
Specialties: Fantasy and high-art straight knives of his design. **Patterns:** Boots, daggers and switch-blade folders. **Technical:** Grinds 440B, 2379 and X90 Cr.Mo.V. 78. **Prices:** $1,500 to $2,500; some to $3,500. **Remarks:** Full-time maker; first knife sold in 1984. **Mark:** Symbol, plus year, month, day and serial number.

STEINBERG, AL, 2499 Trenton Dr., San Bruno, CA 94066/415-583-8281
Specialties: Fancy working straight knives to customer specs. **Patterns:** Hunters, Bowies, fishing and camp knives, push knives. **Technical:** Grinds 01, 440C and 154CM. **Prices:** $60 to $2,500. **Remarks:** Full-time maker; first knife sold in 1972. **Mark:** Signature, city and state.

STEKETEE, CRAIG A., 905 U.S. Hwy. 60 N., Billings, MO 65610/417-744-2770
Specialties: Working straight knives of his design and to customer specs; art and collector knives. **Patterns:** Bowies, daggers, toothpicks, boots, hunters, fillets, miniatures, etc. **Technical:** Forges and stock removal 01, 1095, his Damascus; heat-treats. Engraves; offers filework. Prefers exotic and natural handle materials. **Prices:** $125 to $1,200. **Remarks:** Full-time maker. **Mark:** STEK.

STERLING WORKSHOP (See Reggio Jr., Sidney J.)

STEVENS, BARRY B., Rt. 6, 901 Amherst, Cridersville, OH 45806/419-221-2446
Specialties: Small fancy folders of his design and to customer specs; mini-hunters and fighters. **Patterns:** Fighters, hunters, liner locks, lockback and bolster release folders. **Technical:** Grinds ATS-34, 440C, Damascus and S.S. Damascus. Prefers hand-rubbed finishes and natural handle materials—horn, ivory, pearls, exotic woods. **Prices:** $300 to $1,000; some to $2,500. **Remarks:** Part-time maker; first knife sold in 1991. Doing business as Bare Knives. **Mark:** First and middle initials, last name.

STEWART, CHARLES, 2128 Garrick Ave., Warren, MI 48091/810-757-4418
Specialties: Working knives of his design. **Patterns:** Exotic opening mechanisms for his folders; personally designed and patented release locks; straight knives, some fancy. **Technical:** Forges and grinds 440C, 154CM and ATS-34; offers finishes from gold to blueing. **Prices:** $250 to $11,500; some to $9,500. **Remarks:** Full-time maker; first knife sold in 1968. **Mark:** Stylized initials.

STICE, DOUGLAS, 1901 Elmhurst Dr., Norman, OK 73071/405-360-3957
Specialties: Working straight knives. **Patterns:** Hunters, Bowies, fighters, tantos and fishing knives. **Technical:** Grinds 440C, ATS-34 and D2. **Prices:** $50 to $150; some to $225. **Remarks:** Part-time maker; first knife sold in 1985. **Mark:** Name.

STIPES, DWIGHT, 8089 SE Country Estates Way, Jupiter, FL 33458/407-743-0550
Specialties: Traditional and working straight knives in standard patterns. **Patterns:** Boots, Bowies, daggers, hunters and fighters. **Technical:** Grinds 440C, D2 and D3 tool steel. Handles of natural materials, animal, bone or horn. **Prices:** $75 to $150. **Remarks:** Full-time maker; first knife sold in 1972. **Mark:** Last name.

STODDART, W.B. "BILL", 917 Smiley, Forest Park, OH 45240/513-851-1543
Specialties: Sportsman's working knives and multi-blade folders. **Patterns:** Hunters, camp and fish knives; multi-blade reproductions of old standards. **Technical:** Grinds A2, 440C and ATS-34; makes sheaths to match handle materials. **Prices:** $80 to $300; some to $850. **Remarks:** Part-time maker; first knife sold in 1976. **Mark:** Name, Cincinnati, state.

STOKES, ED, 22614 Cardinal Dr., Hockley, TX 77447/713-351-1319
Specialties: Working straight knives and folders of all designs. **Patterns:** Boots, Bowies, daggers, fighters, hunters and miniatures. **Technical:** Grinds ATS-34, 440C and D2. Offers decorative buttcaps, tapered spacers on handles and finger grooves, nickel silver inlays, hand-made sheaths. **Prices:** $185 to $290; some to $350. **Remarks:** Full-time maker; first knife sold in 1973. **Mark:** First and last name, Custom Knives with apache logo.

STONE BIRDS (See Thompson, Tommy)

STONE, JERRY, P.O. Box 1027, Lytle, TX 78052/512-772-4502
Specialties: Traditional working and using folders of his design and to customer specs; fancy knives. **Patterns:** Fighters, hunters, locking folders and slip-joints. **Technical:** Grinds 440C and ATS-34. Offers filework. **Prices:** $125 to $375; some to $700. **Remarks:** Full-time maker; first knife sold in 1973. **Mark:** Initials.

STOUT, JOHNNY, 1514 Devin Dr., New Braunfels, TX 78130/210-629-1011
Specialties: Working knives, some fancy. **Patterns:** Hunters, fighters, Bowies, automatics, liner locks and folders. **Technical:** Grinds stainless and carbon steels; forges own Damascus. **Prices:** $300 to $650; some to $2,500. **Remarks:** Full-time maker; first knife sold in 1983. **Mark:** Name and city in logo with serial number.

STOVER, TERRY "LEE", 1809 N. 300E., Kokomo, IN 46901/317-457-2809
Specialties: Damascus folders with filework; Damascus Bowies of his design or to customer specs. **Patterns:** Lockback folders and sheffield-style Bowies. **Technical:** Forges 1095, Damascus using 02, 203E or 02, pure nickel. Makes mokume. Uses only natural handle material. **Prices:** $300 to $1,700; some to $2,000. **Remarks:** Part-time maker; first knife sold in 1984. **Mark:** First and middle initials, last name in knife logo; Damascus blades marked in Old English.

STRAIGHT, DON, 3465 Gallows Rd., Falls Church, VA 22042/703-560-6331
Specialties: Traditional working straight knives of his design. **Patterns:** Hunters, Bowies and fighters. **Technical:** Grinds 440C, ATS-34 and D2. **Prices:** $75 to $125; some to $225. **Remarks:** Spare-time maker; first knife sold in 1978. **Mark:** Last name.

STRICKLAND, DALE, 1440 E. Thompson View, Monroe, UT 84754/801-896-8362
Specialties: Traditional and working straight knives and folders of his design and to customer specs. **Patterns:** Hunters, folders, miniatures and utility knives. **Technical:** Grinds Damascus and 440C. **Prices:** $120 to $350; some to $500. **Remarks:** Part-time maker; first knife sold in 1991. **Mark:** Oval stamp of name and city.

STROHECKER, JOHN J., P.O. Box 1411, Riverton, WY 82501/307-856-4139
Specialties: Working and special-order knives. **Patterns:** Hunters and Bowies. **Technical:** Forges 5160 and 52100. Handles made of horn, antlers and exotic woods. Offers pouch-type leather sheaths. **Prices:** $200 to $500; some higher. **Remarks:** Part-time maker; first knife sold in 1984. Studying with Ed. A. Fowler. **Mark:** Stro's.

STRONG, SCOTT, 2138 Oxmoor Dr., Beavercreek, OH 45431/513-426-9290
Specialties: Working knives, some deluxe. **Patterns:** Hunters, fighters, survival and military-style knives, art knives. **Technical:** Forges and grinds 01, A2, D2, 440C and ATS-34. Uses no solder; most knives disassemble. **Prices:** $40 to $350; some to $1,500. **Remarks:** Spare-time maker; first knife sold in 1983. **Mark:** Strong Knives.

STROYAN, ERIC, Box 218, Dalton, PA 18414/717-563-2603
Specialties: Classic and working/using straight knives and folders of his design. **Patterns:** Hunters, locking folders, slip-joints. **Technical:** Forges Damascus; grinds ATS-34, D2. **Prices:** $200 to $600; some to $2,000. **Remarks:** Part-time maker; first knife sold in 1968. **Mark:** Signature or initials stamp.

SUEDMEIER, HARLAN, RFD2, Nebraska City, NE 68410/402-873-4372
Specialties: Working straight knives. **Patterns:** Hunters, fighters and Bowies. **Technical:** Grinds A2, D2, ATS-34 and 440C. **Prices:** $65 to $300; some to $750. **Remarks:** Part-time maker; first knife sold in 1982. Not currently taking orders. **Mark:** First initial, last name.

SUGIHARA, KEIDOH, 4-16-1 Kamori-Cho, Kishiwada City, Osaka, F596 JAPAN

SUMMERS, ARTHUR L., 8700 Brigner Rd., Mechanicsburg, OH 43044/513-834-3776
Specialties: Hunters, Bowies and collectors in drop points, clip points or straight blades. **Patterns:** Fighters, hunters and personal knives. **Technical:** Grinds 440C, ATS-34, D2 and Damascus. **Prices:** $100 to $350; some to $2,000. **Remarks:** Part-time maker; first knife sold in 1987. **Mark:** Last name and serial number.

SUMMERS, DAN, 2675 NY Rt. 11, Whitney Pt., NY 13862

SUMMERS, DENNIS K., 827 E. Cecil St., Springfield, OH 45503/513-324-0624
Specialties: Working/using knives. **Patterns:** Fighters and personal knives. **Technical:** Grinds 440C, A2 and D2. Makes drop and clip point. **Prices:** $75 to $200. **Remarks:** Part-time maker; first knife sold in 1995. **Mark:** First and middle initials, last name, serial number.

SUNDERLAND, RICHARD, Box 248, Quathiaski Cove, British Columbia, CANADA/V0P 1N0/604-285-3038
Specialties: Personal and hunting knives with carved handles in oosic and ivory. **Patterns:** Hunters, Bowies, daggers, camp and personal knives. **Technical:** Grinds 440C, ATS 34 and 01. Handle materials of rosewoods, fossil mammoth ivory and oosic. **Prices:** $150 to $850. **Remarks:** Full-time maker; first knife sold in 1983. Doing business as Sun Knife Co. **Mark:** SUN.

SUN KNIFE CO. (See Sunderland, Richard)

SUTHERLAND KNIVES OUTDOORS WEST (See Sutherland, Greg)

SUTHERLAND, GREG, P.O. Box 23516, Flagstaff, AZ 86002-3516/520-774-6050
Specialties: Classic working/using straight knives of his design and in standard patterns. **Patterns:** Bowies, hunters, fighters, boots, kitchen, duty and utility/camp knives. **Technical:** Grinds ATS-34, 01. Offers occasional filework and some bronze guards and bolsters. Likes Desert Ironwood. Hunting and utility knives come with leather or Kydex sheath. **Prices:** $100 to $1,000. **Remarks:** Full-time maker; first knife sold in 1989. Doing business as Sutherland Knives Outdoors West. **Mark:** Last name, city, state.

SWAIN, ROD, 1020 Avon Place, South Pasadena, CA 91030/818-799-7666
Specialties: Working straight knives, some fancy, of his design and to customer specs. **Patterns:** Outdoor patterns, Bowies and push knives, utility drop-points. **Technical:** Grinds 01, 440C, AEB-L. **Prices:** $75 to $250; some to $450. **Remarks:** Part-time maker; first knife sold in 1981. **Mark:** Last name in logo.

SYSLO, CHUCK, 3418 South 116 Ave., Omaha, NE 68144/402-333-0647
Specialties: High-tech working straight knives. **Patterns:** Hunters, daggers and survival knives; locking folders. **Technical:** Flat-grinds D2, 440C and 154CM; hand polishes only. **Prices:** $175 to $500; some to

$3,000. **Remarks:** Part-time maker; first knife sold in 1978. **Mark:** CISCO in logo.

SZILASKI, JOSEPH, 29 Carroll Dr., Wappingers Falls, NY 12590/914-297-5397
Specialties: Fancy and traditional straight knives of his design, to customer specs and in standard patterns. Many pieces are one-of-a-kind. **Patterns:** Bowies, daggers, fighters and hunters. **Technical:** Grinds 440C and 154CM; forges A2, D2, 01 and Damascus. **Prices:** $95 to $275; some to $2,000. **Remarks:** Full-time maker; first knife sold in 1990. **Mark:** Snake logo.

t

TAGLIENTI, ANTONIO J., P.O. Box 221, Darlington, PA 16115/412-846-5259
Specialties: Working straight knives in standard patterns. **Patterns:** Hunters—likes forefinger radius; Bowies, tantos and camp knives. **Technical:** Grinds D2, 440C and 154CM. Emphasizes full tangs; offers filework. **Prices:** $85 to $200; some to $350. **Remarks:** Part-time maker; first knife sold in 1985. **Mark:** Last name.

TAKAHASHI, HIROHIKO, 3-76-9 Mukai Cho, Turu Mi Ku, Yokohama 230, JAPAN

TAKAHASHI, MASAO, 39-3 Sekine-cho, Maebashi-shi, Gunma 371 JAPAN/0272-34-2223

TALON BLADES (See Knuth, Joseph E.)

TAMBOLI, MICHAEL, 12447 N. 49 Ave., Glendale, AZ 85304/602-978-4308
Specialties: Miniatures, some full size. **Patterns:** Miniature hunting knives to fantasy art knives. **Technical:** Grinds 440C, 154CM and Damascus. **Prices:** $75 to $500; some to $1,000. **Remarks:** Part-time maker; first knife sold in 1978. **Mark:** Initials or last name, city and state.

TASAKI, SEICHI, 24 Shizuwa, Shimotsuga-Gun, Tochigi, JAPAN/0482-55-6066
Specialties: High-tech traditional straight knives and folders. **Patterns:** Variety of hunters, miniatures, interframe folders and more. **Technical:** Forges and grinds 440C and carbon steel. **Prices:** $230 to $850; some to $5,000. **Remarks:** Full-time maker; first knife sold in 1984. **Mark:** Initials connected.

"tat" (See Brack, Douglas D.)

TAY, LARRY C-G, Siglap P.O. Box 315, Singapore 9145, REPUBLIC OF SINGAPORE/65-2419421
Specialties: Working and using straight knives and folders of his design; Marble's Safety Knife with stained or albino Asian buffalo horn and bone or rosewood handles. **Patterns:** Fighters, locking folders and utility/camp knives. **Technical:** Forges and grinds 440C; uses Damascus USA billets, truck leaf springs. **Prices:** $50 to $200; some to $500. **Remarks:** Spare-time maker; first knife sold in 1957. **Mark:** LDA/LAKELL

TAYLOR, BILLY, 10 Temple Rd., Petal, MS 39465/601-544-0041
Specialties: Straight knives of his design. **Patterns:** Bowies, skinners, hunters and utility knives. **Technical:** Flat-grinds 440C, ATS-34 and 154CM. **Prices:** $60 to $300. **Remarks:** Part-time maker; first knife sold in 1991. **Mark:** Full name, city and state.

TAYLOR, C. GRAY, 137 Lana View Dr., Kingsport, TN 37664/423-288-5969
Specialties: High-art display knives; period pieces. **Patterns:** Fighters, Bowies, daggers, locking folders and interframes. **Technical:** Grinds 440C, 154CM and ATS-34. **Prices:** $200 to $3,000; some to $7,000. **Remarks:** Part-time maker; first knife sold in 1975. **Mark:** Name, city and state.

TAYLOR, DAVID, 232 Akard St., Bristol, TN 37620/423-764-3811
Specialties: Folders. **Patterns:** Slip-joint, lock-back and multi-blade folders. **Technical:** Grinds 440C, 154CM and ATS-34. **Prices:** $150 to $550; some higher. **Remarks:** Part-time maker; first knife sold in 1981. **Mark:** Name, city and state.

TAYLOR, SHANE, Rock Springs Rt., Angela, MT 59312/406-354-6551 or 406-232-7175
Specialties: Fancy and working straight knives of his design and to customer specs. **Patterns:** Bowies, daggers, hunters and miniatures. **Technical:** Forges Damascus, cable Damascus and chain. Offers wildlife scrimshaw. **Prices:** $175 to $650; some to $1,500. **Remarks:** Part-time maker; first knife sold in 1982. **Mark:** First name.

TEDDER, MICKEY, Rt. 2, Box 22, Conover, NC 28613/704-464-9002
Specialties: Working folders. **Patterns:** Locking hunters, fighters and boots. **Technical:** Grinds D2, 440C and 154CM. Makes gold miniatures as jewelry. **Prices:** $150 to $300; some to $1,500. **Remarks:** Part-time maker. **Mark:** Last name.

TEDDYBEAR KNIVES (See Luchak, Bob)

TEDDYHAWK (See Goldenberg, T.S.)

TENNESSEE KNIFE MAKER—TKM (See Ward, W.C.)

TERAUCHI, TOSHIYUKI, 7649-13 219-11 Yoshida, Fujita-Cho Gobo-Shi, JAPAN

TERRA-GLADIUS KNIVES (See Reynolds, Dave)

TERRILL, STEPHEN, 21363 Rd. 196, Lindsay, CA 93247/209-562-4395
Specialties: Deluxe working straight knives and folders. **Patterns:** Fighters, tantos, boots, locking folders and axes; traditional oriental patterns. **Technical:** Forges 440C, 1084 and his Damascus. **Prices:** Moderate. **Remarks:** Part-time maker; first knife sold in 1972. **Mark:** Name, city, state in logo.

TERRY KNIVES (See Cohen, Terry A.)

TERZUOLA, ROBERT, Rt. 6, Box 83A, Santa Fe, NM 87501/505-473-1002; FAX: 505-438-8018
Specialties: Working folders of his design; period pieces. **Patterns:** High-tech utility, defense and gentleman's folders. **Technical:** Grinds ATS-34. Offers titanium handles for side-lock folders. **Prices:** $275 to $400; some to $3,000. **Remarks:** Full-time maker; first knife sold in 1980. **Mark:** Mayan dragon head, name and motto meaning "second to none".

THAYER, DANNY, 4504 W. 660 S., Lafayette, IN 47905/317-538-3105
Specialties: Traditional working and using straight knives in standard patterns and to customer specs. **Patterns:** Hunters, Bowies, daggers, utility/camp and kitchen knives. **Technical:** Forges 01, W2 and 5160. **Prices:** $150 to $1,000. **Remarks:** Spare-time maker; first knife sold in 1988. **Mark:** Last name.

THILL, JIM, 10242 Bear Run, Missoula, MT 59803/406-251-5475
Specialties: Traditional and working/using knives of his design. **Patterns:** Fighters, hunters and utility/camp knives. **Technical:** Grinds D2 and ATS-34; forges 10-95-85. Offers hand cut sheaths with rawhide lace. **Prices:** $145 to $350; some to $1250. **Remarks:** Full-time maker; first knife sold in 1962. **Mark:** Running bear in triangle.

THOMAS, DANIEL, 1017 Rollins Dr. SW, Leesburg, VA 22075/703-442-6877
Specialties: Traditional working and using straight knives and folders of his design. **Patterns:** Hunters, slip-joint and locking folders. **Technical:** Grinds ATS-34, D2 and commercial Damascus. Offers fixed blade and folder repair and rebuilding. **Prices:** $125 to $200; some to $350. **Remarks:** Spare-time maker; first knife sold in 1983. **Mark:** Last name, Handcrafted.

THOMAS, DEVIN, 2344 Moonlite Dr., Las Vegas, NV 89115/702-643-6783
Specialties: Traditional straight knives and folders in standard patterns. **Patterns:** Bowies, fighters, hunters. **Technical:** Forges stainless Damascus, nickel and 1095. Uses, makes and sells Mokume with brass, copper and nickel silver. **Prices:** $300 to $1,200. **Remarks:** Full-time maker; first knife sold in 1979. **Mark:** First and last name, city and state with anvil, or first name only.

THOMAS, KIM, 2906 Center Rd., Brunswick OH 44212/216-225-3931
Specialties: Fancy and traditional straight knives of his design and to customer specs; period pieces. **Patterns:** Boots, daggers, fighters, swords. **Technical:** Forges own Damascus from 5160, 1010 and nickel. **Prices:** $135 to $1,500; some to $3,000. **Remarks:** Part-time maker; first knife sold in 1986. Doing business as Thomas Iron Works. **Mark:** Initials.

THOMAS, ROCKY, 204 Columbia Dr., Ladson, SC 29456/803-553-6843
Specialties: Traditional working and using straight knives in standard patterns. **Patterns:** Hunters and utility/camp knives. **Technical:** Grinds 440C, ATS-34 and commercial Damascus. **Prices:** $75 to $125. **Remarks:** Spare-time maker; first knife sold in 1986. **Mark:** First name in script.

THOMPSON, KENNETH, 4887 Glenwhite Dr., Duluth, GA 30136/404-446-6730
Specialties: Traditional working and using knives of his design. **Patterns:** Hunters, Bowies and utility/camp knives. **Technical:** Forges 5168, 01, 1095 and 52100. **Prices:** $75 to $350; some to $600. **Remarks:** Part-time maker; first knife sold in 1990. **Mark:** P/W; or name, P/W, city and state.

THOMPSON, LEON, 1735 Leon Drive, Forest Grove, OR 97116/503-357-2573
Specialties: Working knives. **Patterns:** Locking folders, slip-joints and liner locks. **Technical:** Grinds ATS-34, D2 and 440C. **Prices:** $200 to $600. **Remarks:** Full-time maker; first knife sold in 1976. **Mark:** First and middle initials, last name, city and state.

THOMPSON, LLOYD, P.O. Box 1664, Pagosa Springs, CO 81147/303-264-5837
Specialties: Working and collectible straight knives and folders of his design. **Patterns:** Hunter drop-points, lockbacks and hawkbills. **Technical:** Hollow-grinds ATS-34, D2 and 01. Uses sambar stag and exotic woods. **Prices:** $125 to $400. **Remarks:** Full-time maker; first knife sold in 1985. Doing business as Trapper Creek Knife Co. **Mark:** Name.

THOMPSON, ROBERT L., P.O. Box 23992, Phoenix, AZ 85063/602-846-5102
Specialties: Fantasy and working straight knives of his design; miniatures as jewelry items. **Patterns:** Daggers, fighters and utility knives. **Technical:** Forges own Damascus, cable and meteorite; grinds everything else, including stone. **Prices:** $35 to $350; some to $2,000. **Remarks:** Full-time maker; first knife sold in 1989. **Mark:** Runic figure of initials.

THOMPSON, TOMMY, 4015 NE Hassalo, Portland, OR 97232-2607/503-235-5762
Specialties: Fancy and working knives; mostly liner lock folders. **Patterns:** Fighters, hunters and liner locks. **Technical:** Grinds D2, BG42, CPM 440V and CPM 15V. Handles are either hardwood inlayed with wood banding and stone; shell; or made of agate, jasper, petrified woods, etc. **Prices:** $75 to $500; some to $1,000. **Remarks:** Part-time maker; first knife sold in 1987. Doing business as Stone Birds. **Mark:** First and last name, city and state.

THOM'S CUSTOM KNIVES (See Broome, Thomas A.)

THOUROT, MICHAEL W., T814RR1, RD 11, Napoleon, OH 43545/419-533-6832

Specialties: Working straight knives to customer specs. Designed two-handled skinning ax and limited edition engraved knife and art print set. **Patterns:** Fishing and fillet knives, Bowies, tantos and hunters. **Technical:** Grinds 01, D2, 440C and Damascus. **Prices:** $200 to $5,000. **Remarks:** Part-time maker; first knife sold in 1969. **Mark:** Initials.

THREE CROWNS CUTLERY (See Scofield, Everett)

THUESEN, ED, 10649 Haddington, Suite 180, Houston, TX 77043/713-461-8632; FAX: 713-461-8221
Specialties: Working straight knives. **Patterns:** Hunters, fighters and survival knives. **Technical:** Grinds D2, 440C, ATS-34 and Vascowear. **Prices:** $85 to $250; some to $600. **Remarks:** Part-time maker; first knife sold in 1979. Runs knifemaker supply business. **Mark:** Last name.

THUESEN, KEVIN, 10649 Haddington, Suite 180, Houston, TX 77043/713-461-8632
Specialties: Working straight knives. **Patterns:** Hunters, including upswept skinners, and custom walking sticks. **Technical:** Grinds D2, 440C, 154CM and ATS-34. **Prices:** $85 to $125; some to $200. **Remarks:** Part-time maker; first knife sold in 1985. **Mark:** Initials on slant.

THUNDER MOUNTAIN FORGE CLAIBORNE KNIVES (See Claiborne, Ron)

THUNDERBIRD (See Mendenhall, Harry E.)

THUNDERBOLT ARTISANS (See Hilker, Thomas N.)

TIGHE, BRIAN, RR 1 Ridgeville, L0S 1M0 Ontario, CANADA/905-892-2734
Specialties: Fancy/embellished and high tech folders of his design. **Patterns:** Boots, daggers, locking and slip-joint folders. **Technical:** Grinds 440C, ATS-34 and Damascus. Prefers natural handle material inlay; hand finishes. **Prices:** $350 to $800; some to $1,500. **Remarks:** Part-time maker; first knife sold in 1989. **Mark:** Etched signature.

TILL, CALVIN E. AND RUTH, 405½ N. Maple St., Chadron, Nebraska 69337
Specialties: Fantasy and traditional straight knives of his design and to customer specs. **Patterns:** Bowies, hunters and locking folders. **Technical:** Grinds spring steel only. Full or threaded tangs. Prefers mirror polishes. **Prices:** $80 to $120; some to $250. **Remarks:** Part-time maker; first knife sold in 1986. **Mark:** Name, date and serial number.

TILL, RUTH (See Till, Calvin E. and Ruth)

THE TINKER (See Ladd, Jim S.)

TINKER, CAROLYN D., P.O. Box 5123, Whittier, CA 90607/213-696-9202
Specialties: Working straight knives of her design. **Patterns:** Hunters, kitchen and fishing knives; small tools. **Technical:** Grinds D2, 440C and 154CM. **Prices:** $85 to $125. **Remarks:** Full-time maker; first knife sold In 1974. Currently not taking orders. **Mark:** Name and city in logo.

TINKERMADE KNIVES (See Rachlin, Leslie S.)

T.J.'S CUSTOM KNIVES (See Tyer, Jerry L.)

TKM—TENNESSEE KNIFE MAKER (See Ward, W.C.)

TODD, ED, 9 Woodlawn Rd., Putnam Valley, NY 10579

TOICH, NEVIO, Via Pisacane 9, Rettorgole di Caldogna, Vincenza, ITALY 36030/0444-985065; FAX: 0444-301254
Specialties: Working/using straight knives of his design or to customer specs. **Patterns:** Bowies, hunters, skinners and utility/camp knives. **Technical:** Grinds 440C, D2 and ATS-34. Hollow-grinds all blades and uses mirror polish. Offers hand-sewn sheaths. Uses wood and horn.

Prices: $120 to $300; some to $450. **Remarks:** Spare-time maker; first knife sold in 1989. Doing business as Custom Toich. **Mark:** Initials and model number punched.

TOKAR, DANIEL, Box 1776, Shepherdstown, WV 25443
Specialties: Working knives; period pieces. **Patterns:** Hunters, camp knives, buckskinners, axes, swords and battle gear. **Technical:** Forges L6, 1095 and his Damascus; makes mokume, Japanese alloys and bronze daggers; restores old edged weapons. **Prices:** $25 to $800; some to $3,000. **Remarks:** Part-time maker; first knife sold in 1979. Doing business as The Willow Forge. **Mark:** Arrow over rune and date.

TOLLEFSON, BARRY A., 177 Blackfoot Trail, P.O. Box 1425, Gunnison, CO 303-641-0752
Specialties: Working straight knives, some fancy. **Patterns:** Hunters, skinners, fighters and camp knives. **Technical:** Grinds 440C, ATS-34 and D2. Likes mirror-finishes; offers some fancy filework. Handles made from elk, deer and exotic hardwoods. **Prices:** $75 to $300; some higher. **Remarks:** Part-time maker; first knife sold in 1990. **Mark:** Stylized initials.

TOMES, ANTHONY S., 8190 Loch Seaforth Ct., Jacksonville, FL 32244
Specialties: Working knives and period pieces. **Patterns:** Hunters, daggers, folders and liner locks. **Technical:** Grinds D2 and ATS-34. **Prices:** $50 to $500. **Remarks:** Part-time maker. **Mark:** Initials.

TOMES, P.J., P.O. Box 1921, Orange Park, FL 32067-1921/904-282-7095
Specialties: Scagel reproductions. **Patterns:** Front lock folders. **Prices:** $150 to $750. **Mark:** Last name, USA, MS, stamped in forged blades.

TOMKA ARMOURY (See Kaczor, Tom)

TOMPKINS, DAN, P.O. Box 398, Peotone, Illinois 60468/708-258-3620
Specialties: Working knives, some deluxe, some folders. **Patterns:** Hunters, boots, daggers and push knives. **Technical:** Grinds D2, 440C, ATS-34 and 154CM. **Prices:** $85 to $150; some to $400. **Remarks:** Part-time maker; first knife sold in 1975. **Mark:** Last name, city, state.

TONER, ROGER, 531 Lightfoot Place, Pickering, Ont. L1V 5Z8, CANADA/905-420-5555
Specialties: Exotic sword canes. **Patterns:** Bowies, daggers and fighters. **Technical:** Grinds 440C, D2 and Damascus. Scrimshaws and engraves. Silvercast pommels and guards in animal shapes; twisted silver wire inlays. Uses semi-precious stones. **Prices:** $200 to $2,000; some to $3,000. **Remarks:** Part-time maker; first knife sold in 1982. **Mark:** Last name.

TOPLISS, M.W. "IKE", 1668 Hermosa Ct., Montrose, CO 81401/970-249-4703
Specialties: Working/using straight knives of his design and to customer specs. **Patterns:** Boots, hunters, utility/camp knives. **Technical:** Grinds ATS-34, 440C, D2. Prefers natural hardwoods, antler and Micarta. All sheaths hand-made. **Prices:** $125 to $250; some to $600. **Remarks:** Part-time maker; first knife sold in 1984. **Mark:** Name, city, state.

TOWELL, DWIGHT L., Rt. 1, Box 66, Midvale, ID 83645/208-355-2419
Specialties: Solid, elegant working knives; art knives. **Patterns:** Hunters, Bowies, daggers; folders in several weights. **Technical:** Grinds 154CM; some engraving. **Prices:** $250 to $800; some $3,500 and higher. **Remarks:** Part-time maker; first knife sold in 1970. **Mark:** Last name.

TOWNSEND, J.W., 2073 Highway 200, Trout Creek, MT 59874/406-847-2667
Specialties: One-of-a-kinds. **Patterns:** Fantasy knives and fighters. **Technical:** Grinds 440C, 01, commercial Damascus and ATS-34. **Prices:** $175 to $1,200; some higher. **Remarks:** Full-time maker; first knife sold in 1985. **Mark:** First and middle initials and last name, or stylized last name.

TRABBIC, R.W., 4550 N. Haven, Toledo, OH 43612/419-478-9578
Specialties: Working knives. **Patterns:** Hunters, Bowies, locking hunters and springbacks in standard patterns. **Technical:** Grinds D2, 440C and 154CM. **Prices:** $80 to $250. **Remarks:** Part-time maker; first knife sold in 1973. **Mark:** First and middle initials, last name.

TRACKERS FORGE (See Alderman, Robert)

TRACY, BUD, 15500 Fawn Ln., Reno, NV 89511

TRAPPER CREEK KNIFE CO. (See Thompson, Lloyd)

TRASK RIVER CUSTOM KNIVES (See Woodcock, Dennis "Woody")

TREIBER, LEON, P.O. Box 342, Ingram, TX 78025/210-367-2246
Specialties: Folders of his design and to customer specs. **Patterns:** Locking folders. **Technical:** Grinds CPM T 440V, D2, 440C. **Prices:** $250 to $600. **Remarks:** Part-time maker; first knife sold in 1992. Doing business as Treiber Knives. **Mark:** First initial, last name, city, state.

TREML, GLENN, RR #14, Site 11-10, Thunder Bay, Ontario, CANADA P7B 5E5/807-767-1977
Specialties: Working straight knives of his design and to customer specs. **Patterns:** Hunters, kitchen knives and double-edged survival knives. **Technical:** Grinds 440C, ATS-34 and 01; stock removal method. Uses Pakkawood and Micarta for handle materials. **Prices:** $60 to $400; some higher. **Mark:** Stamped last name.

TRINDLE, BARRY, RR #2, Box 63, Earlham, IA 50072/515-462-1237
Specialties: Engraved folders. **Patterns:** Mostly small folders, classical styles and pocket knives. **Technical:** 440 only. Engraves. Handles of wood or mineral material. **Prices:** $750 and up. **Mark:** Name on tang.

TRITZ, JEAN JOSE, Schopstrasse 23, 20255 Hamburg, GERMANY/040-49 78 21
Specialties: Working/using knives. **Patterns:** Kitchen knives and friction folders. **Technical:** Forges carbon steels, tool steels, ball bearing steel, file steel, San Mai and his own pattern Damascus. Makes own Mokume. Prefers natural handle material; does leatherwork, some exotic. **Prices:** $150 to $1,000; some higher. **Remarks:** Part-time maker; first knife sold in 1989. **Mark:** Initials in monogram.

TRL HANDMADE KNIVES (See Lewis, Tom R.)

TRO KNIVES (See Overeynder, T.R.)

TROLL HAMMER FORGE (See Dube, Paul and Flood, James [Noah])

TRUCKEE KNIFEWORKS (See Fronefield, Mike)

TRUJILLO, THOMAS A., 3001 Tanglewood Dr., Anchorage, AK 99517/907-243-6093
Specialties: Working knives. **Patterns:** Hunters, Bowies, daggers and locking folders. **Technical:** Grinds to customer choice, including rock and commercial Damascus. **Prices:** $150 to $900; some to $6,000. **Remarks:** Full-time maker; first knife sold in 1976. Doing business as Alaska Knife & Service Co. **Mark:** Alaska Knife and/or Thomas Anthony.

TURCOTTE, LARRY, 1707 Evergreen, Pampa, TX 79065/806-665-9369, 806-669-0435
Specialties: Fancy and working/using knives of his design and to customer specs. **Patterns:** Hunters, kitchen knives, utility/camp knives. **Technical:** Grinds 440C, D2, ATS-34. Engraves, scrimshands, silver inlays. **Prices:** $150 to $350; some to $1,000. **Remarks:** Part-time maker; first knife sold in 1977. Doing business as Knives by Turcotte. **Mark:** Last name.

TURECEK, JIM, P.O. Box 882, Derby, CT 06418/203-734-8406
Specialties: Exotic folders, art knives and some miniatures. **Patterns:**

Trout and bird knives with split bamboo handles and one-of-a-kind folders. **Technical:** Grinds and forges stainless and carbon Damascus. **Prices:** $750 to $1,500; some to $3,000. **Remarks:** Full-time maker; first knife sold in 1983. **Mark:** Last initial in script, or last name.

TURNBULL, RALPH A., 5722 Newburg Rd., Rockford, IL 61108/815-398-3799
Specialties: Plain or fancy working knives. **Patterns:** Hunters, fighters, boots, folders and Bowies. **Technical:** Grinds ATS-34, 440C, 154CM, CPM and others, Damascus. Makes wood inlay handles. **Prices:** $100 to $300; some to $2,000. **Remarks:** Full-time maker; first knife sold in 1973. **Mark:** Signature or initials.

TURNER, KEVIN, 17 Hunt Ave., Montrose, NY 10548/914-739-0535
Specialties: Working straight knives of his design and to customer specs; period pieces. **Patterns:** Daggers, fighters and utility knives. **Technical:** Forges 5160 and 52100. **Prices:** $90 to $500. **Remarks:** Part-time maker; first knife sold in 1991. **Mark:** Acid-etched signed last name and year.

TWIG (See Davis, K.M. "Twig")

TWILIGHT FORGE (See Champagne, Paul)

TWISTED NICKEL KNIVES (See Ferguson, Jim [Downey, CA])

TYC, WILLIAM J., 14 Hob St., Newburgh, NY 12550/914-562-5165
Specialties: Traditional and working straight knives of all designs. **Patterns:** Bowies, fighters and utility knives. **Technical:** Grinds 440C, ATS-34 and 01. Satin finishes blades. **Prices:** $80 to $300; some to $500. **Remarks:** Spare-time maker; first knife sold in 1989. **Mark:** First and last name.

TYCER, ART, 3807 Hillside Dr., N. Little Rock, AR 72118/501-753-7637

TYER, JERRY L., HC67, Box 204, Everton, AR 72633/501-427-5393
Specialties: Hunters and utility/camp knives of his design. **Patterns:** Bowies, hunters and utility/camp knives. **Technical:** Forges 5168, 01 and A2; makes own Damascus. Heat-treats. **Prices:** $350 and up. **Remarks:** Full-time maker; first knife was sold in 1982. Doing business as T.J.'s Custom Knives. **Mark:** Stylized initials.

U

UEDA, MASAHARU, B1 Fokuku Seimei Building 2-4, Komatu bara-cho Kita-ku, Osaka City, 530 JAPAN/06-313-2525; FAX: 06-313-2626
Specialties: High-art straight knives of his design. **Patterns:** Hunters, kitchen knives and utility knives. **Technical:** Grinds Cowry X, 440C and ATS-34. **Prices:** $900 to $7,200. **Remarks:** Part-time maker; first knife sold in 1993. Doing business as World Gallery Co., Ltd. **Mark:** NA.

UEKAMA, NOBUYUKI, 3-2-8-302 Ochiai, Tama City, Tokyo, JAPAN

UWHARRIE RATTLER KNIVES (See Rece, Charles V.)

V

VACHON, YVON, 98, Lehoux St., Robertsonville, Quebec, CANADA G0N 1L0/418-338-6601
Specialties: Miniature straight knives and folders in standard patterns. **Patterns:** Automatics, daggers and locking folders. **Technical:** Grinds 440C, 316 and Damascus. Uses exotic wood, malachite, buffalo horn, mother-of-pearl and abalone. **Prices:** $100 to $700; some to $5,600. **Remarks:** Spare-time maker; first knife sold in 1982. Doing business as Creation Yvon Vachon. **Mark:** Initials punched.

VALACHOVIC, WAYNE, P.O. Box 4219, Kailua-Kona, HI 96745
Specialties: Damascus folders in unique designs with Persian influences. **Patterns:** Collectible folders. **Technical:** Forges own Damas-

cus; most knives have filework. **Prices:** Start at $250. **Remarks:** Full-time maker. **Mark:** Last initial with cross.

VALLOTTON, BUTCH AND AREY, 621 Fawn Ridge Dr., Oakland, OR 97462/503-459-2216
Specialties: Heavy-duty folders with complicated mechanisms to customer specs. **Patterns:** Fighters, gentleman's knives and working folders. **Technical:** Grinds ATS-34, 440C, Damascus, titanium, 416 and nickel-silver. Prefers bead-blasted, mirror or anodized finishes. **Prices:** $350 to $2,500. **Remarks:** Full-time maker; first knife sold in 1981. **Mark:** Name, area and state.

VALLOTTON, RAINY D., 1377 Lower Crest Rd., Oakland, OR 97462/503-459-2216
Specialties: Folders and one-handed openers. **Patterns:** Hunters, fighters, folders and sheath knives. **Technical:** Stock removal all steels; uses titanium liners and bolsters; uses all finishes. **Prices:** $250 to $1,000. **Remarks:** Full-time maker. **Mark:** Name.

VALLOTTON, SHAWN, 621 Fawn Ridge Dr., Oakland, OR 97462/503-459-2216
Specialties: Left-hand knives. **Patterns:** All styles. **Technical:** Grinds 440C, ATS-34 and Damascus. Uses titanium. Prefers bead-blasted or anodized finishes. **Prices:** $250 to $1,400. **Remarks:** Full-time maker. **Mark:** Name and specialty.

VALOIS, A. DANIEL, 3552 W. Lizard Ck. Rd., Lehighton, PA 18235/717-386-3636
Specialties: Big working knives; various sized lock-back folders with new safety releases. **Patterns:** Fighters in survival packs, sturdy working knives, belt buckle knives, military-style knives, swords. **Technical:** Forges and grinds A2, 01 and 440C; likes full tangs. **Prices:** $65 to $240; some to $600. **Remarks:** Full-time maker; first knife sold in 1969. **Mark:** Anvil logo with last name inside.

VAN DE MANAKKER, THIJS, Koolweg 34, 575g px Helenaveen, HOLLAND/04g353g3bg

VAN DEN ELSEN, GERT, Purcelldreef 83, 5012 AJ Tilburg, THE NETHERLANDS/013-563200
Specialties: Fancy, working/using, miniatures and integral straight knives of the maker's design or to customer specs. **Patterns:** Bowies, fighters and hunters. **Technical:** Grinds ATS-34 and 440C; forges Damascus. Offers filework, differentially tempered blades and some mokume-gane fittings. **Prices:** $170 to $500; some to $2500. **Remarks:** Part-time maker; first knife sold in 1982. Doing business as G-E Knives. **Mark:** Initials GE in lozenge shape.

VANDERFORD, CARL G., Rt. 9, Box 238B, Columbia, TN 38401/615-381-1488
Specialties: Traditional working straight knives and folders of his design. **Patterns:** Hunters, Bowies and locking folders. **Technical:** Forges and grinds 440C, 01 and wire Damascus. **Prices:** $60 to $125. **Remarks:** Part-time maker; first knife sold in 1987. **Mark:** Last name.

VAN ELDIK, FRANS, Ho Flaan 3, 3632 BT Loenen, NETHERLANDS/31-02943-3095; FAX: 02940-80430
Specialties: Fancy working knives of his design. **Patterns:** Hunters, fighters, boots and folders. **Technical:** Forges and grinds D2, 154CM, ATS-34 and Damascus from Germany. **Prices:** $225 to $1,750; some to $2,500. **Remarks:** Spare-time maker; first knife sold in 1979. **Mark:** Lion with initials and Amsterdam.

VAN HOY, ED, Rt.8 Box 244-A, Greenville, NC 27834/919-830-6636
Specialties: Traditional and working/using straight knives of his design. **Patterns:** Fighters, hunters and utility/camp knives. **Technical:** Grinds ATS-34 and 440V; forges D2. Offers filework, acid etching, mosaic pins, decorative bolsters and custom fitted English bridle leather sheaths. **Prices:** $90 to $350; some to $900. **Remarks:** Full-time maker; first knife sold in 1977. Doing business as Van Hoy Knives. **Mark:** Stamped last initial or Van; acid etched last name, city and state.

VEATCH, RICHARD, 2580 N. 35th Pl., Springfield, OR 97477/503-747-3910
Specialties: Traditional working and using straight knives of his design and in standard patterns; period pieces. **Patterns:** Dagggers, hunters, swords, utility/camp knives and minis. **Technical:** Forges and grinds his own Damascus; uses L6 and 01. Prefers natural handle materials; offers leatherwork. **Prices:** $50 to $300; some to $500. **Remarks:** Full-time maker; first knife sold in 1991. **Mark:** Stylized initials.

VEIT, MICHAEL, Rt. 1, 3070 E. Fifth Rd., LaSalle, IL 61301/815-223-3538
Specialties: Period pieces—fancy straight knives and Damascus folders. **Technical:** Forges his own Turkish Damascus and 01; engraves. **Prices:** Start at $350. **Remarks:** Part-time maker; first knife sold in 1985. **Mark:** Name in script.

VENSILD, HENRIK, Storegade 29, DK-3700 Rønne, DENMARK/+45 56 95 41 91
Specialties: Classic and traditional working and using knives of his design; Scandinavian influence. **Patterns:** Hunters and using knives. **Technical:** Forges Damascus. Hand makes handles, sheaths and blades. **Prices:** $350 to $1,000. **Remarks:** Part-time maker; first knife sold in 1967. **Mark:** Initials.

VIALLON, HENRI, Les Belins, 63300 Thiers, FRANCE/(33)-73-80-24-03
Specialties: Traditional straight knives and folders of his design. **Patterns:** Hunters, folders, boots and utility knives. **Technical:** Forges and grinds 12C27, D2, 440C, ATS-34 and his own Damascus; mosaic Damascus. **Prices:** $175 to $375; some to $1,500. **Remarks:** Full-time maker; first knife sold in 1985. **Mark:** First initial, last name.

VIELE, H.J., 88 Lexington Ave., Westwood, NJ 07675/201-666-2906
Specialties: Folding knives of distinctive shapes. **Patterns:** High-tech folders. **Technical:** Grinds 440C and ATS-34. **Prices:** $350 and up. **Remarks:** Full-time maker; first knife sold in 1973. **Mark:** Last name with stylized throwing star.

VIKING KNIVES (See Eriksen, James Thorlief)

VILLA, LUIZ, R. Com. Miguel Calfat, 398, Itaim Bibi, Sao Paulo, SP-04537-081, BRAZIL/011-8290649
Specialties: One-of-a-kind straight knives of all designs. **Patterns:** Bowies, hunters and utility/camp knives. **Technical:** Grinds D6, Damascus and 440C; forges 5160. Prefers natural handle material. **Prices:** $70 to $200. **Remarks:** Part-time maker; first knife sold in 1990. **Mark:** Last name and serial number.

VILLAR, RICARDO, Al. dos Jasmins, Mairipora, SP-07600-000, BRAZIL/011-4851649
Specialties: Straight working knives to customer specs. **Patterns:** Bowies, fighters and utility/camp knives. **Technical:** Grinds D6 and 420 stainless. **Prices:** $60 to $150. **Remarks:** Part-time maker; first knife sold in 1993. **Mark:** Percor over sword and circle.

VISTNES, TOR, N-6930 Svelgen, NORWAY/047-57795572
Specialties: Traditional and working knives of his design. **Patterns:** Hunters and utility knives. **Technical:** Grinds Uddeholm Elmax. Handles made of rear burls of different Nordic stabilized woods. **Prices:** $300 to $1100. **Remarks:** Part-time maker; first knife sold in 1988. **Mark:** Etched name and deer head.

VIPER (See Emerson, Ernest R.)

VON BOECKMAN, R., P.O. Box 40506, Memphis, TN 38174/800-727-0201
Specialties: Working and using knives of his design. **Patterns:** Straight knives, hunters, fighters, utility and camp knives. **Technical:** Grinds 01, 06, D2, 440C and ATS-34. **Prices:** $75 to $300; some $600 and higher. **Remarks:** Full-time maker; first knife sold in 1987. Doing business as Custom Cutlery. **Mark:** Pyramid logo with RA inside.

VOSS, BEN, 362 Clark St., Galesburg, IL 61401/309-342-6994 **Specialties:** Fancy working knives of his design. **Patterns:** Bowies, fighters, hunters, boots and folders. **Technical:** Grinds 440C, ATS-34 and D2. **Prices:** $35 to $1,200. **Remarks:** Part-time maker; first knife sold in 1986. **Mark:** Name, city and state.

VOTAW, DAVID P., Box 327, Pioneer, OH 43554/419-737-2774 **Specialties:** Working knives; period pieces. **Patterns:** Hunters, Bowies, camp knives, buckskinners and tomahawks. **Technical:** Grinds 01 and D2. **Prices:** $100 to $200; some to $500. **Remarks:** Part-time maker; took over for the late W.K. Kneubuhler. Doing business as W-K Knives. **Mark:** WK with V inside anvil.

VOUGHT JR., FRANK, 115 Monticello Dr., Hammond, LA 70401/504-345-0278 **Specialties:** Distinctive working knives and embellished collectibles. **Patterns:** Bowies, hunters, survival knives, daggers, swords and locking folders. **Technical:** Forges and grinds D2, 440C and ATS-34; has new "field-grade" Outfitter line. **Prices:** $50 to $1,500; some to $15,000. **Remarks:** Full-time maker; first knife sold in 1973. **Mark:** Signature with fleur-de-lis, or Outfitter.

VULTURE CUTLERY (See Goers, Bruce)

VUNK, ROBERT, 4408 Buckeye Ct., Orlando, FL 32804/407-628-3970 **Specialties:** Working knives, some fancy; period pieces. **Patterns:** Variety of tantos, fillet knives, kitchen knives, camp knives and folders. **Technical:** Grinds 01, 440C and ATS-34; provides mountings, cases, stands. **Prices:** $55 to $1,300. **Remarks:** Part-time maker; first knife sold in 1985. Doing business as RV Knives. **Mark:** Initials.

W

WADA, YASUTAKA, Fujinokidia 2-6-22, Nara City Nara prefect, 631 JAPAN/06-313-2525; FAX: 06-313-2626

WADE, JAMES M., Rt. 1, Box 56, Wade, NC 28395/919-483-3548 **Specialties:** Working straight knives. **Patterns:** Gut-hook hunters, boots, Bowies, fighters. **Technical:** Grinds D2, 440C, 154CM and ATS-34. **Prices:** $100 to $450; some to $1,000. **Remarks:** Spare-time maker; first knife sold in 1982. **Mark:** Name.

WAGAMAN, JOHN K., 903 Arsenal Ave., Fayetteville, NC 28305/910-485-7860 **Specialties:** Fancy working knives. **Patterns:** Bowies, miniatures, hunters, fighters and boots. **Technical:** Grinds D2, 440C, 154CM and commercial Damascus; inlays mother-of-pearl. **Prices:** $80 to $340; some to $2,000. **Remarks:** Part-time maker; first knife sold in 1975. **Mark:** Last name.

WAGNER, DAN, 21167 Kansas Ave., Chestertown, MD 21620/410-778-5770; 410-778-5087 **Specialties:** Fantasy and working/using straight knives of his design and to customer specs. **Patterns:** Daggers, fighters, hunters. **Technical:** Grinds ATS-34, 52100, CPM 440V. Offers full or tapered tangs, fancy filework. Uses expensive burls and exotic woods for handles. Offers custom leather work. **Prices:** $75 to $250; some to $650. **Remarks:** Part-time maker; first knife sold in 1991. **Mark:** Oaktree Forge or acorn.

WAHLERS, HERMAN F., Star Rt. Box 1, Austerlitz, NY 12017/518-392-3570 **Specialties:** Straight working knives of his design. **Patterns:** Hunters, camp knives, miniatures and working minis. **Technical:** Grinds D2, 440C and ATS-34. **Prices:** $75 to $200; some higher. **Remarks:** Full-time maker; first knife sold in 1983. Doing business as Harvey Mountain Knives. **Mark:** Initials.

WAHLSTER, MARK DAVID, 1404 N. Second St., Silverton, OR 97381/503-873-3775

Specialties: Automatics, antique and high tech folders in standard patterns and to customer specs. **Patterns:** Hunters, fillets and combat knives. **Technical:** Flat grinds 440C, ATS-34, D2 and Damascus. Uses titanium in folders. **Prices:** $100 to $1,000. **Remarks:** Full-time maker; first knife sold in 1981. **Mark:** Name, city and state or last name.

WALDROP, MARK, 14562 SE 1st Ave. Rd., Summerfield, FL 34491/904-347-9034 **Specialties:** Period pieces. **Patterns:** Bowies and daggers. **Technical:** Uses stock removal. Engraves. **Prices:** Moderate to upscale. **Remarks:** Part-time maker; first knife sold in 1978. **Mark:** Last name.

WALKER, GEORGE A., Star Route, Alpine, WY 83128/307-883-2372 **Specialties:** Deluxe working knives. **Patterns:** Hunters, boots, fighters, Bowies and folders. **Technical:** Forges his own Damascus and cable; engraves, carves, scrimshaws. Makes sheaths. **Prices:** $125 to $750; some to $1,000. **Remarks:** Full-time maker; first knife sold in 1979. Partners with wife. **Mark:** Name, city and state.

WALKER, JIM, Rt. 2 Box 12, Morrilton, AR 72110

WALKER, JOHN W., 10620 Moss Branch Rd., Bon Aqua, TN 37025/615-670-4754 **Specialties:** Straight knives and short daggers. **Patterns:** Hunters, boots, etc., some with precious stones. **Technical:** Grinds 440C, ATS-34, L6, etc. **Prices:** $100 to $450; some to $600. **Remarks:** Part-time maker; first knife sold in 1982. **Mark:** Hohenzollern Eagle emblem with name, or last name.

WALKER, MICHAEL L., Box 2343, Taos, NM 87571/505-758-0233 **Specialties:** High-tech folders of his design. **Patterns:** Locking folders, patent locks, interframes—engraved, scrimmed, anodized in titanium colors, furnished with rich materials. **Technical:** Grinds AEB-L, 6K and commercial Damascus. **Prices:** Start at $800. **Remarks:** Full-time maker; first knife sold in 1980. Has trademarked words "liner lock" for advertising use. Most knives a team effort with Patricia Walker. **Mark:** Walker's Lockers by M.L. Walker, or initials.

WALKER, PATRICIA (See Walker, Michael L.)

WALKER'S LOCKERS (See Walker, Michael L.)

WALLACE, ROGER L., 4902 Collins Lane, Tampa, FL 33603/813-239-3261 **Specialties:** Working straight knives, Bowies and camp knives to customer specs. **Patterns:** Hunters, skinners and utility knives. **Technical:** Forges high-carbon steel. **Prices:** Start at $75. **Remarks:** Part-time maker; first knife sold in 1985. **Mark:** First initial, last name.

WALTERS, A.F., 609 E. 20th St., Tifton, GA 31794/912-382-1282 **Specialties:** Working knives, some to customer specs. **Patterns:** Locking folders, straight hunters, fishing and survival knives. **Technical:** Grinds D2, 154CM and 13C26. **Prices:** Start at $150. **Remarks:** Part-time maker. **Label:** "The jewel knife." **Mark:** J in diamond and knife logo.

WANO KNIVES (See Ware, Tommy)

WARD, CHUCK, 1010 E. North St., Benton, AR 72015/501-778-4329 **Specialties:** Traditional working and using straight knives and folders of his design. **Technical:** Grinds 440C, D2, A2 and 01; uses natural and composite handle materials. **Prices:** $90 to $400, some higher. **Remarks:** Full-time maker; first knife sold in 1990. **Mark:** First initial, last name.

WARD, J.J., 7501 S.R. 220, Waverly, OH 45690/614-947-5328 **Specialties:** Traditional and working/using straight knives and folders of his design. **Patterns:** Hunters and locking folders. **Technical:** Grinds ATS-34, 440C and Damascus. Offers heat-treating and handmade sheaths. **Prices:** $125 to $250; some to $500. **Remarks:** Spare-time maker; first knife sold in 1980. **Mark:** Etched name.

WARD, KEN, P.O. Box 6594, Auburn, CA 95604/916-885-8908

Specialties: Working knives, some to customr specs. **Patterns:** Straight and folding hunters, axes, Bowies, buckskinners and miniatures. **Technical:** Grinds ATS-34, Damascus and 6K stellite. **Prices:** $100 to $700. **Remarks:** Part-time maker; first knife sold in 1977. **Mark:** Name.

WARD, W.C., 817 Glenn St., Clinton, TN 37716/615-457-3568
Specialties: Working straight knives; period pieces. **Patterns:** Hunters, Bowies, swords and kitchen cutlery. **Technical:** Grinds 01. **Prices:** $85 to $150; some to $500. **Remarks:** Part-time maker; first knife sold in 1969. He styled the Tennessee Knife Maker. **Mark:** TKM.

WARDELL, MICK R., 85 Coneybury, White Post, Bletchingley, Surrey RH1 4PR ENGLAND/0883-742918
Specialties: Custom knives. **Patterns:** Hunters, Bowies, tantos and friction folders. **Technical:** Grinds Sandvik 12C27, D2, 01 and 1060. Heat-treats with multiple tempering, clay tempering and hardness testing. Offers filework; makes sheaths. **Prices:** £50 to £400; some to £600. **Remarks:** Full-time maker; first knife sold in 1986. **Mark:** Last name or initials.

WARDEN, ROY A., 275 Tanglewood Rd., Union, MO 63084/314-583-8813
Specialties: Working straight knives of his design and in standard patterns. **Patterns:** Hunters, bird and trout knives, camp knives. **Technical:** Forges 5160. Makes own pattern-welded steel Damascus and mosaic Damascus; Damascus billets rough-forged and patterned to order; makes cable Damascus knives and belt buckles. Heat-treats and embellishes. Makes individual knife display stands from woods, steel and horns. **Prices:** Start at $65. **Remarks:** Part-time maker; first knife sold in 1987. **Mark:** Last name.

WARE, TOMMY, Star Route 4, Box 79, Blanco, TX 78606/512-833-5235
Specialties: Working straight knives of his design or to customer specs. **Patterns:** Hunters, single-blade folding hunters, Bowies, hatchets and camp knives, miniatures. **Technical:** Grinds 440C, ATS-34 and D2; embellishes. **Prices:** $150 to $450; some to $800. **Remarks:** Full-time maker; first knife sold in 1988. **Mark:** Wano Knives, city, state and year in oval logo.

WARENSKI, BUSTER, P.O. Box 214, Richfield, UT 84701/801-896-5319
Specialties: Investor-class straight knives. **Patterns:** Daggers, swords, fighters and Bowies. **Technical:** Grinds, engraves and inlays; offers surface treatments. **Prices:** Upscale. **Remarks:** Full-time maker. Not currently taking orders. **Mark:** First or last name.

WARREN, AL, 1423 Sante Fe Circle, Roseville, CA 95678/916-784-3217
Specialties: Working straight knives and folders, some fancy. **Patterns:** Hunters, Bowies, daggers, short swords, fillets and kitchen knives. **Technical:** Grinds D2, ATS-34 and 440C. **Prices:** $110 to $950. **Remarks:** Part-time maker; first knife sold in 1978. **Mark:** First and middle initials, last name.

WARTHER, DALE, 331 Karl Ave., Dover, OH 44622/216-343-7513
Specialties: Working knives; period pieces. **Patterns:** Kitchen cutlery, daggers, hunters and some folders. **Technical:** Forges and grinds 01, D2 and 440C. **Prices:** $100 to $350; some to $5,000. **Remarks:** Full-time maker; first knife sold in 1967. Takes orders only at shows or by personal interviews at his shop. **Mark:** Warther Originals.

WARREN, DELLANA, P.O. Box 9511, Schenectady, NY 12309/518-370-0101
Specialties: Fancy/embellished and high art folders of her design. **Patterns:** Locking folders. **Technical:** Forges her own Damascus and W2. Engraves; does stone setting, filework and carving. Prefers exotic, high karat gold, silver and gemstone handle material. **Prices:** $1,200 to $3,000; some to $5,000. **Remarks:** Full-time maker; first knife sold in 1994. Doing business as Dellana. **Mark:** Engraved first name, date, name of knife, number.

WARTHER ORIGINALS (See Warther, Dale)

WARZOCHA, STANLEY, 32540 Wareham Dr., Warren, MI 48092/313-939-9344
Specialties: Working straight knives; some period pieces. **Patterns:** Hunters, buckskinners, fighters and fishing knives. **Technical:** Grinds 440C and ATS-34. **Prices:** $125 to $1,200. **Remarks:** Spare-time maker; first knife sold in 1978. **Mark:** Last name.

WATANABE, WAYNE, P.O. Box 3563, Montebello, CA 90640/213-728-6867
Specialties: Straight knives in Japanese styles. One-of-kind designs; welcomes customer designs. **Patterns:** Tantos to katanas, Bowies. **Technical:** Flat grinds A2, 01 and ATS-34. Offers hand-rubbed finishes and wrapped handles. **Prices:** $200 and up. **Remarks:** Part-time maker. **Mark:** Name in characters with flower.

WATER MOUNTAIN KNIVES (See Maneker, Kenneth)

WATSON, BERT, P.O. Box 26, Westminster, CO 80030-0026/303-426-7577
Specialties: Working/using straight knives of his design and to customer specs. **Patterns:** Fighters, hunters, utility/camp knives. **Technical:** Grinds 01, ATS-34, 440C. **Prices:** $50 to $250. **Remarks:** Full-time maker; first knife sold in 1974. Doing business as Game Trail Knives. **Mark:** GTK stamped, sometimes with first name.

WATSON, BILLY, 440 Forge Rd., Deatsville, AL 36022/334-365-1482
Specialties: Working and using straight knives and folders of his design; period pieces. **Patterns:** Hunters, Bowies and utility/camp knives. **Technical:** Forges and grinds his own Damascus, 1095, 5160 and 52100. Copper etches on Damascus. **Prices:** $20 to $900. **Remarks:** Full-time maker; first knife sold in 1970. Doing business as Billy's Blacksmith Shop. **Mark:** Last name.

WATSON, DANIEL, 350 Jennifer Ln., Driftwood, TX 78619/512-847-9679
Specialties: One-of-a-kind knives and swords. **Patterns:** Hunters, daggers, swords and miniatures. **Technical:** Hand-purify and carbonize his own high-carbon steel, pattern-welded Damascus, cable and carbon-induced crystalline Damascus. European and Japanese tempering. **Prices:** $90 to $4,000; swords to $25,000. **Remarks:** Full-time maker; first knife sold in 1979. **Mark:** "Angel Sword" on forged pieces; "Bright Knight" for stock removal.

WATSON, PETER, 66 Kielblock St., La Hoff 2570, SOUTH AFRICA/018-84942
Specialties: Traditional working and using straight knives and folders of his design. **Patterns:** Hunters, locking folders and utility/camp knives. **Technical:** Sandvik and 440C. **Prices:** $120 to $250; some to $1,500. **Remarks:** Part-time maker; first knife sold in 1989. **Mark:** Buffalo head with name.

WATSON, TOM, 1103 Brenau Terrace, Panama City, FL 32405/904-785-9209
Specialties: Lockback folders with coil springs-micarta and pearl inlays. **Patterns:** Folding drop point hunters, folding boot knives, fixed blade hunters, boots and small fighters. **Technical:** Flat-grinds 440C, ATS-34 and A2. Heat-treats with multiple tempering and hardness testing. Prefers satin finishes. **Prices:** Starting at $150. **Remarks:** Full-time maker; first knife sold in 1978. **Mark:** Name and city.

WATT III, FREDDIE, P.O. Box 1372, Big Spring, TX 79721/915-263-6629
Specialties: Working straight knives, some fancy. **Patterns:** Hunters, fighters and Bowies. **Technical:** Grinds A2, D2, 440C and ATS-34; prefers mirror finishes. **Prices:** $150 to $350; some to $750. **Remarks:** Full-time maker; first knife sold in 1979. **Mark:** Last name, city and state.

WATTELET, MICHAEL A., P.O. Box 649, 125 Front, Minocqua, WI 54548/715-356-3069

Specialties: Working and using straight knives of his design and to customer specs; fantasy knives. **Patterns:** Daggers, fighters and swords. **Technical:** Grinds 440C and L6; forges and grinds 01. Silversmith. **Prices:** $75 to $1,000; some to $5,000. **Remarks:** Full-time maker; first knife sold in 1966. Doing business as M&N Arts Ltd. **Mark:** First initial, last name.

WATTS, MIKE, Rt. 1 Box 81, Gatesville, TX 76528

WATTS, WALLY, Rt. 1, Box 81, Gatesville, TX 76528/817-487-2866
Specialties: Unique traditional folders of his design. **Patterns:** One- to four-blade folders and single-blade gents in various blade shapes. **Technical:** Grinds 440C, D2 and ATS-34. **Prices:** $100 to $200; some to $300. **Remarks:** Full-time maker; first knife sold in 1986. **Mark:** Last name.

WEAPONS SHOP (See Brooks, Michael)

WEBB JR., CHARLEY L., 901 Concord Ave., Anderson, SC 29621
Specialties: Traditional and working straight knives and folders of his design and to customer specs. **Patterns:** Boots, Bowies, hunters, utility knives and commemoritives. **Technical:** Grinds 440C, ATS-34, A2 and D2. Prefers mirror polish; heat-treats. Handle materials of exotic woods, Pakkawood and Micarta. Custom handles in bucks and schrades. **Prices:** $75 to $250; some to $600. **Remarks:** Part-time maker; first knife sold in 1991. **Mark:** Initials or name and city.

WEBB, JIM, Rt. 2, Box 435, Joplin, MO 64804/417-781-3434
Specialties: Traditional working and using straight knives and folders of his design and in standard patterns. **Patterns:** Fighters, hunters and locking folders. **Technical:** Grinds 440C. **Prices:** $200 to $375; some to $500. **Remarks:** Full-time maker; first knife sold in 1991. Served apprenticeship in shop of G.W. Stone. **Mark:** Name and serial number.

WEBER, FRED E., 517 Tappan St., Forked River, NJ 08731/609-693-0452
Specialties: Working knives in standard patterns. **Patterns:** Hunters, slip-joint and lock-back folders, Bowies and various-sized fillets. **Technical:** Grinds D2, 440V and ATS-34. **Prices:** $125 to $250; some to $500. **Remarks:** Full-time maker; first knife sold in 1973. **Mark:** First and middle initials, last name.

WEDDLE JR., DEL, 2703 Green Valley Rd., St. Joseph, MO 64505/816-364-1981
Specialties: Working knives; some period pieces. **Patterns:** Hunters, fighters, locking folders, push knives. **Technical:** Grinds D2 and 440C; can provide precious metals and set gems. Offers his own forged wire-cable Damascus in his finished knives. **Prices:** $80 to $250; some to $2,000. **Remarks:** Full-time maker; first knife sold in 1972. **Mark:** Signature with last name and date.

WEHNER, RUDY, Rt. 4, Box 364 A1, Collins, MS 39428/601-765-4997
Specialties: Reproduction antique Bowies and contemporary Bowies in full and miniature. **Patterns:** Skinners, camp knives, fighters, axes and Bowies. **Technical:** Grinds 440C, ATS-34, 154CM and Damascus. **Prices:** $100 to $500; some to $850. **Remarks:** Full-time maker; first knife sold in 1975. **Mark:** Last name on Bowies and antiques; full name, city and state on skinners.

WEILAND JR., J. REESE, 612 Superior Ave., Tampa, FL 33606/813-971-5378 (7:30 a.m.-5:00 p.m.); 813-671-0661 (after 6:00 p.m.); FAX: 813-972-5336
Specialties: Traditional working straight knives and folders; liner locks and Hawk bills. **Patterns:** Hunters, tantos, Bowies, fantasy knives, spears and some swords. **Technical:** Grinds ATS-34 and Damascus bars. Offers titanium hardware on his liner locks and button locks. Distinctive bird-shaped handle on some models. **Prices:** $100 to $4,000. **Remarks:** Full-time maker; first knife sold in 1983. **Mark:** RW slant.

WEILER, DONALD E., P.O. Box 11576, Yuma, AZ 85364/520-782-1159

Specialties: Working straight knives; period pieces. **Patterns:** Dirks, daggers, fighters, survival, throwing and camp knives; scramasax; buckskinner and Norse designs. **Technical:** Forges 01, W2, 5160, ATS-34 and D2. Makes own high-carbon steel Damascus. **Prices:** $80 to $1,000. **Remarks:** Full-time maker; first knife sold in 1952. **Mark:** Last name, city.

WEINAND, GEROME M., 14440 Harpers Bridge Rd., Missoula, MT 59802/406-543-0845
Specialties: Working straight knives. **Patterns:** Bowies, fishing and camp knives, large special hunters. **Technical:** Grinds 01, 440C, ATS-34, 1084 and L6; makes all-tool steel Damascus. Heat-treats. **Prices:** $30 to $100; some to $500. **Remarks:** Full-time maker; first knife sold in 1982. **Mark:** Name, city and state.

WEINSTOCK, ROBERT, Box 39, 520 Frederick St., San Francisco, CA 94117/415-731-5968
Specialties: Fancy and high art straight knives of his design. **Patterns:** Daggers, poignards and miniatures. **Technical:** Grinds A2, 01 and 440C. Chased and hand-carved blades and handles. **Prices:** $1,500 and $4,000; some to $5,000 or $6,000. **Remarks:** Full-time maker; first knife sold in 1994. **Mark:** Carved last name.

WEISS, CHARLES L., 18847 N. 13th Ave., Phoenix, AZ 85027/602-869-0425; FAX: 602-869-0425
Specialties: High-art straight knives and folders; deluxe period pieces. **Patterns:** Daggers, fighters, boots, push knives and miniatures. **Technical:** Grinds 440C, 154CM and ATS-34. **Prices:** $300 to $1,200; some to $2,000. **Remarks:** Full-time maker; first knife sold in 1975. **Mark:** Name and city.

WELCH, WILLIAM H., 8232 W. Red Snapper Dr., Kimmell, IN 46760/219-856-3577
Specialties: Working knives; deluxe period pieces. **Patterns:** Hunters, tantos, Bowies. **Technical:** Grinds ATS-34, D2 and 440C. **Prices:** $100 to $600. **Remarks:** Part-time maker; first knife sold in 1976. **Mark:** Last name.

WERNER JR., WILLIAM A., 336 Lands Mill, Marietta, GA 30067/404-988-0074
Specialties: Fantasy and working/using straight knives. **Patterns:** Bowies, daggers, fighters. **Technical:** Grinds 440C stainless, 10 series carbon and Damascus. **Prices:** $150 to $400; some to $750. **Remarks:** Part-time maker. Doing business as Werner Knives. **Mark:** Last name.

WERTH, GEORGE W., 5223 Woodstock Rd., Poplar Grove, IL 61065/815-544-4408
Specialties: Period pieces, some fancy. **Patterns:** Straight fighters, daggers and Bowies. **Technical:** Forges and grinds 01, 1095 and his Damascus, including mosaic patterns. **Prices:** $200 to $650; some higher. **Remarks:** Full-time maker. Doing business as Fox Valley Forge. **Mark:** Name in logo or initials connected.

WESCOTT, CODY, 5610 Hanger Lake Ln., Las Cruces, NM 88012/505-382-5008
Specialties: Fancy and presentation-grade working knives. **Patterns:** Hunters, locking folders and Bowies. **Technical:** Hollow-grinds D2 and ATS-34; all knives fileworked. Offers some engraving. Makes sheaths. **Prices:** $80 to $300; some to $950. **Remarks:** Full-time maker; first knife sold in 1982. **Mark:** First initial, last name.

WESOLOWSKI, MIKE, 902-A Lohrman Lane, Petaluma, CA 94952/707-762-7564
Specialties: Working knives; display Bowies. **Patterns:** Hunters, utility and using knives, miniatures. **Technical:** Flat-grinds D2, 440C and 154CM; offers finger placement coils. **Prices:** $300 to $600. **Remarks:** Part-time maker; first knife sold in 1973. Doing business as M.W. Knives. **Mark:** Initials, city and state in knife logo.

WEST, CHARLES A., 1315 S. Pine St., Centralia, IL 62801/618-532-2777

Specialties: Classic, fancy, high tech, period pieces, traditional and working/using straight knives and folders. **Patterns:** Bowies, fighters and locking folders. **Technical:** Grinds ATS-34, 01 and Damascus. Prefers hot blued finishes. **Prices:** $100 to $1,000; some to $2,000. **Remarks:** Full-time maker; first knife sold in 1963. Doing business as West Custom Knives. **Mark:** Name or name, city and state.

WEST, PAT, P.O. Box 9, Charlotte, TX 78011/512-277-1290
Specialties: Classic working and using straight knives and folders. **Patterns:** Hunters, kitchen knives, slip-joint folders. **Technical:** Grinds ATS-34, D2 and Vascowear. Offers filework and decorates liners on folders. **Prices:** $300 to $600. **Remarks:** Spare-time maker; first knife sold in 1984. **Mark:** Name.

WESTBERG, LARRY, 305 S. Western Hills Dr., Algona, IA 50511/515-295-9276
Specialties: Traditional and working straight knives of his design and in standard patterns. **Patterns:** Bowies, hunters, utility knives and miniatures. **Technical:** Grinds 440C, D2 and 1095. Heat-treats. Uses natural handle materials. **Prices:** $85 to $600; some to $1,000. **Remarks:** Part-time maker; first knife sold in 1987. **Mark:** Last name.

WHIPPLE, WESLEY A., P.O. Box 47, Thermopolis, WY 82443/307-864-2255
Specialties: Working straight knives, some fancy. **Patterns:** Hunters, Bowies, camp knives, fighters. **Technical:** Forges 5168, 52100, W2; makes cable and pattern Damascus; offers silver-wire inlay. **Prices:** $125 to $450; some higher. **Remarks:** Part-time maker; first knife sold in 1989. **Mark:** Last name.

WHISKERS (See Allen, Mike "Whiskers")

WHITE, GENE E., 1015 Cross Dr., Alexandria, VA 22302/703-671-3997
Specialties: Small utility/gents knives. **Patterns:** Eight standard hunters; most other patterns on commission basis. Currently no swords, axes and fantasy knives. **Technical:** Stock removal 440C and D2; others on request. Mostly hollow grinds; some flat grinds. Prefers natural handle materials. Makes own sheaths. **Prices:** Start at $75. **Remarks:** Part-time maker; first knife sold in 1971. **Mark:** First and middle intials, last name.

WHITE, ROBERT J., RR 1, 641 Knox Rd. 900 N., Gilson, IL 61436/309-289-4487
Specialties: Working knives, some deluxe. **Patterns:** Bird and trout knives, hunters, survival knives and locking folders. **Technical:** Grinds A2, D2 and 440C; commercial Damascus. Heat-treats. **Prices:** $125 to $250; some to $600. **Remarks:** Full-time maker; first knife sold in 1976. **Mark:** Last name in script.

WHITE JR., ROBERT J. "BUTCH", RR 1, Gilson, IL 61436/309-289-4487
Specialties: Working straight knives and folders; some collector pieces; no miniatures. **Patterns:** Hunters, fighters, boots and Damascus miniatures. **Technical:** Forges Damascus; grinds 440C and other tool and stainless steels. **Prices:** $100 to $1,500. **Remarks:** Full-time maker; first knife sold in 1980. **Mark:** Last name in block letters; a block last initial on miniatures.

WHITEHEAD, JAMES D., 204 Cappucino Way, Sacramento, CA 95838/916-641-7309; FAX: 916-641-1941
Specialties: Highly detailed straight and folding miniatures. **Patterns:** Traditional and fancy. **Technical:** Forges and grinds 01 and commercial Damascus. **Prices:** $250 to $2,000. **Remarks:** Part-time maker; first knife sold in 1985. **Mark:** Initials.

WHITLEY, WAYNE, 210 E. 7th St., Washington, NC 27889/919-946-5648
Specialties: Working/using straight knives of his design and to customer specs. **Patterns:** Bowies, hunters, utility/camp knives. **Technical:** Grinds ATS-34, D2, 440C; forges own Damascus and cable and high-carbon tool steels. **Prices:** $65 to $650; some to $1,500.

Remarks: Part-time maker; first knife sold in 1990. Doing business as WW Custom Knives. **Mark:** Name, city, state.

WHITLEY, WELDON G., 6316 Jebel Way, El Paso, TX 79912/915-584-2274
Specialties: Working knives of his design or to customer specs. **Patterns:** Hunters, folders and various double-edged knives. **Technical:** Grinds 440C, 154CM and ATS 34. **Prices:** $150 to $1250. **Mark:** Name, address, road-runner logo.

WHITMAN, JIM, HC 80, Box 5387, 21044 Salem St., Chugiak, AK 99567/907-688-4575; 907-688-4278
Specialties: Working straight knives; some art pieces. **Patterns:** Hunters, especially skinners, Bowies, camp knives, working fighters, swords, hatchets and extreme walking staffs. **Technical:** Grinds AEB-L Swedish, 440C, ATS-34 and commercial Damascus in full convex. Prefers natural and native handle materials—whale bone, antler, ivory and horn. **Prices:** Start at $85. **Remarks:** Part-time maker; first knife sold in 1983. **Mark:** Name, city and state.

WHITMIRE, EARL T., 725 Colonial Dr., Rock Hill, SC 29730/803-324-8384
Specialties: Working straight knives, some to customer specs. **Patterns:** Hunters, fighters, fishing knives and some fantasy pieces. **Technical:** Grinds D2, 440C and 154CM. **Prices:** $40 to $200; some to $250. **Remarks:** Full-time maker; first knife sold in 1967. **Mark:** Name, city, state in oval logo.

WHITTAKER, ROBERT E., P.O. Box 204, Mill Creek, PA 17060
Specialties: Using straight knives. Has a line of knives for buckskinners. **Patterns:** Hunters, skinners and Bowies. **Technical:** Grinds 01, A2 and D2. Offers filework. **Prices:** $35 to $100. **Remarks:** Part-time maker; first knife sold in 1980. **Mark:** Last initial or full initials.

WHITWORTH, KEN J., 41667 Tetley Ave., Sterling Heights, MI 48078/313-739-5720
Specialties: Working straight knives and folders. **Patterns:** Locking folders, slip-joints and boot knives. **Technical:** Grinds 440C, 154CM and D2. **Prices:** $100 to $225; some to $450. **Remarks:** Part-time maker; first knife sold in 1976. **Mark:** Last name.

WICKER, DONNIE R., 2544 E. 40th Ct., Panama City, FL 32405/904-785-9158
Specialties: Traditional working and using straight knives of his design or to customer specs. **Patterns:** Hunters, fighters and slip-joint folders. **Technical:** Grinds 440C, ATS-34, D2 and 154CM. Heat-treats and does hardness testing. **Prices:** $90 to $200; some to $400. **Remarks:** Part-time maker; first knife sold in 1975. **Mark:** First and middle initials, last name.

WIGGINS, HORACE, 203 Herndon, Box 152, Mansfield, LA 71502/318-872-4471 (evenings)
Specialties: Fancy working knives. **Patterns:** Straight and folding hunters. **Technical:** Grinds 01, D2 and 440C. **Prices:** $90 to $275. **Remarks:** Part-time maker; first knife sold in 1970. **Mark:** Name, city and state in diamond logo.

WILCHER, WENDELL L., RR3, Box 3341, Palestine, TX 75801/903-549-2530
Specialties: Fantasy, miniatures and working/using straight knives and folders of his design and to customer specs. **Patterns:** Fighters, hunters, locking folders. **Technical:** Grinds 440C, ATS-34, 01. Some filework. **Prices:** $75 to $250; some to $600. **Remarks:** Part-time maker; first knife sold in 1987. **Mark:** Initials, year, serial number.

WILD BILL & SONS (See Caldwell, Bill)

WILDWOOD STUDIOS (See Rece, Charles V.)

WILLEY, W.G., R.D. 1, Box 235-B, Greenwood, DE 19950/302-349-4070

Specialties: Fancy working straight knives. **Patterns:** Small game knives, Bowies and throwing knives. **Technical:** Grinds 440C and 154CM. **Prices:** $225 to $600; some to $1,500. **Remarks:** Part-time maker; first knife sold in 1975. Owns retail store. **Mark:** Last name inside map logo.

WILLIAMS, DAVID, Box 75, Berea, WV 26327/304-659-3286
Specialties: Working and using straight knives of his design and in Japanese patterns; period pieces. **Patterns:** Daggers, hunters and tantos. **Technical:** Grinds L6 and 01; forges 5160/wrought iron, cable Damascus and David Boye dendritic steel. Trademark look is a rough, pitted black area above the hollow-ground area. Gas forge heat-treats. **Prices:** $75 to $300; some to $500. **Remarks:** Part-time maker; first knife sold in 1980. **Mark:** Bywater Homestead, name, knifemaker.

WILLIAMS, JASON L., P.O. Box 67, Wyoming, RI 02898/401-539-8353
Specialties: Fancy and high-tech folders of his design. **Patterns:** Fighters, locking folders and fancy pocketknives. **Technical:** Forges Damascus and other steels by request. Uses exotic handle materials. Offers inlayed spines and gemstone thumb knobs. **Prices:** Starting at $500. **Remarks:** Full-time maker; first knife sold in 1989. **Mark:** Initials engraved inside case.

WILLIAMS, MICHAEL L., P.O. Box 1145, Broken Bow, OK 74728/405-494-6326
Specialties: Working and dress knives and folders. **Patterns:** Hunters, Bowies, camp knives and specialty knives. **Technical:** Forges 5160, L6, 52100, cable and his own pattern-welded steel. Offers sheaths. **Prices:** $140 and up. **Remarks:** Part-time maker; first knife sold in 1989. **Mark:** Last name, JS.

WILLIAMS JR., RICHARD, 1440 Nancy Circle, Morristown, TN 37814/615-581-0059
Specialties: Working and using straight knives of his design or to customer specs. **Patterns:** Hunters, dirks and utility/camp knives. **Technical:** Forges 5160 and uses file steel. Hand-finish is standard; offers filework. **Prices:** $80 to $180; some to $250. **Remarks:** Spare-time maker; first knife sold in 1985. **Mark:** Last initial or full intials.

WILLIAMS, SHERMAN A., 1709 Wallace St., Simi Valley, CA 93065/805-583-3821
Specialties: Working straight knives in standard patterns. **Patterns:** Hunters, boots, utility knives, unusual trail knives. **Technical:** Forges and grinds ATS-34, 440C, 1095 and 5160. **Prices:** $45 to $500. **Remarks:** Part-time maker; first knife sold in 1983. Doing business as Sherman Knives. **Mark:** First name in crow logo.

WILLIAMSON, TONY, Rt. 3, Box 503, Siler City, NC 27344/919-663-3551
Specialties: Flint knapping—knives made of obsidian flakes and flint with wood, antler or bone for handles. **Patterns:** Skinners, daggers and flake knives. **Technical:** Blades have width/thickness ratio of at least 4 to 1. Hafts with methods available to prehistoric man. **Prices:** $58 to $160. **Remarks:** Student of Errett Callahan. **Mark:** Initials and number code to identify year and number of knives made.

WILLIAMSON II, WALT, 10231 Ashford St., Rancho Cucamonga, CA 91730/714-944-9180
Specialties: Heavy-duty working straight knives of his design. **Patterns:** Bowies, hunters, skinners, capers, bird and fish knives. **Technical:** Hollowgrinds ATS-34 and Damascus; buys Damascus. Provides leather sheaths; offers some semi-precious stones in handles; prefers mirror finishes. **Prices:** $150 to $300. **Remarks:** Full-time maker; first knife sold in 1979. **Mark:** Name, city and state.

THE WILLOW FORGE (See Tokar, Daniel)

WILSON (See Gianluigi, Simonella)

WILSONHAWK (See Wilson, James G.)

WILSON, JAMES G., P.O. Box 4024, Estes Park, CO 80517/303-586-3944
Specialties: Bronze Age knives; 37th century knives—Medieval and Scottish styles; tomahawks. **Patterns:** Bronze knives, daggers, swords, spears and battle axes; 12-inch steel Misericorde daggers, sgian dubhs, "His and Her" skinners, bird and fish knives, capers, boots and daggers. **Technical:** Casts bronze; grinds D2, 440C and ATS-34. **Prices:** $49 to $400; some to $1,300. **Remarks:** Part-time maker; first knife sold in 1975. **Mark:** WilsonHawK.

WILSON, JAMES R., Rt. 2 Box 175HC, Seminole, OK 74868/405-382-7230
Specialties: Traditional working knives. **Patterns:** Bowies, hunters, skinners, fighters and camp knives. **Technical:** Forges 5160, 1095, 01 and his Damascus. **Prices:** Start at $125. **Remarks:** Full-time maker; first knife sold in 1994. **Mark:** First initial, last name.

WILSON, JON J., 1826 Ruby St., Johnstown, PA 15902/814-266-6410
Specialties: Miniatures only. **Patterns:** Bowies, daggers and hunters. **Technical:** Grinds Damascus, 440C and 01. Scrimshands and carves. **Prices:** $65 to $175; some to $250. **Remarks:** Full-time maker; first knife sold in 1988. **Mark:** First and middle initials, last name.

WILSON, MIKE, 2619 Fork Creek Ln., Bowman, GA 30624/706-245-0823
Specialties: Fancy working and using straight knives of his design or to customer specs. **Patterns:** Hunters, Bowies, utility knives, gut hooks, skinners, fighters and miniatures. **Technical:** Hollow-grinds 440C, ATS-34 and D2. Mirror finishes are standard. Offers filework. **Prices:** $70 to $300. **Remarks:** Full-time maker; first knife sold in 1985. **Mark:** Last name.

WILSON, PHILIP C., 1064 Lomitas Ave., Livermore, CA 94550/510-455-9474; 510-422-0503
Specialties: Working knives; emphasis on salt water fillet knives and utility hunters of his design. **Patterns:** Fishing knives, hunters, kitchen knives. **Technical:** Grinds ATS-34, 440C, CPM440V and D2. Prefers hollow grinds and hand-rubbed satin finishes. Heat-treats and Rockwell tests all blades. **Prices:** $120 and up. **Remarks:** Part-time maker; first knife sold in 1985. Doing business as Sea-Mount Knife Works. **Mark:** Signature.

WILSON, R.W., P.O. Box 2012, Weirton, WV 26062/304-723-2771
Specialties: Working straight knives; period pieces. **Patterns:** Bowies, tomahawks and patch knives. **Prices:** $85 to $175; some to $1,000. **Technical:** Grinds 440C; scrimshaws. **Remarks:** Part-time maker; first knife sold in 1966. Knifemaker supplier. **Mark:** Name in tomahawk.

WIMPFF, CHRISTIAN, Rosshaustr. 67, 70597 Stuttgart, 70 GERMANY/711-764324; FAX: 711-7656960
Specialties: High-tech folders of his design. **Patterns:** Boots, locking folders and liner locks. **Technical:** Grinds CPM T 440V, ATS-34 and Schneider stainless Damascus. Offers pantographing and meteorite bolsters and blades. **Prices:** $1,000 to $2,800; some to $4,000. **Remarks:** Full-time maker; first knife sold in 1984. **Mark:** First initial, last name.

WIND RIVER KNIVES (See Bridges, Justin W.)

WINE, MICHAEL, 265 S. Atlantic Ave., Cocoa Beach, FL 32931/407-784-2187
Specialties: Traditional working straight knives. **Patterns:** Fishing, hunting and kitchen knives. **Technical:** Grinds carbon, high-chrome tool steels, stellite; casts 440C. **Prices:** Start at $145. **Remarks:** Spare-time maker; first knife sold in 1971. **Mark:** First initial, last name with palm tree.

WINGO, PERRY, 22 55th St., Gulfport, MS 39507/601-863-3193
Specialties: Traditional working straight knives. **Patterns:** Hunters, skinners, Bowies and fishing knives. **Technical:** Grinds 440C. **Prices:** $75 to $1,000. **Remarks:** Full-time maker; first knife sold in 1988. **Mark:** Last name.

directory

WINKLER, DANIEL, P.O. Box 2166, Blowing Rock, NC 28605/704-295-9156, 704-295-0133 (message); FAX: 704-295-0133 **Specialties:** Period pieces, some made to look old; buckskinner working knives. **Patterns:** Buckskinners, axes, tomahawks, patch knives, daggers, folders, skinners and fighters. **Technical:** Forges and grinds 52100, L6, 01, old files and his Damascus. **Prices:** $200. **Remarks:** Full-time maker; first knife sold in 1984. **Mark:** Initials connected.

WINN, TRAVIS A., 558 E. 3065 S., Salt Lake City, UT 84106/801-467-5957 **Specialties:** Fancy working knives and knives to customer specs. **Patterns:** Hunters, fighters, boots, Bowies and fancy daggers, some miniatures, tantos and fantasy knives. **Technical:** Grinds D2 and 440C. Embellishes. **Prices:** $100 to $500; some higher. **Remarks:** Part-time maker; first knife sold in 1976. **Mark:** TRAV stylized.

WINSTON, DAVID, 1671 Red Holly St., Starkville, MS 39759/601-323-1028 **Specialties:** Fancy and traditional knives of his design and to customer specs. **Patterns:** Bowies, daggers, hunters, boot knives and folders. **Technical:** Grinds 440C, ATS-34 and D2. Offers filework; heat-treats. Engraving by Norvell Foster. **Prices:** $40 to $750; some higher. **Remarks:** Part-time maker; first knife sold in 1984. Offers lifetime sharpening for original owner. **Mark:** Last name.

WISE, DONALD, 304 Bexhill Rd., St. Leonardo-On-Sea, East Sussex TN3 8AL ENGLAND **Specialties:** Fancy and embellished working straight knives to customer specs. **Patterns:** Hunters, Bowies and daggers. **Technical:** Grinds Sandvik 12C27, D2, D3 and 01. Srimshaws. **Prices:** $110 to $300; some to $500. **Remarks:** Full-time maker; first knife sold in 1983. **Mark:** KNIFECRAFT.

WISE, JOHN, P.O. Box 994, Winchester, OR 97495 **Specialties:** Classic high-art straight knives and folders to customer specs. **Patterns:** Daggers, fighters, locking folders, miniatures. **Technical:** Grinds 440C, ATS-34, commercial Damascus. **Prices:** $150 to $350; some to $1,000. **Remarks:** Part-time maker; first knife sold in 1989. **Mark:** Stylized name.

WITSAMAN, EARL, 3957 Redwing Circle, Stow, OH 44224/216-688-4208 **Specialties:** Straight and fantasy miniatures. **Patterns:** Wide variety—Randalls to D-guard Bowies. **Technical:** Grinds 01, 440C and 300 stainless; buys Damascus; highly detailed work. **Prices:** $70 to $200. **Remarks:** Part-time maker; first knife sold in 1974. **Mark:** Initials.

W-K Knives (See Votaw, David P.)

WOLF, BILL, 4618 N. 79th Ave., Phoenix, AZ 85033/602-846-3585 **Specialties:** Investor-grade folders and straight knives. **Patterns:** Lockback, slip joint and sidelock interframes. **Technical:** Grinds ATS-34 and 440C. **Prices:** $650 to $4,000. **Remarks:** Full-time maker; first knife sold in 1989. **Mark:** Name.

WOLF'S KNIVES (See Smit, Glenn)

WOLFE FINE KNIVES (See Loerchner, Wolfgang)

WOMACK, A.M. "BABE", P.O. Box 1397, Coldspring, TX 77331/409-767-8158 **Specialties:** Classic and traditional straight knives and folders of his design. **Patterns:** Hunters, locking folders and utility/camp knives. **Technical:** Grinds ATS-34, 440C and D2. Sheathmaker. **Prices:** $95 to $250; some to $700. **Remarks:** Part-time maker; first knife sold in 1989. **Mark:** Name and city.

WOOD, ALAN, Greenfield Villa, Greenhead, Carlisle, CA6 7NH ENGLAND/016977-47303 **Specialties:** High-tech working straight knives of his design. **Patterns:** Hunters, utility/camp and military knives. **Technical:** Grinds Sandvik 12C27, D2 and 01. Blades are cryogenic treated. Offers Kydex sheaths. **Prices:** $150 to $400; some to $750. **Remarks:** Full-time maker; first knife sold in 1979. **Mark:** First initial, last name and country.

WOOD, BARRY B. and IRIE, MICHAEL L., 3002 E. Gunnison St., Colorado Springs, CO 80909/719-578-9226 **Specialties:** High-tech working folders with patented locking system. **Patterns:** Thirty-four variations of five designs. **Technical:** Blades mainly made of ATS-34, some of commercial Damascus. Handles investment-cast in 17-4PH. **Prices:** $175 to $460; some higher. **Remarks:** Full-time makers; first knife sold in 1969. **Mark:** Two sets of initials in script with linked triangles of arcs.

WOOD, LARRY B., 6945 Fishburg Rd., Huber Heights, OH 45424/513-233-6751 **Specialties:** Fancy working knives of his design. **Patterns:** Hunters, buckskinners, Bowies, tomahawks, locking folders and Damascus miniatures. **Technical:** Forges 1095, file steel and his own Damascus. **Prices:** $125 to $500; some to $2,000. **Remarks:** Full-time maker; first knife sold in 1974. Doing business as Wood's Metal Studios. **Mark:** Variations of last name, sometimes with blacksmith logo.

WOOD, LEONARD J., 16 North St., Beacon, NY 12508/914-838-1637 **Specialties:** Traditional working/using straight knives of all designs. **Patterns:** Boots, Bowies, hunters, miniatures. **Technical:** Grinds ATS-34, 440C, commercial Damascus. **Prices:** $85 to $375; some to $450. **Remarks:** Spare-time maker; first knife sold in 1993. Doing business as Wood's Custom Knives. **Mark:** Last initial with wings.

WOOD, OWEN DALE, P.O. Box 515, Honeydew 2040 (Transvaal), SOUTH AFRICA/011-958-1789 **Specialties:** Fancy working knives. **Patterns:** Hunters and fighters; variety of big knives; sword canes. **Technical:** Forges and grinds 440C, 154CM and his own Damascus. Uses rare African handle materials. **Prices:** $280 to $450; some to $3,000. **Remarks:** Full-time maker; first knife sold in 1976. **Mark:** Initials.

WOOD, WEBSTER, 4726 Rosedale, Clarkston, MI 48348/313-394-0351 **Specialties:** Fancy working knives. **Patterns:** Hunters, survival knives, locking folders and slip-joints. **Technical:** Grinds 01, 440C and 154CM; engraves and scrimshaws. **Prices:** $100 to $500; some to $3,000. **Remarks:** Full-time maker; first knife sold in 1980. **Mark:** Initials inside shield and name.

WOOD, WILLIAM W., P.O. Box 606, Seymour, TX 76380/817-888-5832 **Specialties:** Exotic working knives with Middle-East flavor. **Patterns:** Fighters, boots and some utility knives. **Technical:** Grinds D2 and 440C; buys Damascus. Prefers hand-rubbed satin finishes; uses only natural handle materials. **Prices:** $300 to $600; some to $2,000. **Remarks:** Full-time maker; first knife sold in 1977. **Mark:** Name, city and state.

WOOD'S METAL STUDIOS (See Wood, Larry B.)

WOODCOCK, DENNIS "WOODY", P.O. Box 448, Nehalem, OR 97131/503-368-7511 **Specialties:** Working knives; miniatures. **Patterns:** Hunters, Bowies, skinners, miniatures. **Technical:** Grinds ATS-34, 154CM, D2 and 440C. Offers filework. Scrimshaws; makes sheaths. **Prices:** $45 to $475. **Remarks:** Full-time maker; first knife sold in 1982. Doing business as Knife Emporium. **Mark:** Nickname, last name, city, state.

WOODWORTH, AL, RR #1, P.O. Box 13, Plainville, IL 62365/217-656-4065 **Specialties:** Straight working knives in standard patterns. **Patterns:** Fighters and hunters. **Technical:** Grinds 440C and ATS-34. Makes polyester resin handles. **Prices:** $200 to $600. **Remarks:** Full-time maker; first knife sold in 1987. **Mark:** Initials with cross, Libra sign.

WORKMAN JR., HUBERT L., Tyree Rd., Williamsburg, WV 24991/304-645-4815

custom knifemakers

Specialties: Working knives of his design and to customer specs; period pieces. **Patterns:** Daggers, fighters and hunters. **Technical:** Uses obsidian, flint and chert; prefers natural materials. **Prices:** $25 to $150; some to $250. **Remarks:** Part-time maker; first knife sold in 1989. **Mark:** NA.

WORLD GALLERY CO., LTD. (See Yoshio, Mazaki; Kamada, Yoshikazu; Ueda, Masaharu; Wada, Yasutaka)

WRIGHT, KEVIN, 671 Leland Valley Rd. W, Quilcene, WA 98376-9517/360-765-3589
Specialties: Fancy working or collector knives to customer specs. **Patterns:** Hunters, boots, buckskinners, miniatures. **Technical:** Forges and grinds L6, 1095, 440C and his own Damascus. **Prices:** $75 to $500; some to $2,000. **Remarks:** Part-time maker; first knife sold in 1978. No new orders in 1996. **Mark:** Last initial in anvil.

WRIGHT, TIMOTHY, 4100 W. Grand Ave., Chicago, IL 60651/312-489-4436/4186
Specialties: High-tech working folders and household knives. **Patterns:** Interframe locking folders, straight hunters and special-purpose kitchen cutlery. **Technical:** Grinds A2, ATS-34, BG42 and K190; works with new steels. Makes his own mokume. Makes folders to disassemble; furnishes parts and tools. **Prices:** $75 to $1,000; some to $2,500. **Remarks:** Full-time maker; first knife sold in 1975. **Mark:** Last name.

WW CUSTOM KNIVES (See Whitley, Wayne)

WYATT, WILLIAM R., Box 237, Rainelle, WV 25962/304-438-5494
Specialties: Classic and working knives of all designs. **Patterns:** Hunters and utility knives. **Technical:** Forges and grinds saw blades, files and rasps. Prefers stagg handles. **Prices:** $45 to $95; some to $350. **Remarks:** Part-time maker; first knife sold in 1990. **Mark:** Last name in star with knife logo.

WYVERN (See Ferdinand, Don)

x, y

XYLO (See McGill, John)

YASUTOMO (See Louis G. Mills)

YEATES, JOE A., 730 Saddlewood, Spring, TX 77381/713-367-2765
Specialties: Bowies and period pieces. **Patterns:** Bowies, toothpicks and combat knives. **Technical:** Grinds 440C, D2 and ATS-34. **Prices:** $250 to $1,500; some to $2,000. **Remarks:** Full-time maker; first knife sold in 1975. **Mark:** Last initial within outline of Texas; or last initial.

YORK, DAVID C., P.O. Box 1342, Crested Butte, CO 81224/970-349-5826
Specialties: Working straight knives and folders. **Patterns:** Prefers small hunters and skinners; locking folders, buckskinner and survival knives. **Technical:** Grinds D2 and 440C; buys Damascus. **Prices:** $75 to $300; some to $600. **Remarks:** Part-time maker; first knife sold in 1975. **Mark:** Last name.

YOUNG, BUD, Box 336, Port Hardy, BC V0N 2P0, CANADA/604-949-6478
Specialties: Working straight knives, some fancy. **Patterns:** Hunters from drop-points to skinners. **Technical:** Grinds 01, L6, 1095 and 5160; uses 154CM and ATS-34 when available. Likes satin and glass bead finishes and natural handle materials. **Prices:** $200 to $400; some higher. **Remarks:** Spare-time maker; first knife sold in 1985. **Mark:** Name.

YOUNG, CLIFF, RR #1, Cotnams Island, Pembroke, Ont. K8A 6W2, CANADA/613-638-6401
Specialties: Working knives; some display pieces. **Patterns:** Hunters, fighters, locking folders and fishing knives. **Technical:** Grinds mostly, though does some forging; offers D2, 440C and 154CM. **Prices:** $165 to $350; some to $800. **Remarks:** Part-time maker; first knife sold in 1980. **Mark:** Name, city and province.

YOUNG, ERROL, 4826 Storey Land, Alton, IL 62002/618-466-4707
Specialties: Traditional working straight knives and folders **Patterns:** Wide range, including tantos, Bowies, miniatures and multi-blade folders. **Technical:** Grinds D2, 440C and ATS-34. **Prices:** $75 to $650; some to $800. **Remarks:** Part-time maker; first knife sold in 1987. **Mark:** Last name with arrow.

YOUNG, PAUL A., RR 1 Box 694, Blowing Rock, NC 28605-9746/704-297-4039
Specialties: Working straight knives and folders of his design or to customer specs; some art knives. **Patterns:** Small boot knives, skinners, 18th century period pieces and folders. **Technical:** Forges 01 and file steels. Full-time embellisher—engraves, carves and scrimshaws. **Prices:** $50 to $1,000. **Remarks:** Full-time maker; first knife sold in 1978. **Mark:** Initials in logo.

YUNES, YAMIL R., P.O. Box 573, Roma, TX 78584/512-849-1001
Specialties: Traditional straight knives and folders. **Patterns:** Locking folders, slip-joints, hunters, fighters and utility knives. **Technical:** Grinds 440C, 01 and D2. Has patented cocking design for folders. **Prices:** $45 to $140; some to $300. **Remarks:** Part-time maker; first knife sold in 1975. **Mark:** Last name.

YURCO, MIKE, P.O. Box 712, Canfield, OH 44406/216-533-4928
Specialties: Working straight knives. **Patterns:** Hunters, utility knives, Bowies and fighters, push knives, claws and other hideouts. **Technical:** Grinds 440C, ATS-34 and 154CM; likes mirror and satin finishes. **Prices:** $20 to $500. **Remarks:** Part-time maker; first knife sold in 1983. **Mark:** Name, steel, serial number.

z

Z CUSTOM KNIVES (See McCarty, Zollan)

ZACCAGNINO JR., DON, P.O. Box 583, Pahokee, FL 33476/407-924-7844
Specialties: Working knives and some period pieces of their designs. **Patterns:** Heavy-duty hunters, axes and Bowies; a line of light-weight hunters, fillets and personal knives. **Technical:** Grinds 440C and 17-4 PH—highly finished in complex handle and blade treatments. **Prices:** $165 to $500; some to $2,500. **Remarks:** Part-time maker; first knife sold in 1969 by Don Zaccagnino, Sr. **Mark:** ZACK, city and state inside oval.

ZACK KNIVES (See Zaccagnino Jr., Don)

ZAHM, KURT, 488 Rio Casa, Indialantic, FL 32903/407-777-4860
Specialties: Working straight knives of his design or to customer specs. **Patterns:** Daggers, fancy fighters, Bowies, hunters and utility knives. **Technical:** Grinds D2, 440C; likes filework. **Prices:** $75 to $1,000. **Remarks:** Part-time maker; first knife sold in 1985. **Mark:** Last name.

ZAKABI, CARL S., P.O. Box 3161, Mililani Town, HI 96789/808-623-9661
Specialties: Working and using straight knives of his design. **Patterns:** Fighters, hunters and utility/camp knives. **Technical:** Grinds 440C and ATS-34. **Prices:** $55 to $200. **Remarks:** Spare-time maker; first knife sold in 1988. Doing business as Zakabi's Knifeworks. **Mark:** Last name and state.

ZAKHAROV, CARLOS, R. Sergipe, 68, Rio Comprido, Jacarel, SP-12300-000, BRAZIL/0123-515192; FAX: 0123-515192
Specialties: Using straight knives of his design. **Patterns:** Hunters, kitchen and utility/camp knives. **Technical:** Grinds his own "secret steel". **Prices:** $60 to $200. **Remarks:** Full-time maker. **Mark:** Archip

ZEMBKO III, JOHN, 140 Wilks Pond Rd., Berlin, CT 06037/203-828-3503
Specialties: Working knives of his design or to customer specs. **Patterns:** Variety of working straight knives. **Technical:** Grinds ATS-34, A2

and 01; forges 01. **Prices:** $50 to $400; some higher. **Remarks:** First knife sold in 1987. **Mark:** Name.

ZEMITIS, JOE, 14 Currawong Rd., Cardiff Hts., 2285 Newcastle, AUSTRALIA/049-549907
Specialties: Traditional working straight knives. **Patterns:** Hunters, Bowies, tantos, fighters and camp knives. **Technical:** Grinds 01, D2 and 440C; makes his own Damascus. Embellishes; engraves; scrimshands. **Prices:** $150 to $3,000. **Remarks:** Full-time maker; first knife sold in 1983. **Mark:** First initial, last name and country, or last name.

ZIMA, MICHAEL F., 732 State St., Ft. Morgan, CO 80701/970-867-6078
Specialties: Working straight knives and folders. **Patterns:** Hunters; utility, locking and slip-joint folders. **Technical:** Grinds D2, 440C and ATS-34. **Prices:** $135 to $250; some higher. **Remarks:** Full-time maker; first knife sold in 1982. **Mark:** Last name.

ZINSMEISTER, PAUL D., 315 West San Antonio St., Fredericksburg, TX 78624/210-997-8654

Specialties: Traditional working and using straight knives and folders of his design. **Patterns:** Automatics, hunters, locking folders, slip-joint folders, daggers, Bowies and miniatures. **Technical:** Uses 440C and ATS-34 stainless steel. **Prices:** $85 to $250; some to $1,500. **Remarks:** Full-time maker; first knife sold in 1982. **Mark:** Handmade with stylized last initial.

ZOWADA, TIM, 14141 P. Drive North, Marshall, MI 49068/616-781-2458
Specialties: Working knives, some fancy. **Patterns:** Hunters, camp knives, boots, swords, fighters, tantos and locking folders. **Technical:** Forges 01, W2 and his own Damascus. **Prices:** $200 to $1,000; some to $4,000. **Remarks:** Full-time maker; first knife sold in 1980. **Mark:** Lower case gothic letters for initials.

ZSCHERNY, MICHAEL, 2512 "N" Ave. NW, Cedar Rapids, IA 52405/319-396-3659
Specialties: Folders and daggers. **Patterns:** Slip-joints, lock-back folders, fancy daggers. **Technical:** Grinds 440C and 154CM; prefers natural handle materials. **Prices:** $150 to $1,000; some to $1,700. **Remarks:** Part-time maker. Not currently taking orders. **Mark:** Last name.

knifemakers state-by-state

alabama

Andress, Ronnie	Satsuma
Barrett, R.W.	Huntsville
Batson, James	Madison
Bell, Frank	Huntsville
Bullard, Bill	Andalusia
Coffman, Danny	Jacksonville
Conn Jr., C.T.	Attalla
Connell, Steve	Adamsville
Cutchin, Roy D.	Seale
Daniels, Alex	Town Creek
Edwards, Fain E.	Jacksonville
Faulkner, Allan	Jasper
Fikes, Jimmy L.	Jasper
Fogg, Don	Jasper
Gilbreath, Randall	Dora
Gilpin, David	Alabaster
Hammond, Jim	Arab
Hodge, J.B.	Huntsville
Howard, Durvyn M.	Hokes Bluff
Howell, Len	Opelika
Howell, Ted	Wetumpka
Hulsey Jr., Hoyt	Steele
Lawless, Charles	Arab
Lovestrand, Schuyler	Harvest
Monk, Nathan P.	Cullman
Morris, C.H.	Atmore
Pardue, Melvin M.	Repton
Reeves, James Gary	Gardendale
Roe Jr., Fred D.	Huntsville
Russell, Tom	Jacksonville
Sandlin, Larry	Adamsville
Sinyard, Cleston S.	Elberta
Watson, Billy	Peatsville

alaska

Amoureux, A.W.	Anchorage
Brennan, Judson	Delta Junction
Breuer, Wayne	Wasilla
Broome, Thomas A.	Kenai
Bucholz, Mark A.	Eagle River
Cannon, Raymond W.	Homer
Chamberlin, John A.	Anchorage
Dempsey, Gordon W.	N.Kenai
DuFour, Arthur J.	Anchorage
England, Virgil	Anchorage
Gouker, Gary B.	Sitka
Grebe, Gordon S.	Anchor Point
Hibben, Westley G.	Anchorage
Johnson, David L.	Talkeetna
Kubaiko, Hank	Palmer
Lance, Bill	Eagle River
Little, Jimmy L.	Wasilla
McFarlin, Eric E.	Kodiak
McIntosh, David L.	Haines
Oda, Kuzan	Anchorage
Parrish III, Gordon A.	North Pole
Stegall, Keith	Anchorage
Trujillo, Thomas A .	Anchorage
Whitman, Jim	Chugiak

arizona

Beaver, Devon	Phoenix
Boye, David	Dolan Springs
Cheatham, Bill	Phoenix
Craft III, John M.	Williams
Draper, Bart	Phoenix
Edge, Tommy	Cash
Genovese, Rick	Clarkdale
Goo, Tai	Tucson

Guignard, Gib	Quartzsite
Hancock, Tim	Scottsdale
Hoel, Steve	Pine
Holder, D'Alton	Glendale
Hull, Michael J.	Cottonwood
Kopp, Todd M.	Apache Junction
Lee, Randy	St. Johns
Lively, Tim	Tucson
McFall, Ken	Lakeside
Oliver, Milford	Prescott
Sheehan, Paul P.	Sedona
Snare, Michael	Phoenix
Sutherland, Greg	Flagstaff
Tamboli, Michael	Glendale
Thompson, Robert L. (Bob)	Phoenix
Weiler, Donald E.	Yuma
Weiss, Charles L.	Phoenix
Wolf, Bill	Pheonix

arkansas

Anders, David	Center Ridge
Bogachov, Anatoly	Lockesburg
Brown, Jim	Little Rock
Cook, James Ray	Nashville
Crawford, Pat	West Memphis
Crowell, James L.	Mountain View
Dozier, Robert Lee	Springdale
Dungy, Lawrence	Little Rock
DuVall, Fred	Benton
Ferguson, Lee	Hindsville
Fisk, Jerry	Lockesburg
Flournoy, Joe	El Dorado
Foster, Al	Dogpatch
Frizzell, Ted	West Fork
Gaston, Bert	N. Little Rock
Grigsby, Ben	Mt. View
Hicks, Vernon G.	Bauxite
Lane, Ben	No. Little Rock
Lawrence, Alton	DeQueen
Lile, James B. (Marilyn)	Russelville
Maringer, Tom	Springdale
Martin, Bruce E.	Prescott
Massey, Roger	Texarkana
Ogg, Robert G.	Paris
Polk, Clifton	Van Buren
Price, Jerry L.	Springdale
Quattlebaum, Craig	Searcy
Ramey, Marshall F.	West Helena
Ree, David	Van Buren
Remington, David W.	Lincoln
Russell, A.G.	Springdale
Smoker, Ray	Searcy
Solomon, Marvin	Ferndale
Tycer, Art	N. Little Rock
Tyer, Jerry L.	Everton
Walker, Jim	Morrilton
Ward, Chuck	Benton

california

Alden Jr., Kenneth E.	Ramona
Barlow, Ken	Fortuna
Barron, Brian	San Mateo
Benson, Don	Escalon
Blum, Chuck	Brea
Blum, Ronald	Walnut Creek
Blum, Roy	Covington
Boyd, Francis	Berkeley
Brack, Douglas	Camirillo
Breshears, Clint	Manhattan Beach
Brown, Ted	Downey
Browne, Rick	Upland

Chelquist, Cliff	Arroyo Grande
Cohen, Terry A.	Laytonville
Collins, A.J.	Arleta
Connolly, James	Palermo
Davis, Charlie	Santee
Dillon, Earl E.	Arleta
Dion, Greg	Oxnard
Dixon Jr., Ira E.	Ventura
Donovan, Patrick	San Jose
Doolittle, Mike	Novato
Driscoll, Mark	La Mesa
Eaton, Al	Clayton
Eaton, Rick	Forbestown
Ellis, David	San Diego
Ellis, William Dean	Fresno
Emerson, Ernest R.	Torrance
English, Jim	Jamul
Engnath, Bob	Glendale
Essegian, Richard	Fresno
Ferguson, Jim	Acton
Ferguson, Jim	Downey
Fisher, Ted	Montague
Fox, Jack L.	Citrus Heights
Fraley, Ierek	Dixon
Freeman, Arthur F.	Citrus Heights
Freer, Ralph	Seal Beach
Fronefield, Mike	Truckee
Fulton, Mickey	Willows
Gamble, Frank	Redwood City
George, Tom	Magalia
Gofourth, Jim	Santa Paula
Golding, Robin	Lathrop
Hardy, Scott	Placerville
Harris, Jay	Redwood City
Hartsfield, Phill	Newport Beach
Hayes, Dolores	Los Angeles
Helton, Roy	San Diego
Hermes, Dana E.	Fremont
Herndon, Wm. R. Bill	Acton
Hink, Less	Stockton
Hornby, Glen	Glendale
Hume, Don	Sherman Oaks
Humenick, Roy	Rescue
Jacks, Jim	Covina
Johnson, Dave	Jamul
Jones, Curtis J.	Palmdale
Kozlow, Kelly	Ridgecrest
Kreibich, Donald L.	San Jose
Kruse, Martin	Reseda
LaBorde, Terry	Fallbrook
LeFont, Mark	Hollywood
Leland, Steve	Fairfax
Levine, Norman	Lake Elsinore
Lewis, Mike	Tracy
Likarich, Steve	Colfax
Lockett, Sterling	Burbank
Loveless, R.W.	Riverside
Manabe, Michael K.	San Diego
Martin, Jim	Oxnard
Mattis, James K.	Glendale
Maxwell, Don	Fresno
McClure, Michael	Menlo Park
McLeod, James	Oroville
McMahon, John	Palm Dessert
Meloy, Sean	Lemon Grove
Mendenhall, Harry E.	Milpitas
Middleton, Ken	Carmichael
Mitchell, R.W.	Lake Elsinore
Morgan, Jeff	Santee
Morlan, Tom	Hemet
Packard, Bob	Elverta

Pendleton, Lloyd — Volcano
Perry, Chris — Fresno
Phillips, Randy — Ontario
Pitt, David F. — Pleasanton
Posner, Barry E. — N. Hollywood
Reed, Wyle Fred — Sacramento
Richard, Ron — Fremont
Rust, Charles C. — Palermo
Scarrow, Lin — Bellflower
Scarrow, Will — Bellflower
Schroen, Karl — Sebastopol
Schultz, Richard — San Juan Capistrano
Sibrian, Aaron — Ventura
Sjostrand, Kevin — Visalia
Slobodian, Scott — Pine Grove
Sornberger, Jim — Volcano
Stapel, Chuck — Glendale
Stapel, Craig — Glendale
Steel, Ray — San Diego
Steinberg, Al — San Bruno
Swain, Rod — South Pasadena
Tamboli, Michael — Glendale
Terrill, Stephen — Lindsay
Tinker, Carolyn D. — Whittier
Ward, Ken — Auburn
Warren, Al — Roseville
Watanabe, Wayne — Montebello
Weinstock, Robert — San Francisco
Wesolowski, Mike — Petaluma
Whitehead, James D. — Sacramento
Williams, Sherman A. — Simi Valley
Williamson, Walt — Rancho Cucamonga
Wilson, Philip C. — Livermore
Wylefred, Reed — Sacramento

colorado

Anderson, Mel — Cedaredge
Appleton, Ray — Byers
Barrett, Cecil Terry — Colorado Springs
Booco, Gordon — Hayden
Brock, Kenneth L. — Allenspark
Brown, E.H. — Grand Junction
Campbell, Dick — Conifer
Davis, Don — Loveland
Dawson, Barry — Durango
DeLong, Dick — Aurora
Dennehy, Dan — Del Norte
Dill, Robert, Bonnie and Chris — Loveland
Genge, Roy E. — Eastlake
High, Tom — Alamoso
Hockensmith, Dan — Drake
Hodgson, Richard J. — Boulder
Hughes, Ed — Grand Junction
Hunt, Alex — Fort Collins
Kitsmiller, Jerry — Montrose
Lampson, Frank G. — Fruita
Leck, Dal — Hayden
Letcher, Billy — Fort Collins
Luck, Greg — Greeley
McWilliams, Sean — Bayfield
Miller, Hanford J. — Cowdrey
Miller, M.A. — Thornton
Neeley, Vaughn — Mancos
Nolen, R.D. and George — Estes Park
Olson, Wayne C. — Wheat Ridge
Owens, John — Parker
Peasley, David S. — Alamosa
Pogreba, Larry — Lyons
Robbins, Howard P. — Estes Park
Roberts, Chuck — Westminster
Rollert, Steve — Keenesburg
Sanders, Bill — Mancos
Sasser, Jim — Pueblo

Smith, D. Noel — Canon City
Thompson, Lloyd — Pagosa Springs
Tollefson, Barry A. — Gunnison
Topliss, M.W. "Ike" — Montrose
Watson, Bert — Westminster
Wilson, James G. — Estes Park
Wood, Barry B. — Colorado Springs
York, David C. — Crested Butte
Zima, Michael F. — Ft. Morgan

connecticut

Buebendorf, Robert E. — Monroe
Chapo, William G. — Wilton
Coughlin, Michael M. — Danbury
Hubbard, Arthur J. — Monroe
Jean, Gerry — Manchester
Lepore, Michael J. — Bethany
Martin, Randall J. — Middletown
Mayse, Martin L. — Hamden
Nelson, Roger S. — Central Village
Pankiewicz, Philip R. — Lebanon
Plinkett, Richard — West Cornwall
Putnam, Donald S. — Wethersfield
Rainville, Richard — Salem
Turecek, Jim — Derby
Zembko III, John — Berlin

delaware

Dugan, Brad M. — Milford
Schneider, Karl A. — Newark
Willey, W.G. — Greenwood

district of columbia

Cumming, R.J. — Washington

florida

Adams, Les — Hialeah
Atkinson, Dick — Wausau
Barry, James J. — West Palm Beach
Benjamin Jr., George — Kissimmee
Blackton, Andrew — Bayonet Point
Bradley, John — Pomona Park
Bray Jr., W. Lowell — New Port Richey
Brown, Harold E. — Arcadia
Burns, Dave — Boynton Beach
Cobb, Lowell D. — Daytona Beach
Cox, Colin J. — Apopka
Cross, John M. — Bryceville
Davenport, Jack — Dade City
DeGraeve, Richard — Sebastian
Dietzel, Bill — Middleburg
Ek, Gary Whitney — North Miami
Ellerbe, W.B. — Geneva
Enos III, Thomas M. — Orlando
Farrts, Cal — Altoona
Faulkner, Allan — St. Petersburg
Ferrara, Thomas — Naples
Fowler, Charles R. — Ft. McCoy
Gamble, Roger — St. Petersburg
Garner Jr., William O. — Pensacola
Gibson, Jim — Bunnell
Goers, Bruce — Lakeland
Griffin Jr., Howard A. — Davie
Grospitch, Ernie — Orlando
H&W Knives — Pace
Hancock, Ronald E. — Lecanto
Harris, Ralph Dewey — Brandon
Heitler, Henry — Tampa
Hennon, Robert — Ft. Walton Beach
Hill, Steven E. — Orlando
Hodge III, John — Palatka
Hoffman, Kevin L. — Winter Park
Hughes, Dan — West Palm Beach

Humphries, Joel — Bowling Green
Jernigan, Steve — Milton
Johnson, Durrell Carmon — Sparr
Kelly, Lance — Edgewater
King, Bill — Tampa
Krapp, Denny — Apopka
Lazo, Robert T. — Miami
Levengood, Bill — Tampa
Leverett, Ken — Lithia
Loflin, Bob — Miami Lakes
Long, Glenn A. — Palm Beach Gardens
Lozier, Don — Ocklawaha
Lunn, Larry A. — Safety Harbor
Lyle III, Ernest L. — Orlando
McDonald, Robert J. — Sunrise
Miller Jr., Chris — Gainesville
Miller, Robert — Ormond Beach
Miller, Ronald T. — Largo
Mink, Dan — St. Petersburg
Ochs, Charles F. — Largo
Outlaw, Anthony L. — Panama City
Pendray, Alfred H. — Williston
Price, Joel Hiram — Palatka
Randall, Gary T. — Orlando
Renner, Terry Lee — Bradenton
Robinson, Rex — Leesburg
Rogers, Rodney — Wildwood
Schlomer, James E. — Kissimmee
Schwarzer, James — Pomona Park
Schwarzer, Stephen — Pomona Park
Sharp, Wes & Margie — Milton
Simons, Bill — Lakeland
Smith, Bobbie D. — Bonifay
Smith, Michael J. — Tampa
Smith, W.M. — Bonifay
Stipes, Dwight — Jupiter
Tomes, Anthony — Jacksonville
Tomes, P.J. — Orange Park
Vunk, Robert Bob — Orlando
Waldrop, Mark — Summerfield
Wallace, Roger L. — Tampa
Watson, Tom — Panama City
Weiland Jr., J. Reese — Tampa
Wicker, Donnie R. — Panama City
Wine, Michael — Cocoa Beach
Zaccagnino, Don & Don Jr. — Pahokee
Zahm, Kurt — Indialantic

georgia

Arrowwood, Dale — Sharpsburg
Ashworth, Boyd — Powder Springs
Barker, Robert G. — Athens
Black, Scott — Covington
Bradley, Dennis — Blairsville
Buckner, Jimmie H. — Putney
Carey Jr., Charles W. — Griffin
Chamblin, Joel — Concord
Cofer, Ron — Duluth
Cole, Welborn I. — Atlanta
Cosby, E. Blanton — Columbus
Crockford, Jack — Chamblee
DeYong, Clarence — Kennesaw
Dunn, Charles K. — Shiloh
Ford, Allen — Smyrna
Fuller, John W. — Douglasville
Green, David — Covington
Halligan, Ed and Shawn — Sharpsburg
Hardin, Robert K. — Dalton
Harmon, Jay — Woodstock
Harmon, Joe — Jonesboro
Hawkins, Rade — Red Oak
Hegedus Jr., Lou — Cave Spring
Hegwood, Joel — Summerville

Hensley, Wayne	Conyers
Hinson, R. and Son	Columbus
Holland, John	Calhoun
Hyde, Jimmy	Ellenwood
Johnson, Harold Harry C.	Chickamauga
Kilby, Keith	Jefferson
Kimsey, Kevin	Marietta
King, Fred J.	Cartersville
King, Kemp	Flowery Branch
Kormanik, Chris	Carnesville
Landers, John	Newnan
Lockett, Lowell C.	Woodstock
Lonewolf, J. Aguirre	Demorest
Love, Ed	Stockbridge
McCarty, Zollan	Thomaston
McGill, John	Blairsville
Mitchell, James A.	Columbus
Moore, Bill	Leesburg
North, David	Chickamauga
Parks, John	Jefferson
Pittman, Leon	Pendergrass
Poole, Steve L.	Stockbridge
Poplin, James L.	Washington
Poythress, John	Swainsboro
Prater, Mike	Chickamauga
Ragsdale, James D. Jim	Lithonia
Rogers Jr., Robert P.	Acworth
Roghmans, Mark	Lagrange
Royal, B.M. "Red"	Helen
Scofield, Everett	Chickamauga
Small, Jim	Madison
Smith Jr., James B.	Morven
Snell, Jerry L.	Fayetteville
Stafford, Richard	Warner Robins
Thompson, Kenneth	Duluth
Walters, A.F.	Tifton
Werner, William A. Jr.	Marietta
Wilson, Robert M.	Bowman

hawaii

Dolan, Robert L.	Kula
Evans, Vincent K.	Keaau
Fujisaka, Stanley	Kaneohe
Lui, Ronald	Honolulu
Mayo Jr., Thomas H.	Waialua
Onion, Kenneth J.	Kapolei
Valachovic, Wayne	Kailua-Kona
Zakabi, Carl S.	Mililani Town

idaho

Alderman, Robert	Sagle
Andrews, Don	Coeur D'Alene
Horton, Scot	Buhl
Kranning, Terry L.	Pocatello
Moulton, Dusty	Boise
Mullin, Steve	Sandpoint
Nealy, Ivan F.	Mountain Home
Quarton, Barr	McCall
Reeve, Chris	Boise
Rohn, Fred	Coeur d'Alene
Sawby, Scott	Sand Point
Selent, Chuck	Bonners Ferry
Spragg, Wayne E.	Ashton
Steiger, Monte L.	Genesee
Towell, Dwight L.	Midvale

illinois

Abbott, William M.	Chandlerville
Bloomer, Allan T.	Maquon
Brandsey, Edward P.	Woodstock
Brannan, Ralph	Frankfort
Bridgnardello, E.D.	Beecher
Bulawski, Rick	Sandwich

Cook, Louise	Ozark
Cook, Mike	Ozark
Detmer, Phillip	Breese
Eaker, Allen	Paris
Guth, Kenneth	Chicago
Hill, Rick	Collinsville
James, Peter	Hoffman Estates
Knuth, Joseph E.	Rockford
Kovar, Eugene	Evergreen Park
Lang, Kurt	McHenry
Leone, Nick	Pontoon Beach
Meier, Daryl	Carbondale
Millard, Fred G.	Chicago
Myers, Paul	East Alton
Nowland, Rick	Waltonville
Poag, James	Grayville
Pritchard, Ron	Dixon
Rados, Jerry F.	Grant Park
Schneider, Craig M.	Seymour
Smith, John M.	Centralia
Stalter, Harry L.	Trivoli
Tompkins, Dan	Peotone
Turnbull, Ralph A.	Rockford
Veit, Michael	LaSalle
Voss, Ben	Galesburg
Werth, George W.	Poplar Grove
West, Charles A.	Centralia
White, Robert J. Bob	Gilson
White Jr., Robert J. "Butch"	Gilson
Woodworth, Al	Plainville
Wright, Timothy	Chicago
Young, Errol	Alton

indiana

Allen, Joe	Princeton
Birt, Sid	Nashville
Bose, Tony	Shelburn
Broughton, Don R.	Floyd Knob
Chaffee, Jeff L.	Morriss
Damlovac, Sava	Indianapolis
Darby, Jed	Greensburg
Davis, Ken	Indianapolis
Fitzgerald, Dennis	Fort Wayne
Flynn, Bruce	Middletown
Gutekunst, Ralph	Richmond
Imel, Billy Mace	New Castle
Johnson, C.E. Gene	Portage
Keeslar, Steven C.	Hamilton
Keeton, William L.	Laconia
Largin, Ken	Batesville
Ledford, Bracy R.	Indianapolis
Lutes, Robert	Nappanee
Mayville, Oscar	Marengo
Minnick, Jim	Middletown
Norton, Dennis G.	Fort Wayne
Parsons, Michael R.	Terre Haute
Porter, James E.	Bloomington
Rigney, Willie	Shelbyville
Rubley, James A.	Angola
Shostle, Ben	Muncie
Sokol, Richard	Indianapolis
Stover, Terry "Lee"	Kokomo
Thayer, Danny	Lafayette
Welch, William H.	Kimmell

iowa

Brooker, Dennis	Derby
Brower, Max	Boone
Clark, Howard	Runnells
Lainson, Tony	Council Bluffs
Miller, James P.	Fairbank
Myers, Mel	Spencer
Trindle, Barry	Earlham

Westberg, Larry	Algona
Zscherny, Michael	Cedar Rapids

kansas

Ames, Mickey L.	Lebo
Bradburn, Gary	Wichita
Chard, Gordon R.	Iola
Courtney, Eldon	Wichita
Craig, Roger L.	Topeka
Culver, Steve	Mayetta
Dugger, Dave	Westwood
Dunn, Melvin T.	Rossville
Hegwald, J.L.	Humboldt
Herman, Tim	Overland Park
Kennelley, J.C.	Arkansas City
Kraft, Steve	Abilene
Petersen, Dan L.	Topeka

kentucky

Barr, A.T.	Nicholasville
Baskett, Lee Gene	Eastview
Brumagen, Jerry	Lexington
Bugden, John	Murray
Bybee, Barry J.	Cadiz
Carson, Harold J. Kit	Vine Grove
Clay, J.D.	Greenup
Coil, Jimmie J.	Owensboro
Corbit, Gerald E. "Jerry"	Elizabethtown
Downing, Larry	Bremen
Dunn, Steve	Smiths Grove
Fannin, David A.	Lexington
Fister, Jim	Simpsonville
France, Dan	Cawood
Gevedon, Hanners	Crab Orchard
Hemphill, Jesse	Berea
Hibben, Daryl	LaGrange
Hibben, Gil	LaGrange
Hibben, Joleen	LaGrange
Howser, John C.	Frankfort
Keeslar, Joseph F.	Almo
Pease, W.D.	Ewing
Pierce, Harold L.	Louisville
Pulliam, Morris C.	Shelbyville
Smith, Gregory H.	Louisville
Smith, John W.	West Liberty
Waddle, Thomas	Louisville

louisiana

Black, Tom	Alexandria
Blaum, Roy	Covington
Caldwell, Bill	West Monroe
Camp, Jeff	Ruston
Culpepper, John	Monroe
Dake, C.M.	New Orleans
Douglas, Dale	Ponchatoula
Durio, Fred	Opelousas
Elkins, R. Van	Bonita
Faucheaux, Howard J.	Loreauville
Forstall, Al	Slidell
Gorenflo, James T.	Baton Rouge
Graffeo, Anthony I.	Chalmette
Holmes, Robert	Baton Rouge
Howard, Seth	Baton Rouge
Ki, Shiva	Baton Rouge
Laurent, Kermit	LaPlace
Marks, Chris	Breaux Bridge
Mitchell, Max and Dean	Leesville
Potier, Timothy F.	Oberlin
Provenzano, Joseph D.	Chalmette
Reggio Jr., Sidney J.	Sun
Roath, Dean	Baton Rouge
Sanders, Michael M.	Ponchatoula
Smith, W.F. Red	Slidell

directory

Vought Jr., Frank	Hammond
Wiggins, Horace	Mansfield

maine

Bohrmann, Bruce	Yarmouth
Coombs Jr., Lamont	Bucksport
Courtois, Bryan	Saco
Fuegen, Larry	Wiscasset
Leavitt, Earl F.	E. Boothbay
Oyster, Lowell R.	Kenduskeag
Sayen, Murad	Bryant Pond
Sharrigan, Mudd	Wiscasset

maryland

Antonio, William J.	Golts
Barnes, Aubrey G.	Hagerstown
Barnes, Gary L.	New Windsor
Beers, Ray	Monkton
Bouse, D. Michael	Waldorf
Cohen, N.J. Norm	Baltimore
Freiling, Albert J.	Finksburg
Fuller, Jack A.	New Market
Hendrickson, E.J. Jay	Frederick
Hudson, Robbin C.	Rock Hall
Hurt, William R.	Frederick
Kremzner, Raymond L.	Stevenson
Kretsinger Jr., Philip W.	Boonsboro
McCarley, John	Union Bridge
McGowan, Frank	Sykesville
Merchant, Ted	White Hall
Moran, Wm. F.	Braddock Heights
Nicholson, Kent R.	Phoenix
Rhodes, James D.	Hagerstown
Sentz, Mark C.	Taneytown
Sidelinger, Robert	Bel Air
Smit, Glenn	Aberdeen
Sontheimer, Douglas G.	Potomac
Wagner, Dan	Chestertown

massachusetts

Dailey, G.E.	Seekonk
DaConceicao	Rehoboth
Flechtner, Chris	Fitchburg
Gaudette, Linden L.	Wilbraham
Grossman, Stewart	Clinton
Gwozdz, Bob	Attleboro
Jarvis, Paul M.	Cambridge
Khalsa, Jot Singh	Millis
Kubasek, John A.	Easthampton
Lapen, Charles	W. Brookfield
McLuin, Tom	Dracut
Reed, Dave	Brimfield
Richter, Scott	Watertown
Rua, Gary (Wolf)	Fall River
Siska, Jim	Westfield
Sloan, John	Foxboro
Smith, J.D.	Boston
Tsoulas, Jon J.	Peabody

michigan

Beckwith, Michael R.	New Baltimore
Behnke, William	Lake City
Booth, Philip W.	Ithaca
Buckbee, Donald M.	Clinton Township
Carlisle, Frank	Detroit
Cashen, Kevin R.	Hubbardston
Cook, Mike A.	Portland
Cousino, George	Onsted
Cowles, Don	Royal Oak
Dilluvio, Frank J.	Warren
Enders, Robert	Cement City
Erickson, Walter E.	Warren
Garbe, Bob	Fraser
Gardner, Rob	Ann Arbor
Gottage, Dante and Judy	St. Clair Shores
Hartman, Arlan	N. Muskegon
Hughes, Daryle	Nunica
Kalfayan, Edward N.	Ferndale
Krause, Roy W.	St. Clair Shores
Lankton, Scott	Ann Arbor
Leach, Mike J.	Swartz Creek
Lucie, James R.	Fruitport
Mills, Louis G. Yasutomo	Ann Arbor
Parker, Robert Nelson	Rapid City
Repke, Mike	Bay City
Sakmar, Mike	Rochester
Serven, Jim	Fostoria
Sigman, James P.	Three Rivers
Stewart, Charles Chuck	Warren
Warzocha, Stanley	Warren
Whitworth, Ken J.	Sterling Heights
Wood, Webster	Clarkston
Zowada, Tim	Marshall

minnesota

Dingman, Scott	Bemidji
Dube, Paul N.	Chaska
Fiorini, Bill	LaCrescent
Flood, James Noah	Chaska
Goltz, Warren L.	Ada
Griffin, Thomas J.	Windom
Hagen, Philip L.	Pelican Rapids
Hansen, Robert W.	Cambridge
Johnson, Ronald B.	Clearwater
Knipschield, Terry	Rochester
Lange, Donald G.	Pelican Rapids
McGinnis, Tom	Ozark
Shadley, Eugene W.	Bovey

mississippi

Craft, Richard C.	Jackson
Davis, Jesse W.	Sarah
Greco, John	Bay St. Louis
Hand, James E., M.D.	Gloster
Landrum, Leonard	Lumberton
LeBatard, Paul M.	Vancleave
Roberts, Michael	Clinton
Taylor, Billy	Petal
Wehner, Rudy	Collins
Wingo, Perry	Gulfport
Winston, David	Starkville

missouri

Anderson, Charles B.	Lampe
Bolton, Charles B.	Jonesburg
Burrows, Stephen R.	Kansas City
Cover, Raymond A.	Mineral Point
Davis, W.C.	Raymore
Dearing, John	DeSoto
Dippold, A.W.	Perryville
Driskill, Beryl	Braggadocio
Duvall, Larry E.	Gallatin
Engle, William	Boonville
Frese, William R.	St. Louis
Garcia Jr., Raul	Aberdeen
Glaser, Ken	Purdy
Kennedy, Jerry	Blue Springs
Kinnikin, Todd	House Springs
Knickmeyer, Hank	Cedar Hill
Lane, Ed	Kansas City
Mason, Bill	Excelsior Springs
May, James E.	Auxvasse
McCrackin and Son, V.J.	House Springs
Miller, Bob	Ballwin
Newcomb, Corbin	Moberly
Rardon, A.D.	Polo
Rardon, Archie F.	Polo
Shelton, Paul	Rolla
Steketee, Craig A.	Billings
Warden, Roy A.	Union
Webb, Jim	Joplin
Weddle Jr., Del	St. Joseph

montana

Barnes, Jack	Whitefish
Beam, John R.	Kalispell
Brooks, Steve R.	Big Timber
Brunkhorst, C. Lyle	Helena
Caffrey, Edward J.	Great Falls
Conklin, George	Fort Benton
Crowder, Robert	Thompson Falls
Dunkerley, Rick	Lincoln
Ellefson, Joel	Manhattan
Fassio, Melvin G.	Bonner
Forthofer, Pete	Whitefish
Frank, Heinrich H.	Whitefish
Gallagher, Barry	Lewistown
Gillis, C.R. "Rex"	Great Falls
Harkins, J.A.	Conner
Hill, Howard	Polson
Kauffman, Dave	Helena
Kraft, Elmer	Big Arm
McGuane IV, Thomas F.	Bozeman
Miller, Larry	Missoula
Moyer, Russ	Havre
Peele, Bryan	Thompson Falls
Peterson, Eldon G.	Whitefish
Piorek, James S.	Missoula
Pursley, Aaron	Big Sandy
Reh, Bill	Lolo
Ruana Knife Works	Bonner
Schirmer, Mike	Twin Bridges
Schmidt, Rick	Whitefish
Simonich, Bob	Clancy
Smith, Josh	Lincoln
Taylor, Shane	Angela
Thill, Jim	Missoula
Townsend, J.W.	Trout Creek
Weinand, Gerome W.	Missoula

nebraska

Brown, David B.	Fairbury
Hielscher, Guy	Alliance
Jensen Jr., Carl A.	Blair
Jokerst, Charles	Omaha
Miller, Terry	Seward
Schepers, George B.	Chapman
Suedmeier, Harlan	Nebraska City
Syslo, Chuck	Omaha
Till, Calvin E.	Chadron

nevada

Blanchard, Gary	Las Vegas
Defeo, Robert A.	Henderson
Duff, Bill	Virginia City
Hrisoulas, Jim	Las Vegas
Mecchi, Richard	Las Vegas
Nishiuchi, Melvin S.	Las Vegas
Thomas, Devin	Las Vegas
Tracy, Bud	Reno

new hampshire

Saindon, R. Bill	Claremont

new jersey

D'Andrea, John	Wayne
Grussenmeyer, Paul	Lindenwold
Hetmanski, Thomas S.	Trenton
MacBain, Kenneth	Norwood

McGovern, Jim	Oak Ridge
Polkowski, Al	Chester
Povisils, Karlis A.	Mt. Holly
Pressburger, Ramon	Howell
Slee, Fred	Morganville
Viele, H.J.	Westwood
Weber, Fred E.	Forked River

new mexico

Becket, Norman L.	Farmington
Black, Tom	Albuquerque
Coleman, Keith E.	Los Lunas
Cordova, Joseph G.	Peralta
Digangi, Joseph M.	Santa Cruz
Duran, Jerry T.	Albuquerque
Dyess, Eddie	Roswell
Fisher, Jay	Magdalena
Goode, Bear	Navajo Dam
Hethcoat, Don	Clovis
Homer, Glen	Bloomfield
Jones, Bob	Albuquerque
Lewis, Ron	Edgewood
Lewis, Tom R.	Carlsbad
McBurnette, Harvey	Eagle Nest
Miller, Ted	Santa Fe
Norton, Don	Farmington
Nymeyer, Earl	Hobbs
Pagnard, Philip E.	Albuquerque
Schaller, Antony B.	Albuquerque
Terzuola, Robert	Santa Fe
Walker, Michael	Taos
Wescott, Jim	Las Cruces

new york

Anderson, Edwin	Glen Cove
Baker, Bill	Boiceville
Champagne, Paul	Mechanicville
Cute, Thomas	Cortland
Davis, Barry L.	Castleton
Licata, Steven	Mineola
Loos, Henry C.	New Hyde Park
Ludwig, Richard O.	Maspeth
Maragni, Dan	Georgetown
Martrildonno, Paul	Olivebridge
Meshejian, Marvin	E. Northport
Page, Reginald	Groveland
Pattay, Rudy	Long Beach
Patterson, Karl	Silver Creek
Rachlin, Leslie S.	Elmira
Rappazzo, Richard	Cohoes
Rizzi, Russell	East Setauket
Rotella, Richard A.	Niagara Falls
Scheid, Maggie	Rochester
Schmidt, James A.	Ballston Lake
Serafen, Steven E.	Norwich
Smith, Raymond L.	Breesport
Stahl, John	Baldwin
Summers, Dan	Whitney Point
Szilaski, Joseph	Wappingers Falls
Todd, Ed	Putnam Valley
Turner, Kevin	Montrose
Tyc, William J.	Newburgh
Wahlers, Herman F.	Austerlitz
Warren, Dellana	Schenectady
Wood, Leonard J.	Beacon

north carolina

Barron, David	Etowah
Britton, Tim	Kinston
Brown, Tom	Greensboro
Busfield, John	Roanoke Rapids
Chastain, Wade	Horse Shoe
Clark, Dave	Andrews

Daniel, Travis E.	Winston-Salem
Fox, Paul	Claremont
Gaddy, Gary Lee	Washington
Goguen, Scott	Newport
Goldenberg, T.S.	Fairview
Gross, W.W.	High Point
Gurganus, Carol	Colerain
Gurganus, Melvin H.	Colerain
Guthrie, George B.	Bessemer City
Harless, Walt	Stoneville
Hudson, Tommy	Monroe
King, Randall	Asheville
Livingston, Robert C.	Murphy
Lubrich, Mark	Matthews
Maynard, William N. (Bill)	Fayetteville
McNabb, Tommy	Winston-Salem
Moretz, Jim	Boone
Norris, Mike	Albemarle
Parrish, Robert	Hendersonville
Patrick, Chuck	Brasstown
Patterson, Alan W.	Hayesville
Popp Sr., Steve F.	Fayetteville
Rece, Charles V.	Albemarle
Scholl, Tim	Angier
Sears, Mick	Gastonia
Shuford, Rick	Statesville
Simmons, H.R.	Grantsboro
Sprouse, Terry	Asheville
Tedder, Mickey	Conover
Van Hoy, Ed	Greenville
Wade, J.M.	Wade
Wagaman, John K.	Fayetteville
Whitley, Wayne	Washington
Williamson, Tony	Siler City
Winkler, Daniel	Boone
Young, Paul A.	Vilas

north dakota

Ennis, Ray W.	Grand Forks
Keidel, Gene W.	Dickinson
Keidel, Scott J.	Dickinson

ohio

Babcock, Raymond G.	Vincent
Busse, Jerry	Wauseon
Collins, Harold A.	West Union
Collins, Lynn M.	Elyria
Corwin, Don	Monclova
Cottrill, James I.	Columbus
Darby, Rick	Youngstown
Downing, Tom	Cortland
Downs, Jim	Londonderry
Etzler, John	Grafton
Foster, R.L. (Bob)	Mansfield
Franklin, Mike	Aberdeen
Geisler, Gary	Clarksville
Glover, Ron	Cincinnati
Greiner, Richard	Green Springs
Grubb, Richard A.	Columbus
Guess, Raymond L.	Mechanicstown
Hinderer, R.	Wooster
Imboden II, Howard L.	Dayton
Johnson, W.C. "Bill"	New Carlisle
Kiefer, Tony	Pataskala
Koutsopoulos, George	LaGrange
Koval, Michael T.	New Albany
Layton, Jim	Portsmouth
Longworth, Dave	Hamersville
Maienknecht, Stanley	Sardis
McCarty, Harry	Hamilton
McGroder, Patrick J.	Madison
Mercer, Mike	Lebanon
Messer, David T.	Dayton

Mettler, J. Banjo	No. Baltimore
Morgan, Tom	Beloit
Papp, Robert Bob	Parma
Pratt, Charles	Port Washington
Ralph, Darrel	Reynoldsburg
Salley, John D.	Tipp City
Shinosky, Andy	Warren
Shoemaker, Carroll	Northup
Shoemaker, Scott	Miamisburg
Shushunov, Sergei	Bath
Spinale, Richard	Lorain
Steven, Barry B.	Cridersville
Stoddart, W.B. Bill	Forest Park
Strong, Scott	Beaver Creek
Summers, Arthur L.	Mechanicsburg
Summers, Dennis K.	Springfield
Thomas, Kim	Brunswick
Thourot, Michael W.	Napoleon
Trabbic, R.W.	Toledo
Votaw, David P.	Pioneer
Ward, J.J.	Waverly
Warther, Dale	Dover
Witsaman, Earl	Stow
Wood, Larry B.	Huber Heights
Yurco, Mike	Canfield

oklahoma

Baker, Ray	Sapulpa
Crenshaw, Al	Eufaula
Dill, Dave	Bethany
Englebretson, George	Oklahoma City
Gepner, Don	Norman
Johns, Rob	Enid
Kennedy Jr., Bill	Yukon
Leet, Larry W.	Shawnee
Mitchell, Wm. Dean	Forgan
Nibarger, Charlie	Tulsa
Sanders, Athern Al	Norman
Sisemore, Charles	Hodgen
Spivey, Jefferson	Yukon
Stice, Douglas	Norman
Williams, Michae! L.	Broken Bow

oregon

Alverson, Tim	Klamath Falls
Anderson, Virgil W.	Portland
Bell, Michael	Coquille
Bochman, Bruce	Grants Pass
Buchman, Bill	Bend
Buchner, Bill	Idleyld Park
Coats, Eldon M.	Beatty
Corrado, Jim	Glide
Davis, Terry	Sumpter
Dowell, T.M.	Bend
Draper, Kent	Cheshire
Eck, Larry A.	Terrebonne
Ferdinand, Don	Prospect
Fox, Wendell	Springfield
Goddard, Wayne	Eugene
Harsey, William W.	Creswell
Hilker, Thomas N.	Williams
Horn, Jess	Florence
Huey, Steve	Junction City
Kelley, Gary	Aloha
Lake, Ron	Eugene
Lindsay, Chris A.	Bend
Little, Gary M.	Broadbent
Lum, Robert W.	Eugene
Miller, Michael K.	Sweet Home
Murphy, Dave	Gresham
Osterman, Daniel E.	Junction City
Reed, Del	Beaverton
Saddle Mountain Knife	Vernonia

directory

Schell, Clyde M. — Corvallis
Shoger, Mark O. — Beaverton
Thompson, Leon — Forest Grove
Thompson, Tommy — Portland
Vallotton, Butch — Oakland
Vallotton, Rainy D. — Oakland
Vallotton, Shawn — Oakland
Veatch, Richard — Springfield
Wahlster, Mark David — Silverton
Woodcock, Dennis "Woody" — Nehalem
Wise, John — Winchester
Zeller, Dennis J. — Gresham

pennsylvania

Amor Jr., Miguel — Lancaster
Anderson, Gary D. — Spring Grove
Bartrug, Hugh E. — Elizabeth
Besedick, Frank E. — Charleroi
Candrella, Joe — Warminster
Clark, D.E. Lucky — Mineral Point
Ellenberg, William C. — Melrose Park
Frey Jr., W. Fredrick — Milton
Goldberg, David — Blue Bell
Gottschalk, Gregory J. — Carnegie
Lorditch, Charles Richard — Johnstown
Malloy, Joe — Freeland
Marlowe, Donald — Dover
Milford, Brian A. — Knox
Miller, Rick — Rockwood
Nealy, Bud — Stroudsburg
Nolfi, Tim — Dawson
Parker, J.E. — Clarion
Rupert, Robert — Clinton
Steigerwalt, Ken — Levittown
Stroyan, Eric — Dalton
Taglienti, Antonio J. — Darlington
Valois, A. Daniel — Lehighton
Whittaker, Robert E. — Mill Creek
Wilson, Jon J. — Johnstown

rhode island

Bardsley, Norman P. — Pawtucket
Black, Robert — N. Kingstown
Felfidel, Ralph — Warrich
Gentile, Al — Warwick
Lambert, Ronald S. — Johnston
McHenry, William James — Wyoming
Selvidio, Ralph — N. Kingstown
Williams, Jason L. — Wyoming

south carolina

Barefoot, Joe W. — Liberty
Beatty, Gordon H. — Seneca
Branton, Robert — Awendaw
Brend, Walter J. — Walterboro
Bridwell, Richard A. — Taylors
Cannady, Daniel L. — Allendale
Cox, Sam — Gaffney
Davis, Dixie — Clinton
Defreest, William G. — Barnwell
Easler, Paula — Woodruff
Easler Jr., Russell O. — Woodruff
Fecas, Stephen J. — Anderson
Gainey, Hal — Greenwood
Gaston, Ron — Woodruff
George, Harry — Aiken
Gregory, Michael — Belton
Hendrix, Wayne — Allendale
Herron, George — Springfield
Kaufman, Scott — Anderson
Kay, J. Wallace — Liberty
Kessler, Ralph A. — Marietta
Knott, Steve — Clinton

Langley, Gene H. — Florence
Lee, Tommy — Gaffney
Lewis, K.J. — Lugoff
Lutz, Greg — Greenwood
Montjoy, Claude — Clinton
Owens, Dan — Blacksburg
Page, Larry — Aiken
Parler, Thomas O'Neil — Charleston
Peagler, Russ — Moncks Corner
Poole, Marvin — Anderson
Poston, Alvin — Pamplico
Prince, Joe R. — Moore
Reeves, Winfred M. — West Union
Smith, Ralph L. — Taylors
Thomas, Rocky — Ladson
Webb, Jr., Charley L. — Anderson
Whitmire, Earl T. — Rock Hill

tennessee

Bailey, Joseph D. — Nashville
Baker, Vance — Riceville
Bartlow, John — Norris
Canter, Ronald E. — Jackson
Cargill, Bob — Oldfort
Casteel, Dianna — Monteagle
Casteel, Douglas — Monteagle
Centofante, Frank and Tony — Madisonville
Claiborne, Ron — Knoxville
Clay, Wayne — Pelham
Conley, Bob — Jonesboro
Coogan, Robert — Smithville
Copeland, George A. Steve — Alpine
Corby, Harold — Johnson City
Crisp, Harold — Cleveland
Ewing, John H. — Clinton
Eldridge, Allan L. — Gallatin
Harley, Larry W. — Bristol
Hurst, Jeff — Rutledge
Johnson, Ryan M. — Hixson
Langston, Bennie E. — Memphis
Levine, Bob — Tullahoma
McDonald, W.J. "Jerry" — Germantach
Rhea, David — Lynnville
Rial, Douglas — Greenfield
Ryder, Ben M. — Copperhill
Sampson, Lynn — Jonesborough
Smith, Newman L. — Gatlinburg
Taylor, C. Gray — Kingsport
Taylor, David — Bristol
Vanderford, Carl G. — Columbia
Von Boeckman, R. — Memphis
Walker, John W. — Bon Aqua
Ward, W.C. — Clinton
Williams Jr., Richard T. — Morristown
Wright, Harold C. — Centerville

texas

Adams, William D. — Houston
Allen, Mike Whiskers — Malakoff
Allred, Elvan — Wichita Falls
Anderson, Michael D. — Arlington
Ashby, Douglas — Dallas
Bagwell, Bill — Marietta
Bailey, Kirby C. — Lytle
Barbee, Jim — Ft. Stockton
Barnes, Jim — San Angelo
Batts, Keith — Hooks
Blasingame, Robert — Kilgore
Blum, Kenneth — Brenham
Brayton, Jim — Burkburnett
Brightwell, Mark — Leander
Broadwell, David — Wichita Falls

Brooks, Michael — Lubbock
Bullard, Randall — Canyon
Bullard, Tom — Comfort
Burden, James M. — Burkburnett
Byrd, Don E. — Roanoke
Callahan, F. Terry — Boerne
Carter, Fred — Wichita Falls
Cellum, Tom S. — Willis
Champion, Robert — Amarillo
Chapman, Mike — Houston
Chase, John E. — Aledo
Churchman, T.W. — Amarillo
Clark, Roger — Rockdale
Collett, Jerry D. — Charlotte
Connor, Michael — Winters
Costa, Scott — Spicewood
Crain, Jack W. — Weatherford
Crawford, Larry — Rosenberg
Davis, Vernon — Waco
Dean, Harvey J. — Rockdale
Dominy, Chuck — Colleyville
Edwards, Lynn — West Columbia
Elishewitz, Allen — San Marcos
Eriksen, James Thorlief — Garland
Ferguson, Jim — San Angelo
Fischer, Clyde E. — Nixon
Fowler, Jerry — Hutto
Franks, Joel — Lubbock
Fuller, Bruce A. — Baytown
Gartman, M.D. — Gatesville
Gault, Clay — Lexington
Green, Bill — Garland
Green, Roger M. — Joshua
Griffin, Rendon and Mark — Houston
Hagwood, Kellie — San Antonio
Hajovsky, Robert J. — Scotland
Hamlet Jr., Johnny — Clute
Hand, Bill — Spearman
Hays, Mark — Carrollton
Hesser, David — Dripping Springs
Hoffman, Harold — San Angelo
Hollett, Jeff — Fate
Howell, Robert L. — Kilgore
Hudson, Robert — Humble
Hueske, Chubby — Bellaire
Hughes, Lawrence — Plainview
Jetton, Cay — Winnsboro
Johnson, Gorden W. — Houston
Johnson, Ruffin — Houston
Johnson, Ryan M. — Hixson
Kennedy, Kelly S. — Odessa
Kious, Joe — Kerrville
Klimaszewski, Bernard E. — Killeen
Knipstein, Robert C. — Arlington
Kohler, J. Mark — Sugarland
Ladd, Jim — Deer Park
Ladd, Jimmie L. — Deer Park
Lambert, Jarrell D. — Ganado
LaPlante, Brett — Garland
Laughlin, Don — Vidor
Lay, L.J. — Burkburnett
LeBlanc, John — Winnsboro
Lister Jr., Weldon E. — Boerne
Lott, David — Addison
Luchak, Bob — Channelview
Luckett, Bill — Weatherford
Lyons, Randy — Lumberton
Madsen, Jack — Wichita Falls
Marshall, Glenn — Mason
McConnell Jr., Loyd A. — Odessa
McDearmont, Dave — Lewisville
McElhannon, Marcus — Sugarland
McKissack II, Tommy — Sonora

Merz III, Robert L.	Katy
Miller, R.D.	Dallas
Mills, Andy	Fredericksburg
Neely, Greg	Houston
Moore, James B.	Ft. Stockton
Mount, Don	Horizon City
Ogletree Jr., Ben R.	Livingston
Oliver, Anthony Craig	Ft. Worth
Osborne, Michael	New Braunfels
Osborne, Warren	Waxahachie
Overeynder, T.R.	Arlington
Pate, Lloyd D.	Georgetown
Polzien, Don	Lubbock
Pugh, Jim	Azle
Pullen, Martin	Granbury
Ray, Alan W.	Lovelady
Raymond, Donald	Groveton
Raymond, Mary Jane	Groveton
Richardson Jr., Percy	Milan
Rippy, Robert	Houston
Robinson, Charles	Vega
Ruple, William H.	Charlotte
Schneider, Herman J.	Pittsburg
Scott, Al	Kerrville
Self, Ernie	Dripping Springs
Sims, Bob	Meridian
Sloan, Shane	Newcastle
Smart, Steve	Melissa
Spano, Dominick	San Angelo
Spencer, John E.	Harper
Stokes, Ed	Hockley
Stone, Jerry	Lytle
Stout, Johnny	New Braunfels
Thuesen, Ed	Houston
Thuesen, Kevin	Houston
Treiber, Leon	Ingram
Turcotte, Larry	Pampa
Ware, Tommy	Blanco
Watson, Daniel	Driftwood
Watt III, Freddie	Big Spring
Watts, Mike	Gatesville
Watts, Wally	Gatesville
West, Pat	Charlotte
Whitley, Weldon G.	El Paso
Wilcher, Wendell L.	Palestine
Womack, A.M. "Babe"	Coldspring
Wood, William W.	Seymour
Yeates, Joe A.	Spring
Yunes, Yamil R.	Roma
Zinsmeister, Paul	Fredericksburg

utah

Black, Earl	Salt Lake City
Ence, Jim	Richfield
Erickson, Curt	Ogden
Erickson, L.M.	Liberty
Hatch, Ken	Jensen
Hunter, Hyrum and Kellie	Aurora
Johnson, Steve R.	Manti
Maxfield, Lynn	Layton
Nielson, Jeff	Monroe
Nunn, Gregory R.	Moab
Peterson, Chris	Aurora
Rapp, Steven J.	Salt Lake City
Strickland, Dale	Monroe
Warenski, Buster	Richfield
Winn, Travis A.	Salt Lake City

vermont

Haggerty, George S.	Jacksonville
Kelso, Jim	Worcester

virginia

Ballew, Dale	Bowling Green
Barber, Robert E.	Charlottesville
Batson, Richard G.	Rixeyville
Beverly II, Larry H.	Hartwood
Blakley II, William E.	Fredericksburg
Callahan, Errett	Lynchburg
Chamberlain III, Charles R.	Christiansburg
Compton, William E.	Sterling
Conkey, Tom	Nokesville
Davidson, Edmund	Goshen
Douglas, John J.	Lynch Station
Fielder, William V.	Richmond
Frazier, Ron	Powhatan
Hawk, Jack L.	Ceres
Hawk, Joe	Ceres
Hawk, Joey K.	Ceres
Hedrick, Don	Newport News
Hendricks, Samuel J.	Maurertown
Holloway, Paul	Norfolk
Jones, Barry	Danville
Jones, Enoch	Warrenton
Jones, Phillip G.	Danville
Kellogg, Brian R.	New Market
McCoun, Mark	DeWitt
Metheny, H.A."Whitey"	Spotsylvania
Norfleet, Ross W.	Richmond
Owen, Bill	Monterey
Parks, Blane C.	Dale City
Presley, Vern	Richmond
Richter, John C.	Chesapeake
Ryan, C.O.	Yorktown
Scott, Winston	Huddleston
Straight, Don	Falls Church
Thomas, Daniel	Leesburg
White, Gene E.	Alexandria

washington

Baldwin, Phillip	Snohomish
Ball, Robert	Port Angeles
Ber, Dave	San Juan Island
Blomberg, Gregg	Lopez
Boguszewski, Phil	Tacoma
Brothers, Robert L.	Colville
Chamberlain, John B.	East Wenatchee
Chamberlain, Jon A.	East Wenatchee
Conti, Jeffrey D.	Port Orchard
D'Angelo, Laurence	Vancouver
Davis, K.M. Twig	Monroe
Goertz, Paul S.	Renton
Greenfield, G.O.	Everett
Holland, Dale J.	Issaquah
Mosser, Gary E.	Kirkland
Rice, Adrienne	Lopez Island
Sanderson, Ray	Yakima
Showers, Robert	Longbeach
Wright, Kevin	Quilcene

west virginia

Barnett, Van	New Haven
Bowen, Tilton	Baker
Dent, Douglas M.	South Charleston
Drost, Jason D.	French Creek
Drost, Michael B.	French Creek
Elliott, Jerry P.	Charleston
Liegey, Kenneth R.	Millwood
Maynard, Larry Joe	Crab Orchard
McConnell, Charles R.	Wellsburg
Pickens, Selbert	Liberty
Reynolds, Dave	Harrisville
Sigman, Corbet R.	Liberty
Small, Ed	Keyser

Tokar, Daniel	Shepherdstown
Williams, David	Berea
Williams, Leonard	Meadow Bridge
Wilson, R.W.	Weirton
Workman, Jr., Hubert L.	Williamsburg
Wyatt, William R.	Rainelle

wisconsin

Brdlik, Dan E.	Prescott
Dahl, Cris	Lake Geneva
Davis, Lloyd A.	Jim Falls
Gannaway, Woodson	Madison
Genske, Jay	Fond du Lac
Hanson, Travis	Mosinee
Hembrook, Ron	Neosho
Johnson, Kenneth B.	Mindoro
Kolitz, Robert	Beaver Dam
Lary, Ed	Mosinee
Maestri, Peter A.	Spring Green
Martin, Peter	Waterford
Ricke, Dave	West Bend
Rochford, Michael R.	Dresser
Stafford, Michael	Madison
Wattelet, Michael A.	Minocqua

wyoming

Alexander, Darrel	Ten Sleep
Ankrom, W.E.	Cody
Banks, David L.	Riverton
Bridges, Justin W.	Dubois
Draper, Audra	Riverton
Fowler, Ed A.	Riverton
Friedly, Dennis	Cody
Iiams, Richard D.	Mills
Kinkade, Jacob	Carpenter
Pavack, Don	Edgerton
Rambo, Jay T.	Rock Springs
Rexroat, Kirk	Wright
Reynolds, John C.	Gillette
Ross, Stephen	Evanston
Strohecker, John J.	Riverton
Walker, George A.	Alpine
Whipple, Wesley A.	Thermopolis

foreign countries

argentina

Ayarragaray, Cristian L.	La Paz
Kehiayan, Alfredo	Buenos Aires
Rho, Nestor Lorenzo	Junin B.A.
Schonhals, Gualberto G.	Diamante

australia

Bennett, Peter	Engadine
Brown, Peter	Emerald Beach
Cross, Robert	Tamworth
Crawley, Bruce R.	Croyden
Gerus, Gerry	Cairns
Giljevic, Branko	Queanbeyan
Green, William	View Bank
Harvey, Max	Perth
Husiak, Myron	Altona
Jones, John	Brisbane
Maisey, Alan	Toongabbie
Rowe, Stewart G.	Mt. Crosby
Simmonds, Kurt Barnes	N. Castlemaine
Zemitis, Joe	Cardiff Hts.

belgium

Monteiro, Victor	Brussels

botswana

Dauberman, Desmond P.	Gaborone

brazil

Bodolay, Antal	Belo Horizonte
Boscoli, Melquisede	
Ricci	Presidente Prudente

DeCarvalho, Henrique M.
   Braganca Paulista
Gaeta, Angelo — Jali
Gaeta, Roberto — Sao Paulo
Garcia, Mario Eiras — Sao Paulo
Ikoma, Flavio — Presidente Prudente
Lala, Paulo Ricardo — Presidente Prudente
Lala, Roberto P. — Presidente Prudente
Neto Jr., Nelson — Braganca Paulista
Petean, Francisco — Birigui
Petean, Mauricio — Birigui
Rosa, Pedr
   Guillermo Teles — Presidente Prudente
Villa, Luiz — Sao Paulo
Villar, Ricardo — Mairipors
Zakharov, Carlos — Vanderhoof

canada
Arnold, Joe — Ontario
Beauchamp, Gaetan — Stoneham
Bell, Donald — Bedford
Bourbeau, Jean Yves — Quebec
Cote, Yves — Quebec
DeBraga — Val Belair
Deringer, Christoph — Pike River
Downie, James T. — Port Franks
Dublin, Dennis — Enderby
Fraser, Grant — Foresters Falls
Freeman, John — Cambridge
Garner, Richard — Alberta
Gilbert, Chantal — Quebec
Grenier, Roger — Saint Jovite
Hartmann, Bruce James — Ontario
Hayes, Wally — Orleans
Haynes, Chap — Tatamagouche
Hoffmann, Uwe H. — Vancouver
Jobin, Jacques — Lauzon
Kaczor, Tom — Ontario
Langley, Mick — Qualicum Beach
Lay, R.J. (Bob) — Vanderhoof
Leber, Heinz — Hudson Hope
Lemaire, Denis — Boucherville
Loerchner, Wolfgang — Bayfield
Lyttle, Brian — High River
Macri, Mike — Churchill
Maneker, Kenneth — Galiano Island
Martin, Robb — Ontario
Marzitelli, Peter — Langley
Niro, Frank — Mackenzie
Olson, Rod — High River
Patrick, Bob — Crescent Beach
Pepiot, Stephan — Winnipeg
Piesner, Dean — Ontario
Price, Steve — Kamloops
Rahn, John — Waterloo
Rieger, Chris J. — British Columbia
Roberts, George A. — White Horse
Ross, Tim — Thunder Bay
Schoenfeld, Matthew A. — Galiano Island
Sunderland, Richard — Quathiakski Cove
Tighe, Brian — Ridgeville
Toner, Roger — Ontario
Treml, Glenn — Thunder Bay
Vachon, Yvon — Quebec
Young, Bud — Port Hardy
Young, Cliff — Pembroke

denmark
Andersen, Henrik Lefolii — Fredensborg
Carlsson, Mark — Roskilde

Dyrnoe, Per — Hilleroed
Henriksen, Hans J. — Helsinge
Vensild, Henrik — Renne

england
Boden, Harry — Bonsall
Elliott, Marcus — Llandudno
Farid — Kent
Hague, Geoff — Marlborough
Heasman, H.G. — Llandudno
Henry, Peter and Son — Wokingham
Hitchmough, Howard — London
Jackson, Jim — Berkshire
Jones, Charles Anthony — No. Devon
Lamprey, Mike — Devon
Morris, Darrell Price — Devon
Wardell, Michael Ronald — Bletchingley
Wise, Donald — St. Leonards-On-Sea
Wood, Alan — Greenhead

france
Blum, Michel — Draguignan
Doursin, Gerard — Pernes les Fontainas
Ganster, Jean-Pierre — Strasbourg
Reverdy, Pierre — Valence
Viallon, Henri — Thiers

germany
Balbach, Markus — Weilm nster
Becker, Franz — Marktl/Inn
Borger, Wolf — Graben-Neudorf
Greiss, Jockl — Gutenberg
Fruhmann, Ludwig — Burghausen
Hehn, Richard Karl — Dörrebach
Herbst, Peter — Lauf d.d.Pegn.
Kaluza, Werner — Nurnberg
Kersten, Michael — Berlin
Kressler, D.F. — Puchheim
Rankl, Christian — Munich
Rinkes, Siegfrien — Markterlbach
Steinau, Jurgen — Berlin
Tritz, Jean Jose — Hamburg
Wimpff, Christian — Stuttgart

italy
Albericci, Emilio — Bergamo
Ameri, Mauro — Genova
Bertuzzi, Ettore — Bergamo
Bonassi, Franco — Pordenone
Fogarizzu, Boiteddu — Pattada
Pachi, Francesco — Genoa
Scordia, Paolo — Roma
Simonella, Gianluigi — Maniago
Toich, Nevio — Vicenza

japan
Aida, Yoshihito — Tokyo
Esaki, Shusuke — Osaka City
Fujikama, Shun — Osaka
Fukuta, Tak — Seki-City
Hara, Kovji — Seki-City
Hirayama, Harumi — Warabi City
Ishihara, Nobuhiko — Sakura City
Kagawa, Koichi — Kanagawa
Kanda, Michio — Yamaguehi
Kawasaki, Akihisa — Kobi
Mazaki, Yoshio — Osaka City
Okaysu, Kazou — Tokyo
Sakakibara, Masaki — Tokyo
Shikayama, Toshiaki — Saitama
Sugihara, Keidoh — Osaka
Takahashi, Hirohiko — Yokohama
Takahashi, Masao — Gunma

Tasaki, Seiichi — Tochigi
Terauchi, Toshiyuki — Wakayama-Ken
Ueda, Masaharu — Osaka City
Uekama, Nobuyuki — Tokyo

mexico
Scheurer, Alfredo Faes — Bosque

netherlands
Rijswijk, Aad V. — Spijkenisse
Van de Manakker, Thijs — Helenaveen
Van den Elsen, Gert — A.J. Tilburg
Van Eldik, Frans — Loenen

new zealand
Pennington, C.A. — Christchurch
Reddiex, Bill — Palmerston North
Ross, D.L. (Dave) — Alexandra

norway
Bache-Wiig, Tom — Eivindvik
Holum, Morton — Oslo
Momcilovic, Gunnar — Krokstadelva
Sellevold, Harald — Dreggen
Vistnes, Tor — Kjelhenes

russia
Kharlamov, Yuri — Tula

scotland
McColl, John — Stonehouse

singapore
Tay, Larry C-G — Singapore

slovak republic
Bojtos, Arpad — Lucenec
Pulis, Vladimir — Kremnica

south africa
Bauchop, Peter — Germiston
Bauchop, Robert — Elsburg
Beukes, Tinus — Vereeniging
Bezuidenhout, Buzz — Queensburgh
Boardman, Guy — New Germany
Brown, Robert E. — Port Elizabeth
Burger, Fred — Munster
Frankland, Andrew — Wilderness
Grey, Piet — Silverton
Kojetin, W. — Germiston
Lackovic, Niko — Port Elizabeth
LaGrange, Fanie — Bellville
Lancaster, C.G. — Orkney
Liebenberg, Andre — Bordeaux
Mackrill, Stephen — Pinegowrie
Pienaar, Conrad — Bloemfontein
Rietveld, Bertie — Magaliesburg
Russell, Mick — Port Elizabeth
Schoeman, Corrie — Bloemfontein
Skellern, Dr. M.J. — Munster
Smythe, Ken — Underberg
Watson, Peter — Klerksdorp
Wood, Owen — Honeydew

sweden
Eklund, Rolf — Rosersberg
Embretsen, Kaj — Edsbyn
Lundstrom, Jan-Ake — Dals-Langed
Nordell, Ingemar — Färila
Ryberg, Gote — Norrahammar

switzerland
Soppera, Arthur — Zurich

uruguay
Gonzales, Leonardo Williams — Maldonado

wales
Elliott, Marcus — Llandudno

zimbabwe
Burger, Pon — Bulawayo

knifemakers membership lists

Not all knifemakers are organization-types, but those listed here are in good standing with these organizations.

knifemakers guild

1994 voting membership

a **Yoshihito Aida**, Mike "Whiskers" Allen, R.V. Alverson, Michael Anderson, W.E. Ankrom, Dick Atkinson.

b **Joseph D. Bailey**, Phillip Baldwin, Norman Bardsley, Gary Barnes, Cecil T. Barrett, James Barry III, John Bartlow, Gene Baskett, James Batson, Butch Beaver, Judy T. Beaver, Raymond Beers, Tom Black, Andrew Blackton, Michel Blum, Philip Boguszewski, Dennis Bradley, Edward Brandsey, Clint Breshears, Mark Anthony Brightwell, Tim Britton, David Broadwell, David Brown, Harold Brown, Rick Browne, John Busfield.

c **Bill Caldwell**, Ronald Canter, Bob Cargill, Harold J. "Kit" Carson, Fred Carter, Dianna Casteel, Douglas Casteel, Frank Centofante, William Chapo, Gordon Chard, William Cheatham, Howard F. Clark, Wayne Clay, Lowell Cobb, Keith Coleman, Vernon Coleman, Alex Collins, Blackie (Walter) Collins, Bob Conley, Harold Corby, Joe Cordova, Leonard Corlee, Jim Corrado, Charles Cosgrove, George Cousino, Raymond Cover, Colin Cox, Sam Cox, John Craft III, Pat Crawford, John M. Cross, Bob Crowder, James Crowell, Dan Cruze.

d **Charles M. Dake**, Alex Daniels, Jack Davenport, Edmund Davidson, Barry Davis, Vernon M. Davis, W.C. Davis, Bill DeFreest, Richard DeGraeve, Dan Dennehy, William Dietzel, Robert Dill, Frank Dilluvio, Patrick Donovan, T.M. Dowell, Larry Downing, Tom Downing, Beryl Driskill, Bill Duff, Melvin Dunn, Jerry Duran, Larry Duvall.

e **Paula K. Easler**, Russell Easler, Joel Ellefson, Kaj Embretsen, Jim Ence, Robert Enders, Virgil England, Robert Engnath, Walter Erickson, James T. Eriksen.

f **Stephen Fecas**, Lee Ferguson, Thomas M. Ferrara, Jay Fisher, Jerry Fisk, Joe Flournoy, Don Fogg, Pete Forthofer, Paul Fox, Henry Frank, Michael H. Franklin, Ron Frazier, Dennis Friedly, Larry Fuegen, Stanley Fujisaka, Tak Fukuta, John W. Fuller, Shiro Furukawa.

g **Frank Gamble**, William Garner, Ronald Gaston, Clay Gault, Roy Genge, Richard Genovese, Harry George, James "Hoot" Gibson Sr., Wayne Goddard, Bruce Goers, David Goldberg, Warren Goltz, Dante & Judith Gottage, Greg Gottchalk, Roger M. Green, Rendon & Mark Griffin, Melvin Gurganus, Kenneth Guth.

h **Philip L. "Doc" Hagen**, Robert Hajovsky, Ed Halligan & Son, Jim Hammond, Ronald E. Hancock, James E. Hand, M.D., Walt Harless, Larry Harley, Jay Harmon, Ralph Harris, Joe Hawk, Rade Hawkins, Richard Hehn, Henry Heitler, Roy L. Helton, Earl Jay Hendrickson, Wayne Hensley, Tim Herman, George Herron, Don Hethcoat, Thomas S. Hetmanski, Daryl Hibben, Gil Hibben, Howard Hill, Steven Hill, R. Hinson & Son, Harumi Hirayama, Howard Hitchmough, Richard Hodgson, Steve Hoel, Kevin Hoffman, D'Alton Holder, Jess Horn, Glen Hornby, Durvyn Howard, Arthur Hubbard, Rob Hudson, Steven Douglas Huey.

i **Billy Mace Imel.**

j **Jim Jacks**, Steve Jernigan, Brad Johnson, Durrell C. Johnson, Gorden Johnson, Ronald Johnson, Ruffin Johnson, Steve Johnson, W.C. Johnson, Enoch D. Jones, Robert Jones.

k **Edward N. Kalfayan**, William Keeton, Jim Kelso, Bill Kennedy Jr., Ralph Kessler, Jot Khalsa, Keith Kilby, Bill King, Kemp King, Joe Kious, Jon Kirk, Terry Knipschield, R.C. Knipstein, Mick Koval, Dennis G. Krapp, Roy Krause, D.F. Kressler.

l **Ron Lake**, Jarrell D. Lambert, Frank Lampson, Gene Langley, Scott Lankton, Ken Largin, Edward Lary, Mike Leach, Tommy Lee, Bill Levengood, Norman Levine, Lile Handmade Knives, Robert C. Livingston, Wolfgang Loerchner, R.W. Loveless, Schuyler Lovestrand, William Luckett, Robert Lum, Ernest Lyle, Brian Lyttle.

m **Joe Malloy**, Dan Maragni, Tom Maringer, Randall J. Martin, James May, Harvey McBurnette, Zollan McCarty, Charles McConnell, Loyd McConnell, Ken McFall, J.J. McGovern, Frank McGowan, W.J. McHenry, David McIntosh, Ted Merchant, Robert Merz, James Miller, Louis Mills, Jim Minnick, James B. Moore, Jeff Morgan, C.H. Morris, Steven Mullin, Paul Myers.

n **Bud Nealy**, Corbin Newcomb, Larry Newton, R.D. & George Nolen, Mike Norris, Don Norton.

o **Charles Ochs**, Warren Osborne, T.R. Overeynder, John Owens.

p **Larry Page**, Robert Papp, Melvin Pardue, Russ Peagler, W.D. Pease, Lloyd Pendleton, Alfred Pendray, Eldon Peterson, David Pitt, Leon and Tracy Pittman, Clifton Polk, Al Polkowski, Joe Prince, Jim Pugh, Martin Pullen, Morris Pulliam.

r **Jerry Rados**, James D. Ragsdale, Steven Rapp, A. D. Rardon, Bill Reddiex, Chris Reeve, Pierre Reverdy, John Reynolds, Ron Richard, David Ricke, Willie Rigney, Dean Roath, Howard Robbins, Fred Roe, Rodney Rogers, A.G. Russell.

s **Masaki Sakakibara**, John Salley, Lynn Sampson, A.A. Sanders, Scott Sawby, James Schmidt, Herman Schneider, Maurice & Alan Schrock, Steve Schwarzer, Mark C. Sentz, James Serven, Eugene W. Shadley, Paul Sheehan, Scott Shoemaker, Ben Shostle, Corbet Sigman, Bill Simons, Norman Simons, R.J. Sims, Cleston Sinyard, Jim Siska, Fred Slee, Scott Slobodian, Gregory H. Smith, J.D. Smith, John Smith, Ralph Smith, Red Smith, Jerry Snell, Jim Sornberger, Richard Stafford, Harry Stalter, Ken Steigerwalt, Charles Stewart, Scott Strong, Charles Syslo.

t **Seiichi Tasaki**, David A. Taylor, Gray Taylor, Robert Terzuola, Leon Thompson, Carolyn Tinker, P.J. Tomes, Dan Tompkins, Dwight Towell, Barry Trindle, Jim Turecek, Ralph Turnbull.

v **Wayne Valachovic**, Butch Vallotton, Frans Van Eldik, Michael Veit, Howard Viele, Frank Vought, Robert "Bob" Vunk.

w **Mark Waldrop**, George Walker, Michael Walker, Buster Warenski, Al Warren, Dale Warther, Thomas J. Watson, Reese Weiland, Charles Weiss, Mike Wesolowski, Weldon Whitley, Donnie R. Wicker, R.W. Wilson, Daniel Winkler, Earl B. Witsaman, William Wolf, Webster Wood, Tim Wright.

y **Yoshindo Yoshihara**, Mike Yurco.

z **Don Zaccagnino Jr.**, Tim Zowada.

probationary members, 1994-1995

Joe Arnold (94), A.T. Barr (95), Alan Bloomer (95), Wolf Borger (94), Bobby Branton (95), Judson Brennan (95), Don Broughton (95), Joel Chamblin (95), Paul Champagne (95), David Clark (94), Terry A. David (94), Harvey Dean (94), James Downs (95), Albert Eaton (94), Rick Eaton (94), Allen Elishewitz (94), William Engle (94), Bill Fiorini (95), Kouji Hara (94), Peter Herbst (95), Joel Humphreys (94), Tom Johanning (95), Kermit Laurent (95), Bracy Ledford (95), Steve Linklater (95), Bob Luchak (94), Tommy McNabb (95), Mike Mercer (95), Steve Miller (95), Dan Mink (94), Randy Phillips (94), James Poplin (94), Rex Robinson (95), Charles Roulin (95), Gote Ryberg (94), R. Bill Saindon (95), Mike Sakmar (94), Michael Stafford (94), Jurgen Steinau (94), Kenneth Thompson (94), Leon Treiber (95), Reinhard Tschager (94), Gordon Wilson (94), Christian Wimpff (95), Wood, Irie & Co. (94), Joe Yeates (94)

american bladesmith society

a **Robin Eileen Ackerson**, Bill Adams, Eugene Alexander, Roger Alexander, Jammie C. Allen, Mickey L. Ames, Leroy Amos, David Anders, Autumn D. Anderson, Gary D. Anderson **(MS)**, Ronnie A. Andress, Sr., Alan H. Arrington M.D., Boyd Ashworth

b **Howard D. Baker III**, Vance L. Baker, Robert Ball, David L. Banks, R.G. Barker, Aubrey G. Barnes, Gary Barnes **(MS)**, Marlen R. Barnes, Richard Barney, Todd Barnhart, Al Barton, Hugh E. Bartrug **(MS)**, Ronald L. Bates, James L. Batson **(MS)**, Robert K. Batts, Ray Bear, Geneo Beasley, James S. Beaty III, Gray Beeker, Raymond H. R. Behanna, William H. Behnke, George Benjamin, Jr., C.L. (Larry) Bentley, Dave Ber, Hal Bish, Scott Black, William A. Black, R. Gordon Bloomquist, Michael S. Blue, Kenneth Blum, Leon E. Borgman, Geoffrey W. Boos, Raymond A. Boysen, Garrick A. Bradford, John C. Bradley, Robert Branton, W. Lowell Bray, Jr., Brad Bressie, Don Broughton **(MS)**, Thomas L. Browning, Lisa Broyles, Michael Bubonovich, Jimmie Buckner, Bill Bullard, Jay Burger, Paul E. Burke, Thomas V. Burnhan, Stephan R. Burrows, Jim Butler, John G. Butler, Dee Button-Inman.

c **Buddy Cabe**, Edward J. Caffrey, Terry F. Callahan, John Calmo, Robert W. Calvert, Jeff Camp, Courtenay M. Campbell, Charles W. Carey, Robert D. Carignan, Charles A. Carmahan, Ron Carpenter, Murray M. Carter, Kevin R. Cashen, Chris Cawthorne, Tom S. Cellum, Frank Cherry, Ron Clairborne, Peter John Clapp, Howard F. Clark **(MS)**, Roger L. Clark, Harold A. Collins, Wade Colter, Larry D. Coltrain, Roger Comar, Roger Comes, Ivano Comi, John W. Conner, Michael L. Connor **(MS)**, Charles T. Cook, James R. Cook **(MS)**, George S. Cook, Louise Cook, J. Michael Cook, Joseph G. Cordova **(MS)**, Delbert G. Corella, James H. Corry, Mike Corvin, Houston L. Cotton, Monty L. Crain, John M. Cross **(MS)**, James L. Crowell **(MS)**, William M. Culnon, Steven M. Culver.

d **C.M. Dake**, Mary H. Dake, Benjamin M. Daland, Damascus-USA, Barry Davis, Don Davis, Dudley L. Dawkins, Harvey J. Dean, Jr. **(MS)**, Marco A.M. de Castro, Anthony Del Giorno, John C. Delavan, Richard J. Delotto, Mike de Punte, Christoph Deringer, John Thomas Dewardo, Steven Seweese, Keith Diebold, William J. Dietzel, A.W. Dippold, Charlie Drew, Joseph D. Drouin, Paul Dube, Brad M. Dugan, Vincent E. Dunbar, Rick Dunkerley, Steve Dunn, Fred Durio, Oliver H. Durrell.

e **Robert E. Earhart**, Hugh E. Eddy, Fain E. Edwards, Lynn Edwards, Mitch Edwards, Perry B. Elder Jr., Ronald V. Elkins, Terry W. Ellerbee, Dave Ellis, Shawn Ellis, Kaj Embretsen, James Enebce, David Etchieson, John Etzler, Vincent K. Evans, Wyman Ewing.

f **George Fant Jr.**, Jack S. Feder, Bill V. Fielder, Edward Finn, William R. Fiorini, Clyde E. Fischer, Jerry Fisk **(MS)**, Jim Fister, John W. Fitch Jr., James Flood, Joe E. Flournoy, Jr.**(MS)**, Bruce Floyd, Don Fogg, Gerald J. Fondenot, Charles Ronald Fowler, Ed A. Fowler **(MS)**, Jerry B. Fowler, Wendell Fox, Walter P. Framski, Daniel Frank, Chris Fry, Larry Fuegen **(MS)**, Bruce A. Fuller, Jack A. Fuller **(MS)**.

g **Yvon Gagueche**, Barry Gallagher, Mark S. Gartner, Timothy P. Garrity, Bert Gaston **(MS)**, Thomas Gerner, Ronald J. Gillory Sr., Logwood U. Gion, Kevin S. Givens, Sherwood M. Glotfelty, Wayne L. Goddard **(MS)**, Scott K. Goguen, Jim Gofourth, David Goldberg, Robert Golden, Phillipe Gontier, L.W. Gonzalez, Bear Goode, Gabe Gorenflo, James T. Gorenflo, Greg Gottschalk, Bob Gray, Chris L. Green, Don Greenaway, David Greene, Richard F. Greiner, Lance Gridley, Frank Gunn, Ralph Gutekunst.

h **Philip L. Hagen**, Ed Halligan, Phil Hammond, Timothy J. Hancock **(MS)**, Bill Hand, Scott Hardy, Bob L. Harper, Cass Harris, Jeffrey A. Harris, Dennis M. Harrison, Tom Harrison, Richard E. Hayes, Scotty Hayes, Wally Hayes, Charles E. Haynes **(MS)**, Mary Margaret Haynes, Bob Dale Hays, Earl J. Hendrickson **(MS)**, Shawn E. Hendrickson, Carl E. Henkle, A.J. Hermann, Jay Heselschwerdt, Don Hethcoat, Gene R. Hobart, Dan Hockensmith, Roger A. Hockwalt, David Hodge, Thomas R. Hogan, Bob Hollar, Glen A. Homer, C. Robbin Hudson **(MS)**, Bill R. Hughes, Daryle Hughes, William Hurt.

i **Richard D. Iiams**, Paul R. Inman III., Carole Ivie.

j **Charlton R. (Jack) Jackson**, Jim L. Jackson, William R. Jacobs, Bob J. James, Tom January, C. Ray Johnson, John R. Johnson, Randy Johnson, Robert Johnston, Enoch (Nick) Jones, Shane Justice.

k **Frank D. Keen**, Michael Keeney, Joseph F. Keeslar **(MS)**, Steven C. Keeslar, John C. Keller, Dan A. Kendrick, Jerry Kennedy, Kelly S. Kennedy, Tasman J.C. Kerley, R.W. Kern, Shiva Ki, Keith Kilby **(MS)**, Fred King, Todd Kinnikin, Richard L. Kimberley, Hank Knickmeyer, Kurt Knickmeyer, Charles Ray Knowles, Robert R. Kodama, Christopher R. Kormanik, Lefty Kreh, Bob Kramer, Raymond Kremzner, Phillip W. Kretsinger **(MS)**, Danny L. Kyle.

l **Cliff Lacey**, Curtis J. Lamb, Jarrell D. Lambert, Christopher M. Lander, Leonard Landrum, Bud Lang, Donald G. Lange, Mick Langley **(MS)**, Pierre LaPlante, Sid Latham, Kermit J. Laurent, Charles A. Lawless, Alton Lawrence, Dal Leck, Rick Leeson, Scott B. Lemee, Nick Leone III, Bernard Levine, H. Stephen Lewis, Jack Lewis, Glenn Lillibridge, Guy A. Little, Robert C. Livingston, Lowell C. Lockett, J.A. Lonewolf, Aldo Lorenzi, Eugene F. Loro, Sherry Lott, Mark Lubrich, James R. Lucie, Gerard P. Lukaszevicz, Greg Lutz, William R. Lyons.

m **Michael K. Manabe**, Ken Mankel, James Maples, Dan Maragni **(MS)**, Ken Markley, Chris Marks **(MS)**, Bruce E. Martin, Peter Martin, Paul J. Marx, Alan Robert Massey, Roger D. Massey, James E. May, P. Douglas Mays, Martin L. Mayse, Frederick L. McCoy, Kevin McCrackin, Victor J. McCrackin **(MS)**, Richard McDonald, Robert J. McDonald, Frank McGowan, David Brian McKenzie, Tom McKissack, Tommy McNabb, Dave McWaters, Ronald I. Meekins, Byron M. Mellinger, Keo Khemawong Mengrai, Ted C. Merchant, Mardi Meshecian, Bart Messina, Brian A. Milford, Bob Miller, Hanford J. Miller **(MS)**, Kevin Miller, James P. Miller, Kent Miller, Richard Miller, Dilbert Mills, W. Dean Mitchell **(MS)**, Michael Steven Monods, Billy R. Moore, William F. Moran, Jr. **(MS)**, Dennis L. Morris, Everett A. Morris, Franklin D. Morris, Jan Muchnikoff, Dawn Mulbery, Jack W. Muse, Jan Myhre.

n **Angelo Navagato**, Gregory T. Neely **(MS)**, Bruce W. Nelson, Carl Nelson, Robert M. Newhouse, R. Kent Nicholson, Tim Nolfi.

o **Winston Oakes**, Lee D. Oates, Charles F. Ochs III **(MS)**, Micah Paul Ochs, Clyde O'Dell, Vic Odom, Randy W. Ogden, Michael E. Olive, Mathias Oppersdorff, Ben M. Ortega, Dr. Michael R. Osborne, Stephen H. Overstreet, Donald Owens.

p **Gerard Pacelia**, Jeff Pacelt, Donald Page, Carl R. Palmer, Charles R. Parker, Stephen E. Parker, John David Parks, Jr., Thomas C. Parler, Chuck Patrick, Alan Patterson, Alfred H. Pendray **(MS)**, Frederic Perrin, Jim Perry, Johnny Perry, Dan L. Peterson **(MS)**, Clay C. Peyton, Edward W. Phillips, James M. Phillips, Dean Piesner, Charles O. Piper, David Pitman, Dietnar Pohl, James P. Poling, Andrew Porter, James E. Porter **(MS)**, Michael C. Porter, Timothy F. Potier, Karlis A. Povisils, James Powell, Houston Price, Morris C. Pulliam, Jonathan K. Purviance.

q **Thomas C. Quakenbush,** Craig Quattlebaum.

r **R. Wayne Raley,** Darrel Ralph, Sesh Ramasamy, David Ramsburg, Richard A. Ramsey, Gary Randall, Ralph Randow, Alan W. Ray, Kirk Rexroat, James D. Rhodes, Stephen E. Rice, David M. Rider, E. Ray Roberts, Michael Roberts, Charles R. Robinson, Michael R. Rochford II, Jerry Romig, Eric T. Rose, Bob Rosenfeld, Kenny Rowe, Gary Rua, J. Ken Rudder Jr., Al Runyon, Ronald S. Russ, Raymond B. Rybar Jr., Gerald Rzewnicki.

s **Bill Saindon**, Reisuke Saitoh, Robert Sarkissian, Tom Schilling, James S. Schippnick, James A. Schmidt **(MS)**, Charles E. Schultz, Robert W. Schultz, Steven C. Schwarzer **(MS)**, Barry Scott, Audra L. Scott-Draper, James A. Scroggs, Robert J. Scroggs, W.P. Semon Jr., Mark C. Sentz, Steve Shackleford, Thomas J. Sheehy, Steven Sheets, Malcolm Tiki Shewan, Sergei Shushunov, Tom Siess, Corbet R. Sigman, James P. Sigman, Harland R. Simmons, Roy L. Slaughter, Patrick M. Smail, J.D. Smith, John M. Smith, Joshua J. Smith, Lenerd C. Smith, Raymond L. Smith, Timothy E. Smock, Marvin Solomon, Thomas K. St. Clair, H. Red St. Cyr, Rod Staben, Chuck Stancer, Udo Stegemann, Craig Steketee, Edward L. Stewart, Gary Ken-

neth Stine, Marc Stokeld, Johnnie L. Stout, Howard Stover, Terry Lee Stover, Kenneth J. Straight, Frank Stratton III, Terry Stults, Harlan Suedmeier, Cynthia Ann Summers, Daniel L. Summers, Arthur Swyhart, Mark G. Szarek, Joseph Szilaski, Joseph G. Szopa.

t Shane Taylor, Michael Techow, James L. Temple Jr., Danny Thayer, Jean-Paul Thevenot, Jack W. Thomas, Kenneth Thompson, Fred Thynne, P.J. Tomes **(MS)**, Samuel L. Torgeson, Ed Treanor, Kenneth W. Trisler, Mark A. Tritenbach, Charles Trulove, Donna Turner, Keven Turner, Randall W. Turner, Jerry L. Tyer.

u Tim A. Utton.

v Robert T. Vahle, Wayne Valachovic (MS), Kirby Van De Grick, James N. Van Riper, Jonny David Vasquez, Arthur V. Velasco, Patrik Vogt, William R. Von Bergen, Jr., Lew Von Lossberg, Bruce Voyles.

W Bill Walker, Don Walker, James L. Walker, John Wade Walker III, Roger L. Wallace, Charles B. Ward, Michael B. Ward, Ken Warner, Dellana Warren, Herman Harold Waters, Lu Waters, Billy Watson, Daniel Watson, David Weimer, Haines R. (Dick) Wendell, Randy D. West, Jim Weyer, Kenneth Whaley, Robert R. Wheeler, Wesley Whipple, Daniel J. White, Richard T. White, Lenwood W. Whitley, Randy Whittaker, A.L. Williams, Larry D. Williams, Michael L. Williams, Richard T. Williams, Wayne Willson, George H. Wilson, L. David Wilson, James R. Wilson, George Winier, Daniel Winkler**(MS)**, Donald Witzler, Jim Woods, Randy Wooton, Bill Worthen.

y Yasuhiro Yamanaka, Todd Yelverton, Yoshindo Yoshihara

z William H. Zeanon.

miniature knifemaker's society

Paul Abernathy, Sam Alfano, Mel Anderson, Mary W. Bailey, Paul Charles Basch, Jesse J. Bass, Ray Beers, John Biggers, Blade Magazine, Dennis Blaine, Gerald Bodner, Gary F. Bradburn, Norman W. Bradley, Mary Bray, Brock Custom Knives, Virginia Brock, David Bullard, Barry G. Carithers, Eddie Contreras, Mike Cook, Kenneth W. Corey, Thomas A. Counts, Damascus USA, Gary Demns, Gary Dennis, Diana Duff, Paula K. Easler, Albert & Evelyn Eaton, Allan Eldridge, Gwen Flournoy, William P. Frazee, David Fusco, Jean Pierre Ganster, Wayne Goddard, Tommie F. Guinn, Melvin and Carol Gurganus, Ralph Dewey Harris, Terry Ann Hayes, Richard Heise, Bob Hergert, Charlene C. Herring, Tom Hetmanski, Daryl Hibben, Joleen Hibben, John R. Holmes, John Addison Hoy, Wallace J. Kay, Gary Kelley, Shiva Ki, R.F. Koebbeman, Terry Kranning, Gary Ladd, Bernard Levine, Les Levinson, Jack Lewis, Kenneth R. Liegey, Henry C. Loos, Bob Luchak, Jim Martin, Marlene Marton, Mark Masuda, Ken McFall, McMullen & Yee Publishing, M.C. "Mal" Mele, Mike Mercer, Paul Meyers, Rateep Mosrie, Allen R. Olsen, Charles Ostendorf, Daniel E. Osterman, Gordon Pivonka, Houston Price, Jim Pugh, John Rakusan, Sidney Reggio, Stephan Ricketts, Mark Rogers, Al Sears, Paul C. Sheffield, Glen Paul Smit, Sporting Blades, Harry Stalter, Udo Stegemann, Wilson Streeter, Mike Tamboli, Yvon Vachon, J. Kay Wallace, Rudy Wehner, Jim Weyer, James D. Whitehead, Michael Whittingham, Will Wickliffe, Wendell L. Wilcher, Ron Wilson, Dennis Windmiller, Earl Witsaman, Errol & Mary Young.

professional knifemakers association

Mel & Marylyn Anderson, Don Andrews, Robert Blasingame, Justin Bridges, Robert L. Brothers, C. Lyle Brunckhorst, Jerry Busse, Thomas P. Calawa, Danniel L. Cannady, Raymond W. Cannon, Curt D. Childs, Howard F. Clark, David Clouse, Alex Collins, C.M. Dake, Don Davis, Dan Dennehy, Robert Dill, Melvin T. Dunn, Rick Eaton, Ray W. Ennis, James Thorlief Eriksen, Jay Fisher, Bob Garbe, Paul S. Goertz, Jeff A. Harkins, Kenneth G. Henschel, Tom High, Dan Hockensmith, Scot Horton, Michael J. Hull, Robert James Hunter, R.B. Johnson, Steven R. Johnson, Jerry Kennedy, Frank Lampson, James Largent, Norman Levine, W. Tim Lively, Randy Lyons, Guy MacEwan, Mike Mann, Glenn Marshall, Osa & JB McDowell, David L. McIntosh, Harry E. Mendenhall, J.P. Moss, Dusty Moulton, Bud Nealy, Willard C. Patrick, Eldon G. Peterson, Cecil W. Quier, Wayne A. Reno, Chuck Roberts, Robert Robinson, Steve Rollert, R. Bill Saindon, Michael J. Schirmer, Ernie Self, Eugene W. Shadley, James Sigg, Noel Smith, Craig Steketee, John E. Toner, John W. Townsend, Michael A. Wattelet, Gerome M. Weinand, Charles A. West, Bill Wolf, Barry Wood-Michael L. Irie, Joe A. Yeates.

state/regional associations

midwest knifemakers association
Frank Berlin, Michael Ballinger, Charles Bolton, Gary Bradburn, Steven Burrows, Jim P. Cornelius, Larry Duvall, Jackie Emanual, William Engle, David Feyh, George Gibson, James L. Haynes, Jerry Johnson, Harvey King, George Martoncik, James May, V.J. McCrackin, Dan McCullogh, Gene Millard, William Miller, Clayton E. Morris, Corbin Newcomb, Jon Ossen, Chris Owen, A.D. Rardon, Max Smith, Ed Stewart, Charles Syslo, Ward Westbrook.

new england bladesmiths guild (1995 data)
Phillip Baldwin, Gary Barnes, Paul Champagne, Jimmy Fikes, Don Fogg, Larry Fuegen, Rob Hudson, Midk Langley, Louis Mills, Dan Maragni, Jim Schmidt, Wayne Valachovic and Tim Zowada.

alaska knifemakers association (1995 data)
A.W. Amoureux, John Arnold, Bud Aufdermauer, Robert Ball, J.D. Biggs, Lonnie Breuer, Tom Broome, Mark Bucholz, Irvin Campbell, Virgil Campbell, Raymond Cannon, Christopher Cawthorne, John Chamberlin, Bill Chatwood, George Cubic, Bob Cunningham, Gordon S. Dempsey, J.L. Devoll, James Dick, Art Dufour, Alan Eaker, Norm Grant, Gordon Grebe, Dave Highers, Alex Hunt, Dwight Jenkins, Hank Kubaiko, Bill Lance, Bob Levine, Michael Miller, John Palowski, Gordon Parrish, Mark W. Phillips, Frank Pratt, Guy Recknagle, Ron Robertson, Steve Robertson, Red Rowell, Dave Smith, Roger E. Smith, Gary R. Stafford, Keith Stegall, Wilbur Stegner, Norm Story, Robert D. Shaw, Thomas Trujillo, Ulys Whalen, Jim Whitman, Bob Willis.

arizona knifemakers association (1995 data)
D. "Butch" Beaver, Bill Cheatham, Dan Dagget, Tom Edwards, Anthony Goddard, Steve Hoel, Ken McFall, Milford Oliver, Jerry Poletis, Merle Poteet, Mike Quinn, Elmer Sams, Jim Sornberger, Glen Stockton, Bruce Thompson, Sandy Tudor, Charles Weiss.

arkansas knifemakers association (1995 data)
Hoyt Adcock, Mickey L. Ames, David Anders, Robert Bailey, Cecil Barnes, Keith Batts, Larry Beason, James Black, Jay Black, Joel Bradford, Mike Brannan, J.C. Brown, Richard Brown, Jim Butler, Buddy Cabe, Kendall Carpenter, Alan D. Davis, Jerry Davis, Harvey Dean, Gary Wayne Dumas, Lawrence Dungy, Fred Duvall, Jack East, George Fant Jr., Lee Ferguson, Jerry Fisk, Joe Flournoy, John Fortenbury, Roger Freeze, Dewayne Funderburg, Roger George, Don Greenwaway, Arthur J. Gunn, Jr., L.B. Handly, Monica Hansen, John

Heuston, Don Hicks, Dave Hooper, Nicholas Hulbert, Jerry Husbrecht, Homer Jackson, Terry Johnson, Kenneth Kling, Ben Lane, Alton Lawrence, Bruce Martin, Douglas Mays, John McKeehan, Tom McKissack, Bart Messina, Richard C. Meyer, John Perry, Cliff Polk, Alan Purifoy, Ted Quandt, Craig Quattlebaum, Tim Richardson, Scott J. Robson, Kenny Rowe, James Seale, Andy Shaw, Carroll Shoffner, William Shoffner, Charles Sisemore, Dean Slaughter, Roy Slaughter, Scott Smith, Ray Smoker, Marvin Solomon, Sherman Sparks, Don Thurman, Arthur Tycer, James Walker, Chuck Ward, Jim Watson, Steve White, Mike Williams, Randy Wooton, Jimmy Worden, George Zimmerman.

california knifemakers association
Arnie Abegg, H. David Adams, Kenneth E. Alden, Jr., George J. Antinarelli, Everett Archer, Elmer Art, John Bevans, Dan Bjorklund, Roger Bost, Doug "Tat" Brack, Clint Breshears, Buzz Brooks, Ted Brown, James Bruinsslot, Ken Bruinsslot, David Brunetta, Steven E. Bunyea, David Cavallero, Frank Clay, James N. Copeland, Ewell M. Curtis, Jim Engman, Bob Engnath, Jim Ferguson, John Ferguson, Dave Flowers, Gene Fraley, Ralph M. Freer, Bill Fried, Buster Gaston, Logwood Gion, Tony Goldbach, Richard A. Gutowski, Jerome Harris, Dolores Hayes, Roy Helton, Bill Herndon, Neal A. Hodges, Jim Hrisoulas, Jim Jacks, Charlton R. Jackson, Lawrence Johnson, Curtis J. Jones, Richard D. Keyes, John Kray, Bud Lang, Norman Levine, R.W. Loveless, Lawrence Lund, "KC" Lund, John Mackie, Michael K. Manabe, Thomas Markey, Gene Martin, Rob Martin, Peter H. Matthiessen, James K. Mattis, John McGaughy, Jim Merritt, Jack Mills, Walt Modest, Emil Morgan, Gerald Morgan, William B. Murray, Thomas Orth, Bob Packard, Barry Evan Posner, John Radovich, Terry J. Ramey, Tracey Rinaldi, Jeffrey Robertson, Clark D. Rozas, Brian Saffran, Nick Scarpinato Jr., Larry T. Shiells, H. (Red) St. Cyr, James Stankovich, Chuck Stapel, W.R. Stroman, Kenny Sunada, Don G. Swanston, Tony Swatton, Ken Tallent, Scott Taylor, Carolyn D. Tinker, Tru-Grit Inc., Edward Ujihara, Michael P. Wallace, Jessie C. Ward, Wayne Watanabe, Eric Willis, Harlan M. Willson, Barry B. Wood.

montana knifemaker's association
Bruce Althoff, Lyle Bainbridge, R.J. (Ric) Bosshardt, Chuck Bragg, Paul Bray, Lyle Brunckhorst, Ed Caffrey, Jeff Carlisle, Wade Colter, George Conklin, Jack Cory, Bob Crowder, Rick Dunkerley, Joel Ellefson, Melvin Fassio, Ed Fowler, Barry Gallagher, Wayne Goddard, Bob Gray, Bob Greer, Bob Hollar, Al Kajin, Dave Kauffman, Larry Miller, Russell Moyer, Dan Nedved, Willard Patrick, Brian Peele, Eldon Peterson, Kirk Rexroat, Jim Riddle, Josh Smith, Mark Smith, Shane Taylor, Jim Thill, Jack Todd, J.W. Townsend, Gerome Weinand, Dick Wendell.

north carolina custom knifemakers' guild (1995 data)
Dr. James Batson, Tim Britton, Thomas Brown, Dr. Robert Charlton, Donald Daniel, Travis Daniel, Billy Downs, Gary Gaddy, Major Garris, Mark Gottesman, Robert Grooms, Carol & Melvin Gurganus, George Guthrie, Jack Hyer, Barry Jones, Phillip Jones, Tony Kelly, Charles Ray Knowles, Robert Livingston, Danny Masser, Bill Maynard, Tommy McNabb, Alex Moss, James Parker, Alan Patterson, Charles Rece, Ben Ryder, J.D. Sams, Ellis Sawyer, Tim Scholl, H.R. Simmons, Russel Sutton, Robert Thomas, Mike Weaver, Wayne Whitley, Michael Wise.

ohio knifemakers association (1995 data)
Raymond Babcock, Van Barnett, Harold A. Collins, Larry Detty, Tom Downing, Jim Downs, Patty Ferrier, Jeff Flannery, James Fray, Bob Foster, Raymond Guess, Scott Hamrie, Rick Hinderer, Curtis Hurley, Ed Kalfayan, Michael Koval, Judy Koval, Larry Lunn, Stanley Maienknecht, Dave Marlott, Mike Mercer, David Morton, Patrick McGroder, Charles Pratt, Darrel Ralph, Roy Roddy, Carroll Shoemaker, John Smith, Clifton Smith, Art Summers, Jan Summers, Donald Tess, Dale Warther, John Wallingford, Earl Witsaman, Joanne Yurco, Mike Yurco.

south carolina association of knifemakers (1995 data)
Robert Branton, Richard Bridwell, Dan Cannady, Charles S. Cox, William DeFreest, Paula Easler, Russell Easler, Hal Gainey, Ron Gaston, Harry George, Dick Gillenwater, Mike Gregory, Wayne Hendrix, George Herron, Jerry Hucks, Ralph Kessler, Gene Langley, Dan Owens, Larry Page, Russ Peagler, Alvin Poston, Joe Prince, Ralph Smith, Rocky Thomas.

tennessee knifemakers association (1995 data)
John Bartlow, Doug Casteel, Harold Crisp, Larry Harley, John W. Walker, Harold Woodward, Harold Wright.

canadian knife collectors club (1995 data)
Joe Arnold (London, Ont.), Gary Choppick (Simcoe, Ont.), Alex Daniels (Lynn Haven, FL), George Dmowski (Belle River, Ont.), Harald Moeller (Nanoose Bay, B.C.), Rod Olson (High River, Alb.), George Roberts (Park Hill, Ont.), Tim and Katherine Ross (ThunderBay, Ont.), Suzanne St. Amour (Hillsburgh, Ont.), R. Sunderland (Quathiaski Cove, B.C.), Tom Watson (Panama City, FL), Daniel L. Waugh (Endicott, NY), John Zaal (Kimberley, B.C.), Mike Tierney (Woodstock, Ont.), Mary W. Bailey (Lynn Haven, FL), John Comber (Milton, Ont.).

knife photo index

knives '96

Alderman, Robert: 63
Allred, Elvan: 76
Ames, Mickey L.: 61, 103
Anders, David: 94
Andress, Ronnie: 63, 145
Bache-Wiig, Tom: 91
Bailey, Kirby C.: 97
Ballew, Dale: 116, 118
Barber, Robert E.: 94
Barnes, Aubrey G.: 65
Barr, A.T.: 74, 77, 80, 104
Barron, Brian: 106
Baskett, Lee Gene: 138
Batson, James: 92, 93
Batts, Keith: 61
Beauchamp, Gaetan: 139
Becker, Franz: 112
Behnke, William: 102
Bell, Michael: 57
Bertuzzi, Ettore: 89
Black, Tom: 96, 149
Blasingame, Robert: 76, 145
Bloomer, Alan T.: 73
Blum, Michel: 84
Blum, Roy: 83, 126
Boguszewski, Phil: 74, 81
Bojtos, Arpad: 84
Bonassi, Franco: 90
Booth, Philip W.: 71, 98
Bose, Tony: 71, 72
Bourbeau, Jean-Yves: 84
Branton, Robert: 61, 108
Broadwell, David: 131, 140
Brooks, Steve R.: 145
Broughton, Don R.: 65, 126
Brown, Jim: 103
Busfield, John: 70, 122
Busse, Jerry: 79
Callahan, Errett: 132, 159
Cannady, Daniel L. (Slim): 82
Capdepon, Randy: 105
Carey Jr., Charles W.: 118
Carlsson, Marc Bjorn: 88, 91, 140
Carson, Harold J. "Kit": 80, 150, 153, 155
Carter, Fred: 127
Casteel, Douglas: 54, 98
Centofante, Frank and Tony: 152, 153
Chaffee, Jeff L.: 111
Chapo, William G.: 142
Clark, Howard F.: 63, 66
Clay, Wayne: 68, 150
Coleman, Keith E.: 74, 81
Cook, James Ray: 129
Cook, Louise: 108
Coombs Jr., Lamont: 160
Corbit, Gerald E.: 111
Corbit, Gerald E. and Philip E.: 153, 155
Corby, Harold: Cover
Cordova, Joseph G.: 144
Cousino, George: 107
Crawford, Pat: 80
Cross, John M.: 103
Cutchin, Roy D.: Cover, 129
Dailey, G.E.: 56
Dake, C.M.: 120, 121
Darby, Jed: 105, 107
Darby, Rick: 83
Davenport, Jack: 75, 120, 154
Davidson, Edmund: 96
Davis, Barry L.: 71, 75, 152, 153
Davis, Brad: 153
Davis, Don: 107
Davis, Ken: 79, 82, 107

Dean, Harvey J.: 67, 94, 102
Deringer, Christoph: 134
Dietzel, Bill: 72
Dippold, A.W.: 69
Doursin, Gerard: 89, 141
Doussot, Laurent: 90
Downs, James F.: 128
Draper, Kent: 76
Dunkerley, Rick: 105
Eaton, Al: 139
Eaton, Rick: 66
Elishewitz, Allen: 81
Ellis, David: 82, 128
Emerson, Ernest R.: 80, 75
Ence, Jim: 128
Evans, Vincent K.: 57, 58, 92, 95
Ferrara, Thomas: 121
Farris, Cal: 142
Fister, Jim: 100, 110
Flournoy, Joe: 144
Fogg, Don: 57, 73, 95, 123, 128, 145, 146
Fowler, Charles R.: 103
Fowler, Ed A.: 109, 100
Frankland, Andrew: 85
Franklin, Mike: 77, 79, 81
Freer, Ralph: 104, 142
Friedly, Dennis E.: 97, 137, 157, 163
Fujisaka, Stanley: 100, 127, 149, 151
Gaeta, Angelo: 86
Gallagher, Barry: 104
Ganster, Jean-Pierre: 117, 118
Garbe, Bob: 73, 143
Garcia, Mario Eiras: 63, 86, 134
Gaston, Ron: 59, 150
Gentile, Al: 156
Gerus, Gerry: 141
Getzan, J.: 115
Gilbert, Chantal: 140
Gottage, Judy: 124
Greco, John: 95, 158
Grussenmeyer, Paul G.: 58
Guthrie, George B.: 112, 113, 114
Halligan, Ed: 79, 80, 144
Hancock, Tim: 101, 102, 108, 126, 135, 142
Hands, Barry Lee: 118
Harmon, Jay: 130
Harris, Ralph Dewey: 69, 76
Hartmann, Bruce James: 62, 87, 99
Hartsfield, Phill: 78, 107
Hawkins, Rade: 104
Hayes, Wally: 101
Heitler, Henry: 148
Helton, Roy: 73, 74
Hendrickson, E. Jay: 64, 93, 109
Herman, Tim: 76, 127
Herndon, William R. "Bill": 125
Hethcoat, Don: 106, 128, 146
Hetmanski, Thomas S.: 105
Hibben, Gil: 132, 137
Hinderer, Rick: 71
Hirayama, Harumi: 122
Hoel, Steve: 127, 148
Hoffman, Kevin L.: 78, 121
Hoffman, Uwe H.: 88, 121
Holder, D'Alton: Cover, 110
Holland, John H.: 113
Horn, Jess: 122
Horton, Scot: 74
Howser, John C.: 70
Hudson, C. Robbin: 130
Hughes, Daryle: 64
Hume, Don: 99
Humphreys, Joel: 104, 153, 154

Iiams, Richard D.: 101
Ikoma, Flavio: 57
Irie, Michael L.: 74
Ishihara, Nobuhiko (Hank): 62, 88, 90
Jarvis, Paul M.: 123, 130, 134, 140
Jernigan, Steve: 67
Johnson, C.E. "Gene": 121
Johnson, Steven R.: 112
Jones, Barry M. and Philip G.: 78, 82
Kalfayan, Edward N.: 96, 98, 99
Kawasaki, Akihisa: 86
Keeslar, Joseph F.: 64
Kennedy, Kelly S.: 93
Kilby, Keith: 144
Kious, Joe: 122, 149
Knickmeyer, Hank: 143
Knipstein, R.C. (Joe): 67, 68, 73
Knuth, Joseph E.: 139
Kopp, Todd M.: 96
Kranning, Terry L.: 82, 144
Kubasek, John A.: 75
Lala, Paulo Richardo P.: 87
Lampson, Frank G.: 66, 150
Largin, Ken: 65, 83
Lary, Ed: 58
Lawrence, Alton: 109
Lee, Tommy: 153
Lee, Randy: 97, 160
Leland, Steve: 126
Leoffler, Leo: 137
Levine, Norman: 137
Lewis, Mike: 54, 56
Likarich, Steve: 62, 98, 134
Lile, Marilyn (Jimmy): 152
Loerchner, Wolfgang: 88, 130, 131
Loos, Henry C.: 118
Lovestrand, Schuyler: 157
Lozier, Don: Cover, 135, 141, 151
Lubrich, Mark: 102
Luchak, Bob: 136
Ludwig, Richard O.: 154
Lunn, Larry A.: 55, 129
Manabe, Michael K.: 95, 131
Marks, Chris: 125
Martin, Jim: 117, 124
Martin, Robb: 132
Maxfield, Lynn: 113
Maxwell, Don: 68, 146
McBurnette, Harvey: 75
McClure, Michael: 59
McConnell Jr., Loyd A.: 60, 73, 93, 110
McCrackin and Son, V.J.: Cover, 101, 132
McDonald, W.J. "Jerry": 114
McHenry, William James: 119, 120, 143
McLuin, Tom: 82
Mead, Dennis: 152
Meshejian, Marvin: 142, 143
Michinaka, T.: 87
Middleton, Ken: 56, 139
Milford, Brian A.: 58
Millard, Fred G.: 141
Mills, Andy: 151
Minnick, Jim: 127
Monteiro, Victor: 85, 129
Moulton, Dusty: 105, 117
Nealy, Bud: 135
Neely, Greg: 163
Neering and Mike Repke, Walt: 59, 83
Nishiuchi, Melvin S.: 106
Nordell, Ingemar: 59, 135, 141

Ochs, Charles F.: 99
Ogletree Jr., Ben R.: 114
Osborne, Warren: 71
Page, Larry: 61
Parker, J.E.: 149
Parker, Robert Nelson: 112, 113
Patrick, Bob: 92
Patrick, Chuck: 63, 97, 111
Patterson, Alan W.: 69
Pavack, Don: 98
Pease, W.D.: Cover, 76, 151
Pendleton, Lloyd: 113, 148, 150
Perry, Chris: 106
Peterson, Chris: 140
Peterson, Eldon G.: 146, 151
Plinkett, Richard: 70
Polk, Clifton: 70
Polkowski, Al: 78
Polzien, Don: 55, 95, 125, 156
Porter, James E.: 92, 146, 158
Potier, Timothy F.: 65, 94, 96, 131
Povisils, Karlis A.: 106
Pratt, Charley: 92, 95
Pursley, Aaron: 123
Quattlebaum, Craig: 103
Rados, Jerry F.: 145
Ralph, Darrel: 119, 124
Rardon, A.D.: 152
Reggio, Jr., Sidney J.: 58, 60
Repke and Walt Neering, Mike: 59, 83
Revishvili, Zaza: 55
Rietveld, Bertie: 96
Rigney Jr., Willie: 124
Rippy, Robert: 78, 79
Robinson, Charles (Dickie): 108
Robinson, Rex: 68
Rogers, Rodney: 156
Rochmans, Mark: 101
Rua, Gary (Wolf): 62, 100
Saindon, R. Bill: 120, 121, 143, 157
Sakmar, Mike: 93, 98, 141, 161
Sawby, Scott: 81, 123
Sayen, Murad: 128
Schaller, Anthony B.: 61, 100, 129
Schempp, Ed: 117
Schirmer, Mike: 110, 138
Schoeman, Corrie: 90
Scholl, Tim: 115, 132
Self, Ernie: 59, 70, 107
Sellevold, Harald: 60
Selvidio, Ralph J.: 101
Sentz, Mark C.: 128
Serafen, Steven E.: 114, 138
Shadley, Eugene W.: 70, 71, 72, 134
Sharrigan, Mudd: 60, 64, 132
Sheehan, Paul P.: 99
Sigman, Corbet R.: 163
Siska, Jim: 56
Sjostrand, Kevin: 112
Small, Ed: 64, 97
Smart, Steve: 59, 114
Smith, J.D.: 102, 110, 130, 131, 142
Smith, John W.: 69
Snell, Jerry L.: 126
Solomon, Marvin: 97
Stalter, Harry L.: 117
Stapel, Chuck: 78, 83
Stewart, Charles: 150
Stout, Johnny: 69
Strickland, Dale: 72, 117
Sugihara, Keidoh: 91
Summers, Dan: 65
Sunderland, Richard: 55
Tamboli, Michael: 115, 117
Terauchi, Toshiyuki: 86

directory

Terzuola, Robert: 80
Thayer, Danny: 160
Thomas, Devin: 106, 144
Thomas, Kim: 94
Toich, Nevio: 60
Tomes, P.J.: 65
Topliss, M.W. "Ike": 60, 105, 111
Townsend, J.W.: 138
Treiber, Leon: 68
Trindle, Barry: 123
Tyc, William J.: 93, 136
Tycer, Art: 109
Vachon, Yvon: 115, 116, 119
Vallotton, Butch: 119, 120

Valois, A. Daniel: 159
Van de Manakker, Thijs: 147
Van Rijswijk, Aad: 91
Viallon, Henri: 56, 85, 135
Viele, H.J.: 67, 125
Villa, Luiz: 86
Vistnes, Tor: 86
Voss, Ben: 79, 108
Vought Jr., Frank: 77
Wada, Yasutaka: 84
Walker, Jim: 103, 145
Ward, Chuck: 61, 112
Wardell, Mick R.: 88
Warenski, Buster: 123, 124

Watanabe, Wayne: 78
Watson, Billy: 65
Watts, Mike: 69
Watts, Wally: 67, 72
Webb Jr., Charley L.: 82, 137
Weiland Jr., J. Reese: 139, 154
Weiler, Donald E.: 64
Wescott, Cody: 108
West, Charles A.: 66, 149
Williams, Jason L.: 67, 120, 143
Willson, Harlan M.: 139
Wilson, Philip C.: 100, 126
Winkler, Daniel: IFC
Witsaman, Earl: 116

Wood, Barry B. and Irie, Michael L.: 155
Wood, Leonard J.: 110
Wolf, Bill: 75
Wragg, Samuel: 135
Yeates, Joe A.: 130, 136
Yurco, Mike: 62
Zakabi, Carl S.: 138
Zembko III, John: 62, 146
Zima, Michael F.: 68
Zowada, Tim: 129

engravers

Adlam, Tim: 110
Alfano, Sam: 60, 148
Bates, Billy: 97, 121, 150, 151
Beaver, Judy: 149
Blair, Jim: 151
Churchill, Winston G.: 122
Crowell, Jeff: 150
Davidson, Jere: 151

Dickson, John: 150
Ence, Jim: 148
Foster, Norvell: 142
Hagberg, Ki: 151
Holder, Pat: 115
Iura: 86
Lytton, Simon M.: 87, 149
McCombs, Leo: 128

Meyer, Chris: Cover, 66, 76, 124, 149, 150
Moschetti, Mitch: 127
Nixon, Jimmie L.: 76
Pilkington Jr., Scott: 150
Rudolph, Gil: 74, 124
Shaw, Bruce: Cover, 97, 149, 150, 151

Snell, Barry A.: 113
Sornberger, Jim: 126, 148
Theis, Terry: 148, 151
Trindle, Barry: 123
Wallace, Terry: 113, 148
Warenski, Julie: 123, 124, 135, 150, 151
Whitmore, Jerry: 119

scrimshanders

Bailey, Mary W.: 144
Beauchamp, Gaetan: 116, 155
Boster, Dale: 76
Bourbeau, Jean Yves: 157
Brady, Sandra: 152, 153, 154
Davenport, Susan: 75, 155

Fields, Rick B.: 152, 153, 154, 157
Gemma, John: 156
Hargraves Sr., Charles: 156
Hergert, Bob: 117, 152
Holland, Dennis K.: 156
Karst, Linda K.: 58, 76, 153

Kiracofe, Gary: 156, 157
Lagervall: 59
McClaren, Lou: 115
Mead, Faustina L.: 152, 154
Mitchell, Petria: 157
Morris, Darrell Price: 62

Nelida, Toniutti: 157
Rece, Charles V.: 153, 154
Stuart, Stephen: 153
Williams, Gary: 116, 138, 153, 155

leatherworkers/sheathmakers

Cook, James Ray: 164
Cooper, Harold: 164
Fister, Jim: 164
Foley, Barney: 163
Graves, Dave: 161
Green, Roger M.: 162, 164

Hancock, Tim: 162
Hendrickson, E. Jay: 162
Hughes, Ed: 163
Kennedy, Kelly S.: 162
Kravitt, Chris: 160, 161, 162, 163
Lee, Sonja: 160

McGowan, Liz: 163
McLuin, Tom: 163
Nealy, Bud: 160
Pennington, C.A.: 160
Rowe, Kenny: 160, 163
Schirmer, Mike: 164

Schrap, Robert G.: 161
Shook, Karen: 162
Stout, Johnny: 160

etchers/carvers

Bullard, Tom: 158
Clark, Howard F.: 158
Hergert, Bob: 115
Grussenmeyer, Paul: 158, 159

Hume, Don: 159
Kinnikin, Todd: 158
Kondrla, Denise: 159
Lott, Sherry: 95, 158

Maxfield, Lynn: 159
Rua, Gary (Wolf): 158
Steigerwalt, Ken: 158
Turecek, Jim: 159

Viallon, Henri: 159

handle artisans

Minnick, Joyce: 127

knife photo index

knives '91-'95

The Knife Photo Index includes only the last five editions of photos.

a

Abbott, William M.: *K'91*:91,182; *K'92*:91,176
Aida, Yoshihito: *K'91*:54; *K'92*:63; *K'93*:65,122; *K'94*:130,200; *K'95*:216
Alden Jr., Kenneth E.: *K'94*:200,201; *K'95*:83,128
Allen, Joe: *K'91*:182; *K'92*:176
Allen, Mike "Whiskers": *K'94:149*
Allred, Elvan: *K'95*:140,216
Alverson, Tim: *K'92*:119; *K'95*:217
Ameri, Mauro: *K'92*:95,142; *K'93*:124,204; *K'95*:117
Ames, Mickey L: *K'93*:204; *K'95*:99
Amor Jr., Miguel: *K'92*:67,89,176; *K'93*:104,205; *K'94*:123
Anders, David: *K'95*:93,95,217
Andersen, Henrik Lefolii: *K'91*: 82,182
Anderson, Charles B.: *K'91*:182; *K'92*:149
Anderson, Edwin: *K'91*:182; *K'93*:205
Anderson, Gary D.: *K'92*:176
Anderson, Michael D.: *K'92*:177; *K'95*:87,155
Andrews, Don: *K'91*:162
Ankrom, W.E.: *K'92*:83; *K'95*:127
Appleton, Ray: *K'91*:58,61; *K'92*:81,176
Arnett, Todd J.: *K'93*:109,209; *K'94*:69
Arnold, Joe: *K'94*:200; *K'95*:216
Arrowood, Dale: *K'95*:217
Ashby, Douglas: *K'92*:176; *K'93*:204; *K'94*:68,200
Atkinson, Dick: *K'91*:102,129; *K'92*:79,176; *K'94*:97
Ayarragaray, Cristian L.: *K'94*:200; *K'95*:116
Ayarragaray, Cristian L. and Vuoto, Carlos A.: *K'91*:80,81; *K'92*:97

b

Babcock, Raymond G.: *K'94*:122
Bache-Wiig, Tom: *K'94*:129
Bailey, Joseph D.: *K'92*:177,178; *K'94*:67,137
Bailey, Kirby C.: *K'94*:97; *K'95*:133
Bagwell, Bill: *K'94*:100
Baker, Vance: 217
Baker, Wild Bill: *K'95*:155
Baldwin, Phillip: *K'92*:155; *K'93*:68; *K'94*:79,152; *K'95*:92
Ballew, Dale: *K'91*:73,182; *K'92*:122; *K'93*:112; *K'94*:84
Barber, Robert E.: *K'92*:68; *K'94*:120,201
Bardsley, Norman P.: *K'91*:162,164; *K'92*:68,138; *K'94*:107,117
Barefoot, Joe W.: *K'91*:144
Barnes, Aubrey G.: *K'94*:201
Barnes, Gary L.: *K'95*:134
Barnett, Van: *K'94*:76
Barr, A.T.: *K'93*:98; *K'94*:70,142; *K'95*:83,108,139
Barrett, Cecil Terry: *K'92*:90; *K'93*:74,78
Barrett, R.W.: *K'95*:162
Barry, James J.: *K'91*:126; *K'92*:108
Bartlow, John: *K'91*:148; *K'92*:177
Barton, Almon T.: *K'94*:201
Bartrug, Hugh E.: *K'91*:105,107,163,183; *K'92*:Cover,108,135,176; *K'93*:67; *K'94*:77,98,100,127,136,149
Baskett, Lee Gene: *K'91*:152,155,163; *K'92*:177; *K'93*:136,145,204; *K'95*:146,163
Batson, James: *K'92*:85,89,109,141,177; *K'93*:134; *K'94*:112,118; *K'95*:78,94,103
Batson, Richard G.: *K'95*:96
Batts, Keith: *K'91*: 114; *K'92*:61; *K'93*:122; *K'94*:200; *K'95*:93
Bauchop, Robert: *K'93*:141
Beauchamp, Gaetan: 164
Beaver, D.(Butch): *K'91*:164; *K'93*:153,204
Beaver, Judy: *K'93*:153,204
Beaver, D. Butch and Judy: *K'94*:Cover,67,119
Becker, Franz: *K'91*:82,157; *K'92*:62,96
Beers, Ray: *K'91*:182; *K'92*:63,69; *K'93*:81
Behnke, William: *K'91*:120; *K'92*:178; *K'93*:204; *K'95*:104,122
Bell, Donald: 156,157,216
Bell, Michael: *K'93*:102,104,111

Benjamin Jr., George: *K'91*:148; *K'92*:71,85,177; *K'93*:86
Bennett, Peter: *K'93*:59,204; *K'95*:142
Benson, Don: *K'94*:107
Besedick, Frank E.: *K'94*:85
Beverly II, Larry H.: *K'92*:56,177; *K'94*:91; *K'95*:144
Birt, Sid: *K'91*:99; *K'92*:153; *K'93*:83
Black, Robert: *K'92*:177
Black, T.J.: *K'91*:118,183; *K'93*:103
Black, Tom: *K'91*:156,159; *K'92*:152,178; *K'93*:76,83
Blakley II, William E.: *K'92*:178
Blanchard, Gary: *K'91*:158,159
Bloomer, Alan T.: *K'92*:59,177
Blum, Chuck: *K'92*:178; *K'94*:144
Blum, Kenneth: *K'91*:103,112,146
Blum, Michel: *K'92*:67,95,178; *K'93*:61,83
Boardman, Guy: *K'92*:98
Boden, Harry: *K'91*:79
Bogachov, Anatoly: *K'94*:130; *K'95*:103
Boguszewski, Phil: *K'91*:Cover,67,69; *K'92*:79,80; *K'93*:79; *K'94*:117; *K'95*:81,101,129
Bolton, Charles B.: *K'93*:204
Bonassi, Franco: *K'91*:80; *K'92*:95; *K'93*:61; *K'94*:201
Booco, Gordon: *K'92*:59,179; *K'93*:82,136,205; *K'94*:71,89
Borger, Wolf: *K'92*:96,117; *K'93*:60,80; *K'94*:74,129
Bose, Tony: *K'91*:71,183; *K'93*:75,205; *K'94*:87
Boyd, Francis: *K'94*:103,104
Boye, David: *K'91*:160,183; *K'92*:62,155; *K'94*:68; *K'95*:217
Brack, Douglas D.: *K'91*:94; *K'93*:103,134; *K'95*:65
Bradley, Dennis: *K'92*:89,106,114
Bradley, John: *K'91*:123; *K'93*:133; *K'94*:114
Brady, Sandra: *K'93*:125
Brandsey, Edward P.: *K'90*:134; *K'91*:55; *K'92*:61,87; *K'93*:125; *K'95*:107
Branton, Robert: *K'92*:57,140,178
Brayton, Jim: *K'91*:85
Brdlik, Dan E.: *K'94*:90
Breckenridge, Jack: *K'91*:94
Brend, Walter J.: 161
Brennan, Judson: 78
Breshears, Clint: *K'93*:107
Brightwell, Mark: *K'91*:59; *K'93*:73
Brignardello, E.D.: *K'91*:89
Britton, Tim: *K'91*:103,183; *K'92*:71,79,82,138; *K'93*:106; *K'95*:216
Broadwell, David: *K'91*:90,100; *K'92*:101,179; *K'93*:88,205; *K'94*:93,98,118,146
Brock, Kenneth L.: *K'94*:103
Brooks, Michael: *K'91*:125; *K'92*:65,179
Brooks, Steve R.: *K'92*:65,141; *K'93*:30,204; *K'95*:145,216
Broughton, Don R.: *K'93*:204; *K'95*:91
Brown, Harold E.: *K'91*:150,183; *K'92*:178; *K'93*:98
Brown, Peter: *K'91*:183; *K'93*:98,204
Brown, Rob E.: *K'92*:179; *K'95*:217
Brumagen, Jerry: *K'91*:144
Brunckhorst, C. Lyle: *K'91*:134; *K'93*:145; *K'94*:82
Bryd, Don E.: *K'94*:201
Buckelew, John: *K'92*: 115
Bullard, Bill: *K'94*:200; *K'95*:90
Burrows, Stephen R.: *K'94*:117; *K'95*:167
Busfield, John: *K'91*:64,77,183; *K'92*:74,78,179; *K'93*:66,79; *K'94*:Cover,92,145,146
Byrd, Don E.: *K'95*:110, 119

c

Caffrey, Edward J.: *K'93*:97
Caldwell, Bill: *K'91*:65; *K'92*:181; *K'95*:119
Callahan, Errett: *K'91*:74,109,161,188; *K'92*:Cover,118,121,155; *K'93*:140,206; *K'94*:Inside Cover,115; *K'95*:111,219
Callahan, F. Terry *K'95*:91,120
Candrella, Joe: *K'91*:117,162; *K'92*:179
Cannady, Daniel L.: *K'92*:180; *K'95*:108,219
Cannon, Raymond W.: *K'91*:188; *K'93*:110; *K'94*:202

Cannon, Wes: 166
Canter, Ronald E.: *K'91*:105,189
Carey Jr., Charles W.: *K'93*:116,206; *K'94*:73,203; *K'95*:218
Cargill, Bob: *K'91*:67,188; *K'92*:50; *K'93*:63,68,73
Carlsson, Marc Bjorn: *K'91*:82,162; *K'92*:26,180; *K'93*:136,206; *K'95*:117,126
Carson, Harold J. "Kit": *K'91*:94,119,124,152,154; *K'92*:81,153,180; *K'93*:73,88; *K'94*:90,118,151; *K'95*:Cover,135,146
Carter, Fred: *K'91*:101,189; *K'93*:67,149; *K'94*:94,202; *K'95*:163
Casteel, Dianna: *K'91*:189; *K'92*:90,100,149,153; *K'93*:114; *K'94*:95
Casteel, Douglas: *K'91*:100,188; *K'92*:112,138,180; *K'93*:72,113; *K'95*:78,96
Centofante, Frank and Tony: *K'91*:160,188; *K'92*:73,74,147; *K'93*:145,146,147; *K'95*:127,137,162,164
Chaffee, Jeff L.: *K'91*:189
Chamberlain, John B.: *K'92*:180; *K'93*:107
Chamberlin, John A.: *K'91*:188; *K'92*:103
Chamblin, Joel: *K'94*:86,137,203; *K'95*:129
Champion, Robert: *K'93*:138
Chapman, Mike: *K'91*:149
Chapo, William G.: *K'95*:219
Chard, Gordon R.: *K'91*:66; *K'92*: 90,179; *K'93*:79; *K'95*:92
Chase, John E.: *K'94*:69; *K'95*:219
Cheatham, Bill: *K'91*:Cover,152; *K'92*:76,134,180; *K'93*:65; *K'95*:131
Chesterman, Michael J.: *K'93*:206
Clark, Dave: *K'92*:117,181
Clark, Howard F.: *K'91*:189; *K'92*:127; *K'93*:206; *K'94*:112
Clark, Roger: *K'92*:180; *K'95*:93
Clay, J.D.: *K'91*:86,188; *K'92*:60; *K'95*:83,125
Clay, Wayne: *K'91*:64,158; *K'93*:72
Coats, Eldon: *K'92*:102,103,126; *K'93*:206
Cobb, Lowell D.: *K'93*:86,95,97,100; *K'95*:69
Cofer, Ron: *K'92*:181
Coffman, Danny: *K'95*:137
Cohen, N.J.: *K'91*:188
Coil, Jimmie J.: *K'94*:202
Coleman, Keith E.: *K'92*:181
Collett, Jerry D.: *K'94*:87
Conley, Bob: *K'91*:63; *K'92*:54,75
Connolly, James: *K'93*:82
Connor, Michael: *K'92*:64
Coogan, Robert: *K'91*:149
Cook, James Ray: *K'92*:65,181; *K'93*:95
Cooper, George J.: *K'93*:41
Cooper, J.N.: *K'92*:19,20,21
Copemam, Neil: *K'91*:126
Corby, Harold: *K'91*:93; *K'93*:90,92,206; *K'95*:147
Cordova, Joseph G.: *K'91*:88,130; *K'93*:135; *K'94*:134; *K'95*:105
Corrado, Jim: *K'92*:127; *K'94*:83,202
Corwin, Don: *K'91*:59,71,77; *K'92*:50,51,52,54,78,180; *K'93*:147; *K'94*:98
Cosby, E. Blanton: 133
Cosgrove, Charles G.: *K'91*:148
Cote, Yves: *K'95*:87
Courtois, Bryan: *K'91*:93; *K'92*:180
Cover, Raymond A.: *K'93*:154
Cox, Colin J.: *K'91*:93,189; *K'92*:122,140,181; *K'95*:218
Cox, Sam: *K'92*:146; *K'93*:89
Craft III, John M.: *K'91*:106; *K'92*:104
Craft, Richard C.: *K'91*:125
Crain, Jack W.: *K'91*:120,189
Crawford, Pat: *K'91*:108,189; *K'93*:85,87; *K'94*:99,102
Crockford, Jack: *K'91*:66; *K'93*:78; *K'94*:75
Cross, John M.: *K'92*:76; *K'95*:94
Crosslen, Timothy J.: *K'93*:206
Crowder, Robert: *K'91*:91,159; *K'92*:119,138,181
Crowell, James L.: *K'91*:Cover; *K'92*:113; *K'94*:101
Culver, Steve: *K'93*:121,122
Cumming, R.J.: *K'91*:161,189
Cutchin, Roy D.: *K'95*:126

d

Dahl, Chris W.: *K'91*:101; *K'92*:112
Dake, C.M.: *K'91*:118,146,195; *K'92*:77,190; *K'93*:77; *K'94*:99,103,202; *K'95*:134
D'Andrea, John: *K'92*:94,195
Damagala, John: *K'91*:107
Daniel, Travis E.: *K'91*:115,194
Daniels, Alex: *K'91*:145,155; *K'92*:88; *K'94*:112
Darby, Rick: *K'91*:115,194; *K'95*:121
Dauberman, Desmond P.: *K'94*:123
Davenport, Jack: *K'94*:90,203; *K'95*:Cover,131
Davenport, Steve: *K'91*:194
Davidson, Edmund: *K'91*:103,195; *K'92*:60,87,191; *K'93*:125,148; *K'94*:67; *K'95*:Cover,136
Davidson, Rob: *K'92*:190
Davis, Barry L.: *K'91*:194; *K'92*:84; *K'93*:70,207; *K'95*:219
Davis, Bill: *K'94*:203
Davis, Don: *K'95*:82
Davis, Ken: *K'95*:81
Davis, Terry: *K'91*:72; *K'92*:52,76; *K'93*:74; *K'94*:87,88,93; *K'95*:124
Davis, Vernon M.: *K'91*:145,195; *K'92*:190
Davis, W.C.: *K'91*:86; *K'93*:86
Dean, Harvey J.: *K'91*:96,115; *K'92*:107,191; *K'93*:92,99,207; *K'94*:96,114; *K'95*:123,143
Dearing, John: *K'91*:195
DeBraga, Jose C.: *K'91*:Cover,59,77; *K'92*:66,139; *K'93*:69,112; *K'94*:138; *K'95*:130,219
DeFeo, Robert A.: *K'93*:92,124; *K'94*:112; *K'95*:93
DeFreest, William G.: *K'94*:106
DeGraeve, Richard: *K'92*:191
DeLong, Dick: *K'91*:194
Dempsey, Gordon S.: *K'93*:111
Dennehy, Dan: *K'91*:90; *K'93*:36
Dennehy, John D.: *K'91*:85,86; *K'93*:122,124
DeYong, Clarence: *K'91*:113,145,194; *K'92*:56,190
Dietzel, Bill: *K'92*:143
DiGangi, Joseph M.: *K'92*:137,190
Dill, Robert: *K'92*:154; *K'93*:153
Dilluvio, Frank J.: *K'91*:195; *K'94*:79,203; *K'95*:67,92
DiMarzo, Richard: *K'94*:116
Dion, Greg: *K'91*:130,195; *K'93*:207; *K'94*:127,203; *K'95*:218
Dion, Malcolm: *K'92*:58,86,191
Dippold, A.W.: *K'92*:140,191; *K'94*:134; *K'95*:118
Dominy, Chuck: *K'94*:203; *K'95*:109
Donovan, Patrick: *K'91*:126,194; *K'92*:190; *K'93*:73; *K'95*:131
Doursin, Gerard: *K'95*:115
Doussot, Laurent: *K'93*:63,76,207; *K'95*:115,218
Dowell, T.M.: *K'91*:141; *K'93*:35,80,99,123,207; *K'94*:66,132; *K'95*:218
Downie, James T.: *K'91*:134
Downing, Larry: *K'91*:92,195; *K'92*:74,136; *K'92*:74,136; *K'93*:54,88; *K'94*:95
Downing, Tom: *K'91*:55,122; *K'93*:145; *K'94*:120
Downs, James F.: *K'91*:120,195; *K'92*:91; *K'93*:54,144; *K'94*:127,202; *K'95*:110,138
Dozier, Robert Lee: *K'92*:56,101,191
Draper, Bart: *K'94*:76
Draper, Kent: *K'91*:98,131,146; *K'92*:69,91,190; *K'93*:87,95,149
Driskill, Beryl: *K'91*:194; *K'92*:153; *K'93*:106
Dufour, Arthur J.: *K'93*:94,207
Dungy, Lawrence: *K'94*:77; *K'95*:120
Dunkerley, Rick: *K'94*:203
Dunn, Melvin T.: *K'94*:69; *K'95*:81
Dunn, Steve: *K'92*:191; *K'93*:93; *K'94*:108,113; *K'95*:123,218
Duran, Jerry T.: *K'91*:96; *K'92*:191; *K'93*:87
Duvall, Fred: *K'95*:96
Duvall, Larry E.: *K'91*:108,195; *K'92*:139

e

Easler, Paula: *K'91*:76; *K'92*:126; *K'93*:116
Easler Jr., Russell O.: *K'91*:200; *K'92*:63,147,194; *K'93*:31,144; *K'94*:149,204
Eaton, Al: *K'91*:76,107; *K'92*:122,127; *K'93*:113; *K'95*:86,87,103,123,155
Eaton, Rick: *K'91*:159,200; *K'92*:194; *K'93*:149; *K'95*:158
Edwards, Fain E.: *K'95*:88,89,220

Edwards, Lynn: *K'93*:101,207; *K'94*:204
Eklund, Rolf: *K'91*:83; *K'92*:23
Eldik, Frans Van: *K'95*:72
Eldrige, Allan: *K'92*:93; *K'93*:116
Elishewitz, Allen: *K'92*:194; *K'93*:104,138; *K'95*:80,128,220
Elkins, R. Van: *K'91*:201
Ellefson, Joel: *K'91*:201; *K'92*:194; *K'93*:65; *K'94*:120; *K'95*:156
Elliott, Marcus: *K'94*:204
Ellis, David: *K'91*:200; *K'92*:194; *K'93*:95,98; *K'95*:220
Embretsen, Kaj: *K'91*:83,148,200; *K'92*:24,27; *K'93*:58,70,88,111,207; *K'94*:204; *K'95*:128
Emerson, Ernest R.: *K'91*:68; *K'92*:83,148; *K'93*:78; *K'94*:137; *K'95*:145
Ence, Jim: *K'91*:100; *K'92*:194; *K'94*:Cover,118; *K'95*:77,158
Enders, Robert: *K'91*:64,76; *K'92*:Cover,85,195; *K'93*:159; *K'94*:104,146; *K'95*:125
England, Virgil: *K'93*:96,137; *K'94*:116; *K'95*:73
English, Jim: *K'95*:72
Engnath, Bob: *K'91*:129,130; *K'92*:67,119,135
Enos III, Thomas M.: *K'92*:134; *K'93*:109; *K'95*:69,220
Erickson, Walter E.: *K'92*:113,194; *K'93*:86,109
Eriksen, James Thorlief: *K'91*:54,142,145,200; *K'92*:69,78,108; *K'93*:77,101; *K'94*:121,205; *K'95*:165
Eriksen, Jan: *K'92*:23; *K'93*:121,136
Esaki, Shusuke: *K'94*:71
Essegian, Richard: *K'91*:90
Etzler, John: *K'94*:107,123,205; *K'95*:102,130
Evans, Vincent K.: *K'91*:130,200; *K'92*:105; *K'93*:69; *K'95*:64

f

Fannin, David A.: *K'91*:144; *K'93*:124
Fassio, Melvin G.: *K'91*:154; *K'92*:75
Fecas, Stephen J.: *K'92*:194; *K'93*:147; *K'95*:125
Ferguson, Jim: *K'91*:121,125,141,142,201; *K'92*:89,135,195; *K'93*:154; *K'94*:204; *K'95*:67,221
Fields, Rick B.: *K'93*:Inside Cover
Fikes, Jimmy L.: *K'95*:67
Fiorini, Bill: *K'91*:110,116,140,201; *K'92*:134,195; *K'93*:102,135; *K'95*:221
Fischer, Clyde E.: *K'93*:39
Fisher, Jay: *K'92*:140; *K'93*:124,208; *K'94*:72
Fisher, Theo (Ted): *K'91*:75; *K'92*:126,195
Fisk, Jerry: *K'92*:92,195; *K'93*:Cover,77,133; *K'94*:130; *K'95*:103
Fister, Jim: *K'91*:53,117; *K'92*:86; *K'93*:208; *K'94*:73,205; *K'95*:221
Flechtner, Chris: *K'95*:122
Flournoy, Joe: *K'91*:121,201; *K'92*:Cover,93; *K'93*:84,208; *K'94*:134,204; *K'95*:99
Fogg, (See Kemal),Don: *K'91*:98; *K'92*:109,141,143; *K'93*:67,84,105,152,208; *K'94*:81,132,205; *K'95*:68,74,145,155
Fogle, James W.: *K'91*:151
Forthofer, Pete: *K'92*:62,72,195
Foster, Al: *K'93*:208
Fowler, Ed A.: *K'91*:201; *K'92*:107; *K'93*:132; *K'94*:204; *K'95*:90,221
Fowler, Jerry: *K'93*:101,134
Fox, Paul: *K'91*:201; *K'92*:79; *K'93*:96
Fox, Wendell: *K'94*:102; *K'95*:220
Fraley, Derek: *K'95*:82
Frank, Heinrich H.: *K'91*:63; *K'92*:72; *K'93*:67; *K'95*:71
Frankland, Andrew: *K'93*:208; *K'94*:97,130,134; *K'95*:89,91
Franklin, Mike: *K'93*:100
Freer, Ralph: *K'95*:153,221
Friedly, Dennis E.: *K'91*:108,153,201; *K'92*:149,195; *K'93*:208; *K'94*:148,205; *K'95*:69
Frizzell, Ted: *K'91*:124
Fronefield, Mike: *K'91*:130
Fuegen, Larry: *K'91*:Cover; *K'92*:115,154,195; *K'93*:59,76; *K'94*:100,109,138
Fujisaka, Stanley: *K'91*:159; *K'92*:82,194; *K'94*:92,205; *K'95*:104,221
Fuller, Bruce A.: *K'94*:205; *K'95*:221
Fuller, Jack A.: *K'91*:77,85,97,122,143,200; *K'92*:88,107,142,155,179,195; *K'93*:123
Fuller, John W.: *K'91*:200; *K'93*:208; *K'94*:96,149
Furukawa, Shiro: *K'91*:78

g

Gaddy, Gary L.: *K'95*:155
Gaeta, Roberto: *K'91*:80,204
Gallagher, Barry: *K'95*:222
Gamble, Frank: *K'91*:129; *K'92*:200; *K'95*:131
Gannaway, Woodson: *K'92*:144; *K'94*:129,133
Garbe, Bob: *K'94*:105,206; *K'95*:139,146
Gardner, Rob: *K'92*:69,105
Garner, Bernard: *K'95*:97,223
Garner, Jr., William O.: *K'91*:204; *K'92*:201
Gartman, M.D.: *K'91*:60,71,204; *K'93*:209
Gaston, Bert: *K'92*:201
Gaston, Ron: *K'91*:91,103,154,204; *K'92*:148,153,200; *K'93*:Cover,31,147; *K'94*:109,206; *K'95*:121
Gaugler, Earl W.: *K'92*:136,200; *K'93*:93,209; *K'94*:137
Gault, Clay: *K'92*:54,75,78,200,201; *K'93*:91; *K'95*:121,222
Geisler, Gary R.: *K'91*:115; *K'92*:90
Genge, Roy E.: *K'91*:131
Genovese, Rick: *K'93*:66; *K'95*:77
George, Harry: *K'91*:204; *K'92*:57,200; *K'94*:71
Gerus, Gerry: *K'92*:98,200; *K'93*:59
Gibert, Pedro: *K'91*:80,204
Gilbreath, Randall: *K'91*:204; *K'93*:80; *K'95*:130,156
Giljevic, Branko: *K'91*:79,205; *K'92*:98,201; *K'93*:60; *K'94*:69,75; *K'95*:109,137
Gillenwater, E.E. "Dick": *K'91*:110
Glover, Ron: *K'91*:157
Glucklick, Bob: *K'93*:114
Godby, Ronald E.: *K'93*:224
Goddard, Wayne: *K'91*:144,205; *K'94*:15,20
Godfrey, Steve: *K'91*:205; *K'93*:209
Goers, Bruce: *K'92*:58; *K'93*:94,209
Goertz, Paul S.: *K'91*:204; *K'94*:15,16,140
Goguen, Scott: *K'95*:223
Goldberg, David: *K'91*:76; *K'92*:120,121; *K'94*:121,206
Goldenberg, T.S.: *K'91*:102; *K'92*:89,200; *K'94*:70,113; *K'95*:222
Goltz, Warren L.: *K'92*:90,201
Gonzalez, Leonardo Williams: *K'91*:80,81; *K'92*:97; *K'94*:122
Goo, Tai: *K'93*:135; *K'94*:116
Gottage, Dante and/or Judy: *K'91*:70,89,128,205; *K'92*:74,108; *K'93*:80,151; *K'94*:98,102,206; *K'95*:102,159
Graffeo, Anthony I.: *K'95*:107
Greco, John: *K'91*:91,125,205; *K'92*:67; *K'93*:65,87,97; *K'94*:109,206; *K'95*:82,93,222
Green, Bill: *K'91*:77,79; *K'94*:72
Green, Roger M.: *K'91*:117,205; *K'92*:87; *K'93*:92; *K'94*:82,112,206; *K'95*:89,95
Greenfield, G.O.: *K'95*:154
Greenwood, R.W.: *K'91*:205
Grey, Piet: *K'93*:95,209
Griffin, Rendon: *K'92*:200; *K'94*:103; *K'95*:135
Grossman, Stanley: *K'92*:201
Grossman, Stewart: *K'92*:124; *K'93*:114; *K'94*:84,85,104; *K'95*:87,222
Grussenmeyer, Paul: *K'94*:115
Gurganus, Melvin H.: *K'91*:108,205; *K'92*:201; *K'93*:209; *K'94*:91
Guth, Kenneth: *K'91*:141; *K'92*:201; *K'93*:102

h

Hagen, Phillip L. "Doc": *K'91*:66,210; *K'92*:70,84; *K'93*:75,79,211; *K'94*:85,98; *K'95*:67,98
Hagwood, Kellie: *K'94*:151
Hajovsky, Robert J.: *K'91*:114
Halligan, Ed: *K'95*:81,97,102
Halligan, Ed & Shawn: *K'91*:107,124,210; *K'92*:63,101,207; *K'93*:88,105,111; *K'94*:78,114; *K'95*:222
Hammond, Jim: *K'91*:88; *K'93*:86; *K'94*:109; *K'95*:81,126
Hampton, William W.: *K'95*:107
Hancock, Ronald E.: *K'92*:53; *K'95*:96,112
Hancock, Tim:; *K'93*:104; *K'94*:113,206; *K'95*:223
Hand, Bill: *K'92*:92; *K'94*:67
Hangas, Vic: *K'91*:24-29
Hara, Kouji: *K'93*:61; *K'95*:106
Harkins, J.A.: *K'92*:76,104,113; *K'93*:71; *K'94*:89;

*K'95:*130,132
Harless, Walt: *K'91:*101,123,211; *K'92:*63,116,146,148; *K'93:*147,150
Harley, Larry W.: *K'91:*109,146; *K'92:*71,102,136; *K'93:*54; *K'95:*144
Harmon, Jay: *K'91:*99,210; *K'92:*79,101,102; *K'93:*82,107; *K'94:*137,207; *K'95:*223
Harris, Jay: *K'91:*69; *K'92:*77,108,207; *K'93:*150; *K'94:*89; *K'95:*101,160
Harris, Ralph Dewey: *K'91:*Cover,210; *K'92:*74; *K'95:*135
Harsey, William H.: *K'91:*142
Hartman, Arlan (Lanny): *K'91:*114,150; *K'93:*73; *K'94:*207; *K'95:*138
Hartsfield, Phill: *K'93:*64,103,210; *K'94:*120,207; *K'95:*68,69,86,144
Harvey, Max: *K'91:*79,90,100,210; *K'92:*88; *K'93:*96
Hawk, Jack L.: *K'91:*87; *K'94:*Cover
Hawk, Joe: *K'91:*164; *K'92:*87
Hawk, Joey K.: *K'91:*210
Hawk, Ken: *K'92:*115
Hawkins, Rade: *K'91:*107; *K'93:*106,211; *K'95:*152
Hayes, Dolores: *K'91:*55; *K'92:*139,156,207; *K'93:*63
Hayes, Wally: *K'94:*119
Haynes, Chap: *K'91:*55,128,210
Heasman, H.G.: *K'94:*85
Hedrick, Don: *K'91:*102
Hehn, Richard Karl: *K'91:*82,83,211; *K'94:*118
Heitler, Henry: *K'94:*109
Helgason, E.O.: *K'93:*79
Helton, Roy: *K'91:*62,94; *K'93:*74; *K'94:*91,114,206; *K'95:*125,128
Hendricks, Samuel J.: *K'94:*67,98,207 *K'92:*109,207; *K'93:*107,210
Hendrickson, E. Jay: *K'91:*97,161; *K'94:*73; *K'95:*97
Henriksen, Hans J.: *K'91:*82,83,151; *K'92:*24,26,27; *K'93:*121,136; *K'94:*130,139
Henry, D.E.: *K'91:*30,31
Henry & Son, Peter: *K'91:*161; *K'94:*129
Hensley, Wayne: *K'92:*Cover,126
Herman, Tim: *K'91:*70; *K'92:*73,80; *K'93:*148,210; *K'94:*95,146; *K'95:*76,101
Herndon, Wm. R.: *K'91:*75,89,131,154; *K'92:*136,206; *K'93:*96,136; *K'94:*137; *K'95:*68,94
Hesser, David: *K'95:*86,223
Hethcoat, Don: *K'92:*206; *K'94:*71,207; *K'95:*126
Hetmanski, Thomas S.: *K'93:*115,117,210; *K'95:*129,130
Hibben, Daryl: *K'91:*110; *K'94:*148
Hibben, Gil: *K'91:*11,155; *K'92:*81,122,166,206; *K'94:*85,116,117; *K'95:*Inside Cover,76,147
Hibben, Westley G.: *K'91:*122,206,207
Hicks, Vernon W.: *K'91:*211; *K'92:*51
Hielscher, Guy: *K'95:*156
Hill, Howard E.: *K'91:*149; *K'93:*210
Hill, Steven E.: *K'91:*211; *K'92:*61,115; *K'94:*90,135
Hinderer, Rick: *K'91:*210; *K'92:*207; *K'93:*Cover,132,211; *K'94:*95,100; *K'95:*126,135
Hink, III, Les: *K'91:*62; *K'92:*75,78; *K'93:*75,210; *K'94:*74; *K'95:*124
Hinson & Son, R.: *K'91:*68
Hintz, Gerald J.: *K'93:*153
Hirayama, Harumi: *K'91:*78; *K'92:*99; *K'93:*91; *K'94:*94,128; *K'95:*72
Hitchmough, Howard: *K'91:*82,211; *K'92:*94,207; *K'93:*60,71,90,211; *K'94:*77; *K'95:*118
Hodge, J.B.: *K'91:*211
Hodgson, Richard J.: *K'94:*93
Hoel, Steve: *K'91:*63; *K'92:*51,73,151,170,206; *K'93:*66,67,146; *K'94:*145
Hoffman, Kevin L.: *K'91:*211; *K'92:*183,116,152,206; *K'93:*82; *K'94:*91
Hoffman, Uwe J.: *K'92:*68,102,119; *K'93:*61,101; *K'94:*124,156
Holder, D'Alton: *K'91:*113; *K'92:*137; *K'93:*99; *K'95:*161
Holland, Dale J.: *K'91:*211
Holland, John: *K'95:*128,140
Homer, Glen: *K'91:*150; *K'94:*124
Hopper, Jim: *K'91:*74
Horn, Jess: *K'91:*65; *K'92:*77,151,167; *K'94:*95
Hornby, Glen: *K'91:*211; *K'92:*127,207; *K'94:*87,110
Horton, Scot: *K'92:*207; *K'93:*77; *K'94:*103; *K'95:*129,140
Howard, Seth: *K'93:*57
Howell, Robert L.: *K'94:*103; *K'95:*65

Howser, John C.: *K'92:*54,103
Hoy, Fred W.: *K'93:*42
Hrisoulas, Jim: *K'92:*165
Hudson, C. Robbin: *K'91:*99; *K'92:*134,143; *K'93:*65,70,84; *K'95:*98
Hudson, Robert: *K'92:*207; *K'93:*210
Hudson, Tommy: *K'92:*52,77,118,150,206; *K'93:*74,210,211; *K'94:*80,207
Hueske, Chubby: *K'92:*5
Huey, Steve: *K'91:*91,103; *K'92:*206
Hughes, Ed: *K'91:*124; *K'92:*59; *K'93:*86; *K'94:*107,207; *K'95:*223
Hull, Michael J.: *K'94:*68,106
Hulsey, Hoyt: *K'92:*106; *K'93:*78
Hume, Don: *K'91:*163; *K'92:*64; *K'93:*84
Humenick, Roy: *K'92:*69
Humphreys, Joel: *K'94:*96; *K'95:*123,223
Husiak, Myron: *K'91:*79,210

i

Iiams, Richard D.: *K'92:*212; *K'93:*211
Imboden II, Howard L.: *K'91:*164,216
Imel, Billy Mace: *K'91:*98,217; *K'92:*105; *K'93:*72,115; *K'95:*77,98,100
Ishara, Nobuhiko: *K'95:*224
Ishihara, Hank: *K'93:*61,211

j

Jackson, Jim: *K'91:*104; *K'92:*212; *K'93:*141,212
Jackson, Mark: *K'91:*85
James, Bobby: *K'93:*53
James, Peter: *K'95:*144
Jarvis, Paul M.: *K'95:*96,103,143,155
Jean, Gerry: *K'91:*84,148,216; *K'93:*80
Jernigan, Steve: *K'91:*67,216; *K'92:*80,117,212; *K'93:*Cover,212; *K'94:*92,209; *K'95:*135,224
Jobin, Jacques: *K'92:*212; *K'94:*129,138
Johns, Rob: *K'91:*107
Johnson, Brad: *K'92:*115,212
Johnson, C.E. "Gene": *K'91:*65,216; *K'93:*212; *K'95:*139
Johnson, Durrell Carmon: *K'91:*121,122,216; *K'92:*85,93,213; *K'93:*212; *K'94:*209
Johnson, Gorden W.: *K'94:*113
Johnson, Kenneth R.: *K'93:*141; *K'94:*209
Johnson, R.B.: *K'91:*155,216; *K'92:*148
Johnson, Ruffin: *K'91:*150
Johnson, Ryan M.: *K'93:*133,141,213
Johnson, Steven R.: *K'91:*54,85,89,104,114,159; *K'92:*58,153,213; *K'93:*64,89,212; *K'94:*110,133,209; *K'95:*105,109,119,224
Johnson, W.C. "Bill": *K'91:*216; *K'93:*212; *K'94:*84,208
Jones, Barry M.: *K'94:*124,208
Jones, Barry M. and Phillip G.: *K'95:*82,224
Jones, Bob: *K'91:*72; *K'92:*54; *K'94:*88,99; *K'95:*140
Jones, Charles Anthony: *K'91:*82,83; *K'92:*51; *K'95:*224
Jones, Curtis J.: *K'91:*92,109,125,216; *K'92:*138,212; *K'93:*212; *K'94:*81,209
Jones, John: *K'91:*86,96
Jones, Paul: *K'94:*115
Jones, Phillip G.: *K'94:*124,208
Jones, Thomas L.: *K'91:*102

k

Kagawa, Koichi: *K'92:*99
Kalfayan, Edward N.: *K'91:*216; *K'92:*212,213; *K'93:*90,105,110,145,213; *K'94:*66,209; *K'95:*95,164,225
Kaluza, Werner: *K'94:*130; *K'95:*104,159,225
Kamada, Yoshikazu: *K'93:*62
Kanda, Michio: *K'95:*154
Kato, Kioshi: *K'93:*58,135
Kauffman, Dave: *K'92:*53,142; *K'94:*Cover,208; *K'95:*225
Kaufman, Scott: *K'95:*105
Kay, J. Wallace: *K'94:*85
Keeslar, Joseph F.: *K'91:*120; *K'92:*89,92,213; *K'93:*81,112,213
Keeslar, Steven C.: *K'94:*80,208

Keeton, William L.: *K'91:*66,90,126; *K'92:*213
Kehiayan, Alfredo: *K'91:*80,81,146,148; *K'93:*61
Keidel, Gene: *K'95:*162
Kelley, Gary: *K'91:*74; *K'92:*119; *K'93:*140
Kelly, Lance: *K'91:*101,217
Kelso, Jim: *K'93:*141; *K'94:*126; *K'95:*72
Kemal: *K'92:*70
Kennedy, Kelly S.: *K'93:*29,213; *K'95:*225
Kessler, Ralph A.: *K'93:*77; *K'94:*108; *K'95:*94
Khalsa, Jot Singh: *K'92:*152,170; *K'93:*83,148; *K'95:*160
Kharlamov, Yuri: *K'95:*114
Kiefer, Tony: *K'93:*213
Kilby, Keith: *K'91:*97,121,217; *K'92:*92,152; *K'93:*151,213; *K'94:*101,122,147,208; *K'95:*91,119,225
Kimsey, Kevin: *K'94:*124
King, Bill: *K'91:*62
King, Fred: *K'91:*217; *K'92:*142,213; *K'94:*209
King, Kemp: *K'91:*112; *K'95:*140
King, Randall: *K'93:*90
King Jr., Harvey G.: *K'94:*77
Kious, Joe: *K'92:*73,213; *K'93:*116
Kneubuhler, W.K.: *K'94:*25
Knickmeyer, Hank: *K'92:*69; *K'93:*99,134; *K'94:*80,136; *K'95:*Cover,118,152
Knight, Jim: *K'94:*82
Knipschield, Terry: *K'92:*60,102; *K'94:*132
Knipstein, R.C. "Joe": *K'91:*217; *K'92:*60
Knuth, Joseph E.: *K'93:*110,134; *K'94:*81,208; *K'95:*67,113
Kohler, J. Mark: *K'94:*99
Kojetin, W.: *K'94:*128; *K'95:*143
Kopp, Todd M.: *K'94:*208; *K'95:*224
Kormanik, Chris: *K'92:*213; *K'93:*213
Koutsopoulos, George: *K'92:*212; *K'94:*107; *K'95:*156
Kozlow, Kelly:: *K'93:*107
Kranning, Terry L.: *K'91:*77,217; *K'94:*84,209; *K'95:*85,225
Krapp, Denny: *K'92:*68,69,147
Kravitt, Chris: *K'92:*114,116; *K'93:*120,121
Kremzner, Raymond L.: *K'91:*54,129,141,142; *K'93:*106
Kressler, D.F.: *K'92:*62
Kretsinger, Jr., Phillip W.: *K'91:*118,120,217; *K'93:*98
Kubaiko, Hank: *K'92:*57,213
Kubasek, John A.: *K'91:*97,120,217; *K'92:*106

l

La Grange, Fanie: *K'93:*58,68,215
Lainson, Tony: *K'92:*59,118,219
Lake, Ron: *K'91:*63,104; *K'93:*120; *K'94:*146,147; *K'95:*74,125
Lambert, Jarrell D.: *K'93:*214; *K'95:*90
Lambert, Ronald S.: *K'94:*121
Lamprey, Mike: *K'95:*146
Lampson, Frank G.: *K'91:*222; *K'92:*78; *K'94:*77; *K'95:*132,143
Lance, Bill: *K'92:*118
Landrum, Leonard "Len": *K'93:*215; *K'94:*73,210
Lang, Kurt: *K'91:*110,142; *K'92:*92,118,134
Lange, Donald G.: *K'92:*86; *K'93:*215; *K'94:*211
Langley, Gene H.: *K'91:*107; *K'93:*74
Langley, Mick: *K'91:*98
Langston, Bennie E.:: *K'93:*78,215; *K'94:*210
Lankton, Scott: *K'92:*104,219; *K'94:*81,136
Lapen, Charles: *K'93:*111
Laplante, Brett: *K'94:*74,105; *K'95:*127,139
Largin, Ken: *K'92:*113; *K'93:*54; *K'95:*80
Lary, Ed: *K'91:*153; *K'93:*146
Laurent, Kermit: *K'94:*66,72
Lawrence, Alton: *K'94:*76; *K'95:*88
Lazo, Robert T.: *K'92:*116,137
Leach, Mike J.: *K'91:*222; *K'93:*87; *K'94:*211; *K'95:*226
Leavitt, Jr., Earl F.: *K'91:*109,117; *K'92:*115,137,142
LeBatard, Paul M.: *K'92:*218; *K'94:*72,211
Leber, Heinz: *K'92:*58,70; *K'95:*121,139
LeBlanc, John: *K'92:*218; *K'93:*77,214; *K'94:*138,210; *K'95:*133,138
Leck, Dal: *K'94:*111; *K'95:*122
Ledford, Bracy R.: *K'91:*111,222; *K'92:*105,154,219
Lee, Randy: *K'92:*218; *K'93:*92; *K'94:*73,210; *K'95:*107,123,176,226

Lee, Tommy: *K'91*:92,99; *K'92*:114; *K'93*:69; *K'94*:151,211
LeFaucheux, J.V.: *K'92*:96
LeFont, Mark: *K'91*:75,106
Leland, Steve: *K'95*:103
Lemaire, Denis: *K'94*:103
LePore, Michael J.: *K'91*:158,223; *K'92*:218; *K'93*:72,97
Letcher, Billy: *K'93*:214
Levengood, Bill: *K'91*:116,122; *K'92*:59,62,116,147,149,219; *K'93*:82,93; *K'94*:90,211
Leverett, Ken: *K'94*:121
Levine, Bob: *K'95*:127
Levine, Norman: *K'91*:223; *K'92*:70,136,139,154,219; *K'93*:214; *K'94*:69,135,210; *K'95*:226
Lewis, K.J.: *K'93*:130,131
Lewis, Mike: *K'91*:106,107; *K'92*:113; *K'93*:111,213; *K'94*:80; *K'95*:64,66
Lewis, Tom R.: *K'92*:60,218; *K'94*:76,210
Liebenbert, Andre: *K'93*:109
Likarich, Steve: *K'91*:129,149,222; *K'92*:71,106,139; *K'93*:96,137,214; *K'94*:116,125,133,211; *K'95*:120,147
Lile, Marilyn (Jimmy): *K'91*:92,118,134,150; *K'92*:5; *K'93*:38,90,125; *K'94*:70; *K'95*:93,122
Lister, Jr., Weldon E.: *K'91*:62; 151,218
Little, Jimmy L.: *K'91*:108
Livingston, Robert C.: *K'91*:144,223; *K'92*:218; *K'93*:215
Lockachiev, Alexander: *K'95*:146
Loerchner, Wolfgang: *K'91*:100,128,156; *K'92*:Inside Cover, 104,218; *K'93*:83,151,214; *K'94*:119; *K'95*:74,100,101,163,167
Lohman, Fred: *K'95*:66
Lonewolf, J. Aguirre: *K'93*:153; *K'95*:167
Long, Glenn A.: *K'95*:226
Lorey: *K'92*:218
Love, Ed: *K'93*:99,101,137,214
Loveless, R.W.: *K'92*:100; *K'93*:100,125; *K'94*:73,120; *K'95*:120
Lovestrand, Schuyler: *K'95*:163
Lovett, Mike: *K'91*:113,223; *K'92*:103,108,124,140
Lozito, Joseph F.: *K'91*:73,75
Lubrich, Mark: *K'94*:210
Luchak, Bob: *K'93*:94,101,137,214; *K'94*:72
Luck, Gregory: *K'91*:85; *K'92*:116,218; *K'93*:122
Luckett, Bill: *K'91*:93,123
Ludwig, Richard O.: *K'95*:226
Lui, Ronald M.: *K'92*:68; *K'94*:92; *K'95*:137
Lum, Robert W.: *K'91*:102,114,116; *K'93*:69,82
Lunn, Larry A.: *K'94*:80
Lutes, Robert: *K'91*:109,116,150; *K'92*:219; *K'93*:115; *K'94*:149
Lyle III, Ernest L.: *K'91*:223; *K'92*:88; *K'94*:211
Lyons, Randy: *K'95*:102,123
Lyttle, Brian: *K'91*:99,121,135; *K'92*:105,151,218; *K'93*:149; *K'95*:95,104,159

m

MacBain, Kenneth C.: *K'92*:118; *K'93*:85,152; *K'95*:227
Malloy, Joe: *K'91*:124,223; *K'92*:221; *K'94*:124,138,213; *K'95*:127
Manabe, Michael K.: *K'94*:127,212,213; *K'95*:99,120,227
Mar, Al: *K'95*:160
Maragni, Dan: *K'95*:98
Marak, George: *K'93*:97
Mariacher, Robert R.: *K'94*:212
Maringer, Tom: *K'91*:106,108,179; *K'92*:113,141; *K'93*:140,216; *K'94*:108; *K'95*:58,59,60,62
Marks, Chris: *K'92*:93; *K'93*:92,104
Marshall, Glenn: *K'91*:66,90,134; *K'95*:138
Martin, Bruce E.: *K'91*:96; *K'92*:93; *K'92*:221
Martin, Randall J.: *K'93*:89,90,138,217
Martrildonno, Paul: *K'91*:59,69,76,111,131; *K'92*:67, 119,156; *K'93*:80,89,116,137; *K'94*:212; *K'95*:227
Marzitelli, Peter: *K'91*:123; *K'92*:61; *K'93*:123; *K'95*:144
Mason, Arne: *K'93*:120
Mason, Joel: *K'95*:66
Mattis, James K.: *K'95*:150,151
Maxfield, Lynn: *K'91*:223; *K'92*:221; *K'93*:94,217; *K'94*:212

Maxwell, Don: *K'93*:100,217; *K'94*:91; *K'95*:82
May, James E.: *K'91*:131,222; *K'94*:114
Maynard, William N.: 212
Mayo, Jr., Tom: *K'92*:63
Mayville, Oscar L.: *K'91*:119
McBurnette, Harvey: *K'91*:65,69; *K'92*:74,221; *K'93*:216; *K'94*:93; *K'95*:77,227
McClung, Kevin: *K'93*:139
McClure, Michael: *K'95*:118
McConnell, Jr., Loyd A.: *K'91*:92; *K'92*:89,146,148, 156,220; *K'93*:71,88; *K'95*:79,105,162,227
McCrackin, Kevin: *K'93*:95
McCrackin and Son, V.J.: *K'91*:123; *K'92*:64,84,86,221; *K'93*:216; *K'94*:83,114,212
McDonald, Robert J.: *K'92*:71,91; *K'93*:216; *K'94*:79,150,151; *K'95*:89,99,226
McFall, Ken: *K'91*:145; *K'93*:148; *K'95*:137
McGovern, Jim: *K'92*:221
McGowan, Frank E.: *K'91*:223; *K'92*:154,221; *K'94*:213
McHenry, William James: *K'92*:77,79,142; *K'93*:106,108,149,216; *K'94*:101,213; *K'95*:134
McKissack II, Tommy: *K'91*:68,71; *K'92*:53,75,220; *K'93*:74; *K'94*:75,79
McNabb, Tommy: *K'92*:115,194
McWilliams, Sean: *K'91*:89; *K'93*:87; *K'94*:213
Mecchi, Richard: *K'91*:55; *K'92*:137
Meier, Daryl: *K'91*:Inside Cover; *K'92*:145
Mendenhall, Harry E.: *K'91*:94; *K'92*:150,220; *K'93*:96
Mercer, Mike: *K'91*:77,222; *K'92*:121,122,124; *K'93*:113; *K'94*:82; *K'95*:84,86
Merchant, Ted: *K'92*:221
Merz III, Robert L.: *K'91*:67,105,118; *K'92*:78,220; *K'93*:68; *K'94*:74,99,213
Messer, David T.: *K'92*:124
Mettler, J. Banjo: *K'91*:60; *K'92*:51
Meyers, Paul: *K'92*:219
Middleton, Ken: *K'94*:111
Millard, Fred G.: *K'94*:124
Miller, Bob: *K'91*:144; *K'92*:220; *K'93*:132,141; *K'94*:119
Miller, Clark: *K'93*:82
Miller, Hanford J.: *K'91*:98; *K'92*:64; *K'94*:141
Miller, James K.: *K'93*:217
Miller, James P.: *K'91*:95,223; *K'92*:65,106,219
Miller, Jim H.: *K'91*:217
Miller, Larry: *K'91*:134,222; *K'92*:220
Miller, R.D.: *K'92*:220; *K'94*:74
Miller, Robert: *K'93*:65,107
Miller, Ronald T.: *K'92*:82; *K'93*:94
Mills, Andy: *K'91*:64,69
Minnick, Jim: *K'91*:161; *K'92*:104; *K'93*:216; *K'94*:Cover; *K'95*:227
Mitchell, Dean: *K'94*:110,135,212
Mitchell, Max, Dean and Ben: *K'93*:84
Mitchell, Wm. Dean: *K'95*:65,89
Moeller, Harald: *K'91*:108
Monteiro, Victor: *K'94*:156; *K'95*:128
Montjoy, Claude: *K'91*:62,129,154,222; *K'92*:220; *K'93*:85,106,110,150,217
Moore, James B.: *K'91*:72
Moran, Jr., Wm. F.: *K'91*:6,97,128,137; *K'92*:62, 70,92; *K'93*:99,121,217; *K'94*:71,114; *K'95*:71
Morgan, Jeff: *K'92*:219
Morris, C.H.: *K'93*:216
Morseth, Harry: *K'93*:38
Mosci, Carlos Roberto: *K'91*:81
Moulton, Dusty: *K'94*:108,120,213; *K'95*:85,94
Mount, Don: *K'92*:138; *K'94*:117; *K'95*:147
Mullin, Steve: *K'91*:98,141; *K'93*:70
Murphy, Dave: *K'92*:43
Myers, Paul: *K'91*:152,153; *K'92*:124

n

Nealy, Bud: *K'91*:230; *K'92*:58,68,107,150,155; *K'93*:Cover,63; *K'95*:228
Neeley, Vaughn: *K'93*:160,161
Neely, Greg: *K'92*:92; *K'94*:141
Newcomb, Corbin: *K'91*:124; *K'95*:228
Newton, Larry: *K'95*:132,228
Nielson, Jeff V.: *K'93*:218; *K'94*:214; *K'95*:85,228
Nishiuchi, Melvin S.: *K'91*:87,230; *K'92*:229; *K'94*:107,136,214

Nolen, R.D. and George: *K'91*:160,162,164,230; *K'92*:153,156,229; *K'93*:151,154,218; *K'94*:214
Nolfi, Tim: *K'91*:144,230; *K'92*:64,136,139,228; *K'93*:85,135; *K'94*:121
Nordell, Ingemar: *K'92*:24,26; *K'93*:59,98; *K'95*:117
Norris, Mike: *K'91*:230
North, David and Prater, Mike: *K'91*:230; *K'92*:228
Norton, Dennis: *K'91*:125,131
Norton, Don: *K'91*:230; *K'92*:146,228; *K'94*:70,215
Nowland, Rick: *K'92*:228; *K'93*:218; *K'95*:85
Nunn, Gregory: *K'91*:230; *K'95*:111

o

Ochs, Charles F.: *K'91*:96,122; *K'92*:65,109,228; *K'93*:76,85; *K'94*:70,112; 95,119,143,229
Ogg, Robert G.: *K'95*:162
Okaysu, Kazou: *K'95*:157
Oliver, Anthony Craig: *K'91*:230
Olson, Wayne C.: *K'94*:70
Onion, Kenneth J.: *K'95*:119,229
Osborne, Warren: *K'91*:65,231; *K'92*:73,170,228; *K'93*:67; *K'94*:86; *K'95*:75,158,229
Osterman, Daniel E.: *K'93*:68,113,114,117,218; *K'94*:82,83,94; *K'95*:84,85
Outlaw, Anthony L.: *K'91*:231
Overeynder, T.R.: *K'91*:117; *K'92*:74,228; *K'95*:75
Owens, Dan: *K'91*:64,113; *K'93*:138,218; *K'94*:76
Oyster, Lowell R.: *K'91*:72,109; *K'92*:51,119; *K'93*:75; *K'94*:87,211

p

Padilla, Gary: *K'93*:219; *K'95*:228
Page, Larry: *K'93*:219
Page, Reginald: *K'91*:110
Papp, Robert: *K'91*:91
Pardue, Melvin M.: *K'91*:63,70; *K'94*:215
Parker, J.E.: *K'95*:154
Parks, John: *K'92*:141; *K'93*:219
Parsons, Michael R.: *K'91*:111,143,158,159,231; *K'92*:150; *K'93*:149
Pate, Lloyd D.: *K'04*:215; *K'95*:119,143
Patrick, Bob: *K'95*:108,228
Patrick, Chuck: *K'91*:60,109,231; *K'92*:85,136,229; *K'93*:63,133; *K'95*:152
Patterson, Alan W.: *K'93*:71,122; *K'94*:78; *K'95*:66,113,145
Patterson, Karl: *K'92*:57
Pavack, Don: *K'91*:231; *K'93*:219; *K'94*:215; *K'95*:122,138
Peagler, Russ: *K'91*:104; *K'92*:68; *K'95*:108,229
Pease, W.D.: *K'92*:73; *K'93*:62,72; *K'94*:95; *K'95*:84,136
Peele, Bryan: *K'93*:121
Pendleton, Lloyd: *K'91*:114; *K'94*:68,214
Pendray, Alfred H.: *K'92*:70; *K'93*:105,219; *K'94*:126
Petersen, Dan L.: *K'92*:90,92,229
Peterson, Chris: *K'94*:123,214; *K'95*:228
Peterson, Eldon G.: *K'91*:152,157,231; *K'92*:72, 152; *K'93*:66,151; *K'94*:94,214; *K'95*:76,101,160
Peterson, Jack V.: *K'92*:121
Phillips, Randy: *K'91*:104,231; *K'92*:80,82; *K'94*:150; *K'95*:165
Pienaar, Conrad: *K'93*:98,219; *K'94*:121
Pitt, David F.: *K'91*:88
Pittman, Leon: *K'91*:157
Poag, James: *K'91*:156
Pogreba, Larry: *K'94*:74
Polk, Clifton: *K'93*:75
Polkowski, Al: *K'91*:231; *K'92*:82,103; *K'93*:86,100; *K'94*:107; *K'95*:108
Poole, Marvin: *K'94*:69; *K'95*:229
Popp, Sr., Steve: *K'92*:88,126
Porter, James E.: *K'91*:92,95,113; *K'92*:65,103,107; *K'93*:110,125,153; *K'94*:118,214; *K'95*:68,167
Potier, Timothy F.: *K'92*:101,229; *K'93*:93,121; *K'94*:49,51,215; *K'95*:94
Poythress, John: *K'92*:229
Prater, Mike: *K'94*:215
Pratt, Charles: *K'92*:106,229; *K'93*:123; *K'94*:66,83,215; *K'95*:Cover
Price, Steve: *K'91*:90; *K'92*:91; *K'93*:219
Prince, Joe R.: *K'95*:129,229

Pugh, Jim: *K'91*:163; *K'92*:82
Pullen, Martin: *K'93*:228; *K'94*:75,95,125,134
Pulliam, Morris C.: *K'91*:96,231; *K'93*:93,121
Pursley, Aaron: *K'91*:116,158; *K'92*:77,118,229; *K'93*:219; *K'94*:94

q

Quarton, Barr: *K'92*:104,238
Quattlebaum, Craig: *K'92*:236; *K'93*:220; *K'95*:136,230

r

Rados, Jerry F.: *K'91*:69,105,143,154,238; *K'92*:238; *K'93*:132; *K'94*:89,216
Ragsdale, James D.:; *K'93*:221; *K'94*:96,216; *K'95*:136
Rahn, John: *K'94*:110,111,134,216; *K'95*:98,102
Rambo, J.T.: *K'91*:150
Randall Made Knives: *K'94*:148
Randall, W.D. and (Bo) Gary T.: *K'91*:52,112; *K'92*:87,147,156,238
Rapp, Steven J.: *K'91*:93,100,238; *K'92*:238; *K'93*:221; *K'94*:113; *K'95*:143,231
Rappazzo, Richard: *K'91*:238; *K'92*:84; *K'93*:71; *K'94*:100
Rardon, A.D.: *K'91*:72,238; *K'92*:55,77; *K'93*:69,116,220; *K'94*:87; *K'95*:87,127,135,231
Ray, Alan W.: *K'91*:71,240; *K'92*:55,59,107; *K'94*:81,216; *K'95*:89,123,230
Rece, Charles V.: *K'93*:144
Reddiex, Bill: *K'91*:79,241; *K'92*:98,127,238; *K'93*:61,221; *K'94*:216
Ree, David: *K'91*:240
Reeve, Chris: *K'91*:42,45,60,238; *K'92*:81,82,238; *K'93*:87,162; *K'95*:80,83
Reinhardt, Hank: *K'92*:168
Remington, David W.: *K'94*:216
Reverdy, Pierre: *K'92*:95,135; *K'95*:153
Rexroat, Kirk: *K'95*:161,230,231
Rho, Nester Lorenzo: *K'94*:123,216; *K'95*:115
Rhodes, James D.: *K'95*:97
Richard, Ron: *K'91*:67,238; *K'93*:109
Richardson, Jr., Percy: *K'93*:220
Richter, John C.: *K'93*:135
Richter, Scott: *K'95*:97
Ricke, Dave: *K'91*:238; *K'92*:56,237; *K'94*:216
Rietveld, Bertie: *K'93*:220; *K'94*:216; *K'95*:101
Rigney, Willie: *K'91*:101,238; *K'92*:146,236; *K'93*:83,220; *K'94*:216; *K'95*:96,230
Rijiswijk, Aad Van: *K'95*:72,114,230
Rinkes, Siegfried: *K'95*:160,231
Rippy, Robert: *K'95*:80,83
Rippy, Robert and Bonnie (The Rippys): *K'91*:91, 115; *K'92*:59,100,102,237; *K'93*:123,138,220; *K'94*:216
Rizzi, Russell J.: *K'92*:58,236; *K'93*:221; *K'95*:110,231
Robbins, Howard P.: *K'92*:236; *K'93*:221; *K'95*:231
Roberts, Chuck: *K'93*:138
Robinson, Charles: *K'95*:91
Roe, Jr., Fred D.: *K'91*:130,240
Rogers, Rodney: *K'91*:119,155; *K'92*:63,101,109, 148,236; *K'94*:148,151; *K'95*:92,121
Rollert, Steve: *K'92*:237
Rowe, Kenny: *K'91*:84; *K'93*:122,125
Rua, Gary (Wolf): *K'94*:79; *K'95*:111
Ruana, Rudolph H.: *K'91*:24-29; *K'93*:25,26,27
Rubley, James A.: *K'94*:137,216; *K'95*:91
Rupert, Robert: *K'95*:101,113
Ruple, William H.: *K'92*:55,237; *K'93*:221
Russ, Joe: *K'93*:221
Russell, A.G.: *K'92*:166; *K'94*:19
Russell, Mick: *K'95*:104,230
Rychetnik, Joe: *K'94*:24

s

Saindon, R. Bill: *K'94*:97,150,218
Sakakibara, Masaki: *K'95*:131
Sakmar, Mike: *K'93*:222; *K'94*:219; *K'95*:90,153
Salisbury, Joel: *K'93*:134
Salley, John D.: *K'91*:60,239; *K'93*:144; *K'94*:219;

K'95:232
Sampson, Lynn: *K'91*:62; *K'92*:83; *K'94*:90
Sandberg, Dale: *K'93*:51
Sanders, A.A.: *K'91*:240
Sanders, Bill: *K'92*:60,150,236
Sanders, Michael M.: *K'91*:129; *K'92*:239; *K'93*:103; *K'94*:218; *K'95*:109
Sandlin, Larry: *K'95*:88
Sawby, Scott: *K'91*:66; *K'93*:66,76,145; *K'94*:92,145,133; *K'95*:75,130
Sayen, Murad: *K'93*:105,137,152,213; *K'94*:119; *K'95*:74,155
Scarrow, Will: *K'91*:240
Schaller, Anthony B.: *K'95*:232
Schepers, George B.: *K'93*:133
Scheurer, Alfredo E. Faes: *K'95*:147
Schirmer, Mike: *K'93*:222; *K'94*:108,120; *K'95*:120
Schmidt, James A.: *K'91*:241; *K'93*:70; *K'94*:118; *K'95*:74
Schmidt, Rick: *K'94*:69,113
Schneider, Herman J.: *K'92*:152,239; *K'93*:33,34
Schoeman, Corrie: *K'93*:76; *K'95*:117
Schoenfeld, Matthew A.: *K'91*:131,241
Scholl, Tim: *K'95*:122
Schonhals, G.G.: *K'92*:97
Schroen, Karl: *K'95*:145
Schwarzer, Stephen: *K'91*:134,239; *K'92*:84,85, 135,143,239; *K'93*:134; *K'94*:136; *K'95*:152
Scordia, Paolo: *K'93*:59; *K'94*:111,219
Scott, Al: *K'95*:161
Selent, Chuck: *K'93*:116
Self, Ernie: *K'94*:75,98
Sellevold, Harald: *K'91*:87; *K'92*:22,25,27; *K'94*:129,138
Selvidio, Ralph J.: *K'93*:108; *K'94*:89,219; *K'95*:125,134,156,233
Semich, Peter: *K'91*:119
Sentz, Mark C.: *K'91*:97,239; *K'92*:115
Serafen, Steven E.: *K'95*:232
Serven, Jim: *K'91*:60,241; *K'92*:80; *K'94*:102
Shadley, Eugene W.: *K'92*:52,64; *K'94*:88,94
Shaffer, Russell: *K'95*:110
Sharrigan, Mudd: *K'95*:112,154
Sheehan, Paul P.: *K'91*:55,126,240; *K'93*:117
Shinosky, Andy: *K'94*:93; *K'95*:165,233
Shoemaker, Scott: *K'91*:110; *K'92*:Cover; *K'93*:110; *K'94*:119
Shoger, Mark O.: *K'91*:95,239; *K'92*:85,239; *K'94*:219
Shostle, Ben: *K'92*:236; *K'95*:78
Sidelinger, Charles: *K'95*:Cover
Sidelinger, Robert: *K'92*:53; *K'93*:222; *K'94*:219
Sigman, Corbet R.: *K'91*:49,62,241; *K'92*:237,239; *K'93*:37,69,222; *K'94*:92; *K'95*:129
Simmonds, Kurt Barnes: *K'93*:73,223
Simonella, Gianluigi: *K'95*:116
Simons, Bill: *K'92*:55,83,117; *K'93*:77
Sims, Bob: *K'91*:64; *K'92*:52,54,55
Sinyard, Cleston S.: *K'92*:87,237; *K'93*:109,223; *K'94*:219; *K'95*:232
Sisemore, Charles: *K'95*:233
Siska, Jim: *K'91*:89,240; *K'92*:88,236; *K'93*:120,132,222; *K'95*:233
Slee, Fred: *K'91*:65,241; *K'94*:125; *K'95*:232
Sloan, Shane: *K'92*:76,91
Slobodian, Scott: *K'92*:66,67,134,239; *K'93*:103,104,109,223; *K'94*:81,83,113,126; *K'95*:66,152,157
Small, Ed: *K'91*:240
Smit, Glenn: *K'92*:120; *K'93*:97
Smith, D. Noel: *K'94*:116
Smith, Gregory H.: *K'91*:119
Smith, J.B.: *K'92*:93
Smith, J.D.: *K'92*:105,239; *K'93*:92,105,133,223; *K'94*:79,91,101,121,126,127,141; *K'95*:105
Smith, John M.: *K'91*:121; *K'95*:154
Smith, Raymond L.: *K'95*:126
Smith, W.F. (Red): *K'91*:241
Snell, Jerry L.: *K'91*:239; *K'92*:101,239; *K'93*:223; *K'94*:96,125,218; *K'95*:80,109,232
Solomon,Marvin: *K'93*:222; *K'95*:96
Solydwood: *K'91*:106
Sonntag, Carl: *K'94*:20
Soppera, Arthur: *K'92*:94,96; *K'93*:60,64,223; *K'94*:102
Sornberger, Jim: *K'91*:128,158,163; *K'92*:75,236; *K'95*:140,233

Spano, Dominick W.: *K'95*:83,110
Spinale, Richard: *K'91*:157; *K'92*:73; *K'93*:67,223; *K'95*:76
Stafford, Michael: *K'94*:115
Stafford, Richard: *K'91*:114,239; *K'92*:237,238; *K'93*:140
Stalter, Harry L.: *K'91*:76,94; *K'92*:125,239; *K'93*:117
Stapel, Chuck: *K'91*:89,113,134,239; *K'93*:108,222; *K'94*:218; *K'95*:81
Stegall, Keith: *K'91*:103; *K'92*:238
Steigerwalt, Ken: *K'91*:70,241; *K'93*:70,71; *K'95*:101
Steinau, Jurgen: *K'92*:96,138; *K'93*:222
Steinberg, Al: *K'92*:238
Stewart, Charles (Chuck): *K'91*:65,239; *K'92*:73, 80; *K'93*:72,75,80; *K'94*:89,94,102; *K'95*:134
Stewart, Patrick C.: *K'92*:120,238
Stockdale, Walt: *K'95*:162
Stokes, Ed: *K'94*:67,77,218; *K'95*:82,90,233
Strong, Scott: *K'91*:100,116,240; *K'92*:140,237; *K'93*:85; *K'94*:72,111,218
Stuart, V. Pat: *K'92*:114
Stumpff, Jr., George: *K'91*:241
Suedmeier, Harlan: *K'91*:94; *K'93*:223
Sullivent, Loyd: *K'92*:121,237; *K'93*:54
Summers, Arthur L.: *K'95*:161,233
Sunderland, Richard: *K'91*:161; *K'92*:236
Swain, Rod: *K'93*:89,138
Szilaski, Joseph: *K'94*:218; *K'95*:102

t

Taglienti, Antonio J.: *K'92*:93
Takahashi, Masao: *K'94*:66,68
Tamboli, Michael: *K'91*:77,246; *K'92*:127; *K'93*:73,115; *K'94*:86,220
Tasaki, Seichi: *K'91*:78
Tay, Larry: *K'92*:99
Taylor, C. Gray: *K'91*:68,72; *K'92*:83; *K'94*:Cover,93; *K'95*:74,159
Taylor, David: *K'93*:225; *K'94*:86,221; *K'95*:132
Taylor, Shane: *K'94*:83,221; *K'95*:120,235
Terzuola, Robert: *K'91*:68; *K'92*:83,140,247; *K'94*:90,138; *K'95*:75
Thayer, Danny: *K'91*:97; *K'92*:247; *K'94*:109,221
Thomas, Kim: *K'95*:89
Thompson, Kenneth: *K'93*:225; *K'94*:221
Thompson, Leon: *K'91*:68; *K'92*:76,246; *K'93*:225; *K'94*:87,220; *K'95*:235
Thompson, Randy: *K'95*:175
Thompson, Robert L.: *K'95*:113,234
Thourot, Michael W.: *K'91*:246; *K'92*:57,61; *K'93*:225; *K'94*:68,76,221; *K'95*:111
Toich, Nevio: *K'94*:220; *K'95*:234
Tollefson, Barry A.: *K'92*:247
Tokar, Daniel: *K'93*:125,137
Tomes, Anthony S.: *K'91*:246
Tomes, P.J.: *K'91*:152,155,246; *K'92*:109; *K'93*:Cover,146; *K'94*:148
Toner, Roger: *K'92*:156; *K'93*:85,152,223,224; *K'95*:234
Topliss, M.W.: *K'95*:235
Towell, Dwight L.: *K'91*:64,246; *K'94*:75
Townsend, J.W.: *K'91*:94; *K'92*:88,139,246; *K'93*:108; *K'94*:117,119,136
Treiber, Leon: *K'94*:74,97; *K'95*:132,234
Treml, Glenn: *K'92*:246; *K'93*:94,224
Trindle, Barry: *K'91*:66,246; *K'92*:72,246; *K'93*:224; *K'95*:161
Tuoteet, Lauri: *K'91*:11
Turcotte, Larry: *K'94*:220; *K'95*:102
Turecek, Jim: *K'91*:246; *K'92*:106,247; *K'93*:64; *K'94*:101,105
Turnbull, Ralph A.: *K'91*:58,88,104,144,246; *K'92*:54,126,246,247; *K'93*:224; *K'94*:96,105; *K'95*:234
Turunen, Pentti: *K'92*:25
Tyc, William J.: *K'93*:87
Tyer, Jerry L.: *K'94*:124,221

u

Ueda, Masaharu: *K'94*:104
Uekama, Nobuyuki: *K'93*:89
Ulrich, Micheal H.: *K'91*:86
Urstadt, E.W.: *K'91*:247

directory

v

Valachovic, Wayne: *K'91*:70,247; *K'92*:84,247; *K'93*:225; *K'94*:100; *K'95*:235
Vallotton, Butch: *K'93*:224; *K'94*:134; *K'95*:135
Vallotton, Shawn: *K'93*:224
Valois, A. Daniel: *K'92*:137,246
Van Eldik, Frans: *K'91*:83,247; *K'93*:58,99; *K'94*:128,220
Van Elkins, R.: *K'92*:93
Veatch, Richard: *K'93*:117
Veit, Michael: *K'91*:68,101,156; *K'92*:75,246; *K'94*:93,133,221
Vensild, Henrik: *K'92*:25
Viallon, Henri: *K'91*:83,247; *K'92*:94,135,149; *K'93*:60,225; *K'94*:101,129,220; *K'95*:151,235
Vistnes, Tor: *K'94*:133,220
Von Boeckman, R.: *K'91*:247; *K'92*:107,246
Voss, Ben: *K'91*:246; *K'92*:90,247; *K'93*:76,100,225; *K'94*:106
Vought, Jr., Frank: *K'91*:92,102,105,115,247; *K'92*:57,102,246; *K'93*:65,225; *K'94*:108; *K'95*:121
Vunk, Robert: *K'91*:85,130,247; *K'92*:67,105,148,149; *K'93*:103,132

w

Waddle, Thomas: *K'91*:63,250
Wagaman, John K.: *K'91*:123,145; *K'92*:253; *K'93*:227
Waldrop, Mark: *K'92*:70
Walker, George A.: *K'91*:153
Walker, John W.: *K'95*:110,236
Walker, Michael L.: *K'91*:67,157; *K'92*:143,151; *K'95*:70,124
Wallace, Roger L.: *K'92*:253
Walters, Brian K.: *K'91*:250
Ward, Chuck: *K'94*:223; *K'95*:107
Wardell, Michael Ronald: *K'94*:122
Warden, Roy A.: *K'91*:250; *K'92*:253; *K'93*:133; *K'94*:222; *K'95*:236
Warenski, Buster: *K'91*:70,99,250; *K'92*:104,152,252; *K'93*:105,151,226; *K'94*:80,76,92,147; *K'95*:69,71

Warren, Al: *K'91*:119,250
Watanabe, Wayne: *K'94*:126,222; *K'95*:237
Watson, Billy: *K'94*:73; *K'95*:113,237
Watson, Daniel and Billy: *K'92*:141; *K'93*:226
Watson, Tom: *K'91*:251; *K'92*:144; *K'93*:100,146
Wattelet, Michael A.: *K'93*:110
Watts, Wally: *K'91*:71,250; *K'92*:76; *K'93*:74,78; *K'94*:88
Webb Jr., Charley L.: *K'95*:107,237
Webb, Jim: *K'94*:123,222
Wegner, Tim: *K'93*:123
Wehner, Rudy: *K'94*:223
Weiland, Jr., J. Reese: *K'91*:251; *K'92*:253; *K'93*:147,227; *K'94*:222; *K'95*:67,92,164
Weiler, Donald E.: *K'91*:250; *K'93*:84; *K'94*:110,127
Weinand, Gerome W.: *K'91*:251; *K'92*:64,65,253; *K'93*:105,227; *K'94*:70,136
Weiss, Charles L.: *K'91*:101,117,251; *K'92*:87,252; *K'93*:145; *K'95*:97,153
Werner Jr., William A.: *K'95*:154
Werth, George W.: *K'95*:113
Wescott, Cody: *K'91*:251; *K'93*:150,227; *K'94*:77,99
West, Pat: *K'92*:253
Westberg, Larry: *K'93*:227
Whipple, Wesley A.: *K'92*:71
White, Gene E.: *K'94*:68,84,223; *K'95*:237
White, Robert J.: *K'91*:60
White, Jr., Robert J. "Butch": *K'91*:59; *K'92*:253
Whitehead, James D.: *K'91*:75,250; *K'92*:121; *K'93*:113,115; *K'95*:86
Whitley, Weldon G.: *K'92*:252
Wilder, Barry: *K'91*:87
Willey, W.G.: *K'91*:160
Williams, David: *K'93*:102; *K'94*:127,133
Williams, Jason L.: *K'95*:131,144,237
Williams, Leonard: *K'95*:99,108,144
Williams, Sherman A.: *K'91*:251; *K'92*:60,103,252; *K'93*:124
Willson III, George H.: *K'93*:226
Wilson, Jon J.: *K'94*:84
Wilson, Mike: *K'95*:110,236
Wimpff, Christian: *K'95*:116,237
Wingo, Perry: *K'92*:253
Winkler, Daniel: *K'91*:59,86,95,153,251; *K'92*:

84,252; *K'93*:140,141,154,226; *K'94*:Cover,100,112; *K'95*:112,163
Winn, Travis A.: *K'92*:71
Witsaman, Earl: *K'91*:75; *K'92*:122,124; *K'93*:113,117,128,226; *K'94*:83,84,222; *K'95*:86,87
Wolf, Bill: *K'92*:58,61,91,252; *K'93*:72,79; *K'95*:92,132,137
Wood, Alan: *K'94*:130,222
Wood, Owen Dale: *K'93*:59,69,137,226
Wood, Webster: *K'92*:252; *K'95*:103,138
Wood, William W.: *K'91*:157; *K'93*:106,150; *K'94*:85
Workman Jr., Hubert L.: *K'94*:115
Wright, Adam: *K'94*:67
Wright, Kevin: *K'91*:76,251; *K'93*:143
Wright, Timothy: *K'92*:141
Wyatt, Alan: *K'91*:72

y

Yeates, Joe A.: *K'92*:124; *K'93*:93,115; *K'94*:110,223; *K'95*:90,236
Young, Bud: *K'91*:105
Young, Errol:; *K'93*:114
Young, J.A.:; *K'93*:75
Yurco, Mike: *K'91*:93,126,254; *K'92*:255; *K'94*:104,223

z

Zaccagnino, Don: *K'91*:119,149,254; *K'93*:94; *K'94*:71,223; *K'95*:95,109
Zakabi, Carl S.: *K'93*:89,136; *K'94*:222; *K'95*:121,146
Zembko III, John: *K'91*:254; *K'92*:255; *K'95*:237
Zemetis, Joe: *K'91*:79,254; *K'92*:98; *K'93*:93,227; *K'94*:223; *K'95*:114,165,236
Zima, Michael F.: *K'91*:254; *K'92*:55,255; *K'93*:104,227; *K'94*:86,96
Zinsmeister, Paul D.: *K'92*:255; *K'93*:79,227
Zowada, Tim: *K'92*:112,134,136,255; *K'93*:88,132; *K'94*:97; *K'95*:98,122,236
Zscherny, Michael: *K'91*:63

engravers

Alfano, Sam: *K'93*:Cover; *K'94*:120
Allred, Scott: *K'95*:140
Bates, Billy: *K'91*:102; *K'92*:50,153; *K'93*:73; *K'94*:149; *K'95*:137,138,139,162
Beaver, Judy: *K'95*:159
Becker, Franz: *K'91*:157
Blair, Jim: *K'95*:158,161
Blanchard, Gary: *K'91*:158,159,163; *K'92*:74
Boster, A.D.: *K'91*:Cover,99; *K'92*:152; *K'93*:147,150,151; *K'94*:96,147
Butler, Martin: *K'91*:100,128,156; *K'92*:74,104,151; *K'93*:151; *K'95*:74,158,167
Carter, Fred: *K'91*:90,101; *K'93*:67,149
Churchill, Winston: *K'91*:63; *K'94*:145,147
Collins, David: *K'92*:170
Collins, Michael: *K'91*:112; *K'95*:140
Cover, Jr., Raymond A.: *K'93*:154; *K'94*:146
Davidson, Jere: *K'93*:148; *K'95*:Cover,76,101,160
Dean, Bruce: *K'95*:109,137
Draper, Kent: *K'93*:149
Dubben, Michael: *K'94*:95
Dubber: *K'93*:88
Eaton, Rick: *K'93*:149; *K'94*:145; *K'95*:158,160
Eldridge, Allan: *K'91*:125
Ence, Jim: *K'93*:150
Erhardt, Arnold: *K'93*:153
Flannery, Jeff: *K'91*:70,121; *K'92*:153; *K'93*:73; *K'94*:118
Fogle, James W.: *K'93*:151
Foster, Norvell:; *K'93*:73
Fracassi, Firmo: *K'93*:146
French, J.R.: *K'94*:95; *K'95*:108,139
Foster, Norvell: *K'91*:59
Galleazzi, A.: *K'92*:151
George, Tim: *K'95*:159
George, Tim and Christy: *K'92*:73; *K'93*:66,67,72
Glimm, Jerome C.: 152

Goodwin, Dan: *K'92*:72
Gournet, Geoffroy R.: *K'92*:150; *K'93*:63; *K'94*:95
Graf, Don: *K'95*:139
Harrington, Fred A.: *K'92*:51,74,150; *K'93*:75,106,151; *K'94*:102,146; *K'95*:125,159
Henderson, Don: *K'95*:138
Henderson, Fred D.: *K'91*:63
Hendricks, Frank E.: *K'92*:75
Herman, Tim: *K'91*:70; *K'93*:148; *K'94*:95
Holder, Pat: *K'93*:73; *K'95*:161
Horvath, Kurt: *K'93*:66
Hudson, Tommy: *K'92*:52,150; *K'93*:74
Hurst, Ken: *K'92*:74
Jacobs, Yuri: *K'93*:90
Johns, Bill: *K'95*:140
Kaluza, Werner: *K'95*:159
Kelly, Lance: *K'91*:101
Kelso, Jim: *K'93*:67
Lageose, Tony: *K'92*:72; *K'93*:151
LaPage, Tony: *K'91*:116
Lee, Ray: *K'91*:103
Leschorn, Tony: *K'91*:112; *K'93*:148
Limings, Jr., Harry: *K'91*:92; *K'92*:74,126; *K'93*:145
Lindsay, Steve: *K'91*:64; *K'93*:148; *K'94*:93,146,147
Lister, Weldon: *K'91*:62,71; *K'92*:75,151; *K'93*:88
Lyttle, Brian: *K'92*:151; *K'93*:149; *K'94*:145; *K'95*:159
Lytton, Simon M.: *K'91*:159; *K'92*:63,73,94,98; *K'93*:85,150
Marek, George: *K'91*:89
McCombs, Leo: *K'95*:138
McHenry, William James: *K'93*:149
McKenzie, Lynton: *K'92*:51,151,153; *K'93*:66,83
Mendenhall, Harry E.: *K'91*:69; *K'92*:79,108,150; *K'93*:150; *K'95*:101,160
Meyer, Chris: *K'91*:157
Morton, David A.: *K'94*:77,94,102; *K'95*:161
Nixon, Jim: *K'94*:149

Oberdorfer, Fritz: *K'95*:104,160
Old Dominion Engravers: *K'91*:70,72,157,158,159; *K'92*:153; *K'93*:72,92
Parsons, Michael R.: *K'91*:158,159; *K'92*:150; *K'93*:149
Pederson, Rex: *K'93*:73
Pedini, Marcello: *K'93*:73
Perdue, David: *K'94*:130; *K'95*:160
Pilkington, Jr., Scott: *K'91*:62,64,158; *K'92*:73; *K'93*:72; *K'94*:146; *K'95*:160
Poag,James:; *K'91*:156
Pursley, Aaron: *K'91*:116,158; *K'94*:94
Raftis, Andrew: *K'92*:152
Robyn, Jon: *K'91*:65,104; *K'92*:170; *K'93*:72
Rudolph, Gil: *K'92*:75
Rundell, Joe: *K'93*:105; *K'94*:102
Sanchez, Lewis B.: *K'91*:62,116; *K'92*:62; *K'93*:114; *K'94*:107
Scharnagel: *K'91*:82
Schmidt, R.: *K'93*:58
Scott, Alvin: *K'91*:64; *K'95*:161
Selent, Chuck: *K'92*:75
Shaw, Bruce: *K'91*:157,159; *K'92*:68; *K'93*:73,148,154; *K'95*:137,154
Sherwood, George: *K'91*:66,91; *K'92*:118; *K'93*:82
Shostle, Ben: *K'91*:91,163; *K'92*:150,153; *K'93*:Cover,72,89,149; *K'94*:109,144,147; *K'95*:76
Sinclair, W.P.: *K'93*:150; *K'95*:160
Skaggs, R.E.: *K'91*:64,101,156; *K'92*:152; *K'93*:66,148; *K'94*:Cover; *K'95*:Inside Cover,75,77,96,98,100,125,159
Smith, Ron: *K'91*:117; *K'92*:170; *K'94*:144; *K'95*:75
Sornberger, Jim: *K'91*:158
Spinale, Richard: *K'91*:157; *K'93*:67; *K'94*:144
Stewart, James: *K'92*:71; *K'93*:125
Stoltz, Stanley: *K'92*:150
Swartley, Robert D.: *K'95*:75

Takeuchi, Shigetoshi: *K'93*:58
Taylor, David: *K'94*:147
Theis, Terry: *K'91*:64,69; *K'93*:150; *K'95*:139
Tomlin, Lisa: *K'92*:73; *K'93*:72; *K'94*:95; *K'95*:84
Trindle, Barry: *K'91*:94; *K'95*:161
Valade, Robert: *K'91*:131
Vancura: *K'92*:70
Vinnecombe: *K'91*:79

Vos, Eduard: *K'91*:83; *K'93*:58
Waldrop, Mark: *K'93*:72; *K'95*:136
Walker, Patricia: *K'91*:58,61,67,157; *K'92*:81,151
Warenski, Buster: *K'91*:70,99; *K'94*:144
Warenski, Julie: *K'91*:89,101,159; *K'92*:152; *K'93*:67,83,105,151; *K'94*:147; *K'95*:69,77,158
Warren, Kenneth: *K'91*:156,159; *K'92*:152; *K'93*:76
Wescott, Cody: *K'93*:150

Wessinger, Rose: *K'95*:94
Whitehead, James D.: *K'93*:113,115
Whitener, Nellie: *K'95*:161
Wilkerson, Dan: *K'93*:100; *K'94*:146
Williams, Gary: *K'93*:113
Winkler, Armin: *K'93*:58
Wood, Mel: *K'91*:99; *K'93*:151

scrimshanders

Bailey, Mary W.: *K'91*:155; *K'92*:148,149; *K'93*:146
Barrett, R.W.: *K'94*:149; *K'95*:162
Beauchamp, Gaetan: *K'95*:164
Bellet, Connie: *K'93*:145
Bonshire, Benita: *K'94*:149
Bowles, Rick: *K'91*:112,152,155; *K'92*:147; *K'93*:146; *K'94*:148
Brady, Sandra: *K'91*:154; *K'93*:145,146,147; *K'94*:148,150,151; *K'95*:164,165
Burdette, Bob: *K'93*:92,147; *K'95*:108,147
Clark, Chris: *K'91*:116; *K'92*:147,149
Collins, Michael: *K'91*:112
Cosimini, Rene Danielle: *K'94*:150,151
Cover, Jr., Raymond A.: *K'91*:152
Cox, Andy: *K'92*:146
Dolbare, Elizabeth: *K'94*:151
Engnath, Bob: *K'91*:104,152,153,154; *K'92*:149; *K'94*:148,149
Erickson, Linda: *K'92*:68
Fields, Rick B.: *K'91*:78,154,155; *K'92*:74,146,147,148; *K'93*:145,146,147;

K'94:148; *K'95*:162,163,164
Fisk, Dale: *K'94*:150
Fracassi, Firmo: *K'93*:146
Garbe, Sandra: *K'95*:139
Hargraves, Sr., Charles: *K'91*:155; *K'92*:148; *K'93*:144; *K'94*:148,151; *K'95*:162
Harless, Star: *K'92*:146,148; *K'93*:147
Hergert, Bob: *K'93*:114,144; *K'95*:162,165
Himmelheber, David R.: *K'95*:164
Holland, Dennis K.: *K'92*:146; *K'94*:149; *K'95*:140
Karst, Linda K.: *K'91*:153; *K'92*:50,84,146,148,149; *K'93*:68,84,144,145,147; *K'95*:Cover,139,162,165
Keidel, Gene: *K'95*:162
Kondrla, Denise: *K'92*:126,147; *K'93*:Cover,116,144
McFall, Ken: *K'95*:164
McGrath, Gayle: *K'91*:109,116; *K'93*:115,146; *K'94*:149
McLaran, Lou: *K'93*:73
Mead, Faustina L.: *K'93*:147; *K'95*:163,164
Minnick, Joyce: *K'91*:161

Morris, Darrel: *K'94*:150; *K'95*:165
Ochonicky, Michelle: *K'91*:155
Petree, Linda A.: *K'91*:73; *K'92*:68
Purvis, Hilton: *K'91*:154
Rece, Charles V.: *K'92*:147; *K'93*:144; *K'94*:151
Raoux, Serge: *K'92*:149
Rizzini, Aldo: *K'92*:149
Russ, Joann: *K'93*:75
Selent, Chuck: *K'91*:154; *K'93*:116,145; *K'94*:150
Semrich, Alice: *K'91*:119
Smuck, Bruce: *K'93*:85
Talley, Mary Austin: *K'91*:152,153; *K'92*:124
Walker, Karen: *K'91*:153; *K'92*:149,252
Williams, Gary: *K'91*:75,77,94,152,154; *K'93*:136,144,145; *K'94*:83,151; *K'95*:Inside Cover,76,146,163
Young, Mary: *K'93*:114
Zemitis, Jolanta: *K'95*:165

etchers/carvers

Anderson, Jim: *K'93*:153
Bartrug, Hugh E.: *K'93*:152
Beaver, Judy: *K'91*:164; *K'93*:153
Bourbeau: *K'95*:166
Boye, David: *K'92*:155
Burrows, Stephen R.: *K'95*:167
Casteel, Doug: *K'95*:166
Cover, Jr., Raymond A.: *K'93*:154
DeBraga, Jose C.: *K'93*:152; *K'95*:167
DiMarzo, Richard: *K'92*:126,154; *K'94*:116; *K'95*:167
Ellefson, Joel: *K'95*:167
Eubanks, Mary Ann: *K'91*:164
Evans, Dale: *K'93*:154
Ferguson, Jim: *K'92*:154; *K'93*:154; *K'94*:152
Fuegen, Larry: *K'92*:154

Fuller, Jack A.: *K'92*:155
Greco, John: *K'95*:166
Grussenmeyer, Paul:: *K'93*:152,153,154; *K'94*:115,152; *K'95*:166,167
Harrison, Lou: *K'93*:96
Hayes, Dolores: *K'92*:156
Hoffman, Kevin L.: *K'93*:153
Hudson, C. Robbin: *K'94*:152
Imboden II, Howard L.: *K'91*:164; *K'92*:155; *K'93*:154
Kalyna, Greg: *K'93*:152
Kelso, Jim: *K'92*:155; *K'94*:152; *K'95*:166
Leibowitz, Leonard: *K'91*:158,160; *K'92*:156; *K'93*:72; *K'94*:152
Leschorn, Tom: *K'92*:156
Lonewolf, J. Aguirre: *K'93*:153; *K'94*:152; *K'95*:167

MacBain, Ken: *K'93*:152
Martrildonno, Paul: *K'92*:156
McConnell, Loyd: *K'92*:156
Meyers, Ron: *K'92*:154
Myers, Ron:: *K'93*:148; *K'94*:152
Nealy, Bud: *K'92*:155
Nolfi, Tim: *K'93*:154
Olsen, Geoff: *K'95*:166
Quarton, Barr: *K'92*:154
Ramsey, Dale: *K'92*:154
Rothenburger Waffeneck: *K'91*:83
Russell, Michael: *K'92*:154
Sornberger, Jim: *K'95*:167
Toner, Roger: *K'92*:156

leatherwork/sheathmakers

Barnett, Jack: *K'94*:25
Barr, A.T.: *K'94*:142
Cashen, Kevin R.: *K'95*:170
Davidson, Hal: *K'95*:149
Dawkins, Dudley: *K'94*:141; *K'95*:168
Defeo, Robert A.: *K'95*:170
Dennehy, John D.: *K'94*:141
Dunn, Melvin T.: *K'95*:169
Fister, Jim: *K'95*:169
Foley, Barney: *K'95*:168,170

Frey, Jim: *K'95*:111
Halligan, Ed: *K'95*:168
Layton, Jim: *K'94*:20
Lee, Sonja: *K'95*:169
Lile, Jimmy: *K'95*:169
Lozier, Don: *K'95*:170
Polkowski, Al: *K'94*:142; *K'95*:169,170
Potier, Timothy: *K'94*:51
Reeve, Chris: *K'95*:168
Rippys, The: *K'94*:142

Rowe, Kenny: *K'94*:141; *K'95*:93,96,170
Schrap, Robert G.: *K'94*:141; *K'95*:170
Sellevold, Harald: *K'94*:142
Shook, Karen: *K'95*:112
Stuart, Pat: *K'94*:141
Tierney, Mike: *K'94*:141
Turner, Kevin: *K'94*:142
Wegner, Tim: *K'94*:19,20,140
Weiler, Donald E.: *K'94*:142

handle artisans

Crosslen, T.J.: *K'92*:169
Davidson, Hal: *K'95*:148,149
DiMarzo, Richard: *K'91*:163
Eubanks, Mary Ann: *K'92*:156
Hirayama, Harumi: *K'92*:170
Holder, Pat: *K'93*:115

Jones, Paul: *K'94*:115
Katz, Brian: *K'92*:141
Kelso, Jim: *K'94*:79,152
Lane, Tom: *K'94*:97
Marvis, Paul M.: *K'93*:105
Miller, Robert: *K'93*:105

Myers, Ron: *K'92*:156
Paranto, Craig: *K'93*:153
Rardon, A.D.: *K'93*:116
Sayen, Murad: *K'93*:152

specialty cutlers

The firms listed here are special in the sense that they make or market special kinds of knives made in facilities they own or control either in the U.S. or overseas. Or they are special because they make knives of unique design or function.

ACE OF BLADES
P.O. Box 3336
Fairfax, VA 22038
Phone: 703-904-8629
Specialties: Discreet personal defense cutlery by John Mitchell, owner and designer.

ADAMS INTERNATIONAL KNIFEWORKS
(See Importers & Foreign Cutlers)

AMERICAN WILDERNESS
P.O. Box 25208
Colorado Springs, CO 80936
Phone: 719-574-4462
FAX: 719-574-4462
Specialties: Multi-functional survival tools.

ANZA FILE KNIVES
(See Blair Blades & Accessories—Mail-Order Sales)

B&D TRADING CO.
3935 Fair Hill Rd.
Fair Oaks, CA 95628
Phone: 916-967-9366;800-334-3790
FAX: 916-967-4873
Specialties: Carries the full line of Executive Edge—Brazil's locking folders.

BARTEAUX MACHETES, INC.
1916 S.E. 50th St.
Portland, OR 97215
Phone: 503-233-5880
FAX: 503-233-5838
Specialties: Machetes of high-carbon and stainless steel. Line greatly expanded of late.

BECKER KNIFE and TOOL CO. (See Blackjack Knives)

BENCHMADE KNIFE CO. INC.
15875-G SE 114th St.
Clackamas, OR 97015
Phone: 503-655-6004
FAX: 503-655-6223
Specialties: Balisong knives, tactical patterns in folders, axes and big knives. U.S. production.

BENCHMARK KNIVES (See Gerber Legendary Blades— General Cutlers)

BERETTA U.S.A. CORP.
17601 Beretta Dr.
Accokeek, MD 20607
Phone: 301-283-2101
Specialties: A variety of Beretta-only designs, including folding tactical knives.

BLACKJACK KNIVES
Also Condor Sport Knives, Becker Knife and Tool Co., Ek Commando Knive Co., Cripple Creek Knives
1307 W. Wabash Ave.
Effingham, IL 62401
Phone: 217-347-7700
FAX: 217-347-7737
Specialties: High-tech self-defense and adventure patterns with names like Mamba, Trail Guide, Halo; also high-end hunters and a variety of specialty patterns. Has own factory in Effingham.

BROWNING
Rt. 1
Morgan, UT 84050
Phone: 800-333-3288
Specialties: Has its own name on sports knives of all kinds, all in Browning finish.

BRUNTON CO.
620 E. Monroe St.
Riverton, WY 82501
Phone: 307-856-6559
FAX: 307-856-1840
Specialties: Heavy-duty sports knives, straight and folding, on a distinctive design theme.

COLD STEEL, INC.
2128-D Knoll Dr.
Ventura, CA 93003
Phone: 800-255-4716
FAX: 805-642-9727
Specialties: Variety of urban survival instruments—big in tantos. Bowie and Hunter; several new and exclusive specialty designs.

COLONIAL KNIFE CO., INC. (See General Cutlers)

CONDOR SPORT KNIVES (See Blackjack Knives)

CRIPPLE CREEK KNIVES (See Blackjack Knives)

CTECH PLASTICS ENGINEERING
Shaun Cavanaugh
207B Calle De Los Molinos
San Clemente, CA 92672
Phone: 714-492-7305

FAX: 714-492-9665
Specialties: Knives in thermosets and thermoplastics. Custom injection molding, prototype tooling and engineering services.

EK COMMANDO KNIFE CO. (See Blackjack Knives)

EQUIP USA
666 Grand Ave.
Mancos, CO 81328
Phone: 303-533-7982
Specialties: Vaughan Neely designs, such as the Timberlite, plus Timberline knives.

F&H MARKETING, INC.
3165 A-2 S. Campbell
Springfield, MO 65807
Phone: 417-886-CUTT
Specialties: Manufacturer of the Honeycomb.

GT KNIVES
7716 Arsons Dr.
San Diego, CA 92126
Phone: 619-566-1511
FAX: 619-530-0734
Specialties: High-tech machined folders.

HANDMADE CLASSICS
P.O. Box 578373
Chicago, IL 60657
Phone: 312-944-4307
Specialties: Authentic hand-forged replicas of period pieces, currently doing Scagel, Bowie, and Early File knife. Brochure $1.

H&B FORGE CO.
Rt. 2, Geisinger Rd.
Shiloh, OH 44878
Phone: 419-895-1856
Specialties: Tomahawks and throwing knives.

IMPERIAL SCHRADE CORP. (See General Cutlers)

IRON MOUNTAIN KNIFE CO.
1270 Greg St.
Sparks, NV 89431-6005
Phone: 702-356-3632
FAX: 702-356-3640
Specialties: Line of fixed-blade hunters based on special patented handle shape.

KATZ KNIVES, INC.
P.O. Box 730
Chandler, AZ 85224
Phone: 602-786-9334
FAX: 602-786-9338

KERSHAW/KAI CUTLERY CO.
25300 SW Parkway
Wilsonville, OR 97070
Phone: 503-682-1966
Specialties: Former Gerber designer's heavy-duty sports knives made overseas; also smaller "pocket jewelry"; handsome scrimshaw; new designs in using knives.

KNIVES OF ALASKA, INC.
P.O. Box 675
Cordova, AK 99574 (Northern office)
715 N. Tone
Denison, TX 75020 (Southern office)
Phone: 800-572-0980
FAX: 903-463-7165
Specialties: Husky edged tools for big game hunting and fishing.

LAKOTA U.S.A. (See Brunton/Lakota U.S.A.)

LEATHERMAN TOOL GROUP, INC.
12106 NE Ainsworth Cir.
P.O. Box 20595
Portland, OR 97220
Phone: 503-253-7826
FAX: 503-253-7830
Specialties: All-in-one pocket tool in two sizes.

MAR KNIVES, INC., AL
5755 SW Jean Rd., Suite 101
Lake Oswego, OR 97035
Phone: 503-635-9229
Specialties: Founded by the late Al Mar, a designer, the company continues to market Mar's designs under the direction of Ann Mar.

MISSION KNIVES, INC.
P.O. Box 1616
San Juan Capistrano, CA 92693
Phone: 714-661-3879
Specialties: Titanium blade knives and all titanium folders. Currently supplying certified non-magnetic SPECWAR knives to the U.S. Navy SEALS and EOD teams.

MORTY THE KNIFE MAN, INC.
60 Otis St.
West Babylon, NY 11704

Phone: 516-491-5764/800-247-2511
Specialties: Everything for the fish trade; own and make both U.S. and import brands; includes many working knives not easily found, as well as chain mesh protection gloves and aprons.

MUSEUM REPLICAS LTD.
2143 Gees Mill Rd., Box 840XZ
Conyers, GA 30207
Phone: 404-922-3703
Specialties: Authentic edged weapons of the ages, battle-ready—over 50 models; subsidiary of Atlanta Cutlery; catalog $2.

MYERCHIN MARINE CLASSICS
P.O. Box 911
Rialto, CA 92376
Phone: 714-875-3592
FAX: 909-874-6058
Specialties: The Myerchin Offshore System—a quality cutlery package for the yachtsman or deep water sailor; supplier to the U.S. Navy and Coast Guard.

OUTDOOR EDGE CUTLERY CORP.
2888 Bluff St., Suite 130
Boulder, CO 80301
Phone: 303-652-8212
FAX: 303-652-8238
Specialties: All-in-one tools for preparing game and all-purpose field use.

PILTDOWN PRODUCTIONS
Errett Callahan
2 Fredonia Ave.
Lynchburg, VA 24503
Phone: 804-528-3444
Specialties: Makes obsidian scalpels and knives; replicates Stone Age tools and weapons—all types—for museums and academia. $3 for catalog.

REMINGTON ARMS CO., INC.
1011 Centre Rd.
Delle Donne Corp. Ctr.
Wilmington, DE 19805
Phone: 800-243-9700
Specialties: Old and new patterns in the Remington style and more to come.

SANTA FE STONEWORKS
3790 Cerrillos Rd.
Santa Fe, NM 87505
Phone: 505-471-3953
FAX: 505-471-0036
Specialties: Embellished personal and gift cutlery and desk accessories.

SOG SPECIALTY KNIVES, INC.
P.O. Box 1024
Edmonds, WA 98020
Phone: 206-771-6230
Specialties: High-quality folding and combat knives, and a multi-tool, as well.

SOQUE RIVER KNIVES
P.O. Box 880
Clarksville, GA 30523
Phone: 706-754-8500
FAX: 706-754-7263
Specialties: Manufacturers of uniquely designed folding knives, beginning with the Lev-R-Lok, a quick-opener.

SPYDERCO, INC.
P.O. Box 800
Golden, CO 80402
Phone: 303-279-8383
FAX: 303-278-2229
Specialties: Clipit folding knives; sharpening gear. Has kitchen and diving knives and new stuff every year.

SWISS ARMY BRANDS LTD.
(See Importers & Foreign Cutlers)

TRU-BALANCE KNIFE CO.
2155 Tremont Blvd., NW
Grand Rapids, MI 49504
Phone: 616-453-3679
Specialties: The late Harry McEvoy's full line of throwers—a design for any throwing job. Can provide custom-made throwing knives. Catalog and throwing instructions can be had with a SASE.

WENOKA SEA STYLE
P.O. Box 10969
Riviera Beach, FL 33419-0969
Phone: 407-845-6155
FAX: 407-842-4247
Specialties: First a full line of divers' knives; now a beefy folder.

WYOMING KNIFE CORP.
101 Commerce Dr.
Ft. Collins, CO 80524
Phone: 303-224-3454
Specialties: A tool for dealing with game animals—gutting and skinning. Also makes a short folding saw, and the Powder River folders.

general cutlers

These are, plain and simple, knife factories. Some are giants; some not so big; some are a century old; some just two decades in existence. All market very complete lines of knives, generally through standard mercantile channels.

ALCAS CUTLERY CORP. (See Cutco Cutlery)

AMERICAN CONSUMER PRODUCTS, INC.
  (See Ka-Bar Knives)

BEAR MGC CUTLERY
1111 Bear Blvd. SW
Jacksonville, AL 36265
Phone: 205-435-2227
FAX: 205-435-9348
Specialties: General line of traditional folders and belt knives—wide range of patterns.

BUCK KNIVES
1900 Weld Blvd.
El Cajon, CA 92020
Phone: 619-449-1100
Specialties: Creators of the belt folder syndrome; sturdy, solid working knives widely sold.

CAMILLUS CUTLERY CO.
54 Main St.
Camillus, NY 13031
Phone: 315-672-8111
Specialties: Long-time competitor in all phases of cutlery; military knife contractor; some neat pocketknife designs. Makes and markets Western knives.

CASE & SONS CUTLERY CO., W.R.
Owens Way
Bradford, PA 16701
Phone: 814-368-4123
FAX: 814-368-5369
Specialties: At the same old stand producing the good base patterns, and widely advertised these days.

CHICAGO CUTLERY CO.
1536 Beech St.
Terre Haute, IN 47804
Phone: 800-457-2665
Specialties: Solid utility knives; a full line of kitchen cutlery; owned by General Housewares Corp.

COAST CUTLERY (See Importers & Foreign Cutlers)

COLONIAL KNIFE CO., INC.
Steve Paolantonio
Agnes at Magnolia St.
Providence, RI 02909
Phone: 800-556-7824
FAX: 401-421-2047
Specialties: Commercial pocketknives for competitive pricing; some belt knives.

CUTCO CUTLERY
P.O. Box 810
Olean, NY 14760
Phone: 716-372-3111
Specialties: Kitchen cutlery—American-made shears, steak knife sets, some sportsman knives. Parent company—Alcas Cutlery Corp.

FISKARS (See Gerber Legendary Blades)

GERBER LEGENDARY BLADES
14200 SW 72nd Ave.
Portland, OR 97281
Phone: 503-639-6161
FAX: 503-684-7008
Specialties: Well-known sports and dining cutlery line, plus Fiskars cutlery and Benchmark specialty knives.

GIESSER MESSERFABRIK GMBH, JOHANNES (See Importers & Foreign Cutlers)

IMPERIAL SCHRADE CORP.
7 Schrade Ct.
Ellenville, NY 12428
Phone: 914-647-7600
FAX: 914-647-8701
Specialties: Probably the biggest; owns Imperial and Schrade. Sells many labels in several brands, U.S.-made and imported.

KA-BAR KNIVES
Ka-Bar Knives, Collectors Division

31100 Solon Rd.
Solon, OH 44139
Phone: 216-248-7000; 800-321-9316 (Ext. 329)
FAX: 216-348-8051
Specialties: Sells working sports cutlery. Made the first WWII Marine Corps knife, a design still in service. Imports Sabre knives. Collectors division specializes in commemoratives and special models. A division of American Consumer Products, Inc.

ONTARIO KNIFE CO.
P.O. Box 145
Franklinville, NY 14737
Phone: 716-676-5527
FAX: 716-676-5535
Specialties: Some pocketknives; many styles of utility knives for household and restaurant use. Brands, both Hickory and Colonial Forge. Excellent values.

QUEEN CUTLERY
P.O. Box 500
Franklinville, NY 14737
Phone: 716-676-5527
FAX: 716-676-5535
Specialties: Old name. The line is growing, moving toward collector appeal.

SCHRADE CUTLERY CORP. (See Imperial Schrade Corp.)

SWISS ARMY BRANDS LTD.
  (See Importers & Foreign Cutlers)

UTICA CUTLERY CO.
820 Noyes St.
Utica, NY 13503
Phone: Outside NY 800-888-4223; 315-733-4663
FAX: 315-733-6602
Specialties: Nice line of pocketknives, including Barlows and hunters and working pattern knives. Brands: Kutmaster, Walco.

WESTERN CUTLERY (See Camillus Cutlery Co.)

importers & foreign cutlers

Knives are imported by almost every sort of commercial cutler, but the names here are those whose specialty is importing, whether it be their brand, famous overseas brands, or special knives for special purposes best made overseas. Every effort is made to keep the list updated, but importing is sometimes an uncertain endeavor.

ADAMS INTERNATIONAL KNIFEWORKS
8710 Rosewood Hills
Edwardsville, IL 62025
Phone: 618-656-9868
FAX: 618-656-9868
Specialties: Antique or current automatic knives designed for law enforcement, military and collectors. Largest dealer of Linder-Solingen, Germany knives; offers Muela, Cold Steel, SOG, Kershaw, Ka-Bar-Boker and Henckels to name a few.

AITOR-CUCHILLERIA DEL NORTE, S.A.
P.O. Box No. 1
48260 Ermua (Vizcaya)
SPAIN
Phone: 34-43-17 00 01
Specialties: Full range of Aitor products from jungle knives to folding pocketknives.

ARISTOCRAT
  (See Degen Knives, Inc.)

ATLANTA CUTLERY CORP.
2143 Gees Mill Rd., Box 839XZ
Conyers, GA 30207
Phone: 404-922-3700
Specialties: Carefully chosen inventory from all over the world; selected Indian, Pakistani, Spanish, Japanese, German, English and Italian knives; often new ideas—a principal source for kukris.

B&D TRADING CO.
3935 Fair Hill Rd.
Fair Oaks, CA 95628
Phone: 916-967-9366/800-334-3790
FAX: 916-967-4873
Specialties: The Executive Edge, folders made in Brazil.

BAILEY'S
P.O. Box 550
Laytonville, CA 95454
Specialties: Importers of Tuatahi brand axes from New Zealand.

BAKER, B.W.
  (See Svord Knives)

BELTRAME, FRANCESCO
Coltellerie F.lli Beltrame F&A
di Francesco & Armando snc
Via dei Fabbri 15
33085 Maniago (PN)
ITALY
Phone: 0427-71338
FAX: 0427-71338

BOKER USA, INC.
1550 Balsam St.
Lakewood, CO 80215-3117
Phone: 303-279-5997
FAX: 303-279-5919
Specialties: Tree Brand knives and a host of new knives in the Boker USA label.

CAMPOS, IVAN DE ALMEIDA
Custom and Old Knives Trader
R. Stelio M. Loureiro, 206
Centro, Tatui
BRAZIL
Phone: 0152-512102 or 51-6952
FAX: 0152-514896
Specialties: Knives of all Brazilian makers.

C.A.S. IBERIA, INC./MUELA
650 Industrial Blvd.
Sale Creek, TN 37373
Phone: 615-332-4700
Specialties: Knives made in Spain by people with an eye on U.S. custom makers.

CATOCTIN CUTLERY
P.O. Box 188; 17 S. Main St.
Smithsburg, MD 21783
Phone: 301-824-7416
FAX: 301-824-6138
Specialties: Full line of Aitor knives from Spain, others from Italy, Germany, the Philippines; wholesale only. Has own brands—Fox and Koncept, the latter U.S.-made.

CHRISTOPHER MFG., E.
  (See Knifemaking Supplies)

COACH MARKETING
1701 W. Wernsing Ave.
Effingham, IL 62401
Phone: 217-347-2668
Specialties: Imports Degen Knives, locking folders and multi-function outdoorsman knives; and Aristocrat knives, premium sports and action cutlery made in the U.S. and in Seki, Japan.

COAST CUTLERY
2045 SE Ankeny St.
Portland, OR 97214
Phone: 503-234-4545
FAX: 503-234-4422
Specialties: Long-time large wholesaler now national Puma reps; exclusive Puma importer.

COLUMBIA PRODUCTS CO.
P.O. Box 1333
Sialkot 51310
PAKISTAN
Phone: 92-432-86921
FAX: 92-432-558417
Specialties: See Columbia Products Int'l.

COLUMBIA PRODUCTS INT'L
P.O. Box 8243
New York, NY 10116-8243
Phone: 201-854-8504
FAX: 201-854-7058
Specialties: Lockblade and slip-joint folders in old and new U.S.-style patterns; heavy-duty belt knives; low prices.

COMPASS INDUSTRIES, INC.
104 E. 25th St.
New York, NY 10010
Phone: 212-473-2614; 800-221-9904
Specialties: Imports for dealer trade from all over at many price and quality levels; two hot brands are Silver Falcon and Sportster.

CONAZ COLTELLERIE
dei F.lli Consigli-Scarperia
Via G. Giordani, 20
50038 Scarperia (Firenze)
ITALY
Phone: 055-846197

FAX: 055-846603
Specialties: Handmade, handsharpened knives with horn handles.

CONFEDERATE STATES ARMORY
2143 Gees Mill Rd.
Box 839XZ
Conyers, GA 30207
Phone: 800-241-3664
Specialties: Replicas of Confederate arms of the Civil War.

CONSOLIDATED CUTLERY CO., INC.
696 NW Sharpe St.
Port St. Lucie, FL 34983
Phone: 407-878-6139/800-288-6288
Specialties: Hunting knives, wood-carving tools, stag-handled steak/carving sets, camping axes, knife sharpening steels.

CRAZY CROW TRADING POST
P.O. Box H-K96
Pottsboro, TX 75020
Phone: 903-463-1366
FAX: 903-463-7734
Specialties: Mountain man cutlery and fixings. Knife blades, books, knifemaking supplies; $3 for catalog.

DEGEN KNIVES, INC. (See Coach Marketing)

EKA (See Nichols Co.)

EMPIRE CUTLERY CORP.
12 Kruger Ct.
Clifton, NJ 07013
Phone: 201-472-5155; 800-325-6433
FAX: 201-779-0759
Specialties: Imports Frost knives from Mora in Sweden, including the new Swedish soldier's knives. Knives are priced to sell.

EXECUTIVE EDGE (See B&D Trading Co.)

FALLKNIVEN AB
Box 46
S-960 30 Vuollerim
SWEDEN
Phone: Int. +46-976-10468
FAX: +46-976-10505
Specialties: Folders and hunting knives.

FORSCHNER GROUP, INC., THE
(See Swiss Army Brands Ltd.)

FREDIANI COLTELLI FINLANDESI
Via Lago Maggiore 41
I-21038 Leggiuno, ITALY
Phone: 0039 332 647 362
Specialties: Purveyors from Italy of fine Finnish knives, some with Italian decorative touches.

FROST CUTLERY CO. (See Mail-Order Sales)

FROSTS KNIFE MANUFACTURING (Mora, SWEDEN) (See Scandia International)

GIESSER MESSERFABRIK GMBH, JOHANNES
P.O. Box 168
D-71349 Winnenden
GERMANY
Phone: 0049-7195-1808-0
FAX: 0049-7195-6 44 66
Specialties: Manufacturer of professional and kitchen cutlery. See Illinois Cutlery and Markuse Corp.

GOODWIN ENTERPRISES
P.O. Box 4124
Chattanooga, TN 37405
Phone: 615-267-5071
Specialties: Imports German cutlery, including exclusive Red Stag pocketknives—jigged bone, etched blades in colors, and more.

GREEN HEAD GAME CALL CORP.
R.R. 1, Box 33
Lacon, IL 61540
Phone: 309-246-2155/800-247-8279
Specialties: Distributor of Canadian-made D.H. Russell belt knives; some two-bladed folders. Game calls also.

GUTMANN CUTLERY, INC.
1100 W. 45th Ave.
Denver, CO 80211
Phone: 303-433-6506
Specialties: Edge Mark, Explorer, Hen & Rooster, Opinel and Russell Green River are the leading names in a selection of over 300 knives sold through retail stores and through the mail.

HENCKELS ZWILLINGSWORK, INC., J.A.
9 Skyline Dr., Box 253
Hawthorne, NY 10532
Phone: 914-592-7370
FAX: 914-592-7384
Specialties: U.S. office of world-famous Solingen cutlers—high-quality pocket and sportsman's knives with the "twin" logo.

HIMALAYAN IMPORTS
225 W. Moana Ln., Suite 226
Reno, NV 89509
Phone: 702-853-3464
Specialties: Just one: Nepalese-made kukris, which they spell *khukuri*, hand-forged in that mountain kingdom.

HOFFRITZ/CUTLERY WORLD
515 W. 24th St.
New York, NY 10011
Phone: 212-924-7300
FAX: 212-627-5922
Specialties: Selected chef's kitchen and carving cutlery; elegant gentlemen's pocketknives; sports knives of all kinds, most with Hoffritz's own name; all sold in 80 Hoffritz stores and through catalog.

ILLINOIS CUTLERY
P.O. Box 607
Barrington, IL 60011-0607
Phone: 708-426-5002
FAX: 708-426-4942
Specialties: U.S. agent for Johannes Giesser Messerfabrik GmbH line of professional knives (butchers/cooks/household).

JOY ENTERPRISES
801 Broad Ave, P.O. Box 314
Ridgefield, NJ 07657
Phone: 201-943-5920
FAX: 201-943-1579
Specialties: Sporting and combat-style cutlery under the Fury label—full range. Folders and swords. Wholesale only.

KA-BAR KNIVES, Collector's Division
(See General Cutlers)

KEN'S FINN KNIVES
Rt. 1, Box 338
Republic, MI 49879
Phone: 906-376-2132
Specialties: Puukkos and other Finnish knives. Brochure $2.

KNIFE COLLECTORS ASSN.-JAPAN
(See Murakami, Ichiro)

KNIFE IMPORTERS, INC.
P.O. Box 1000
Manchaca, TX 78652
Phone: 512-282-6860
FAX: 512-282-7504
Specialties: Eye Brand cutlery.

KOPROMED, USA
1701 Broadway, Suite 282
Vancouver, WA 98663
Phone: 360-695-8864
FAX: 360-690-8576
Specialties: U.S. distributor for Kopromed forged 440C hunting knives and table cutlery from Poland.

LEISURE PRODUCTS CORP.
P.O. Box 1171
Sialkot-51310
PAKISTAN
Phone: 92-432-86921/562009
FAX: 92-432-561030/558417
Specialties: A wide range of lockblade and slip-joint folders in old and new U.S.-style patterns; heavy-duty belt knives; low prices.

LINDER, CARL NACHF.
Erholungstr. 10
42699 Solingen
GERMANY
Phone: 0212-330856
FAX: 0212-337104

MARKUSE CORP., THE
10 Wheeling Ave.
Woburn, MA 01801
Phone: 617-932-9444
FAX: 617-933-1930
Specialties: U.S. agent for Johannes Giesser Messerfabrik GmbH's "Creative Collection" range of knives.

MARTO U.S.A.
2874 Hartland Rd., Dept. FC1
Falls Church, VA 22043
Specialties: Oriental and historical swords.

MARTTIINI KNIVES
P.O. Box 44
96101 Rovaniemi 10, FINLAND
Phone: 358-60-21751
Specialties: Finnish knives straight from Finland's biggest cutler. Includes fancy Finn-type hunters.

MATTHEWS CUTLERY
4401 Sentry Dr., Suite K
Tucker, GA 30084
Phone: 404-939-6915
Specialties: Wholesalers only. Carries all major brands which include over 2,800 patterns. Has U.S. distribution for Linder-Solingen and others. Catalog $2.

MUELA (See C.A.S. Iberia, Inc./Muela)

MURAKAMI, ICHIRO
Knife Collectors Assn. Japan
Tokuda Nishi 4 chome, 76 banchi, Ginancho
Hashimagun, Gifu
JAPAN
Phone: 81 58 274 1960
FAX: 81 58 273 7369
Specialties: Buys collector-grade and commercial U.S.

knives for sale in Japan.

MUSEUM REPLICAS LIMITED
2143 Gees Mill Rd., Box 839 XZ
Conyers, GA 30207
Phone: 404-922-3703
Specialties: Battle-ready hand-forged edged weapons. Carry swords, daggers, halberds, dirks and axes. Catalog $2.

NICHOLS CO.
P.O. Box 473
#5 The Green
Woodstock, VT 05091
Phone: 802-457-3970
FAX: 802-457-2051
Specialties: Importer/distributor of precision-engineered EKA pocketknives from Sweden; also fixed-blade knives from Norway and Finland.

NORMARK CORP.
1710 E. 78th St.
Minneapolis, MN 55423
Phone: 612-933-7060
FAX: 612-933-0046
Specialties: Scandinavian-made sturdy knives for fishermen; puuko-style belt knives for hunters; fillet knives. Good stainless steel.

PRECISE INTERNATIONAL
15 Corporate Dr.
Orangeburg, NY 10962
Phone: 800-431-2996
Specialties: Wenger Swiss Army knives.

PRO CUT
P.O. Box 2189
Downey, CA 90242
Phone: 800-356-8507
FAX: 310-803-4261
Specialties: Wholesale only. Imports historical medieval and samurai swords; armor and weapons, over 100 different models.

PUUKKO CUTLERY (See Suomi Shop)

PUMA CUTLERY (See Coast Cutlery)

REFLECTIONS OF EUROPE
Peter Ward
151 Rochelle Ave.
Rochelle Park, NJ 07662
Phone: 201-845-8120
FAX: 201-843-8419
Specialties: Importer for Eberhard Schaff kitchen cutlery and professional chef knives.

RUSSELL CO., A.G.
1705 Highway 71 North
Springdale, AR 72764
Phone: 501-751-7341
Specialties: Morseth knives; Russell-marked special designs—"Woods Walker," Sting, CIA letter opener, Russell One-Hand knives, lots more every year.

SCANDIA INTERNATIONAL
118 English Neighborhood Rd., P.O. Box 218
East Woodstock, CT 06244-0218
Phone: 203-928-9525
FAX: 203-928-1179
Specialties: U.S. importer of Frosts Knife Manufacturing AB of Mora, Sweden—over 800 models.

SPYDERCO, INC. (See Specialty Cutlers)

STAR SALES CO., INC.
1803 N. Central St., P.O. Box 1503
Knoxville, TN 37901
Phone: 615-524-0771
FAX: 615-524-4889
Specialties: New collector pocketknives; imports Star knives and Kissing Crane knives.

SUOMI SHOP
P.O. Box 303
Wolf Lake, MN 56593
Phone: 218-538-6633
FAX: 218-538-6633
Specialties: A full and complete Finnish cutlery line, including the Puukko cutlery line, all custom/hand-forged. Offers Scandinavian or Nordic expertise on makers and knife values.

SVORD KNIVES
Smith Rd., RD 2
Waiuku, South Auckland
NEW ZEALAND
Phone: +64 9 235 8846
FAX: +64 9 298 7670
Specialties: New Zealand private cutler makes belt knives and commercial knives.

SWISS ARMY BRANDS LTD.
The Forschner Group, Inc.
One Research Drive
Shelton, CT 06484
Phone: 800-243-4032
FAX: 800-243-4006
Specialties: This is the Victorinox headquarters in the U.S.; all current production comes through here; manages service center also. Group also manages flow of excellent Forschner commercial and household cutlery.

TAYLOR CUTLERY
P.O. Box 1638
1736 N. Eastman Rd.
Kingsport, TN 37662
Phone: 615-247-2406, 800-251-0254
FAX: 615-247-5371
Specialties: Taylor-Seto folders and straight knives, a line of scrimshaw knives, stag handles and many other imports.

UNITED CUTLERY CORP.
1425 United Blvd.

Sevierville, TN 37862
Phone: 615-428-2532
FAX: 615-428-2267
Specialties: Wholesale only. Purchases for resale only; manufacture a number of items in the U.S. now.

VALOR CORP.
5555 N.W. 36th Ave.
Miami, FL 33142
Phone: 305-634-4536
Specialties: Emphasizes lockback folders from overseas in

popular styles. Over 100 knife models imported.

ZEST INTERNATIONAL
1500 NE Jackson St.
Minneapolis, MN 55413
Phone: 800-453-8937/612-781-5036
FAX: 612-781-1452
Specialties: Full line of sports cutlery—dozens of models—with Zest trademark in 440A steel.

knifemaking supplies

The firms listed here specialize in furnishing knifemaking supplies in small amounts. Professional knifemakers have their own sources for much of what they use, but often patronize some of these firms. All the companies listed below have catalogs of their products, some available for a charge. For information about obtaining one, send a self-addressed and stamped envelope to the company. Firms are listed here by their request. New firms may be included by sending a catalog or the like to our editorial offices. We cannot guarantee the company's performance.

ACME SUPPLY CO.
2504 N. Augusta St.
Staunton, VA 24401
Phone: 703-885-8782
Specialties: Specialized sharpening and serrating; repair, restoration; distributor of Bader grinders, Baldor buffers and motors, specialty tools.

AFRICAN IMPORT CO.
20 Braunecker Rd.
Plymouth, MA 02360
Phone: 508-746-8552
FAX: 508-746-0616
Specialties: Exotic African handle materials such as elephant and fossil ivory; exotic skins and leathers.

ARCTIC WILDERNESS ADVENTURES (See Eklund)

ART JEWEL ENTERPRISES, LTD.
460 Randy Rd.
Carol Stream, IL 60188
Phone: 708-260-0400
FAX: 708-260-0486
Specialties: Handles—stag, ivory, pearl, horn, rosewood, ebony.

ATLANTA CUTLERY CORP.
2143 Gees Mill Rd., Box 839XE
Conyers, GA 30207
Phone: 800-241-3595
Specialties: Many blades and fixings to choose from; occasional special buys in cutlery handles, pocketknife blades and the like; complete kits for buckskinner knives, small pocketknives. Catalog $2.

BILL'S CUSTOM CASES
P.O. Box 2
Dunsmuir, CA 96025
Phone: 916-235-0177
FAX: 916-235-4959
Specialties: Soft knife cases made of Cordura, Propex and leather.

BLADEMASTER GRINDERS
P.O. Box 812
Crowley, TX 76036
Phone: 817-473-1081
Specialties: Manufactures knifemaking machine called "Blademaster." Wholesale and retail.

BLADES "N" STUFF
1019 E. Palmer Ave.
Glendale, CA 91205
Phone: 818-956-5110
FAX: 818-956-5120
Specialties: Full line of supplies and equipment, including excellent selection of tropical woods. Does big business in custom-ground heat-treated blades in dozens of shapes. Catalog $5.

BOONE TRADING CO., INC.
562 Coyote Rd.
Brinnon, WA 98320
Phone: 206-796-4330
Specialties: Exotic handle materials including elephant, fossil walrus, mastodon, warthog and hippopotamus ivory. Also sambar stag, oosic, impala and sheephorn.

BORGER, WOLF/IMPORT-EXPORT
Benzstrasse 8
76676 Graben-Neudorf
GERMANY
Phone: 07255-8314
FAX: 07255-6921
Specialties: Supplies European knifemakers, and others. German text catalog—write for details.

BOYE KNIVES
P.O. Box 1238
Dolan Springs, AZ 86441
Phone: 520-767-4273
FAX: 520-767-3030

Specialties: Casts dendritic blades and bar stock for knifemaking. Information $1.
BRIAR KNIVES
Darrel Ralph
7032 E. Livingston Ave.
Renoldsburg, OH 43068
Phone: 614-577-1040, 614-241-9793 (pager)
Specialties: Sells commercial Damascus.

CHARLTON, LTD. (See Damascus-USA)

CHRISTOPHER MFG., E.
P.O. Box 685
Union City, TN 38281
Phone: 901-885-0374
FAX: 901-885-0440
Specialties: Knife supplies for buckskinners; much early American hardware; catalog $5 (outside U.S. $6). Also has knives made overseas, including Bowie replicas.

CUSTOM KNIFEMAKER'S SUPPLY
Bob Schrimsher
P.O. Box 308
Emory, TX 75440
Phone: 903-473-3330
FAX: 903-743-2235
Specialties: Big catalog full of virtually everything for knifemaking. Their 21st year in business.

CUSTOM KRAFT
14919 Nebraska Ave.
Tampa, FL 33613
Phone: 813-972-5336
Specialties: Knifemakers Ron Miller and Reese Weiland make up Custom Craft; they specialize in hard-to-find knifemaking supplies like titanium naltex, safety gear, mills, taps, Fuller brand files, and Allen/spline drive screws, to name a few. Catalog $1.

CUTLERY SPECIALTIES
22 Morris Ln.
Great Neck, NY 11024
Phone: 516-829-5899
FAX: 516-773-8076
Specialties: Offers polishes, cleaners, glues, sealants and epoxy.

DAMASCUS-USA
Deans Farm Rd.
Tyner, NC 27980-9718
Phone: 919-221-2010
FAX: 919-221-2009
Specialties: Manufactures carbon and stainless Damascus bar stocks and blanks.

DAN'S WHETSTONE CO., INC.
130 Timbs Place
Hot Springs, AR 71913
Phone: 501-767-1616
FAX: 501-767-9598
Specialties: Traditional sharpening materials and abrasive products.

DIAMOND MACHINING TECHNOLOGY, INC.
85 Hayes Memorial Dr.
Marlborough, MA 01752
Phone: 508-481-5944
FAX: 508-485-3924
Specialties: Quality diamond sharpening tools to hone all knife edges, including a unique serrated knife sharpener for all serration sizes.

DIXIE GUN WORKS, INC.
P.O. Box 130
Union City, TN 38281
Phone: 901-885-0700
FAX: 901-885-0440
Specialties: Knife division sold to E. Christopher Mfg.

EKLUND
P.O. Box 483

Nome, AK 99762-0483
Phone: NA
Specialties: Exotic handle materials like fossil walrus ivory, fossil whale and mammoth bone, mammoth ivory, oosic horn and antler. Eskimo artifacts and trophy tusks; price sheet $1.

EZE-LAP DIAMOND PRODUCTS
3572 Arrowhead Dr.
Carson City, NV 89706
Phone: 800-843-4815
Specialties: Diamond-coated sharpening instruments, various sizes.

FIELDS, RICK B.
26401 Sandwich Pl.
Mt. Plymouth, FL 34761
Phone: 904-383-6270
Specialties: Fossil walrus and mammoth ivory.

FLITZ INTERNATIONAL, LTD.
821 Mohr Ave.
Waterford, WI 53185
Phone: 414-534-5898
Specialties: General line of polishers.

FORTUNE PRODUCTS, INC.
HC 04, Box 303
Hwy. 1431 E. (Smithwick)
Marble Falls, TX 78654
Phone: 210-693-6111
FAX: 210-693-6394
Specialties: "Accu-sharp" sharpeners.

GILMER WOOD CO.
2211 NW St. Helens Rd.
Portland, OR 97210
Phone: 503-274-1271
FAX: 503-274-9839
Specialties: They list 112 varieties of natural woods.

GOLDEN AGE ARMS CO.
115 E. High St.
P.O. Box 366
Ashley, OH 43003
Phone: 614-747-2488
Specialties: Many types of blades; stag for handles; cast items—much for the buckskinner. Catalog $4.

GRS CORP.
Don Glaser
P.O. Box 748
Emporia, KS 66801
Phone: 316-343-1084 (Kansas); 800-835-3519
FAX: 316-343-9640
Specialties: Engraving products such as the Gravermeister and the Gravermax.

HAWKINS CUSTOM KNIVES & SUPPLIES
P.O. Box 400
Red Oak, GA 30272
Phone: 404-964-1177
FAX: 404-306-2877
Specialties: Various size steel blanks, belts, buffing compounds and wheels; stag and drill bits.

HAYDU, THOMAS G.
2507 Bimini Lane
Ft. Lauderdale, FL 33312
Phone: 305-792-0185
Specialties: Deluxe boxes for knives that stay at home—some from Tomway Corp. have tambour covers.

HOUSE OF MUZZLE LOADING, THE
(See Blades "N" Stuff)

HOUSE OF TOOLS LTD.
#136, 8228 MacLeod Tr. S.E.
Calgary, AB T2H 2B8
CANADA
Phone: 403-258-0005
FAX: 403-252-0149

Specialties: 440C and ATS34 handle and bolster material, sand belts, buff wheels and a large selection of tools.

INDIAN RIDGE TRADERS (See Koval Knives, Inc.)

JOHNSON, R.B.
I.B.S. Int'l.
Box 11
Clearwater, MN 55320
Phone: 612-558-6128
Specialties: Folder supplies, threaded pivot pins, stainless and black oxide screws, taps and compasses.

JOHNSON WOOD PRODUCTS
RR 1
Strawberry Point, IA 52076
Phone: 319-933-4930 or 933-6504
Specialties: Fancy domestic and imported knife handle woods.

KNIFE & CUTLERY PRODUCTS, INC.
P.O. Box 12480
N. Kansas City, MO 64116
Phone: 816-454-9879
Specialties: Offers 14 pages of knifemaking supplies such as exotic woods, wheels, bar stock and blades in a variety of shapes. Catalog $2; list of pocketknives $1.

KNIFE AND GUN FINISHING SUPPLIES
(See Mail-Order Sales)

KNIVES, ETC.
2522 N. Meridian
Oklahoma City, OK 73107
Phone: 405-943-9221
FAX: 405-943-4924
Specialties: Exotic woods; variety of blade steels; stag.

KOVAL KNIVES, INC.
5819 Zarley St.
New Albany
Columbus, OH 43054
Phone: 614-855-0777
FAX: 614-855-0945
Specialties: Full range of Micarta and other materials for handles; brass, nickel silver, steels; machines and supplies for all knifemaking; some knife kits; catalog.

KWIK-SHARP
350 N. Wheeler St.
Ft. Gibson, OK 74434
Phone: 918-478-2443
Specialties: Ceramic rod knife sharpeners.

LINDER-SOLINGEN KNIFE PARTS
4401 Sentry Dr., Suite K
Tucker, GA 30084
Phone: 404-939-6915
Specialties: German-made knifemaking parts and blades. Wholesale catalog—send $2.

LITTLE GIANT POWER HAMMER
420 4th Corso
Nebraska City, NE 68410
Phone: 402-873-6603
Specialties: New headquarters for Little Giant/Mayer Bros. power hammer parts, information and advice.

LOHMAN CO., FRED
3405 N.E. Broadway
Portland, OR 97232
Phone: 503-282-4567
FAX: 503—288-3533
Specialties: Sword polishing and handle wrapping service, quality replacement parts, for the restoration of Japanese-style swords, both new and old. Catalog $5.

MARKING METHODS, INC.
301 S. Raymond Ave.
Alhambra, CA 91803-1531
Phone: 818-282-8823
FAX: 818-576-7564
Specialties: Manufacturer of electro-chemical etching equipment and supplies for the knifemaking trade—power units & kits, long life photo stencils, and accessories.

MASECRAFT SUPPLY CO.
170 Research Pkwy #3
P.O. Box 423
Meriden, CT 06450
Phone: 800-682-5489
FAX: 203-238-2373
Specialties: Handle materials.

MEIER STEEL
Daryl Meier
RR 4
Carbondale, IL 62901
Phone: 618-549-3234
Specialties: Supplier and creator of "Meier Steel." Contact for available sizes and prices of his Damascus.

MOTHER OF PEARL CO.
D.A. Culpepper
P.O. Box 445
401 Old GA Rd.
Franklin, NC 28734
Phone: 704-524-6842;
FAX: 704-369-7809

Specialties: Pearl, black pearl, abalone, pink pearl, sheephorn, bone, buffalo horn, stingray skin, exotic leathers, snake skin.

NORTHWEST KNIFE SUPPLY
621 Fawn Ridge Dr.
Oakland, OR 97462
Phone: 503-459-2216
FAX: 503-459-4460
Specialties: Coote grinders, Klingspor abrasives, exotic woods, Micarta, stag, other supplies. Catalog $2; foreign $4.

OREGON ABRASIVE & MFG. CO.
11303 NE 207th Ave.
Brush Prairie, WA 98606
Phone: 206-254-5400
FAX: 206-892-3025
Specialties: Sharpening stones made under their own roof, and sharpening systems based on those.

OZARK KNIFE
3165 S. Campbell
Springfield, MO 65807
Phone: 417-886-2888
FAX: 417-886-CUTT
Specialties: Offers list of custom knives for sale, plus general cutlery collectibles; Randall knives, shining Wave Damascus and mokume.

PARAGON INDUSTRIES, INC.
2011 South Town East Blvd.
Mesquite, TX 75149-1122
Phone: 800-876-4328; 214-288-7557
FAX: 214-222-0646
Specialties: Manufacturer of knifemaker's heat-treating furnaces in five available sizes.

POPLIN, JAMES/POP KNIVES & SUPPLIES
103 Oak St.
Washington, GA 30673
Phone: 404-678-2729
Specialties: Sanding belts, handle screws, buffing wheels and compound woods for knife handles, etc.

PUGH, JIM
917 Carpenter St., Azle, TX 76020
P.O. Box 711, Azle, TX 76098
Phone: 817-444-2679
FAX: 817-444-5455
Specialties: Kydex sheath material; limited.

RADOS, JERRY
Mlg: P.O. Box 531
Grant Park, IL 60940
Shpg: 7523E 5000 N. Rd.
Grant Park, IL 60940
Phone: 815-472-3350
FAX: 815-472-3944
Specialties: Offers many distinct patterns of Damascus in forged-to-shape blades or customer designs.

REACTIVE METALS STUDIO, INC.
P.O. Box 890
Clarkdale, AZ 86324
Phone: 520-634-3434
FAX: 520-634-6734
Specialties: Phil Baldwin heads up another business and this is a source for titanium and like exotic metals plus the equipment for coloring or anodizing them.

REAL WOOD
36 Fourth St.
Dracut, MA 01826
Phone: 508-957-4899
Specialties: Exotic wood for knife handles; carry over 60 different species and are always adding more; catalog $1.

REPRODUCTION BLADES
17485 SW Pheasant Ln.
Beaverton, OR 97006
Phone: 503-848-9313
Specialties: Custom cast blades.

RIVERSIDE MACHINE
Rt. 1, Box 488
DeQueen, AR 71832
Phone: 501-642-7643
FAX: 501-642-4023
Specialties: Grinders, belts, wood, steel, blade stamps, Riverside Stampmaster, trip hammer repair, parts and sales.

ROCKY MOUNTAIN KNIVES
George L. Conklin
P.O. Box 902, 615 Franklin
Ft. Benton, MT 59442
Phone: 406-622-3268
FAX: 406-622-5670
Specialties: Knife sharpening; supplies.

SANDPAPER, INC. OF ILLINOIS
270 Eisenhower Ln. N., Unit 5B
Lombard, IL 60148
Phone: 708-629-3320
FAX: 708-629-3324
Specialties: Coated abrasives in belts, sheets, rolls, discs or any coated abrasive specialty.

SCHELL, CLYDE M.
4735 N.E. Elliott Circle
Corvallis, OR 97330

Phone: 503-752-0235
Specialties: Knife and exotic wood material.

SCHEP'S FORGE
Box 83
Chapman, NE 68827
Phone: 308-986-2444
Specialties: Damascus steel made in Nebraska.

SHEFFIELD KNIFEMAKER'S SUPPLY, INC.
P.O. Box 141
Deland, FL 32721
Phone: 904-775-6453
FAX: 904-774-5754
Specialties: Steels and handle material; N/S, brass, copper, H16, aluminum, abrasive products and much more.

SHINING WAVE METALS
P.O. Box 563
Snohomish, WA 98290-0563
Phone: 206-334-5569
Specialties: Phil Baldwin makes and sells mokume, Damascus and a variety of Japanese alloys (for furniture, not blades) to order or from stock. Wholesale only.

SMITH WHETSTONE, INC.
1700 Sleepy Valley Rd.
Hot Springs, AR 71901
Phone: 501-321-2244
FAX: 501-321-9232
Specialties: Sharpeners of every kind, ceramic sharpeners, oils, kits and polishing creams.

SUEDMEIER, HARLAN "SID"
(See Little Giant Power Hammer)

TEXAS KNIFEMAKERS SUPPLY
10649 Haddington, Suite 180
Houston, TX 77043
Phone: 713-461-8632
FAX: 713-461-8221
Specialties: Bar stock, factory blades, much handle material; offers heat-treating; catalog $2.

THOMAS CUTLERY, CHARLES B.
(See Acme Supply Co.)

TRIPLE GRIT (See Oregon Abrasive & Mfg. Co.)

TRU-GRIT, INC.
760 E. Francis St. #N
Ontario, CA 91761
Phone: 909-923-4116
Specialties: Complete selection of 3M, Norton, Klingspor and Hermes belts for grinding and polishing, also Burr-King and square wheel grinders, Baldor buffers and an excellent line of machines for knifemakers; ATS-34 and 440C steel.

TUDOR II, HUGH SANFORD (SANDY)
Box 92
Vail, AZ 85641
Phone: NA
Specialties: Purveyor of desert ironwood.

WASHITA MOUNTAIN WHETSTONE CO.
P.O. Box 378
Lake Hamilton, AR 71951
Phone: 501-525-3914
Specialties: Knife sharpeners.

WILD WOODS
Jim Fray
P.O. Box 104
Monclova, OH 43542
Phone: 419-866-0435
FAX: 419-867-0656
Specialties: Stabilized woods in a variety of colors in four grades.

WILSON, R.W.
113 Kent Way
Weirton, WV 26062
Phone: 304-723-2771
Specialties: Full range of supplies, but sells nothing he doesn't use himself.

WOOD CARVERS SUPPLY, INC.
P.O. Box 7500
Englewood, FL 34295-7500
Phone: NA
Specialties: Carving tools, etc.

WYVERN INDUSTRIES
229 Flounce Rock Dr.
Prospect, OR 97536
Phone: 503-560-3355
Specialties: Purveyors of the hard-to-get for those who use anvils in their work.

ZANOTTI, ALAN (See African Import Co.)

ZOWADA, TIM
14141 P. Drive North
Marshall, MI 49068
Phone: 616-781-2458
FAX: 616-781-2458
Specialties: Damascus bars and billets, mokume and gas forge kits.

mail-order sales

The firms listed here have come to our attention over a period of years. All publish lists or catalogs. Their specialties are listed; send a self-addressed and stamped envelope for information. Firms are included here upon request. New firms wishing to be included should send a catalog or the like to our editorial offices. We cannot guarantee the company's performance.

A&J ENTERPRISES
P.O. Box 6071
Branson, MO 65615
Phone: 417-335-2170
FAX: 417-335-2011
Specialties: Buys, sells and trades collector-grade knives by mail and at major shows.

ADAMS INTERNATIONAL KNIFEWORKS
    (See Importers & Foreign Cutlers)

AFRICAN IMPORT CO..
    (See Knifemaking Supplies)

AMERICAN TARGET KNIVES
1030 Brownwood NW
Grand Rapids, MI 49504
Phone: 616-453-1998
Specialties: Throwing knives

AMSPACHER, BRUCE
P.O. Box 9527
Newport Beach, CA 92658
Phone: 800-821-3985; 714-250-3187
FAX: 714-250-4412
Specialties: Sells, buys, trades custom-made, investment-grade knives; offers a free weekly price list.

ARIZONA CUSTOM KNIVES
Jay and Karen Sadow
10721 East Terra Dr.
Scottsdale, AZ 85258
Phone: 602-661-2142
Specialties: Collector quality handmade knives.

ARTHUR, GARY B.
Rt. 7 Box 215
Forest, VA 24551
Phone: 804-525-8315
FAX: 804-525-8364
Specialties: Sells, buys and trades custom-made, invest-ment-grade knives.

ATLANTA CUTLERY CORP.
2143 Gees Mill Rd., Box 839XZ
Conyers, GA 30207
Phone: 404-922-3700
Specialties: Catalog on request; wide selection of knives; aims to provide working-quality knives and give good value; showroom. Catalog $2.

ATLANTIC BLADESMITHS
32 Bradford St.
Concord, MA 01742
Phone: 508-369-3608
Specialties: Factory and custom-made knives, over 100 in stock at all times, for immediate sale. List $3.

BALLARD CUTLERY
1495 Brummel Ave.
Elk Grove Village, IL 60007
Phone: 708-228-0070
FAX: 708-228-0077
Specialties: Special-purchase knives, all types. Tries for good buys.

BARRETT-SMYTHE, LTD.
127 East 69th St., 1A
New York, NY 10021
Phone: 212-249-5500
FAX: 212-249-5550
Specialties: One-of-a-kind folding knives on sale in uptown Manhatten at prices suitable for their station.

BASCH ENTERPRISES, PAUL CHARLES
111 W. Del Amo Blvd., Suite 1
Long Beach, CA 90805
Phone: 310-423-5362
FAX: 310-423-5792
Specialties: Buys, sells and trades handmade knives only; large stock; sets up 45 shows a year.

BECK'S CUTLERY SPECIALTIES
748F East Chatham St.
Cary, NC 27511
Phone: 919-460-0203
Specialties: South African Peter Bauchop's tactical designs; other U.S. big-ticket tactical names.

BELL SR., R.T. "BOB"
P.O. Box 690147
Orlando, FL 32869
Phone: 407-352-1082
Specialties: Wide range of quality knives.

BILL'S CUSTOM CASES (See Knifemaking Supplies)

BLADES "N" STUFF (See Knifemaking Supplies)

BLAIRS BLADES & ACCESSORIES
531 Main St., Suite 651

El Segundo, CA 90245
Phone: 310-322-1063
FAX: 310-322-3112
Specialties: Sales reps for Anza File Knives.

BLUE RIDGE KNIVES
Rt. 6, Box 185
Marion, VA 24354-9351
Phone: 703-783-6143
FAX: 703-783-9298
Specialties: Wholesale only; top brand knives.

BOONE TRADING CO., INC.
P.O. Box BB
Brinnon, WA 98320
Phone: 206-796-4330
Specialties: Ivory; catalog features scrimshawed and carved ivory-handled knives.

CARMEL CUTLERY
Dolores & 6th; P.O. Box 1346
Carmel, CA 93921
Phone: 408-624-6699
FAX: 408-624-6780
Specialties: Knife retailer; factory and custom knives.

CHRISTOPHER MFG., E. (See Knifemaking Supplies)

CLASSIC CUTLERY QUARRY
39 Roosevelt Ave.
Hudson, NH 03051-2828
Phone: 603-883-1199
FAX: 603-883-1199
Specialties: Factory knives and accessories, all discount-ed. Also custom, rare and discontinued knives. Genuine stone handle materials, jigged bone and mother-of-pearl; from the common to the unusual. Huge catalog $5 (refund-able).

CREATIVE SALES & MFG.
Box 550
Whitefish, MT 59937
Phone: 406-862-5533
Specialties: Patent knife sharpeners.

CUTLERY SHOPPE
5461 Kendall St.
Boise, ID 83706
Phone: 208-376-0430; 800-231-1272
Specialties: Discounts; custom and unusual balisongs; fight-ing and military-type knives; catalog $1.

DAMASCUS-USA (See Knifemaking Supplies)

DENTON, J.W.
102 N. Main St., Box 429
Hiawassee, GA 30546
Phone: 706-896-2292
FAX: 706-896-1212
Specialties: Buys and sells Loveless knives—has lists.

EDGE CO. KNIVES
P.O. Box 826
Brattleboro, VT 05302
Phone: 800-732-9976
FAX: 802-257-1967
Specialties: A variety of opportunity knives.

FAZALARE, ROY
P.O. Box 1335
Agoura Hills, CA 91376
Phone: 818-879-6161
Specialties: Purveyor of five folders, especially multi-blade traditional patterns.

FROST CUTLERY CO.
P.O. Box 22636
Chattanooga, TN 37422
Phone: 615-894-6079
FAX: 615-894-9576
Specialties: Domestic and imported cutlery, especially folders and pocketknives; Hen & Rooster brand.

GENUINE ISSUE, INC.
949 Middle Country Rd.
Selden, NY 11784
Phone: 516-696-3802
FAX: 516-696-3803
Specialties: Representing the Digby line.

GILMER WOOD CO. (See Knifemaking Supplies)

GODWIN, INC., G. GEDNEY
2139 Welsh Valley Rd.
Valley Forge, PA 19481
Phone: 610-783-0670
Specialties: Reenactment gear—18th and 19th century com-plete.

GOLDEN AGE ARMS CO.
    (See Knifemaking Supplies)

GOLDEN EDGE CUTLERY
16350 S. Golden Rd.
Golden, CO 80401
Phone: 800-828-1925
FAX: 303-278-2057
Specialties: Carry full line of Spyderco products, as well as many other quality knife companies.

HANDMADE CLASSICS
P.O. Box 578373
Chicago, IL 60657
Phone: 312-944-4307
Specialties: Scagel, Bowie, early file knife recreations, authentic and fully useable.

HAWKINS CUSTOM KNIVES & SUPPLIES
    (See Knifemaking Supplies)

HERITAGE ANTIQUE KNIVES
P.O. Box 22171
Chattanooga, TN 37422
Phone: 423-894-8319
Specialties: Bruce Voyles dealing in old knives, mostly U.S. and English and mostly folders; some Bowies. List.

HOUSE OF TOOLS LTD.
#136, 8228 MacLeod Tr. SE
Calgary, Alberta
CANADA T2H 2B8
Phone: 403-258-0005
FAX: 403-252-0149
Specialties: 440C and ATS-34 handle and bolster mate-rial, sand belts, buff wheels and a large selection of tools.

HUNTER SERVICES
P.O. Box 14241
Parkville, MD 64152
Phone: 816-587-9959
FAX: 816-746-5680
Specialties: Quality antique pocketknives and related items. Select custom and military cutlery. $6 for four lists per year, refunded on first order.

JARVIS, PAUL M.
30 Chalk St.
Cambridge, MA 02139
Phone: 617-547-4355
FAX: 617-491-2900
Specialties: Custom knives, Japanese sword fittings, metal carving.

JENCO SALES, INC.
P.O. Box 1000
Manchaca, TX 78652
Phone: 800-531-5301
FAX: 800-266-2373
Specialties: Full line distributor of knives and sharpeners.

KEN'S FINN KNIVES
Rt. 1, Box 338
Republic, MI 49879
Phone: 906-376-2132
Specialties: Puukko and Finnish-made knives. Brochure $2.

KENEFICK, DOUG
29 Leander St.
Danielson, CT 06239
Phone: 203-774-8929
Specialties: Excellent selection of Randall Made knives and custom knives at list prices; catalog on request.

KNIFE-AHOLICS UNANIMOUS
P.O. Box 831
Cockeysville, MD 21030
Phone: 410-628-6262
Specialties: David Cohen—purveyor of custom knives.

KNIFE & CUTLERY PRODUCTS, INC.
P.O. Box 12480
North Kansas City, MO 64116
Phone: 816-454-9879
Specialties: Sells brand-name commercial cutlery, some col-lectibles; 14-page list $2

KNIFE & GUN FINISHING SUPPLIES
P.O. Box 458
Lakeside, AZ 85929
Phone: 520-537-8877
FAX: 520-537-8066
Specialties: Complete line of machine and materials for knife-making and metal finishing. Specializing in rare and exotic handle materials—oosic, ivory, rare hardwoods, horn, stag. Catalog $2.

KNIFE IMPORTERS, INC.
P.O. Box 1000
Manchaca, TX 78652
Phone: 512-282-6860
FAX: 512-282-7504
Specialties: Eye Brand cutlery.

KNIFEMASTERS/J&S FEDER
P.O. Box 2419
Westport, CT 06880
Phone: 203-226-5211
FAX: 203-226-5312
Specialties: Write for details.

KRIS CUTLERY
P.O. Box 133
Pinole, CA 94564
Phone: 510-758-9912
Specialties: Medieval swords and daggers, Indonesian and Moro krisses, Damascus balisongs.

LES COUTEAUX CHOISSIS DE ROBERTS
Ron Roberts
P.O. Box 273
Mifflin, PA 17058
Phone: 717-436-5010
FAX: 717-436-9691
Specialties: Handles all types of manufacturers knives and related items for collectors and users.

LONDON, RICK
P.O. Box 21303
Oakland, CA 94620
Phone: 510-482-2775
Specialties: Purveyor of collectible knives. A special eye for fine crafted folders.

LOVELESS KNIVES (See Denton, J.W.)

MATTHEWS CUTLERY
4401 Sentry Dr., Suite K
Tucker, GA 30084
Phone: 404-939-6915
Specialties: Wholesale only. Carries major brands; monthly sale lists. Catalog (96 pages) $2.

MORTY THE KNIFE MAN
60 Otis St.
West Babylon, NY 11704
Phone: 516-491-5764; 800-247-2511
FAX: 516-491-6325
Specialties: The world's fish knives—all of them.

MURAKAMI, ICHIRO (See Importers & Foreign Cutlers)

MUSEUM REPLICAS LTD.
2143 Gees Mill Rd.
Box 840XZ
Conyers, GA 30207
Phone: 404-922-3703
Specialties: Authentic edged weapons of the ages, battle-ready—over 50 models; subsidiary of Atlanta Cutlery; catalog $2.

NASHOBA VALLEY KNIFEWORKS
373 Langen Rd., Box 35
Lancaster, MA 01523
Phone: 508-365-6593
FAX: 508-368-4171
Specialties: Custom sales, emphasis on Guild members

knives, plus Randall and Ruana. Large inventory; 6 lists a year. List $2.

NORDIC KNIVES
1634CZ Copenhagen Dr.
Solvang, CA 93463
Phone: 805-688-3612
Specialties: Custom and Randall knives; custom catalog $3; Randall catalog $2; both catalogs $4.

PEN AND THE SWORD LTD., THE
1833 E. 12th St.
Brooklyn, NY 11229
Phone: 718-382-4847
FAX: 718-376-5745
Specialties: Custom knives in a wide price range.

PLAZA CUTLERY, INC.
3333 Bristol St.
Costa Mesa, CA 92626
Phone: 714-549-3932
Specialties: List of custom knives for collectors, many top names every time; $1.

POMPER, OTTO
135 S. Wabash Ave.
Chicago, IL 60603
Phone: 312-372-0881
FAX: 312-372-0882
Specialties: Premier fine cutlery, gifts and gadgets.

R&C KNIVES AND SUCH
P.O. Box 1047
Manteca, CA 95336
Phone: 209-239-3722
FAX: 209-825-6947
Specialties: Custom knives for collectors. Wide variety. Send stamps; can call anytime. Catalog $2.

RAMSHEAD ARMOURY
P.O. Box 385
Maryville, IL 62062-0385
Phone: 618-288-3031
Specialties: Stocks swords, daggers and such for the Renaissance dragon-slaying-tournament trade. Catalog $2.

REPRODUCTION BLADES
  (See Knifemaking Supplies)

RIVERSIDE MACHINE (See Knifemaking Supplies)

ROBERTSON'S CUSTOM CUTLERY
P.O. Box 211961
Augusta, GA 30917
Phone: 706-650-0982
Specialties: Investment grade fighters, sub-hilt fighters, Bowies and Daggers.

RUSSELL CO., A.G.
1705 Highway 71 North
Springdale, AR 72764
Phone: 501-751-7341; 800-255-9034
Specialties: Regularly lists custom knives by all makers; sold on

consignment; also commemoratives, Russell and Morseth knives.

SHAW, GARY
24 Central Ave.
Ridgefield Park, NJ 07660
Phone: 201-641-8801
Specialties: Investment-grade knives of all kinds.

SMOKY MOUNTAIN KNIFE WORKS
P.O. Box 4430
Sevierville, TN 37864
Phone: 800-251-9306
Specialties: Retail and wholesale sales of all kinds of knives and supplies.

STIDHAM'S KNIVES
Stidham, Rhett
P.O. Box 570
Roseland, FL 32957-0570
Phone: 407-589-0618
FAX: 407-489-3162
Specialties: Randalls, most of all; other high-end straight collectibles—keeps large inventory.

STODDARD'S, INC.
Copley Place
100 Huntington Ave.
Boston, MA 02116
Phone: 617-536-8688
FAX: 617-357-8263
Specialties: Oldest cutlery retailer in the country; handmade and Randall knives, other fine production knives—Spyderco and Al Mar knives, etc. Manager: Steven Weingrad. Two additional stores in MA area.

STONEWORKS
P.O. Box 211961
Augusta, GA 30907
Phone: 706-650-0982
Specialties: Exclusively designed custom knives with exotic stone handles.

SWORD AND LANCE, THE
21031 Parthenia St., Apt. 140
Canoga Park, CA 91304-2074
Specialties: Provides swords, knives, axes, polearms in ancient, medieval and fantasy pieces. Catalog (60 pages) $2.

THOMAS CUTLERY, CHARLES B.
2504 N. Augusta St.
Staunton, VA 24401
Phone: 703-885-8782
Specialties: Fine selected factory knives from U.S., Germany and Switzerland; discount priced; showroom.

VOYLES, BRUCE (See Heritage Antique Knives)

WASHITA MOUNTAIN WHETSTONE CO.
P.O. Box 378
Lake Hamilton, AR 71951
Phone: 501-525-3914
Specialties: Manufactures sharpening stones and wood products for custom wood boxes for many knife companies.

knife services

engravers

Alfano, Sam, 36180 Henry Gaines Rd., Pearl River, LA 70452/504-863-3364; FAX: 504-863-7715

Alpen, Ralph, 7 Bentley Rd., West Grove, PA 19390/215-869-9493

Allard, Gary, Creek Side Metal & Wood, 2395 Battlefield Rd., Fishers Hill, VA 22626/703-465-3903

Allred, Scott, 2403 Lansing Blvd., Wichita Falls, TX 76309/817-691-9563

American Etching & Engraving Co. (See Miller, James K. and Vicky)

Baron Technology, Inc., 62 Spring Hill Rd., Trumbull, CT 06611/203-452-0515; FAX: 203-452-0663

Bates, Billy, 2302 Winthrop Dr. SW, Decatur, AL 35603/205-355-3690

Beaver, Judy, 48835 N. 25 Ave., Phoenix, AZ 85027/602-465-7831; FAX: 602-465-7077

Becker, Franz, Am Kreuzberg 2, 84533 Marktl/Inn, GERMANY/08678-8020

Bettenhausen, Merle L., 17358 Ottawa, Tinley Park, IL 60477/708-532-2179

Blair, Jim, P.O. Box 64, 58 Mesa Verde, Glenrock, WY 82637/307-436-8115

Blanchard, Gary, 3025 Las Vegas Blvd. S., Las Vegas, NV 89109/702-733-8333; FAX: 702-732-0333

Bleile, C. Roger, 5040 Ralph Ave., Cincinnati, OH 45238/513-251-0249

Bonshire, Benita, 1121 Burlington, Muncie, IN 47302/317-282-9073

Boster, A.D., 3744 Pleasant Hill Dr., Gainesville, GA 30504/404-535-8811

Bratcher, Dan, 311 Belle Aire Place, Carthage, MO 64836/417-356-1518

Brgoch, Frank, 1580 S. 1500 East, Bountiful, UT 84010/801-295-1885

Brooker, Dennis B., Rt. 1 Box 12A, Derby, IA 50068/515-533-2103

Butler, Martin, 305 Robin Rd., London, Ont. N6J 1S5, CANADA/519-641-0652

Churchill, Winston G., RFD P.O. Box 29B, Proctorsville, VT 05153/802-226-7772

Coffey, Barbara, RR 3 Box 662, Monroe, VA 24574-9600

Cole, Larry R., P.O. Box 82, Broadbent, OR 97414-0082

Collins, David, Rt. 2 Box 425, Monroe, VA 24574/804-922-7465

Collins, Michael, Rt. 3075, Batesville Rd., Woodstock, GA 30188/404-475-7410

Creekside Metal & Wood (See Allard, Gary)

Cupp, Alana, P.O. Box 207, Annabella, UT 84711/801-896-4834

Dashwood, Jim, 255 Barkham Rd., Wokingham, Berkshire RG11 4BY, ENGLAND/0734-781761

Davidson, Jere, Rt. 1, Box 132, Rustburg, VA 24588/804-821-3637

Dean, Bruce, 13 Tressider Ave., Haberfield, N.S.W. 2045, AUSTRALIA/02-797-7608

DeLorge, Ed, 2231 Hwy. 308, Thibodaux, LA 70301/504-447-1633

Dibben, Melissa, Rt. 1, Box 80, Harrisville, MO 64701

Dolbare, Elizabeth, 39 Dahlia, Casper, WY 82604/307-266-5924

Drain, Mark, SE 3211 Kamilche Pt. Rd., Shelton, WA 98584/206-426-5452

Duarte, Carlos, 108 Church St., Rossville, CA 95678

Dubben, Michael, 414 S. Fares Ave., Evansville, IN 47714

Dubber, Michael W., P.O. Box 4365, Estes Park, CO 80517-4365/303-586-2388

Duguet, Thierry D., Rt. 250 W., Box 288, Ivy, VA 22945/804-977-4138

Eaton, Rick, 5560 Forbestown Rd., Forbestown, CA 95941/916-675-1632

Eldridge, Allan, 1424 Kansas Lane, Gallatin, TN 37066/615-452-6027

Engel, Terry (Flowers), P.O. Box 96, Midland, OR 97634/503-882-1323

Eyster, Ken, Heritage Gunsmiths, Inc., 6441 Bishop Rd., Centerburg, OH 43011/614-625-6131

Fisher, Jay, 104 S. Main St., P.O. Box 267, Magdela, NM 87825/505-854-2407

Flannery Engraving Co., Jeff, 11034 Riddles Run Rd., Union, KY 41091/606-384-3127

Foster Enterprises, Norvell Foster, P.O. Box 200343, San Antonio, TX 78220/210-333-1675

Fountain Products, 492 Prospect Ave., West Springfield, MA 01089/413-781-4651; FAX: 413-733-8217

French, J.R., 1712 Creek Ridge Ct., Irving, TX 75060/214-254-2645

George, Tim and Christy, Rt. 1, Box 45, Evington, VA 24550

Gilliam, Bill, 4078 Valley Fair, Simi Valley, CA 93063/805-527-7534

Glimm, Jerome C., 19 S. Maryland, Conrad, MT 59425/406-278-3574

Gournet, Geoffroy, 820 Paxinosa Ave., Easton, PA 18042/215-559-0710

Hand Engravers Emporium (See Maki, Robert E.)

Hands Engraving, Barry Lee, 26192 E. Shore Rt., Bigfork, MT 59911/406-837-0035

Harrington, Fred A., Winter: 3725 Citrus, St. James City, FL 33956/813-283-0721; Summer: 2107 W. Frances Rd., Mt. Morris, MI 48458/810-686-3008

Henderson, Fred D., 569 Santa Barbara Dr., Forest Park, GA 30050/404-968-4866

Hendricks, Frank, HC03, Box 434, Dripping Springs, TX 78620/512-858-7828

Heritage Gunsmiths, Inc. (See Eyster, Ken)

Holder, Pat, 4412 W. Diana Ave., Glendale, AZ 85302/602-435-9589; FAX: 602-939-4408

Hudson, Tommy, P.O. Box 2046, Monroe, NC 28110/704-283-8556

Ingle, Ralph W., #4 Missing Link, Rossville, GA 30741/404-866-5589

Johns, Bill, Rt. 4 Box 220, Fredericksburg, TX 78624/210-997-6795

Kelly, Lance, 1723 Willow Oak Dr., Edgewater, FL 32132/904-423-4933

Kelso, Jim, RD 1, Box 5300, Worcester, VT 05682/802-229-4254

Kostelnik, Joe and Patty, RD #4, Box 323, Greensburg, PA 15601/412-832-0365

Kraft, Brenda, Box 1143, Polson, MT 59860

Kudlas, John M., 622 14th St. SE, Rochester, MN 55904/507-288-5579

Lee, Ray, 209 Jefferson Dr., Lynchburg, VA 24502/804-237-2918

Letschnig, Franz, RR1, Martintown, Ont., CANADA/613-528-4843

Limings Jr., Harry, 959 County Rd. 170, Marengo, OH 43334-9625

Lindsay, Steve, RR2 Cedar Hills, Kearney, NE 68847/308-236-7885

Lister, Weldon, Rt. 1, Box 1517, Boerne, TX 78006/210-755-2210

Lyttle, Brian, Box 5697, High River, AB T1V 1M7, CANADA/403-558-3638

Lytton, Simon M., 19 Pinewood Gardens, Hemel Hempstead, Herts. HP1 1TN, ENGLAND/01442-255542

McCombs, Leo, 1862 White Cemetery Rd., Patriot, OH 45658/614-256-1714

McDonald, Dennis, 8359 Brady St., Peosta, IA 52068/319-556-7940

McKenzie, Lynton, 6940 N. Alvernon Way, Tucson, AZ 85718/602-299-5090

Mendenhall, Harry E., 1848 Everglades Dr., Milpitas, CA 95035/408-263-0677

Meyer, Chris, 39 Bergen Ave., Wantage, NJ 07461

Miller, James K. and Vicky, Rt. 2 Box 1-A, Tuscumbia, AL 35674/205-381-1747

Morgan, Tandie, P.O. Box 693, 30700 Hwy. 97, Nucla, CO 81424/303-864-7985

Morton, David A., 1110 W. 21st St., Lorain, OH 44052/216-245-3419

Moschetti, Mitch, P.O. Box 27065, Denver, CO 80227/303-733-9593

Mountain States Engraving (See Warren, Kenneth)

Nelida, Toniutti, via G. Pasconi 29/c, Maniago 33085 (PN), ITALY

Nixon, Jimmie L., 5043 Byrd Ln., Tyler, TX 75707/903-592-1157

Norton, Jeff, 2009 65th St., Lubbock, TX 79412/806-744-2436

Parsons, Michael R., 1600 S. 11th St., Terre Haute, IN 47802-1722/812-234-1679

Patterson, W.H., P.O. Drawer DK, College Station, TX 77841/409-846-9257

Perdue, David L., Rt. 1 Box 657, Gladys, VA 24554/804-283-5300

Pilkington Jr., Scott, P.O. Box 97, Monteagle, TN 37356/615-924-3475

directory

Poag, James, RR1, Box 212A, Grayville, IL 62844/618-375-7106
Potts, Wayne, 912 Poplar St., Denver, CO 80220/303-355-5462
Poulakis, Jon, 58 Redfern Dr., Rochester, NY 14620-4618
Rabeno, Martin, Spook Hollow Trading Co., 92 Spook Hole Rd., Ellenville, NY 12428/914-647-4567
Raftis, Andrew, 2743 N. Sheffield, Chicago, IL 60614/312-871-6699
Reed, Chris, 4399 Bonny Mede Ct., Jackson, MI 49201/517-764-4387
Roberts, J.J., 7808 Lake Dr., Manassas, VA 22111/703-330-0448
Robidoux, Roland J., DMR Fine Engraving, 25 N. Federal Hwy. Studio 5, Dania, FL 33004/305-926-8040; FAX: 305-926-7955
Robyn, Jon, 232 Meriweather Rd., Lynchburg, VA 24503/804-384-7240
Rosser, Bob, Hand Engraving, 1824 29th Ave. South, Suite 214, Birmingham, AL 35209/205-870-4422
Rudolph, Gil, 386 Mariposa Dr., Ventura, CA 93001/805-643-4005
Rundell, Joe, 6198 Frances Rd., Clio, MI 48420/810-687-0559
Schönert, Elke, 18 Lansdowne Pl., Central, Port Elizabeth, SOUTH AFRICA
Shaw, Bruce, P.O. Box 545, Pacific Grove, CA 93950/408-646-1937
Sherwood, George, 46 North River Dr., Roseburg, OR 97470/503-672-3159
Shostle, Ben, 1121 Burlington, Muncie, IN 47302/317-282-9073
Silver Fox Studio, Silver Images, 21 E. Aspen Ave., Flagstaff, AZ 86001/602-774-6604
Sinclair, W.P., 3, The Pippins, Warminster, Wiltshire BA12 8TH, ENGLAND/U.K. Code (44-1985) 218544; FAX: (44-1985) 214111
Smith, Jerry, 7029 East Holmes Rd., Memphis, TN 38125/901-755-2648
Smith, Ron, 5869 Straley, Ft. Worth, TX 76114/817-732-6768

Snell, Barry A., 172 Sexton Lane, Clinton, TN 37716/615-457-9138
Swartley, Robert D., 2800 Pine St., Napa, CA 94558/707-255-1394
Theis, Terry, P.O. Box 535, Fredericksburg, TX 78624/210-997-6778
Thierry, Ivan, 15 Côte de Villancé, 28350 Saint-Lubin-des-Joncherets, FRANCE/33-32582865; FAX: 33-32583831
Valade Engraving, Robert B., 931 3rd Ave., Seaside, OR 97138/503-738-7672
Waldrop, Mark, 14562 SE 1st Ave. Rd., Summerfield, FL 34491/904-347-9034
Walker, Patricia, P.O. Box 2343, 555 Este Es Rd., Taos, NM 87571/505-758-0233; FAX: 505-758-4133
Wallace, Terry, 385 San Marino, Vallejo, CA 94589/707-642-7041
Warenski, Julie, P.O. Box 214, Richfield, UT 84701/801-896-5319
Warren, Kenneth W., Mountain States Engraving, P.O. Box 2842, Wenatchee, WA 98807-2842/509-663-6123
Watson, Silvia, 350 Jennifer Lane, Driftwood, TX 78619/512-847-9679
Wessinger, Louise, 268 Limestone Rd., Chapin, SC 29036
Whitehead, James D., 204 Cappucino Way, Sacramento, CA 95838/916-641-7309; FAX: 916-641-1941
Wildwood Studios (See Rece, Charles V.)
Williams, Gary, 221 Autumn Way, Elizabeth, KY 42701
Willig, Claus, Siedlerweg 17, 8720 Schweinfurt, GERMANY/01149-09721-41446
Winn, Travis A., 585 E. 3065 S., Salt Lake City, UT 84106/801-467-5957
Wood, Mel, P.O. Box 1255, Sierra Vista, AZ 85636/602-455-5541
Young, Paul A., Rt. 1, Box 139-A, Vilas, NC 28692/704-297-4039
Zietz, Dennis, 5906 40th Ave., Kenosha, WI 53144/414-654-9550

heat-treaters

American Etching & Engraving Co. (See Miller, James K. and Vicky)
Barbee, Jim, P.O. Box 1173, Fort Stockton, TX 79753/915-336-2882
Bay State Metal Treating Co., 6 Jefferson Ave., Woburn, MA 01801/617-935-4100
Bos Heat Treating, Paul, Shop: 1900 Weld Blvd., El Cajon, CA 92020/619-562-2370; Home: 2320 Yucca Hill Dr., Alpine, CA 91901/619-445-4740
El Monte Steel, 355 SE End Ave., Pomona, CA 91766
Hauni Richmond, Inc., 2800 Charles City Rd., Richmond, VA 23231/804-222-5262
Holt, B.R., 1238 Birchwood Dr., Sunnyvale, CA 94089/408-736-8500
Lamprey, Mike, 32 Pathfield, Great Torrington, Devon EX38 TBX, ENGLAND/01805-622651

Metal Treating, Inc., 710 Burns St., Cincinnati, OH 45204/513-921-2300; FAX: 513-921-2536
Miller, James K. and Vicky, Rt. 2 Box 1-A, Tuscumbia, AL 35674/205-381-1747
O&W Heat Treat, Inc., One Bidwell Rd., South Windsor, CT 06074/203-528-9239; FAX: 203-291-9939
Texas Heat Treating, Inc., 303 Texas Ave., Round Rock, TX 78664/512-255-5884
Texas Knifemakers Supply, 10649 Haddington, Suite 180, Houston, TX 77043/713-461-8632
The Tinker Shop, 1120 Helen, Deer Park, TX 77536/713-479-7286
Valley Metal Treating, Inc., 355 S. East End Ave., Pomona, CA 91766/909-623-6316; FAX: 909-620-7304
Wilson, R.W., P.O. Box 2012, Weirton, WV 26062/304-723-2771

leatherworkers

Andre, John, Beadwork & Buckskin, 3955 NW 103 Dr., Coral Springs, FL 33065/305-345-0447
Anonymous Leather & Mfg., Vary Ltd., 519 Castro St., #M38, San Francisco, CA 94114/415-431-4555
The Astorian Ltd. (See Noone, George S.)
Baker, Don and Kay, 5950 Foxfire Dr., Zanesville, OH 43701/614-849-3044
Beadwork & Buckskin (See Andre, John)
Blade-Tech (See Wegner, Tim)
Cheramie, Grant, 4260 West Main, Rt. 3, Box 940, Cut Off, LA 70345/504-632-5770
Clements' Custom Leathercraft, Chas, 1741 Dallas St., Aurora, CO 80010-2018/303-364-0403; FAX: 303-364-0403
Congdon, David, Congdon Blade Leather, 1063 Whitchurch Ct., Wheaton, IL 60187/708-665-8825
Cooper, Harold, 136 Winding Way, Frankfort, KY 40601/502-227-8151
Cooper, Jim, 2148 Cook Place, Ramona, CA 92065-3214/619-789-1097
Cow Catcher Leatherworks, 3006 Industrial Ave., Raleigh, NC 27609/919-833-8262
Custom Leather Knife Sheath Co. (See Schrap, Robert G.)

Dawkins, Dudley, 221 N. Broadmoor, Topeka, KS 66606/913-235-0468
Dennehy, John D. Custom Leatherworks, P.O. Box 431, 3926 Hayes, Wellington, CO 80549/303-568-9055
Fannin, David A., 2050 Idle Hour Center #191, Lexington, KY 40502
Foley, Barney, 8241 262nd St., Floral Park, NY 11004-1512/718-347-1646
Genske, Jay, 262½ Elm St., Fond du Lac, WI 54935/414-921-6505
Graves, Dave, Miracle Valley Leather, P.O. Box 383, Lerona, WV 25971/304-384-9137
Harris, Tom, 519 S. 1st St., Mount Vernon, WA 98273/206-336-2713
Hawk, Ken, Western Leather, Rt. 1, Box 770, Ceres, VA 24318-9630/703-624-3219
Homyk, David N., 8047 Carriage Ln., Wichita Falls, TX 76306/817-855-8425
John's Custom Leather (See Stumpf, John R.)
Kravitt, Chris, Treestump Leather, 18 State St., Ellsworth, ME 04605/207-667-8756
Lamprey, Mike, 32 Pathfield, Great Torrington, Devon EX38 7BX, ENGLAND/0805-622651
Lay, Judy M., RR #2 Braeside Rd., Vanderhoof B.C. VOJ 3AO CANADA/604-567-3856

Layton, Jim, 2710 Gilbert Ave., Portsmouth, OH 45662/614-353-6179
Lee, Sonja, P.O. Box 1873, St. Johns, AZ 85936/520-337-2594
Lefaucheux, Jean-Victor, Saint-Denis-Le-Ferment, 27140 Gisors, FRANCE/16.32.55-1410; FAX: 16.32.55-5087
Luck, Gregory, P.O. Box 2255, Greeley, CO 80632/303-686-7223
Mason, Arne, Mesa Case, 125 Wimer St., Ashland, OR 97520/503-482-2260; 800-326-9078
McGowan, Liz, 12629 Howard Lodge Dr., Sykesville, MD 21784/410-489-4323
Mesa Case (See Mason, Arne)
Metheny, H.A.“Whitey”, 7750 Waterford Dr., Spotsylvania, VA 22553/703-582-3228
Miller, Michael K., M&M Kustom Krafts, 28510 Santiam Highway, Sweet Home, OR 97386/503-367-4927
Milton Gomes Cristine, Jose, R. Natal Meira de Barros, 194, Jd. Aricanduva, Sao Paulo, SP-03454-030, BRAZIL/011-8866895
Miracle Valley Leather (See Graves, Dave)
M&M Kustom Krafts (See Miller, Michael K.)
Morrissey, Martin, 4578 Stephens Rd., Blairsville, GA 30512
Niedenthal, John Andre, Beadwork & Buckskin, Studio 3955 NW 103 Dr., Coral Springs, FL 33065-1551/305-345-0447
NQ Leatherworks (See Qvist, Niels)
Poag, James H., RR #1 Box 212A, Grayville, IL 62844/618-375-7106
Pratt, Charles, 1953 Fillmans Bottom Rd., Port Washington, OH 43837/614-498-5404
Qvist, Niels, Leestrupvej #2, Hyllede, DK-4683 Roennede, DENMARK/(45)53 82 57 52
Ravon Industries, P.O. Box 670, Denton, TX 76202/817-382-1831
Red's Custom Leather, Ed Todd, 9 Woodlawn Rd., Putnam Valley, NY 10579/914-528-3783

Riney, Norm, 6212 S. Marion Way, Littleton, CO 80121/303-794-1731
Rowe, Kenny, Rowe's Leather, 1306 W. Ave. C, Hope, AR 71801/501-777-2974, 501-777-8216
Rowe's Leather Goods (See Rowe, Kenny)
Ruiz Industries, Inc., 1513 Gardena Ave., Glendale, CA 91204/818-242-4239
Schrap, Robert G., Custom Leather Knife Sheath Co., 7024 W. Wells St., Wauwatosa, WI 53213-3717/414-771-6472; FAX: 414-784-2996
Spragg, Wayne E., P.O. Box 508, Ashton, ID 83420/915-944-9630
Strahin, Robert, 401 Center Ave., Elkins, WV 26241/304-636-0128
Stuart, V. Pat, Rt. 1, Box 447-S, Greenville, VA 24440/703-377-2596
Stumpf, John R., John's Custom Leather, 523 S. Liberty St., Blairsville, PA 15717/412-459-6802
Tierney, Mike, 447 Rivercrest Dr., Woodstock, ON N4S 5W5, CANADA/519-539-8859
Todd, Ed (See Red's Custom Leather)
Treestump Leather (See Kravitt, Chris)
Turner, Kevin, 17 Hunt Ave., Montrose, NY 10548/814-739-0535
Velasquez, Gil, 7120 Madera Dr., Goleta, CA 93117/805-968-7787
Watson, Bill, #1 Presidio, Wimberly, TX 78676/512-847-2531
Wegner, Tim, Blade-Tech Industries Inc., 8818-158th St. E., Puyallup, WA 98373/206-840-0447; FAX: 206-840-0447
Western Leather (See Hawk, Ken)
Whinnery, Walt, 1947 Meadow Creek Dr., Louisville, KY 40218/502-458-4361
Wilder, W. Barry (See Cow Catcher Leatherworks)
Williams, Sherman A., 1709 Wallace St., Simi Valley, CA 93065/805-583-3821

photographers

A Bar V Studio (See Rhoades, Cynthia J.)
Alfano, Sam, 36180 Henery Gaines Rd., Pearl River, LA 70452
Allen, John, Studio One, 3823 Pleasant Valley Blvd., Rockford, IL 61114
Berchtold, Robert, Berchtold Studios, 820 Greenbriar Circle, Suite #26, Chesapeake, VA 23320/804-366-0653; FAX: 804-366-0122
Berchtold Studios (See Berchtold, Robert)
Berisford, Bob, 505 West Adams St., Jacksonville, FL 32202/904-356-4780
Bittner, Rodman, 3444 North Apache Circle, Chandler, AZ 85224/602-730-5088
Bloomer, Peter L., Horizons West, 427 S. San Francisco St., Flagstaff, AZ 86001/602-779-1014
Bogaerts, Jan, Regenweg 14, 5757 Pl., Liessel HOLLAND/04934-1580; FAX: 04934-2664
Box Photography, Doug, 1700 West Main, Brenham, TX 77833/409-836-1700
Brian Photography, Inc., 412 S. 5th St., Dade City, FL 33525/904-567-7569
Brown, Charles, P.O. Box 671, Clayton, NC 27520/919-553-4688
Brown, Tom, 6048 Grants Ferry Rd., Brandon, MS 39042-8136
Buffaloe, Edwin, 104 W. Applegate, Austin, TX 78753/512-837-9746
Burdette, Roger W., Custom Images, 2421 Logan Ave., Des Moines, IA 50317/515-266-4743
Burger, Gunter, Horststr. 55, 44581 Castrop-Rauseel GERMANY/02305-77145
Butman, Steve, P.O. Box 5106, Abilene, TX 79608/915-695-2341
Calidonna, Greg, 205 Helmwood Dr., Elizabethtown, KY 42701/502-769-2463
Carter, Art, 818 Buffin Bay Rd., Columbia, SC 28210/802-772-2148
Casey, Robert, 3590 Polk Ave., Ogden, UT 84403/801-394-9114
Catalano, John D., 56 Kingston Ave., Hicksville, NY 11801/516-938-1356
Chastain, Christopher, B&W Labs, 1462 E. Michigan St., Orlando, FL 32806/407-898-0266
Clark, John W., 604 Chevry St., Des Moines, IA 50309/515-280-3954
Cook, John, P.O. Box 642, Nambour 4560, AUSTRALIA
Corbett Photography, Charles, 126 Wilcocks Rd., Bloemfontein 9301, REPUBLIC OF SOUTH AFRICA/051-366-565; FAX: 051-366-565

Cotton, William A., 749 S. Lemay Ave. A3-211, Fort Collins, CO 80524/303-221-5071
Country Visions Photography (See Wells, Carlene L.)
Courtice, Bill, P.O. Box 1776, Duarte, CA 91010-4776/818-358-5715
Criscooli, Walter, Via Aquilzia 14, 33100 Udine, ITALY/0432-26819
Crosby, Doug, RFD 1, Box 1111, Stockton Springs, ME 04981
Custom Images (See Burdette, Roger W.)
Davis, Marshall B., P.O. Box 3048, Austin, TX 78764/512-443-4030
Durant, Ross, 316 E. 1st Ave., Vancouver, B.C. V5t 1A9, CANADA/604-872-2717
Earley, Don, 1241 Ft. Bragg Rd., Fayetteville, NC 28305/910-485-6660
Ehrlich, Linn M., 2643 N. Clybourn Ave., Chicago, IL 60614/312-472-2025
Ellison, Troy, 3709 19th, Box 436, Lubbock, TX 79410/806-793-7777
Elvens Foto AB (See Eriksson, Stig)
Eriksson, Stig, Elvens Foto AB, Box 103, S-828 00 Edsbyn, SWEDEN/0271-20197
Etzler, John, 11200 N. Island Rd., Grafton, OH 44044/216-748-3980
Everett, David, White Lotus Studio, 258 Hartford Ave., Newington, CT 06111-2077
Fahrner Photographics, Dave, 1623 Arnold St., Pittsburgh, PA 15205/412-921-6861
Faul, Jan W., 903 Girard St. NE, Rr. Washington, DC 20017/202-526-1122; FAX: 202-526-0905
Fedorak, Allan, 28 W. Nicola St., Amloops, B.C. V2C 1J6, CANADA/604-372-1255
Fisher, Jay, P.O. Box 267, Magdalena, NM 87825
Fitzgerald, Dan, P.O. Box 198, Beverly Hills, CA 90213/818-507-8418
Forster, Jenny, 1112 N. McAree, Waukegan, IL 60085/708-244-7928
Foster's, Star Rt., Box 259A, Topton, NC 28781/704-321-3561
Fox, Daniel, Lumina Studios, 2570 Superior Ave., Cleveland, OH 44114/216-589-9090
Gardner, Chuck, 116 Quincy Ave., Oak Ridge, TN 37830/615-483-9411
Gawryla, Don, 1105 Greenlawn Dr., Pittsburgh, PA 15220/412-344-0787
Godby, Ronald E., 204 Seven Hollys Dr., Yorktown, VA 23692/804-898-4445

Goffe Photographic Associates, 3108 Monte Vista Blvd., N.E., Albuquerque, NM 87106/505-262-1421

Gray, Corey, 760 Warehouse Rd., Suite D, Toledo, OH 43615/419-382-3222

Griggs, Dennis, Tannery Hill Studios, Inc., RR 1 Box 44A, Topsham, ME 04086-9705/207-725-5689

Gustavsson, Hakan, Box 182, S-828 00 Edsbyn, SWEDEN/0271-236 00

Hansen, Claus Stahnke, Kastrupvej 75, 1 tv., 2300 Copenhagen KBH S, DENMARK/01 58 54 78

Hanusin, John, 3306 Commercial, Northbrook, IL 60062/708-564-2706

Hardy Photographics, Scott, 639 Myrtle Ave., Placerville, CA 95667/916-622-5780

Hays, James A., 9515 W. 118th St. #10, Overland Park, KS 66210-3174/816-363-1344

Hodge, Tom, P.O. Box 4444, Highland Park, NJ 08904/201-247-8869

Holter, Wayne V., 125 Larking Ave., Boonsboro, ND 21713

Horizons West (See Bloomer, Peter L.)

Impress by Design, 304 Timberidge Dr., Martinez, GA 30907/706-650-0982

Integrated Arts (See Bradley, Steven)

Kelley Photography, Gary, 17485 SW Pheasant Lane, Aloha, OR 97006/503-848-9313

Kerns, Bob, 18723 Birdseye Dr., Germantown, MD 20874/301-916-9092

Korsnes, Egil, Brakehaugen 2A, N-5050 Nesttun, NORWAY/55-135630

LaFleur, Gordon, 111 Hirst, Box 1209, Parksville, BC, CANADA V0R 270/604-248-8585

Landis, George E., Landis Associates, Inc., 16 Prospect Hill Rd., Cromwell, CT 06416/203-635-4720

Lasting Images Photography (See Stittleburg, Jan)

Lautman, Andy, 4906 41st N.W., Washington, D.C. 20016

Lear Photography, Dale, 234 Broadway St., Jackson, OH/614-286-6767

LeBlanc, Paul, No. 3 Meadowbrook Cir., Melissa, TX 75454/214-838-4290

Lenz Photography, 939 S. 48th St., Suite 206, Tempe, AZ 85281/602-894-1229

Lester, Dean, 2801 Junipero Ave, Suite 212, Long Beach, CA 90806-2140/310-426-3960

Levinson, Lester, 13038 S. Brandon Ave., Chicago, IL 60633/312-646-1060

Lewis, K.J., 374 Cook Rd., Lugoff, SC 29078

Long, Gary W., 3556 Miller's Crossroad Rd., Hillsboro, TN 37342/615-596-2275

Long, Jerry, 402 E. Gladden Dr., Farmington, NM 87401

Lum, Billy, 16307 Evening Star Ct., Crosby, TX 77532/713-328-3521

Lumina Studios (See Fox, Daniel)

Marshall Arts Photography (See Davis, Marshall B.)

McClintock, Robert, 111 Main St., Brattleboro, VT 05301/802-257-1100

McCollum, Tom, P.O. Box 933, Lilburn, GA 30226/404-972-8552

McCrackin, Kevin, 3720 Hess Rd., House Springs, MO 63051/314-677-6066

Moake, Jim, 18 Council Ave., Aurora, IL 60504/312-898-7184

Moya, Inc., 4212 S. Dixie Hwy., West Palm Beach, FL 33405/407-832-8457

Nevada Commercial Photography (See Parker, T.C.)

Newton, Thomas D., 136 1/2 W. 2nd St., Reno, NV 89501/702-232-0971

Norman's Studio, 322 S. 2nd St., Vivian, LA 71082/318-375-2932

Owens, William T., Box 99, Williamsburg, WV 24991/304-645-4114

Palmer Studio, 2008 Airport Blvd., Mobile, AL 36606/205-471-3523

Parker, T.C., Nevada Commercial Photography, 1720 Pacific, Las Vegas, NV 89104/702-457-0179

Parsons, 15 South Mission, Suite 3, Wenatchee, WA 98801/509-662-9576

Payne, Bob, 2385 Tyler Lane, Louisville, KY 40205/502-459-9602

Payne, Robert G., P.O. Box 141471, Austin, TX 78714/512-272-4554

Peders, Foto Atelier, Markevn 4A, 5012 Bergen, NORWAY/55-90-00-44

Photographic Multi-Services (See Smith, Earl W.)

Randall, William, 2525 N. Alvernon #F6, Tucson, AZ 85712

Rasmussen, Eric L., 1121 Eliason, Brigham City, UT 84302/801-734-9710

Reinders, Rick, 1707 Spring Place, Racine, WI 53404/414-634-1246

Rhoades, Cynthia J., A Bar V Studio, Box 195, Clearmont, WY 82835/307-758-4380

Rice Photography, Tim, 310 Wisconsin, Whitefish, MT 59937/406-862-5416

Richardson, Kerry, 2520 Mimosa St., Santa Rosa, CA 95405/707-575-1875

Ridolfi's Photographics, 830 Central Ave., Tracy, CA 95376/209-835-7551; 209-835-7587

Rogo, Penny L., Silhouettes Studio, 4400 140th Ave. N. Suite 150, Clearwater, FL 34622-3813

Ross, Bill (See Ross Commercial Photographics)

Ross Commercial Photographics, P.O. Box 413, 405 Second Ave., Gallipolis, OH 45631/614-446-6700

Rubicam, Stephen, 14 Atlantic Ave., Boothbay Harbor, ME 04538-1202/207-633-4125

Ruby, Tom, Holiday Inn University, 11200 E. Goodman Rd., Olive Branch, MS 38654/601-895-2941

Rush, John D., 2313 Maysel, Bloomington, IL 61701/309-663-6766

Scadlock, David V., 406 Oak St., Mt. Horeb, WI 53572/608-437-4434

Schreiber, Roger, 429 Boren Ave. N., Seattle, WA 98109/206-622-3525

Sellick, Rachel, 92 The Glebe, Glebe Estate, Norton, Stockton-On-Tees, Cleveland, TS20 1RL ENGLAND

Semmer, Charles, 7885 Cyd Dr., Denver, CO 80221/303-429-6947

Silhouettes Studio (See Rogo, Penny L.)

Silver Fox Studio, Silver Images Photography, 21 E. Aspen Ave., Flagstaff, AZ 86001/520-774-6604; FAX: 520-774-7408

Sims Photography, 461 Breezy Dr., Marietta, GA 30064/404-428-1698

Slobodian, Scott, 13570 Norma Ct., Pine Grove, CA 95665/209-296-3809; FAX: 209-296-3828

Smith, Earl W., Photographic Multi-Services, 5121 Southminster Rd., Columbus, OH 43221/614-771-6487

Smith, Randall, 1720 Oneco Ave., Winter Park, FL 32789/407-628-5447

Storm Photo, 334 Wall St., Kingston, NY 12401

Strauss, Hans J., Bahnhofstr. 2, D-8262 Altotting, GERMANY/086 71-6979

Studio Elfin, Box 515, Bethlehem 9700, SOUTH AFRICA/058-3034830; FAX: 058-3038287

Surles, Mark, P.O. Box 147, Falcon, NC 28342/919-483-8814

Tardiolo, Photo, 9381 Wagon Wheel, Yuma, AZ 85365/602-248-1302

Teger, Allan I., 248 Tremont St., Newton, MA 02158/617-527-0798

Terra Photographic, P.O. Box 978, Newport, NH 03773/603-863-7735

Third Eye Photos, 140 E. Sixth Ave., Helena, MT 59601/406-443-4688

Tighe, Brian, RR 1, Ridgeville, Ontario, LOS 1MO CANADA/905-892-2734

Tocci, Tony, 41 Ellwood Rd., East Brunswick, NJ 08816/908-238-2289

Towell, Steven L., 1124 Wedgewood Dr., Franklin, TN 37064/615-794-9893

Troutman, Harry, 107 Oxford Dr., Lititz, PA 17543/717-626-0685

Tsutsumi, Naganori, World Photo Press, 3-39-2, Nakano, Nakano-ku, Tokoyo 164, JAPAN/03-5358-1341; FAX: 03-5385-1347

Valley Photo, 2100 Arizona Ave., Yuma, AZ 85364/602-783-3522

Vallini, Massimo, Via Dello Scalo 2/3, 40131 Bologna ITALY/011-39-51-522.087

Vara, Lauren, P.O. Box 13511, Arlington, TX 76094/817-861-4299

Verhoeven, Jon, 106 San Jose Dr., Springdale, AR 72764-2538/501-751-5040

Wabnik, Jochen, Otto-Dix-Ring 66, 01219 Dresden, GERMANY/275-3035

Wells, Carlene L., Country Visions Photography, 1060 S. Main, Sp. 52, Colville, WA 99114/509-684-2954

Weyer International, 2740 Nebraska Ave., Toledo, OH 43607/419-534-2020; FAX: 419-534-2697

White Lotus Studio (See Everett, David)
Wildwood Studios, 1949 E. Main St., Albemarle, NC 28001/704-982-1178

Wise, Harriet, 242 Dill Ave., Frederick, MD 21701
Worley, Holly, 4186 W. Grand Ave., Littleton, CO 80123/303-794-5832
Ziegler, Larry, 303 Oakwood Dr., Mt. Holly, NC 28120/704-827-6598

scrimshanders

American Etching & Engraving Co. (See Miller, James K. and Vicky)
Anderson, Terry Jack, 10076 Birnamwoods Way, Riverton, UT 84065-9073
Art of Scrimshaw (See Velasquez, Gil)
Bailey, Mary W., 3213 Jonesboro Dr., Nashville, TN 37214/615-889-3172
Baker, Duane, 2145 Alum Creek Dr., Cambridge Park Apt. #10, Columbus, OH 43207/614-236-0915
Barrett, R.W., 3214 Montrose Dr., Huntsville, AL 35805/205-539-3439
Barrows, Miles, 524 Parsons Ave., Chillicothe, OH 45601/614-775-9627
Beauchamp, Gaetan, 125, de la Riviere, Stoneham, PQ CANADA
Beaver, Judy, 48835 N. 25 Ave., Phoenix, AZ 85027/602-465-7831; FAX: 602-465-7077
Bellet, Connie, Fickle Finger Flats, P.O. Box 111, Ringling, MT 59642/406-547-2272
Benade, Lynn, 2567 Edgewood Rd., Beechwood, OH 44122/216-464-0777
Bonshire, Benita, 1121 Burlington Dr., Muncie, IN 47302/317-282-9073 (Phone & FAX)
Boone Trading Co., Inc., P.O. Box BB, Brinnon, WA 98320/206-796-4330
Bouchard, Judy, 1808 W. Pleasant Ridge Rd., Hammond, LA 70403/504-345-2456
Bowles, Rick, 1416 Debbs Rd., Chesapeake, VA 23320
Brady, Sandra, P.O. Box 104, Monclova, OH 43542/419-866-0435; FAX: 419-867-0656
Burdette, Bob, 4908 Maplewood Dr., Greenville, SC 29615/803-288-0976
Byrne, Mary Gregg, 1018 15th St., Bellingham, WA 98225-6604/206-676-1413
Cable, Jerry, 332 Main St., Mt. Pleasant, PA 15666/412-547-8282
Capocci-Christman, Lynda, RR 4, Box 289A, Wabash, IN 46992/219-563-4634
Caudill, Lyle, 7626 Lyons Rd., Georgetown, OH 45121/513-876-2212
Collins, Michael, Rt. 3075, Batesville Rd., Woodstock, GA 30188/404-475-7410
Cosimini, Rene (See McDonald, Rene Cosimini-)
Courtnage, Elaine, Box 473, Big Sandy, MT 59520/406-378-2492
Cover Jr., Raymond A., Rt. 1, Box 194, Mineral Point, MO 63660/314-749-3783
Cox, J. Andy, 116 Robin Hood Lane, Gaffney, SC 29340/803-489-1892
Cricchio, Barbara, P.O. Box 91, Hackensack, NJ 07602-0091
Curtis, Jean E., 2809 Midwood, Lansing, MI 48910/517-393-9316
Davenport, Susan, 36842 W. Center Ave., Dade City, FL 33525/904-521-4088; FAX: 904-521-4088
DeYoung, Brain, 4140 Cripple Creek Way, Kennesaw, GA 30144/404-928-8051
DiMarzo, Richard, 2357 Center Place, Birmingham, AL 35205/205-252-3331
Dolbare, Elizabeth, 39 Dahlia, Casper, WY 82604/307-266-5924
Eldridge, Allan, 1424 Kansas Lane, Gallatin, TN 37066/615-452-6027
Engel, Terry (Flowers), P.O. Box 96, Midland, OR 97634/503-882-1323
Engnath, Bob, 1217 Crescent Dr., Apt. B, Glendale, CA 91205/818-241-3629
Eubank, Mary Ann, Rt. 1, Box 196, Pottsboro, TX 75076/903-786-3596; FAX: 903-786-3501
Evans, Rick M., 2717 Arrowhead Dr., Abilene, TX 79606/915-698-2620
Fields, Rick B., 26401 Sandwich Pl., Mt. Plymouth, FL 32776/904-383-6270; FAX: 904-383-6270
Fisk, Dale, Box 252, Council, ID 83612/208-253-4582

Foster Enterprises, Norvell Foster, P.O. Box 200343, San Antonio, TX 78220/210-333-1675
Fountain Products, 492 Prospect Ave., West Springfield, MA 01089/413-781-4651; FAX: 413-733-8217
Frazier, W.C., RR 3, Box 8720, Mansfield, LA 71052/318-872-1732
Garbe, Sandra, 1246 W. Webb, DeWitt, MI 48820/517-669-6022
Gemma, John, 24 Vermont St., Johnston, RI 02919/401-831-5427
Gill, Scott, 925 N. Armstrong St., Kokomo, IN 46901/317-452-3657
Halligan, Ed & Shawn, 14 Meadow Way, Sharpsburg, GA 30277/404-251-7720 (Phone & FAX)
Hargraves Sr., Charles, RR 3 Bancroft, Ontario, CANADA/613-339-2302
Harless, Star, c/o Arrow Forge, P.O. Box 845, Stoneville, NC 27048-0845/910-573-9768
Harrington, Fred A., Winter: 3725 Citrus, St. James City, FL 33956/813-283-0721; Summer: 2107 W. Frances Rd., Mt. Morris, MI 48458/810-686-3008
Hawkins, Stan, 2230 El Capitan, Arcadia, CA 91006/818-445-3054
Henry, Michael K., Intarsia and Scrimshaw Art, P.O. Box 735, East Moriches, NY 11940/516-878-2063
Hergert, Bob, 12120 SW 9th, Beaverton, OR 97005/503-641-6924
Hielscher, Vickie, HC34, P.O. Box 992, Alliance, NE 69301
High, Tom, Rocky Mountain Scrimshaw & Arts, 5474 S. 112.8 Rd., Alamosa, CO 81101/719-589-2108; FAX: 719-589-2826
Himmelheber, David R., 11289 40th St. N., Royal Palm Beach, FL 33411/407-795-1264
Holland, Dennis K., 4908-17th Place, Lubbock, TX 79416/806-799-8427
Hoover, Harvey, 14536 Asheville Dr., Magalia, CA 95954/916-873-3546
Images In Ivory (See Stahl, John)
Imboden II, Howard L., 620 Deerville Dr., Dayton, OH 45429/513-439-1536
Johnson, Corinne, W3565 Lockington, Mindora, WI 54644/608-857-3035
Johnston, Kathy, W. 1134 Providence, Spokane, WA 99205/509-326-5711
Journey Artistic Creations (See Nelson, Judith K.)
Karst, Linda K., 402 Hwy. 27 E., Ingram, TX 78025/210-367-3350
Kelso, Jim, RD 1, Box 5300, Worcester, VT 05682/802-229-4254
Kiracofe, Gary, 1012 Trillium Ln., Sister Bay, WI 54234
Kirk, Susan B., 1340 Freeland Rd., Merrill, MI 48637/517-839-9131
Kostelnik, Joe and Patty, RD #4, Box 323, Greensburg, PA 15601/412-832-0365
Kudlas, John M., 622 14th St. SE, Rochester, MN 55904/507-288-5579
Land, John W., P.O. Box 917, Wadesboro, NC 28170/704-694-5141, 704-694-2001
Lemen, Pam, 3434 N. Iroquois Ave., Tucson, AZ 85705/520-887-3095
Letschnig, Franz, RR1, Martintown, Ont., CANADA/613-528-4843
Little, Mary M., HC 34, Box 10301, P.O. Box 156, Broadbent, OR 97414/503-572-2656
Lovestrand, Erik, 1211 Yorkshire St., Prattville, AL 36067-6821/912-275-7932
Martin, Diane, 28220 N. Lake Dr., Waterford, WI 53185/414-662-3629
McCullough, Larry E., Box 556, Mocksville, NC 27028/704-634-5632
McDonald, Rene Cosimini-, 2300 N.W. 81 Avenue, Sunrise, FL 33322/305-748-5090
McFadden, Berni, 1402 E. Best Ave., Coeur d'Alene, ID 83814/208-664-2686
McGowan, Frank, 12629 Howard Lodge Dr., Sykesville, MD 21784/410-489-4323
McGrath, Gayle, 12641 Panasoffkee, N. Ft. Meyers, FL 33903/813-997-2215

McKissack II, Tommy, P.O. Box 991, Sonora, TX 76950/915-387-3253

McLaran, Lou, 603 Powers St., Waco, TX 76705/817-799-2234

McWilliams, Carole, P.O. Box 693, Bayfield, CO 81122/303-884-0320

Mead, Faustina L., 2550 E. Mercury St., Inverness, FL 34453-0514/904-344-4751

Mendenhall, Harry E., 1848 Everglades Dr., Milpitas, CA 95035/408-263-0677

Miller, Anita, 450 S. 1st, Seward, NE 68434/402-643-4726

Miller, James K. and Vicky, Rt. 2 Box 1-A, Tuscumbia, AL 35674/205-381-1747

Minnick, Joyce, 144 N. 7th St., Middletown, IN 47356/317-354-4108

Mitchell, James, 1026 7th Ave., Columbus, GA 31901/404-576-4014

Moore, James B., 1707 N. Gillis, Stockton, TX 79735/915-336-2113

Morris, Darrel, 29 Hawksmoor, Aliso Viejo, CA 92656

Nelson, Judy, 8170 S. Eastern Ave., Suite 4-124, Las Vegas, NV 89123

Ochonicky, Michelle "Mike", Stone Hollow Scrimshaw Studio, 31 High Trail, Eureka, MO 63025/314-938-9570

Ochs, Belle, 124 Emerald Lane, Largo, FL 34641/813-530-3826

Parish, Vaughn, 103 Cross St., Monaca, PA 15061/412-495-3024

Peck, Larry H., 4021 Overhill Rd., Hannibal, MO 63401/314-221-5994

Peterson, Lou, 514 S. Jackson St., Gardner, IL 60424/815-237-8432

Petree, Linda A., Rt. 14, Box 2364A, Kennewick, WA 99337/509-586-9596

Poag, James H., RR #1 Box 212A, Grayville, IL 62844/618-375-7106

Polk, Trena, 4625 Webber Creek Rd., Van Buren, AR 72956/501-474-3828

Purvis, Hilton, P.O. Box 371, Noordhoek, 7985, REP. OF SOUTH AFRICA/021-891114

Rece, Charles V., P.O. Box 868, Paw Creek, NC 28130/704-391-0209

Riffe, Glen, 4430 See Saw Cir., Colorado Springs, CO 80917/719-574-8568

Roberts, J.J., 7808 Lake Dr., Manassas, VA 22111/703-330-0448

Rocky Mountain Scrimshaw & Arts (See High, Tom)

Rundell, Joe, 6198 Frances Rd., Clio, MI 48420/810-687-0559

Satre, Robert, 518 3rd Ave. NW, Weyburn, Sask. S4H 1R1, CANADA/306-842-3051

Schulenburg, E.W., 25 North Hill St., Carrollton, GA 30117

Schwallie, Patricia, 4614 Old Spartanburg Rd. Apt. 47, Taylors, SC 29687/803-292-8975

Selent, Chuck, P.O. Box 1207, Bonners Ferry, ID 83805/208-267-5807

Semich, Alice, 10037 Roanoke Dr., Murfreesboro, TN 37129/615-890-5146

Sherwood, George, 46 North River Dr., Roseburg, OR 97470/503-672-3159

Shostle, Ben, 1121 Burlington, Muncie, IN 47302/317-282-9073 (Phone & FAX)

Sinclair, W.P., 3, The Pippins, Warminster, Wiltshire BA12 8TH, ENGLAND/U.K. Code (44-1985) 218544; FAX: (44-1985) 214111

Smith, Jerry, 7029 East Holmes Rd., Memphis, TN 38125/901-755-2648

Smith, Peggy, 676 Glades Rd., Shop #3, Gatlinburg, TN 37738/615-436-3322; 615-436-3567

Smith, Ron, 5869 Straley, Ft. Worth, TX 76114/817-732-6768

Stearns, Glen, 209 N. Detroit St., Kenton, OH 43326

Stahl, John, Images in Ivory, 2049 Windsor Rd., Baldwin, NY 11510/516-223-5007

Stalter, Harry L., 2509 N. Trivoli Rd., Trivoli, IL 61569/309-362-2306

Stone Hollow Scrimshaw Studio (See Ochonicky, Michelle "Mike")

Stuart, Stephen, 8080 Sunrise Lakes Dr. N., Building 28, Apt. 106, Sunrise, FL 33322/305-748-5151

Talley, Mary Austin, 2499 Countrywood Parkway, Cordova, TN 38018/901-372-2263

Thompson, Larry D., 23040 Ave. 197, Strathmore, CA 93267/209-568-2048

Tisdale, Gerald, 10013 Album Ave., El Paso, TX 79925-5442/915-590-4188

Tong, Jill, P.O. Box 572, Tombstone, AZ 85638/602-457-9268

Toniutti, Nelida, Via G. Pascoli, 33085 Maniago-PN-, Italy/24-0594

Velasquez, Gil, Art of Scrimshaw, 7120 Madera Dr., Goleta, CA 93117/805-968-7787

Walker, Karen, Star Route, Alpine, WY 83128/307-883-2372

Walker, Patricia, P.O. Box 2343, 555 Este Es Rd., Taos, NM 87571/505-758-0233; FAX: 505-758-4133

Warren, Al, 1423 Santa Fe Circle, Roseville, CA 95678/916-784-3217

Williams, Gary, (Garbo), 221 Autumn Way, Elizabethtown, KY 42701/502-765-6963

Winn, Travis A., 585 E. 3065 S., Salt Lake City, UT 84106/801-467-5957

Young, Mary, 4826 Storeyland Dr., Alton, IL 62002/618-466-4707

Zima, Russell, 7291 Ruth Way, Denver, CO 80221/303-657-9378

miscellaneous

custom grinders

American Etching & Engraving Co. (See Miller, James K. and Vicky)

Engnath, Bob, 1019 E. Palmer Ave., Glendale, CA 91205/818-956-5710; FAX: 818-956-5120

Ferguson, Jim, Twisted Nickel Knives, P.O. Box 40247, Downey, CA 90239/310-862-7461 (evenings)

Forosisky, Nicholas, R32 Clover St., Johnstown, PA 15902/814-288-4543

High, Tom, Rocky Mountain Scrimshaw & Arts, 5474 S. 112.8 Rd., Alamosa, CO 81101/719-589-2108; FAX: 719-589-2826

Holden, Larry, 1544 Strecker St., Ridgecrest, CA 93555/619-377-3579

Imboden II, Howard L., 620 Deerville Dr., Dayton, OH 45429/513-439-1536

Kwik-Sharp Optronics, Inc., 350 N. Wheeler St., Ft. Gibson, OK 74434/918-683-9514

Lamprey, Mike, 32 Pathfield, Great Torrington, Devon EX38 TBX, ENGLAND/01805-622651

Largin, Ken, 67 Arlington Dr., Batesville, IN 47006

McGowan Manufacturing Company, 25 Michigan Ave., Hutchinson, MN 55350/612-587-2222; FAX: 612-587-7966 (mfg. sharpeners)

McLuin, Tom, 36 Fourth St., Dracut, MA 01826/508-957-4899

Miller, James K. and Vicky, Rt. 2 Box 1-A, Tuscumbia, AL 35674/205-381-1747

Peele, Bryan, The Elk Rack, 215 Ferry St., P.O. Box 1363, Thompson Falls, MT 59873/406-827-4633

Rece, Charles V., P.O. Box 868, Paw Creek, NC 28130/704-391-0209

Twisted Nickel Knives (See Ferguson, Jim)

Wilson, R.W., P.O. Box 2012, Weirton, WV 26062/304-723-2771

custom handle artisans

American Etching & Engraving Co. (See Miller, James K. and Vicky)

Anderson, Mel, 1718 Lee Ln., Cedaredge, CO 81413/970-856-6465

Beaver, Judy, 48835 N. 25 Ave., Phoenix, AZ 85027/602-465-7831; FAX: 602-465-7077

Clements' Custom Leathercraft, Chas, 1741 Dallas St., Aurora, CO 80010/303-364-0403

Cooper, Jim, 2148 Cook Place, Ramona, CA 92065-3214/619-789-1097

Cover Jr., Raymond A., Rt. 1, Box 194, Mineral Point, MO 63660/314-749-3783

DiMarzo, Richard, 2357 Center Pl. S., Birmingham, AL 35205/205-252-3331

Draghi, Juan Jose, Gral Alvear 345, CP 2760-San Antonio de Areco, Pcia. de Bs Aires, ARGENTINA

Eccentric Endeavors, J. Michel Santos, P.O. Box 13, Port Costa, CA 94569

Eldridge, Allan, 1424 Kansas Lane, Gallatin, TN 37066/615-452-6027

Eubank, Mary Ann, Rt. 1 Box 196, Pottsboro, TX 75076/903-786-3596

Ferguson, Jim, Twisted Nickel Knives, P.O. Box 40247, Downey, CA 90239/310-862-7461 (evenings)

Francis, Roger, 5419 Miller Ave., Dallas, RX 75206/214-824-8468 or 214-387-1209

Grussenmeyer, Paul G., 101 S. White Horse Pike, Lindenwold, NJ 08021-2304/609-435-1500; FAX: 609-435-3786

Harrison, Ed, 10125 Palestine, Houston, TX 77029/713-673-6893

High, Tom, Rocky Mountain Scrimshaw & Arts, 5474 S. 112.8 Rd., Alamosa, CO 81101/719-589-2108; FAX: 719-589-2826

Hill, Russell S., 2384 Second Ave., Grand Island, NY 14072/716-773-0084

Holden, Larry, 1544 Strecker St., Ridgecrest, CA 93555/619-377-3579

Holder, Pat, 4412 W. Diana Ave., Glendale, AZ 85302/602-435-9589; FAX: 602-939-4408

Holland, Dennis K., 4908-17th Place, Lubbock, TX 79416/806-799-8427

Imboden II, Howard L., 620 Deerville Dr., Dayton, OH 45429/513-439-1536

Kelso, Jim, RD 1, Box 5300, Worcester, VT 05682/802-229-4254

Kemp, Mel, Scottsdale Casting, Inc., P.O. Box 130, Rimrock, AZ 86335-0130

Knack, Gary, 309 Wightman, Ashland, OR 97520/503-482-2108

Lee, Ray, 209 Jefferson Dr., Lynchburg, VA 24502/804-237-2918

Lefaucheux, Jean-Victor, Saint-Dennis-Le-Ferment, 27140 Gisors, FRANCE/32-55-1410; FAX: 32-55-5087

Letschnig, Franz, RR1, Martintown, Ont., CANADA/613-528-4843

Lott, Sherry, 5611 Long Creek Ln., Houston, TX 77088-5525/713-820-7973

Marlatt, David, 67622 Oldham Rd., Cambridge, OH 43725/614-432-7549

Mead, Dennis, 2250 E. Mercury St., Inverness, FL 34453-0514/904-344-4751

Mendenhall, Harry E., 1848 Everglades Dr., Milpitas, CA 95035/408-263-0677

Miller, James K. and Vicky, Rt. 2 Box 1-A, Tuscumbia, AL 35674/205-381-1747

Miteaif, Oleg, Oboronnay 46/2, 300007 Tula, RUSSIA

Myers, Ron, 6202 Marglenn Ave., Baltimore, MD 21206/301-866-8435

Northwest Knife Supply (See Vallotton, A.)

Sayen, Murad, P.O. Box 127, Bryant Pond, ME 04219/207-665-2224

Smith, Glen, 1307 Custer Ave., Billings, MT 59102/406-252-4064

Smith, D. Noel, P.O. Box 1363, Canon City, CO 81215-1363/719-275-2574

Snell, Barry A., 172 Sexton Ln., Clinton, TN 37716/615-457-9138

Twisted Nickel Knives (See Ferguson, Jim)

Vallotton, A., Northwest Knife Supply, 621 Fawn Ridge Dr., Oakland, OR 97462/503-459-2216

Watson, Silvia, 350 Jennifer Lane, Driftwood, TX 78619/512-847-9679

Williams, Gary, (GARBO), 221 Autumn Way, Elizabethtown, KY 42701/502-765-6963

Willson, Harlan M., 641 University Dr., Lompoc, CA 93436

display cases and boxes

American Display Company, 55 Cromwell St., Providence, RI 02904/401-331-2464

Bill's Custom Cases, P.O. Box 2, Dunsmuir, CA 96025/916-235-0177; FAX: 916-235-4959 (soft knife cases)

Clements', Chas, Custom Leathercraft, 1741 Dallas St., Aurora, CO 80010-2018/303-364-0403

Dennehy, John D., Custom Leatherworks, P.O. Box 431, 3926 Hayes, Wellington, CO 80549/303-568-9055

Gimbert, Nelson, P.O. Box 787, Clemmons, NC 27012/919-766-5216

Haydu, Thomas G., Tomway Corp., 2507 Bimini Lane, Ft. Lauderdale, FL 33312/305-792-0185; FAX: 305-792-0115

The Long Island Sutlers, 2169 Jones Ave., Wantagh, NY 11793/516-742-9495

M&M Kustom Krafts (See Miller, Michael K.)

Mason, Arne (See Mesa Case)

Mesa Case, Arne Mason, 125 Wimer St., Ashland, OR 97520/503-4872-2260

Miller, Michael K., M&M Kustom Krafts, 28510 Santiam Highway, Sweet Home, OR 97386/503-367-4927

Miller, Robert, P.O. Box 2722, Ormond Beach, FL 32176/904-676-1193

Retichek, Joseph L., W9377 Co. TK. D, Beaver Dam, WI 53916/414-887-8061

S&D Enterprises, 304 W. Second St., Manchester, OH 45144/513-549-2709 or 513-549-2603, 513-549-2602

Tomway Corp. (See Haydu, Thomas G.)

etchers

American Etching & Engraving Co. (See Miller, James K. and Vicky)

Baron Technology, Inc., 62 Spring Hill Rd., Trumbull, CT 06611/203-452-0515; FAX: 203-452-0663

David Boye Knives Gallery (See Martin, Francine)

Eubank, Mary Ann, Rt. 1, Box 196, Pottsboro, TX 75076/903-786-3596; FAX: 903-786-3501

Fountain Products, 492 Prospect Ave., West Springfield, MA 01089/413-781-4651; FAX: 413-733-8217

Hayes, Dolores, P.O. Box 41405, Los Angeles, CA 90041/213-258-9923

Holland, Dennis, 4908 17th Place, Lubbock, TX 79416/806-799-8427

Kelso, Jim, RD1, Box 5300, Worcester, VT 05682/802-229-4254

Lefaucheux, Jean-Victor, Saint-Denis-Le-Ferment, 27140 Gisors, FRANCE/16-32-55-14-10; FAX: 16-32-55-50-87

Leibowitz, Leonard, 1025 Murrayhill Ave., Pittsburgh, PA 15217/412-361-5455

MacBain, Kenneth C., 30 Briarwood Ave., Norwood, NJ 07648/201-768-0652

Martin, Francine, David Boye Knives Gallery, P.O. Box 81, Davenport, CA 95017/408-426-6046

Miller, James K. and Vicky, Rt. 2 Box 1-A, Tuscumbia, AL 35674/205-381-1747

Myers, Ron, 6202 Marglenn Ave., Baltimore, MD 21206/301-866-8435

Northwest Knife Supply (See Vallotton, A.)

Sayen, Murad, P.O. Box 127, Bryant Pond, ME 04219/207-665-2224

Smith, Glen, 1307 Custer Ave., Billings, MT 59102/406-252-4064

Vallotton, A., Northwest Knife Supply, 621 Fawn Ridge Dr., Oakland, OR 97462/503-459-2216

Watson, Silvia, 350 Jennifer Lane, Driftwood, TX 78619/512-847-9679

knife appraisers

Clements' Custom Leathercraft, Chas, 1741 Dallas St., Aurora, CO 80010-2018/303-364-0403; FAX: 303-364-0403

Levine, Bernard, P.O. Box 2404, Eugene, OR 97402/503-484-0294

Russell, A.G., 1705 Hwy. 71 North, Springdale, AR 72764/501-751-7341

Vallini, Massimo, Via Dello Scalo 2/3, 40131 Bologna ITALY/011-39-51-522.087

organizations & publications

organizations

AMERICAN BLADESMITH SOCIETY
c/o E. Jay Hendrickson, President
4204 Ballenger Creek Pike
Frederick, MD 21701
Phone: 301-663-6923
If you're interested in the forged blade, you are welcome here. The Society has a teaching program, East and West, and awards stamps to Journeymen and Master Smiths after they pass tests—tough tests at a hot forge. You don't have to make knives to belong. A list of knifemaker members appears on page 278.

THE CANADIAN KNIFE COLLECTORS CLUB
c/o John Comber, President
2410 Lower Base Line, RR #1
Milton, Ont., L9T 2X5 Canada
Phone: 416-878-4955
One umbrella organization—the Canadian Knife Collectors Club—serves collectors and craftsmen alike. The CKCC holds its own shows and has a semi-annual newsletter.

JAPANESE SWORD SOCIETY OF THE U.S.
P.O. Box 712
Breckenridge, TX 76424
They publish a newsletter bi-monthly and a bulletin once a year.

KNIFEMAKERS GUILD
c/o Frank Centofante, President
P.O. Box 928
Madisonville, TN 37354-0928
Phone: 615-442-5767
This continues to be the big one. The Guild has prospered, as have its members. It screens prospects to ensure they are serious craftsmen; and it runs a big show in Orlando each July where over 250 Guild members show their best work, all in one room. Not all good knifemakers belong; some joined and later left for their own reasons; the Guild drops some for cause now and again. The Knifemakers Guild is an organization with a function. A list of Guild members appears on page 277.

KNIFEMAKERS GUILD OF CANADA
c/o George A. Roberts
149 Mill St.
Parkhill, Ont. N0M 2KO Canada
Phone: 519-294-0267
Newly formed group—1994.

MIDWEST KNIFEMAKERS ASSOCIATION
c/o Corbin Newcomb, President
628 Woodland Ave.
Moberly, MO 65270
Phone: 816-263-4639
The MKA currently has a membership of 49 makers from 10 states in the Midwest; a list appears on page 279.

MINIATURE KNIFEMAKER'S SOCIETY
c/o Gary F. Bradburn
1714 Park Pl.
Wichita, KS 67203
Phone: 316-269-4273
The MKS is dedicated to improving the quality of custom miniature knives. The MKS welcomes miniature makers and collectors as members, publishes a bi-monthly newsletter, and awards miniature collectors who publicly show their collections. Send $1 for a list of members and an application. A list of knifemaker members appears on page 279.

PROFESSIONAL KNIFEMAKERS ASSOCIATION
1450 Prospect Ave., Suite 222
Helena, MT 88271
Phone: 406-449-8827

REGIONAL ASSOCIATIONS
There are a number of state and regional associations with goals possibly more directly related to promotion of their members' sales than the Guild and the ABS. Among those known to us are the American Knife Throwers Alliance; Arizona Knifemakers Association; the Arkansas Knifemakers Association; the California Knifemakers Association; the Montana Knifemaker's Association; the South Carolina Association of Knifemakers; the Midwest Knifemakers Association; the New England Bladesmiths Guild; North Carolina Knifemaker's Guild; Ohio Knifemakers Association; and the Association of Southern Knifemakers. Lists of members of most of these may be found on page 279.

publications

THE BLADE MAGAZINE
Krause Publications
700 E. State St.
Iola, WI 54945
Phone: 800-272-5233
Editor: Steve Shackleford. Eight times yearly. Official magazine of the Knifemakers Guild. $3.25 on newsstand; $17.99 per year. Also publishes *Edges*, a quarterly ($12.95 for six issues); *Blade Trade*, a cutlery trade magazine; and knife books.

DBI BOOKS, INC.
4092 Commercial Ave.
Northbrook, IL 60062
Phone: 708-272-6310
FAX: 708-272-2051
In addition to this *Knives* annual, DBI publishes *Gun Digest Book of Knives*, by Jack Lewis and Roger Combs, *Knifemaking*, also by Lewis and Combs, and *Levine's Guide to Knives and Their Values*, by Bernard Levine.

FIGHTING KNIVES
P.O. Box 16598
N. Hollywood, CA 91615-9962
Phone: 818-760-8963
Publisher: Larry Flynt. Editor: Greg Walker. $3.95 newsstand; $14.95 subscription (6 issues). Covers knives from military/para-military point of view; wide-ranging commentary.

KNIFE WORLD
P.O. Box 3395
Knoxville, TN 37927
Phone: 800-828-7751
Editor/Publisher: Houston Price. Monthly. Tabloid size on newsprint. Covers custom knives, knifemakers, collecting, old factory knives, etc. General coverage for the knife enthusiast. Subscription $15 year.

KNIVES ILLUSTRATED
774 S. Placentia Ave.
Placentia, CA 92670
Phone: 714-572-2255
Editor: Bud Lang. $3.50 on newsstands; $14.95 for six issues. Plenty of four-color, all on cutlery; concentrates on handmade knives.

NATIONAL KNIFE MAGAZINE
P.O. Box 21070
Chattanooga, TN 37424
Phone: 615-899-9456
Editor: Lisa Broyles. Monthly. Four-color cover. For members of the National Knife Collectors Association. Lots of ads. Emphasis on pocketknife collecting, but has broadened coverage to include all phases of knife interest. Membership $30 year; $35 for new members.

TACTICAL KNIVES
Harris Publications
1115 Broadway
New York, NY 10010
Phone: 212-807-7100
FAX: 212-627-4678
Editor: Steve Dick. Aimed at emergency-service knife designs and users, this new publication has made a great start. Price: $4.95; $14.95 for six issues. On newsstands.

WEYER INTERNATIONAL BOOK DIVISION
2740 Nebraska Ave.
Toledo, OH 43607
Phone: 419-534-2020
FAX: 419-534-2697
Publishers of the *Knives: Points of Interest* series. Sells knife-related books at attractive prices; has other knife-publishing projects in work.